THE LAW RELATING TO PARENT AND CHILD IN SCOTLAND

THE LAW RELATING TO PARENT AND CHILD IN SCOTLAND

by

A. B. WILKINSON
Q.C., M.A., LL.B.
Sheriff of Glasgow and Strathkelvin

and

KENNETH McK. NORRIE
LL.B., PH.D.
Senior Lecturer at the University of Strathclyde

Published under the auspices of
THE SCOTTISH UNIVERSITIES LAW INSTITUTE

W. GREEN/Sweet & Maxwell
EDINBURGH
1993

First published 1993

ISBN 0 414 01044 2

A catalogue record for this book
is available from the British Library

Typeset by Tradespools Ltd., Frome
Printed in Great Britain by Hartnolls Ltd.,
Bodmin, Cornwall

CONTENTS

CHAPTER 3

ANTE-NATAL ISSUES

CHAPTER 4

CONSTITUTION OF THE PARENT-CHILD
RELATIONSHIP

CHAPTER 5

PARENTAL RESPONSIBILITIES AND RIGHTS: GENERAL

CHAPTER 6

PARTICULAR PARENTAL RESPONSIBILITIES AND RIGHTS

CHAPTER 7

CHAPTER 8

CHAPTER 9

CHAPTER 12

EDUCATION OF CHILDREN   322

PREFACE

There has been no book devoted to a comprehensive treatment of the Scots law of Parent and Child since the third edition of Lord Fraser's classic work was published under the editorship of James Clark in 1906. Some of the law of which Fraser wrote survives, perhaps to a surprising extent, if in a transitional or vestigial form, but the most marked feature of the intervening years has been the radical and far-reaching effect of legislative change. The concept of legitimacy which was central to the older law is obsolescent, the law of guardianship and legal capacity of children has been largely, but no entirely, recast, questions of custody and aliment are governed by new statutory criteria and modern medical technology has given rise to new legal problems in the constitution of the parent and child relationship itself. At the same time the public law regulation of the care and protection of children, the law of adoption and aspects of the law of education now require a place, which they did not previously occupy, in any adequate discussion of the law of parent and child. Questions of boundaries inevitably arise. We have tried to avoid drawing these boundaries narrowly and artificially and to cover all aspects of the law which have a close bearing on the parent and child relationship. We have not, however, discussed, except incidentally, topics which more appropriately fall within the scope of other specialist works. Thus we have dealt, sometimes quite extensively, with questions of succession and criminal liability where that was required by the context but we have not attempted a comprehensive discussion of the cognate aspects of the law of succession or criminal law or of revenue and social security law.

There are many to whom gratitude is due. Professor I. D. Willock, Mr. J. J. Robertson and Dr. Brian Davis generously made available research materials which they had gathered. Mr. Simon Bowie, Mr. Craig Harvie, and Mr. Amish Amin provided useful technical assistance. Most of the text was read in an earlier version by the late Lord Dunpark, Dr. E. M. Clive and Mr. Niall Whitty and we are very grateful to them for the invaluable suggestions they made as we are to Mr. Russel P. Meek and Professor J. M. Thomson for comments on the chapters on compulsory measures of care and custody respectively. We are similarly indebted to the Honourable Lord Caplan, Sheriff Mark Sischy and Professor Alastair Bissett-Johnson who read the text in virtually its final form, to successive directors of the Scottish Universities' Law Institute for their guidance and forbearance and, in particular, to the present Director, Professor W. W. McBryde, who was instrumental in bringing about our collaboration and has done much to ease the path to publication. Lord Dunpark gave abundantly not only of his learning and practical judgment but of his interest and support. It is a matter of particular regret that he has not lived to see the publication of a book he did so much to encourage.

We have endeavoured to state the law as at 31st July 1993.

A. B. Wilkinson
Kenneth McK. Norrie

TABLE OF CASES

xix

TABLE OF STATUTES

TABLE OF STATUTES

TABLE OF STATUTORY INSTRUMENTS

SELECTED ABBREVIATIONS AND AUTHORITIES

A.C.	Law Reports, Appeal Cases (England)
Adam	Adam's Justiciary Cases
All E.R.	All England Law Reports
A.L.R.	American Law Reports (Annotated)
Anton & Beaumont	A. E. Anton and P. R. Beaumont, *Private International Law*, 2nd ed. (1990)
App. Cas.	Appeal Cases (House of Lords)
Balfour	Sir James Balfour of Pittendreich, *Practicks: or a System of the More Ancient Law of Scotland* (Stair Society, vols. 21 & 22)
Bankton	Andrew McDouall, Lord Bankton *Institute of the Laws of Scotland in Civil Rights* 1751–1753
Bell	G. J. Bell, *Principles of the Law of Scotland*
B.M.J.	British Medical Journal
Camb. L.J.	Cambridge Law Journal
Ch.	Law Reports, Chancery Division (England)
Clive	E.M. Clive, *The Law of Husband and Wife in Scotland* 3rd ed. (1992)
C.L.Y.	Current Law Yearbook
Cox C.C.	Cox's Criminal Cases
Crim. App. Rep.	Criminal Appeal Reports
Crim. L.R.	Criminal Law Review
D.	Dunlop (Session Cases)
D.L.R.	Dominion Law Reports (Canada)
E.H.R.R.	European Human Rights Reports
Enc.	*Stair Memorial Encyclopaedia of the Laws of Scotland*
Erskine	John Erskine, *An Institute of the Law of Scotland*
F.	Fraser (Sessions Cases)
Fam.	Law Reports, Family Division (England)
Fam. L.	Family Law
F.C.	Faculty Collection
F.L.R.	Family Law Reporter
Fraser	Lord Fraser *The Law of Scotland Relative to Parent and Child*, 3rd ed. (1906)
Hume	Hume's Decisions
Hume, Comm.	Baron David Hume, *Commentaries on the Law of Scotland, Respecting Crimes*
Hume, Lect.	Baron David Hume, *Lectures on the Law of Scotland* (Stair Society)
I.C.L.Q.	International and Comparative Law Quarterly

I.R.	Irish Reports
Irv.	Irvine's Justiciary Cases
Jac.	Jacob (English Reports, vol. 37)
J.A.M.A.	Journal of the American Medical Association
J. Fam. L.	Journal of Family Law
J.L.S.S.	Journal of the Law Society of Scotland
J.P.	Justice of the Peace Reports
J.R.	Juridical Review
K.B.	Law Reports, King's Bench (England)
Law Com.	Law Commission (England)
L.G.R.	Local Government Reports
L.Q.R.	Law Quarterly Review
L.T.	Law Times
M.	Macpherson (Session Cases)
Macl. & Rob.	Maclean and Robinson (English Reports, vol. 9)
Macq.	Macqueen (House of Lords, Scotland)
Mod. L.R.	Modern Law Review
Mor.	Morison's *Dictionary of Decisions*
Mor. Supp.	Brown's *Supplements to Morison's Dictionary of Decisions*
New L.J.	New Law Journal
N.I.L.Q.	Northern Ireland Legal Quarterly
N.S.W.L.R.	New South Wales Law Reports
N.Y.U.L.R.	New York University Law Review
N.Z.L.R.	New Zealand Law Reports
P.	Law Reports, Probate Division (England)
Pat.	Paton's Reports (House of Lords)
Q.B.	Law Reports, Queen's Bench (England)
R.	Rettie (Session Cases)
R.C.	Rules of the Court of Session 1965
S.	Shaw (Session Cases)
S.A.L.R.	South African Law Reports
S.C.	Session Cases
S.C.C.R.	Scottish Criminal Case Reports
Sc. Jur.	Scottish Jurist
S.C.L.R.	Scottish Civil Law Reports
Scot. Law Com.	Scottish Law Commission
Sh. Ct. Rep.	Sheriff Court Reports
S.L.R.	Scottish Law Reporter
S.L.T.	Scots Law Times
S.N.	Session Notes
Sol. J.	Solicitors Journal
Stair	Sir James Dalrymple, Viscount Stair, *Institutions of the Law of Scotland*
T.L.R.	Times Law Reports
Thomson	J. M. Thomson, *Family Law in Scotland* 2nd ed. (1991)
Univ. Tor. L.J.	University of Toronto Law Journal

W.L.R.   Weekly Law Reports
W. &. S.   Wilson & Shaw (House of Lords Reports, Scotland)
Yale L.J.   Yale Law Journal

CHAPTER 1

GENERAL INTRODUCTION

INTRODUCTORY

The Parent-Child Relationship

"Child" may mean (1) the off-spring of particular human parents ("child of X") and in that sense is the correlative of "parent" and (2) the young of the human species from birth, or even before, to about the age of adolescence. In the first sense, age is irrelevant, although for most purposes other than succession the legal significance of the parent and child relationship ends, or is much reduced, when the child attains majority. The word "child" when used in the second sense was not a term of art for the common law which spoke rather of pupils, *i.e.* children under the legal age of puberty, 12 in the case of a girl and 14 in the case of a boy, and minors between these ages and majority. The tendency of modern statute has been to apply the term child to everyone under the age of 16,[1] perhaps a rather later age than common usage would justify, and in some contexts child is defined as extending to persons up to the age of 18 or even beyond.[2] That there should be two distinct but related senses in which the word child may be used represents, however, more than an accident of language. The relationship of parent and child and the extensions flowing from it provide the primary means to which human societies have looked for the nurture, care and upbringing of their younger members and that means may be seen, despite occasional attempts to dispense with it, as founded on nature. This work takes as its starting-point the legal recognition and regulation of the relationship of parent and child and goes on to consider legal provision for substitute and supplementary arrangements for the care and upbringing of children and associated questions of the management of children's property, the capacity of children to act and the function of guardianship.

Common Law Classification

The common law made radical distinctions between (1) legitimate children, *i.e.* those born or conceived in wedlock or subsequently legitimated,[3] and illegitimate children; and (2) between pupils and minors in the sense indicated above. Confusingly, but perhaps more properly, the term minor was also often used to embrace all persons, including pupils, under the age of majority.[4] For clarity, the expression minor *pubes* could be used when the case of a person be-

---

[1] See for example the Social Work (Scotland) Act 1968, s. 30(1); Law Reform (Parent and Child (Scotland) Act 1986, s. 8.

[2] See, for example Family Law (Scotland) Act 1985, s. 1(5), and the definition of child for the purposes of parental rights other than guardianship, custody and access in the Law Reform (Parent and Child) (Scotland) Act 1986, s. 8.

[3] See *post* at pp. 10–26.

[4] As in reduction of transactions on the ground of minority and lesion.

tween pupillarity and majority was under consideration, to distinguish its position from that of persons under majority generally.

Although for some limited purposes the natural relationship between an illegitimate child and its parents was recognised, by imposing an obligation of aliment on the father and, at least in the later development of the law, by giving the right of custody to the mother, it was only the relationship between a legitimate child and its parents that was treated as being in the full sense a relationship of parent and child recognised by law and to which the whole body of common law rules relating to that relationship applied. Legitimate children were subject to the *patria potestas* or paternal power of their father which in the case of pupil children was so extensive that it was called, if slightly misleadingly, a right of dominion.[5] In the case of minors it was much reduced and might be lost by the minor's forisfamiliation.[6] Although on the failure of the father by death or otherwise certain rights which he had exercised as part of the *patria potestas* might accrue or be transferred to relatives, the child's mother or others, the *patria potestas* as such was regarded as vesting in the father alone and was inalienable. The mother's position in respect of custody and guardianship was considerably improved, if in a piecemeal fashion, by a series of enactments from the mid-nineteenth century onwards, but the rule that, in principle, the *patria potestas* belonged to the father alone remained the law until as late as 1973.[7] The guardians who on the failure of the father of a legitimate pupil child might be entrusted with the management of his estate and, unless the court ordered otherwise, with his personal care and custody were known as tutors. Pupil children had no legal capacity to act or to manage their own affairs. Minors had such capacity, but for many transactions the concurrence of the minor's father, if alive, or if he had guardians (known as curators) the concurrence of his guardians, was necessary. In contrast with pupils, however, neither the father nor the curators of a minor could take over the management of his estate or act without his authority on his behalf. A father had certain but limited powers of personal control of a minor; curators had none. In relation to contracts and legal proceedings fathers were often referred to as tutors of their pupil, and curators of their minor, children; but such language was no more than descriptive of the role and did not imply any distinct office—they so acted by virtue of the *patria potestas*.

Statutory Development

This work treats of a number of topics—local authority involvement in care, assumption of parental rights and powers, compulsory measures of care, regulation of fostering and child-minding, and adoption—which are the creatures of modern statute designed to address familial and social problems which the common law did not address. They bear on the law of parent and child primarily as remedies for the malfunction of the parent and child relationship or as a means

---

[5] See *post* at pp. 37–38; 70–71.

[6] See *post* at pp. 44–45.

[7] Guardianship Act 1973, s. 10 (now repealed by the Law Reform (Parent and Child) (Scotland) Act 1986, Sched. 2 and superseded by s. 2 of that Act).

of regulating alternative or substitute provision in the event of its failure. Their legislative history, where it is important for the understanding of the modern law, is given later in its appropriate context. From the mid-nineteenth century onwards there has also been a series of statutes, particularly in the fields of custody, guardianship and the position of illegitimate children, which served to modify, extend and ameliorate the common law in the light of developing perceptions. Although some of these statutes effected fairly radical revision of common law tenets, they left the common law framework substantially in place. Since 1985, however, the effect of legislation such as the Family Law (Scotland) Act 1985, the Law Reform (Parent and Child) (Scotland) Act 1986, and the Age of Legal Capacity (Scotland) Act 1991, has been to bring about in large measure the replacement of common law by statute. Legitimacy, and with it illegitimacy, has been virtually swept away; the law of custody and aliment is embodied in statutory rules; the ancient distinction between pupils and minors *puberes* has been abolished and replaced by a sharp distinction, for the purposes of the legal capacity of persons who have not attained majority, between those under 16 years of age and those over that age; curatory and tutory have been abolished, although the latter, abolished only in name, has been replaced by guardianship of those under the age of 16. The process is not, however, complete. There is as yet no comprehensive statutory code[8] and even where, as for custody and aliment, the law is entirely, or almost entirely, statutory, it is enacted against a common law background without some knowledge of which the statute law cannot be fully understood. Moreover, common law rules retain some transitional or incidental importance. Although legitimacy has become a largely outmoded concept, its application to heritable titles, coats of arms, honours and dignities, remains in principle part of the law: declarators of legitimacy and illegitimacy are still competent. More importantly, the law on legitimacy still requires to be considered for the purposes of successions opening before the commencement of the Law Reform (Parent and Child) (Scotland) Act 1986[9] and for the construction of deeds executed before that commencement and of references in deeds, even if executed thereafter, to a legitimate and illegitimate person or relationship. Similarly, the law on pupils and minors and their guardianship remains applicable to any transactions entered into before the date of commencement of the Age of Legal Capacity (Scotland) Act 1991.[10]

This chapter contains a brief consideration of historical sources and a discussion in some detail of the law of legitimacy, and there follows thereafter a chapter containing a consideration of the appointment of tutors and curators, of the legal capacity of pupils and minors before 1991 and of custody (particularly in relation to the statutory development of the common law) before 1986. Because the guardian of a person under the age of 16 years has in relation to him and his estate the powers and duties which, immediately before the commencement of the Age of Legal Capacity (Scotland) Act 1991, a tutor had in relation to his pu-

---

[8] To which, however, the Scottish Law Commission is gradually moving: see Scot. Law Com. No 135, *Report on Family Law*, May 1992, para. 19.4, in which they set out a proposed Draft Outline of a future Scottish Child and Family Law Code, which will gather together current and future legislation in one harmonious whole.

[9] Dec. 8, 1986.

[10] Sept. 25, 1991.

pil,[11] the substantive law of tutory is discussed later in the context of the contemporary law of guardianship.[12]

Historical Sources

The main historical sources of the Scots law of parent and child are the civil law (in the sense of the civilian tradition developed from the Roman law of Justinian), canon law and to some extent, particularly in questions of guardianship, feudal law. The historical development of the law and the influence of these sources are discussed later in the context of the particular aspects of the modern law to which they are relevant. For a wider discussion, reference should be made to other works which are readily available.[13] Only canon law, because of its importance for doctrines of legitimacy which were central to much of the common law of parent and child and because it has been a subject of some controversy, requires brief separate treatment here.

Canon Law

In the medieval period questions of status, including legitimacy, were exclusively within the jurisdiction of the ecclesiastical courts, which applied canon law, and these questions were referred to them even if they arose in the course of proceedings in the secular courts.[14] After the Reformation the jurisdiction of the medieval ecclesiastical courts was taken over by the courts of the commissaries, which continued to apply canon law insofar as it was compatible with statute and protestant views. But latterly, and well before 1830 when the jurisdiction of the commissaries was transferred to the Court of Session[15] (to which appeal from the commissaries had lain since their institution after the Reformation), it seems to have been a matter of the commissaries' following their own precedents which embodied canon law principles rather than their making direct reference to canon law sources. At least for some time after the Reformation, familiarity with canon law was expected of entrants to the Faculty of Advocates.[16] Against that background it would have been surprising if canon law had not been a formative force in the development of those aspects of Scots law to which it had relevance. It is, however, often difficult, because of the interaction between them, to distinguish clearly between civil law and canon law influences except where civil law influence can definitely be excluded, as in distinctively canonist doctrines such as putative marriage. Also, there was, particularly in the nineteenth century, a tendency to ascribe directly to the civil law doctrines such as legitimation by subsequent marriage which had found their way into Scots law through the canon law. That tendency may have been due to a prejudice which had developed against canon law despite its use by the commissaries and the institutional writers. In 1772 it was referred to in the Court of Session as "a fouler source."[17] By 1811 familiarity with canon law had so declined that in

---

[11] s. 5(1).

[12] See *post* at pp. 357–375.

[13] Baird Smith, "Roman Law", Stair Society Vol. I, pp. 171–182 and "Canon Law", *ibid.*, pp. 183–192; Girvan, "Feudal Law", *ibid.*, pp. 193–206; Anton, "Parent and Child", Stair Society Vol. XX, pp. 116–124; Montgomery, "Guardian and Ward", *ibid.*, pp. 125–129; Clive, *Husband and Wife*, (3rd ed.), Chap. 1.

[15] Court of Session Act 1830, s. 33.

[16] Baird Smith, *op. cit.* at p. 191.

[17] *Scrutton* v. *Gray* (1772) *Hailes' Reports*, i, 499.

Brymer v. *Riddell*[18] counsel (shortly afterwards to be elevated to the Bench as Lord Gillies) could profess complete ignorance of it. Yet in 1775 Lord President Dundas had said: "The Canon law is in great measure the law of Scotland."[19] Perhaps, however, it is difficult to improve on Lord Hailes' summary: "The Canon law is not the law of Scotland; but the law of Scotland contains much of the Canon law. This is so certain, that in many cases we determine according to the Canon law without knowing it."[20]

LEGITIMACY AND LEGITIMATION

Significance of Legitimacy

In common with most other European legal systems, a person's status in law, and the nature of his relationship with his parents, was for long dependent upon whether that person was legitimate or illegitimate. The reason for this was, according to Fraser,[21] and the same was true in other countries, that: "it is the policy of law to discourage every other connection than that of marriage, by not acknowledging, as to any legal effect, the relations which spring from connections unsanctioned by marriage. The rights and privileges of husband and wife, of parent and child, it reserves for those who are known to the law in these relations." Yet the mere fact of parenthood has always been sufficient in Scotland to give rise to a degree of legal recognition of the parent-child relationship. Although that relationship received, until recently, its full and typical expression only in the case of the legitimate child, there always existed a certain, albeit limited, legal relationship between an illegitimate child and his parents and, more particularly, between an illegitimate child and his mother. The expression *filius nullius*, although often used, always was an inadequate, and in some degree an inept, description of the status of the illegitimate child.[22] In reference to the authority which parents have over their children, Stair says: "This native authority reacheth all children, whether procreate of lawful marriage or not, so they be truly known to be children."[23] What for Stair was true of authority was also true for him of the whole nexus of rights and obligations between parents and children and had its ground "in the common nature that man hath with other animals."[24] As a description of the actual state of the law, rather than the dictates of the law of nature on which he took the law of Scotland to be based, Stair's state-

---

[18] Feb. 19, 1811, Fergusson's *Consistorial Law*, 212; Robert Bell, *Report on a Case of Illegitimacy* (1825), pp. 102 and 139. Lord Gillies had, it seems, sought to supply the gap in his knowledge from the extensive Canon law collection in the Advocates' Library, only to be overcome by the bulk of the material.

[19] *Maxwell* v. *Gordon* (1775) *Hailes' Reports*, i, 624.

[20] *Ibid.*

[21] *Parent and Child, Guardian and Ward*, (3rd ed.) at p. 144.

[22] That the child had a legal relationship with its natural parents can be seen, for example, in the rules that the mother of the illegitimate child had the right of custody during pupillarity, and that both parents owed obligations of aliment to the child. Any radical justification for the use of the phrase *filius nullius* in Scotland depended on the making of a somewhat artificial distinction between a legal relationship and the legal recognition of a natural relationship: see *Clarke* v. *Carfin Coal Co.* (1891) 18. R(H.L.) 63. The only truly accurate use of the expression was in relation to questions of succession.

[23] I, v, 6.

[24] I, v, 1.

ment puts the matter too broadly, but it sufficiently points the legal recognition of the natural relationship.

At common law the illegitimate child laboured under a number of civil disabilities, of which the most important, at least in at all recent times, was that he lacked testamentary capacity unless he had issue of his own. That particular disability was removed by the Bastards (Scotland) Act 1836. Moreover, at common law the illegitimate child's legal relationship with his parents was sufficiently different from that enjoyed by the legitimate child to add an inferior legal status to the other social disadvantages from which he might suffer, and this has taken much longer to disappear from the law. The trend of modern statute has, however, been to assimilate the legal position of legitimate and illegitimate children in very nearly all respects. The most important statute to effect this change was the Law Reform (Parent and Child) (Scotland) Act 1986, the aim of section 1 of which was to rid the law for as many purposes as then possible of the differences between the legitimate and the illegitimate child. Previous statutes had been working towards that aim, though in a piecemeal and partial fashion, and dealing with discrete areas of law. These, and similar developments, are described in the following paragraphs.

Custody

At common law, while custody of the legitimate child inhered in the father, as an aspect of his *patria potestas*, the right of custody of the illegitimate child belonged with some qualification exclusively to the mother.[25] The legal position of the mother of the legitimate child was improved by statute and she was given parity of rights with the father by the Guardianship Act 1973. The Guardianship of Infants Act 1925 allowed the court to make custody awards if this was for the welfare of the child, but there was some doubt originally whether this covered illegitimate children. By section 2(1) of the Illegitimate Children (Scotland) Act 1930 the court was empowered, on the application by the mother or the father of any illegitimate child, or in any action of aliment for any illegitimate child, to make such order as it thought fit regarding the custody of such a child, having regard to the welfare of the child, to the conduct of the parents and to the wishes as well of the mother as of the father. Since the coming into force of the Law Reform (Parent and Child) (Scotland) Act 1986 all mothers have had the right of custody of their children whether or not they are or have been married to the father, and the father has had the right of custody if he is married to the mother or was married to her at the time of the child's conception or subsequently.[26] While in its terms this provision deals with parental rights rather than the child's status, its effect is to retain a significant legal difference between the child who before 1986 was called legitimate and the child who before 1986 was called illegitimate. The Scottish Law Commission have proposed that all fathers be given parental responsibilities and rights on the same terms as all mothers,[27] and it is

---

[25] See *Corrie* v. *Adair* (1860) 22 D. 897; *Weepers* v. *Heritors of Kennoway* (1844) 6 D. 1166. See also *post*, pp. 70–71.

[26] Law Reform (Parent and Child) (Scotland) Act 1986, s. 2(1).

[27] Scot. Law Com. No. 135, *Report on Family Law*, May 1992, para. 2.50.

only when this is given legislative effect that all children will be subject to the same rules in relation to custody.

Guardianship

As an aspect of the *patria potestas*, the father of a legitimate child had at common law the right of guardianship, that is, the rights of tutory and curatory. By the Guardianship Act 1973[28] the mother of a legitimate child was given the same rights and authority as the law allowed to the father. It was a serious defect in the law that neither the father nor the mother of an illegitimate child had the right of guardianship[29] nor, following from this, the right to appoint by testamentary deed or otherwise a guardian to act on their death.[30] Court order was the only way in which an illegitimate child could obtain a tutor or curator. This defect was not cured until the passing of the Law Reform (Parent and Child) (Scotland) Act 1986, under which the right of tutory and curatory (now guardianship) is granted to the mother of the child whether or not she is or was married to the child's father, and to the father of the child if he is or was married to the mother of the child at the date of the child's conception or at any date thereafter. As in cases of custody, this provision was seen as dealing with parental rights rather than the child's status, but in effect it perpetuated the difference between children born within and children born outwith wedlock. This difference too will remain until the proposal of the Scottish Law Commission, noted under "Custody," is given legislative effect.

Succession

In relation to succession, the common law had provided that an illegitimate child could not succeed to the estate of either of his parents, nor they to his[31]: in this area at least the description of the illegitimate child as *filius nullius* was completely accurate. The first inroad to this principle came with the Legitimacy Act 1926, under section 9 of which an illegitimate child was given the same right of succession to the estate of his mother as if he had been legitimate, but only if the mother died intestate and without lawful issue; and the mother of an illegitimate child was given the same right of succession to the estate of that child as if the child had been legitimate and she the only surviving parent, but only if the child died intestate. By the Law Reform (Miscellaneous Provisions) (Scotland) Act 1968 illegitimate children were given the same rights of succession in the estates of both parents, though not of remoter ascendants or collaterals, as legitimate children.[32] This did not apply to the construction of deeds executed prior to November 25, 1968. The effect of the Law Reform (Parent and Child) (Scotland) Act 1986 is to remove all distinctions between the legitimate and illegitimate child in relation to succession, except that (i) it does not affect the right of *legitim* out of, or the right of succession to, the estate of any person who died before the commencement of the Act (December 8, 1986) and

---

[28] s. 10.
[29] Erskine, I, vi, 55; *Cunningham* v. *Smith* (1880) 7 R. 424.
[30] *Brand* v. *Shaws* (1888) 16 R. 315.
[31] Erskine, III, x, 8.
[32] Law Reform (Miscellaneous Provisions) (Scotland) Act 1968, ss. 1–3 (amending the Succession (Scotland) Act 1964).

(ii) it does not apply to, or affect the succession to or devolution of, any title, coat of arms,[33] honour or dignity transmissible on the death of the holder.

Damages for Death

There is little authority on the question of whether at common law a parent could sue for damages for the negligently-caused death of an illegitimate child, or whether an illegitimate child could sue for damages for the negligently-caused death of a parent. In relation to loss of support, the question would seem to resolve into the question of whether the one owed an obligation of aliment to the other, for that was the basis of the common law claim in relation to legitimate children.[34] Both parents were alimentary debtors to their illegitimate children[35] and the negligently-caused death of either parent would seem, in principle, to have given the child a right of action for loss of support. The illegitimate child owed no obligation of aliment to the father,[36] and therefore the father could not claim damages for the death of the child.[37] The position in relation to the mother was at one time more doubtful,[38] and was never resolved at common law, but it would appear to follow from *Clarke* v. *Carfin Coal Co.*[39] that a mother's claim for damages for loss of support would be incompetent on the same principles as a father's. Statute now governs the matter. Under the Law Reform (Miscellaneous Provisions) (Scotland) Act 1940 illegitimate children could recover damages from anyone wrongfully causing the death of either parent,[40] and by the Law Reform (Damages and Solatium) (Scotland) Act 1962 the parents were given a reciprocal right.[41] The law is today contained in the Damages (Scotland) Act 1976 which gives the right to sue to "relatives" as there defined. Parent and child are both within the definition[42] and, in the Act as originally passed, "an illegitimate person shall be treated as the legitimate child of his mother and reputed father."[43] This provision has now been replaced by the requirement to read the Act in accordance with the provisions of the Law Reform (Parent and Child) (Scotland) Act 1986,[44] under which the fact that a person's parents are not or have not been married to one another shall be left out of account in establishing the legal relationship between the person and any other person.[45] The result is that for the purposes of the Damages (Scotland) Act 1976 the legitimacy or illegitimacy of the child is irrelevant.

---

[33] The Scottish Law Commission, at the suggestion of the Lord Lyon, have recommended that the reference to coats of arms be removed from this provision, so that the transmission thereof is unaffected by a person's legitimacy or illegitimacy: see Scot. Law Com. No. 135, *Report on Family Law*, May 1992, para. 17.11.

[34] Fraser (3rd ed.) at p. 136.

[35] Bankton, I, v, 64; Erskine, I, vi, 56.

[36] *Anderson* v. *Kirk Session of Lauder* (1848) 10 D. 960; *Corrie* v. *Adair* (1860) 22 D. 897.

[37] *McNeill* v. *McGregor* (1901) 4 F. 123.

[38] Fraser, (3rd ed.) at p. 157.

[39] (1891) 18R. (H.L.) 63.

[40] Law Reform (Miscellaneous Provisions) (Scotland) Act 1940, s. 2(2).

[41] Law Reform (Damages and Solatium) (Scotland) Act 1962, s. 2.

[42] Damages (Scotland) Act 1976, Sched. 1, para. 1(*b*).

[43] *Ibid.*, para. 2(*b*).

[44] Law Reform (Parent and Child) (Scotland) Act 1986, Sched. 1, para. 15.

[45] *Ibid.* s. 1(1).

Domicile

A child's domicile was and remains dependent on his or her status of legitimacy or illegitimacy. A child's domicile of origin is that of the father if the child is legitimate and that of the mother if illegitimate.[46] This rule, though well-established, suffers the disadvantage that a child's domicile is thus said to depend upon its legitimacy, while its legitimacy (being a question of status) will depend upon its domicile. As will be seen later[47] the problem was resolved in England by concentrating on the validity of the parents' marriage rather than the legitimacy of the child. However, the fact that this solution allows no place for the concept of putative marriages means that it cannot be the law of Scotland. An alternative solution would be to favour the domicile of the father, but that can scarcely be defended today. The better solution is, therefore, simply to state a preference for the law, either of the mother's or of the father's domicile, which favours legitimacy.[48]

In the Law Reform (Parent and Child) (Scotland) Act 1986 domicile is expressly excepted from the general proposition that the illegitimate child is to be treated as if the parents were or had been married to one another, and the Act did not affect the rule whereby a child born out of wedlock takes the domicile of his mother as a domicile of origin or dependence.[49] The Scottish and English Law Commissions recommended shortly thereafter that the domicile of a child under 16 should be the country with which he or she is for the time being most closely connected, there being a presumption that that country is the country in which the child has a home with one or both parents.[50] This was to apply to all children whether legitimate or illegitimate, and the recommendation was repeated in the Scottish Law Commission's *Report on Family Law*.[51] If this recommendation is accepted by Parliament, domicile, like almost everything else, will not be affected by a person's legitimacy or illegitimacy.

Remaining Effects of Illegitimacy

Since 1986 the only significant remaining legal differences between the legitimate and the illegitimate child, other than those of transitional significance, concern the child's domicile and the succession to titles, coats of arms, honours and dignities transmissible on the death of the holder. In addition, the father's marriage to the mother affects his parental rights in relation to the child. As noted above, the effects in relation to domicile, to succession to coats of arms, and in relation to fathers' responsibilities and rights will disappear if the proposals of the Scottish Law Commission are enacted. This will have the result that legitimacy will have content in the future only in relation to succession to titles, honours and dignities transmissible on death. However, the old law of le-

---

[46] *Udny* v. *Udny* (1869) 7 M. (H.L.) 89, *per* Lord Westbury at p. 99. A posthumous child takes the domicile of its mother: Anton and Beaumont at p. 130.

[47] *post* at p. 29.

[48] Though the reasoning in *Smijth* v. *Smijth*, 1918 1 S.L.T. 156 is not entirely clear, the result in that case is consistent with the proposition advanced in the text. See *post* at pp. 31–32.

[49] Law Reform (Parent and Child) (Scotland) Act 1986, s. 9(1)(*a*).

[50] Scot. Law Com. No. 107; Law Com. No. 168, *Report on the Law of Domicile* (1987), paras. 4.14–4.20.

[51] Scot. Law Com. No. 135, May 1992, para. 17.13.

gitimacy and illegitimacy will remain of greater significance than that for some time, because rights vested or acquired before the new law takes effect will be preserved,[52] both in relation to succession and property matters and in relation to the validity of the exercise of parental rights.[53] Deeds coming into effect before the final abolition of illegitimacy will continue to be construed according to the law then in force, and intentional limitations of rights based on the outmoded concept of illegitimacy will continue to be given effect.

Legitimacy Through Lawful Marriage of the Parents

According to Erskine,[54] "lawful children are those who are either procreated in marriage, or who are afterwards legitimated or made lawful." Stair is to like effect, referring to "a lawful child begotten of persons lawfully married."[55] So far as children born legitimate were concerned, Erskine's and Stair's definitions were preferable to Bell's: "a lawful child, according to the law of Scotland, is one born in wedlock, or within a certain time after the dissolution of the marriage,"[56] which concentrated attention on birth rather than conception in wedlock as the source of legitimacy and was open to the interpretation that a child born of a married woman was, by operation of law, legitimate and moreover that there was an arbitrary determination of the period of time between dissolution of marriage and the birth of a child which would be consistent with the child's legitimacy. Birth of a married woman gave rise, however, to no more than a presumption, although a very strong presumption, of legitimacy and the legitimacy of a child born after the dissolution of a marriage depended not on the length of time which had elapsed, although that may have been relevant to proof, but on whether or not he or she was procreated in marriage. Erskine's and Stair's definitions were, however, defective in overlooking the case of the child whose parents married subsequent to his or her conception but before his or her birth. Such cases were not instances of legitimation by subsequent marriage, which was properly applicable only to children born before the marriage of their parents, but the legitimacy of children born of such intervening marriage was undoubted. Nor, it is submitted, was that result affected by the death of the father or the divorce of the parents before the child's birth. A legitimate child could therefore be defined as a child of parents between whom a lawful marriage subsisted at the time of the child's conception or birth or at any intervening time.[57]

The legitimacy of children conceived as a result of artificial insemination has not been the subject of judicial consideration in Scotland or England. Where insemination was with the semen of the husband, a child so conceived was, however, "procreated in marriage"[58] and "begotten of persons lawfully married"[59]

---

[52] See *Wright's Trs.* v. *Callander* 1992 S.L.T. 498.
[53] See Scot. Law Com. No. 135, draft Bill, cl. 44.
[54] I, vi. 49.
[55] III, iii, 42.
[56] *Prin.* para. 1624.
[57] *Cf.* today the presumption of paternity contained in s. 5(1)(*a*) of the Law Reform (Parent and Child) (Scotland) Act 1986.
[58] Erskine, *ibid.*
[59] Stair, *ibid.*

no less than a child conceived in the normal way, and was clearly legitimate. By parity of reasoning, where the donor was a third party the child was illegitimate.[60] It was never doubted that the legitimacy of children conceived as a result of fecundation *ab extra* depended on whether or not fecundation was attributable to the husband and there is no sound principle on which such cases can be distinguished for this purpose from artificial insemination. This position was not affected by the passing of the Human Fertilisation and Embryology Act 1990. That Act provides[61] that the husband of a woman who gives birth as a result of artificial insemination (or certain other infertility treatments) will be deemed to be the father of the child for all purposes, if certain conditions are satisfied,[62] and that the man to whom the treatment is provided "together" with the woman will be deemed the father of the child for all purposes, if certain conditions are satisfied.[63] The section deems paternity, not legitimacy: the husband or partner is deemed father and the child's legitimacy will therefore depend not on whether his sperm was used to create the child but on whether the man deemed father is married to the mother at the appropriate time.

Legitimacy Without Lawful Marriage of the Parents

Although the subsistence of a lawful marriage between parents, whether at the time of conception or at sometime thereafter so as to effect legitimation, was normally a necessary condition of the legitimacy of their offspring, children of marriages which were declared null could nonetheless be legitimate. That could be so both in the case of a putative but void marriage and in the case of a voidable marriage.

Putative Marriages—General

Fraser defines a putative marriage as "one where the parties, or either of them, *bona fide* believing that they could marry, had entered into the contract, while there was an unknown impediment, arising from relationship, previous marriage, or other irritant nullity, which prevented a valid marriage."[64] Although such marriages are null, the effect of the *bona fides* of the parties (or either of them) was to confer the status of legitimacy on children of the union conceived while that *bona fides* subsisted.

At one time some doubt existed as to whether the doctrine of legitimacy derived from putative marriage formed part of the law of Scotland. That doubt

---

[60] That does not detract from the view, affirmed in *MacLennan* v. *MacLennan*, 1958 S.C. 105, that the artificial insemination of a married woman with the semen of a third party donor is not adultery. Adultery has no necessary connection with procreation and in cases of adultery the *de quo* is whether there was carnal connection. In questions of legitimacy it is, however, parenthood that is in issue, and the absence of carnal connection is as irrelevant to a question of legitimacy as the absence of procreative, as distinct from copulative, action is irrelevant to adultery.

[61] s. 28.

[62] For which see *post* at pp. 136–140.

[63] For which see *post* at pp. 140–141. s.29(5) excepts the case of succession to titles, coats of arms, honours or dignities, to which the previous rules ascertaining legitimacy continue to apply.

[64] at p. 27. It is convenient to use this definition which postulates the *bona fides* of at least one of the parties, although in ordinary usage the expression "putative marriage" may be applied, irrespective of *bona fides*, to any reputed or supposed but actually invalid marriage.

arose from the division of judicial opinion in *Brymer* v. *Riddell*,[65] in which the judges were equally divided between those who held that the *bona fide* belief of either party in the validity of the marriage was sufficient to confer the status of legitimacy on the children of the union and those who held the contrary.[66] The case was adjourned for the opinion of an additional judge, but a decision was never reached because the child died in the interval. *Brymer* v. *Riddell* suffers, in any event, from the defect that, although there was an elaborate discussion of principle, relevant Scottish authorities, in particular decisions of the commissaries, were not cited. Every other consideration points to the acceptance of the doctrine as part of the law of Scotland. It was and is part of the canon law into which it was introduced by a rescript of Innocent III[67] and rather earlier it is mentioned in the writings of Peter Lombard.[68] It was a commonplace of medieval consistorial practice in Scotland.[69] The canon law view was taken over by the commissaries after the Reformation as can be seen from *Dunbar* v. *Adair*[70] and *Hamilton* v. *Burrell*,[71] in both of which, although the decision was against legitimacy, the doctrine of legitimacy from putative marriage was clearly accepted; and in the Court of Session it was observed in *Campbell* v. *Cochran*[72] that "whatever was the issue of this question [the validity of a putative marriage] the daughter would be legitimate from the mother's *bona fides*." The *locus classicus* for the doctrine in Scots law is Craig's *Jus Feudale*,[73] and although Stair[74] and Erskine[75] have been described as "reserved on the subject,"[76] their citation of Craig without comment carries a clear implication of approval. Bankton[77] endorses Craig in more positive terms. The matter may be considered to have been put beyond doubt by *Purves's Trs.* v. *Purves*[78] in which, although the decision was against legitimacy, the doctrine of legitimacy from putative marriage was expressly accepted and which has been followed in the Outer House cases of *Petrie* v. *Ross*[79] and *Smijth* v. *Smijth*.[80]

Error Founding Putative Marriages

The application of the doctrine is dependent on the error of one or both parties

---

[65] February 19, 1811, Fegusson's *Consistorial Law*, 212; Robert Bell, *Report of a Case of Legitimacy under Putative Marriage*, Hume's *Session Papers*, Vol. CVIII, No. 20.

[66] Lords Newton (Senior), Robertson and Polkennet had held that legitimacy could not be derived from a putative marriage, while Lord Justice-Clerk Hope and Lords Meadowbank (Senior) and Glenlee had affirmed the doctrine. Fraser, at p. 32, is clearly surprised that doubt should have been entertained and attributes it to neglect of the Commissary decisions—a neglect which may be attributed to their being available only in manuscript.

[67] Decr. IV, xvii, 14. Decr. IV, xvii, 2 is probably also to be explained on this ground.

[68] *Sententiae*, IV, D, 11.

[69] Fraser (3rd ed.) at pp. 28–31.

[70] May 20, 1573.

[71] Jan 7, 1702.

[72] (1747) Mor. 10456.

[73] II, 18 and 19 (Clyde's trans. at pp. 763 and 766–767).

[74] III, iii, 42.

[75] I, vi, 51.

[76] Hume's *Lectures*, Vol. 1, p. 199.

[77] I, v, 51.

[78] (1895) 22 R. 513.

[79] (1896) 4 S.L.T. 63.

[80] 1918 1 S.L.T. 156.

to the marriage having been made in good faith. The nature and degree of error consistent with *bona fides* was extensively canvassed in the pleadings in *Dunbar* v. *Adair* but has never been the subject of authoritative judicial exposition. The error must, however, be due to justifiable ignorance and, therefore, if knowledge could easily have been obtained, ignorance resulting from failure to obtain it will not be sufficient. To adopt the language of Roman law, the ignorance must be induced: *errore acerrimo non affectato insimulatove.*[81] According to Fraser,[82] the error must be one of fact and not of law. In *Purves's Trs.* v. *Purves* it was held that averments that a woman had gone through a ceremony of marriage, invalid under the law as it then stood,[83] with the husband of her deceased aunt had done so in the *bona fide* belief that such a marriage was lawful, were irrelevant in a question as to the legitimacy of the woman's son and therefore could not be admitted to probation. The decision proceeded on the view that "everyone is bound to know as much of the law as is necessary to regulate his conduct in the ordinary relations of life, and it cannot be said in this case that there was a popular sentiment or opinion that such marriages were legal which might have induced the parties to think that they were not disobeying the law when they entered into this marriage."[84] That appears to leave open the question of whether *bona fides* relevant for the purposes of legitimacy from putative marriage could arise from an error of law consisting in ignorance of some recondite or obscure point of law or founded on popular sentiment.

Fraser cited Boehmer's *Jus Ecclesiasticum Protestantium*[85] and Hertius' *De Matrimonio Putativo*[86] in support of his view; and indeed it was solely on them that he relied. They do not, however, vouch his proposition. Both these commentators allowed an exception for the *dubium jus*,[87] and in his *Institutiones Juris Canonici*,[88] published after his *Jus Ecclesiasticum Protestantium*, Boehmer allowed that error *juris* might be sufficient ground for *bona fide* belief. The predominant trend of canonist and of civilian doctrine has been to distinguish between excusable and inexcusable error rather than between error of fact and error of law, and that distinction seems particularly apt to questions of good or bad faith. In England, where there was no common law doctrine of putative marriage and the statutory test for the legitimacy of children of a void marriage was whether the parents or either of them reasonably believed that the marriage was valid,[89] it was enacted,[90] to remove earlier doubts, that a reasonable belief

---

[81] Code, V, v, 4.

[82] at p. 34.

[83] *Fenton* v. *Livingstone* (1861) 23 D. 366.

[84] *per* the consulted judges (the Lord President, Lord Adam, Lord McLaren, Lord Kinnear and Lord Wellwood) at p. 536.

[85] IV, xvii, 34, 35 and 36.

[86] s. 17.

[87] Boehmer, *ibid.* while laying down the general rule that error of law does not excuse "*quia culposus et affectatus censetur*" allows an exception where other circumstances occur and at IV, xvii, 35 allows that error as to *dubium jus* may suffice as an exception. Hertius at pp. 367–375 (esp. pp. 368–370) treats the effect of error of law as debatable and favours the view that error as to *dubium jus* is excusable. Error as to natural law does not excuse.

[88] IV, xvii, 1: *Matrimonii legitimi effectus est ut liberi nascantur legitimi, si vel maxime nulliter, bona fide tamen et publice initum errore etiam juris interveniente.*

[89] Legitimacy Act 1976, s. 1 (and before that the Legitimacy Act 1959, s. 2).

[90] *Ibid.* s. 1(3), added by the Family Law Reform Act 1987, s. 28(2).

could flow from an error in law as well as an error in fact. While in Scotland it is
now decided that under the *condictio indebiti* an error of law will not justify recovery,[91] the relevant considerations are not identical and it seems that in the
more closely analogous case of homologation of a voidable marriage, reliance
may be placed on ignorance of law.[92] In *Purves's Trs*. Lord Kincairney, although bowing to the authority of Lord Fraser, rejected the application of the
maxim *ignorantia juris neminem excusat* and thought that the texts supported
the argument that an error on a question of *dubium jus* was enough to save the
legitimacy of the children,[93] and the opinion of the consulted judges is consistent with that view.[94] It is submitted that the comment on *Purves's Trs*. made by
the editor of the third edition of Fraser is sound: "It is thought that the door is not
closed by the opinions in this case against a decision modifying to some extent
the view of Lord Fraser, that the error must be 'an *error facti* as opposed to an
error juris.' "[95] Accordingly, although any case of error of law must be treated
with considerable reserve, where the error of law relates to a question of *dubium
jus* or is supported by popular belief, it remains an open question whether the
children of a putative marriage *bona fide* entered into under such error would be
legitimate.[96]

Publicity of Putative Marriages

In a passage quoted with approval by Lord Kincairney in *Purves's Trs*.[97]
Fraser lays down that in order to constitute a putative marriage so as to save the
legitimacy of the children it would seem to be necessary that the marriage had
been entered into publicly and after due proclamation of banns.[98] That view accorded with the general doctrine of the canon law,[99] which was designed to enforce ecclesiastical legislation, on marriage *in facie ecclesiae* and after the
publication of banns, stemming from the Fourth Lateran Council of 1215. Analogous considerations of policy may have lain behind the observations in *Irving*
v. *Ker and Others*[1] that "she [the second wife] was married, if she was ever married, without proclamation of banns, which certainly takes from her all excuse
of ignorance," but the more probable meaning of these words is to cast doubt on

---

[91] *Glasgow Corporation* v. *Lord Advocate*, 1959 S.C. 203.
[92] *A.B.* v. *C.B.* 1961 S.C. 347; *C.B.* v. *A.B.* (1885) 12 R.(H.L.) 36, *per* Lord Selborne L.C. at p. 38.
      Knowledge will, however, be imputed in the absence of evidence of ignorance: *A.B.* v. *C.B.*,
[93] *per* Lord Kincairney (Ordinary) at p. 518.
[94] Of the remaining judges Lord Low, with whom Lord Kyllachy and Lord Stormonth-Darling con-
      curred, confined himself to saying that the averments upon which the plea was based were plainly
      irrelevant and insufficient. Lord Young concurred in the result arrived at without expressing any
      opinion on the question of error. Lord Rutherfurd Clark concurred with the Lord Ordinary. Lord
      Trayner considered the law settled for three centuries.
[95] p. 35.
[96] In *Philp's Trs.* v. *Beaton*, 1938 S.C. 733 Lord Jamieson (Ordinary) held that an error *juris*, even
      where it is related to a *dubium jus*, could not form the basis of *bona fides* for the purposes of puta-
      tive marriage. On a reclaiming motion the Lord Ordinary's interlocutor was reversed on grounds
      which did not require consideration of the question of putative marriage, but both Lord President
      Normand (at p. 747) with whom Lord Fleming concurred and Lord Moncrieff (at p. 750)
      expressly reserved their opinions.
[97] at p. 517.
[98] p. 33.
[99] Sanchez, III, xii, 1; *Corpus Juris Canonici* 3, X, iv, 3; 2, X, iv, 17; 14, X, iv, 17.
[1] August 6, 1693; Fraser at p. 34.

the party's *bona fides*. The general canon law requirement was relaxed in Scottish practice before the Reformation and the legitimacy of children born of parents who had *bona fide* entered into an irregular marriage which proved to be void was upheld.[2] Later authority was to the same effect.[3] Fraser's argument, that in order to confer legitimacy the purported marriage must have been entered into publicly and after due proclamation of banns, is based "on the principle that a regular marriage infers a presumption of *bona fides*, on account of the publicity of the transactions while, on the other hand, parties who clandestinely marry do themselves afford the strongest proof that there could not be *bona fides* in their proceedings." That argument goes to proof rather than to substance. It is submitted that Bankton[4] put the matter in proper perspective when he said "such *bona fides* will be the more easily presumed, if the marriage was publicly solemnised than when it was clandestine," and that where the objections to *bona fides* can as a matter of fact be overcome despite the clandestine or irregular nature of the purported marriage, there is no reason that such *bona fides* should not be accepted for the purpose of conferring legitimacy on the children of the union.

Onus of Proof

In England, where legitimacy from putative marriage, at first recognised and then rejected by the common law, was reintroduced by the Legitimacy Act 1959,[5] it was held that the onus of proof lies on the party asserting legitimacy and that reasonable belief in the validity of the marriage must be shown on an objective standard.[6] It is thought that in neither respect was that the law of Scotland.[7] It is readily intelligible that the onus of establishing a claim to a right conferred by statute must rest upon the person asserting it, but legitimacy from putative marriage in Scotland was part of the common law of legitimacy with the result that the common law presumption of legitimacy applied. Moreover, where the conduct of the parties would in the absence of *bona fide* belief have been criminal, as in bigamy or incest, their innocence was to be presumed. While, therefore, the evidential onus of adducing sufficient evidence to put the question of putative marriage fairly in issue may have been on the party asserting legitimacy, the legal onus which came into place once that had been done rested on the contradictor although, of course, the circumstances of the particular case of putative marriage may have weakened the presumption of legitimacy or even shifted the provisional onus.[8] Similarly, English law was not concerned in this context with *bona fides* as such but with the meaning of reas-

---

[2] *Kinlocht* v. *Powre* (1543) *Liber Officialis Sancti Andree*, 87 No. 135; *Bisset* v. *Lychtone* (1543), *ibid.* 88 No. 136.

[3] *Campbell* v. *Cochran*; *Petrie* v. *Ross: Smijth* v. *Smijth, supra.* Erskine I, vi, 51 follows the Canon law as laid down in the Decretals.

[4] I, v, 51.

[5] See now the Legitimacy Act 1976.

[6] *Hawkins* v. *Attorney-General* [1966] 1 W.L.R. 978.

[7] And in any event was changed in England by the Family Law Reform Act 1987, s. 28, which added a new s. 1(4) to the Legitimacy Act 1976 to the effect that it shall be presumed, unless the contrary be shown, that one of the parties to the void marriage reasonably believed it to be valid.

[8] For the distinction between the legal and the provisional onus see *Brown* v. *Rolls Royce Ltd.*, 1960 S.C.(H.L.) 22 at pp. 27–28, *per* Lord Denning.

onable belief in the terms of the statute. While objective criteria may form part of the background to an assessment of the credibility of protestations of good faith, the question of whether or not a person acted in good faith must ultimately be the subjective one of his actual state of mind and not the state of mind which might be imputed to the reasonable man in the circumstances. Any abuse to which this view might have been open was sufficiently counteracted by the requirement that the error must have been due to justifiable ignorance.

Effect of Putative Marriages

The effect of putative marriage was to confer on the children the status of legitimacy in relation to a parent *in mala fide* as well as the parent *in bona fide*. There was, however, a qualification so far as a parent *in mala fide* was concerned: he could not benefit from his own wrong. He was under all the obligations of a parent of a legitimate child but he had none of the parental rights and powers.[9] Thus although he had an alimentary liability to the child he had no reciprocal right to aliment. The child and the child's issue could succeed to his estate and to the estates of ancestors and collaterals traceable through him, but no corresponding rights of succession enured to the *mala fide* parent or those who traced their relationship through him. It seems that the *mala fide* parent could not even take advantage of the statutory provisions governing parental rights of succession to the estate of an illegitimate child which, since the effect of putative marriage was to confer legitimacy, were inept to cover his case.

It was at one time much disputed whether a putative marriage could operate so as to legitimise children conceived before the marriage was contracted. The predominant civilian opinion which Fraser[10] adopted was that it could not do so, at any rate where, as in the common case, the parties had not been free to marry each other at the time of conception. The fact that parents had not been free to marry at the time of conception was, however, commonly considered to be a bar to legitimation at common law even where the subsequent marriage was valid. The Legitimation (Scotland) Act 1968 which *inter alia* removed any objection to legitimation arising from impediment at the time of conception provided that a putative marriage should have the same effect as a valid marriage for the purpose of legitimation.[11] The somewhat anomalous result was that where unmarried parents, between whom there was unknown to them an impediment to marriage, procreated a child, they could, so long as their ignorance persisted, effect his legitimation by going through a form of marriage but as soon as their ignorance was dispersed the opportunity for legitimation flew off.

Analogous Cases—Concubinage; Rape

An extension of the doctrine of *bona fides* was canvassed so as to bring about the legitimacy (a) of children procreated in incestuous concubinage in the *bona fide* but erroneous belief of their parents that no impediment existed to their subsequent marriage and consequent legitimation of their issue, and (b) of children

---

[9] Fraser, *Husband and Wife* (2nd ed.), I, p. 152.
[10] *Parent and Child* at p. 33.
[11] Legitimation (Scotland) Act 1968, s. 8(1).

born as a result of rape.[12] The former case derived some colour from the circumstances surrounding the succession of Robert III to the throne of Scotland, but neither his succession nor his legitimacy depended on this view of the law.[13] The case of children born of rape was scarcely one of *bona fides* at all but could be advanced out of regard for the innocence of the mother. There is no Scottish authority in point and it may be argued that legitimacy from putative marriage did not have as its function the providing of a generalised remedy for injustice or wronged innocence in cases of illegitimacy—all illegitimacy may, in a real sense, be said to be unjust from the standpoint of the child and seduction, short of rape, may also be a wrong on the innocence of the mother—but the more limited function of approximating the effects of a void marriage, entered into *in bona fide* and under excusable error, to those of a valid marriage. There is, however, some strength in the contrary contention that cases of rape lay, from the mother's standpoint, *a fortiori* of cases of good faith. It is important to remember when one speaks of putative marriage that there is in truth no marriage at all. The doctrine was founded not on respect for purported marriages but on respect for good faith. As Fraser says, "a contrary judgment would, in effect, impose a punishment without a crime, and entail rigorous hardship on individuals, which it is good policy, if possible, to avoid."[14] The victim of rape was a fit beneficiary of that policy no less than the *bona fide* participant in a pretended but invalid marriage. The protection which the law gave to the *bona fides* of the latter could therefore be extended to the innocence of the former. The further advantage would follow that although the perpetrator of the rape would incur liabilities of a father of a legitimate child he would be deprived, on principles discussed above, of any rights in relation to the child. Against these arguments it can, however, be said that they would impose on the mother a legal relationship with her child which might be contrary to her wishes and which in the circumstances she should be entitled to repudiate. If the child was treated as illegitimate, it remained open to the mother to regularise the relationship, if she so wished, by adoption.

Voidable Marriages

Section 4(1) of the Law Reform (Miscellaneous Provisions) Act 1949 provides:

> "Where a decree of nullity is granted in respect of a voidable marriage, any child who would have been the legitimate child of the marriage if at the date of the decree it had been dissolved, instead of being annulled, shall be deemed to be their legitimate child."

In England marriage may be voidable on a number of grounds and it was primarily with a view to the English position that the legislation was passed. In Scotland the only ground on which marriage is voidable, as distinct from void, is where one of the parties is *incapax copulandi* at the time of the ceremony and

---

[12] Fraser, pp. 35–36.
[13] *Ibid.*
[14] at pp. 27–28.

that incapacity is permanent and incurable.[15] There will be children of such marriages only where there has been *fecundation ab extra* or artificial insemination with the semen of the husband. In the latter case the children would usually have been legitimate in any event on the ground that declarator of nullity is barred by homologation[16]; in some cases of *fecundation ab extra* that will also be so.[17] Even apart from homologation children of a voidable marriage were, however, probably legitimate at common law. They were undoubtedly legitimate as long as the marriage subsisted unchallenged and indefeasibly so once it was dissolved by death or divorce. To allow that status once acquired to be lost would be productive of anomaly. Moreover, such marriages are nearly always entered into in the *bona fide* belief of at least one spouse in their permanent validity (where that is not so there may be personal bar against seeking declarator of nullity), and children of such marriages might therefore have been treated as legitimate on the principle of putative marriage.

Legitimation by Subsequent Marriage at Common Law

Children procreated out of wedlock and therefore illegitimate were for long able to acquire legitimate status by the subsequent intermarriage of their parents. The time of the introduction of this doctrine into the law of Scotland cannot be traced with precision. It was repudiated in the *Regiam Majestatem*, although the authenticity of the passage has been doubted,[18] and it was also repudiated by Craig.[19] Clear indications of the reception of the doctrine in Scotland are, however, to be found by the early sixteenth century, and Anton has conjectured a much earlier date as likely.[20] In cases to which the Legitimation (Scotland) Act 1968[21] applied the common law rules were superseded. The earliest date with effect from which an illegitimate person could be legitimated under the Act was, however, June 8, 1968. The law in force before the commencement of the Act will remain applicable where any question turns on legitimation before June 8, 1968, and in particular to successions opening before that date.

Legitimation by subsequent marriage as an institution of the canon law is first encountered in rescripts of Pope Alexander III issued in 1171 and 1180 and recorded in the Decretals of Gratian.[22] There can be little doubt that canon law was the vehicle by which it found its way into the law of Scotland, but the civil law came to be regarded as its authentic source.[23] Nonetheless, canon law influences

---

[15] Clive, (3rd ed.) at pp. 100–105. And see Norrie, "Transsexuals, the Right to Marry and Voidable Marriages in Scots Law," 1990 S.L.T. (News) 353.

[16] *A.B.* v. *C.D.* 1961 S.C. 347.

[17] But see Clive, (3rd ed.) at p. 104.

[18] Reg. Maj., II, c, 50, 51; Fraser at p. 38.

[19] II, xvii, 8.

[20] Stair Society, vol. xx, pp. 117–118.

[21] See *post* at pp. 20–25.

[22] Decr., IV, xvii, 1 and 6.

[23] For the view that the doctrine was introduced from the Canon law, see *Kerr* v. *Martin* (1840) 2 D. 752, *per* Lord Fullerton at p. 794; Fraser, p. 38, n. 6; Hume's *Lectures* at p. 202. In *Rose* v. *Ross* (1826) 5 S. 605, however, Lord Gillies said at p. 648: "The Civil law forms in truth the law of Scotland on this point," and although dicta in *Kerr* v. *Martin* acknowledge the Canon law influence the decision is more readily reconciled with a Civil law source. For a summary history of the Roman law, see Voet, XXV, vii, 6; Fraser at p. 37; Hume, *ibid.*

cannot be discounted. The Roman law afforded the benefits of legitimation by subsequent marriage only to children conceived in concubinage but Scots law followed the canon law in extending the scope of the doctrine to children of casual unions. Canon law theorists had explained the doctrine by a fictional drawing-back of the sacramental effects of marriage to the date of conception or birth, as was indeed suggested by the wording of one of Alexander III's rescripts: *tanta est enin vis sacramenti ut qui antea sunt geniti post contractum matrimonium habeantur legitimi.*[24] The parents were deemed *fictione juris* to have been married at the earlier date. In *Rose* v. *Ross*[25] and the leading case of *Kerr* v. *Martin*[26] fictional views were, however, rejected and the doctrine was placed, consistently with what appears to have underlain its Roman law origins, on a basis of justice and expediency. In *Munro* v. *Munro*[27] it was said that legitimation

> "has been thought to be recommended by these considerations of equity and expediency, that it tends to encourage the conversion of what is at first irregular and injurious to society into the honourable relation of lawful matrimony, and that it prevents those unseemly disorders in families, which are produced where the elder born children of the same parents are left under the stain of bastardy, and the younger enjoy the status of legitimacy."

The fictional theory had been difficult to reconcile with the operation of legitimation where either of the parents had been married to a third party in the interval between the birth of the child and their subsequent marriage, and it had also excluded legitimation where a diriment impediment to the marriage of the parents existed at the time of conception or birth. On the latter point the law until 1968 was, consistently with the civil as well as the canon law, generally understood to be that children could not be legitimated if their parents were not free to marry at the time of the conception whether by reason of a subsisting marriage or otherwise. "Incestuous and adulterine bastards" could not therefore be legitimated, although the *ratio* of *Kerr* v. *Martin* is, as pointed out by some of the judges, difficult to reconcile with that view.[28] In that case the other consequence of the fiction—that an intervening marriage constituted a mid-impediment to legitimation—was rejected.

At one time a regular marriage was thought to be necessary in order to bring about legitimation but it was later settled that an irregular marriage was suffi-

---

[24] Decr., IV, xvii, 6.

[25] (1826) 5 S. 605, *per* Lord Gillies at p. 648.

[26] (1840) 2 D. 752.

[27] (1837) 16 S. 18 at p. 30, *per* Lords Glenlee, Medwyn, Moncrieff and Cockburn.

[28] At least until *Kerr* v. *Martin* this was undoubted law (Craig, II, xiii, 16; Bankton, I, v, 54; Erskine, I, vi, 52; Bell, *Prin.* 1627; *Irving* v. *Kerr* August 6, 1693) but it rests heavily on the fictional theory which was rejected in *Kerr* v. *Martin*. Lord Justice-Clerk Boyle, Lords Glenlee, Meadowbank, Medwyn and Moncrieff said (at p. 773): "If the retroacting presumption is to be cut down, it is not easy to see a solid reason, in legal principle, why children begotten in adultery should be incapable of legitimation, after the parents become free to marry. It is only because there cannot be a capacity in them to marry at the time of the connexion, in order to admit the presumption of a consent to marry at that time, that all the laws, civil, canon, French, and Scotch except that case." This was assumed to be the law by an Extra Division of the Inner House (consisting of Lords Allanbridge, Cullen and Brand) in *Wright's Trs.* v. *Callander*, 1992 S.L.T. 498.

cient.[29] It was undecided whether, at common law, putative or voidable marriage effected legitimation but with those possible exceptions, nothing short of a valid marriage would suffice.[30] The will of the parents, however expressed, if it fell short of actual marriage, could not result in legitimation and equally, if there was marriage, the contrary will of the parents could not prevent legitimation. Although legitimation put a child under potential alimentary obligations which he would not otherwise have had, could affect the intestate succession of his estate, and subjected the child under age to the full parental power of both parents, it did not (in contrast on this point with the Roman law) depend on the consent of the child even if above pupillarity.[31] A child could be legitimated after its death with the consequent accrual to its issue of rights of succession in and through their grandparent's estate, but in these circumstances legitimation did not affect rights which had vested or impose liabilities which did not exist at the time of the child's death.[32] Subject to such vested rights, legitimation had the effect that the child was in law the legitimate child of the parents with all the rights and obligations consequent thereon and was so in equality with all other lawful children of its parents although, where there had been an intervening marriage, it would, in any question dependent on primogeniture or seniority, be postponed to the children of the intervening marriage.[33] Legitimation took place immediately on marriage without the necessity of declarator[34] and the child was deemed to have been legitimate from birth.[35]

Statutory Legitimation by Subsequent Marriage

Legitimation by the subsequent marriage of the parents was put on to a statutory basis by the Legitimation (Scotland) Act 1968, s. 1 of which provided that where the parents of an illegitimate person married each other after the com-

---

[29] *Walker* v. *McAdam* (1807) Mor. App. 1, Proof No. 4, affd. 1 Dow 148.

[30] *Cf.* Legitimation (Scotland) Act 1968, s. 8(1).

[31] *Hume and Anor.* v. *Macfarlane* 1908 16 S.L.T. 123. Fraser (3rd ed at p. 44) conjectures that the ceremony of the caircloth by which children born before the marriage were placed under the *nuptial pallium* extended over both parents at the time of the marriage ceremony may originally have been intended as a sign of the children's consent to legitimation. It is, however, perhaps better explained as an acknowledgment by the husband of his paternity of the children so as to effect their legitimation. Anton suggests (Stair Society Vol. XX, p. 117) that the Canon law may have done no more than give recognition and approval to an ancient customary rule embodied in the caircloth ceremony.

[32] *Kerr* v. *Martin*, *per* Lord Justice-Clerk Boyle, Lords Glenlee, Meadowbank, Medwyn and Moncreiff at p. 771, and *per* Lord Fullerton at p. 796; *Rose* v. *Ross* (1827) 5 S. 605, *per* Lord Meadowbank at p. 634; Bankton, I, v, 58; Bell, *Prin.*, 1627; More's *Notes on Stair*, XXXIII; Voet XXV, vi, 7. More holds that such posthumous legitimation is effective for all purposes of succession. It will not, however, affect vested rights (*McNeill* v. *McGregor* (1901) 4 F.123, *per* Lord Moncreiff at pp. 128–129). Where, therefore, an illegitimate child was killed through the fault of another, his parents could not, by marrying thereafter, qualify a title to sue for solatium (*McNeill* v. *McGregor*).

[33] Opinions in *Kerr* v. *Martin*; Craig, II, xviii, 12; Bankton III, iii, 97; Erskine, I, vi, 52; Bell, *Prin.* 1627. For a contrary view, see Voet, XXV, vii, 11.

[34] *Beddie* v. *Middleton* (1903) 10 S.L.T. 513.

[35] This follows from the fictional theory and survives the rejection of that theory in *Kerr* v. *Martin* where it underlies the opinions of the majority of the judges no less than of the minority. Were that not so the dicta, albeit *obiter*, that children of an intervening marriage were not to be prejudiced would be redundant. The authorities on posthumous legitimation cannot satisfactorily be reconciled with any view other than that legitimation applies retroactively so as to confer legitimate status from birth: Fraser at p. 46.

mencement of the Act (June 8, 1968) the marriage rendered that person legitimate from the date of the marriage, so long as, at that date, (i) the father was
domiciled in Scotland and (ii) the child was living. The marriage could be regular or irregular,[36] and (resolving one of the undecided matters at common law)
included putative marriages and voidable marriages.[37] Although the common
law was not expressly abrogated, the effect of the Act was to replace the common law by a statutory code applicable to all cases referable to the law in force
at or after the commencement of the Act. Rights which had vested or which are
ascertainable by reference to the law in force before then were not affected.

In no respect, therefore, was the Act truly retrospective but, in cases referable
to the law in force since the commencement of the Act, legitimising effect was
given from June 8, 1968 to marriages contracted before that date: (1) where the
child had died before the marriage of its parents,[38] and (2) where the marriage
did not at common law have the effect of making the child legitimate because of
the existence of an impediment at the time of conception.[39] Although in these
cases the Act applied to marriages before the commencement of the Act, rights
accrued under the Act with effect only from the date of marriage or the date of
commencement, whichever was the later.[40] The broad result is that where, for
the assertion of any right or obligation, it was sufficient that legitimation should
have been effected on or after June 8, 1968, a child born illegitimate would be
regarded as having been legitimated by the subsequent marriage of his parents
no matter when the marriage took place and irrespective of the existence at any
time of an impediment to intermarriage and of whether or not he was alive at the
time of the marriage. Legitimation cannot be effected at common law from June
8, 1968 but rights may, of course, continue to be enjoyed and to accrue as a result of earlier legitimations at common law and, in relation to intestacies arising
or deeds becoming operative before June 8, 1968, with the common law
effects.[41]

Effects of the Act

The central provisions of the Act are contained in sections 1, 3 and 4. Section 1
covers all legitimations effected by marriages on or after June 8, 1968 other
than posthumous legitimations. It enacts that where the marriage is after the
commencement of the Act and the child was living at the date of the marriage,
the marriage, with effect from that date, rendered the child legitimate and conferred on him the rights and imposed on him the obligations of a legitimate person. Section 3 caters for and removes any doubts which at common law may
have surrounded the case of an illegitimate person who died before the marriage
of the parents.[42] In such a case the provisions of the Act apply for the purpose of

---

[36] In which case the date of the marriage for the purposes of the Act, as for other purposes, was the
date specified in the decree of declarator or otherwise ascertained by the court.

[37] Legitimation (Scotland) Act 1968, s. 8(1).

[38] *Ibid.*, s. 3. This did no more than remove such doubts as there may have been at common law.

[39] *Ibid.* s. 4.

[40] *Ibid.*, ss. 1, 3 and 4.

[41] ss. 3 and 4 are not free from ambiguity on this point but they do not derogate from the general presumption that a statute is not retrospective (*Gardner* v. *Lucas* (1878) 5 R.(H.L.) 105; *Henshall* v.
Porter [1923] 2 K.B. 193).

[42] These doubts were in fact insubstantial: see *ante* at p. 20.

determining the rights and obligations of any person living at or after the date of the marriage, if that was on or after June 8, 1968, as if the illegitimate person had been legitimated with effect from the date of the marriage. If the marriage was before the commencement of the Act the provisions apply for the purpose of determining the rights and obligations of any person living at or after June 8, 1968 as if that was the effective date of legitimation. The provisions apply irrespective of whether the death of the illegitimate person, or the marriage of the parents, or both, preceded the commencement of the Act, but they do not, of course, apply to successions opening or deeds becoming operative before that date. They do not in any event affect any right which has indefeasibly vested before legitimation, or confer any status or rights or impose any obligation in respect of any time previous thereto.

The scope of rights and obligations arising out of legitimation are spelled out in some detail. Legitimation enures, as at common law, to the benefit not only of the person legitimated but to claimants whose rights depend on his legitimacy.[43] Rules are enacted for some matters which are in any event covered by the provisions of the Act on the effective date of legitimation and by the presumption against retrospection respectively. This duplication should not, however, be read as detracting either from the generality of these provisions or from the application of the presumption. Some of the specific rules can by their nature be applied only to legitimations under the Act; others apply to all legitimations provided the right or obligation at issue was one to which the Act applies.

It is specifically provided that legitimation shall not confer any status or right, or impose any obligation, on any person in respect of any time previous to the legitimation[44] and that no one shall be entitled, by virtue of his own legitimation or the legitimation of any other person, to any right in the intestate estate or legitim out of the estate of any person dying after the commencement of the Act and before the date of the legitimation.[45] Legitimation does not affect any right under a deed coming into operation after the commencement of the Act if the right has become indefeasibly vested in someone other than the person legitimated before the date of legitimation.[46] Subject to that, however, a legitimated person is entitled to any right under a deed coming into operation after the commencement of the Act, being a right his entitlement to which depends on his legitimacy, and a person other than the legitimated person is entitled to any right under such a deed, being a right his entitlement to which depends on the legitimacy of the legitimated person.[47] This provision is not restricted to deeds coming into operation after legitimation and accordingly a legitimated person can acquire rights under deeds which came into operation before legitimation. The right itself must, however, have been one that vested on or subsequent to legitimation as to hold otherwise would be to undermine the fundamental principle of the Act that legitimation is effective only from the date on which it takes place (*i.e.* the date of marriage). Any reference in any deed coming into opera-

---

[43] Legitimation (Scotland) Act 1968, s. 2(7).
[44] *Ibid.*, s. 2(1).
[45] *Ibid.*, s. 2(2).
[46] *Ibid.*, s. 2(3).
[47] *Ibid.*, s. 2(4).

tion after the commencement of the Act to a child, or to issue, of a marriage is to be construed as including a reference to any child legitimated by that marriage.[48] Where any such reference is to issue, it is to be construed as including a reference to the issue, being legitimated persons, of any child of that marriage (including such issue of any child legitimated by the marriage).[49] The statutory wording "issue, being legitimated persons" might give rise to the inference that a reference to issue is not to include issue, being persons born legitimate, of any child legitimated by the marriage, but that anomalous result is avoided by ordinary rules of construction on the meaning of issue. It is a common feature of these provisions on the interpretation of references to children and issue that they should be construed along with s. 4(2) and so, provided there is no prejudice to rights which have indefeasibly vested, they apply even if the deed came into operation before legitimation. Special provision is made for the case of rights or obligations, whether created by operation of law or by any deed coming into operation after the commencement of the Act, which are conferred or imposed by reference to the relative seniority of the members of a class consisting of legitimate persons only. In such a case, a legitimated person ranks as if he had been born on the date of his legitimation except that where two or more members of the class are legitimated persons they rank *inter se* in accordance with their respective times of birth.[50] This provision applies only to classes consisting of legitimate persons only. Where a class is so defined as to include illegitimate persons, legitimated persons rank, as do others, according to time of birth. All provisions of section 2, which deal with the scope of rights and obligations arising on legitimation, are so expressed as to apply only to legitimations by or under the Act or to successions opening or deeds coming into operation after the commencement of the Act and leave the effects of legitimation at common law unaltered in other cases.[51] There is also separate provision by which the common law rules are specifically preserved in relation to deeds which came into operation before the commencement of the Act.[52] The operation of any deed is affected by the Act only in so far as on the construction of the deed no contrary intention appears.[53] Overall, it can be said that despite the change from birth to marriage as the effective date of legitimation, the effects of legitimation under the Act are not, when regard is had to the provisions of the common law regarding vested rights and seniority, materially different from the effects at common law insofar as these were settled.

Statutory Legitimation and Adoption Orders

In view of the rule, as commonly understood, that the existence at the time of conception of a diriment impediment to the intermarriage of the parents barred legitimation at common law, it frequently happened after adoption was intro-

---

[48] *Ibid.*, s. 2(5)(*a*).

[49] *Ibid.*, s. 2(5)(*b*).

[50] *Ibid.*, s. 2(6). The use of the word "time" rather than "date" indicates the application of the rule to cases where more than one child, as in the case of twins, are born on the same day.

[51] s. 2(1) when read along with s. 2(8) and the references to the commencement of the Act in s. 2(2)–(7).

[52] *Ibid.*, s. 7(3).

[53] *Ibid.*, s. 7(1).

duced into the law of Scotland[54] that a child conceived at a time when his parents could not intermarry was adopted by his parents if they married after the removal of the impediment. This conferred parental rights and obligations on both parents and, since 1975,[55] legitimate status on the child. Since the coming into force of the Legitimation (Scotland) Act 1968, such children would automatically be legitimated by the intermarriage of their parents, with effect from the commencement of the Act or the date of the marriage, whichever was later. As the consequences of legitimation were, until recently, rather more far-reaching than those of adoption, even when adoption was by both parents, legitimation would, with effect from the relevant date, effectively supersede the adoption order. The adoption order remained, however, technically in force and accordingly provision was made in these circumstances for revocation of an adoption order by the court which made it.[56] An application could be made by any of the parties concerned and so by the child as well as by the parents. Similar provisions had previously been made by the Adoption Act 1958[57] for adoptions by one parent. Revocation does not affect the operation of the provisions of the Succession (Scotland) Act 1964 governing succession by and to adopted children in relation to any intestacy which occurred or any deed which became operative before revocation.[58] The importance of this provision is in excluding any retroactive operation of the revocation so as to affect rights which have arisen between the date of the adoption order and the date of legitimation. These results are extended to revocations under the Adoption (Scotland) Act 1978 as well as to those under the Legitimation Act itself.[59]

Titles, Honours and Dignities

Where a question of succession to or devolution of any title, honour, or dignity arises after the commencement of the Legitimation (Scotland) Act 1968, the Act has effect in relation to the right in question as if it were a right under, and as if the title, honour or dignity devolved in accordance with, a deed coming into operation after the commencement of the Act.[60] Were it not for that provision, persons who could not have been legitimated at common law but who were legitimated under the Act would have been cut off from succession to titles, honours, or dignities created by letters patent or other deeds before the commencement of the Act. This is an exception to the general principle that such succession is governed by the common law.

Children Conceived Before but Born After the Marriage

It is clear from the fact that legitimation is effective from the date of the marriage[61] and from the reference in sections 1 and 4 to persons living at the date of the marriage that the Act cannot readily be construed so as to make legitimate

---

[54] Adoption of Children (Scotland) Act 1930.
[55] Children Act 1975, Sched. 2 para. 3.
[56] Legitimation (Scotland) Act 1968, s. 6(1).
[57] Adoption Act 1958, s. 26.
[58] Legitimation (Scotland) Act 1968, s. 6(2).
[59] *Ibid.*, s. 6(3).
[60] *Ibid.*, s. 8(4).
[61] *Ibid.*, s. 1.

children conceived before but born after the marriage of their parents. The common law rules on legitimation were in general ousted by section 1 so far as marriages after the commencement of the Act are concerned. That section applies, however, only where the person to be legitimated was living at the date of the marriage. It accordingly has no application to the case of children conceived before but born after the marriage, and in such cases the common law doctrine of legitimation or, perhaps better, principles akin to that doctrine still apply.[62] Such children are legitimate from the date of their birth, at any rate where no impediment existed to the intermarriage of their parents at the time of conception, and it is submitted that that will be so even if the death of the father or, if such a case can be conjectured, the divorce of the parents had intervened between marriage and birth.[63] In *Kerr* v. *Martin*[64] a strong body of judicial opinion thought it inconsistent with the eventual *ratio* of that case that an impediment to the intermarriage of parents at the time of conception should constitute a barrier to legitimation by subsequent marriage. The considerations of expediency which pointed to the dispensing of this barrier[65] in cases of the legitimation of children born before marriage had added force in relation to the legitimacy of children conceived before but born after the marriage. After the passing of the Legitimation (Scotland) Act 1968 these considerations are compelling and probably result in such children being regarded as legitimate even if there was a barrier to the intermarriage of their parents at the time of conception.

Other Forms of Legitimation

In the developed Roman law legitimation could be effected *per rescriptum principis*.[66] This form of legitimation is usually ascribed to two novels of Justinian,[67] but exceptional instances are to be found earlier. In the medieval papacy letters of legitimation on the Roman imperial model were granted by the popes but were rare in Scotland. It is not clear that they were ever accepted as having civil effect, although it is likely that the ecclesiastical courts recognised them in questions of succession to moveables with which they were concerned. These papal letters of legitimation are to be distinguished from dispensations *de defectu natali* which were common but did no more than exempt from certain ecclesiastical disabilities.[68] Scots law took over the Roman practice although in a highly modified form. The Roman imperial rescript conferred full legitimation and accordingly it was not granted where the parent of the illegitimate child had legitimate issue, for to do so would have been to prejudice their rights. Royal letters of legitimation in Scotland had, however, only a limited effect. They conferred on the illegitimate person no rights of succession and were no more than a waiver of the rights of the Crown. They gave, therefore, capacity to test to an illegitimate person who, until 1836, could not make a will unless he had legitimate issue of his own and they might also, but only if they contained a special

---

[62] See *ante* at p. 10.
[63] *Ibid.*
[64] (1840) 2, D. 752 at p. 773.
[65] See *ante* at p. 19, note 28.
[66] Fraser (3rd ed.) at p. 51.
[67] Nov. 74, c. 1 and 2; 89, c. 9.
[68] Anton, Stair Society, Vol. xx at p. 118.

clause to that effect, create rights of intestate succession in the illegitimate's estate.[69] Legitimation *per rescriptum principis* has been regarded as obsolete since illegitimate persons acquired full capacity to test. Although collaterals and ascendants of an illegitimate person, other than his parents, had no rights *ab intestato* in his estate until 1986,[70] the rescript did not survive as a means of creating rights in intestacy.

Declarator of Legitimacy and Illegitimacy

Jurisdiction and Procedure

A declarator may be raised to determine the legitimacy or illegitimacy of any person whose status is in dispute. Jurisdiction is now regulated by statute and subsists if the child was born within the territorial jurisdiction of the court or the alleged or presumed parent or the child (a) is domiciled there when the action is brought or (b) was habitually resident there for not less than one year immediately preceding the bringing of the action or (c) died before the bringing of the action and was domiciled there at the date of death or had been habitually resident there for not less than one year immediately preceding that date.[71]

Actions of declarator of legitimacy or illegitimacy were formerly competent only in the Court of Session. They are consistorial actions which at common law fell within the jurisdiction of the commissaries to the exclusion both of the Court of Session and the sheriff court, except that the former might review the commissaries' decisions by way of advocation, and which were transferred to the exclusive jurisdiction of the Court of Session when the consistorial jurisdiction of the commissaries was abolished by the Court of Session Act 1830.[72] Actions, the direct or main object of which was to determine the personal status of individuals, were expressly excluded from the general jurisdiction in declarators given to the sheriff court by the Sheriff Courts (Scotland) Act 1907.[73] By the Law Reform (Parent and Child) Scotland Act 1986, jurisdiction in declarators of legitimacy, legitimation and illegitimacy is, however, given to the sheriff court as well as the Court of Session.[74]

An action of declarator without any further conclusion is competent.[75] A declaratory conclusion may, however, be combined with other conclusions and may, in particular, be a preliminary to petitory conclusions.[76] Questions of status, including legitimacy and illegitimacy, may, without declarator, be determined where they arise incidentally to the enforcement of other rights.[77] In that

---

[69] Erskine, III, x, 7; Stair, III, iii, 45; Hume's *Lectures* I, 201–202; Fraser at pp. 51–52.

[70] Law Reform (Parent and Child) (Scotland) Act 1986.

[71] *Ibid.*, s. 7(2).

[72] s. 33.

[73] s. 5(1).

[74] s. 7(2).

[75] Walker, *Civil Remedies*, p. 116; *Magistrates of Ayr* v. *Lord Advocate*, 1950 S.C. 102; *McLay* v. *Farrell*, 1950 S.C. 149; *Fife County Council* v. *Lord Advocate*, 1950 S.C. 314.

[76] Walker, *Civil Remedies*, p. 114.

[77] *McDonald* v. *Mackenzie* (1891) 18 R. 502; *Mackie* v. *Lyon* (1943) 59 Sh.Ct.Rep. 130 & 133; *Turnbull* v. *Wilsons & Clyde Coal Co.*, 1935 S.C. 580; In *Hamilton's Trs.* v. *Wright and Sharp* (1880) 7 R. 460 the competency of raising the action in the sheriff court was affirmed on the view that it might be unnecessary to determine the question of status but when, after having been remitted to the sheriff court, the case again came before the Court of Session the sheriff's interlocutor

event, jurisdiction is determined by the principal subject-matter and not by the statutory rules just noted. Judgment in such an action will, however, be *res judicata* only between the parties and to the extent necessary for determination of the dispute between them.[78] A declarator will be necessary where it is desired to obtain a judgment *in rem* on the question of status and, generally, where status is a major issue in controversy. Whether that declarator should be sought by means of combining a declaratory conclusion with others or by means of a separate action is dependent on the particular circumstances but, whichever course is followed, the statutory requirements for jurisdiction must be satisfied. A separate action will be appropriate if defenders are to be called to the declarator who would not otherwise be convened to the process or if the question of status would be best disposed of independently of the other issues.[79] A pending action may be sisted to enable a separate declarator to be raised.

Conclusions for declarator of legitimacy or illegitimacy, where it is expedient to do so, may be combined with conclusions for declarator of marriage or of divorce as the case may be.[80] A conclusion for putting to silence, normally associated with a declarator of freedom from marriage, is competent against any false claims to personal status and so may be combined with, and follow on, a declarator of illegitimacy.[81] It is available against a parent who makes a false claim to the legitimate relationship as well as against the child.[82] As declarators of marriage and actions of putting to silence remain within the exclusive jurisdiction of the Court of Session, they can, of course, be combined with declarators of legitimacy and illegitimacy only in that court.

Title to Sue

Any person who has a legally enforceable interest which turns on a question of legitimacy has a title to sue a declarator.[83] That parents and the child have such an interest is self-evident. They have a clear title to sue. A declarator must have at least the possibility of present legal consequences and it will not be granted where the sole interest is in some future or contingent right.[84] Accord-

---

was recalled and the sheriff-substitute's finding on the question of status restored without any discussion of competency. The jurisdiction of the sheriff court to entertain questions of status incidentally to the enforcement of other rights exists at common law independently of s. 5(1) of the Sheriff Courts (Scotland) Act 1907 which is concerned solely with actions of declarator and is to broadly the same effect in relation to them as is the common law rule in relation to other actions. The doctrine has been applied in actions of affiliation and aliment (*Fleming* v. *Farmer* (1922) Sh.Ct.Rep. 73) For Court of Session practice see *Swinton* v. *Swinton* (1862) 24 D. 833.

[78] *Turnbull* v. *Wilsons and Clyde Coal Co., supra.*

[79] *Rackstraw* v. *Douglas*, 1919 S.C. 354.

[80] *X.* v. *Y.* 1921 1 S.L.T. 79; *Brown* v. *Brown*, 1972 S.L.T. 143; see also *Jamieson* v. *Jamieson*, 1969 S.L.T. (Notes) 11.

[81] *Imre* v. *Mitchell*, 1958 S.C. 439.

[82] *Ibid.*

[83] *Shedden* v. *Patrick* (1849) 11 D. 1333; (1853) 15 D. 379; *Benson* v. *Benson* (1854) 16 D. 555; *Morley* v. *Jackson*, (1888) 16R. 78; *Grant* v. *Countess of Seafield*, 1926 S.C. 274; *Bosville* v. *Lord Macdonald*, 1910 S.C. 597.

[84] Walker, *Civil Remedies*, pp. 113–114. The rule admits substantial exceptions (see *Mackay's Manual*, p. 375) and where there is a proper contradictor, a future, or even a contingent legal right can be made the subject of declarator (*Fleming* v. *McLagan* (1876) 6 R. 588, *per* Lord Young at 598). It is thought, however, that the scope afforded by such exceptions cannot extend to the raising of actions by parties whose sole interest is one which may emerge only on the death of a party having a present and primary interest.

ingly, while the parents and child are all alive, it will be rarely, if ever, that others have a title to sue a declarator of legitimacy. On the death of any of them, an interest and consequent title to sue may, however, emerge in others. It was at one time thought that only the Crown or persons whose right was derived from the Crown had a title to sue a declarator of bastardy,[85] probably because the possibility of other interests had not been considered, but such actions have been entertained, not only at the instance of a parent, but of parties with a remoter interest unconnected with the Crown,[86] and it may now be taken as settled that title to sue for declarator of a person's illegitimacy depends on the same principles as those applicable to declarators of legitimacy.

For the purposes of declarator, legitimation is but a means by which legitimacy may be achieved and there is properly no separate species of declarator of legitimation. Title to sue is accordingly determined as in other cases of legitimacy. There is, moreover, no warrant for the specialty which has been suggested that legitimation cannot be the subject-matter of declarator after the death of the child[87] and there is abundant authority to the contrary.[88] Even the more limited proposition, that legitimation cannot be founded on as the basis of legitimacy if both the declarator and the marriage follow the death of the child, cannot be maintained in cases to which the Legitimation (Scotland) Act 1968 applies[89] and is probably, as a general proposition, also unsound at common law.[90] *McNeill* v. *McGregor,*[91] cited in support of this view, is directed solely to the effect of legitimation on the vested interests of third parties and no doubt a declarator cannot be entertained at the instance of parties whose sole interest in establishing legitimation is to trench on such rights.

International Aspects of Legitimacy and Legitimation

Choice of Law: General

In the classic formulation of Lord Westbury in *Udny* v. *Udny*

> "Civil status is governed universally by one specific principle. Domicil or the place of settled residence of an individual is the criterion established by law for the purpose of determining the civil condition of the person, for it is on this basis that the personal rights of the parties—that is, the law which determines his majority or his minority, marriage, succession, testacy or intestacy—must depend."[92]

The only exception which need be noted to that general proposition is that of succession to immoveables in which the law of the domicile yields to the *lex*

---

[85] Stair IV, xii, 1; IV, xii, 7 & 8.
[86] *Imre* v. *Mitchell*, 1958 S.C. 439; *Smith* v. *Dick* (1869) 8 M. 31.
[87] Walker, *Civil Remedies*, p. 120.
[88] *e.g., Rose* v. *Ross, Munro* v. *Munro, Kerr* v. *Martin, Bosville* v. *Lord Macdonald, cit. supra.*
[89] s. 3. See *ante* p. 21.
[90] See *ante* p. 21 and footnote 87.
[91] (1901) 4 F. 123.
[92] (1869) 7 M. (H.L.) 89 at 99.

situs.[93] Questions of legitimacy or illegitimacy are, therefore, determined by the law of the domicile of the person whose status is in issue.

Lord Westbury's speech in *Udny* v. *Udny*, a case of legitimation, echoes Lord Wensleydale's in the earlier legitimacy case of *Fenton* v. *Livingston*:

> "The law of the domicile regulates also the personal qualities which take effect from birth, such as legitimacy or illegitimacy, or absolutely as to the succession of personal property, but subject to a qualification as to realty to be afterwards explained, and the qualities which arise after birth, such as majority and minority. The laws of the State affecting the personal status of its subjects travel with them wherever they go, and attach to them in whatever country they are resident."[94]

Although the principle that choice of law for determining questions of legitimacy, including legitimation, should follow the domicile of the child is clear, the application of that principle has been obscured and to some extent frustrated by the apparent *circulus inextricabilis* involved in ascertaining the domicile of a child before his status has been established. That problem was circumvented in a line of English authority, now somewhat discredited and including the much criticised House of Lords case of *Shaw* v. *Gould*,[95] by the expedient of resolving the question of legitimacy into one of whether or not the child's parents had been validly married. The choice of law rules were, therefore, those applicable to validity of marriage. That device had the advantage of simplicity but the disadvantage that it was applicable only to cases of legitimacy at birth, and not to legitimation, and accordingly required that legitimacy at birth and legitimation be treated on distinct rather than on consonant principles. Whatever its merits or demerits it is in any event clear that it is not part of the law of Scotland. It allows no place for putative marriage. It has, moreover, been suggested that it relies on notions of the indelibility of bastardy which underlay English judicial thinking on the international private law of legitimacy, at least until the Legitimacy Act 1926, and which have no counterpart in Scots law and are irreconcilable with the longstanding institution of legitimation.[96] In this more than most areas of international private law, English authority is an unsure guide.

The alternative solution to the *circulus inextricabilis*, favoured by the leading Scottish cases[97] and at least one English case of legitimacy[98] at birth and by the cases in both jurisdictions on legitimation,[99] is to substitute the domicile of the father for the domicile of the child. The substitution is usually explained on the

---

[93] See *post* p. 125.

[94] (1859) 3 Macq. 497 at 547–548.

[95] (1868) L.R. 3 H.L. 55; see Cheshire, *Private International Law*, 9th ed., pp. 442–448; Graveson, *Private International Law*, 7th ed., pp. 355 & 367.

[96] Anton and Beaumont, 2nd ed. at pp. 486–487.

[97] *Fenton* v. *Livingstone, cit. supra; Beattie* v. *Beattie* (1866) 5 M. 181; *sed contra, Smijth* v. *Smijth*, 1918 1 S.L.T. 156.

[98] *Re Bischoffsheim* [1948] Ch. 79.

[99] *e.g. Bowes* v. *Bowes* (1871) 6 Paton 645; *Rose* v. *Ross* 4 W. & S. 289; *Munro* v. *Munro* (1840) 1 Rob. 492; *Countess of Dalhousie* v. *McDouall* (1840) 1 Rob. 475; *McDouall* v. *Adair* (1852) 14 D. 525; *Maitland* v. *Maitland* (1885) 12 R. 899; *Re Goodman's Trusts* (1881) 17 Ch.D. 266; *Re Andros* (1883) 24 Ch.D. 667; *Re Grove* (1887) 40 Ch.D. 216; *Re Grey's Trusts* [1892] 3 Ch. 88.

basis of a presumption of legitimacy[1] although Anton has attempted both to modify the doctrine in a way which would admit of reference to the domicile of the mother and to explain it on different grounds.[2]

Although it is evident that reference to the father's domicile is in substitution for and is a means of overcoming the difficulties of ascertaining the child's domicile, most judicial *dicta* and textbook discussion treat legitimacy as determinable by the father's domicile as if that were an independent criterion. That may be defended in cases of legitimacy at birth, other than cases of posthumous children, since the domicile of the father will be identical with the domicile of the child at that time on the assumption that the child is legitimate. That would also be true of legitimations of the type with which all the Scottish and most of the English authorities are concerned (*e.g.* Scottish common law legitimations) by which the effect of legitimation is drawn back to the birth of the child so as to make the child legitimate from birth. Where, however, the question is of domicile at the time of the marriage, the child's domicile cannot be assumed to be the same as the father's as by then the child may have acquired a separate domicile of choice or a different dependent domicile. It is, however, clear both on principle and from the *dicta* of Lord Wensleydale and Lord Westbury cited above, that it is the child's domicile which is the ultimate governing factor. The father's domicile is but a route to a goal which might otherwise be unattainable. It is the child's status and not the father's which is in issue. Accordingly, the father's domicile should not be substituted for the child's where the child's domicile can be ascertained without deciding the question of legitimacy.

Where the contention is that a child has been legitimated under rules which provide for legitimation to be effective only from the date of the marriage, as is now the case under statute both in Scotland and England,[3] there is no doubt as to the child's domicile of origin. It is the domicile of the mother at the time of the child's birth. The domicile of the child at the time of its parents' marriage is also ascertainable. It is the domicile of origin or a subsequent domicile of dependence or a domicile of choice which the child has by then acquired. It is submitted that in such cases the proper reference is to the child's domicile and not to the father's.

For the purposes of the Legitimation (Scotland) Act 1968 a child is, however, legitimated if its father was domiciled in Scotland at the date of the marriage,[4] but no corresponding rule is laid down for the recognition of foreign legitimations.[5] It is submitted that the Act applies only to the legitimation of persons domiciled in Scotland.

Choice of Law—Legitimacy at Birth

Even where the domicile of the child has to be ascertained at birth, it is doubtful if the automatic invocation of the father's domicile is justified. Where, by the

---

[1] Cheshire (4th ed.), p. 385.
[2] Anton (1st ed.), p. 346. The discussion in the second edition is much abbreviated.
[3] Legitimation (Scotland) Act 1968, ss. 1, 3 and 4; Legitimacy Acts 1926 and 1959.
[4] s. 1.
[5] See footnote 15, *infra*.

law of the father's domicile the child would be legitimate, but illegitimate by the law of his mother's domicile, the choice of either can be defended as resulting in an internally coherent solution. In that situation: "The reasonable solution is to presume his (the child's) legitimacy and to regard him as domiciled, at least temporarily, with his father."[6] Faced with an otherwise irreconcilable dilemma, a preference is exercised in favour of the solution that will result in the child's legitimacy. By parity of reasoning, however, in cases where the law of the father's domicile points to illegitimacy and that of the mother's domicile to legitimacy, the invocation of the father's domicile can be justified only on the basis of a preference for illegitimacy. Moreover, in that situation, whichever choice is made, the resultant solution lacks internal coherence. If the law of the father's domicile is applied, the child is held illegitimate by the application of a law which is relevant to his status only if he is legitimate. Equally, if the law of the mother's domicile is applied, legitimacy is affirmed by the application of a law which is irrelevant unless the child is illegitimate. Logic has broken down and the application of neither system of law can be defended on logical grounds. The child must, however, have a domicile and that domicile must, in its origin, be the domicile of one or the other of its parents. It is difficult to see how in that situation the claims of the law of the father's domicile can be put higher than the mother's and, therefore, the universal application of the law of the father's domicile can scarcely be defended. Cheshire, indeed, seems to have recognised that: "If legitimacy is denied to him by the *lex domicilii* of the father, he would then follow the mother into whatever domicile she may have."[7] The consequence of the child's following the mother into her domicile is, however, in the type of case under consideration, that the child will be held to be legitimate. If, however, that is the result reached by applying the law of the father's domicile and then discarding it when it points to illegitimacy, the same result can be achieved by saying quite simply that as between the law of the father's domicile and the mother's there is a preference for the law which favours legitimacy. That simple view is the ultimate justification for applying the law of the father's domicile and then discarding it if it points to illegitimacy and it is preferable to the anomalies inherent in applying the law of the father's domicile regardless of the result produced. It is a view which is consistent with Scottish authority. In *Smijth* v. *Smijth*[8] Lord Anderson rejected an argument that the law of the father's domicile (the law of England under which, at that time, the children would have been illegitimate) should be applied and applied instead the law of Scotland which he took to be the law of the domicile of the children derived from their mother. Indeed, he regarded that as undoubted and in one passage it seems that the only question which troubled him was the effect of a subsequent change in domicile. The reasoning is not, however, altogether clear. Much stress is placed on considerations of equity and humanity.

"If this law is not applicable, then the pursuer will never succeed in having the stigma of illegitimacy removed, as I assume that the law of

---

[6] Cheshire (4th ed.) *ibid.*.
[7] *Ibid.*
[8] 1918 1 S.L.T. 156.

England will not give them the remedy which they seek. When it is kept in mind that the pursuer's claim, if conceded, will not have any patrimonial consequences, that the remedy sought flows from considerations of 'equity and humanity', and that no other law, save that of this country, can be successfully invoked, a strong case for the application of the Law of Scotland is made out.

"I am unable to appreciate in what respect the father's domicile affects the present application. Neither his former status nor his succession will be affected by decree being granted as craved by the pursuer. Sir William (the father) was the party who was in bad faith in connection with the pu-tative marriage. Why should the domicile of the guilty party be regulative of the matter?"[9]

Consistently with that equitable approach, Lord Anderson acknowledges that it may be that no general rule can be laid down and that the law which is applic-able may depend on the facts of the particular case. It is submitted, however, that although equitable exceptions may be allowed in special circumstances, it is unsatisfactory that there should be no general rule. Such a general rule can be found, consistently with the decision in *Smijth* v. *Smijth* and with the equitable objects Lord Anderson had in mind, in a preference, as between the law of the father's domicile and of the mother's, for the law pointing to legitimacy (*i.e.* the child will be legitimate if that would be the result under either of the two poten-tially applicable legal systems).

Choice of Law—Legitimation

In cases of legitimation by subsequent marriage there may be a question of validity of marriage to be determined by the law appropriate to such questions.[10] Given a valid marriage, the question arises as to which system of law deter-mines whether or not the marriage has had legitimising effect. All the au-thorities affirm that the relevant law is the law of the father's domicile.[11] These authorities are, however, entirely concerned with common law legitimations. In such legitimations which are retroactive to the time of birth, the father's domi-cile at the time of marriage would, if legitimation were to be affirmed, necessar-ily be identical with the child's[12] except in the case, which appears not to have arisen for consideration, of the child's having acquired a separate domicile of choice before its parents' marriage. It can scarcely be maintained that where the child has acquired a domicile of choice at the time of the marriage in a country which does not recognise legitimation by subsequent marriage, he is nonethe-less to be regarded as legitimate because he would be so regarded by the law of his father's domicile at that time. As Lord Armadale said in *Shedden* v. *Patrick*:

---

[9] *Ibid.*

[10] *Starkowski* v. *Attorney-General* [1952] P. 135.

[11] See footnote 99, *supra*.

[12] This is a necessary and logical result of the retroactive principle and with an exception for the val-idity of legal acts which have intervened there is no reason to deny it effect. See *contra*, Anton, p. 168.

"The whole question is, whether he be legitimate or not. The question of his status must be resolved by the law of his own country."[13]

The question left open is whether in such a case it is necessary that it should accord with the law of both the father's and the child's domicile. References to the power or capacity or will of the father to legitimate his children are inept because, according at least to Scottish notions, legitimation does not depend on the father's will, other than his consent to marriage, but is a result that flows *ipso jure* from marriage. It is submitted that in this, as in other questions of status, the law of the domicile of the person whose status is in issue is the sole and sufficient criterion. The point, as has been noted above, may be more acute in statutory legitimations which have no retroactive effect and in which the child's domicile throughout may well be different from the father's. The Legitimation (Scotland) Act 1968 does not, as already submitted, apply to the legitimation of persons not domiciled in Scotland. In the case of a person domiciled in Scotland it is, however, also necessary for legitimations under the Act that the father should have been domiciled in Scotland at the date of the marriage.[14] As already noted, no corresponding rule is laid down for the recognition of foreign legitimations.[15]

In England it has been laid down, although not without dissent, that legitimation can be affirmed only if it accords with the law of the domicile both at the time of the child's birth and at the time of the marriage. That view, however, although it has been expressed subsequent to the Legitimacy Act 1926 as well as before it, is much influenced by notions of the indelibility of bastardy which are rejected in Scotland. Although it had not been a matter of decision, Scottish judicial opinion even before the Legitimation (Scotland) Act 1968 had, with the exception of the opinion of Lord Robertson in *Blair* v. *Kay's Trustees*,[16] been uniformly to the effect that where there is a conflict between the law of the domicile at the time of the child's birth and the law of the domicile at the time of the marriage, the latter should prevail.[17] The relevant domicile is that at the time at which the status was created. That view is now confirmed by statute for all Scottish legitimations taking place on or after June 8, 1968, although by reference to the father's rather than the child's domicile.[18]

Foreign cases of legitimation by paternal recognition or by letters of legitimation or their equivalent have not arisen for decision in Scotland. The analogy with legitimation by subsequent marriage is, however, sufficiently close to

---

[13] (1808) 5 Paton 194 at 202.

[14] s. 1.

[15] The Scottish Law Commission had recommended that recognition of foreign legitimations be governed by the law of the father's domicile at the time of the marriage and that recommendation was reflected in the Bill. It was, however, dropped—it is believed with the concurrence of the Scottish Law Commission and as a result of the decision of the House of Lords in *Indyka* v. *Indyka* [1969] 1 A.C. 33 which was seen as opening the door to recognition of decrees determining status on grounds of "real and substantial connection" as well as domicile. Section 5(2) of the Act precludes the court, in a question of recognition, from having regard to the father's domicile at any time prior to the marriage. A person cannot be recognised as having been legitimated from a date earlier than that on which the legitimation occurs (s. 5(3)).

[16] 1940 S.L.T. 464.

[17] *Munro* v. *Munro* (1840) 1 Rob. 492 at 504 and 615; *Aikman* v. *Aikman* (1859) 21 D. 757 *per curiam* (Lord Cowan) at 767.

[18] s. 5(2).

suggest that similar principles should apply. Accordingly, the question should be determined by reference to the law of the child's domicile at the time when paternal recognition took place or the letters of legitimation were granted. There is, however, a stronger argument in cases of paternal recognition than in cases of legitimation by subsequent marriage that, where the father's domicile at the material time differs from the child's, regard should be had to the former as well as, or instead of, the latter. Legitimation by recognition clearly depends on the father's will to recognise, and therefore on his capacity to do so. It is however submitted, although with diffidence, that in this case too, regard should be had only to the law of the domicile of the person whose status is in issue. It is sufficient that that law gives effect to the act of recognition.[19]

Change of Domicile

Judicial decision has been concentrated on domicile at the time of birth, or, in the case of legitimation, at the time of marriage. It is clear that when legitimacy can be affirmed by reference to the law of the domicile at these times, it is unnecessary to have regard to domicile at any other time and that legitimacy, once conferred, cannot be lost by a change of domicile.[20] It is not, however, equally clear that, if notions of indelibility of bastardy are rejected, a child cannot by a change of domicile acquire a status of legitimacy which was not open to it by the law of the relevant domicile at the time of birth or, where its parents have subsequently married, at the time of their marriage. Yet, where legitimation is not in issue, questions of legitimacy are once and for all questions to be determined at the time of birth and there is little to be said for invoking a legal system unconnected with domicile at that time. These considerations do not, however, apply to legitimation by subsequent marriage. Marriage has continuing effects. There seems to be no fundamental reason that where the law of the domicile at the time of the marriage does not recognise legitimation by subsequent marriage, it should not be possible, by a subsequent change of domicile during the subsistence of the marriage, to create the status of legitimacy. In the case of legitimation by paternal recognition or by letters of legitimation, the time of the legal act in question can be the only relevant *tempus inspiciendum* and that cannot be affected by a subsequent change of domicile.

Legitimacy as an Incidental Question

As an exception to the rule that the law of the domicile alone determines questions of legitimacy, such questions arising in connection with succession to immoveables are decided by reference to the *lex situs*.[21] Accordingly, a person universally regarded as legitimate for all other purposes, may be treated as illegitimate for the purpose of succession to immoveables if the *lex situs* so re-

---

[19] In *Re Luck's Settlement Trusts* [1940] Ch. 864 the Court of Appeal held by a majority that regard had to be paid to the law of the father's domicile at the time both of the child's birth and of the act of recognition. It is submitted, however, that on the analogy with cases of subsequent marriage the Scottish courts would not have regard to domicile at the time of birth.

[20] *Shedden* v. *Patrick* (1808) 5 Paton 194, *per* Lord President Campbell at 199.

[21] *Fenton* v. *Livingstone* (1859) 21 D. (H.L.) 10.

quires. On the other hand, it will not avail him that the *lex situs* concedes his legitimacy if the *lex domicilii* does not.[22]

The role accorded to the *lex situs* on succession to immoveables raises the question of whether issues of legitimacy which arise in connection with succession to moveables should be subsumed to the *lex successionis*. If the succession is governed by the law of a foreign country, should that law (including, if, but only if, the relevant law so provides, its rules of international private law) determine any questions of legitimacy which arise in connection with the succession, subject only to such exceptions as the public policy of the forum may require? This is the problem of the incidental or subsidiary question.[23] The same problem, if in rather different form, arises when the *lex successionis* is the law of Scotland. In that case is the domestic law of the forum to be applied or, where there is a conflict between them, its rules of international private law for determining the choice of law applicable to legitimacy? It has been argued that the domestic law should apply,[24] and, despite some criticisms which have been made of it,[25] that argument has force. It is difficult to see why the intestate succession to the estate of someone who died domiciled within the jurisdiction of the forum should be enlarged or reduced by the accidents of foreign law. Similarly, where the law of the forum applies to the construction of a will, there is much to be said for the view that the words of the will should not be construed so as to enlarge or restrict the class of beneficiaries beyond that which these words would have implied in the contemplation of the domestic law of the forum unless, by the ordinary rules of construction, the testator's intention can be shown to have been to the contrary.[26] Some English authority can be cited in support of this view[27] and there is no Scottish authority clearly against it. It has the advantage of avoiding anomalies which may arise from determining questions of legitimacy by a legal system other than that governing the succession. It has the disadvantages that persons may be regarded as legitimate for one purpose and not for another, (perhaps not of practical importance and, in any event, already a result of the law regarding succession to immoveables) and that persons may be cut off from the succession on the sole ground that the domestic law of the forum does not recognise a relationship recognised by the only law with which they have any real connection. The rigid application of this view would, for ex-

---

[22] *Rose* v. *Ross* (1830) 4 W. & S. 289.

[23] Anton and Beaumont, 2nd ed., at pp. 85–89.

[24] R. S. Welsh; "Legitimacy in the Conflict of Laws" (1947) 63 L.Q.R. 65.

[25] Anton (1st ed.), p. 347.

[26] It is submitted that the sharp distinction between questions of construction and questions of status made by Romer J. in *Re Bischoffsheim* [1948] Ch. 79 at 86 ("The only relevant rule of construction is that a bequest in an English will to the children of A means to his legitimate children and that does not carry the matter very far, for the question remains who are his legitimate children, and that is not a question of construction at all, it is a question of law.") and by Kay J. in *Re Andros* (1883) 24 Ch.D. 637 at 639, is artificial. The *de quo* is to give effect to the testator's intention as expressed in his will. If "child" is glossed under rules of construction as meaning "legitimate child" or if the testator expressly says "legitimate child" it is in both cases a question of construction to determine what is meant in context by "legitimate child". Whom did the testator intend to benefit?

[27] *Birtwhistle* v. *Vardill* (1835) 2 Cl. & Fin. 571 and (1839) 7 Cl. & Fin. 895. *Boyes* v. *Bedale* (1863) 1 H. & M. 798; *Re Goodman's Trusts* (1880) 14 Ch.D. 619 and (1881) 17 Ch.D. 266; *sed contra Re Andros; Re Bischoffsheim*, cit. *supra*.

ample, exclude children legitimated by paternal recognition and children of polygamous marriages from succession to a domiciled Scotsman, although their relationships with the parent through whom the claim to succession was made was regular and legitimate by their own law. It seems that on balance the arguments for determining legitimacy by the *lex successionis* should be rejected.

Children of Polygamous Marriages

The legitimacy of children of polygamous marriages requires further consideration. There is no Scottish authority in point but guidance may be obtained from the House of Lords Committee on Privileges, which has accepted polygamous marriages for the purpose of a hereditary qualification to sit as a peer of the United Kingdom as well as by recent English decisions,[28] the consistent trend of which has been to recognise the status of legitimacy derived from polygamous marriage where that was consistent with the law of the domicile.

---

[28] *Sinha Peerage Case* (1939) 171 Lords Journal 350; [1946] 1 All E.R. 348; *Baindail* v. *Baindail* [1946] P. 122; *Bamgbose* v. *Daniel* [1955] A.C. 107.

CHAPTER 2

HISTORICAL DEVELOPMENT OF MAJOR ASPECTS

Scope of this Chapter

Various rules previously in force, though statutorily abolished, will be of continuing relevance and importance for some years to come: this is particularly so in relation to reduction on the ground of minority and lesion, abolished for transactions after September 25, 1991,[1] but still applicable to transactions that occurred before then. This chapter examines the common law, and the history of the statutory development, in relation to tutory and curatory, legal capacity of children, and custody. The current law in these areas is found elsewhere in this work.

TUTORY AND CURATORY

Introduction

Scots law originally followed Roman law in recognising two forms of guardianship over children, the difference lying in the age of the child subject to guardianship. Tutor was the name give to the guardian of a pupil child. The guardian of a child above the age of pupillarity, a minor *pubes*, was known as its curator. The two offices were distinct, and because of the radical difference in respect of capacity and legal competence which the law marked between a pupil and a minor *pubes*, the powers and functions of a tutor differed greatly from those of a curator. When a pupil reached the age of legal puberty, 12 for a girl and 14 for a boy, his or her tutor became his or her curator. "Guardian" was not a term of art in Scots law except for certain specific statutory purposes for which it had the meaning ascribed by the particular statute.[2]

The meaning of tutory was derived from the Latin *tueri*, to protect or defend. It was "a power and faculty to govern the person, and to manage the estate of a pupil."[3] Curatory, derived from the Latin *curare*, to care for or look after, was sometimes described as the power of managing a minor's estate.[4] That description was accurate in so far as it omitted any reference to power over the minor's person, for a curator had no such power.[5] It was, however, misleading if the power of management was understood in the same sense as the virtually complete power of management enjoyed by a tutor. The duty of curators was "to see

---

[1] Age of Legal Capacity (Scotland) Act 1991, s. 1(5).

[2] See, *e.g.* Social Work (Scotland) Act 1968, s. 94; Adoption (Scotland) Act 1978, s. 65; Guardianship Act 1973, s. 13; Education (Scotland) Act 1980, s. 135. "Guardian" today has become a term of art, with the meaning ascribed to it that "tutor" had at common law: s. 5(1), Age of Legal Capacity (Scotland) Act 1991. And see further, *post* at pp. 357–361.

[3] Erskine, I, vii, 1.

[4] *Ibid.*

[5] Stair, I, vi, 35; Erskine, I, vii, 1 and 33; Bell, *Prin.*, para. 2090.

to the minor's affairs, that they get no detriment,"[6] but they could not undertake positive acts of management independently of the minor. Their powers were limited to consenting to, or withholding consent from, transactions that required such consent to be legally valid.

The parents of a legitimate child (originally only the father) were the primary guardians, whether tutors or curators. On their failure there were a number of methods by which a tutor or curator could be given to a child, and these will be considered in the following paragraphs. An illegitimate child had no guardians unless appointed by the court.

Appointment of Non-Parental Tutors

Tutors at common law were divided into three classes according to the manner of their appointment—tutors-nominate (or tutors-testamentar), tutors-legitim (or tutors-at-law or tutors-of-law), and tutors-dative. Tutors-nominate were those appointed by the will or other testamentary deed of a deceased parent; tutors-legitim were those on whom the office devolved by operation of law; and tutors-dative were those appointed by the court.

Tutors-Nominate

Because of the respect accorded to the wishes of the deceased parent, tutors-nominate were the preferred class of tutors. A tutor-nominate by his acceptance excluded a tutor-legitim or a tutor-dative even if they had taken up the appointment.[7] The right of nomination was derived from the parental power which extended to naming persons to look after a pupil child after its parent's death. It was not necessary that the nomination should be in a formal or testamentary deed; it could be by means of any writing the parent chose which was sufficient to indicate his wishes.[8] Being testamentary in character the nomination was ambulatory and so open to revocation or variation at any time during the parent's lifetime.[9] At common law the right of nomination could be exercised only by the father of a legitimate child.[10] By section 5 of the Guardianship of Infants Act 1925 the mother of a pupil child could, by deed or will, appoint any person to be tutor of the child after her death. In a provision which seems rather unnecessary in relation to the tutory of legitimate children the section gave the same right to the father of a pupil child. There is no doubt that the effect of the words used was to give the mother of a legitimate child the same right to appoint tutors-nominate as the father possessed at common law, but it was undecided whether the section conferred the right to make such appointments on the fathers and mothers of illegitimate children. A natural construction[11] would suggest that the provision embraced illegitimate children and their fathers and mothers as well

[6] Stair, I, vi, 36.
[7] Erskine, I, vii, 3.
[8] Stair, I, vi, 6; Bankton I, vii, 6; Mackenzie, I, vii, 3; Erskine, I, vii, 2.
[9] Stair, I, vi, 6; Erskine, I, vii, 2; *Scott* v *Wilson* (1773) Mor. 6585.
[10] Craig, II, 27; Bankton, 1, vii, 2; Erskine, I, vii, 2; *Murray* v. *Merschall* (1555) Mor. 16226.
[11] It was held in *J*. v. *C*. [1970] A.C. 668 that a natural construction of s. 1 of the 1925 Act was to be adopted: *per* Lord Guest at p. 697 and Lord MacDermott at p. 710.

as legitimate, but it is doubtful if such a radical reversal of the common law was intended, at least in the case of fathers.

Tutors-Legitim

Long obsolescent even before its final abolition, the office of tutor-legitim entitled a person to the right of guardianship of a pupil child, if he chose to exercise his right, on the death of both parents and the failure, through death, declinature to act, or incapacity, of tutors-nominate. The tutor-legitim (so called because he took office not by appointment but by operation of law) was, at common law, the nearest male agnate to the pupil child. The exclusion of females was based on the view that the office was *officium virile*, but that view probably fell with the passing of the Sex Disqualification Removal Act 1919. In Scots law a person's agnates are those, male or female, related to him through his father and, in contrast with the Roman law, they have that character even if intervening links in the relationship are traced through females. In ascertaining the nearest agnate for the purposes of appointment as tutor-legitim relations of the full blood, although more remote, were preferred to those of the half blood. If there were several agnates in the same degree the office fell on the person who would have been heir-at-law to the pupil under the rules for succession to heritage applicable before the Succession (Scotland) Act 1964.[12] If the nearest agnate so ascertained was disqualified on account of non-age or otherwise, the office fell to the person nearest in succession thereafter. If, however, the nearest agnate was duly qualified but declined to accept office the next agnate could not take his place and the way was open for the appointment of a factor *loco tutoris* or a tutor-dative.

Appointment as tutor-legitim was by way of petition for a brieve issued from chancery and directed to a sheriff before whom the inquest was to take place and by whom the brieve was to be returned.[13] The tutor-legitim was excluded if he sought appointment more than a year and a day from the death of the child's surviving parent and a tutor-dative had been appointed in the interval. The only matter which the petitioner required to prove was that he was the nearest agnate and was of full age, but it could be urged in objection to the service that he was not provident of his own affairs nor able or capable to manage the affairs of others. Before retour of the brieve could be extracted the tutor-legitim had to lodge a bond of caution for his intromissions with the pupil's estate and until that was done he had no power to act. A tutor-legitim's title to act was constituted by letters of tutory for which the extract of the retour was the warrant. Erskine[14] says that he had to take the oath *de fideli administratione*, presumably before the letters of tutory were issued or, at any rate, before he acted, but the need for the oath to be taken was denied by Fraser[15] on the authority of Mackenzie and Bankton.

---

[12] Erskine, I, vii, 5.
[13] The procedure is fully described by Fraser, at pp. 253–258.
[14] I, vii, 7.
[15] at p. 256.

Tutors-Dative

In the event of failure of tutors-nominate and tutors-legitim, a tutor-dative could be appointed by the court. Jurisdiction to make the appointment rested with the Court of Session as successor to the Court of Exchequer in the exercise of the right of the Crown as *pater patriae*.[16] No appointment could be made within a year and a day from the death of the surviving parent or failure of any tutor-nominate if the person qualified to be tutor-legitim objected. An appointment made within that time was, however, valid and effectual if, on the expiry of a year and a day, the tutor-legitim had not served. There was no objection to the appointment of a tutor-dative within less than a year and a day if there were no tutors-nominate, or the tutors-nominate declined to act, and the tutor-legitim renounced office.[17] It was held that where more than one tutor-dative was appointed the appointment was joint,[18] so that it fell on the death of any one tutor unless the appointment specifically provided otherwise. But under the Trusts (Scotland) Act 1921[19] a majority accepting and surviving is a quorum and, in any event, the appointment would normally be expressed in favour of survivors.

Procedure was by way of petition which had to be intimated to the next of kin and to the Crown.[20] The reason for the latter requirement was that the appointment of tutors-dative was part of the Crown prerogative as *parens patriae*. The purpose of intimation to the next of kin was "that they may offer and inform concerning the fittest persons to be tutors."[21] Any person could be appointed, but from 1925 this was subject to the requirement that the welfare of the child was the first and paramount consideration.[22] Stair indicated a preference for a relative, or those whom it could be shown that the parents would have wished to have appointed. A tutor-legitim who declined to serve could, nonetheless, be appointed tutor-dative.

Appointment by Donor

It was sometimes said, by way of apparent exception to the rule that no one other than a parent could nominate tutors, that the donor of property given to a pupil could nominate a tutor to the donee. Some writers and some early decisions[23] supported the usage but tutor was a misnomer in these cases. The appointee could be a trustee or factor of the property which was the subject of the gift, on the principle that a donor is entitled to attach to a gift conditions for the management of the property given so long as these are not repugnant to the gift, but only to that extent was there any abridgment of the parental power during the life of the parents or, after their death, of the power of tutors-nominate appointed by them.[24] It was undecided whether a donor, by express stipulation

---

[16] Erskine, 1, vii, 8.

[17] *Martin* (1859) 22 D. 45; *Simpson* (1861) 23 D. 1292, *Wilson* (1857) 19 D. 286.

[18] *Stewart* v. *Baikie* (1829) 7 S. 330; *Scot* v. *Stewart* (1834) 7 W. & S. 211.

[19] s. 3(c).

[20] Court of Exchequer (Scotland) Act 1856, s. 19; *Wilson* (1857) 19 D. 286; *Graham, Petr.* (1881) 8 R. 996.

[21] Tutors and Curators Act 1672, c. 2.

[22] Guardianship of Infants Act 1925, s. 1.

[23] Craig, II, xx, 7; *Dishington* v. *Hamilton* (1558) Mor. 8913.

[24] Stair, I, vi, 6; Bankton I, vii, 7; Erskine I, vii, 2.

adjected to his gift, could make the gift conditional on his appointee having full powers of a tutor in respect of the donee's entire property and person to the exclusion of parents and tutors nominated by them, but it is submitted that such a condition would have been null as contrary to public policy. In any event, if, as a result of such a gift, any question was raised regarding the custody of the pupil or management of his property it had to be resolved, at least since 1925, with regard to the welfare of the child, rather than the terms of the gift, as the first and paramount consideration.

Factors Loco Tutoris

These were judicial factors within the meaning of the Judicial Factors Acts, and as such subject to the duties and liabilities contained therein. Like tutors-dative they were, of course, appointed by the court, but factors *loco tutoris* differed from tutors-dative in two main respects: (1) their office was not gratuitous and so, unlike tutors (other than tutors-nominate for whose remuneration the appointing parent had made provision), they were entitled to be remunerated by way of commission for their services[25]; and (2) they had no right of custody of the pupil[26] even in the limited and *prima facie* sense in which the later law allowed such a right to tutors.[27] Nonetheless a factor *loco tutoris* could apply to the court for protection of the child's person and regulation of his custody and, in a suitable case, an award of custody could even be made in his favour.[28]

At common law a factor *loco tutoris* could not be appointed during the father's lifetime unless there were special circumstances justifying his supersession in the exercise of his powers.[29] The same principle later applied to an appointment during the lifetime of the mother. The common law also did not envisage the appointment of a factor *loco tutoris* unless, again, there were special grounds so long as there was anyone acting, or entitled to act, as tutor.[30] After the Guardianship of Infants Act 1925, when the welfare of the child became the first and paramount consideration, appointment was appropriate wherever it could be shown to be for the welfare of the child. Where, as after 1973, both parents were tutors and one of them was unable to act or was disqualified, the appointment of a factor *loco tutoris* did not thereby become necessary, or even competent while the other parent was able to act, unless the welfare of the child so demanded. Subject to that qualification, insanity of a parent,[31] the absence of a parent abroad and in embarrassed circumstances,[32] and conflict of interest[33] between parent and child were all indications for the appointment of a factor

---

[25] Judicial Factors Act 1849, s. 13.
[26] *Macleod* v. *Hill* (1833) 5 Sc.Jur. 271; *Robertson* v. *Elphinstone* May 28, 1814, F.C. 631.
[27] See *post* at p. 72.
[28] *Gulland* v. *Henderson* (1878) 5 R. 768; *Couper* v. *Riddell* (1872) 44 Sc.Jur. 484; *Bonnar* v. *Allen's Trs.* (1869) 41 Sc.Jur 617; *Muir* v. *Milligan* (1868) 6 M. 1125; *Denny* v. *Macnish* (1863) 1 M. 268. See also *Moncreiff* (1891) 18 R. 1029, and *Paul* (1838) 16 S. 822.
[29] See *Cochrane, Petr.* (1891) 18 R. 456, *per* Lord Young at p. 458.
[30] *Morrison, Petr.* (1770) Hailes 359. Compare *Murray* v. *Murray* (1847) 10 D. 194. It was, however, otherwise if the validity of a tutor's appointment was disputed: *Barwick* v. *Barwick* (1855) 17 D. 308.
[31] *Fleming* (1850) 13 D. 951.
[32] *Moncreiff* (1891) 18 R. 1029.
[33] *Cochrane, Petr.* (1891) 18 R. 456; *Macalister* v. *Crawford's Trs.*, 1909 1 SLT 232.

loco tutoris although, in the last instance, his powers could, if the conflict was limited, be restricted to the matter to which it related. Mere poverty,[34] or even the fact that a parent was an undischarged bankrupt, was held not to be enough,[35] but bankruptcy could be sufficient if combined with other circumstances inferring a risk to the pupil's property, such as the fact that the parent was enjoying occupation of the property rent-free or was of no fixed abode.[36] In one case it was held to be enough that single management was needed of a small estate in which another family was interested.[37] Cases of tutors refusing to act, or being contumacious, or being incapable, also afforded grounds for the appointment of a factor, as did cases where tutors-legitim refused to serve or renounced after service.[38] In an action for reparation in which a pupil child was awarded damages or became entitled to them by virtue of an extra-judicial settlement, the Court of Session might appoint a responsible person as factor[39] if there was no one otherwise available to grant a full and valid discharge or if the court was satisfied that the administration of the damages for the benefit of the child could not otherwise be reasonably secured. The appointment, which could not be made in an action raised by a tutor other than a parent, was not formally that of a factor *loco tutoris* and a factor might, in similar conditions, be appointed in the case of a minor. The corresponding provision in the sheriff court was that the sum awarded had, unless otherwise ordered, to be paid into court.[40]

Factors *loco tutoris* could be appointed by the Court of Session or by the sheriff court in the sheriffdom in which the pupil child resided. In the Court of Session procedure was by way of petition presented to the Outer House.[41] In the sheriff court it was by petition "as nearly as may be in the form in use in ordinary actions in that court"[42] (*i.e.* by initial writ). The class of petitioners was not restricted by any formal requirement although no doubt the petitioner's title had to be supported by some connection with the child, either personally or by way of interest in his estate. Service of the petition had to be made on all those who, because they were acting as, or entitled to be, tutors, had an interest to oppose the petition.[43] Similarly, where the child's estate, or part of it, was the subject of a trust, there had to be service on the trustees, including, it seems, trustees who had declined to accept office. Service was also required on other persons who, although they had no entitlement to act as tutors or to manage the pupil's estate, might, because of their connection with the child, have a concern to see that an appointment was made. Thus, where the parents were dead, the petition had to

---

[34] *Wardrop* v. *Gossling* (1860) 7 M. 532; *Stevenson's Trs.* v. *Dumbreck* (1857) 19 D. 462; (1861) 4 Macq. 86. Caution could, however, be required in respect of a particular fund.

[35] *Walton* (1850) 12 D. 192, *Saunders* (1821) 1 S. 115.

[36] *Johnstone* v. *Wilson* (1822) 1 S. 558; *Fleming* (1850) 13 D. 951.

[37] *McWhirter* (1852) 14 D. 761.

[38] *Barwick* v. *Barwick, supra*; *Russell* (1855) 17 D. 1005; *Edgar* v. *Fisher's Trs.* (1893) 21 R. 325; *MacIntyre* (1850) 13 D. 951; *Black & Ors., Petrs.* (1839) 1 D. 676; *Munnoch* (1837) 15 S. 1267.

[39] See Rule of Court 131 (Court of Session).

[40] Sheriff Courts (Scotland) Act 1907 Sched. 1, r. 128.

[41] Rule of Court 189 (*a*)(i).

[42] Judicial Factors (Scotland) Act 1880, s. 4, as amended by the Law Reform (Miscellaneous Provisions) (Scotland) Act 1980, s. 14, which abolished the former financial restrictions on sheriff court jurisdiction.

[43] *Robertson, Petrs.* (1865) 3 M. 1077; *Russell* (1855) 17 D. 1005, *Fowlds* v. *Hodges* (1836) 15 S. 244.

be served on the child's next-of-kin,[44] and where an appointment was sought in relation to an illegitimate child, there had to be service on the child's mother.[45] Service was not required where the person concerned concurred in the petition, and it could be dispensed with in the case of anyone whose whereabouts were unknown or who was abroad or was a minor.[46]

A factor *loco tutoris* could not be appointed to a child before he was born. Occasionally, however, problems could arise about the management of property in which children, not yet born, might have had an interest. In these circumstances a judicial factor could be (and still can be) appointed with powers in relation to the property in question.[47]

Parents as Curators

Parents, who were given the designation of tutors and administrators at law to their pupil children, were, when their children reached puberty, designed as curators.[48] As with tutory, so, however, with curatory, the designation was not the mark of a separate office in the parent but merely served to indicate an aspect of the exercise of parental power. It was competent for the donor of a bequest or a gift to a minor child to exclude the curatorial power of the child's parent, but, with that exception, a parent had curatorial power over the whole of the minor's estate.[49] The rule at common law was that the right of a father of a legitimate minor child to act as the minor's curator was, with certain exceptions, indefeasible and exclusive of all others so that the minor himself could not, during his father's lifetime, choose curators.[50] In 1973 the mother was given by statute the same right as the father to be curator of her legitimate minor child[51] and the right of the one was exercisable by him or her without the other.[52]

Displacement of Parents as Curators

Curatory was a parental right and, as stated above, indefeasible and exclusive of all others. This was, however, only the general rule and the law permitted a number of exceptions thereto. These are discussed in the following paragraphs.

Curators Chosen by the Child

A minor child could not choose new curators to displace a parent against the parent's wishes, but a parent could consent to his minor child choosing curators[53] (which the child could do by petitioning the court for an appointment[54]). There was no clear principle which excluded such consent from taking effect so as to enable curators, chosen by the minor, to act along with the consenting parent or parents, but it seems that consent was treated as an implied resignation of

---

[44] *Logan, Petr.* (1828) 6 S. 477; *Fowlds* v. *Hodges, supra.*
[45] *Buckie, Petr.* (1847) 9 D. 988.
[46] *Carmichael, Petr.* (1848) 10 D. 1286; *MacIntyre* (1850) 13 D. 951.
[47] *Montignani, Petr.* (1866) 4 M. 461; *Gowans, Prentice, Petrs.* (1849) 11 D. 1028.
[48] Stair, I, v, 12 and I, vi, 35; Erskine, I, vi, 54.
[49] Erskine, *ibid.*
[50] Erskine, *ibid.*
[51] Guardianship Act 1973, s. 10.
[52] *Ibid.*
[53] Stair, *ibid.*; Erskine, *ibid.*
[54] Administration of Justice (Scotland) Act 1933, s. 12(1).

the parental right.[55] The Guardianship Act 1973 (which gave mothers equal rights with fathers) did not make it clear what happened if one parent gave consent and the other did not. If an appointment of curators could competently be made in such circumstances, it seems that the appointed curators on the one hand, and the parent who did not consent to the appointment on the other, each had curatorial powers exercisable by the one without the other. It is submitted, however, that the better view was that the parental power was such that it excluded the appointment of curators during the lifetime of a non-consenting parent even if the other parent consented.

Curators Ad Litem

Where both parents refused to concur with a minor child who had raised an action,[56] or where it appeared that a parent had an interest adverse to that of his minor child, the court would appoint a curator *ad litem*.[57] After both parents were given equal curatorial rights[58] it must follow that it was necessary to appoint a curator *ad litem* only where both parents had an adverse interest or refused to concur.

Court Removal and Replacement of Parent

Where a parent was unfit by reason of conduct or character, or was incapable of acting as curator, the court could replace him either by appointing a curator on the minor's application,[59] or by appointing a curator *bonis*.[60] It was held to be sufficient for this purpose that the father was bankrupt and in prison, or where his circumstances were such that denuding of the minor's estate might be feared.[61] It has been said that the court would more readily supersede a parent in the exercise of curatorial than of tutorial rights,[62] but the reason for that is not altogether clear as the wider scope of tutorial powers carried with it a greater risk of damage to the ward's estate. Where the objection was to only one parent, the proper course after 1973 was to supersede that parent in the exercise of his or her powers leaving the other parent as sole curator.

Forisfamiliation

A minor child could escape from the restrictions inherent in curatory by being forisfamiliated, that is, being emancipated from the parental power inherent in the *patria potestas*. Forisfamiliation was inferred from marriage, from the child living separately from its parents and managing its own affairs, from unnatural treatment or neglect by the parents, and, probably, from the minor's taking up employment although still living in the same house as his parents if that employment was distinct from his parents and afforded sufficient means for

---

[55] Fraser (3rd ed.) at p. 450.
[56] *McConochie* v. *Binnie* (1847) 9 D. 791.
[57] See further, *post* pp. 403–404.
[58] Guardianship Act 1973, s. 10.
[59] *Barclay, Petr.* (1698) 4 Mor. Supp. 405.
[60] *McNab* v. *McNab* (1871) 10 M. 248.
[61] *Barclay, Petr., supra.*
[62] *Robertson, Petrs.* (1865) 3 M. 1077, *per* Lord Justice-Clerk Inglis at p. 1079.

support.[63] Bankton doubted if marriage had this effect,[64] but the preponderance of institutional authority was against him. It appears, however, from *Anderson v. Cation and Husband*[65] that marriage might not have been sufficient at common law to amount to forisfamiliation if the other circumstances were inconsistent with the minor's independence; and if, as Fraser contends, the ending of curatory by forisfamiliation rested on notions of the parent's consent and implied resignation, a marriage against the will of a parent could not, of itself, have been effective to bring curatory to an end. Latterly, however, by statute the parent's curatory ended when a minor married.[66] If, however, the marriage was dissolved by divorce or death of the spouse before the minor attained majority it seems that the curatory revived unless the minor was, as would frequently be the case, also forisfamiliated on common law principles. The rule that a woman on marriage passed into the curatory of her husband, retained for a time in the case of minor wives,[67] was completely abolished in 1984.[68]

Appointment of Non-Parental Curators

There were two ways in which, on the failure of parents, curators could be appointed: (1) by testamentary deed, and (2) by the court on petition of the minor.

Testamentary Nomination

The common law, following the Roman law, did not give fathers the power of nominating curators to their children.[69] The reasoning was that, while it was in the nature of the *patria potestas* that a father should enjoy curatorial rights, the independence in law of a minor whose father was dead was such that curators could not be imposed on him, on the father's death or other failure, even by the will of the father. That reasoning took rather scant account, however, of the minor's need for protection in his business affairs after his father's death, or of the view that the minor might not be well qualified to make a wise choice of curators for himself. Accordingly, the Tutors and Curators Act 1696[70] gave fathers the right of nominating curators to their minor children who could be imposed on the minors even against their will. Originally the nomination had to be made in *liege poustie* and so could not be made on deathbed, but that restriction was later abolished.[71] It was an omission from the Guardianship Act 1973 that no such power was given to the mother of a legitimate minor child, and the gap was not filled until the passing of the Law Reform (Parent and Child) (Scotland) Act 1986,[72] which also gave parents who have parental rights the right to appoint curators to children when they were not and had not been married to each other. The appointment, being testamentary in character, could be revoked at any time during the parent's lifetime, but was effective only if the parent at the time of

---

[63] Stair, I, v, 13; Erksine, I, vi 53 and 55.
[64] I, vi, 8.
[65] (1828) 7 S. 78.
[66] Law Reform (Husband and Wife) (Scotland) Act 1984, s. 3(1).
[67] Married Women's Property (Scotland) Act 1920, s. 2.
[68] Law Reform (Husband and Wife) (Scotland) Act 1984, s. 3(2) and (3).
[69] Erskine, I, vii, 11.
[70] c. 8.
[71] 34 and 35 Vict. c. 81.
[72] ss. 2(1) and 4(1).

death was the tutor or curator of the child. The rules regarding appointments *sine quo non* or with provision for a quorum, or subject to the occurrence of a condition, were the same as those applicable to tutors.[73]

Appointment by Petition

Where both parents were dead and there had been no testamentary nomination of curators or those nominated had failed, a minor could petition the court for the appointment of a curator or curators.[74] This procedure, introduced by the Administration of Justice (Scotland) Act 1933,[75] replaced the action of choosing curators which was the procedure formerly available where a minor sought to choose curators for himself. The minor's freedom to choose his own curators on the death or other failure of his father (and latterly also of his mother) was ancient and, as has already been noted, the Tutors and Curators Act 1696 was an innovation in enabling the imposition of curators on a minor by his father's testamentary nomination. Actions of choosing curators were competent in the sheriff court, but the procedure by the 1933 Act was confined to the Court of Session and was by way of petition to the Outer House. The court could appoint anyone eligible for the office who was resident in Scotland, or anyone not so resident if he found security and prorogated the jurisdiction.

The rules of eligibility for appointment as curator, whether under a parent's nomination or by the court, were the same as for tutors and are analogous to the rules discussed later in relation to present day guardians.[76]

Acceptance and Entry into Office

No one could be compelled to accept the office of curator,[77] and all nominees were free to accept or decline. Acceptance by a testamentary curator could be expressed in the same way as in the case of a tutor nominate or implied on the same grounds.[78] In the case of curators appointed by the court, there could be no doubt of their acceptance unless, perhaps, in the case of fraud or like defect apt to nullify the proceedings, because they must have declared in advance their willingness to accept. The Tutors and Curators Act 1696 had envisaged that testamentary curators should accept before the Judge Ordinary (the sheriff) as a condition of their entering into their office. That requirement had long been neglected in practice and had probably fallen into desuetude before curatory was abolished. It appears, however, that a less formal acceptance, as by initialling a Minute of Acceptance, would not have been effectual if, for a protracted period thereafter, the testamentary curators did not exercise their office. So, in *Bruce* v. *Hamilton*,[79] where there had been such an acceptance but the curators had not

---

[73] They are discussed in relation to the current law, *post* at pp. 385–387.

[74] The father's nomination excluded election of curators by a minor (*Pitcairn* v. *Curators* (1731) Mor. 16339; *cf. Primrose* v. *Earl of Roseberry* (1715) Mor. 16335, and *Drumore and Ors. Petrs.* (1744) Mor. 16349. *A fortiori* the election of curators was excluded during the lifetime of the parents. To the extent, however, that a parent's curatory was excluded, a minor might have been free to petition for the appointment of curators (More's Notes on Stair D. 15, p. x1).

[75] s. 12.

[76] *Post* at pp. 382–384.

[77] Stair, I, vi, 30; Bankton, I, vii, 49; Erskine, I, vii, 20.

[78] *Ante*, at pp. 38–39.

[79] (1854) 17 D. 265.

acted for a period of more than eight years, it was held that they were not to be regarded as having accepted office in terms of the statute so as to render their consent essential to the validity of a deed executed by the minor to whom they had been nominated curators. The rules regarding taking the declaration *de fideli administratione*, finding caution and entry into office were the same for curators appointed by the court as for tutors dative.[80] Testamentary curators, like tutors nominate, did not require to make the declaration or to find caution. Unlike tutors, curators were not, however, subject to the Judicial Factors Act 1849, and so they required to make up inventories in terms of the Tutors and Curators Act 1672[81] as a precondition of their being entitled to act. The duties of the office, however, vested on acceptance.[82]

Powers, Duties and Liabilities of Curators

By the Age of Legal Capacity (Scotland) Act 1991 curatory of minors was abolished. Persons under the age of 16 are now subject to guardianship equivalent to the tutory of the previous law; persons of or over that age have legal capacity to enter into any transaction and are not by reason of age alone subject to curatory or, indeed, any form of guardianship. New rules, superseding the previous rules on the capacity of pupils and minors, govern the legal capacity of children under 16. As, however, nothing in the 1991 Act applies to transactions entered into before September 25, 1991, the curatory of minors and the capacity of minors and pupils have continuing application to such transactions and are considered in the pages that follow. As the modern guardians have the same powers and duties as did a tutor before the commencement of the Act, the powers and duties of a tutor are considered later in the context of guardianship.[83]

Curators' Limited Powers

The curator had none of the amplitude of power possessed by the tutor. Not only did he have no control over the person of his ward, but, far from being a manager of the ward's property as was a tutor, his rôle was confined to giving or withholding that concurrence to the minor's acts which, in many types of transaction, was necessary for validity. The minor himself was, therefore, properly the manager of his own property, although the need for his curator's concurrence meant that he could not alone carry that management into full effect. So, although a curator was a trustee within the meaning of the Trusts Acts,[84] many of the powers which were ordinarily enjoyed by trustees did not attach to a curator because they were inconsistent with the nature of his office. Indeed, a curator had no power whatsoever to act positively in relation to the minor's estate. "After he has attained the age of puberty, it is properly [the minor] himself who acts; the curator does nothing more than concur with him, or consent to his deeds; and consequently a deed signed by the curator only, without the minor, is as truly void as one subscribed by the minor only, without his curator."[85] So,

---

[80] See *ante* at p. 40 and *post* at pp. 390–394.
[81] c. 2; Erskine, I, vii, 21.
[82] Erskine, I, vii, 20 and 23.
[83] *Post* at pp. 357–375.
[84] Trusts (Scotland) Act 1921, s. 2.
[85] Erskine, I, vii, 14.

while curators were given to minors "for the right managing of their goods and affairs,"[86] their contribution to that management was by a negative control, for they could not act for their minors but could only authorise them and act with them by consenting to their deeds.

So absolute was the invalidity of any act of the curator alone that the defect could not be cured unless the act was adopted by the minor. The court had no power to authorise such acts in advance nor to validate them after the event.[87] The rule applied to ordinary acts of administration as well as to alienations and other major transactions. So not only were curators unable to grant leases but they could not uplift rents and their discharge was ineffectual to release a debtor from his obligation.[88] In an accounting with the minor, however, a discharge by a curator might be good if granted for full consideration and it was proved that the proceeds were applied *in rem versum* of the minor.[89] And possession by curators might be held the equivalent of possession by the minor where that was to the minor's advantage.[90] Similarly, other acts, such as the recovery of title deeds, undertaken by curators alone, might be sustained if the minor did not object and they were evidently for his benefit.[91] Although, properly, the minor acted with the consent of his curators and not the curators with his consent, it seems that the subsequent consent of the minor would validate his curator's acts. Where the minor acted alone in a case where his curator's concurrence was required, that concurrence might be given so as to render the transaction effectual even after an interval but probably not after the minor's death.[92]

Curators' Duties and Liabilities

The scope of a curator's duties extended beyond those which the rather passive character of his powers might suggest. The duty of curators, Stair says,

> "is to see to the minor's affairs, that they get no detriment. . .And therefore they must not only be counsellors to the minors by showing them what they ought to do, and requiring them to do the same; but especially they must cause them constitute factors, and grant procuratories for pursuing their actions, and putting them to execution, and for uplifting their money."[93]

Stair, therefore, saw the curator as having an active rôle in causing his ward to act in certain ways for the ingathering and preservation of his estate. So far as Stair's view rested on accountability and consequent liability for mere omissions, it was later superseded but, with that qualification, remained apt. The dilemma, however, was that in the absence of power to compel, the only way in which the curator could cause the minor to act was by counsel and suasion. Faced with the obduracy of his ward, the remedies of the curator were obscure.

---

[86] Stair, I, vi, 35.
[87] *Drummond* v. *Murray* (1744) Mor. 8903.
[88] *McIntosh* v. *Fraser* (1675) Mor. 11239; *Bute* v. *Campbell* (1725) Mor. 16338.
[89] *Stark* v. *Tennant* (1843) 5 D. 542 and (1846) 8 D. 1001.
[90] *Jamieson* v. *Spottiswoode's Trs.* December 6, 1808, F.C. 33.
[91] *McKirdy* v. *McLachlan* (1840) 2 D. 949.
[92] Fraser, (3rd ed.,) p. 472.
[93] I, vi, 36.

In the eighteenth century, the view seems sometimes to have been entertained that the court might compel the minor to act, or authorise the act in his place, but the preponderance of opinion was against that.[94] The only remedy which the institutional writers suggest was that the curator should crave to be exonerated.[95]

Although a curator to a minor was not a judicial factor, within the meaning of the Judicial Factors Acts, his duties in the ingathering and preservation of the estate corresponded to those of tutors and other judicial factors but always subject to the qualifications inherent in the restricted nature of his powers. He had to see, so far as he could, that his ward took appropriate steps for the ingathering and preservation of his estate and was under a duty to consent to acts necessary for that end.[96] Failure to consent to necessary acts of administration afforded ground for removal.[97] Curators were judicial factors within the meaning of the Trusts (Scotland) Act 1921,[98] although not of the Judicial Factors Act 1849[99] and could not resign office without judicial authority; nor had they power to assume new curators.[1] Curators appointed by a parent's testamentary deed might, on the other hand, resign subject to the restrictions imposed by the Trusts (Scotland) Act 1921 and might assume new curators. Because the Judicial Factors Acts did not apply to curators, they would seem to have continued to be subject to a duty to make up inventories in accordance with the requirements of the Tutors and Curators Act 1672[2] at the sight of the court and after citation of the next-of-kin, but the practice is thought to have fallen into abeyance. An informal inventory might suffice for the purposes of an eventual accounting with the minor but the difficulty remained that, without an inventory compiled in accordance with the statutory requirements, the curator had no title to act[3] and, if he did so, incurred the liabilities of a pro-curator.[4] Parents exercising their curatorial function in relation to their children's estate did not require to compile inventories.[5] On the termination of the curatory, the accounting between curator and minor might be extra-judicial, but failing that was effected by an action of count and reckoning. The action might be brought by the curator to secure his discharge as well as by the minor.[6] Where a curator had been required to find caution he might, after an extra-judicial discharge, present a petition for delivery of his bond.[7] Failure to make up inventories, or failure to find caution, would not justify the reopening of an accounting which had been settled at majority, at least where the curator acted *bona fide* and for the minor's advantage.[8]

---

[94] Fraser, (3rd ed.) at p. 476.

[95] Stair, I, vi, 36; Erskine, I, vii, 29; Bankton, I, vii, 49 and 55.

[96] Stair, *ibid.*; Erskine, I, vii, 24.

[97] Fraser, (3rd ed.) at p. 477.

[98] s. 2.

[99] s. 1.

[1] Trusts (Scotland) Act 1921, s. 3(3).

[2] c. 2.

[3] Tutors and Curators Act 1672.

[4] For which, see *post* at pp. 399–402.

[5] Erskine, I, vi, 55. Under the Guardianship of Infants Act 1886, s. 12, fathers were *qua* tutors made subject to the provisions of the Judicial Factors Act 1849, including those requiring the lodging of a rental and inventory, but that enactment did not extend to them *qua* curators.

[6] *Stark* v. *Tennant* (1843) 5 D. 542.

[7] *Rintoul, Petr.* (1861) 23 D. 357; *Young & Ors., Petrs* (1864) 2 M. 695.

[8] *Williamson* v. *Williamson*, June 30, 1815, F.C.

At common law curators, like tutors, were liable *singuli in solidum* and, despite their lack of power to act on their own or to compel the minor to action, were liable for omissions.[9] A father in appointing curators nominate might, however, exclude such liability,[10] and statute eventually laid down that, unless the contrary was expressly provided, a curator was liable only for his own acts and intromissions and was not liable for omissions.[11] The change in liability did not, however, it is thought, alter the nature and scope of the curator's duties. As in the case of tutors, a curator might be liable for the acts of his co-curators to the extent to which he had authorised them either expressly or by acquiescence, and freedom from liability for omissions was construed rather narrowly with the result that liability remained for many instances of neglect.

Auctor In Rem Suam

The principles governing the actings of a trustee who was *auctor in rem suam* applied generally to curators[12] but, because of the peculiarities of the curatorial office, had certain specialties. Where a curator was *auctor in rem suam* in concurring to a deed for which his consent was required, the deed was treated as the minor's alone and, as it then lacked the concurrence necessary for its validity, was null.[13] So a minor could not effectively grant a lease to his curator or enter into any contract with him for which the curator's concurrence was required; still less could a minor take on a gratuitous obligation to his curator, or make any substantial donation to him. A minor might, however, make a will in favour of his curator provided it was free from any taint of undue influence,[14] and that raises the question of whether the curator was free to take a benefit from any kind of voluntary act by the minor for which the curator's concurrence was not required. Might the minor, for example, apprentice himself to his curator, or, if in business, enter into business transactions with him? The question was undecided. It is arguable that in matters in which he was free to act alone, the minor should have been free to benefit, or enter into relations with, his curator if he so chose and that the curator could not be said to be *auctor in rem suam* in a matter for which his concurrence was not required; but the better view probably was that the curator's duty to counsel his ward extended beyond matters for which his concurrence was required and that any transaction in which he had an interest was null in a question with him unless, perhaps, it could be shown to be for the minor's evident advantage. The taking of a benefit from the minor's testamentary deed was, on that view, a special case justified by the absence of any prejudice to the minor during his lifetime.

Termination of Curatory

Just as tutory ended when the pupil reached the legal age of puberty, so cur-

---

[9] Stair, I, vi, 36; Erskine, I, vii, 27.

[10] Tutors and Curators Act 1696, c. 8.

[11] Trusts (Scotland) Act 1921, s. 3(*d*).

[12] Erskine, I, vii, 19. And see further, *post* at pp. 372–373.

[13] *McGibbon* v. *McGibbon* (1852) 14 D. 605.

[14] *Yorkston* v. *Burn* (1691) Mor. 8950; *Craick* v. *Napier* (1739) Mor. 4325 and 16342; *Stevenson* v. *Allans* (1680) Mor. 8949; Bankton, I. vii, 59.

atory ended when the minor attained majority, originally at 21, later at 18.[15]
Curatory would also be ended by the death of the minor or curator, by the occurrence of a condition to which the appointment was subject, by resignation and
by removal of the curator as suspect. The same principles applied to the termination of curatory as to the corresponding cases of termination of tutory, and
are analogous to the principles discussed later in relation to termination of present-day guardianship.[16]

Guardians Today

The methods of appointing tutors to pupil children described above[17] were all
effectively abolished by the Age of Legal Capacity (Scotland) Act 1991, and in
the case of factors *loco tutoris* expressly so.[18] So too is the whole notion of curatory of children, for that Act extends the common law notion of tutory to
guardianship of all children under the age of 16 years, regardless of sex, and
provides that no person shall, by reason of age alone,[19] be subject to the curatory
of another person. Tutory has therefore become the only form of guardianship
of children, though the name itself is dropped in place of, simply, guardianship.
The 1991 Act provides no new name to replace "pupil," which is now as inappropriate as "tutor," except to state[20] that any reference in any rule of law, enactment or document to the tutor of a pupil child shall be construed as a reference to
the guardian of a person under the age of 16 years. The nomenclature of "ward"
is sanctioned by usage[21] and will be used in this work to refer to the child under
16 subject to the guardianship of persons other than his parents.

The 1991 Act greatly simplifies the law in relation to the appointment of
guardians, and provides[22] that as from the commencement of the Act (September 25, 1991) no guardian of a person under the age of 16 years shall be appointed except under section 3 (orders relating to parental rights) or section 4
(power of parent to appoint guardian) of the Law Reform (Parent and Child)
(Scotland) Act 1986.[23] An appointment of a guardian under section 3 is effectively the statutory successor to the appointment of a tutor-dative and the appointment of a guardian under s. 4 is effectively the statutory successor to the
appointment of a tutor-nominate: consequently many of the principles and rules
applicable thereto will, subject to the regulation of the 1986 Act, remain relevant today. The discussion above concerning factors *loco tutoris* remains relevant also, since that office is effectively subsumed into the general office of
judicial factor and may still be used as such in appropriate circumstances. It is to

---

[15] Age of Majority (Scotland) Act 1969.
[16] See *post* at pp. 394–399.
[17] *Ante* at pp. 38–43.
[18] Age of Legal Capacity (Scotland) Act 1991, s. 5(4). It should perhaps be noted here that tutors-
dative and tutors-legitim can still be appointed to mentally incapax adults, and indeed the practice
has recently been revived: see Ward "Revival of Tutors-Dative," 1987 S.L.T. (News) 69, "Tutors
to Adults: Developments" 1992 S.L.T. (News) 325; and see *Britton* v. *Johnstone*, 1992 S.C.L.R.
947, in which Lord Abernethy confirmed the competency of an appointment of a tutor-at-law
under the Curators Act 1585.
[19] So retaining the law on guardianship of the incompetent.
[20] s. 5(1).
[21] See, *e.g.* the title of Fraser's work: *Parent and Child, Guardian and Ward.*
[22] s. 5(2).
[23] The latter of which provisions is itself amended by Sched. 1, para. 41 of the 1991 Act.

be remembered that the rules to be discussed later relating to guardian and ward were evolved in the context of tutor and pupil; but references thereto are now to be taken to be references to guardians of persons under the age of 16 years.[24] The remedy of reduction of transactions on the ground of minority and lesion has also been abolished,[25] and guardians today can transact on behalf of their wards, in accordance with the principles discussed later,[26] without that fact (together with lesion) giving a ground for challenge.

LEGAL CAPACITY OF CHILDREN

Introduction

The capacity of persons for legal acts was determined by Roman law according to a refined system of gradation according to age. There were four main stages: infancy, until the age of seven; pupillarity, which lasted from infancy until the age of 12 for boys and 14 for girls; minority, which extended from the end of pupillarity until majority; and majority, which was reached at the age of 25. Within the stage of pupillarity, distinction was made between those *proximi infantiae* and those *proximi pubertati*. Erskine said that the law of Scotland made some difference in respect of each of the stages of life marked by Roman law, but infancy had little legal significance distinct from pupillarity and distinctions within pupillarity were little regarded.[27] The three stages for Scots law were, in effect, pupillarity which lasted from birth until 12 in the case of a girl and 14 in the case of a boy, minority or puberty which lasted thereafter until majority, and majority which under the law obtaining until January 1, 1970 was reached at the age of 21 and thereafter at 18.[28] Minority was also sometimes applied, as in the doctrine of minority and lesion, as a generic term for all those under the age of majority. A sharp distinction, from the standpoint of capacity, marked off each stage from the others.

Unless a person was incapacitated by virtue of his mental condition, or disqualified on some extraneous ground, legal capacity turned entirely on whether the person concerned was pupil, minor or major. It was not affected by his physical maturity, or, short of mental disability, by the degree of his understanding, or by his age within any of the three classes, nor by his position or condition in life. A capacity otherwise lacking could not be conferred by judicial or other act nor could judicial decree, or even the royal prerogative, dispense with defects of capacity.[29] Age, for this purpose, was at common law calculated *de momento in momentum* so that it was precisely on the 21st or, later, the 18th anniversary, measured to the minute from the moment of birth, that the minor attained majority and so also with the passage from pupillarity to minority.[30] It is perhaps for this reason that Scottish birth certificates record the exact time of birth. In thus allowing no place for the maxim *dies inceptus pro completo habetur* Scots law

---

[24] *Ibid.*, s. 5(1).
[25] *Ibid.*, s. 1(5).
[26] *Post* at pp. 367–368.
[27] Erskine, I, vii, 1.
[28] Age of Majority (Scotland) Act 1969, s. 1.
[29] Craig, *Jus Feudale*, II, xx, 2; Bankton, I, vii, 103.
[30] Stair, I, vi, 33; Erskine, I, vii, 36.

followed Roman law and was in some contrast with the law of England. Statute now provides that the time at which a person attains a particular age shall be taken to be the beginning of the relevant anniversary of the date of his birth, but anniversaries occurring before September 25, 1991 remain subject to the common law rule.[31] Evidence of age is at large, but in nearly all cases now proof will be satisfied by the evidence of the Register of Births. Where no better evidence is available, reputation may have some presumptive force. A minor might bar himself from claiming the privileges of minority if he had induced another to contract with him by a fraudulent representation that he was major.[32] Where, however, it was shown that the minor had acted under a mistake as to his age, it was held to be no answer to a plea of minority that the minor had, on other occasions, asserted himself to be major thus inducing a belief that he was such,[33] and that principle applied equally to an erroneous statement made in connection with the transaction in question—*errantibus non fallentibus subveniunt jura*.

The expressions "perfect age," "complete age," and "lawful age" are sometimes encountered in statutes and deeds. Their interpretation must depend on the context, and no rule of universal application can be laid down. The primary meaning of "lawful age" is, however, it is submitted, that age at which it is lawful to do the particular act in question, and it is in that sense that Stair says of tutors-legitim, who under the law as it then was could not take office until 25: "lawful age is not to be understood by his majority, but by his being 25 years complete."[34] In the absence of some such specialty, lawful age will bear the meaning of majority as will "perfect age" and "complete age." A legacy payable at "perfect age" has, however, been held to be payable at puberty[35] and a statutory privilege available under bankruptcy legislation to parties "not under-age" has been held to be capable of exercise by anyone above pupillarity.[36]

Legal Capacity of Pupils

Contractual Capacity

It has been asserted in strong and apparently absolute terms that a pupil had no legal personality. Thus Erskine says: "a pupil has no person, in the legal sense of the word. He is incapable of acting, or even of consenting"[37]; and in *Dalgleish* v. *Hamilton*[38] in 1752 it was said: "the tutor acts for the pupil, who is himself considered nobody."[39] Stair, however, put the matter more guardedly, and it is submitted more correctly, when he spoke of the pupil as "not capable of contracting"[40] or as "having no discretion."[41] As will be seen, there are a number

---

[31] Age of Legal Capacity (Scotland) Act 1991, s. 6. see further p. 379.

[32] Erskine, I, vii, 36.

[33] *Sutherland* v. *Morson* (1825) 3 S. 449.

[34] IV, iii, 9.

[35] *Goldman* v. *Grieve* (1626) Mor. 8969.

[36] *Miller* v. *Aitken* (1840) 2 D. 1112.

[37] I, vii, 14.

[38] (1752) Mor. 2184.

[39] Even in modern times Lord Cameron can be found saying, "in our law a pupil is without legal personality": *Finnie* v. *Finnie* 1984 S.L.T. 439 at p. 441.

[40] I, vi, 4.

[41] I, vi, 35.

of important respects in which legal personality was to be attributed to a pupil. He might be the subject of liability in delict and crime and of remedies in recompense; he had, if in a highly qualified sense, personality for the purposes of the conduct of legal proceedings; even his lack of contractual capacity was not absolute, and he had an extensive passive capacity as recipient and title-holder of property.[42] It may be better to say, not that a pupil lacked personality but that in general he lacked capacity to act so as to bind himself. To put the matter that way has the advantage of directing attention to the purpose of the law, which was to provide for the pupil's protection.

Hume, after remarking on the pupil's incapacity to act, adds: "It is otherwise on those occasions when a right is to be acquired by the pupil, or something to be done by others in his favour, for here where there is no need for a choice or decision, but acquiescence may be presumed, the pupil appears in his own person and the thing is done in his own name."[43] Thus, as Fraser points out, the proper mode of conveying a right in favour of a pupil was by disponing it directly to himself, and not to the tutor for the pupil's behoof.[44] So the interposition of a tutor was not necessary for the validity of a gift or bequest to a pupil or of a deed granted in his favour without any reciprocal obligation on his part, and the title to all such acquisitions and rights so conferred was properly taken in his name.[45] The reason was that as there could be no question of prejudice to the pupil there was no need for the interposition of the tutor. The need for protection arose, however, as soon as any active role was in question, including dealing with property acquired. And so a pupil could not enter into a contract or grant any deed by which he might be bound or on which diligence against his estate might be done or discharge any obligation due to him. All such acts required to be done by the tutor on the pupil's behalf.

Of the pupil's general incapacity for contracts and legal acts there was no doubt. Erskine, however, posited one exception to that incapacity. He says that all deeds or contracts of a pupil at his own hand were null, in respect that they had no effect against him but were obligatory on the other contractors who might be compelled to perform their parts if the contract were judged to be beneficial to the pupil.[46] He explains the rule, while acknowledging it to be contrary to the nature of contracts, as being based in favour of pupils, "to whom the law has not denied the power of making their condition better, though they cannot make it worse" and also "*in poenam* of those who would impose upon their weakness."[47] Erskine's doctrine was adopted by Fraser[48] and, although general observations about the absolute incapacity of pupils in institutional and other writers and judicial dicta can be cited against it, it was judicially approved, al-

---

[42] Since the commencement of the Age of Legal Capacity (Scotland) Act 1991, the capacity of pupil children has been extended to all children under the age of 16, and s. 1(3)(*e*) of that Act provides that nothing in it shall 'prevent any person under the age of 16 years from receiving or holding any right title or interest." This provision represents, it is submitted, no change in the law.

[43] Hume's *Lectures*, Vol. 1, p. 256.

[44] (3rd ed.) at p. 205.

[45] *Drummond's Trs.* v. *Peel's Trs.* 1929 S.C. 484, *per* Lord President Clyde at p. 493.

[46] I, vii, 33.

[47] *Ibid.*

[48] (3rd ed.) at pp. 205–206.

beit *obiter*, in *Drummond's Trs.* v. *Peel's Trs.*[49] It consisted with the protective function of the law and is unequivocally vouched by its Roman law origins.[50] Without it, ready money transactions with pupils, which must often have occurred, would have been wholly insecure and difficult to explain. The criticism that the mutuality of obligation in the contract was undermined does not have much weight, as the same argument could be urged against other doctrines for the protection of pupils and minors such as reduction on proof of minority and lesion, and it was a risk which those who contracted with pupils must be deemed to have undertaken. It was, of course, implicit in this doctrine of *negotium claudicans* that if the pupil sought to enforce the obligation he must himself have been willing to perform his part. The decision to enforce the obligation for the pupil's benefit was therefore a decision which only the tutor could take. Where performance by both parties had taken place at the time of the contract, as in a ready money transaction, the tutor could affirm or reject the bargain at least if *restitutio in integrum* were possible. The rule accords with the English rule that "an infant's contract is at common law generally voidable at the instance of the infant, though binding upon the other party."[51]

Under the Sale of Goods Act 1979[52] a pupil was liable to pay a reasonable price for goods supplied to him which were necessaries, and which were suitable to his condition of life and his actual requirements at the time of sale and delivery. A pupil had, therefore, a capacity to contract for such necessaries although whatever the bargain might say he would be bound to pay no more than a reasonable price. More generally, where a pupil had benefited from work done or goods supplied under a purported contract which was null because of his incapacity, he might be liable *quantum lucratus* on principles of recompense.[53]

Judicial Proceedings

It was commonly said that a pupil had no *persona standi in judicio*. That could, however, be accepted, if at all, only in a highly qualified sense.[54] There was no radical incompetency in an instance in the name of a pupil. Beyond that the authorities, although reasonably clear in their particular applications, might be thought not to yield any coherent general doctrine. The correct view, it is submitted, was that a pupil had *persona standi* but lacked capacity to enter into *litis contestation*. For practical purposes, however, the particular rules sufficed, even if they showed some obscurities or inconsistencies in the doctrine they represented.

Actions in right of a pupil who had tutors were properly brought by the tutors in their capacity as such. Where the child's tutors were his parents, as would usually be the case after 1974[55] where both parents were alive, the instance

---

[49] 1929 S.C. 484.
[50] Inst., I, 21: "*unde in his causis ex quibus obligationes mutuae nascuntur. . .si tutoris auctoritas non interveniat, ipsi quidem, qui cum his contrahunt, obligantur, at invicem pupilli non obligantur*".
[51] Halsbury's *Laws of England* (4th ed.), p. 168, s. 407.
[52] s. 31 (original text); now amended by the Age of Legal Capacity (Scotland) Act 1991.
[53] Stair, I, viii, 6.
[54] *Drummond's Trs.* v. *Peel's Trs.*, 1929 S.C. 484, *per* Lord President Clyde at p. 493.
[55] Guardianship Act 1973, s. 10(1), commenced May 8, 1974.

might be taken in the name of either parent as tutor and administrator-in-law or of both. In other cases of a plurality of tutors, it would be a question of the terms of their appointment whether the action had to be raised in name of all the tutors, or of a majority, or of a quorum. There was, however, no fundamental nullity in proceedings in name of the pupil alone,[56] and where an action had been raised in the pupil's own name, the tutor might subsequently be sisted as pursuer.[57] An instance in the name of the pupil with consent or concurrence of the tutor was not in proper form but had been allowed as substantially sufficient.[58]

There were a number of situations in which an action would, and should, have been raised in the name of the pupil himself. That was the only course open where the pupil had no tutors. Thus, proceedings in right of an illegitimate pupil child had to be raised in the name of the pupil himself and the same was true in all other cases where a pupil had no tutor.[59] Even, however, where a pupil did have tutors, proceedings might, and should, have been raised in name of the pupil himself if (a) the action was against the tutor,[60] or (b) the tutor had an adverse interest,[61] or (c) the tutor was unable because of mental or physical infirmity to act,[62] or (d) communication with the tutor was impossible (as where he had disappeared),[63] or (e) the tutor refused to sue.[64]

In all cases in which an action was raised in name of the pupil alone, a curator *ad litem*[65] would be appointed to take over the conduct of the proceedings on the pupil's behalf and his appointment cured any defect in the instance.[66] The defender might insist *in limine* that such an appointment be made, unless, where there were tutors and they did not have an adverse interest or other disqualification, the tutors agreed to be sisted to the process. The protection of the defender was not, however, the sole, or even the main, matter at stake and if there were no tutors, or they did not compear, it was *pars judicis* to appoint a curator *ad litem*.[67] A question remained of who might instruct proceedings to be raised in the name of a pupil alone. For the pupil himself to have done so would seem to impute to him a capacity for the management of his affairs which the law did not recognise and would, in any event, often be impossible by reason of his lack of understanding or of the circumstances in which he was placed. The tutors themselves might, it is conceived, have instructed proceedings in his name even if they were not themselves to appear, or were to appear as defenders, but they might have been unwilling or unable to do so and, of course, the problem remained of what was to be done if there were no tutors. It may be that anyone having an interest in the pupil's welfare might take the initiative, although in

---

[56] *Drummond's Trs.* v. *Peel's Trs., supra.*

[57] Fraser (3rd Ed,) at p. 208.

[58] *Keith* v. *Archer* (1836) 15 S. 116.

[59] Maclaren, *Court of Session Practice*, pp. 168–169.

[60] *MacNeil* v. *MacNeil* (1798) Mor. 16384; *Keith* v. *Archer, supra, per* Lord Balgray at p. 118.

[61] *Bogie* v. *Bogie* (1840) 3 D. 309; *Park's Trs.* v. *Park* (1876) 3 R. 850; *Ross* v. *Tennant's Trs.* (1877) 5 R. 182.

[62] *Rankine and Anr., Petrs.* (1821) 1 S. 118.

[63] *Carrigan* v. *Clelland* (1907) 15 S.L.T. 543.

[64] *McConochie* v. *Binnie* (1847) 9 D. 791.

[65] For the current law relating to curators *ad litem*, see *post*, pp. 403–404.

[66] Fraser (3rd ed.), pp. 208–209; Maclaren, *Court of Session Practice*, p. 169; *Drummond's Trs.* v. *Peel's Trs., supra.*

[67] Fraser, p. 208.

doing so such a person incurred a risk of liability to the defender should the proceedings not be adopted by the curator *ad litem*. A curator *ad litem* could not be
appointed before the action was raised and a particular appointment had to be
made for each action—not a general appointment to pursue and defend processes in respect of the pupil.[68]

Where a pupil was sued both he and his tutors had to be called as defenders. If
a pupil had tutors and they were not called as defenders, any decree taken in the
action was null. The defect could be cured by amendment calling the tutors as
defenders, but short of such amendment it seems that citation of the tutors and
even the appointment of a curator *ad litem* did not serve to validate the instance.[69] Erskine thought it supererogatory to cite "his tutors if he has any"
when it was known that the pupil had none, and explained the practice as having
been adopted merely "to cut off all ground of cavilling."[70] Such citation was,
however, later held to be necessary,[71] but the effect of failure was undecided.

If a tutor appeared in the process the court would not appoint a curator *ad
litem* unless the tutor was under a disability or was disqualified because of a
conflict of interest or on like ground.[72] Where there was an appearance in process for tutors who had been properly called and cited, any decree pronounced
was a valid decree *in foro* binding also the pupil child.[73] The same result followed where there was appearance for the pupil alone and a curator *ad litem* was
appointed and undertook the defence of the action.[74] Failure to appoint a curator
ad litem in such a case would result in the nullity of any decree pronounced.[75]
On the principle that a party could not be compelled to appear *in judicio* it was at
one time thought that the court would not appoint a curator *ad litem* to a pupil
for whom no appearance had been entered.[76] Any decree pronounced in these
circumstances was a decree in absence, and that might be to the pupil's advantage rather than a decree *in foro* which might result from the imposition of a curator *ad litem*. The appointment of a curator *ad litem* to a non-compearing pupil
defender was, however, competent and would be made where it was for the pupil's evident advantage.[77]

A compearing parent or other tutor of a pupil child had full management of
the process in the child's interest and might compromise it.[78] He could grant a
valid discharge for any sums awarded to the pupil and was entitled to demand
payment of them on the pupil's behalf,[79] unless in an appropriate case a factor
was appointed by the Court of Session or in the sheriff court moneys were ordered to be paid into court. He was personally liable for any expenses awarded[80]

---

[68] Fraser, p. 209; *Baird, Petrs.* (1741) Mor. 16346; *Drummond's Trs.* v. *Peel's Trs., supra.*
[69] Maclaren, *Court of Session Practice*, p. 170.
[70] IV, i, 8.
[71] Fraser, p. 212; *Calderhead's Trs.* v. *Fyfe* (1832) 10 S. 582.
[72] *Stuart* v. *Moore* (1861) 23 D. 595.
[73] Maclaren's *Court of Session Practice*, p. 170.
[74] *Ibid.*
[75] *Ibid.*
[76] Fraser, p. 214; Maclaren, p. 171.
[77] *Drummond's Trs.* v. *Peel's Trs.*, 1929 S.C. 484.
[78] *Gow* v. *Henry* (1899) 2 F. 48.
[79] *Murray's Trs.* v. *Bloxsom's Trs.* (1887) 15 R. 233.
[80] *White* v. *Steel* (1894) 21 R. 649.

with a right of relief, where they had been properly incurred, against the pupil's estate. A curator *ad litem*, too, was *verus dominus litis* and as such had the entire management of the case and could compromise it.[81] He could not, however, grant a valid discharge for any sum awarded and so it was necessary for a factor to be appointed or, in the sheriff court, for the moneys to be paid into court.[82] He was never personally liable for expenses and had a right to his own expenses which was construed as favourably to him as was consistent with the rights of other parties.[83] Where appointed because of a conflict of interest between parent and child, the court might order his expenses to be paid by the parent or out of the child's estate in order to enable the action to proceed.[84]

Legal Capacity of Minors

There was a marked contrast in respect of legal capacity between a pupil and a minor *pubes*. Whereas a pupil lacked, with certain exceptions which have been noticed, all legal capacity, minors were in principle *sui juris* and capable of legal acts. In *Hill* v. *City of Glasgow Bank*[85] Lord President Inglis said:

> "a minor *pubes* is certainly subject to no legal incapacity. Incapacity ends with the attainment of the age of puberty, and it may be said, generally, that after that time a minor is just as capable of contracting obligations and of doing any other thing incurring liability as is a person of full age."

The reference to puberty was, of course, to the legal age at which puberty was deemed to be attained, 12 in the case of a girl and 14 in the case of a boy. There were, however, a number of qualifications which had to be made to that statement and which distinguished a minor from a person who was major. These qualifications were as follows:

(1) A minor either or both of whose parents were alive and who had not been forisfamiliated remained in some degree subject to parental power and to that extent his personal freedom was limited.[86]

(2) Where a minor had curators his contractual capacity was with some exceptions dependent on their concurrence (in the case of parents, the concurrence of either parent). His capacity to raise or defend legal proceedings was similarly restricted. But a minor who had no curators might contract as if he were major and sue and be sued in his own name.

(3) All contracts and legal acts of minors, whether made on the minor's own account where he had no curators or with the consent and concurrence of his curators, were open to reduction at the minor's instance on proof of enorm lesion provided that proceedings to that end were taken

---

[81] *McCuaig* v. *McCuaig*, 1909 S.C. 355, *per* Lord President Dunedin at p. 357; *Dewar* v. *Dewar's Trs.* (1906) 14 S.L.T. 238. Authority to compromise was regarded as uncertain in *Drummond's Trs.* v. *Peel's Trs., supra*, but is, it is thought, now in modern practice treated as settled.

[82] Maclaren, *Court of Session Practice*, p. 186.

[83] *Fraser* v. *Pattie* (1847) 9 D. 903; *Dunlop* v. *Brown & Ors.* (1903) 11 S.L.T. 522.

[84] *Studd* v. *Cook* (1883) 10 R. (H.L.) 53; *cf. Crum Ewing's Trs.* v. *Bayly's Trs.*, 1910 S.C. 994.

[85] (1879) 7 R. 68.

[86] *Post* at pp. 68–70.

within four years of the attainment of majority.[87] The same privilege
had been open in relation to tutors' acts in name of pupils but its principle significance was the protection of minors above the age of
pupillarity.

Minors Without Curators

The contractual capacity of a minor who had no curators was as extensive as
if he were major.[88] The minor could therefore act as he pleased in granting
leases[89] and uplifting rents and interest,[90] petitioning as a creditor in a sequestration or himself being rendered bankrupt and sequestrated,[91] selling his property
heritable and moveable by his own deed without judicial authority or other consent[92] and gifting his moveable property.[93] The only limitation was a practical
one: that in some transactions persons might hesitate to contract with a minor
because of the risk of reduction on the ground of minority and lesion. Some
comment is, however, appropriate on two matters which were sometimes regarded as possible exceptions to the general amplitude of the minor's contractual capacity: (1) the gratuitous alienation of heritage, and (2) the uplifting and
discharge of debts.

According to Fraser, a gratuitous alienation of heritage by a minor was *ipso
jure* null.[94] His discussion of the matter was, however, mainly related to a minor's incapacity to test over heritage which was abolished by statute in 1964,[95]
and it seems that the objection to an *inter vivos* gratuitous alienation of heritage
arose only if its sole object was to alter the succession. Once a minor had capacity to test over heritage that objection could scarcely be urged and there was no
other ground for regarding gratuitous alienations of heritage as null although
they were, of course, as was any substantial alienation of moveables, vulnerable
to reduction on the ground of lesion.

Fraser canvassed some contradictory decisions about a minor's powers to uplift debts due to him. "The difficulty here," he says, "arises from the hardship
that would be imposed upon the debtor who has paid his debt, were he afterwards subjected to second payment, on the first being reduced from facility and
lesion."[96] The risk arose from the fact that even where the debt was paid in full
there might be lesion sufficient for reduction if thereafter the money paid was
not profitably employed for the minor's behoof. In *Jack* v. *North British Rail-
way Co.*[97] the authorities were reviewed and Erskine's statement that "every
deed of a minor who has no curators is as effectual as if he had curators, and had
acted with their consent" was approved subject to the qualification given by

---

[87] *Post* at pp. 63–68.
[88] Stair, I, vi, 32; Erskine, I, vii, 33.
[89] Erskine, *ibid.*
[90] *MacNab* v. *Culdairs* (1695) 4 Mor. Supp. 237.
[91] *McDonald, Petr.* (1789) Mor. 9038; *Dempster* v. *Potts* (1837) 15 S. 364.
[92] Stair, I, vi, 44; Erskine, I, vii, 33; *Thomson* v. *Stevenson* (1666) Mor. 8982.
[93] Fraser (3rd ed.), p. 437; *Kincaid* (1561) Mor. 8979.
[94] Fraser (3rd ed.) at p. 442.
[95] Succession (Scotland) Act 1964, s. 28.
[96] Fraser (3rd ed.) at p. 438.
[97] (1886) 14 R. 263.

More,[98] who says: "Where minors have no curators they may act by themselves, and payments made to them by their debtors will be valid and effectual. But the Court of Session will not in every instance compel a debtor to pay to a minor who has no curators, at least without his giving security to keep the debtor indemnified, thus indirectly compelling the minor, though this appears to be necessary for his own protection, to have curators appointed to him." The result appears to be that a debtor of a minor who had no curators might insist as a condition of payment on the minor's giving security to keep him indemnified or petitioning for and obtaining the appointment of curators. That was so only in relation to the payment of capital; it did not apply to the uplifting of interest or other income.

The capacity of a minor who had no curators to raise and defend judicial proceedings was in principle the same as his contractual capacity. That principle was, however, qualified in that although the minor might sue in his own name, the defender might insist on the appointment of a curator *ad litem*. The minor himself might also after the action was in court seek the appointment of a curator *ad litem*.[99] A curator *ad litem* to a minor did not take over the whole conduct of the proceedings as he did when appointed to a pupil; his function was to advise the minor and to exercise his management indirectly by giving or withholding his concurrence which was necessary for the validity of the minor's acts. Similarly, where a minor who had no curator was called as a defender, the proper course was for a curator *ad litem* to be appointed to him but failure to do so did not nullify the proceedings although they might on that account be more open than they would otherwise have been to reduction on the ground of lesion.[1] The minor was properly called alone as defender if he had no curators and it was unnecessary to call or cite "his tutors and curators, if he any has," although it might have been prudent to do so if there was any doubt whether he had curators. If the minor did not enter appearance it was not competent for the pursuer to move for the appointment of a curator *ad litem* to him.[2]

Minors With Curators

The position of a minor whose curators concurred in his acts was identical with that of a minor who had no curators. So their concurrence made perfect his capacity which without it would have been defective, and he could then act with the same freedom as one who was major. Nor was he essentially in a different position from a minor who had no curators with regard to the reduction of his acts on the ground of minority and lesion. The concurrence of curators might make reduction less likely but did not exclude it. Stair says that "curators may not authorise their minors, where hazard predomines,"[3] but the sense seems to have been that the curators might thereby have become personally liable for any loss that ensued and that the transaction would have been particularly open to

---

[98] *Lectures*, I, p. 110.
[99] Maclaren, *Court of Session Practice*, p. 173.
[1] *Ibid.*, pp. 175–176; *Cunningham* v. *Smith* (1880) 7 R. 424.
[2] Maclaren, p. 176.
[3] I, vi, 36.

the risk of reduction on the ground of lesion; and the same would seem to be the correct interpretation, at least in the later law, of old authorities to the effect that a minor could not, even with the consent of his curators, make donations or gratuitously discharge debts.

Where a minor who had curators acted without concurrence in relation to any part of his property, the general rule was that the transaction was null.[4] The nullity was, however, pleadable only at the instance of the minor and not of the party with whom he had contracted. There was, therefore, a *negotium claudicans* and the minor might if he so elected insist on performance. Fraser[5] so states the law, and although in one passage it is contraverted by Bell[6] it is supported by Stair[7] (who says that deeds done without the consent of curators were null by exception in a context which clearly indicates exception at the instance of the minor), as well as by Erskine[8] and Bankton.[9] Where the minor elected to enforce the contract he was, of course, obliged to carry out his part of the bargain.

The rule that the deeds of a minor who had curators were null if the curators had not concurred and the minor did not elect for performance admitted of one general and several particular exceptions. The general exception was that the contract would not be treated as null if performance had taken place and it had turned out to the minor's advantage. The minor could not seek reduction of a deed which was *in rem versum* of himself; minor *tenetur in quantum locupletior factus*.[10] Similarly a minor could not have a deed treated as null if he had acted fraudulently by falsely holding himself out as major.[11] These exceptions were based on personal bar. The particular exceptions, particular in the sense that they related to particular types of transaction, were that a minor might without consent of his curators enter into contracts of employment or apprenticeship,[12] might if he was in trade or business enter into contracts in the course of that trade or business,[13] and might contract for necessaries consistent with his condition in life.[14] So far as necessaries were concerned, the common law was supplemented by a statutory rule that a minor was bound to pay a reasonable price for goods supplied to him which were suitable to his condition of life and his actual requirements at the time of the sale and delivery.[15] There seems also to have been a rule of practice that the court would not give effect to a plea of nullity where to do so would have conferred no apparent advantage on the minor and the transaction was of little consequence.[16] In an old case, the purchase of a horse was held valid, although the curators had not concurred,[17] and Craig says:

---

[4] Stair, I, vi, 33.
[5] (3rd ed.), p. 495.
[6] *Prin.*, para. 2089. But see *Comm.* 7th ed., Book I, p. 129.
[7] I, vi, 33.
[8] I, vii, 33.
[9] I, vii, 56.
[10] Erskine, I, vii, 33; Stair, I, vi, 33: Fraser (3rd ed.) at p. 491; Gloag, *Contract* (2nd ed.) at p. 83.
[11] Fraser, *ibid.*.
[12] *McFeetridge* v. *Stewarts and Lloyds Ltd.*, 1913 S.C. 773.
[13] *O'Donnell* v. *Brownieside Coal Co.*, 1934 S.C. 534.
[14] Gloag, *op. cit.* at p. 83.
[15] Sale of Goods Act 1979, s. 3 (before amendment by the Age of Legal Capacity (Scotland) Act 1991); Sale of Goods Act 1893, s. 2.
[16] Fraser, (3rd ed.) at p. 493.
[17] *Brown* v. *Nicolson* (1629) Mor. 8940.

"I have seen it decided in court, in things not of great moment, as the rents of a single year, that discharge of them were valid, though granted by the minor without consent of his curators."[18]

Because the concurrence of curators with a minor was generally necessary for the validity of the latter's acts, a discharge of a debt owed to a minor was ineffectual unless granted both by him and his curators.[19] It seems never to have been doubted that a minor could, with the concurrence of his curators, uplift debts, although, as will be seen, that concurrence did not provide complete security against reduction on the ground of lesion.[20] At one time it was held that a minor could not, even with the concurrence of his curators, gratuitously alienate heritage so as to alter his succession, but, as already noticed in relation to minors who did not have curators, once that was no longer the law so far as testamentary deeds were concerned it could scarcely be supported in relation to *inter vivos* deeds.[21]

If a curator concurred in a deed in which he was *auctor in rem suam* the deed would be treated as if he had not concurred and would therefore be null unless it could be shown to be *in rem versum* of the minor.[22] That would be so although a third party was involved in the transaction if he had knowledge that the deed was granted for behoof of the curator.[23] There was, however, no objection to the granting of a benefit to a curator where the deed was of a kind that did not require his concurrence, as in a testamentary bequest, but unfair means must not have been employed to obtain the benefit and it seems that reduction would be granted more readily than in other cases of undue influence.[24]

Because the lack of concurrence of curators did not constitute a radical defect in a minor's capacity, it was for the defender to object if he was convened to an action in which the minor sued alone. Without such objection, the instance of a minor suing alone was good and could not, if decree passed, be challenged thereafter by the defender. If decree passed against a defender without his having taken objection to the instance, he was thereafter barred *personali exceptione* from challenging the decree on the ground of lack of concurrence by curators. The decree was also valid against the minor in such circumstances, but might be reduced on the ground of lesion. A curator *ad litem* would be appointed at the request of the defender or of the minor if the curator refused to concur, or had an adverse interest, or was incapacitated. It was not competent for a curator to a minor to sue without the minor's consent. In proceedings against a minor in which the minor did not appear, any decree was a decree in absence even if his curators appeared. If the minor appeared and his curators did not, any decree pronounced would be a decree *in foro* only if the curator *ad litem* concurred in defending the process.[25]

---

[18] *Jus Feudale*, II, xx, 16.
[19] Erskine, I, vii, 24 and 37; *Cuningham* v. *Curators* (1707) Mor. 16325.
[20] *Post* at pp. 63–68.
[21] *Ante* at p. 59.
[22] *McGibbon* v. *McGibbon* (1852) 14 D. 605.
[23] *Thomson* v. *Pagan* (1781) Mor. 8985.
[24] Bankton, I, vii, 59; *Stevenson* v. *Allans* (1680) Mor. 8949; *Yorkston* v. *Burn* (1697) Mor. 8950; Fraser (3rd ed.), p. 490.
[25] Maclaren, *Court of Session Practice*, pp. 172–174.

Reduction on the Ground of Minority and Lesion

Following the Roman law, the common law of Scotland allowed for the reduction of transactions entered into by persons below the age of majority or on their behalf if these transactions resulted in severe prejudice, or "enorm lesion."[26] The reduction was justified merely by the injury and did not depend upon proof of fraud or any other intrinsic nullity of the transaction. Indeed, it was no defence that the other party had acted in good faith. By minority, in this connection, was meant the whole period of non-age and so relief might be granted against deeds entered into by tutors on behalf of pupils as well as against deeds executed in puberty and the deeds of a minor *pubes* were reducible both where the minor, having no curator, acted alone and where he had curators and acted with their concurrence. There were therefore three classes of case to which such challenge was available: (1) transactions by tutors on behalf of pupils; (2) transactions by minors without curators acting on their own behalf; and (3) transactions by minors acting with their curators' consent. In each case the requirements were the same in principle although where curators had concurred, and also where a tutor had acted on behalf of a pupil, proof of lesion might be more difficult to establish. There was, of course, no need for this remedy where the transaction was absolutely null as in nearly all contracts of pupils acting alone and most contracts of a minor who had curators but acted without their concurrence.

The transaction had to be challenged before the end of the *quadriennium utile*, that is, the four-year period after the attaining of majority, and though there was some conflict of authority as to whether the challenge could be made before majority, reduction was sought before majority, and not denied for that reason, in *McFeetridge* v. *Stewarts and Lloyds Ltd.*,[27] and in *Patrick* v. *William Baird & Co.*[28] In *Young* v. *Evans*,[29] where an extra-judicial settlement was pleaded in defence to an action on behalf of a pupil, the curator *ad litem* pleaded in replication that the settlement was to his ward's enorm lesion but the point was not decided. Where a person to whom the privilege was competent died before invoking it, the right to do so passed to his representatives.[30] Unless they were themselves minor, they had to take proceedings for reduction within a *quadriennium utile* running from the date of the deceased's death or, if the deceased had passed majority, within the unexpired period of the *quadriennium utile* available to him immediately before his death; they could not take advantage of any unexpired part of the deceased's minority. Where they were themselves minor, they had the use in their own right of any unexpired portion of their own minority but could take advantage of the *quadriennium utile* only to the extent that it would have been available to the deceased immediately before his death. In short, the *quadriennium utile* was available to the extent, and only to the extent, that it would have been available to the deceased himself and no time was allowed for the unexpired years of minority of the deceased; but a rep-

---

[26] Erskine, I, vii, 34; Fraser (3rd ed.), pp. 498–541.
[27] 1913 S.C. 773.
[28] 1926 S.N. 101.
[29] 1968 S.L.T. (Notes) 57.
[30] Stair, I, vi, 44; Erskine, I, vii, 47.

resentative who was himself minor might add the unexpired years of his own minority in his own right.[31] These rules represented a somewhat uneasy compromise between putting the successor in the place of the deceased on the one hand, and consideration for the minority of a minor successor on the other. They were also properly adapted only to the case of a single heir and their application, where there were several representatives of the deceased, some major and some minor, was obscure. The privilege might be invoked by creditors and assignees on conditions similar to those applying to personal representatives.[32]

Unchallengeable Transactions

There were certain circumstances in which transactions could not be reduced on the ground of minority and lesion. These were as follows:

(1) Where the loss was caused not by the minority of the child but by some extraneous factor, such as *damnum fatale*.[33]

(2) Where the transaction was in the course of the minor's trade, business or profession.[34]

(3) Where the transaction created an obligation to tradesmen for necessaries.[35]

(4) Where the minor induced the other party to enter into the contract by fraud.

(5) Where the contract was ratified or homologated by the minor after attaining majority in the knowledge of his right of reduction.[36]

(6) Where the transaction was of its nature unchallengable on this ground alone (*e.g.* the marriage or the testament of the minor could not be reduced on the ground of minority and lesion).

The privilege remained open in respect of the deeds of a minor engaged in trade which were not connected with his trade, but there was a presumption that bills of exchange accepted by a minor engaged in trade represented sums advanced to him in the course of his business although the bills did not on their face disclose the cause,[37] and, where a minor engaged in trade borrowed money, he had, contrary to the ordinary rules in a case of loan, the onus of proving lesion.[38] The ordinary rules applied, however, where credit was given to a minor for a purely speculative transaction[39] or where a minor entered into a cautionary obligation beyond the demands of his business.[40]

Facts to be Proved, Presumptions

To justify reduction only two facts had to be proved: (1) minority, and (2) lesion to the requisite degree. Age short of majority, even if by only a day, was ir-

---

[31] Erskine, I, vii, 42.

[32]; Fraser (3rd ed.,) p. 502; *Harkness* v. *Graham* (1833) 11 S. 760.

[33] Stair, I, vi, 44; Bankton, I, vii, 77; Erskine, I, vii, 36; *Edgar* v. *Executors of Edgar* (1614) M. 8986.

[34] *McFeetridge* v. *Stewarts and Lloyds Ltd.*, 1913 S.C. 773.

[35] Fraser (3rd ed.) at p. 525.

[36] Stair, I, vi, 44; Bankton, I, vii, 90.

[37] *Craig* v. *Grant* (1732) Mor. 9035; Erskine, I, vii, 38.

[38] *Macdonald* (1789) Mor. 9038.

[39] *Dennistoun* v. *Mudie* (1850) 12 D. 613.

[40] *Wall* v. *Brownlee* (1724) Mor. 9035; Fraser (3rd ed.,) p. 521.

relevant, as were the intellectual capacities of the minor or that he was forisfamiliated,[41] except to the extent that these facts might, in some circumstances, affect proof of lesion. Erskine says, of the degree of lesion required for reduction: "if it be inconsiderable, restitution is excluded; for actions of reduction are extraordinary remedies, not to be applied but on great and urgent occasions."[42] So the lesion must have been enorm but there was no exact general definition of what constituted enorm lesion. Much depended on the nature of the transaction. Certain transactions were presumed to be to the minor's lesion and generally, if transactions were to be secure against reduction, they must not have gone beyond the limits of a fair bargain. But where there were competing considerations, the court would not weigh the balance of advantage nicely. Where curators had concurred with a minor or if a tutor had acted for a pupil, there required to be "the clearest evidence of lesion in order to set aside the deed; otherwise the commerce with minors, which is frequently necessary, would be too much embarrassed."[43] The same would be so where the transaction received judicial sanction. Where the minor had acted alone, comparatively little might suffice to instruct a case. The lesion was to be ascertained as at the time of the transaction and not the proceedings for reduction.[44] That can, however, be reconciled with cases in which money had been squandered by the minor only on the view that that result must be taken to have been an evident risk at the time of the transaction.

Principal among those instances in which lesion was presumed were donations and cautionary obligations. In these cases the presumption was irrebuttable and gave rise to an immediate right of restitution.[45] To come within this rule, the donation need not have been direct or have involved the transfer of money or property. The discharge of a debt never paid, the waiving of a right and, it is thought, entering into any gratuitous obligation, fell into this category. Modest gifts, within the ordinary course of social and family relations, including in one case a provision for the maintenance of brothers and sisters, were, however, excepted.

The borrowing of money was presumed to be to the minor's lesion. The presumption was rebuttable but the fact that the loan was contracted by a tutor or with the concurrence of curators did not suffice for rebuttal. Nor, despite the general rule that lesion was to be ascertained as at the time of the transaction, was it enough to show that the loan, when contracted, seemed to be a reasonable provision in the minor's interests. In order to escape reduction, the creditor had to show that the money had, in fact, been employed *in rem versum* of the minor, *i.e.* that he had, in fact, obtained benefit from it as in the paying off of his debts, improving his estate, providing for his education and maintenance, or for setting him up in business.[46] If, to the contrary, the money had been squandered by the minor or embezzled by his tutors or curators, the bond would be reduced.

---

[41] *Dundas* v. *Allan* (1711) Mor. 9034; *Anderson* v. *Caution and Husband* (1828) 7 S. 58 and (1832) 11 S. 10.

[42] I, vii, 36.

[43] Erskine, I, vii, 34.

[44] Fraser (3rd ed.), p. 504.

[45] *Ibid.*, p. 516.

[46] *Ibid.*, p. 517.

Accordingly, a creditor was entitled to proof of the beneficial application of money lent and might demand repayment even short of the due term if that proof was not forthcoming.

Sales of a minor's heritage and assignations of his personal rights were also presumed to be to his lesion.[47] In a sale, it was for the purchaser to show that the price had been applied to the minor's benefit and reduction would be granted although the minor could not refund the price because it had been squandered or embezzled. That would be so even if the sale was sanctioned by the court.

Where the transaction did not fall within a class in which lesion was presumed, the onus of proof rested on the minor and where the nature of the obligation was in dispute, the onus was on the minor to prove that it was, in fact, of a kind in which lesion was presumed. Proof of lesion was achieved if the minor proved that he had not benefited to the full value of the consideration given for the obligation.[48] So a bond granted by a sister in favour of her brother in consideration of the latter's trouble and expense in connection with legal proceedings on her behalf was reduced as going beyond proper recompense, while any claim that the brother might properly have was reserved.[49] Marriage contracts, although not marriage itself, might be reduced on the ground of lesion, and it seems that in an old case the view was entertained that lesion to the children of the marriage might be equivalent to lesion to the minor spouse.[50] Leases, unlike sales of heritage, did not fall into the category in which lesion was presumed, but they might be reduced on proof of lesion.[51]

Pursuing the Action

Reduction had to be pursued within the *quadriennium utile*, which was calculated *de momento in momentum* and so permitted the raising of an action on the last day provided it was done before the time of expiry.[52] It was essential that an action be raised, and no private act signifying revocation would suffice.[53] If the *quadriennium* expired without an action being raised, reduction on the ground of lesion was thereafter forever barred. That did not, of course, prevent reduction on other grounds, such as that a deed was impetrated by fraud or was fundamentally null. The requirement that an action for reduction be raised did not apply where reduction was sought *ope exceptionis*. In that event, the plea had to be stated before the *quadriennium* expired. There was some controversy as to the extent to which reduction *ope exceptionis* was competent.[54] A similar controversy attended the use of suspension without reduction. In *McFeetridge* v. *Stewarts and Lloyds Ltd.*[55] the incidental setting aside of an award of compensation and receipts was considered competent, and it seems that the law came to

---

[47] *Ibid.*, p. 518.
[48] *Ibid.*, p. 504; *Anderson* v. *Caution and Husband* (1832) 11 S. 10.
[49] *Rose* v. *Rose* (1821) 1 S. 154; Stair, I, vi, 44; Erskine, I, vii, 38; Fraser (3rd ed.), p. 508.
[50] *Davidson* v. *Hamilton* (1632) Mor. 8988.
[51] Fraser (3rd ed.), at p. 511; *Monro* v. *Monro* (1735) Elchies, v. "Minor" 1.
[52] Stair, I, vi, 44; Erskine, I, vii, 35; Bankton, I, vii, 74.
[53] *Stewart* v. *Snodgrass* (1860) 23 D. 187.
[54] Fraser (3rd ed.), p. 537.
[55] 1913 S.C. 773.

be that reduction *ope exceptionis* might be allowed in cases of minority and lesion on the same principles as in other cases.

If an action of reduction was raised, all persons with an interest to defend required to be called as defenders. It was not necessary to call tutors and curators.[56] If the right which was to be reduced had been assigned, the assignee and not the cedent had to be called as defender.[57] In the case of an assignation there might, however, be a question of whether reduction was competent. It would be granted in a question with universal successors and with singular successors where the assignation was gratuitous. Where a personal right had been transferred to a singular successor for an onerous consideration, the maxim *assignatus utitur jure auctoris* still applied, so that the assignee could take no higher right than his cedent and the minor's remedy against him remained entire.[58] The maxim did not, however, apply to those to whom heritage was transferred for a valuable consideration,[59] for there the disponee rested upon the faith of the records and so might disregard all rights granted by his author upon which an infeftment had not taken place before that which proceeded on his own disposition; nor did it apply to a purchaser of corporeal moveables.[60] Where, therefore, a real right had been transferred to a singular successor for onerous consideration, the minor's remedy of reduction was cut off except where the transferee took his title in the knowledge that it was derived from a minor or was otherwise *in mala fide*.

Both Parties Minors

Special problems attended the reduction of a transaction in which both parties were minors when they entered into it. In *pari casu* neither could be restored against the other because both had equal privilege. If, however, only one had suffered lesion he might be restored against the other to the extent that the latter was *lucratus*.[61] Where both had suffered lesion they were relieved from further performance. So where one minor had borrowed from another and squandered the money he was not bound to repay. The equity of this rule, though applauded by Erskine,[62] Bankton[63] and Fraser,[64] seems doubtful.

Restitution

Where a deed was reduced on the ground of minority and lesion, restitution ought, so far as possible, to be mutual and complete. So where matters were entire there should be *restitutio in integrum* so that parties were restored to their former state. Thus on the reduction of sale of heritage, the purchaser was obliged not only to restore to the minor his property but had to account for any profits the subjects had yielded in the interval, while the minor was bound not only

---

[56] Erskine, I, vii, 34; *Blantyre* v. *Walkinshaw* (1667) Mor. 2215.
[57] *Blantyre* v. *Walkinshaw, supra.*
[58] Erskine, I, vii, 40.
[59] Erskine, *ibid.*; *Scottish Widows' Fund* v. *Buist* (1876) 3 R. 1078.
[60] *Scottish Widows' Fund* v. *Buist, supra.*
[61] Erskine, I, vii, 40.
[62] *Ibid.*
[63] I, vii, 92.
[64] (3rd ed.) at p. 539.

to repay the price received by him with interest but to reimburse the purchaser for expenditure by him on the property in so far as that had conduced to a higher yield of profits.[65] Where, however, events had intervened so as to make *restitutio in integrum* impossible, the minor had to be restored to his former state even though no corresponding restitution could be made to the other party. That was justified on the principle that the privilege was for the benefit of minors, and that those who contracted with them did so at the risk that if the transaction enured to the minor's lesion, restitution might be at the expense of loss to themselves. So, if a sale was reduced, the minor might take the subjects without repaying the price if the price had been squandered or misappropriated, and where a loan to a minor was reduced the money borrowed needed to be repaid only if it had been applied *in rem versum* of the minor. As this principle rested on the voluntary assumption of risk by the party contracting with the minor it did not apply where that party had contracted *ex necessitate*. In such a case, which could however in modern conditions seldom occur, there was no restitution to the minor unless the other party could also be restored to his former position.

Fraser says that the principle of restitution applied to all cases where a minor had suffered wrong even if the wrong be one of omission and that consequently "he will have redress against injuries sustained from having been prevented from acquiring property, as much as from having been injured in any transaction into which he had actually entered."[66] But in *Cooper* v. *Cooper's Trs.* it was said that "not to gain what but for the contract would have been got is one thing, to lose that which was taken away by the contract is quite another, and this last is…the only lesion recognised as a ground of reduction."[67] There is, however, strength in Lord Rutherfurd Clark's dissenting opinion, that there was neither reason nor legal principle on which that distinction could be maintained.[68]

Legal Capacity of Child Since 1991

The Age of Legal Capacity (Scotland) Act 1991 applies to transactions and legal acts occurring after September 25, 1991, and it provides that, in general, the child below 16 lacks legal capacity (subject to various exceptions) and the child above 16 has full legal capacity (subject to the right of reduction of certain transactions undertaken while the person is 16 or 17 years of age). The substantive rules are considered in some detail in Chapter 13.

CUSTODY

Custody at Common Law

At common law, custody was properly applicable only to pupil children.[69]

---

[65] Erskine, I, vii, 41.

[66] (3rd ed.) at p. 515.

[67] (1885) 12 R. 473, *per* Lord Craighill at p. 493.

[68] *Ibid.*, at p. 495.

[69] The pupil child was not *sui juris* and so could be subjected not only to the dominion of his father but, on the failure of his father, to the custody of others. In contrast, the minor *pubes* was *sui juris* in relation to his personal freedom except in so far as that was restrained by the *patria potestas*. The institutional writers are at variance as to how long that restraint was effective to give the father a right of custody. Stair (I, v, 13) thought there was no doubt that, unless the child was forisfamiliated or the father had abused his power, children could be compelled to remain with their

The *patria potestas* which belonged to the father and could not in its fullness be conferred on anyone else, admitted, however, of such control over minors above the age of pupillarity that they could, if in a somewhat weaker sense than in the case of pupils, be said to be in their father's custody. After remarking that a minor whose father was dead, or was emancipated, was, subject to some quali-fications, a person *sui juris* and free to choose his place of residence (something inconsistent with his being in the custody of another), the consulted judges in *Craig* v. *Greig and McDonald*[70] said: "No doubt, if his father be alive, and the minor be not emancipated, there is greater restraint upon his personal liberty by reason of the influence of the *patria potestas*. . .he is not free to choose his place of residence, as a minor is who is subject only to the guardianship of curators." The extent of this paternal restraint on the minor *pubes* was not clearly defined. It grew weaker as the minor advanced in years and discretion but, during the lifetime of the father, it was not completely lost until majority or foris-familiation. Until then, at least the vestiges of what could be characterised as custody might be said to remain. Accordingly cases are to be found in which a father sought to assert a claim to the custody of his child who was a minor *pubes*.[71] In contrast, however, with a father's claim to the custody of his pupil children, which might be refused only if to grant it would place the children's moral or physical welfare in serious jeopardy, his claim to the custody of a mi-nor *pubes* might be refused on "good and sufficient grounds" among which the reasonable wishes of the child were a material element.[72]

The pure doctrine of the common law was that the minor *pubes*, again in con-trast with a pupil child, could not be subjected to the custody of anyone other than his father. The source of all claims to his custody was in the *patria potestas* which was inalienable. Apart from the *patria potestas* his personal freedom was subject to no restraint—once beyond pupillarity *intellegitur venisse in suam tutelam et esse in sua ipsius custodia*.[73] In two cases in the last decade of the nineteenth century[74] applications for the custody of minors were, however, en-tertained, although in neither was the petitioner the minor's father. They were refused on their merits without consideration of the question of competency. Such willingness as they show to contemplate applications by persons other than the minor's father may be ascribed to an awareness that cases might occur in which there was no alternative consonant with the increased emphasis which

---

parents even after majority. To him therefore only the father's death or forisfamiliation could bring custody to an end; but no later authority supports that view. Erksine (I, vii, 1) thought that the compelling power of the father over his issue lasted only until majority. Bankton (I, vi, 1), while allowing an extensive authority of the father over his children, even if major, so long as they remained in his house, held that the father could not after their pupillarity detain them in his family against their will; custody therefore ended with pupillarity. More (Notes on Stair, p. xxxi; *Lectures*, I, p. 87) was of the same opinion as Bankton. By the mid-19th century the question had been resolved as indicated in the text.

[70] (1863) 1 M. 1172, *per* Lord Justice-Clerk Inglis, Lords Benholme and Mackenzie at p. 1179.
[71] *Harvey* v. *Harvey* (1860) 22 D. 1198; *Edgar* v. *Fisher's Trs.* (1894) 21 R. 1076.
[72] *Edgar* v. *Fisher's Trs., supra, per* Lord McLaren at p 1079; Fraser, p. 76, note 1.
[73] *Newton* v. *Ker* (1533) Mor. 16218; *Mathieson* v. *Wedderby* (1534) Mor. 16218 (note); *Graham* v. *Graham* (1780) Mor. 8934; *Harvey* v. *Harvey, supra, per* Lord Justice-Clerk Inglis at p. 1208; *Craig* v. *Greig & McDonald, supra, per* Lord Justice-Clerk Inglis, Lord Benholme and Macken-zie at p. 1179.
[74] *Flannigan* v. *Muir* (1892) 19 R. 909; *Morrison* v. *Quarrier* (1894) 21 R. 1071.

was by then placed on the welfare of the child. To take an extreme but apt example, the difficulty was evident of turning away as incompetent a custody application by a relative of a 12-year-old girl which was the only means of saving her from grave moral of physical danger. Yet the court's powers were seen as clearly circumscribed. It needed "a very strong case"[75] to justify intervention against the will of the minor. In general, the opposition even of a 12-year-old girl was a "supreme difficulty."[76]

Primacy of Father of Legitimate and Mother of Illegitimate Child

At common law the effect of the *patria potestas* was such that during the father's lifetime there was only very limited scope for custody disputes. His right to custody of his legitimate child could be denied only on proof of serious physical or moral danger to the child.[77]

What was true of the father of a legitimate child was, despite the absence of any equivalent of the *patria potestas*, largely true, so far as custody was concerned, of the mother of an illegitimate child.[78] When the child reached what was regarded as an appropriate age, usually, in the absence of special circumstances, seven in the case of a boy and 10 in the case of a girl, the putative father might discharge his obligation to pay aliment by making a suitable offer to take over responsibility for the care of the child whether in his own home or in the home of someone nominated by him. The consequence of refusal was that, unless the offer could be shown not to be genuine or otherwise to be unsuitable, the father's liability to aliment ceased but the mother's right to custody remained intact. An agreement by the mother to commit the custody of the child to others, whether the father or strangers, was revocable even if declared permanent and custody might be reclaimed,[79] as was the case with such agreements by parents

---

[75] *Flannigan* v. *Muir, supra, per* Lord President Robertson at p. 912.

[76] *Morrison* v. *Quarrier, supra, per* Lord President Robertson at p. 1074.

[77] *Leys* v. *Leys* (1886) 13 R. 1223; *Lang* v. *Lang* (1869) 7 M. 445; *Steuart* v. *Steuart* (1870) 8 M. 821; *Pagan* v. *Pagan* (1883) 10 R. 1072; *Nicholson* v. *Nicholson* (1869) 7 M. 1118.

[78] The law as here stated is as laid down in *Corrie* v. *Adair* (1860) 22 D. 897, especially *per* Lord Justice-Clerk Inglis at p. 900 and Lord Cowan at p. 901, and subsequent cases. See also *Simpson* v. *Cassels* (1865) 3 M. 396; *Grant* v. *Yuill* (1872) 10 M. 511; *Westlands* v. *Pirie* (1887) 14 R. 763; *McCarroll* v. *Kerr* (1877) 15 S.L.R. 106; *Brown* v. *Halbert* (1896) 23 R. 733; *Millar* v. *Melville* (1898) 1 F. 367; *Moncrieff* v. *Langlands* (1900) 2 F. 1111. Before that, although the preponderant view was the same, there had been some conflict of judicial opinion. According to one view, the mother's custody of the child was not a matter of law but merely a recognition of the generally appropriate natural arrangement. On that view the mother properly had no right and custody could be regulated according to the circumstances under the general superintendence of the court. Sometimes it was said, with surprising modernity, that the only question was what was best for the child. Therefore the putative father, although he too properly had no right, could apply for custody and, if he could show that he would make superior arrangements, might be preferred. The conflict in judicial opinion is seen in three cases all reported in 4 S.: *Whitson* v. *Speid* (1825) 4 S 42, *Baxter* v. *Dougal's Trs.* (1825) 4 S. 139, and *Fairweather* v. *Lyall* (1826) 4 S. 614. See also generally *Burges* v. *Halliday* (1758) Mor. 1357, *Oliver* v. *Scott* (1778) Mor. 444, *Caldwell* v. *Stewart* (1773) 5 Mor. Supp. 390, *Kidston* v. *Smith* (1778) 5 Mor. Supp. 390, *Ballantyne* v. *Malcolm* (1803) Hume 425, *Wilson* v. *Bowie* (1810) Hume 426, *Goadby* v. *Macandys* July 7, 1815, F.C., 482; *Hunter's Trs.* v. *Speed*, Dec. 2, 1820, F.C., 211; *Keay* v. *Watson* (1825) 3 S. 561, *Rankine* v. *AB* (1833) 5 Sc.Jur. 363, *Pott* v. *Pott* (1833) 12 S. 183, *Weepers* v. *Heritors of Kennoway* (1844) 6 D. 1166.

[79] *Kerrigan* v. *Hall* (1901) 4 F. 10, *Macpherson* v. *Leishman* (1887) 14 R. 780.

of legitimate children, unless to do so would be to create a danger to the child's life or health or raise a similar serious objection relating to the child's physical or moral welfare.[80] At one time it had been held that testamentary trustees appointed by the father of an illegitimate child, if they held funds for behoof of the child, might obtain custody if that were necessary for the proper application of funds for the purpose of the child's education.[81] The principle was capable of extension to trustees acting under any trust deed with appropriate purposes whether *inter vivos* or *mortis causa* and whether granted by the father or a stranger because it did not depend on any legal relationship between the father and his illegitimate child (there were none other than that of an alimentary debtor); and in *Johnston* v. *Clark*[82] it was said that "if a person bestows an estate on a child who has not a lawful father, he may appoint a guardian to that child, to the effect of directing his education, as well as of taking charge of his estate." It is, however, doubtful if the authority of these decisions survived in its entirety later developments in the common law although it may, until statute intervened, have remained the law that a child could not benefit from a settlement without fulfilling the conditions as to custody express or implicit in it.

Custody on Failure of Father of Legitimate Child

Because of the supremacy of the paternal right questions of who other than the father might be entitled to custody could arise at common law if the father died or became disqualified as custodian (because to enforce his right would involve serious physical or moral danger to the child) or, on a temporary basis, in the event of his inability or unwillingness to exercise his right. In the event of the father's disqualification or incapacity it was usually to the mother, if she was alive, that custody passed.[83] Beyond that, in cases other than on the death of the father, the law provided no clear rules. Once the *patria potestas* was laid aside there was room for judicial discretion. It consists, however, with the rules applicable on the death of the father that in the event of his disqualification or incapacity, the mother's relatives should, on the failure of the mother, have been preferred in a competition with others.[84] On the death of the father, the general rule was that custody of the children under seven years of age passed to the mother.[85] There was a strong presumption on which the rule was based, that that was in the interests of the child. Even over the age of seven, the mother would have custody unless some special cause was shown that to give her custody would be disadvantageous to the child.[86] These rules, however, suffered some

---

[80] *Sutherland* v. *Taylor* (1887) 15 R. 224. There are dicta in *Mackenzie* v. *Keillor* (1892) 19 R. 963 which put the regard to be paid to the child's welfare more broadly.

[81] *Whitson* v. *Speid* (1825) 4 S. 42; *Hunter's Trs.* v. *Speed*, Dec. 2, 1820, F.C., 211; *Baxter* v. *Dougal's Trs.* (1825) 4 S. 139.

[82] (1785) Fac.Dec. 369; Mor. 16374.

[83] *A.B.* v. *C.D.* (1850) 12 D. 1297. Cf. *Cameron, Petr.* (1847) 9 D. 1401; *Baillie* v. *Agnew* (1775) 5 Mor.Supp. 526; *Craig* v. *Thompson* (1829) 1 Sc.Jur. 201.

[84] For the practice on the father's death and failure of mother and tutors, see *Higgins* v. *Boyd* (1821) 1 S. 50, and *Gibson* v. *Dunnett* (1824) 3 S. 249. Even during the father's lifetime cognates might be preferred to agnates because of the latters' interest in succession.

[85] The rule is ancient: *Foreman* v. *Oliphant* (1527) Mor. 16216; *Durie* v. *Laird of Dowhill and Lochlevin* (1517) Mor. 16216; *The King and Tullibarden* v. *Laird of Wedderburne* (1516) Mor. 16216. See also *Scot* v. *Scot*, (1759) 5 Mor.Supp. 872; *Borthwick* v. *Dundas* (1845) 8 D. 318.

[86] Erskine, I, vii, 7; *Campbell* v. *Campbell* (1833) 11 S. 544; Fraser, pp. 288 and 289.

exceptions if the mother remarried,[87] and were largely superseded if the father had left directions as to custody. The policy of the law in the latter event was to give effect to the father's wishes and so to give custody to his nominee.[88] By 1845, however, it was doubted whether the father's specific direction must prevail so as to deprive the mother of custody in the case of a child under seven[89] and it was not enough to defeat the mother's claim that the father had nominated tutors.[90] On the failure of the mother, for whatever cause, and in the absence of any express direction by the father, custody passed to the child's tutors. The law took, however, an unsentimental and cautious view of human nature in relation to the custody of tutors. A tutor who was next in succession to the child was deemed to be an admirable guardian of the child's estate which he had every interest to preserve, but to be wholly unfit to be a guardian of the child's person as his interest ran contrary to the continuance of the child in life. Indeed Fraser, borrowing from Blackstone,[91] says that to give custody to such a person would be "*agnum lupo committere ad devorandum.*" Accordingly not only tutors who took office by operation of law in the absence or failure of the father's nomination (tutors-at-law) but also tutors appointed by the court (tutors-dative) and tutors nominated by the father (tutors-nominate) were excluded from custody if they stood next in succession or had the same interest in the ward's estate as a person next in succession would have.[92] Moreover, there was a wider field for the exercise of judicial discretion in the control of the custody of tutors and, in deciding on applications by them in competition with other claimants, than there was for interference with the father's powers during his lifetime.[93] A tutor disqualified from taking actual custody might, nonetheless, be entitled to fix a suitable place of residence for the pupil.[94] If the tutor was disqualified, the nearest cognate was preferred.[95] Neither tutors nor any other person to whom custody might pass on the father's death had the *patria potestas*, and although the rules on custody of children on the father's death were regarded as rules of law, their implementation was subject to the general superintending control of the court.[96]

Custody on Failure of Mother of Illegitimate Child

The common law had no rules for determining custody on the death or other

---

[87] Erskine, *ibid.*; *Fullerton* v. *Boyne* (1675) Mor. 16291; *Langshaw* v. *Muir* (1629) Mor. 16252; *Finnie* v. *Oliphant* (1631) Mor. 406; but the rule applied only in a question with tutors qualified to have custody. See *Johnston* v. *Otto* (1849) 11 D. 718; *McCallum* v. *McDonald* (1853) 15 D. 535.

[88] *A.* v. *B.* (1553) Mor. 16224; Balfour, CXXIII, p. 336.

[89] *Borthwick* v. *Dundas* (1845) 8 D. 318, *per* Lords Mackenzie, Fullerton and Jeffrey at p. 320; *contra, per* Lord President Boyle at p. 319.

[90] *Borthwick* v. *Dundas, supra*, on this point in contrast with the earlier rule (*Langshaw* v. *Muir, supra*).

[91] Fraser, (3rd ed.) at p. 292; Blackstone, I, c., 17; *Robertson* v. *Elphinstone* May 28, 1814, F.C. 631, *per* Lord Meadowbank at p. 636.

[92] Stair, I, vi, 15; Erskine, I, vii, 7; Bankton, I, vii, 28; Craig, II, xx, 6; Reg. Maj., II, xlvii, 4; Balfour, CXXVI, p. 337, citing *Clepan* v. *Laird & Wymis* (1551) Mor. 16227 and *Dishington* v. *Hamilton* (1558) Mor. 8913; *Chalmers* v. *Gadgirth* (1611) Mor. 16239; *Edgar* v. *Inglis* (1606) Mor. 16237; *Dury* v. *Dury* (1666) Mor. 16277; *Taylor* v. *Forrester* (1622) Mor. 16242.

[93] *Black* v. *Ferguson* (1866) 4 M. 807, *per* Lord Deas at p. 809.

[94] *Walker* v. *Walker* (1824) 2 S. 788.

[95] *Higgins* v. *Boyd* (1821) 1 S. 50; *Gibson* v. *Dunnett* (1824) 3 S. 249.

[96] *Borthwick* v. *Dundas, supra, per* Lord President Boyle at p. 319.

failure of the mother of an illegitimate child. The illegitimate child had no tutors at law and it was undecided whether the mother could nominate tutors or other persons to act as custodians after her death.[97] The interest of trustees holding estate for the child has already been noticed. Although neither the father nor, after his death, his relatives[98] had any right to custody during the mother's lifetime, they might make a claim after her death, but were not entitled to any special consideration. The law did not recognise any familial relationship between the illegitimate child and others apart from the natural bond with the mother and the obligation of the father to aliment. In strict contemplation of the law the illegitimate child had no relatives and, in the absence of the mother, responsibility for the care of the child rested, subject to the father's alimentary obligation, with the community as a whole—*filius nullius filius populi*. In the event of claimants for custody coming forward, a choice could, therefore, be made in the free exercise of a judicial discretion.

Statutory Modifications of the Common Law

The common law has now been almost entirely superseded by statute, and the matter today, like other issues of parental rights, is governed by the Law Reform (Parent and Child) (Scotland) Act 1986. Instead of concentrating on a right of custody, and determining the strengths of competing rights, the law today determines the matter from the child's, rather than the parents' point of view, in particular by applying the welfare principle. This position came about only gradually.

Custody of Children Under 16

By the Custody of Children Act 1939[99] the power of any court to make orders as to the custody of (or maintenance or education of, or access to) pupil children was extended to minor children under the age of 16. The restraints of the common law on the making of custody orders in respect of a minor *pubes* were therefore removed provided the minor was under 16. This remains the position today, for under the Law Reform (Parent and Child) (Scotland) Act 1986, "child" is there defined, in relation to guardianship, custody and access as a child under the age of 16 years.[1] The natural interpretation of that provision, although the matter could have been more clearly expressed, is that a custody order, being an order relating to parental rights, can be made, and if made endures, until the child reaches the age of 16. A minor was entitled to be heard regarding his custody and where the application was by petition was cited as respondent.[2] It is unclear what, if any, effect changes in the legal capacity of children[3] have on this rule, but it is good practice to take account of the views of older children[4] and a child of sufficient understanding to form and communicate a view prob-

---

[97] *Brand* v. *Shaws* (1888) 15 R. 449, *per* Lord President Inglis at p. 454.
[98] *Goadby* v. *Macandys*, July 7, 1815, F.C. 482.
[99] s. 1(1).
[1] s. 8, as amended by the Age of Legal Capacity (Scotland) Act 1991, Sched. 1, para. 43 and Sched. 2.
[2] *Morrison, Petr.*, 1943 S.C. 481.
[3] Age of Legal Capacity (Scotland) Act 1991.
[4] See *post* at pp. 214–216.

ably has a right to be heard or, at the very least, an interest which it would be wrong to disregard.[5]

Modifications of Father's Rights

The first inroad on the pre-eminent right of the father of the legitimate child was made by the Conjugal Rights (Scotland) Amendment Act 1861, which originally provided[6] that in any action for separation or divorce the court might make such provision "as to it shall seem just and proper" with respect to the custody, maintenance, and education of any pupil children of the marriage. This was amended by the Law Reform (Parent and Child) (Scotland) Act 1986[7] to consist with that statute, and re-enacted as section 20 of the Court of Session Act 1988, which now provides that in such actions the court may make with respect to any child of the marriage any such order (including an interim order) as it thinks fit relating to parental rights. "Child" is given the same meaning as under the 1986 Act, that is, in relation to custody (and access), a child under the age of 16[8]; "child of the marriage" is defined to include any child who (i) is the child of both parties to the marriage or (ii) is the child of one party to the marriage and has been accepted as a child of the family by the other party.[9] By the (now repealed[10]) Guardianship of Infants Act 1886[11] the court was empowered, on the application of the mother or of the father of any pupil child (later child under the age of 16) to make such order as it might think fit regarding the child's custody having regard to the welfare of the child and to the conduct of the parents and to the wishes as well of the mother as of the father. By the Guardianship of Infants Act 1925[12] (also now repealed[13]) the welfare of the child was made the first and paramount consideration in deciding *inter alia* questions of custody or upbringing in any proceeding. By the Guardianship Act 1973[14] the mother was given equality of parental rights and authority with the father. Finally, by the Law Reform (Parent and Child) (Scotland) Act 1986, custody, being within the defini-

---

[5] An analogy can be found in s. 12(8) of the Adoption (Scotland) Act 1978, as amended by the Age of Legal Capacity (Scotland) Act 1991, s. 2(3), which obliges the court to obtain the child's consent to an adoption order if the child is over 12 years. The *Report on Family Law*, Scot. Law Com. No. 135, May 1992, suggests that before a person reaches a major decision concerning the child the views of the child should be taken into consideration (bearing in mind the child's age and maturity), and that it should be presumed that a child aged 12 or over has sufficient maturity to express a reasonable view: paras. 2.60–2.66, draft Bill, cl. 6. This would give effect to art. 12 of the UN Convention of the Rights of the Child (28 *International Legal Materials* 1448), ratified by the UK on Dec. 16, 1991, which provides that children are to have the right to express their own view and that due weight should be given to these views, in accordance with the age and maturity of the child. See *post* at pp. 000.

[6] s. 9.

[7] Sched. 1, para. 2.

[8] Court of Session Act 1988, s. 20(2)(*a*).

[9] *Ibid.*, s. 20(2)(*b*). The court has no power under this provision to make a custody award over a child accepted as a child of the family by both parties to the marriage, but the natural child of neither: *Bradley* v. *Bradley*, 1987 S.C.L.R. 62, because the parents would not otherwise have the right to be heard.

[10] Law Reform (Parent and Child) (Scotland) Act 1986, Sched. 2.

[11] s. 49.

[12] s. 1.

[13] Law Reform (Parent and Child) (Scotland) Act 1986, Sched. 2.

[14] s. 10, repealed by the Law Reform (Parent and Child) (Scotland) Act 1986, Sched. 2.

tion given in that statute of "parental rights,"[15] is automatically conferred on the mother of the child, whether or not she is or has been married to the child's father, and on the father of the child so long as he is married to the child's mother or was married to her at the time of the child's conception or subsequently.[16] The court may make such order relating to parental rights as it thinks fit,[17] but in any proceedings relating to parental rights the court shall regard the welfare of the child involved as the paramount consideration and shall not make any order relating to parental rights unless it is satisfied that to do so will be in the interests of the child.[18] The custodial power belongs to each parent and is exercisable by either without the other, unless any decree or deed conferring the right otherwise provides.[19] On the death of either parent the surviving parent with parental rights is sole custodian.[20]

Illegitimate Children

Custodial rights relating to children whose parents are not married to each other have also been modified by statute although less radically (except in the important sense that they are both now treated more or less equally) than in the case of legitimate children. By the Illegitimate Children (Scotland) Act 1930[21] the right of the father of an illegitimate child to meet a claim for aliment by the mother by an offer to assume custody of the child was abolished. By the same Act,[22] the court was empowered on an application by the mother or by the father to make such order as it may think fit regarding custody of an illegitimate child having regard to the welfare of the child and to the conduct of the parties and to the wishes as well of the mother as of the father. The law is now contained in the Law Reform (Parent and Child) (Scotland) Act 1986, s.1 of which provides for the legal equality of children whether or not their parents are or have been married to each other. Section 2 confers parental rights (including the right of custody) on the mother whether or not she is or has been married to the child's father and on the father if he is married to the child's mother or was married to her at the time of the child's conception or subsequently. The mother who is not married to the father thus retains the primary right to custody, and in the absence of a court order hers is the sole right recognised by law, but the father may make an application for custody under s. 3(1) of the 1986 Act, which will then be determined by the welfare test laid down in s. 3(2) of that Act. Section 3(1) provides that "any person claiming interest' may make an application for an order relating to parental rights, and this clearly envisages that orders may be made in

---

[15] s. 8.

[16] Law Reform (Parent and Child) (Scotland) Act 1986, s. 2.

[17] *Ibid.*, s. 3(1).

[18] *Ibid.*, s. 3(2).

[19] *Ibid.*, s. 2(4).

[20] This, it is submitted, is the consequence of equality of parental rights and authority. The parental power cannot be conferred on anyone other than a parent, and a guardian nominated by the deceased parent under s. 4 of the 1986 Act cannot encroach on the parental right of custody of the surviving parent, for the right of guardianship does not carry with it the right of custody.

[21] s. 2(2). The whole Act was repealed by the Law Reform (Parent and Child) (Scotland) Act 1986, Sched. 2.

[22] s. 2(1).

favour of other persons.[23] A modern court would not, it is submitted, disturb existing arrangements for the custody of a child in order to give effect to proposals of the father's testamentary trustees[24] unless these proposals had merits from the standpoint of the child's welfare which outweighed the harmful effects of removal, and that would normally only be so if the existing arrangements were seriously unsatisfactory. A condition in a bequest which, in effect, seeks to fetter the court's freedom, in the exercise of its duty to determine custody by reference to the welfare of the child as the paramount consideration, is, it is submitted, null on ground of public policy.

Welfare Prior to 1925

The importance and centrality given by the Guardianship of Infants Act 1925 to the welfare of the child was at that time an innovation. To some extent, however the way had been prepared for the 1925 Act by earlier legislation and by judicial decision. The Conjugal Rights (Scotland) Amendment Act 1861,[25] the Guardianship of Infants Act 1886[26] and the Custody of Children Act 1891[27] were all in terms which enlarged the powers of the court in the cases to which they applied so as to enable it, where appropriate, to modify or set aside the rights of the father and give greater weight to *inter alia* the welfare of the child. Although it had been held in the Court of Session that the effect of the 1861 Act was purely jurisdictional and did not give the court any wider powers than it possessed at common law[28] that view is irreconcilable with the decision and with the preponderance of the speeches in *Symington* v. *Symington*[29] in which Lord Cairns L.C. said that:

> "the Act of Parliament has given the Court the widest and the most general discretion, and has purposely done so.... It must be the duty of the Court in every case to consider the whole of the circumstances of the particular case before it—the circumstances of the misconduct which leads to a separation no doubt, the circumstances of the general character of the father, the circumstances of the general character of the mother, and, above all, it should be the duty of the Court to look to the interest of the children."[30]

In practice, however, after 1861 and even after the decision of the House of Lords in *Symington*, great weight was attached to the father's right and it was often no less conclusive than it would have been at common law.[31] The 1886 Act was more influential than its predecessor both in enlarging the claims of the mother as against the father of a legitimate child and in the stress to be put on the child's welfare to which, unlike the 1861 Act, it explicitly referred. Lindley L.J.

---

[23] *F.* v. *F.*, 1991 S.L.T. 357, discussed *post* at pp. 203–204.
[24] See *ante*, at pp. 40–41.
[25] s. 9. See now the Court of Session Act 1988, s. 20.
[26] s. 5 (repealed by the 1986 Act, Sched. 2).
[27] s. 3 (repealed by the Children Act 1989, Sched. 15).
[28] *Lang* v. *Lang* (1869) 7 M. 445; *cf. Steuart* v. *Steuart* (1870) 8 M. 821.
[29] (1875) 2 R. (H.L.) 41.
[30] *Ibid.* at p. 43.
[31] *e.g. Lang* v. *Lang, supra; Steuart* v. *Steuart, supra; Bowman* v. *Graham* (1883) 10 R. 1234; *Beattie* v. *Beattie* (1883) 11 R. 85. *Cf. Ketchen* v. *Ketchen* (1870) 8 M. 952, *contra.*

could say "the dominant matter for the consideration of the Court is the welfare of the child"[32] and that "it is essentially a mother's Act."[33] These observations were, of course, only true in questions between father and mother which were the questions with which the Act was concerned. After some hesitation[34] a similar view prevailed in Scotland. "The first consideration," the Lord President said in *Reid* v. *Reid*,[35] "is the welfare of the children, though no doubt the wishes of the spouses are also to be taken into account." The Act so interpreted gave expression to what had in any event been a trend in judicial decision. At common law the rights of the father, although often strictly applied, were open to some latitude of interpretation. Danger to physical or moral welfare was a question of degree. It ordinarily could arise only if there were fault on the part of the father but again culpability was a question of degree. There was occasional opportunity, which some judges took, for what was essentially a welfare judgment. In *Smart* v. *Smart*[36] Lord Hobhouse ascribed to judicial decision as well as to legislative action and general opinion a tendency in family questions "to bring the marital duty of the husband and the welfare of the children into greater prominence; in both respects diminishing the powers accorded to the husband and the father." That tendency was aided by an indirect influence of the legislation even in cases to which it did not in terms apply. In such a case the statute was not "to be altogether laid aside" but was occasion for administering the law "within temperate limits so as to adapt it to modern views."[37]

There was, however, a competing line of authority which led to results little different from those of the older cases. Some judges were persuaded that the 1886 Act had made little difference to the common law except, perhaps, in giving the mother a rather stronger claim in a question with the father. That conclusion could be reached by allowing that there had been some development in the common law while, at the same time, interpreting the 1886 Act so as to retain a prominent place for the primary right of the father. Thus in *Sleigh* v. *Sleigh*[38] Lord McLaren said:

"Under the Guardianship of Infants Act 1886 the Court has an unqualified discretion to deal with applications as to the custody of the children, the guiding consideration being 'the interests of the children'. I think that in laying down for us this principle the statute has not at all displaced the common law as interpreted in the decisions, because it is a matter very clear on the historical development of the law of this subject that the interest of the children has been treated as the ruling consideration. It was no doubt kept in view that the father, as head of the family, had powers and rights over the children, who looked to him on their part for support and advancement in life. Now, while the statute gives to the Court a large dis-

---

[32] In *Re McGrath (Infants)* [1893] 1 Ch. 143 at p. 148.
[33] In *Re A. and B. Infants* [1897] 1 Ch. 786 at p. 790. *Cf.* Rigby L.J. at p. 792: "The Act goes very far indeed in diminution of the rights of the father, and in conferring new rights—I will not say equal rights, but new and important rights—upon the mother."
[34] See *Stevenson* v. *Stevenson* (1894) 21 R. 430, overruled (1894) 21 R. (H.L.) 96.
[35] (1902) 3 F. 330 at p. 332.
[36] [1892] A.C. 425 at p. 432.
[37] *Brand* v. *Shaws* (1888) 16 R. 315, *per* Lord Shand at p. 323.
[38] (1893) 30 S.L.R. 272 at p. 275.

cretion according to what appears to be the interest of the children, it does not alter the position of the father as head of the family. We therefore approach a case of this class with this fact to begin with, that the father is the guardian, and cannot be displaced from that position except on sufficient legal grounds".

In *Mackellar* v. *Mackellar*,[39] however, he accepted "that the doctrine of the father's right was carried to a great length under the common law, and that it has a much more restricted application under the statute."[40] "The statute," he said, "has made this alteration of the law, that the Court is directed to consider the conduct and wishes of the parents and the welfare of the children, the direction being given in such terms as to indicate that in considering the question no preference is given to one spouse over the other."[41] The result was the same as in *Sleigh*: the custody of the children was given to the father. Both cases can be regarded as quite extreme instances of assertion of a paternal right despite the passing of the 1886 Act and neither, despite some discussion of the Act, shows, in the result, any material departure from the common law. And there was, indeed, a view on which even the strictest standards of the common law could be reconciled with the statute. The father's right to custody, although, as part of the *patria potestas*, derived from the Roman law and ultimately from an archaic concept of the family, had for long been justified on the view that it was for the child's welfare. The father, it was held, was the best judge of what was in the interests of the child. The court interfered only where the child's welfare was seriously endangered by the father's conduct, not because the law was otherwise neglectful of the interests of the child but because, unless there was clear evidence that the father was abusing his position, interference by the court would be to substitute an inferior for a superior view of where those interests lay.[42] Considerations of that kind were seldom expressly avowed in judicial opinions after 1886 but their persisting influence lurks behind many of the decisions. The law before 1925 presents, therefore, a somewhat confused picture so far as custody disputes between parents of legitimate children are concerned. Statute had opened the way for a wider consideration of the child's welfare and the claims of the mother and judicial dicta had laid some stress on both, but the interpretation had often been such as to retain a strong position for the primacy of the father's right and many of the decisions showed little advance on the common law.

The Guardianship of Infants Act 1886 applied only to disputes between parents of legitimate children. In a question with third parties, the father's right was before 1925 unaffected by statute except that, under the Custody of Children Act 1891[43] where a parent had abandoned or deserted his child or allowed his child to be brought up by another person, at that person's expense, for such a length of time and under such circumstances as to satisfy the court that the par-

---

[39] (1898) 25 R. 883.

[40] *Ibid.*, at p. 885.

[41] *Ibid.*, at p. 884.

[42] That this is still, at least, a starting-point can be seen from the following comment of Lord Fraser of Tullybelton in *Gillick* v. *West Norfolk and Wisbech Area Health Authority* [1985] 3 All E.R. 402 at p. 412: "Nobody doubts, certainly I do not doubt, that in the overwhelming majority of cases the best judges of a child's welfare are his or her parents."

[43] s. 3.

ent was unmindful of his parental duties, the onus shifted to the parent of showing that he was a fit person to have the custody of the child. In considering
whether that onus had been discharged regard had to be had to the welfare of the
child. With that exception, there was, before 1925, little move away from the
nearly absolute nature of the father's right in a question with third parties.

So far as illegitimate children were concerned, there was also little change
before 1925. Their position was not affected directly by statute, apart from the
1891 Act.[44] In *Campbell* v. *Croall*[45] under the 1891 Act and in *Sutherland* v.
Taylor[46] at common law (each case at the instance of the mother of illegitimate
children) custody was refused on grounds that stressed children's interests as a
central consideration but the circumstances of each case were such, in respect of
the danger to the children's health, that refusal would have been the likely result
even at an earlier period of the law's development. As late as 1921 arrangements for the care of an illegitimate child, which had lasted, without any cause
for complaint, for over 10 years, were disturbed and custody granted to the
child's mother after some inquiry into whether the mother was in a position to
make effectual plans for the child's welfare but without further consideration of
where the child's interest lay; and one of the judges was of the opinion that the
prayer of the petition ought to have been granted *de plano*.[47]

Welfare Since 1925

The most significant statutory departure from the common law was the
Guardianship of Infants Act 1925, s. 1 of which required that the court regard
the welfare of the child as the first and paramount consideration and also that it
was not to take into consideration whether from any other point of view the
claim of the father was superior to that of the mother or the claim of the mother
was superior to that of the father. As originally enacted, the section also excluded from consideration, otherwise than from the point of view of the child's
welfare, any right at common law possessed by the father, but that was deleted
as no longer necessary by the Guardianship Act 1973.[48] Not only, therefore, was
consideration of the child's welfare given precedence over all other questions
but, in disputes between father and mother, regard for the welfare of the child
was in future to be the sole basis for giving preference to the one or the other on
general grounds.

It appeared, however, that, if only rarely, preference could still be given to
one parent or the other on grounds other than welfare according to the circumstances of the particular case. Matters such as the conduct of the spouses to each
other or responsibility for the breakdown of the marriage were primarily to be
considered in the context of the child's welfare[49] and usually that would exhaust
the scope for their consideration. Exceptionally, however, although always
postponed to and subject to consistency with the child's welfare, they were in-

---

[44] The Guardianship of Infants Act 1886 "does not apply to illegitimate children": *Brand* v. *Shaws*
(1888) 16 R. 315 at pp. 320 and 323.
[45] (1895) 22 R. 869.
[46] (1887) 15 R. 224.
[47] *Walter* v. *Culbertson*, 1921 S.C. 490.
[48] s. 10(8).
[49] *Christison* v. *Christison*, 1936 S.C. 381; *McLean* v. *McLean*, 1947 S.C. 79.

dependently taken into account. It was also implicit, and accords in general with the interpretation given to the section, that the welfare of the child was to be assessed according to the circumstances of each case rather than by any *a priori* principle of preference. The result overall was, therefore, such an extensive departure both from the common law and from the general pattern of interpretation of previous statutes and decisions under them that it is only in exceptional cases that, on the merits of custody disputes, any assistance can be derived from pre-1925 authorities. Moreover, the expression of the welfare principle in general terms of wide application left little scope for refined interpretation; and judicial decisions even after 1925, being decisions on the facts of each case, can seldom be precedents.[50] A number of cases under the 1925 Act, however, continue to provide useful illustrations of the working of the principle and indicate the considerations which may bear on welfare.

Section 1 of the Guardianship of Infants Act 1925 applied in any proceeding before any court where *inter alia* the custody or upbringing of a child was in question. Despite the generality of these words, a number of cases proceeded on the view, or at least on the assumption, that the section applied only to disputes between parents of legitimate children.[51] A similar view had been taken in England.[52] That view was based on the concluding words of the section which could only be applied to disputes between parents and on the requirement[53] that the Act be construed as one with the Guardianship of Infants Act 1886 whose custody provisions were confined to disputes between parents.[54] In *J* v. *C*,[55] however, it was held that the words of the section must receive their natural meanings so as to apply to disputes between parents and third parties as well as between parents *inter se*. It was applicable, as it says, to any proceedings before any court where the custody or upbringing of a child is in question irrespective of whether or not the claimants, or any of them, are parents and irrespective of whether or not the child is legitimate. Originally the Act only applied to pupil children[56] but it was later extended to children under 16 years of age.[57]

The Law Reform (Parent and Child) (Scotland) Act 1986

Section 3(2) of the 1986 Act requires that the court, in actions relating to parental rights, regard the welfare of the child as the paramount consideration and also that it shall not make any order relating to parental rights unless it is satis-

---

[50] *Townsend* v. *Townsend* (1973) 4 Fam. L. 127, *per* Davies L.J. at p. 128.

[51] *Hume* v. *Hume*, 1926 S.C. 1008; *McLean* v. *Hardie*, 1927 S.C. 344; *Pow* v. *Pow*, 1931 S.L.T. 485; *Nicol* v. *Nicol*, 1953 S.L.T.(Notes) 67 ("Assuming that s. 1 of the 1925 Act does not apply"); *McNaught* v. *McNaught*, 1955 S.L.T. (Sh.Ct.) 9; *Macallister* v. *Macallister*, 1962 S.C. 406.

[52] In *Re Carroll* [1931] 1 K.B. 317, *per* Scrutton L.J. at pp. 335–337, and Slesser L.J. at pp. 355 and 362.

[53] s. 11(2).

[54] That the 1886 Act was so restricted was reasonably clear from its terms. In *Brand* v. *Shaws* (1886) 16 R. 315 it was held that the 1886 Act had no application to an illegitimate child: see *ante*, at p. 77.

[55] [1970] A.C. 668.

[56] s. 11 incorporating the Guardianship of Infants Act 1886, s. 8.

[57] Custody of Children (Scotland) Act 1939, s. 1(1).

fied that to do so will be in the interests of the child. The effect of this section is for all intents and purposes the same as that of section 1 of the 1925 Act, this notwithstanding that the welfare of the child is stated to be "the paramount consideration" rather than "the first and paramount consideration."[58] The substantive law on custody since the passing of the 1986 Act is considered in some detail in Chapter 7.

---

[58] The Scottish Law Commission were of the view that the words "first and" added nothing, and could indeed be described as unnecessary, obscure and question-begging: see Scot. Law Com. No. 82, *Report on Illegitimacy* (1984), para. 9.17.

CHAPTER 3

ANTE-NATAL ISSUES

INTRODUCTORY

The most significant event in the creation of the parent-child relationship is birth. To the layman it is from the moment of birth that motherhood or father-hood commences. The man who says, "I have just become a father" is saying that a child has just been born; the woman who says, "I am going to be a mother" is saying that she is pregnant but has not yet given birth. The law however does not precisely reflect this, and in some respects the parent-child relationship may be constituted before birth. At least certain aspects of that relationship come into existence as soon as an embryo or foetus[1] comes into being. For example, the law of Scotland has long recognised that an unborn child[2] has a claim for le-gitim from the estate of a parent who dies before the child is born,[3] which must be an aspect of the parent-child relationship since legitim cannot be claimed in the absence of that relationship. There is indeed modern statutory authority for the proposition that at least in some circumstances and for some purposes the parent-child relationship may come into existence before birth. If a pregnancy is constituted by means of one of the medical procedures governed by the Human Fertilisation and Embryology Act 1990, then, "the woman who *is carrying* or has carried a child. . .is to be treated as the mother of the child."[4] If a woman is treated as a mother for all purposes while she is still pregnant then she has the parental rights and duties of the mother of a born child. However, the courts are unlikely to accept the full consequences of this ill-thought-out definition.[5]

The unborn child has no legal personality in any meaningful sense of that phrase.[6] It has no ability to own property, or to sue or to be sued, nor can legal acts be performed on its behalf. But its existence is not without legal con-sequence, which, in some respects, involves parental rights and obligations. Of course most of the parental rights and obligations will, in practical terms, be meaningless during the pregnancy; but that in itself does not deny their exist-ence. The parent-child relationship is one of shifting content throughout its sub-sistence, and many aspects of it are meaningless at particular times. A parental obligation to aliment a child, or to feed and nurture it, is largely meaningless un-til after the child is born; but that is no more strange than the fact that the par-

---

[1] These terms may have precise medical meanings, depending upon the state of development of the potential human life. They are used here interchangeably to mean any living human entity be-tween the completion of the process of fertilisation and the completion of the process of birth.

[2] The phrase "unborn child" is here used as shorthand and not as indicating the moral or legal status imputed to the child before its live birth.

[3] *Jervey* v. *Watt* (1762) Mor. 8170. See further, *post* at p. 91.

[4] Human Fertilisation and Embryology Act 1990, s. 27(1).

[5] See further, *post* at pp. 121–125.

[6] See Yorke, "The Legal Personality of the Unborn Child," 1979 S.L.T. (News) 158.

ental right to determine a child's religious upbringing has no content for a significant period after birth, nor the fact that the parental duty to provide education is directly enforceable only between the ages of five and 16.[7] In English law a parental right to withhold consent to marriage is no right in any meaningful sense until the child is old enough legally to marry. But it is a parental right from the moment the relationship is constituted, though for practical reasons it cannot immediately be exercised. When the child attains adulthood most, but not all, of the consequences of the parent-child relationship disappear—consequences that remain include succession rights, and the consequences relating to the laws of incest and the forbidden degrees of marriage.[8]

This shifting relationship cannot exist before an embryo comes into being, and it cannot survive the death of either the parent or the child. Its consequences vary with time. The question, "When is the parent-child relationship established?" is then ultimately as (legally) meaningless as is the question, "When does human life begin?" Rather, the question is, what precise consequences does the law recognise as flowing from the existence of particular entities (embryos or foetuses), and the answer to that depends upon the stage of development of the embryo or foetus. The unborn child, no less than the born child, has a developing and changing status in relation to its parents, and to society as a whole. A child after birth has a different status, and varying legal personality, at different ages: so the born child before the age of 16 can own property but cannot normally sue in his own name; the child above that age can both own property and sue. There is nothing in principle to deny the child before birth some legal status which has less content than that of the child, just as the pupil had at common law a legal status which had less content than that of a minor. Just like the living human being, the unborn child goes through a number of stages, at each of which its position in law may be quite different.

THE STAGE BEFORE PREGNANCY

From Production of Gametes to Fertilisation

The creation of new human life requires as a first essential the production of gametes of a human male and a human female. The mere production of these, and the making of them available for reproduction through sexual intercourse, has no significance for the law either in relation to any parent-child relationship or in relation to the creation of any entity whose existence has consequences recognised by the law. The destruction of sperm and eggs that have not yet joined together is legally innocuous.

However, when sperm and eggs are produced and intended to be used for any of the forms of infertility treatment governed by the Human Fertilisation and Embryology Act 1990, the person whose body produced them does have certain legally recognised rights of control, in the sense that their consent to such use has to be obtained.[9] The producer of the gametes must provide consent if they

---

[7] Education (Scotland) Act 1980, ss. 30 and 31.

[8] On which, see Norrie, "Incest and the Forbidden Degrees of Marriage in Scots Law" (1992) 37 J.L.S. 216.

[9] Human Fertilisation and Embryology Act 1990, Sched. 3.

are to be stored (*i.e.* frozen) either as gametes or after they have been used to create embryos,[10] or if they are to be donated for the treatment of others,[11] or if they are to be used to bring about the creation of embryos, in which last case the producer must be made aware of whether the embryo is for treatment or for research.[12] When gametes are donated, "proper arrangements" have to be made for their keeping and disposal by the person licensed to keep and use them.[13] Directions as to the keeping of gametes may be given to the licence holder by the Human Fertilisation and Embryology Authority[14] set up by the 1990 Act.

From Fertilisation to Implantation

Once the sperm and egg have joined together, in the sense of the former fertilising the latter, there exists what is variously called (depending upon the stage of development) a fertilised ovum, a zygote, a blastocyst, a pre-embryo, an embryo, a foetus, or an unborn child. Whatever it is called, and this is true for the later stages also, its name is irrelevant to its position in law, which depends upon status rather than nomenclature.

Status of the Pre-implantation Embryo

Once the process of fertilisation has been completed,[15] the embryo must find its way, naturally or with medical assistance, to a woman's uterus, and be implanted there. This process in natural conditions takes up to a week; the embryo may exist in that state for far longer if it is created *in vitro*, or is removed from the woman's body before implantation. The status of the embryo between its coming into being and the completion of the process of implantation has long given rise to controversy. It has frequently been argued that the pre-implantation embryo cannot be destroyed, because its destruction would infringe the criminal law prohibition of abortion.[16] Whether this is so is undecided in Scotland, although the court might well take the view that, since abortion is concerned primarily with the termination of pregnancy,[17] and pregnancy will not have commenced before implantation, the destruction of pre-implantation embryos will not amount to abortion in Scots law.[18] Clearly, such destruction

---

[10] *Ibid.*, Sched. 3, paras. 2 and 8.

[11] *Ibid.* at para. 5.

[12] *Ibid.* at para. 6.

[13] *Ibid.*, s. 17(1)(c).

[14] *Ibid.* s. 24(3).

[15] For the purposes of the Human Fertilisation and Embryology Act 1990 the completion of the process of fertilisation is defined as the moment at which a two-cell zygote appears: s. 1(1)(b).

[16] See, *e.g.* Smith & Hogan, *Textbook on Criminal Law* (6th ed., 1988) at p. 367; Tunkel, "Modern Anti-pregnancy Techniques and the Criminal Law" [1974] Crim. L.R. 461, and "Abortion: How Early, How Late and How Legal?" (1979) 2 B.M.J. 253; Keown, " 'Miscarriage': A Medico-Legal Analysis" [1984] Crim. L.R. 604. All of these writers were arguing on the basis of the English statutory provisions, which have no analogy in Scotland.

[17] And so in Scotland it is no crime to attempt to abort a woman who is not pregnant: *H.M.A.* v. *Semple*, 1937 J.C. 41; *H.M.A.* v. *Anderson*, 1928 J.C. 1. But these cases do not address the question of the pre-implantation embryo. Cf. Gordon, *Criminal Law of Scotland*, 2nd ed. at p. 812: "Abortion may be committed at any stage between conception and birth". It might be argued that abortion is the ending of the life of a developing entity, of which termination of pregnancy is only a typical example.

[18] This matter is more fully discussed by Norrie in *Family Planning Practice and the Law* (1991) at pp. 48–59. See also Douglas, *Law, Fertility and Reproduction* (1991), at pp. 27–36.

cannot amount to any form of homicide, for the law of homicide in Scotland requires a living, breathing, human person to exist[19]: while a fertilised egg may arguably have humanity, the law will not recognise it as having personality.[20] It is also undecided whether its destruction can amount to a civil wrong. In the U.S. case of *Del Zio* v. *Presbyterian Hospital*[21] a civil action for damages was raised against a hospital director who had terminated an infertility treatment programme in which the plaintiffs were taking part, by destroying the embryo that had been created *in vitro* from the husband's sperm and the wife's egg. The couple were awarded damages after the court found that the defendant had acted wrongfully. But on a close examination of the case, it is clear that damages were awarded on the basis of the emotional shock suffered by the plaintiffs (a well-recognised ground of action) and that the destruction of the embryo was merely the medium through which that shock was caused. The question remains, however, of whether persons whose gametes have been used to create an embryo may have such an interest in the embryo's continued existence and development as to make its destruction by another an actionable wrong in respect of which, quite apart from any emotional shock, they may sue.

In Vitro Embryos

In factual terms we can today distinguish between eggs that have been fertilised naturally in a woman's body, and those fertilised artificially outwith a woman's body and *in vitro*. In relation to the latter the Human Fertilisation and Embryology Act 1990 regulates their treatment. Section 3(1) of that Act provides that no person may bring about the creation of an embryo[22] or keep or use an embryo except in pursuance of a licence granted by a committee of the Human Fertilisation and Embryology Authority. A licence cannot authorise the keeping or using of an embryo after the appearance of the primitive streak,[23] which is taken to have appeared in an embryo not later than the end of the period of 14 days beginning with the day when the gametes were mixed, not counting any time during which the embryo is stored.[24] To "store" an embryo means to preserve it by cryopreservation (freezing) or in any other way[25]: this presumably means any other way that similarly arrests the development of the embryo. A licence cannot authorise the placing of an embryo in any species of animal.[26]

During the period of 14 days the licence holder may do to the embryo anything that the licence authorises, and in addition to use for infertility treatment, the licence may authorise the creation, keeping and using of embryos for the

---

[19] *H.M.A.* v. *McAllum* (1858) 3 Irv. 187; Macdonald, *Criminal Law of Scotland* (5th ed., 1948) at p. 87; Gordon, *Criminal Law of Scotland* (2nd ed., 1978) at p. 727.

[20] See *post* at pp. 98–99.

[21] 74 Civ. 3588 (Nov. 14, 1978, U.S. District Court for the Southern District of New York).

[22] Which means a live human embryo where fertilisation is complete, and references to an embryo include an egg in the process of fertilisation: Human Fertilisation and Embryology Act 1990, s. 1(1).

[23] *Ibid.*, s. 3(3).

[24] *Ibid.*, s. 3(4).

[25] *Ibid.*, s. 2(2). Cryopreservation is the only method possible today by which a living embryo can be stored, but the Act clearly does not wish to inhibit future developments.

[26] *Ibid.*, s. 3(3)(b).

purposes of a project of research specified in the licence.[27] This, it appears, will
include destruction, though that is not stated in so many words in the Act itself
(except when human sperm is mixed with the egg of a hamster or other animal
in order to test the sperm's fertility, in which case the resulting form must be
destroyed when the research is completed and, in any event, not later than the
two-cell stage[28]). If a person does something that is not or cannot be authorised
by a licence he shall be guilty of an offence and liable on conviction on indictment to imprisonment for up to 10 years or a fine or both.[29] It follows that no embryo may lawfully be in existence after 14 days unless it has been implanted into
a woman (or was there naturally in the first place).

Rights Over In Vitro Embryos

For an embryo that is artificially and lawfully created, the question arises as
to whether the woman whose egg, and the man whose sperm, was used in its
creation have any rights or obligations, parental or otherwise, over it. That questions did not arise for the common law. The common law recognition of children before birth was limited to those described as "*in utero*" or "*en ventre sa
mere.*" The destruction of pre-implantation embryos by means of so-called
"morning-after contraception" has been said not to be abortion.[30] Unless common law principles applicable to children *in utero* can be extended to embryos
in vitro, any rights or obligations over such embryos must be contained in the
Human Fertilisation and Embryology Act 1990. By Schedule 3, paragraph 6(1)
a person's gametes may not be used to bring about the creation of an embryo *in
vitro* unless there is an effective consent by that person to any embryo being
used (a) to provide infertility treatment services to that person, (b) to provide infertility treatment services to another person, or (c) for the purposes of any research project. Likewise an embryo created *in vitro* cannot be stored without the
consent of those whose gametes were used in its creation.[31] An embryo fertilised naturally and taken from a woman cannot be used for any of the above purposes,[32] nor stored without that woman's consent[33]: in these circumstances the
consent of the man whose sperm fertilised the egg is not required. These provisions for consent cannot, it is submitted, be characterised as "parental" rights of
consent, because the Act envisages consent to research upon and consequent
destruction of embryos up until 14 days. The validity of the exercise of any parental right depends upon the satisfaction of the welfare test,[34] which will normally be incompatible with research and will certainly be incompatible with
destruction. The provisions in the 1990 Act are therefore best regarded as imposing statutory control on the use of embryos without in any way creating parental rights and obligations. It is to be noted that similar consent provisions are

---

[27] *Ibid.*, s. 11(1) and Sched. 2, para. 3(1).
[28] *Ibid.*, Sched. 2, para. 3(5).
[29] *Ibid.*, s. 41(1).
[30] This was the view of the English Attorney-General, expressed to Parliament: May 10, 1983, H.C.
    Written Answers, Vol. 42, col. 236–237. See further, Norrie, *Family Planning Practice and the
    Law* (1991), Chap. 4.
[31] Sched. 3, para. 8(2).
[32] *Ibid.*, para. 7(1).
[33] *Ibid.*, para. 8(3).
[34] See *post* at pp. 206–209.

laid down for the use and storage of gametes[35] and it cannot be argued that a person has any "parental" control over his or her own gametes.

DURING GESTATION

Introduction

Once the process of implantation in the uterus has been completed, the embryo attains a very different status in law from the one it had previously, and its existence entails a very large number of consequences. Without question the most important and most contentious of these is that it is protected from destruction by the law prohibiting abortion, and this issue will therefore be discussed first. It is not the only consequence, as will be seen.

Abortion

The Nature of Abortion

Abortion is the destruction[36] of an unborn child by the termination of pregnancy. It is a common law crime according to the law of Scotland,[37] though it has been recognised that there may be circumstances in which it is a lawful act, such as when it is "a necessary medical operation."[38] Abortion remains a common law crime today. "Abortion in the sense of the criminal law is held to be criminal because its successful accomplishment results in the destruction of potential human life."[39] Potential human life is deemed worthy of protection by the law, though the crime of abortion would be committed only after a pregnancy has commenced, if abortion is defined as the termination of a pregnancy, or the inducing of a miscarriage. The important moment for the commencement of pregnancy is the completion of the process of implantation.[40] This is not to say, however, that the High Court of Justiciary could not declare criminal, even if it be not abortion, the destruction of potential human life before implantation.

---

[35] *Ante* at pp. 83–84.

[36] It has been argued that abortion does not necessarily presuppose destruction and that there may well be an ethical duty to carry out the abortion in such a manner as gives the abortus the best chance of survival: see McLean, "Abortion Law: Is Consensual Reform Possible?" (1990) 17 J. Law & Soc. 106. If such a duty exists in ethics, it does not exist in law, and, in any case, would apply only to a few very late abortions. A surgeon carrying out an abortion must do so in such a way as serves the best interests of his patient, *i.e.* the pregnant woman: see Norrie, *Family Planning Practice and the Law*, at p. 57. The U.S. Supreme Court held in *Thornburgh* v. *American College of Obstetricians and Gynecologists* (1986) 106 Sup.Ct. 2169 that a Pennsylvania statute providing that abortion had to be carried out in the way best designed to give the foetus the greatest chance of survival was unconstitutional since it might involve subjecting the woman to greater risk.

[37] Macdonald, *Criminal Law of Scotland*, at p. 114; Gordon, *Criminal Law*, at p. 812.

[38] Anderson, *Criminal Law of Scotland* (2nd ed., 1904) at p. 156; Jones & Christie, *Criminal Law*, at p. 188. As a rule of law this view is unsupported by judicial decision but it represents the practice of the prosecuting authorities.

[39] *Per* Lord Anderson in *H.M.A.* v. *Anderson*, 1928 J.C. 1 at p. 4.

[40] See Yen & Jaffe, *Reproductive Endocrinology, Physiology, Pathophysiology and Clinical Management* (2nd ed.), at p. 200; "Post-Coital Contraception" (1983) 1 *Lancet* 853. This is confirmed for the purposes of the Human Fertilisation and Embryology Act 1990 by s. 2(3) thereof, which provides that "a woman is not to be treated as carrying a child until the embryo has become implanted."

Once a woman becomes pregnant, she has the right to seek an abortion (though not a right to demand an abortion, as in, for example, the United States of America, where the right to an abortion—if it can be afforded—is currently constitutionally protected as part of the right of privacy[41]) and must clearly consent to that act being done upon her. The woman's consent to that act is not the exercise of any parental right that she may have over the foetus, because parental rights must be exercised consistently with the welfare of the child, and the abortion decision may be taken for reasons other than the welfare of the child and in any event will normally be against the interests of the unborn child.

Defences to the Crime of Abortion

The potential human life is protected by the prohibition of abortion, but that protection is not absolute, and the embryo may be aborted (that is, destroyed) if carried out by a registered medical practitioner and two registered medical practitioners are of the view, formed in good faith, that one of the grounds laid down in s. 1(1) of the Abortion Act 1967[42] is satisfied. The grounds are as follows:

(1) that the continuance of the pregnancy would involve risk, greater than if the pregnancy were terminated, of injury to the physical or mental health of the pregnant woman or any existing children of her family (though this ground is available only when the pregnancy has not exceeded 24 weeks in duration);

(2) that the termination is necessary in order to prevent grave permanent injury to the physical or mental health of the pregnant woman (in which case there is no limit of time as in (1) above);

(3) that the continuance of the pregnancy would involve risk to the life of the pregnant woman, greater than if the pregnancy were terminated (in which case there is no limit of time as in (1) above); and

(4) that there is a substantial risk that if the child were born it would suffer from such physical or mental abnormalities as to be seriously handicapped (in which case there is no limit of time as in (1) above).

In relation to the first two grounds, account may be taken of the pregnant woman's actual or reasonably foreseeable environment.[43]

It is important to note that the ground need not exist in fact nor in law: all that is required is that two registered medical practitioners believe in good faith that one or more of the grounds exists, and the court's role is limited to an investigation of that good faith.[44]

Time Limits for the Abortion Defences

As originally enacted, the 1967 Act did not contain limits in time to the avail-

---

[41] *Roe* v. *Wade* (1973) 410 U.S. 113; *Doe* v. *Bolton* (1973) 410 U.S. 179.

[42] As amended by s. 37 of the Human Fertilisation and Embryology Act 1990. See also the Abortion Regulations 1991 (S.I. 1991 No. 499).

[43] Abortion Act 1967, s. 1(2).

[44] *Per* Scarman L.J. in *R.* v. *Smith* [1974] 1 All E.R. 376, at p. 381; and Baker P. in *Paton* v. *Trustees of the British Pregnancy Advisory Service* [1978] 2 All E.R. 987 at p. 991. See also *Rance* v. *Mid Downs Health Authority* [1991] 1 All E.R. 801.

ability of the abortion defences in Scotland[45] (so long as the destruction was carried out during the subsistence of the pregnancy). That remains the case today only in relation to the second, third and fourth of the above-listed grounds. In relation to the first ground, the pregnancy must not exceed 24 weeks in duration. This may seem to be a significant tightening up of the old law, but it is unlikely to be wholly effective since, if a pregnancy is of more than 24 weeks duration, then it may be possible to use the second or the third ground instead of the first. In relation to the second ground, that is "grave permanent injury," it is to be remembered that account may be taken of the pregnant woman's actual or reasonably foreseeable environment.[46] This was the provision which, after the 1967 Act was originally passed, allowed "social" abortions, and it will continue to do so, notwithstanding the apparent tightening up of the words, so long as the courts limit their role to a determination of whether or not the doctors granting the required certificates were acting in good faith. In relation to the third ground, that is, "risk to life," there is nothing in the Act which expressly qualifies or restricts the interpretation of that phrase given by McNaghten J. in *R*. v. *Bourne*,[47] in which he directed the jury that, life depending upon health, and health including mental as well as physical health, risk to life included risk to physical or mental health. To apply that interpretation to "risk to life" in the Act would, where the risk is to the pregnant woman, subsume the first ground, with its time limit, under the third ground, which has no time limit.[48] It is is submitted that the scheme of the Act is to distinguish between risk to life and risk to health and that a broad interpretation of risk to life, which would destroy that distinction, should not be adopted.

Another difficulty which the statute creates but does not address is that it imposes a time limit in some circumstances but gives no indication as to when the 24 weeks start running. It might be assumed that this is taken to refer to how the medical profession count the weeks, but in Britain the medical profession treats a pregnancy as commencing on the date of the woman's last menstrual period, with the result that the pregnancy as a whole runs for 40 weeks. This is of course factually inaccurate, indeed impossible, and is adopted merely for convenience. A pregnancy "that has not exceeded its 24th week" is a pregnancy that in fact is less than 24 weeks old. The Human Fertilisation and Embryology Act 1990, which introduces this phrase into the 1967 Act, provides in another section that for the purposes of that Act pregnancy commences on implantation of the embryo,[49] which will normally be about a week after fertilisation, and this might indicate that the 24 weeks are to be counted from the completion of implantation. However, medical science is not yet able to determine precisely when implantation in the womb has occurred, not least because the creation of life is a developing process rather than a series of discrete events. A doctor who in good faith certifies that a pregnancy is less than 24 weeks old, using the accepted

---

[45] Unlike the position in England: for an examination of this and other differences between the two systems between 1967 and 1990, see Norrie, "Abortion in Great Britain, One Act, Two Laws," 1985 Crim. L.R. 475.

[46] Abortion Act 1967, s. 1(2).

[47] [1938] 3 All E.R. 615.

[48] See further, Norrie, "British Abortion Rules Altered: Or Are They?" 1992 S.L.T. (News) 41.

[49] Human Fertilisation and Embryology Act 1990, s. 2(3).

medical method of counting these weeks, is unlikely to be found to be in breach of the law.[50] It is to be remembered that abortion, being a criminal act, must be proved beyond reasonable doubt, and this standard of proof would also have to be satisfied by a prosecutor arguing that an abortion had been carried out too late in law.

Selective Reduction

Particularly with infertility treatment, when a number of embryos are frequently placed into a woman, in order to maximise the chances of at least one of them implanting successfully, the medical practice known as "selective reduction" is often performed whereby one or more of the implanted embryos is destroyed in order to benefit the remaining embryo or embryos. There had been doubt in English law as to whether this amounted to an offence under the relevant legislation,[51] since the statute prohibits inducing "miscarriage"[52]: this is not wholly appropriate as a description of the destruction of very early embryos *in utero* (which would be absorbed into the woman's body by the process of phagocystosis rather than being expelled out of her body). The matter was put beyond all doubt by the amendment of section 5(2) of the 1967 Act by section 37 of the Human Fertilisation and Embryology Act 1990, and the destruction of any embryo or embryos implanted in a woman can be done only when authorised by s. 1 of the 1967 Act.

Succession

It is in relation to succession that the civil law of Scotland has most clearly recognised that the existence of a conceived but unborn child can have significant consequences. The proposition taken from the *Digest*,[53] in a translation approved by the House of Lords,[54] is wide in its scope: "An unborn child is taken care of just as much as if it were in existence, in any case in which the child's own advantage comes into question; though no one else can derive any benefit through the child before its birth." In Scotland this principle has been expressly applied only in succession matters,[55] but in that field it is widely accepted by the institutional writers and others.[56] The basis of the principle is the presumption that a parent would desire to provide for children conceived but unborn at the

---

[50] *Cf. Rance* v. *Mid Downs Health Authority* [1991] 1 All E.R. 801. For a further discussion of the difficulty, see Jacob, *Current Law Annotations* of the Human Fertilisation and Embryology Act 1990 (c. 37), s. 37. The same problem appears in the Registration of Births, Deaths and Marriages (Scotland) Act 1965, s. 56(1), as amended by the Still-Birth (Definition) Act 1992, s. 1(2), which provides for the registration of the birth of children still-born after 24 weeks' gestation.

[51] Offences Against the Person Act 1861, ss. 58 and 59.

[52] See Kennedy & Grubb, *Medical Law: Text and Materials* (1989) at pp. 793–796.

[53] 1, v, 7: "*Qui in utero est, perinde ac si in rebus humanis esset, custoditur, quoties de commodis ipsius partus quaeritur: quanquam alii, antequam nascatur, nequaquam prosit.*"

[54] In *Elliot* v. *Joicey* 1935 S.C.(H.L.) 57 at p. 70.

[55] Though in Canada, for example, the same passage was used to justify awarding damages to a child negligently injured while it was *in utero*: see *Montreal Tramways* v. *Leveille* [1933] 4 D.L.R. 337. In *Cohen* v. *Shaw*, 1992 S.L.T. 1022, Lord Cullen could see no reason why it should be limited to succession.

[56] Stair, III, v, 50; Erskine, III, viii, 76; Bankton, I, ii, 7, p. 47; Bell, *Prin.* 1642; Fraser (3rd ed.) at p. 220; McLaren at p. 696; *Enc.*, 10, 1015–1020; 25, 660–662.

date of his or her death,[57] and as such it has the same foundation as the *conditio si testator sine liberis decesserit*.[58] It has extensive application in the law of succession. So, for example, it has been held that a child born subsequently to her father's death was entitled to legitim from his estate,[59] that a legacy in favour of "children" included a child *in utero* but not yet born,[60] and that a posthumous child can in appropriate circumstances take benefit from the application of the *conditio si testator sine liberis decesserit*.[61] A lengthy discussion may be found in what is considered to be the leading decision of *Mountstewart* v. *Mackenzie*,[62] though that case is ultimately unhelpful since a living heir was allowed to be served before the birth of an unborn child, though subject to holding the estate in trust for a child if born. It is interesting to note that in that case there was no allegation that there was an unborn child, merely that there might be.

The extent to which the principle can be taken even in the face of apparently unambiguous words in a will can be seen from the case of *Cox's Trs.* v. *Cox*,[63] in which the residue of an estate was directed to be divided between certain "descendants alive at the time of [the testator's] death." Four such descendants were *in utero* at the date of the testator's death. The First Division held that they were included in the gift. Lord Carmont said this:

> "The particular principle, which from a very early time has guided the Courts in this country in regard to the interpretation of such words of gift as these, has been favourable to including those children who were *in utero* in order to let them share in such gifts, and that is based upon the view that an equitable interpretation of such words used in such testamentary deeds should be given to them. From Roman times we find that the posthumous child has been given its place along with the other children, and that on the fiction that although not born at the time specified in the settlement the child should be deemed to have been so born."[64]

The Qualifications

While the principle itself is well established, equally settled are two qualifications, which are mentioned by nearly all the authorities cited above. The first is that the principle applies only when to do so directly benefits the child itself. No one else can claim a right through the child, until such time as the child is born alive. So, for example, in *Elliot* v. *Joicey*[65] a truster set up a trust for the benefit of her children who were to take the income for 21 years. If any child should die

---

[57] Technology now allows a dead woman's corpse to be artificially ventilated in such a way as to provide a gestation environment for her unborn child: *The Independent*, Oct. 17, 1992, reports such a case involving a 15-week-old foetus growing in the ventilated corpse of its deceased mother.

[58] Fraser, *ibid.*; *Enc.*, 25, 751.

[59] *Jervey* v. *Watt* (1762) Mor. 8170.

[60] *Hardman* v. *Guthrie* (1826) 6 S. 920. See also *Melrose* v. *Melrose's Trs.* (1869) 7 M. 1050.

[61] *Findlay's Trs.* v. *Findlays* (1886) 14 R. 167; *Enc.*, 25, 753.

[62] (1707) Mor. 14903.

[63] 1950 S.C. 117.

[64] *Ibid.*, at p. 121. The rule was resisted by the court in *Burns' Trs.* v. *Burns*, 1916 2 S.L.T. 318, but that case must now be regarded as no longer good law.

[65] 1935 S.C.(H.L.) 57. See also *Villar* v. *Gilbey* [1907] A.C. 139 (in which to apply the fiction would have given the child a right to a liferent instead of a right to the fee).

within that period without issue the share would accrue to the other children. One child did die within the 21 years, leaving a child *in utero* (which was later born alive). If that (grand)child had been deemed to be born at the date of his parent's death, then the benefit from his grandparent's estate would go to his parent's estate, and not to the posthumous child himself. The House of Lords held that in these circumstances the principle could not be applied. The fact that the child's parent's estate would be increased, so increasing the child's share in legitim, was too remote and speculative a benefit: "the *commodum* of the post-humous child must be a direct *commodum* to itself resulting from the instrument under construction by virtue of the application to that instrument of the benevol-ent fiction in question."[66]

The second qualification to the principle is that the child must subsequently be born alive. The right to benefit that vests in the child while it is still in the womb is, effectively, a benefit with a resolutive condition attached, which means that it may be subject to defeasance by the child's failure to attain live birth.[67] While there is no Scottish decision turning on this point, this is almost certainly because the position is so well settled, and the qualification unques-tioned.[68] Indeed, it may be correct, as Meston suggests,[69] that this second quali-fication is simply an example of the first. A child who dies in the womb cannot enjoy the benefit it is to take and clearly to apply the doctrine in relation to such a child is to apply it for the benefit of someone else.

Effect of the Succession (Scotland) Act 1964

The Succession (Scotland) Act 1964 has no effect on this rule,[70] though the Act itself makes no reference to it. Difficulties might arise in relation to section 9, which provides that the value of a spouse's prior rights will differ depending upon whether the intestate is "survived by issue" or not. If there is issue *in utero*, it may be argued that the intestate is "survived" by the child which is sub-sequently born alive, because the child is alive at a time after the deceased's death. In *Elliot* v. *Joicey*[71], however, Lord Macmillan disapproved a similar ar-gument in relation to a testamentary deed using the word "surviving," on the ground that this goes against the ordinary meaning of the word "survive", which is taken to imply "in life at the moment of death." A child *in utero* may well later

---

[66] *Ibid.* at p. 72, *per* Lord Macmillan.

[67] It is interesting to note that the statutory formulation of the rule found in Quebec was character-ised by the Supreme Court of Canada as a suspensive condition, and the argument was rejected that it was a "resolutory" condition: *Tremblay* v. *Daigle* (1989) 62 D.L.R. (4th) 634 at p. 656. This was done to answer the proposition that if the right vested before the birth but was subject to a resolutive condition, the foetus would have legal personality. This does not necessarily follow, however. The vesting is as fictional as the unborn child's existence, and it can be defeated by the same event as defeats the child's legal existence, *i.e.* its death before live birth.

[68] See, *e.g.* Bell, *Prin.*, 1641 and 1642; Bankton, 1, ii, 8; *Enc.*, 25, 662.

[69] "Succession Rights of Posthumous Children" (1970) 15 J.L.S. 33.

[70] s. 1(1)(*b*) provides that a person's intestate succession will devolve according to the rules in that Act and to "any enactment or rule of law in force immediately before the commencement of this Act which is not inconsistent with those provisions." The rule is inconsistent with no provision in the Act.

[71] 1935 S.C.(H.L.) 57 at p. 69.

succeed, but it is not yet in life.[72] It would seem to follow that the child *in utero* must be ignored in relation to section 9, because it does not survive the deceased since it is not in life at the moment of the deceased's death. It may, however, be doubted if that is consistent with the policy of the Act. The purpose of differentiating in the value of prior rights according to whether or not issue survive is that, where there are issue more of the estate should be available for distribution to them. It would be anomalous to deny that benefit to a child *in utero* at the time of death.

Effect of the Human Fertilisation and Embryology Act 1990

Under section 14(4) of the Human Fertilisation and Embryology Act 1990 embryos may be stored for up to five years[73]; there is no legal limit on how long sperm can be stored. It follows that it is possible for a child to be born many years after the death of its genetic father. An embryo in storage is not to be regarded as an embryo *in utero* for the purposes of the law of succession, nor is it to receive the benefit of the civilian fiction described above. If the genetic father of an embryo dies while it is in storage, then the child subsequently born will have no succession rights in that man's estate. This is a consequence of section 28(6)(*b*) of the 1990 Act, which provides that where the sperm of a man is used after his death, or any embryo created with his sperm is used after his death, that man is not to be treated as the father of the child, and a man not treated as the father is not to be treated as the father "for any purpose,"[74] which includes succession purposes. This avoids the possibility of the distribution of the estate of the genetic father being held up until any potential child is born alive, possibly five or more years after death. This only applies if the sperm or embryo is "used" after his death, which means used to bring about a pregnancy that will continue with normal gestation. So if the putative father of an artificially created embryo dies during its gestation the later born child will have all normal succession rights, including the benefit of the civilian fiction, even although his conception was by a method governed by the 1990 Act; but if the father dies before the woman begins to carry the child (*i.e.* before the embryo has become implanted[75]) then the posthumous child will have no succession rights in his genetic father's estate.

The Act does not completely obviate succession difficulties, however. In its terms it is limited to denying the genetic father of the child any legal consequence of paternity. It might be argued that the Act only cuts off succession rights of the genetic father or to his estate and does not affect other succession claims, for example by grandparents and grandchildren. If this were so, then a trust set up, say, for "all my grandchildren" could benefit a grandchild who was born some years after the death of his or her genetic father. An estate in which such a provision were made could not be finally distributed until there are no gametes or embryos in existence capable of producing the testator's genetic

---

[72] In *Cohen* v. *Shaw*, 1992 S.L.T. 1022 Lord Cullen, in an action for damages, distinguished between a posthumous child and what he described as "surviving children" (p. 1024I).

[73] A period which may be increased by regulations: Human Fertilisation and Embryology Act 1990, s. 14(5).

[74] *Ibid.*, s. 29(2).

[75] *Ibid.*, s. 2(3).

grandchild. The only way of avoiding this result is to hold that the breaking of
the father-child link also breaks any link traced through the father. An analogy
with the adoption legislation is apt. The Adoption (Scotland) Act 1978 provides[76] that a child who is subject to an adoption order is in law to be treated as
the child of the adopter and of no other person. That too in its terms does not affect grandparents, but it has never been suggested that a legal connection between natural grandparents and an adopted child survives the adoption. To
apply similar reasoning to the Human Fertilisation and Embryology Act 1990
would consist with the policy of the Act and ought, it is submitted, to be done. If
the genetic father is not to be treated as the father for any purpose, he is not the
father for the purpose of any link traced through him.

There is no provision similar to that in s. 28(6)(*b*) made in relation to the genetic mother of an embryo, for none is needed since the Act elsewhere provides
that for all purposes of law the woman who carries the child shall be the
mother.[77] The child therefore will never have succession rights in the estate of
its genetic mother if she is not the woman who carries it during gestation, and
her death before its birth is therefore legally irrelevant to the child.

Aliment

The alimentary needs of the child before birth are, in the nature of the case,
met by the mother but there is no reason that financial support should not be provided in respect of these needs on the same principles as for a child who has
been born. Such "inlying expenses" are of an essentially alimentary character
and are so recognised by statute.[78] Section 2(5) of the Family Law (Scotland)
Act 1985 provides that a woman, whether married or not, may bring an action
for aliment on behalf of her unborn child as if the child had been born, but no
such action can be heard by the court or disposed of until the child is actually
born. Payments in advance of the birth are now no longer possible, as they were
under the Illegitimate Children (Scotland) Act 1930.[79] The position of the pregnant woman is therefore rather less protected than it used to be, in that she may
be unable to purchase articles for the baby before its birth but the eventual
award of aliment may be backdated to the date of bringing of the action or, on
special cause shown, to an earlier date. Starting proceedings before the birth
may have the effect of preventing the father dissipating his assets in order to defeat the claim for aliment.[80]

Aliment Jure Representationis

From the point of view of the living child, aliment from his parent's estate is
an entitlement[81] and that entitlement can accrue, like the right to claim legitim,
before birth (though defeasibly for the same reasons). So if a parent dies before
the child is born, that child is entitled to claim aliment from the parent's estate,

---

[76] Adoption (Scotland) Act 1978, s. 39.
[77] Human Fertilisation and Embryology Act 1990, ss. 27 and 29.
[78] See further, *post* at pp. 280–286.
[79] s. 3(1), repealed by the Family Law (Scotland) Act 1985, Sched. 2.
[80] See Nichols, *The Family Law (Scotland) Act 1985* (2nd ed., 1991) at p. 14.
[81] *Beaton* v. *Beaton's Trs.* 1935 S.C. 187.

so long as he is subsequently born alive.[82] In *Spalding* v. *Spalding's Trs.*[83] the First Division held that an obligation to aliment a child was a debt that was preferred to the beneficiaries under a trust disposition and settlement, and that "it became a debt so soon as the child was begotten."[84] The same conditions will attach to this right as to the rights of succession. After the birth of the child the action for aliment can be brought on his behalf by the parent or guardian of the child, or a person entitled to, seeking or having custody or care of the child.[85]

Aliment of "Accepted Child"

Section 1(1)(*d*) of the Family Law (Scotland) Act 1985 provides that a person owes an obligation of aliment to a child "who has been accepted by him as a child of his family," and the question arises whether a child can be accepted as such before it has been born. The issue is of importance only when such acceptance has become impossible or is purposely retracted by the time the child is born, for example if the putative acceptor has died or has left the family. In England an affirmative answer to that question was given in the case of *Caller* v. *Caller*.[86] There, a man married a pregnant woman, knowing that she was pregnant and knowing that he was not the father of the child. He deserted the wife before the child was born. The court held that the husband had clearly agreed to take over responsibility for the unborn child, that a "family" had come into (an admittedly brief) existence on the marriage, and that the husband had therefore "accepted [the unborn child] as one of the family." Consequently, the child was entitled to aliment from the husband. This case was not followed in *A.* v. *A. (Family: Unborn Child)*,[87] but there the relevant statutory provision[88] involved a child being "treated" rather than being "accepted" as part of the family. Bagnall J. held that the two concepts are quite different, and that "to treat" means "to act or behave towards," which cannot be done to an unborn child. "Acceptance" can be directed towards the other parent, and so can be done before the birth of the child. "Treatment" involves behaviour, "acceptance" involves attitude. The Family Law (Scotland) Act 1985 uses the word "accepted"[89] rather than "treated"[90] and *Caller* v. *Caller* is therefore the relevant authority. Section 1(1) (*d*) demands acceptance by a person of the child "as a child of *his* family," rather than, as the English statute had it, "as a child of *the* family"; but this change in terminology has no significance and it is submitted that the English case ought to be followed. There is nothing in the Scottish Act to suggest that the acceptance can occur only after birth. The fact that the Act states that the obligation is owed to a "child" who has been accepted, and that "child" is defined as "a per-

---

[82] *Hastie & Ker* v. *Hastie* (1671) Mor. 416.
[83] (1874) 2 R. 237.
[84] *Per* Lord Deas at p. 251.
[85] Family Law (Scotland) Act 1985, s. 2(4)(*c*), as amended by the Age of Legal Capacity (Scotland) Act 1991, Sched. 1, para. 40 and Sched. 2.
[86] [1966] 2 All E.R. 754.
[87] [1974] 1 All E.R. 755.
[88] Matrimonial Proceedings and Property Act 1970, s. 27(1).
[89] s. 1(1)(*d*).
[90] Which is used, for example, in s. 2B of the Sexual Offences (Scotland) Act 1976, which makes sexual intercourse between step-parent and step-child a crime if the latter has been "treated as a child" of the former's family, and in s. 2(1A)(*b*) of the Marriage (Scotland) Act 1977.

son under the age of 18 years"[91] suggests no more than that the claim for aliment can be made only when the child reaches personhood (*i.e.* on birth[92]) and not that the acceptance as a member of the family has to be done during the child's personhood.

Delict: General

The existence of an unborn child can have important consequences in relation to the law of delict. The fact that a child is unborn (indeed that it is not conceived) does not prevent a person from owing a duty of care towards it. A duty of care can be directed to all those who may foreseeably be harmed by its breach, and there is no requirement that the subject be identified or even identifiable at the time of the breach; nor is there any requirement that the injured person is in existence at that time. Thus the manufacturer of baby food will be liable to the newborn child injured by contaminated food notwithstanding that the food was manufactured before the baby's birth or conception.[93] Whether a defender is liable for injuries inflicted before birth or for breaches of duty committed before birth or before conception is a matter that has given rise to some controversy. It has, however, long been generally accepted in Scotland that the law places no bar to allowing recovery.[94] However, the dearth of direct authority leaves many areas in doubt, such as whether the injured child can sue his or her mother as well as third parties, and whether interdict is ever available to prevent the harm occurring. These (and other) matters will be examined separately in the following paragraphs.

Damages Against a Third Party

There is no reported Scottish decision in which a child has sued someone for personal injuries caused by acts done to it before its birth. It has been assumed that, at least where the defender is a third party (*i.e.* not the mother), such a claim

---

[91] s. 1(5)(*a*).

[92] *Cf.* s. 2(5) which provides that an action can be brought before birth, but the action cannot be heard or disposed of until after birth.

[93] The statement in the text is one of principle: the precise facts given would now, of course, be governed by the Consumer Protection Act 1987.

[94] See Scot. Law Com., *Report on Liability for Antenatal Injury* Cmnd. 5371 (1973); Walker, *Delict* (2nd ed.) at pp. 88–89; Walker, "The Rights of the Unborn Child to Reparation" (1954) 70 S.L.R. 125; Stewart, *Delict* at p. 130. Oblique statutory recognition that this is correct can be found in s. 35 of the Human Fertilisation and Embryology Act 1990. Due to doubts about the position in English law (see Law Com., *Report on Injuries to Unborn Children*, Cmnd. 5709 (1974)) the Congenital Disabilities (Civil Liability) Act 1976 was passed in order to recognise liability to the unborn child; this Act was not extended to Scotland on the assumption that it would be otiose to do so. The 1976 Act was amended by the 1990 Act: s. 35(1) provides for the obtaining in England of information relating to genetic parenthood when this is required to raise an action under the 1976 Act; s. 35(2) provides for the obtaining in Scotland of information relating to genetic parenthood when this is required to raise any action for damages in which the damages claimed consist of or include damages or solatium in respect of personal injury. This assumes that the common law of Scotland recognises the actionability of antenatal injuries that was statutorily recognised in England in the 1976 Act. Similarly, s. 44 of the 1990 Act adds into the 1976 Act a new s. 1A which provides that a child born as a result of infertility treatment can sue if an act or omission in the course of selecting, keeping or using embryos or gametes causes injury to the child when born: again this is not extended to Scotland, presumably because Scots common law provides a remedy already.

would be relevant,[95] and that assumption has been accepted *obiter* in three Outer House decisions and one Inner House decision.[96] Until a case is decided on the precise issue it remains uncertain what the juridical basis of the liability for antenatal injuries is in Scots law, but there are at least three possibilities.

The Civilian Fiction Theory

First, one might use an analogy with the civilian fiction applied in the law of succession, discussed above, that in all things to the child's benefit a child not born at the appropriate date is to be regarded as having been born, so long as it later achieves live birth. This approach has been adopted in some civilian jurisdictions. So in a decision based on the Civil Code of Quebec,[97] damages were awarded (and upheld on appeal) to a child who suffered injury as a result of the defendant's negligence which caused the child's mother, when pregnant with the pursuer, to fall while descending from a tram. The passages from the *Digest* which in Scots law have been used to justify an unborn child's claims in succession were founded upon in that case. However, as Rodger points out,[98] the relevant passages[99] are clearly not intended by their authors to be extended into the field of delict. Certainly the rule has been regarded by the judges who have applied it in succession cases as no more than a rule of construction[1] (of wills, trust deeds and statutes). Walker, after stating that the civilian fiction is accepted in Scots law for succession purposes, warns: "it is not, however, safe to infer that the same principle would necessarily apply in a case of reparation."[2] On the other hand, as Winfield points out, "to limit this proposition[3] to property rights is to rate property higher in the scale of legal values than life and limb."[4] While the policy attractions of that statement cannot be denied, the Roman law authority for adopting this approach in Scotland is, at best, fragile. Nevertheless this approach does receive support in *Cohen* v. *Shaw*,[5] in which Lord Cullen could see no reason in principle why the civilian fiction should be limited to succession cases, and he opined that there was nothing in the law of Scotland to suggest that the fiction should have less than general application. He awarded damages to a child whose father had been killed before the child's birth on the

---

[95] See n. 94 above.

[96] *Cohen* v. *Shaw*, 1992 S.L.T. 1022, *per* Lord Cullen; *Hamilton* v. *Fife Health Board*, 1992 S.L.T. 1026, *per* Lord Prosser; *McWilliams* v. *Lord Advocate*, 1992 S.L.T. 1045, *per* Lord Morton of Shuna; *Hamilton* v. *Fife Health Board*, 1993 S.L.T. 624 *per* Lords McCluskey, Caplan and Wylie. These cases were raised under the Damages (Scotland) Act 1976, and are discussed *post* at pp. 108–109 and 110–111.

[97] *Montreal Tramways* v. *Leveille* [1933] 4 D.L.R. 337.

[98] "Report of the Scottish Law Commission on Antenatal Injury," 1974 J.R. 83 at pp. 89–90.

[99] D. 1, v. 7 and D. 1, v. 26.

[1] See in particular *Villar* v. *Gilbey* [1907] A.C. 139, *per* Lord Loreburn L.C. at p. 144.

[2] (1954) 70 S.L.R. 125. In England, Dillon L.J. in *Burton* v. *Islington Health Authority* [1992] 3 All E.R. 833 at p. 839 considered that it would be open to the English courts to apply the civilian fiction in a claim for damages, but held it unnecessary to do so, since the same result was achieved by adopting the approach whereby the claim crystallises on the birth of the child: see *post* at p. 100.

[3] *i.e.* that in D. 1, v. 26.

[4] "The Unborn Child" (1944) 8 Camb. L.J. 76 at p. 90. The Court of Appeal in England seem to have been persuaded by this in *Burton* v. *Islington Health Authority, De Martell* v. *Merton and Sutton Health Authority* [1992] 3 All E.R. 833, in which the English common law was said to accept the civilian fiction in the field of tort liability.

[5] 1992 S.L.T. 1022 at p. 1024F.

ground that the civilian fiction allowed him to deem the unborn child to be born at the date of death.[6]

The Legal Personality Theory

Secondly, it might be argued that the unborn child has legal personality and as such can be the subject of a reparable injury. This approach is adopted in some jurisdictions in the USA, where, after an initial reluctance to recognise the competency of claims for antenatal injuries,[7] such claims are now usually accepted.[8] In some US jurisdictions the constitutional right to life is recognised in, and statutorily granted to,[9] the unborn child, usually from the point of viability,[10] but sometimes even before.[11] Some other jurisdictions also accept this.[12] This approach cannot be followed in Scotland. There is no constitutionally protected "right to life" guaranteed an unborn child at any stage of development, and while Article 2 of the European Convention on Human Rights does guarantee "everyone" a right to life, it has been held by the European Commission on Human Rights that "everyone" does not include the unborn child.[13] Similarly, the UN Convention on the Rights of the Child[14] defines "child" in Article 1 as "every human being below the age of 18 years." The neutral phrase "human being" was chosen to allow individual states to decide whether to include the unborn. In Scotland the unborn child, though its existence has legal consequences, has no legal personality.[15] That does not mean that its existence before birth is

---

[6] See further, *post* at pp. 108–109. Lord Prosser in *Hamilton* v. *Fife Health Board*, 1992 S.L.T. 1026 at p. 1028, accepted this and assumed that the child in *Cohen* would have been unsuccessful without the use of the fiction. However, Lord Morton of Shuna in *McWilliams* v. *L.A.*, 1992 S.L.T. 1045 at p. 1048I, did not accept that the civilian fiction was either appropriate or necessary, and Lord Prosser's decision was later overruled: 1993 S.L.T. 624. See *post*, at p. 111.

[7] See particularly the influential decision of Holmes J. in *Dietrich* v. *Inhabitants of Northampton* (1884) 138 Mass. 14.

[8] The turning point came in the case of *Bonbrest* v. *Kotz* (1946) 65 F.Supp. 138.

[9] See *e.g.* s. 184 of the California Penal Code which confers on the foetus legal personality for the purposes of the criminal law (allowing it, for example, to be the victim of the crime of murder).

[10] *i.e.* the commencement of the third trimester in the context of the abortion decision in *Roe* v. *Wade* (1973) 410 US 113. So in *Jefferson* v. *Griffin Spalding County Hospital* (1981) 274 SE 2d 457 the Supreme Court of Georgia held that a viable foetus had legal personality and was entitled to the full protection of the law granted to any other human being.

[11] The US Supreme Court has held that it is not unconstitutional for a state legislature to declare legislatively that human life begins on conception: *Webster* v. *Reproductive Health Services* (1989) 106 L. Ed., 2d 410. In *Davis* v. *Davis* (1990) 59 U.S.M.L. 2205 a trial judge had held that seven embryos created with the gametes of a married couple were children and he awarded custody of them to the mother during divorce proceedings. The Tennessee Court of Appeals reversed this decision, and on June 1, 1992 the Supreme Court of Tennessee upheld the Court of Appeals, on the ground that human embryos are neither "persons" nor "property": (1992) 842 S.W. (2d) 588.

[12] See the decision of the Supreme Court of New South Wales, reported as *Lynch* v. *Lynch*, *The Independent*, Aug. 7, 1991.

[13] *X.* v. *United Kingdom* (1990) 3 E.H.R.R. 408. See also *Trembley* v. *Daigle* (1990) 62 D.L.R. (4th) 634, a decision of the Supreme Court of Canada, to the same effect, interpreting the Quebec Civil Code.

[14] (1989) 28 *International Legal Materials* 1448, adopted Nov. 28, 1989 and ratified by the UK on Dec. 16, 1991.

[15] "Prior to being born, a child is not a person," *per* Lord Prosser in *Hamilton* v. *Fife Health Board*, 1992 S.L.T. 1026 at p. 1028E. In relation to English law it was said by Baker P. that this proposition "permeates the whole of the civil law of this country": *Paton* v. *Trs. of the British Pregnancy Advisory Service* [1978] 2 All E.R. 987 at p. 989. This was approved by the Court of Appeal in *Re F. (In Utero)* [1988] 2 W.L.R. 1288, *per* May L.J. at p. 1301. The definition of "embryo" given in

devoid of legal protection, nor does it mean that the term "person" may never be used to describe an unborn child, but it does mean that legally protected interests accruing before birth cannot be explained on a theory of legal personality.

The Crystallisation of Damage Theory

Thirdly, it might be argued that an injury caused by a negligent act committed while the child is unborn does not cause any legally recognised loss, injury or damage until such time as the child acquires the capacity (in law) to suffer such loss, injury or damage. In other words, an antenatal act can only ever cause latent damage, which becomes patent on live birth.[16] It is submitted that this is the approach that ought to be adopted by the Scottish court. It has long been held in Scotland that liability in negligence does not arise simply from the negligent act, but rather from the loss, injury or damage that the negligent act causes. A breach of a duty of care is a continuing wrong, which continues for so long as the wrongful act retains the ability to cause direct or foreseeable hurt. "The ground of any action based on negligence is the concurrence of breach of duty and damage, and I cannot see how there can be that concurrence unless the duty still exists and is breached when the damage occurs."[17] "The fact that the negligent act which caused the injury was not contemporaneous with the injury itself is not a bar to recovery."[18] *Donoghue* v. *Stevenson*[19] itself provides an example. Given this unchallengeable fact it can be seen that it is irrelevant when the breach of duty occurs so long as it also causes damage to occur and that damage is visited upon a living person. It would follow that if a child is injured *in utero* by an act committed then or even before its conception, this is, as it were, latent damage which becomes patent when the child attains such legal personality as allows its injuries to be recognised, *i.e.* the moment of live birth. If that injury is caused by negligence, liability arises at that moment. This is the approach that the Scottish Law Commission (founding on *Watson*) thought that the courts would adopt.[20] However, Rodger[21] considers this "a remarkable feat of redefinition." His argument is that the injury is suffered when the harm is caused and not when title to sue upon it is acquired. In *Cohen* v. *Shaw*[22] Lord Cullen expressly reserved his opinion as to whether this approach would commend itself to the Scottish court; and in *Hamilton* v. *Fife Health Board*[23] Lord Prosser dismissed a

---

the Human Fertilisation and Embryology Act 1990 is careful to avoid the possibility of including within its terms the status of personhood. See also the Canadian cases of *Trembley* v. *Daigle*, *supra*, and *Re A (In Utero)* (1990) 72 D.L.R. (4th) 722 (Ontario Family Court).

[16] This is the conceptual reason why actions for "wrongful life" (see *post* at p. 104) cannot ever succeed, for such actions postulate a duty on the part of the defender to terminate life (or prevent its occurring) before birth, so preventing the claim ever crystallising: the pursuer is effectively founding upon his right not to have his right crystallised. See further, Norrie, "Wrongful Life in Scots Law: No Right, No Remedy," 1990 J.R. 205.

[17] *Per* Lord Reid in *Watson* v. *Fram Reinforced Concrete (Scotland) Ltd.*, 1960 S.C.(H.L.) 92 at p. 109.

[18] *Per* Potts J. in *Burton* v. *Islington Health Authority* [1991] 1 All E.R. 825 at p. 831, upheld [1992] 3 All E.R. 833.

[19] 1932 S.C.(H.L.) 31.

[20] Scot. Law Com., *Report on Liability for Ante-Natal Injury* (1973) at p. 6.

[21] "Report of the Scottish Law Commission on Antenatal Injury," 1974 J.R. 83 at p. 84.

[22] *Supra.*

[23] *Supra.*

claim under the Damages (Scotland) Act 1976 on the ground that an antenatal injury had been "sustained" by a foetus and not by a child at the moment of birth.[24] Both these judges preferred to recognise a child's right to sue on the basis of the civilian fiction as discussed above. On the other hand, Lord Morton rejected the need to rely upon the fiction and accepted the approach postulated here.[25]

However, this third approach has much, it is submitted, to commend it. Not only is it favoured by the Scottish Law Commission but it has been adopted in cases from other common law jurisdictions. So in *Watt* v. *Rama*[26] the Supreme Court of Victoria, founding upon *Donoghue* v. *Stevenson*[27], allowed a case to go to trial having rejected the argument that the breach of duty was spent by the time the injury was suffered at birth. Two members of the court said this: "On the birth the relationship crystallised and out of it arose a duty on the defendant in relation to the child."[28] This case was followed by the Ontario Court of Appeal,[29] by the Supreme Court of British Columbia,[30] by the New South Wales Court of Appeal,[31] and by the English Court of Appeal in *Burton* v. *Islington Health Authority, de Martell* v. *Merton and Sutton Area Health Authority*.[32] In *Burton*, a child born in 1967[33] claimed damages from a health authority which had performed an operation upon her mother while pregnant with the plaintiff, which operation allegedly caused her various injuries and allegedly ought not to have been carried out upon a pregnant woman. Potts J. at first instance held that the claim disclosed a reasonable cause of action, for this reason:

> "The circumstances created a contingent or potential duty on the defendants which crystallised on birth of the injured child. The wrong to the child was then complete, she having been born alive physically damaged as a result of the defendants' earlier neglect. On birth, the child acquired legal status and legal rights. Thus her cause of action in negligence was complete and accrued to her when she was a 'legal person who could sue or be sued,' and when 'she was a legal person having a legal right' to whom another 'legal person' could owe at that time a corresponding legal duty."[34]

This, and an identical claim, were upheld on appeal.[35]

---

[24] This decision was, however, overruled: 1993 S.L.T. 624. See *post* at pp. 110–111.

[25] *McWilliams* v. *L.A.*, 1992 S.L.T. 1045.

[26] [1972] V.R. 353.

[27] 1932 S.C.(H.L.) 31.

[28] at p. 360, *per* Winneke C.J. and Pape J.

[29] *Duval et al.* v. *Seguin et al.* (1973) 40 D.L.R. (3d) 666.

[30] *Cherry* v. *Borsman* (1991) 75 D.L.R. (4th) 668.

[31] *X.* v. *Pal* (1991) 23 N.S.W.L.R. 26.

[32] [1992] 3 All E.R. 833.

[33] The case was heard in 1990, but because the birth was in 1967, the Congenital Disabilities (Civil Liability) Act 1976 did not apply. The limitation period does not commence running until child plaintiffs—and pursuers—attain majority.

[34] [1991] 1 All E.R. 825 at p. 833. It was in relation to this reasoning that Lord Cullen in *Cohen* v. *Shaw* said: "I reserve my opinion as to whether the way in which the question of breach of duty was addressed and answered in that case was one which would commend itself to a Scottish court", 1992 S.L.T. at p. 1024E.

[35] [1992] 3 All E.R. 833. In *McWilliams* v. *L.A.* Lord Morton said: "the reasoning of Potts J. commends itself to me" (1992 S.L.T. 1045 at p. 1048H).

This approach accords with the Scottish view of delict, as exemplified in *Watson* v. *Fram Reinforced Concrete (Scotland) Ltd.* and in *Donoghue* v. *Stevenson* itself. It also accords with the approach of Scots criminal law.[36] *Donoghue* v. *Stevenson* was used by Lord McCluskey in *Hamilton* v. *Fife Health Board*[37] as the basis for actionability and he said that "doctors engaged in the medical work of assisting in the delivery of a child can obviously foresee that a failure to exercise due care and skill by them may result in injuries to the foetus, being injuries which will cause the child to suffer loss". This is an acceptance of the crystallisation of damage theory, as is made plain in this case by Lord Caplan (whose comments are accepted by Lord McCluskey). He stated expressly that injuries can be said to have been "sustained" at the moment of birth even if inflicted before that moment. The civilian fiction was dismissed as unnecessary, and the approach in *Burton* approved. Though these comments were, ultimately, *obiter*, they indicate the approach likely and, it is submitted, properly to be followed.

There may be practical difficulties in establishing that an unborn child is a reasonably foreseeable subject of negligently caused injury, particularly if the allegedly negligent act occurs before conception[38]; but that is not a conceptual difficulty and there are many situations in which unborn children are as foreseeable as living persons.[39] It should also be noted that if the unborn child dies before its live birth, the latent damage cannot become patent, and the breach of duty becomes legally innocuous.[40]

Damages Against the Mother

In English law, due to the doubts about whether there ever could be liability for antenatal injury (which doubts were brought to public attention by the Thalidomide tragedy)[41] it was deemed necessary to put the matter on a statutory basis, and this was done with the Congenital Disabilities (Civil Liability) Act 1976. However, that statute contained an important qualification in section 1(1) by excluding from liability the child's own mother, unless[42] the injuries she causes the child are caused as a result of her negligent driving of a motor vehicle while pregnant. (The reason for this exception to the qualification is that otherwise the child would be denied insurance compensation.[43]) The Act does not ap-

---

[36] *McCluskey* v. *HMA* 1989 S.L.T. 175.

[37] 1993 S.L.T. 624.

[38] The fact that the negligence occurred before conception is as irrelevant as is the fact that it occurred before birth so long as there is a causal link between the negligence and the injuries suffered by the child once born: *Renslow* v. *Mennonite Hospital* (1977) 367 N.E. 2d 1250; *Bergstresser* v. *Mitchell* (1978) 577 F2d 22.

[39] In *Bourhill* v. *Young's Exr.*, 1941 S.C. 395, Lord Justice-Clerk Aitchison (diss. in the Court of Session) said at p. 438 that the fact that a woman may be pregnant "is an easily foreseeable fact; it might almost be described as an obvious fact." See also Winneke C.J. and Pape J. in *Watt* v. *Rama* [1972] V.R. 353 at p. 360, Potts J. in *Burton* v. *Islington Health Authority* [1991] 1 All E.R. 825 at pp. 831 and 833 and Lord McCluskey in *Hamilton* to similar effect.

[40] This follows, it is submitted, from the comments of Potts J. in *Burton* v. *Islington Health Authority* [1991] 1 All E.R. 825 at p. 833. See also *Smith* v. *Fox* [1923] 3 D.L.R. 785 (Ont. Sup. Ct.). *Cf. Bagley* v. *North Herts Health Authority* (1986) 136 New L.J. 1014.

[41] But which doubts proved groundless in the first case raised under the common law: *B.* v. *Islington Health Authority, supra.*

[42] Congenital Disabilities (Civil Liability) Act 1976, s. 2.

[43] Law Com., *Report on Injuries to Unborn Children* (1974).

ply in Scotland, but the reasoning behind the maternal exclusion may be equally applicable here also. The sentiment clearly is that if a child could sue its own mother for injuries she inflicts upon it during its gestation within her, this would disrupt family harmony and create an unwelcome adversarial atmosphere between the two.[44] It is to be noted that family harmony is not so protected by the English statute that a father is also given immunity from liability.[45] A rather more plausible *rationale* for excluding a mother is that otherwise her freedom would be unduly restricted during pregnancy, with the concurrent effect of over-emphasising women's child-bearing role in society. This reasoning is not wholly convincing either. We all have duties not to injure others, and as a result our freedom is restricted—but that is no reason to deny the existence of the duty. And besides, an award of damages is a retrospective remedy (unlike interdict, which will be discussed shortly) and the argument that its availability is incompatible with personal freedom is, for that reason, less strong. Alternatively, it could be argued that if a woman were subject to actions for damages arising from how she conducts herself during pregnancy, she might be encouraged to avoid them completely by undergoing an abortion and so preventing her breaches of duty from causing compensable loss. This argument is not fully persuasive in a legal system, like Scotland, in which there is no "right" to an abortion, although the ease with which abortion can be obtained gives it some force.

There is no authority one way or the other in Scotland on the question, but it is suggested that if liability can be imposed upon a mother by the application of the general principles of delictual liability, then any limitation or denial should come from Parliament. If it is accepted, as was argued above, that there is liability on third parties, it is difficult to see how, in the absence of statute, liability of the mother can be denied.[46]

Circumstances in which a Mother might be held Liable

It is disturbingly easy to visualise circumstances in which a pregnant woman can do things that will cause suffering to her child once it is born. The most obvious example is drug abuse, though alcohol and tobacco usage may also be cited as examples (though with these causation will be somewhat more difficult to prove). In order to establish liability in negligence, the Scottish courts have traditionally demanded proof on the balance of probabilities of the existence of

---

[44] It was primarily for this reason that the early American cases denied liability in such cases: see, *e.g. Stanford* v. *St Louis-San Francisco Ry.* (1926) 214 Ala. 611.

[45] Besides, if family autonomy were so important, this would justify preventing the living child suing its parents for postnatal injury, which has never been suggested. In *Young* v. *Rankin*, 1934 S.C. 499 it was held competent for a minor child to sue his father for damages for personal injuries caused by the father's negligence; and in *Wood* v. *Wood*, 1935 S.L.T. 431 a mother was held entitled to sue her son for damages for personal injuries, this even at a time when spouses could not sue each other (see *Harper* v. *Harper*, 1929 S.C. 220). In the latter case the Lord Ordinary rejected the contention that the claim should be dismissed for reasons of public policy. Statutorily, husbands and wives are now able to sue each other in delict, as if they were not married to each other: Law Reform (Husband and Wife) Act 1962, s. 2(1).

[46] In the New South Wales case of *Lynch* v. *Lynch*, *The Independent*, Aug. 7, Dec. 12, 1991, a child successfully sued its mother for the injuries it received while *in utero* due to the mother's negligent car driving. The decision was, however, expressly limited to situations in which there is compulsory insurance, for reasons of policy identical to those that led to s. 2 of the Congenital Disabilities (Civil Liability) Act 1976 in England (see, *ante* at p. 101).

damnum injuria datum, or damage wrongfully caused, this being derived from the *lex aquilia*.[47] Damage, following the position with third party defenders described above, is the injury suffered by the child once it has been born alive. Wrongfulness lies in the breach of a duty of care owed by the defender to the pursuer. Applying the basic principles of negligence in determining whether there exists a duty of care, it seems undeniable that the foetus in the womb is a neighbour of the pregnant woman (or at any rate that the child when born—a foreseeable event to a pregnant woman—is a neighbour) and thus is a person (when born) so closely and directly affected by the woman's acts or omissions that she ought reasonably to have it in contemplation as being so affected when she is directing her mind to the acts or omissions which are called in question. Whether that duty has been breached depends upon whether the woman has taken "reasonable care." Walker says[48] in relation to reasonable care: "It is fixed by what we should expect in the like case from a man of ordinary sense, knowledge, care and prudence, having regard to what such a person must be taken to have known and what he should have foreseen." The test being objective must refer to the reasonable pregnant woman, and not the reasonable pregnant drug addict or alcoholic. If the court were to hold that a reasonable pregnant woman would not subject her child to risk of injury by taking drugs or alcohol, then to do so will be a breach of the duty of care. Causation between that breach and the injury suffered would then have to be established in order to complete the requirements. In most cases this will be the most difficult element, and would probably deny the child damages based for example on the mother's smoking— while there is scientific evidence to suggest that there is a link between smoking by pregnant women and low birth weight, the pursuer would have to prove that the defender's smoking actually did cause, or at least materially contributed to,[49] his own low birth weight (assuming for the sake of argument that that would amount to a compensable injury). The same difficulties would be faced if a child alleged that his mother's excessive exercise, or sexual activity, or alcohol consumption, led to his injury. On the other hand there are situations in which causation might more easily be established. If for example the pregnant woman continued to abuse narcotic drugs while she was pregnant, and the child was born with a drug dependency,[50] or if the pregnant woman was an alcoholic and the child was born with foetal alcohol syndrome,[51] then causation might more easily be established. The pain and suffering of such children are clearly of a compensable nature, and for that reason alone it is difficult to see why liability should be denied (if fault can also be proved). There are examples in other jurisdictions in which such claims have been successful. So for example in *Grodin* v. *Grodin*[52] a child successfully sued his mother and the manufacturer of a

---

[47] See Smith, "Designation of Delictual Actions: Damn Iniuria Damn," 1972 S.L.T. (News) 125; "Damn Iniuria Again," 1984 S.L.T. (News) 85; *McKendrick* v. *Sinclair*, 1972 S.L.T. 110.

[48] *Delict* (2nd ed.) at p. 199.

[49] *McGhee* v. *National Coal Board*, 1973 S.C.(H.L.) 37.

[50] Cf. *D. (A Minor)* v. *Berkshire County Council* [1987] 1 All E.R. 20 (H.L.); *Re Superintendant of Family and Child Service and McDonald* (1982) 135 D.L.R. (3d) 330; both cases arising from attempts to remove the child from its parents after birth because of its suffering from drug dependency. See further, *post* at pp. 115–118.

[51] Cf. *Re Children's Aid Society for the District of Kenora and J.L.* (1982) 134 D.L.R. (3d) 249.

[52] (1980) 301 N.W. 2d 869 (Michigan Appeal Court).

drug which the mother took during pregnancy and which blackened the child's teeth.

"Wrongful Life"

Liability will only be established if the harm *to that particular child* could have been avoided by the mother exercising reasonable care. A mother will not be liable for harm caused to a child through some genetic defect or a disease such as HIV infection that the mother passed on to the child and which she knew or ought to have known that she could pass on. In that situation the child would be claiming that had there been no negligence (*i.e.* had the mother taken sufficient precautions against passing on the defect) he would not have been born at all, and possibly that some other child would have been born: this would therefore be an action for "wrongful life," which has been denied in England both at common law[53] and by statute,[54] and would, it is submitted, be denied in Scotland.[55] For the same reason, a child born with defects could not sue its mother who knew of these defects and refused to abort the child.[56]

Interdict

Interdict against Third Parties

While damages is a retrospective remedy designed to provide reparation to the person who has suffered loss, injury or damage as a result of a civil wrong, interdict is a prospective remedy designed to prevent the injury occurring in the first place. It is however wrong to see the two remedies as being different sides of the same coin, and it certainly does not follow that interdict would have been available in all circumstances to prevent events that give rise to a claim for damages. The remedies are different in a number of respects. First, damages can normally be claimed as of right if the pursuer proves his case; interdict on the other hand is a discretionary remedy: it is "of the nature of an extraordinary remedy, not to be given except for urgent reasons, and even then not as a matter of right, but only in the exercise of a sound judicial discretion."[57] Secondly, damages is a remedy for which the court must look to the past; with interdict the court must look to the future. Thirdly, with damages for ante-natal injury the court is granting a remedy to someone already in existence, albeit in relation to events that occurred before the pursuer achieved existence; the court in which an interdict is sought to prevent ante-natal injury is however being asked to grant a remedy on behalf of someone who has not yet achieved legal existence.

The difficulty with interdict is identifying whether anyone can claim it when, *ex hypothesi*, the "person" who is threatened does not yet have any legal existence. Of course if the interdict is sought against a third party, then this problem

---

[53] *McKay* v. *Essex Area Health Authority* [1982] Q.B. 1166.

[54] Congenital Disabilities (Civil Liability) Act 1976, s. 4(5).

[55] The matter is fully discussed by Norrie, "Wrongful Life in Scots Law: No Right, No Remedy," 1990 J.R. 205.

[56] This is of course only one of the reasons for this particular conclusion: the overwhelming reason of policy is that there can never be a duty to do something that is *prima facie* a criminal offence.

[57] *Per* Lord Deas in *Kelso School Board* v. *Hunter* (1874) 2 R. 228 at p. 232.

can be avoided easily: the pregnant woman will inevitably be affected by any threat to her unborn child, and she would therefore have both title and interest to seek an interdict to prevent the threat eventuating. It must, however, be remembered that in these circumstances she would be suing on her own behalf to prevent injury to her own person. Even in the (difficult to imagine) situation of a threatened injury that affects the unborn child but not the pregnant woman herself, her right to seek an interdict would be preserved by her own right to be protected from the emotional trauma that injury to her child could cause her. If the pregnant woman were unconscious or otherwise incapax and thus unable to raise the action, title would inhere in the guardian of the incapax, again because the threat is to be regarded as directed towards the woman and not her unborn child, and no legal specialties arise from the fact that she is carrying an unborn child.

Interdict against the Mother

A far greater difficulty in relation to interdict arises when the threat comes from the pregnant woman herself, and she cannot therefore act as pursuer. In this situation the question—does the unborn child have a right not to be injured?—arises in a pure form. The issue has been extensively canvassed in other jurisdictions when the threat to the child has come from its mother who wishes to have an abortion.[58] These cases, however, may well be *sui generis* and ought not to be relied upon in other situations. Abortions in the cases cited were legal acts and their accomplishment would not have led to criminal penalties nor to civil damages. Abortion leads to the destruction of the unborn child who can therefore never be the subject of legal rights. But if the threat is itself a wrongful act and is a threat of less than destruction these arguments do not apply. In relation to awarding damages, the English court has recognised that a breach of duty of care can create "a contingent or potential duty on the defendants,"[59] the entitlement to damages crystallising when the hurt is suffered, *i.e.* on birth.[60] The right to seek an interdict does not need harm before it crystallises—it merely needs a threat. It is therefore submitted that the court could recognise the contingent or potential existence of the unborn child as giving it a right not to be injured, which right could be the basis of a claim for interdict. The fact that the court would have to predict that the child will later be born alive and so suffer the injury is no more a conceptual difficulty in relation to interdict than the fact that the court always has to predict that the threat it is interdicting will otherwise eventuate.

Subject to certain qualifications, a living child has no title to sue until it reaches the age of 16.[61] To ascribe to an unborn child even the limited *persona*

---

[58] See, *e.g.* in England, *Paton* v. *Trs. of the British Pregnancy Advisory Service* [1978] 2 All E.R. 987, *C.* v. *S.* [1987] 2 W.L.R. 1108; in Australia, *Attorney-General of Queensland, ex rel. Kerr* v. *T.* (1983) 46 A.L.R. 275; in Canada, *Medhurst* v. *Medhurst* (1984) 9 D.L.R. (4th) 252, *Medhurst* v. *Medhurst* (1984) 7 D.L.R. (4th) 335, *Borowski* v. *Attorney-General for Canada* (1987) 39 D.L.R. (4th) 731, (1989) 57 D.L.R. (4th) 231, *Tremblay* v. *Daigle* (1990) 62 D.L.R. (4th) 634; and in New Zealand, *Wall* v. *Livingstone* [1982] 1 N.Z.L.R. 734.

[59] *Per* Potts J. in *Burton* v. *Islington Health Authority* [1991] 1 All E.R. 825 at p. 833.

[60] See *ante* at pp. 99–101.

[61] See *post* at pp. 353 and 368–369.

standi in judicio which, in some circumstances, a child under 16 may have would be to confer on it a legal personality which it almost certainly does not possess. An interdict against a pregnant woman could only be sought by persons with title to sue either on their own behalves or on behalf of the unborn child. In relation to attempts to prevent pregnant women undergoing abortions, it has been held in England that a husband and potential father had no title to seek an injunction on behalf of the unborn child his wife was carrying[62]; and it has further been held that the "personal interest" of a potential father who was not married to the pregnant woman gave him no independent title to sue in his own name.[63] In relation to these men's title to sue not in their own names but on behalf of the unborn child, it has been held that the foetus has no right to life and therefore no one can sue on its behalf to prevent its abortion.[64] Yet, again, these cases were inextricably linked to the specialities of the abortion situation and even in that context are not wholly persuasive on the question of title to sue. A father has, it is submitted, sufficient title and interest to interdict potential harm to a child in respect of whom, if born, he would have important responsibilities and rights.

In the normal case, the court is able to appoint a curator *ad litem* to look after the interests of those who, in a court case—and it need not be the parties—cannot look after their own interests. Might the Scottish courts be persuaded to appoint a curator *ad litem* to an unborn child? In South Africa it has been held that a curator *ad litem* could not be appointed over an unborn child in order to prevent its abortion.[65] The Family Court in Nova Scotia did appoint a guardian *ad litem* over an unborn child for just that reason,[66] but that decision is inconsistent with a later ruling of the Supreme Court of Canada[67] and clearly can no longer be relied upon. In England it has been held that the wardship jurisdiction does not extend to the unborn child,[68] even in circumstances in which the court considered that the child did need protection from its mother and in which the threat was less than destruction by abortion. These cases are strong and persuasive authority against the existence of a power of the court to appoint a curator *ad litem* over an unborn child. In Scotland the question has never directly arisen, but there is old authority for the proposition that a tutor can be appointed to an unborn child.[69] This case has never been overruled, and is quoted more recently as good authority by Fraser.[70] The report of the case is, however, brief to the point of opacity, and it probably means no more than that a testamentary appointment of a guardian to a posthumous child is as valid as a testamentary gift

---

[62] *Paton* v. *Trs. of the British Pregnancy Advisory Service* [1978] 2 All E.R. 987.

[63] *C.* v. *S.* [1987] 2 W.L.R. 1108.

[64] *Paton, supra; X.* v. *United Kingdom* (1980) 3 E.H.R.R. 408, in which the European Commission on Human Rights rejected Paton's application based on the unborn child's right to life; *Tremblay* v. *Daigle* (1990) 62 D.L.R. (4th) 634 (Supreme Court of Canada) (though in that case the court stated *obiter* that if it had held that the foetus did have such a right, the father would be a person with as much right to speak on its behalf as anyone else: at p. 649).

[65] *Christian League of Southern Africa* v. *Rall*, 1981 (2) S.A.L.R. 821.

[66] *Re Simms and H.* (1979) 106 D.L.R. (3d) 435.

[67] *Tremblay* v. *Daigle* (1990) 62 D.L.R. (4th) 634.

[68] *Re F. (In Utero)* [1988] 2 All E.R. 193.

[69] *Murray* v. *Merschall* (1555) Mor. 16226 (cited with approval in Balfour's *Practicks* at p. 116). See also D. xxvii, 10, 8.

[70] Fraser (3rd ed.) at p. 220.

to a posthumous child.[71] It is likely that the Scottish courts will follow the approach in England, Canada, and South Africa in the cases cited above.

One other possibility is that the Lord Advocate, representing the public interest, may raise the action. In a case aimed at preventing an abortion, the Attorney-General of Queensland stepped in on behalf of the public and took over an application for injunction initially raised by the putative father of an unborn child.[72] And in the Republic of Ireland the Attorney General sought (and at first instance obtained) an injunction preventing a 14-year-old leaving Ireland for the purpose of obtaining an abortion in England.[73] This obviated the title-to-sue problem. In Scotland the Lord Advocate, representing the public interest, might have title to raise an interdict, though he would do so only in the most exceptional of circumstances, in which the *public* interest is threatened.

However, even if the title problem could be resolved, say by the Lord Advocate stepping in, it is by no means certain that an interdict would—or indeed should—be granted. Interdict, as pointed out above, is a discretionary remedy, which the court is not bound to grant if there are policy reasons for withholding it.[74] In the abortion cases[75] the view has consistently been expressed that the granting of a remedy in such circumstances would involve too great a limitation on the pregnant woman's freedom of action, which would be against public policy. So, for example, in *Attorney-General of Queensland, ex rel. Kerr* v. *T.*[76] Gibbs C.J. pointed out that: "There are limits to the extent to which the law should intrude upon personal liberty and personal privacy in the pursuit of moral and religious aims. Those limits would be overstepped if an injunction were to be granted in the present case."

Due to the very peculiar position of abortion in the law it may well be, as already argued, that one cannot rely too heavily on these cases, but the same policy considerations have been held determinative in quite different situations. In the English case of *Re F (In Utero)*[77] a local authority, concerned that a pregnant woman who led a nomadic existence, who was mentally disturbed and whom they believed to be incapable of caring for her child either after its birth or before, applied for leave to issue a summons making the unborn child a ward of court. The application was refused, and the refusal upheld on appeal. At one level the decision was based merely on the definitional point that an unborn child is not a "minor" as that term was used in the relevant statute.[78] But there was also a deeper *rationale* for the decision: it was clear that the court could not exercise the wardship rights, powers and duties over the foetus without controlling the mother's actions, and that the court was not willing to undertake such control. According to May L.J.[79]: "Until the child is actually born there must necessarily be an inherent incompatibility between any projected exercise

---

[71] A rule presently embodied in s. 4 of the Law Reform (Parent and Child) (Scotland) Act 1986.

[72] *Attorney-General of Queensland, ex rel. Kerr* v. *T.* (1983) 46 A.L.R. 274.

[73] *The Times*, March 6, 1992.

[74] See n. 57 *supra*.

[75] See n. 58 *supra*.

[76] (1983) 46 A.L.R. 275 at pp. 277–278.

[77] [1988] 2 W.L.R. 1288. See Fortin, "Can You Ward a Foetus?" (1988) 51 Mod. L.R. 768.

[78] Family Law Reform Act 1969, s. 1.

[79] [1988] 2 W.L.R. 1288 at p. 1298.

of wardship jurisdiction and the rights and welfare of the mother." Similarly, Balcolme L.J. said,[80] "the only purpose of extending the [wardship] jurisdiction to include a foetus is to enable the mother's actions to be controlled."[81] The Court of Appeal were deeply unhappy about the implications of that. Any conflict between the interests of the child and the interests of the mother would have to be resolved in favour of the child, because the whole aim of the wardship court is to protect the interests of the ward rather than its mother. May L.J. pointed out that if an order were made concerning the child and the mother disagreed, the order would have to be enforced against her wishes:

> "I think that there would be insuperable difficulties if one sought to enforce any order in respect of an unborn child against its mother, if that mother failed to comply with the order. I cannot contemplate the court ordering that this should be done by force, nor indeed is it possible to consider with any equinimity that the court should seek to enforce an order by committal."[82]

A court in Scotland wishing to interdict a woman whose behaviour constituted a threat to her unborn child would have to be willing to enforce its order, or to imprison a woman who failed to comply with it. It is difficult to visualise the Scottish court being willing to take these sorts of steps. Anything less than real and severe threat would not found an interdict, since the court would have to balance the rights of the pregnant woman with the interests of the child who may potentially be born, and the rights and liberties of a woman are not lost nor even diminished by her becoming pregnant.

Suing for the Antenatal Death of a Parent

A child who is born alive is entitled to damages for the antenatal death of his parent (by which is normally meant, in practical terms, his father[83]). He is entitled under section 1(1) of the Damages (Scotland) Act 1976 to reparation as being a relative, which includes[84] a "child of the deceased,"[85] and under section 1(4) to a loss of society award,[86] though not to solatium for pain and suffering.[87] In *Cohen* v. *Shaw*[88] the Lord Ordinary (Cullen) held that the word "child" as used in the 1976 Act should on any view be taken as including one in the womb

---

[80] *Ibid.* at p. 1305.

[81] See also Staughton L.J. at p. 1306.

[82] *Ibid.* at p. 1301. *Cf.* the Canadian decision of *Re A (In Utero)* (1990) 72 D.L.R. (4th) 722 in which it was held by the Ontario Family Court that a foetus has no status as a legal person and thus no rights to child protection under the Ontario Child and Family Services Act 1984. But see the bizarre decision in *Re S. (Adult: Refusal of treatment)* [1992] 3 W.L.R. 806, discussed *post* at p. 113.

[83] Though not always. It is possible to keep a woman who is brain-dead "alive" with life-support machines until her unborn child has reached term: see the news report in *The Independent*, Oct. 17, 1992, which reports of the corpse of a dead woman being ventilated in order to provide a gestation environment for a foetus of 15 weeks old.

[84] Sched. 1.

[85] Sched. 1, para. 1(*b*).

[86] *Cohen* v. *Shaw*, 1992 S.L.T. 1022.

[87] This was the case at common law: see *Moorcraft* v. *Alexander & Sons*, 1946 S.C. 466; *Connachan* v. *Scottish Motor Traction Co.*, 1946 S.C. 428; *Leadbetter* v. *N.C.B.*, 1952 S.L.T. 179; *Riddell* v. *James Longmuir & Sons Ltd.*, 1971 S.L.T. (Notes) 33.

[88] *Supra.*

at the time of death, but subsequently born alive. He was unable to envisage any reason that those drafting the 1976 Act might have had for distinguishing the unborn child from surviving children. However, because "relative" is defined to include a person who "was" a child of the deceased, he concluded that the *tempus inscipiendum* was the date of death, and that the pursuer could only be described as a child of the deceased at that date by applying the civilian fiction that in all things to the child's benefit the unborn child is treated as already born. Alternatively, the crystallisation theory discussed above may be invoked. It is also relevant to note that in some of the other definitions of relative a time is expressly stated when the relationship must exist: there is no such time for the relationship of parent and child.[89] However the matter is regarded it is sufficient that the pursuer was a child of the deceased after birth and the fact that the wrongful act took place before birth is irrelevant for the same reason as that fact is irrelevant when the child is claiming damages for its own injuries.[90]

A child who dies *in utero* or is still-born has no claim for the death of a parent whenever that occurs, because the activation of any right he may have is conditional on birth. A child whose conception was brought about by one of the reproductive techniques governed by the Human Fertilisation and Embryology Act 1990 and whose gestation *in utero* commenced after the death of its genetic father has no claim, because a man is not to be treated as father of a child for any purpose (this including a claim for damages under the Damages (Scotland) Act 1976) if his sperm or an embryo created with his sperm is used after his death.[91] If the genetic mother dies before or after the embryo created with her egg is implanted into another woman, the later born child has no claim since the woman who carries him and no other woman is to be treated as mother for all purposes,[92] including a claim for damages under the 1976 Act.

Suing for the Death of a Child in Utero

At Common Law

A quite separate issue to those considered above is that of a third party suing for damages as a result of the death of the unborn child. There are examples from other jurisdictions of damages being awarded to parents for the still-birth of their children, caused as a result of the defenders' negligence.[93] The injury suffered in these cases was nervous shock of the parents. In Scotland damages for nervous shock as a result of the death of another are recognised,[94] though there may be problems in establishing that the killing of a child *in utero* amounts to causing the death of another. However, it is submitted that the later the pregnancy is, the more attached the mother (and indeed the father) is likely to be to

---

[89] Damages (Scotland) Act 1976, Sched. 1, para. 1(*b*), as compared with paras. 1(*a*) and 1(*aa*).

[90] See *ante* at pp. 96–101.

[91] Human Fertilisation and Embryology Act 1990, ss. 28(6)(*b*) and 29(2).

[92] *Ibid.*, ss. 27 and 29.

[93] See, *e.g.* the early New Zealand case of *Stevenson* v. *Basham* [1922] N.Z.L.R. 225, and the more recent New Jersey case of *Giardina* v. *Bennet* (1988) 545 A2d 139.

[94] See Walker, *Delict* at pp. 671–680; *Brown* v. *Glasgow Corporation*, 1922 S.C. 527. See also the lengthy discussion by the 2nd Division in *Bourhill* v. *Young's Exr.*, 1941 S.C. 395.

the unborn child, and the more foreseeable her nervous shock at its destruction will be.[95] If the parents of an unborn child which dies *in utero* or is still-born[96] can prove that they have suffered nervous shock as a consequence of that event, it is submitted that they ought to be awarded damages in reparation. If personal injuries are caused to a pregnant woman as a result of the defender's negligence, she may sue for damages for these personal injuries, and if a miscarriage is caused by these injuries, this would be a relevant head of damages.[97]

Under the Damages (Scotland) Act 1976

Section 1 of the Damages (Scotland) Act 1976 provides that "where a person dies in consequence of personal injuries sustained" through the delict of another person, then damages will be payable to certain "relatives" specified in Schedule 1 to the Act, which includes any person who was a parent of the "deceased." Damages could be claimed by a parent of an unborn child negligently killed before its birth only if the child were within the meaning of the words "person" as used in section 1 and "deceased" as used in Schedule 1. Neither of these words is defined, and their normal meaning is therefore to be ascribed to them: the law regards a "person" as someone who has had a living existence independently of his mother,[98] and a "deceased" as someone who was in that state and no longer is so. It would follow that damages cannot be claimed under this statute for any delict that causes the unborn child to die *in utero*.

Suing for the Postnatal Death of a Child Injured in Utero

It may happen that a child is injured while *in utero*,[99] but is born alive and then dies of its injuries. There was a conflict of Outer House authority as to whether, in that situation, parents can sue under the Damages (Scotland) Act 1976 for a

---

[95] *Cf.* the New York case of *Del Zio* v. *Presbyterian Hospital*, 74 Civ. 3588 (Nov. 14, 1978) in which damages were recovered by parents of an *in vitro* embryo when they suffered mental shock because the director of the hospital terminated their treatment programme by destroying the embryo. While not suggesting that the Scottish court would go so far, it is to be noted that in *Alcock* v. *Chief Constable of South Yorkshire* [1991] 4 All E.R. 907 the House of Lords held that the class of persons to whom a common law duty may be owed is not limited by reference to a particular relationship to the deceased, although it must be to someone within the defendant's contemplation.

[96] A still-born child is one that dies *in utero* after 24 weeks' or more gestation: Registration of Births, Deaths and Marriages (Scotland) Act 1965, s. 56(1), as amended by the Still-Birth (Definition) Act 1992, s. 1(2).

[97] In *Bourhill* v. *Young*, 1942 S.C.(H.L.) 78 damages were claimed for, *inter alia*, a miscarriage, though that was the result, rather than the cause, of the mental shock (allegedly) suffered in that case. If a miscarriage can found an action for damages when it is the result of mental shock, it should also be able to found an action when it is the cause of the mental shock. Causation might of course prove difficult (as it did in *Bourhill*: see the decision of the Inner House, 1941 S.C. 395, where the evidential difficulties are more fully discussed than in the House of Lords), but that in itself is no reason not to allow the pursuer to attempt to prove his or her case.

[98] "In law a foetus is not yet a person, and is no more a person at [a] late stage than at any other stage from conception onwards": *per* Lord Prosser in *Hamilton* v. *Fife Health Board*, 1992 S.L.T. 1026 at p. 1030. Again, "a 'person' denotes someone who is living, not someone who has yet to be born": *per* Woolf L.J. in *D (A Minor)* v. *Berkshire County Council* [1987] 1 All E.R. 20 at p. 30.

[99] This is taken to include the child in the course of the process of being born, because of the law's simplistic view of the process of creation: Lord Prosser accepted in *Hamilton* v. *Fife Health Board*, *supra* at p. 1028E, that "at any given moment of time a child must be either born or not born, living or not living, and that prior to being born, a child is not a 'person'." In that case the alleged negligence occurred during the birth process, and the child was treated as not being a person at that point.

loss of society award. In *McWilliams* v. *Lord Advocate*,[1] Lord Morton of Shuna held that parents could sue for the death of a child as a result of injuries it had sustained *in utero*. He found it unnecessary to depend upon the civilian fiction whereby an unborn child can be treated as having been born when that is to its advantage, holding instead that the terms of the 1976 Act were satisfied: a child which had been born alive and later died as a result of prenatal injuries was clearly "a person" at the date of death and, since damage caused before birth crystallised at live birth, the child had at that point "sustained" injury. On the other hand, Lord Prosser in *Hamilton* v. *Fife Health Board*[2] held that injuries sustained in the womb could not be said to have been "sustained" by a "person" as required by the 1976 Act, because personality is not achieved until the moment of live birth. Consequently, because the terms of the Act were not satisfied, the parents could not sue for damages for loss of society.[3] Lord Prosser's decision, however, has now been overturned.[4] The Inner House held that the phrase in the 1976 Act, "personal injury sustained by him" was apt to cover injuries to the person of a child before birth which continue to have effects after birth by impairment of physical condition. It was pointed out by Lord Caplan that it was difficult to identify what policy objectives Parliament could have been trying to achieve if Lord Prosser's view was correct, since it would mean distinguishing parents whose child had died through injury inflicted shortly before birth from those whose child had died through injury inflicted shortly after birth. The result of this decision is that relatives of a child that dies can sue the person responsible for inflicting the fatal injuries, whether those injuries are sustained before or after birth, so long as the child is a living person (*i.e.* has been born alive) before its death from the injuries. The basis for this liability is not an extended application of the civilian fiction but the terms of the Damages (Scotland) Act 1976.

Parental Responsibilities

As will be seen in detail in Chapter 5, one of the inevitable consequences of the parent-child relationship is the imposition upon the parent of various responsibilities, duties and obligations towards their children. Failure in these responsibilities can lead to criminal prosecution[5] and to civil liability in damages. One of the most important of these responsibilities is to care for the child and to provide it with necessaries for its life. So, for example, a parent is obliged to ensure that the child receives proper medical treatment. A pregnant woman has almost total physical control over the child she is carrying, and it is in a very real sense in her care. The question must be asked whether her parental responsibilities to care for the child arise on its conception and can be enforced before its birth. The question may be of great importance if for example some medical procedure requires carrying out for the welfare of the child before it has an existence independent of its mother.

---

[1] 1992 S.L.T. 1045.
[2] 1992 S.L.T. 1026.
[3] See further, Norrie, "Liability for Injuries Caused Before Birth" 1992 S.L.T. (News) 65.
[4] *Hamiltion* v. *Fife Health Board*, 1993 S.L.T. 624, *per* Lords McCluskey, Caplan and Wylie.
[5] Children and Young Persons (Scotland) Act 1937, s. 12.

A pregnant woman is not merely the means of the unborn child's survival (even although she is essential for it), and it is submitted that she could not be forced to do something that infringed her own right to bodily integrity. A threat even to the life of the unborn child would not be sufficient to overcome the woman's own rights. So if for example it were discovered that a woman in the final stages of pregnancy was suffering from complete placenta praevia,[6] with the prognosis that there was a 99 per cent chance of foetal death and a 50 per cent chance of maternal death if natural childbirth were attempted, and at the same time there was an almost 100 per cent chance of both foetal and maternal survival if the child were delivered by Caesarian section, the woman would be entitled to refuse the invasion of her own bodily privacy that such an operation would constitute, and she would not be in breach of any parental obligation. Treatment without her consent would amount to an assault, and the threat to the unborn child would not be an emergency such as to render her consent unnecessary.[7] It has been said that any other answer would involve the court being willing to contemplate the use of force to manacle a resisting woman on to the hospital bed so that she could be forcibly anaesthetised and then cut open.[8] The example given is not fanciful, and the facts are those of *Jefferson* v. *Griffin Spalding County Hospital Authority*,[9] a case in which the Supreme Court of Georgia ordered a woman 39 weeks pregnant to undergo a Caesarian section in order to save the life of the child.[10] Nor is this case unique, and there is a growing number of similar decisions in the United States involving compulsory Caesarian sections, compulsory blood transfusions, and detention in hospital.[11] In the legally unsatisfactory and emotionally disturbing case of *Re A.C.*[12] the Court of Appeals of the District of Columbia overturned the decision of a lower court that had ordered a terminally ill pregnant woman to undergo a Caesarian section. The woman had only a few days to live and her unborn child would certainly die with her, although it would have a chance of survival, though slim, if it were removed immediately from the woman's body. A Caesarian section would shorten the woman's life by a few hours. That operation was carried out by order of the lower court, and both mother and child died. The Court of Appeals then overruled the decision, though on the basis that the evidence had not estab-

---

[6] "The placenta attached...to the lower uterine segment thus impairing the normal delivery of a baby by obstruction and by inevitable haemorrhage": *Faber Pocket Medical Dictionary*.

[7] And in any case emergency can justify medical treatment without consent only when the patient's wishes cannot be ascertained, and not when the patient expressly does not give consent.

[8] It has been reported that this was precisely what happened in a case in Chicago: see Gallagher, "Prenatal Invasions and Interventions: What's Wrong with Fetal Rights" (1987) 10 Harv. Women's L.R. 9 at pp. 9–10.

[9] (1981) 274 S.E. 2d 457.

[10] At the end of the day, the woman, in defiance of the court order, gave birth naturally, with no ill-effects either for herself or her child.

[11] There is also a burgeoning literature on the issue. See Kolder *et al.*, "Court Ordered Obstetrical Interventions" (1987) 316 New Eng. J. Med. 1192; Gallagher, *op. cit.*; Johnsen, "The Creation of Fetal Rights: Conflicts with Women's Constitutional Rights to Liberty, Privacy and Equal Protection" (1986) 95 Yale L.J. 599; Nelson and Milliken, "Compelled Medical Treatment of Pregnant Women: Life, Liberty and Law in Conflict" (1988) 259 J.A.M.A. 1060; Myers, "Abuse and Neglect of the Unborn: Can the State Intervene?" (1984) 23 Duquesne L.R. 1; Rhoden, "The Judge in the Delivery Room: The Emergence of Court-Ordered Cesareans" (1986) 74 Calif. L.R. 1951.

[12] (1990) 573 A 2d 1235.

lished whether the woman was capable of consenting or not, nor indeed satisfactorily whether she had in fact withheld consent. However, the importance of the case is that the court refused to rule out completely the possibility of overruling a pregnant woman's decision, holding merely that "in *virtually* all cases the decision of the patient will control." The court said: "We do not quite foreclose the possibility that a conflicting state interest may be so compelling that the patient's wishes must yield, but we anticipate that such cases will be extremely rare and truly exceptional. This is not such a case."[13]

These cases are unlikely to be followed in Scotland. The comments of Balcombe L.J. in the English case of *Re F (In Utero)* in relation to the U.S. decisions are in point: it would be "intolerable" for the courts to have to make such decisions without statutory guidance as to the principles upon which the decision should be based.[14] He continued: "in such a sensitive field, affecting as it does the liberty of the individual, it is not for the judiciary to extend the law."Nevertheless, in a short and clearly hurried judgment, the president of the Family Division of the High Court in England, Stephen Brown P., granted a declaration that a Caesarian section performed against the wishes of a competent pregnant woman would be lawful if the operation were necessary in the patient's best interests and to protect the vital interests of the unborn child.[15] The American cases are based expressly on the constitutional point that the state has an interest in the life of a viable foetus[16] which justifies intervention by the state, and that is not an argument that can be raised in Scotland. In principle these American cases should be resisted. A child in the womb is entitled to certain protections in Scots law, from criminal abortion,[17] from delictual injury,[18] and from parents who misuse or abuse it.[19] But these protections are justified only in so far as they do not conflict with any other important legal principle. To force a woman to undergo an operation upon her body when she does not wish to consent conflicts sharply with the principle of autonomy, which finds legal expression in the right of self-determination. This is so even when the interference is designed to protect the life or well-being of another. It is not true to say that the Abortion Act 1967 subordinates a woman's right of decision to the welfare of the child (*e.g.* by prohibiting abortions over 24 weeks except for certain limited reasons[20]): a woman has no "right" in the abortion situation, for that act remains a criminal

---

[13] It should be pointed out that even within the United States, these cases remain highly exceptional and in most jurisdictions the courts have refused to make such orders. Academic opinion is strongly opposed to court-ordered medical treatment against the wishes of the pregnant woman: see the articles cited in note 00 above. See also Mason, *Medico-Legal Aspects of Reproduction and Parenthood* (1990), Chap. 6.

[14] [1988] 2 W.L.R. 1288 at p. 1306.

[15] *Re S. (Refusal of Medical Treatment)*. [1992] 3 W.L.R. 806. The child died.

[16] This argument is based, somewhat tenuously (see Gallagher, *op. cit.* at pp. 15–18, 32–37), on the reasoning in *Roe* v. *Wade*, which recognised that state interest could prohibit abortion completely during the third trimester of pregnancy (*i.e.* after the foetus has attained viability). Because the argument is based on the state interest in viable foetuses, there is no such case in the USA involving a previable foetus. That this distinction is not made in English (or Scots) law is made clear in *Re F. (In Utero)* [1988] 2 W.L.R. 1288 at p. 1301, *per* May L.J. and p. 1304, *per* Balcolme L.J. (and indeed is under increasing challenge in the USA).

[17] *Ante*, pp. 87–90.

[18] *Ante*, pp. 96–104.

[19] *Post*, pp. 115–118.

[20] *Ante*, pp. 88–89.

offence and all the statute does is to provide certain defences. The law in Scotland has for long refused to sanction the idea of compulsory blood testing in order to determine paternity,[21] this on the ground that it would be an unwarranted invasion of a person's private right; and while the court now has the power to request a party to any civil proceedings to provide a sample of blood or other body fluid or tissue, it may not direct that such be taken and it is limited to drawing such adverse inferences as is appropriate from any refusal.[22] If the Scottish courts are unwilling, indeed unable, to order blood tests, they must be far more unwilling, and equally unable, to order compulsory medical operations of a far more invasive nature. It would follow that in Scotland if an operation upon a pregnant woman were necessary in order to save the life or health of her unborn child, and she refused consent to that operation, she could not be forced to undergo the operation, and the unborn child would have to suffer the risk. No breach of parental responsibility would have been committed.

The Mentally Incapax Woman

Slightly different considerations would apply if the pregnant woman were for some reason unable to provide or withhold consent to medical treatment that is necessary for her unborn child's welfare and which would inevitably involve interference upon her body. If the woman were unable to consent to her own medical treatment, the justification for carrying it out would be emergency, or immediate necessity facing the woman, and a doctor carrying out such treatment without consent would not be liable in damages for assault.[23] However, this provides a justification for non-consensual medical treatment only when the emergency faces the patient herself, and would provide no help if the emergency faced not her but her unborn child. It could be argued, however, that the woman's own emotional well-being demands that her child's life be saved, and in that sense the emergency could be said to face her also. Some help in that argument may be obtained from a line of US cases. In *Strunk* v. *Strunk*[24] a kidney was taken from a mental incompetent to save the life of his brother who was dying from kidney disease, this being justified on the argument that the brother's existence was important for the well-being of the incompetent and to save his life would therefore save the incompetent from "serious emotional impact." And in *Lausier* v. *Pescinski*[25] the court refused to order a kidney to be removed from an institutionalised catatonic man to save the life of his sister, this on the ground that the sister's previous lack of interest in her brother suggested that her survival would not be likely to benefit the donor. If this argument is accepted in relation to a mentally incapax pregnant woman, then an operation to save the life of her unborn child would be justified on the ground of emergency if it is concluded that the child's survival would save her serious emotional impact. However, it is clear that this argument could not be used in all cases. If the wo-

---

[21] See *post* at p. 152.

[22] Law Reform (Miscellaneous Provisions) (Scotland) Act 1990, s. 70; see *post* at pp. 152–154.

[23] *F.* v. *West Berkshire Health Authority* [1989] 2 All E.R. 545 (H.L.).

[24] (1969) 445 S.W. 2d 145. See also *Hart* v. *Brown* (1972) 289 A. 2d 386.

[25] (1975) 226 N.W. 2d 180. These cases are discussed by Gallagher, *op. cit.* at pp. 26–28, and by Norrie, in "Human Tissue Transplants: Legal Liability in Different Jurisdictions" [1985] 34 I.C.L.Q. 442 at pp. 454–455.

man were so incompetent that she would never enjoy the existence of her child, it could only be said in the most tenuous of ways that its potential non-existence would be a threat to her wellbeing. Or in a case similar to that of *Re A.C.*,[26] where the woman was going to die in a few days in any case, it is somewhat false to say that the benefit of her child's life is necessary for her own wellbeing. (It may well have been for this reason that the court in that case preferred to justify such operations on a "substituted judgment" test, whereby the court determines whether to give consent on behalf of the incompetent by making the decision which the evidence shows the incompetent would have made had she been competent.) It may however be that the court would be willing to stretch the concept of necessity to cover these situations, where no other competing interest is significantly affected.

Consent on Behalf of the Unborn Child

It may be doubted whether consent to medical treatment is required on behalf of the unborn child itself, for example to the performance of some surgical procedure while it is still in the womb. Whether such consent is required or not, however, the medical treatment would be justified on the basis of emergency, so long as the emergency faced the unborn child. A doctor performing an operation on an unborn child could not be sued for assault on the ground of lack of consent so long as the treatment were necessary in the sense of being a response to an emergency situation.

Care Proceedings and Removal of the Child

A further consequence of the existence of a foetus in the womb is that it will be recognised as being entitled to the protection granted to children who have been born, to the extent that if it is not properly looked after, it may be subject to care proceedings and be removed from its parents. Of course this removal can only take place once the child has been born alive, but once it has been born, things done to it by its parents may justify its removal from their care under the provisions of the Social Work (Scotland) Act 1968.[27] There is no reason why the court may not look at matters that occurred before the birth of the child in determining whether it is in need of compulsory measures of care.

Though the matter has not yet been discussed in a Scottish case, it has arisen in a number of cases from other jurisdictions. In England, for example, the House of Lords in the case of *D (A Minor)* v. *Berkshire County Council and Others*[28] were faced with the question of whether a child born suffering from drug withdrawal symptoms, directly referrable to the mother's drug addiction and continued drug-taking during pregnancy, was a child whose proper development was being avoidably prevented by the mother's actions, even although the child had never been in the care of the mother at any time after its birth. A juvenile court had made a care order under section 1(2)(*a*) of the Children and Young Persons Act 1969 on the ground that the child's proper development was

---

[26] *Supra* note 12.
[27] Discussed fully in Chap. 17.
[28] [1987] 1 All E.R. 20. See Bainham, "Protecting the Unborn—New Rights in Gestation?" (1987) 50 Mod. L.R. 361.

being avoidably prevented or neglected or its health was being avoidably impaired or neglected or it was being ill-treated. This was challenged on the ground that the statute demanded that the child "is being" ill-treated, etc., and that this requirement could never be satisfied once the child had been removed from its parents. The House of Lords held that the phrase "is being" denoted a continuing rather than an instant situation and that the court was entitled to look at the past as well as the present, and indeed at the future, though this last only in a hypothetical way by looking to see whether the situation which began earlier and was still continuing at the point of time immediately before the process of protecting the child was put in motion would, if that process had not been put in motion, have been likely to continue further.[29] Consequently, in the words of Lord Goff of Chieveley,[30] "it can be said that a child is being ill-treated if it has been cruelly beaten in the past, and there is a likelihood that it will continue to be cruelly beaten in the future." He went on:

> "It is not enough that something has avoidably been done or omitted to be done in relation to the child in the past which has, for example, impaired its health, and that the symptoms or effects still persist at the relevant time; for it cannot be said in such circumstances that, at the relevant time, the child's health *is being* avoidably impaired: all that can be said is that its health has been avoidably impaired in the past."[31]

It is important to note that this case was decided on the precise terms of the English statutory provisions, and this must be borne in mind in reading all such cases. There are similar examples from North America, which again turn on the precise terms of the statute in question. So, for example, in *Re Superintendant of Family and Child Service and McDonald*[32] the question was whether a child born drug addicted was "a child in need of protection" within the context of the British Columbia Family and Child Service Act 1980. The British Columbia Supreme Court said: "It would be incredible to come to any other conclusion than that a drug-addicted baby is born abused. That abuse has occurred during the gestation period"[33]; and it was held that a child "is" in need of protection when it is born drug-addicted and has never been in the care of its parents.[34]

In Scotland the relevant statute is the Social Work (Scotland) Act 1968, s. 32(2) of which lays down the conditions which have to be satisfied for a child to be in need of compulsory measures of care (which may include its removal from its parents by the imposition of a supervision requirement requiring the child's residence to be away from its parents[35]). A number of these conditions can apply to an unborn child. So, for example, under section 32(2)(*c*) a child may be in need of compulsory measures of care if there is a lack of parental care that is

---

[29] *Per* Lord Brandon of Oakbrook at p. 41.

[30] *Ibid.* at p. 44.

[31] *Ibid.*

[32] (1982) 135 D.L.R. (3d) 330.

[33] *Ibid.* at p. 335.

[34] See also *Re Children's Aid Society for the District of Kenora & J.L.* (1982) 134 D.L.R. (3d) 249, in which the Provincial Court of Ontario held that a child born with foetal alcohol syndrome was a "child in need of protection" within the meaning of the Ontario Child Welfare Act 1980.

[35] Social Work (Scotland) Act 1968, s. 44(1).

likely to cause him unnecessary suffering or seriously to impair his health or development. This ground is analogous to, but different in important respects from, the ground involved in the English case of *D (A Minor)* v. *Berkshire County Council.*[36] The problem in that case was whether a child in the womb could be said to satisfy a ground that it "is being" subject to impairment of health or development. The wording of the Scottish statute, with its emphasis on "likelihood,"[37] more clearly refers to a future danger from present or past events; and it has been held in the Inner House that this ground can be satisfied even when the child has never been in the care of the parent[38] (the exact situation in *D (A Minor)* and in the two Canadian cases cited above).

Applying that to drug or alcohol addiction by the mother during pregnancy, it can be stated that such addiction will in some cases clearly amount to habits and modes of life which yield the reasonable inference that the parents are unlikely to care for the child properly. However, it should be noted that the mere suffering of the child from drug withdrawal symptoms or foetal alcohol syndrome will not be sufficient on its own to satisfy this ground. This will be strong evidence, but the test is not the suffering of the child at its birth, but whether the lack of parental care is likely to cause the child unnecessary suffering in the future or seriously to impair his health or development. "The principal focus of attention is therefore the situation of the now living child and not the mother's behaviour while pregnant."[39] So a woman who is able to break her habit of addiction sometime during the pregnancy, but who has already caused her foetus some impairment in its health or development, will not have the child removed under this ground.[40]

Under section 32(2)(*dd*) of the 1968 Act a child may be in need of compulsory measures of care if he is, or is likely to become, a member of the same household as a person who committed certain offences. The words "is likely to become" are sufficient to include a child who is not yet born but who, if born, would be a member of the same household as the person who committed the offences. Again, the offences could be in the past, and at a time when the child was not yet born (nor even conceived).[41]

As well as compulsory measures of care authorised by the Social Work (Scotland) Act 1968, that Act also permits the immediate removal of children from their parents and their taking to a place of safety.[42] This provision may sometimes be used to authorise the removal of a child immediately on its birth, for example under section 37(2)(*c*) (that the child is or is likely to become a member of the same household as a person who has committed certain offences) or under section 37(2)(*e*) (that the child is likely to be caused unnecessary suffering or serious impairment of health because there is, or is believed to be, a lack of parental care).

---

[36] [1987] 1 All E.R. 20.

[37] See further, pp. 450–451.

[38] *McGregor* v. *L.,* 1981 S.L.T. 194.

[39] Bainham, *op. cit.* at p. 364.

[40] *Per* Lord Goff of Chieveley in *D. (A Minor)* v. *Berkshire County Council* [1987] 1 All E.R. 20 at pp. 44–45.

[41] *A* v. *Kennedy,* 1993 S.C.L.R. 107.

[42] Social Work (Scotland) Act 1968, s. 37. See *post* at pp. 457–459.

It follows from the above that the parents' actions before the birth of the child can be relevant in determining whether a child is in need of compulsory measures of care. This does not constitute any untoward limitation on the parent's freedom and liberty, for it is in all senses on a par with the limitations placed on parents whose children have already been born. The fear that to allow the court to look at events before birth will unduly restrict a pregnant woman's liberty is therefore unfounded in this context, since her actions would have to be such as would justify removal of a living child. These provisions could not be used to prevent a pregnant woman from, say, smoking tobacco or drinking moderate alcohol, or to ensure that she gave birth in a hospital rather than at home. While arguably failure to follow medical advice might amount to lack of parental care, it should be remembered that lack of parental care on its own is not sufficient to activate the care provisions in the Social Work (Scotland) Act 1968. Rather, it must be established that such lack "is likely to cause [the child] unnecessary suffering or *seriously* to impair his health or development."[43] Evidence that smoking leads to low birth weight would not be sufficient to satisfy this ground, because that may not be considered to be a "serious" impairment of health or development; and in any case causation would have to be established in the sense of showing that the smoking was the likely cause of that particular child being of low birth weight.

THE BIRTH PROCESS

The final stage in the process of the creation of human life is the birth process itself. This may be taken to commence at the point when spontaneous or induced labour commences, and to be completed at the moment when the umbilical chord is severed. During that time the child will have somewhat greater protection than that granted during its period of gestation in the womb. Destruction of a child during the process of birth is not abortion in Scots law, but nor is it homicide. In *H.M. Advocate* v. *McAllum*[44] the panel was accused of murder when she allegedly strangled the child she was giving birth to. The Lord Justice-Clerk (Inglis) expressly distinguished between abortion and destruction during birth, but he described them both as "very serious offences."[45] If the destruction of a child in the course of being born is a crime but it is not abortion, then the defences to the crime of abortion laid down in the Abortion Act 1967 cannot be utilised. However, it is likely that the law would recognise a common law defence if the child were destroyed in order to preserve the life of the mother.[46]

As far as the parent-child relationship goes during the birth process, it is likely that the most significant consequence of that relationship that practically would arise would be the parental obligation to care for the welfare of the child. This may impose on a woman giving birth the duty to seek medical help if the child's potential life is at risk, and if her failure to do so injures the child she may

---

[43] Social Work (Scotland) Act 1968, s. 32(2)(c).

[44] (1858) 3 Irv. 187.

[45] *Ibid.* at p. 200.

[46] In the English case of *R.* v. *Bourne* [1939] 1 K.B. 687 it was held that this would be a defence to the analogous, statutory, English offence of child destruction. The defence there was given a wide interpretation.

be sued for damages, and may have the child removed, on the conditions discussed above.

Once the umbilical chord is severed, the child can be said to have an existence independent of its mother, and if it is alive at that moment, for however short a period, it is a full human person in law, and therefore entitled to all the protections the law affords to human persons. Its destruction will not be countenanced in order to preserve the life of someone else.[47] The parent-child relationship will for all intents and purposes be fully constituted and all the normal rights and obligations flowing from that relationship which have not already arisen will come into existence at that moment.

Conclusion

While for most purposes the parent-child relationship will come into existence at birth, it is to be borne in mind that that relationship exists in law only in the context of the consequences it gives rise to. Some of these consequences, such as those relating to succession and the claiming of damages, certainly occur before birth (and this is not affected by the survival rule); others may possibly occur before birth, such as the imposition of duties of care and nurture. Most will arise on birth, but some will arise after that, such as the obligation to provide suitable education.[48] After a number of years the relationship will gradually lose significance as the child approaches adulthood. Though parental rights and obligations may disappear, the relationship will remain one of legal significance until the death of one of the parties.

The fear of recognising the existence of the unborn child, and of allowing legal consequences to follow, is that the pregnant woman will be unduly restricted in her own rights and liberties and in her self-determination, which are not to be denied just because she is pregnant. While this risk is certainly real, it is suggested that the balance struck by the law of Scotland is an acceptable and sensible one. Cases in which a pregnant woman will act against the interests of her unborn child will be few indeed (though they will never be completely unknown in any society in which women of child-bearing age are subject to the risk of drug addiction). If the law protects the child by allowing its removal on birth for actions the woman does during pregnancy, and by allowing the child to sue its mother or father or anyone else who causes it injury before or after its birth, then that is probably sufficient and acceptable deterrent. To go further and to allow a pregnant woman to be interdicted from certain activities, and to enforce such interdict, would be to go too far. It would be too great an interference in the woman's liberties and fundamental freedoms and would reduce the pregnant woman to the status of an incubator for future generations, and to sanction that would be contrary to public policy.

---

[47] Cf. R. v. *Dudley & Stevens* (1884) 14 Q.B.D. 273.
[48] Education (Scotland) Act 1980, ss. 30 and 31.

CHAPTER 4

CONSTITUTION OF THE PARENT-CHILD RELATIONSHIP

Scope of this Chapter

The law of parent and child in Scotland used to be concerned primarily with the status of the child as determined by its legitimacy or illegitimacy, which in turn was determined by its parents' relationship to each other.[1] Fraser opens his work on *Parent and Child*[2] with the statement: "Legitimacy is the status of a party who has been born in a lawful manner, that is, in a manner approved of by the law". Since the coming into force of the Law Reform (Parent and Child) (Scotland) Act 1986, it is no longer true that the major concern of the law is with the child's status: in general the thrust of the law is to give all children the same status, which will alter only with age.[3] Nowadays the major concern of the law is the relationship between the child and its parents, the nature of that relationship, how it is constituted, and its consequences in law. The consequences of the existence of the parent-child relationship will be examined more fully in other parts of this book, and the main purpose of this chapter is to show how that relationship will, apart from the adoption process, come about in the eyes of the law. This relationship in law is no longer necessarily established by proving, to an extent sufficient to satisfy the burden of proof, a genetic parental link between two persons. That may frequently be essential, and will usually be sufficient, but there are now some cases in which it is not even relevant. Very different considerations arise in trying to establish the legal relationship of mother and child from that of father and child, and consequently they must be considered separately.

ESTABLISHING MATERNITY

Mater semper certa est etiamsi vulgo conceperit; pater vero is est, quem nuptiae demonstrant.[4] The passage from the Digest is absolute in its terms but both fact and law admit of a relative judgment. It points, however, to the comparative certainty of proof of maternity, demonstrable as it often is by direct evidence, and the uncertainty of proof of paternity, which until recently had to rely almost entirely on inference. Once maternity is established, the mother today has the full

---

[1] *Ante*, at pp. 10–26.

[2] 3rd ed. (1906) at p. 1.

[3] The only exception to this is with adopted children who for certain limited purposes have a separate status: see Chap. 19. However it is probably better to regard these differences more as exceptions that arise from the alterations to a child's legal parentage rather than as the defining characteristics of a different category of children.

[4] Digest, II, 4, 5: "The mother is always indentifiable even if the son has been conceived in promiscuity; the father indeed is declared by the marriage" (Mommsen, Krueger & Watson, eds., 1985).

complement of both parental rights and parental obligations in relation to her child, this flowing simply from her maternity.[5]

Defining Maternity

The certainty which usually attaches to maternity is based on the assumption that a child is conceived of the woman who bears it. Any other view would until recently have seemed absurd. Indeed, it was not so much a question of making an assumption as of drawing a factual inference of unassailable certainty. Modern medical procedures have, however, given rise to exceptions. It is now possible to take an egg from one woman, to fertilise it externally, and to implant it into another woman who will carry it for the necessary gestation period, and then give birth to a child. Similarly, it is possible to remove an egg that has been fertilised naturally in one woman from that woman's body and to implant it into another woman, with the same aim and result. These are, respectively, egg donation and embryo transfer, which are two of the technological methods of alleviating infertility that were hardly dreamed of until the later years of the twentieth century. There are many others,[6] but the two mentioned have this in common, that they both result in the genetic mother (*i.e.* the person whose egg was fertilised to be developed into a child) being different from the "carrying" or "nurturing" mother (*i.e.* the woman in whose uterus the child gestates and who goes through the process of giving birth to the child). Where these procedures are employed the question, not previously possible, arises of whether it is the person from whose egg the child has been conceived ("the genetic mother") or the person who nurtures the child in the womb and bears it ("the carrying or nurturing or gestational mother") who is to be regarded as the child's mother for the purposes of the law. Further complications to the question may arise if the purpose of implantation into a nurturing mother is to create a child not for her to bring up but for another person to bring up as a member of that other person's family. This is referred to as surrogate maternity.[7]

There has been much academic (and in other countries judicial) discussion of the question of defining "mother" in the face of these techniques,[8] and some attempts to identify the criteria adopted by the common law for defining mother-

---

[5] This is to be compared with the establishment of paternity (see *post* at pp. 126–141), which does not necessarily import the full complement of parental rights and obligations on the father unless he be married to the mother, though it will automatically give rise to some (such as, for example, succession rights).

[6] See the more complete discussion than is possible here in D. J. Cusine, *New Reproductive Techniques: A Legal Perspective* (1988).

[7] Though it is, in fact, only one form of surrogacy. The more usual is when a woman carries a child created by the fertilisation of her own egg, the intention being that she gives up the child on birth to another woman. Commercial surrogacy was made a criminal offence by the Surrogacy Arrangements Act 1986, which was amended by s. 36 of the Human Fertilisation and Embryology Act 1990 to make clear that all surrogacy arrangements, legal and illegal, commercial and non-commercial, are unenforceable in law. S. 30 of the 1990 Act allows the court to make an order providing for a child to be treated as the child of the parties to the marriage when the child has been carried by a woman other than the wife of the marriage and the child has been created using the gametes of either the husband or the wife or both (see *post*). This avoids the need for, but has the same effect as, adoption: see *Re Adoption Application (Surrogacy)* [1987] 2 All E.R. 826.

[8] See, for example Cusine, *op. cit.* at pp. 59–72; Rosettenstein, "Defining a Parent: The New Biology and Rebirth of the *Filius Nullius*" (1981) 131 New L.J. 1095; McKenzie, "Who Are a Child's Parents?" 1986 S.L.T. (News) 303.

hood have been made. Where there is no legislation, these attempts are probably futile, because the common law had no need to distinguish between a woman's genetic contribution to the creation of a child and a woman's nurturing contribution: as there was no need for such a distinction, none was made.

However, because there can now be a distinction in fact between the genetic mother and the nurturing mother, there has arisen the need for the law to define what it means by "mother" rather more precisely, that is, what criteria it uses in determining maternity. It could be argued, on an analogy with establishing paternity, that it is the biological or genetic rather than the nurturing connection that is the important one. One may find corroboration for this suggestion by pointing to the law's preference for "blood-links" in other areas, such as in the law of succession, as well as to the fact that, generally, paternity will depend upon genetic connection. This is the approach that was used in the American case of *Calvert* v. *Johnston*,[9] in which a surrogate, who had carried a foetus created by the egg of another woman and the sperm of that woman's husband, was held by the California Court of Appeal to have no statutory or constitutional right to be declared mother of the child since she had no genetic connection with it.[10] It may be that this approach is too simplistic, in that while the father's contribution is solely genetic, the mother's contribution is both genetic and nutritive: it does not therefore follow that only one aspect of the mother's contribution should be used to the exclusion of the other. When the Warnock Committee in the United Kingdom considered the matter,[11] the majority there did not follow the analogy with establishing paternity, and preferred to draw an analogy with sperm donation, which the committee had previously suggested should be dealt with by severing completely all legal links between the donor and the child[12]: the result would be that the woman who provided the gestative environment would be the legal mother of the child rather than, if different, the woman who provided the genetic material. The courts have not pronounced on the matter,[13] and the proposals of the Warnock Committee were accepted by Parliament, and given effect in the Human Fertilisation and Embryology Act 1990. Section 27 of the 1990 Act provides as follows:

> "The woman who is carrying or has carried a child as a result of the placing in her of an embryo or of sperm and eggs, and no other woman, is to be treated as the mother of the child."

This applies whether the woman was in the United Kingdom or elsewhere at the time of the placing in her of the embryo or of the sperm and eggs.[14]

The result of this is that the woman who carries the child in her womb and

---

[9] (1991) 60 U.S.L.W. 1069.

[10] The decision was confused a little by the judge at first instance also holding, in the action for custody, that he had to decide what was in the best interests of the child, which was to go to the commissioning couple rather than the surrogate. This aspect of the case was not commented upon by the Court of Appeal.

[11] Committee of Inquiry into Human Fertilisation and Embryology (the Warnock Committee), Cmnd. 9314 (1984), at paras. 6.6–6.8.

[12] *Ibid.* at para. 4.22.

[13] Though the opportunity could have been taken, but was not, in the English case of *Re W. (Minors) (Surrogacy)* [1991] 1 F.L.R. 385.

[14] Human Fertilisation and Embryology Act 1990, s. 27(3).

who gives birth to it will be treated as the mother of that child. This means that the person will be treated "in law" as the mother of the child "for all purposes,"[15] and "references to any relationship between two people in any enactment, deed, or other instrument or document (whenever passed or made) are to be read accordingly."[16] This is not a presumption, but is rather an irrebuttable deeming provision and it will not matter where the egg came from that was used to bring about the creation of the embryo that led to the child, nor how the egg was implanted. The genetic link between child and egg-producer is irrelevant for the law, and proof that it exists will be meaningless: the donor of the egg, if different from the nurturing mother, is not to be treated in law as being the mother of the child for any purpose.[17] It follows that in a situation similar to that in *Calvert* v. *Johnston* the surrogate would be considered in law the mother, and the "commissioning mother" would have no parental rights whatsoever; though she and her husband would be entitled to apply for an order under section 30 of the 1990 Act that they be treated as parents.[18]

Exceptions

There are a number of qualifications to this general principle. First, according to section 27(2) the carrying woman will not be considered in law to be the mother of the child where the child is treated by virtue of adoption as not being the child of any person other than the adopter or adopters. This is not a true exception to the general principle, but rather keeps the law in line with the adoption legislation, which provides[19] that when the adoptive relationship comes into being no person other than the adopter or adopters is to be regarded as the parent of the child.

Secondly, the carrying woman will not be considered in law to be the mother of the child for the purposes of section 2 of the Human Organ Transplants Act 1989, which contains restrictions on organ transplantations between persons who are not genetically related.[20] These restrictions refer to a genetic link, and their purpose would be undermined if any form of genetic parent-child relationship did not come within their terms. Consequently the parent-child relationship otherwise created by the 1990 Act is deemed not to be effective for the purposes of the Human Organ Transplants Act 1989. It may be noted here that there is no exception made in relation to the laws on incest or the forbidden degrees of marriage,[21] where genetics are otherwise seen as having a significance.[22] This means that a child born through artificial reproductive technology may have

---

[15] *Ibid.*, s. 29(1).

[16] *Ibid.*, s. 29(3). It would, however, remain open to the person executing a deed expressly to exclude from his definition of "mother" or "father" persons deemed mother and father by these provisions. S. 29(3) is so worded that nothing short of express terms or necessary implication will, however, suffice. A surrogacy contract, being unenforceable in any case, cannot be used to exclude s.29(3).

[17] *Ibid.*, ss. 27(1) and 29(2).

[18] See *post* at pp. 143–145.

[19] Adoption (Scotland) Act 1978, s. 39(1).

[20] Human Fertilisation and Embryology Act 1990, Sched. 4, para. 8.

[21] Notwithstanding a plea in the House of Lords from the Chief Rabbi that such an exception be made: H.L. Dec. 7, 1989, col. 1074.

[22] Though the extent of that significance can be questioned: see Norrie, "Incest and the Forbidden Degrees of Marriage in Scots Law" (1992) 37 J.L.S. 216.

sexual intercourse with and may marry a person to whom he or she is genetically related.[23] Due to the secrecy that is written into other parts of the 1990 Act it is, in any event, unlikely in the extreme that it would ever be discovered that a child born through these means was genetically related to someone he or she wished to marry or have sex with.

Thirdly, it is provided[24] that the provision deeming maternity from the fact of gestation does not apply to any title, coat of arms, honour or dignity transmissible on the death of the holder thereof or affect the succession thereto or the devolution thereof; and where the terms of any deed provide that any property or interest in property shall devolve along with a title, coat of arms, honour or dignity, nothing in the provision deeming maternity shall prevent the property or interest from so devolving. This is in line with the general principle that succession to any such title or dignity is governed by the common law of parentage and must be legitimate[25] and that in relation to the devolution of these interests, the genetic link between the holder and the child remains determinative.[26] A child born to a woman other than its genetic mother will have its legitimacy determined by the nature of the relationship between its genetic mother and its genetic father. If the gametes have been donated, as will normally be the case, proof of legitimacy (and therefore the right to inherit dignities and honours) will be almost impossible to establish. That the courts have traditionally favoured presuming legitimacy in the absence of evidence to the contrary will seldom save such a child's legitimacy for the purposes of this form of succession since proof that the child developed from an embryo that was created by unknown donors will usually be sufficient to rebut the presumption of legitimacy and will certainly do so if either the nurturing mother or her husband can be excluded as a provider of gametes. In unusual cases, an embryo may be created using the gametes of a married couple, to be carried by another woman: in that situation the carrying mother will be mother for all other legal purposes, including general succession, but the child will succeed to the titles, coats of arms, honours or dignities transmissible from its genetic parents, together with any property or interest in property that devolves along with them.

Fourthly, though the matter is not dealt with in the Act, it may be that the

---

[23] This may be compared with the adoption legislation which also creates a parent-child relationship in the absence of a genetic link (see Chap. 19). S. 41(1) of the Adoption (Scotland) Act 1978 (as amended by the Incest and Related Offences (Scotland) Act 1986, Sched. 1, para. 5) has the effect of bringing the child and the adopter within the forbidden degrees in respect of the law relating to both marriage and incest, but it does not take the child outwith the forbidden degrees in relation to its natural genetic parents, and other relations.

[24] Human Fertilisation and Embryology Act 1990, s. 29(5).

[25] Legitimation *per subsequens matrimonium* will however suffice. The Legitimation (Scotland) Act 1968, s. 8(4), has the effect of allowing persons legitimated under the Act to succeed to titles and dignities, even although they would not be legitimated at common law: see *ante* at p. 24.

[26] This reflects the position under s. 9(1)(c) of the Law Reform (Parent and Child) (Scotland) Act 1986, and s. 37(1)(a) of the Succession (Scotland) Act 1964 which prevents anyone succeeding to such interests through the operation of, respectively, the Law Reform (Parent and Child) (Scotland) Act 1986 (which otherwise removes the distinction between the legitimate and the illegitimate child) and the Adoption (Scotland) Act 1978 (which creates a parent-child relationship in the absence of any genetic link). It should be noted however that the exclusion in the 1990 Act, which covers property or interests devolving along with the title or honour, is rather wider than the exclusion contained in either of these other Acts, which does not include such property or interest. *Cf.* the position under the Legitimation (Scotland) Act 1968, *supra*, n. 25.

mother-child relationship will not be recognised if the question arises incidentally to a question of succession abroad. Entitlement to succeed to immoveables is generally a matter for the *lex situs*,[27] which will even determine a person's status for that purpose.[28] It would follow from these authorities that if the *lex situs* does not recognise the nurturing mother as the legal mother, then she and the child would have no succession rights in each other's immoveable estate. However, the 1990 Act states that the nurturing mother is to be legal mother "for all purposes,"[29] which, literally, must include succession to immoveables abroad. In this context, then, it may be argued that the 1990 Act has overturned the traditional rule in the international private law of succession. On the other hand, succession to immoveables abroad is not and cannot be governed by Scots law, and the 1990 Act is part of Scots law. If succession to immoveables is governed by another legal system it is that other legal system that has the power, at the end of the day, to say who succeeds. If the foreign system refers that question back to one of the legal systems which contains the 1990 Act, then section 27 will give the rule, but if the foreign legal system is willing to answer the question itself, then that is the answer that ultimately must be accepted. The contrary can be maintained only on an argument, which it is submitted is unsound, that the relevant provisions of the 1990 Act are restricted to questions of proof, which are matters for the *lex fori*, and do not affect the substantive law. International private law issues relating to the determination of parentage are discussed at the end of this chapter.

Proof of Maternity

It is only very rarely that, in the absence of the medical procedures previously discussed, there is any dispute as to who a child's mother is. Problems can sometimes occur, however, as when it is alleged that a child has been infiltrated into a family or that there has been confusion in a hospital at birth. They may also arise if a quest is made for the origins of a child who has been abandoned. And a like effect may follow from deliberate concealment as where, due to the social stigma attaching to illegitimacy, a child born to a young unmarried girl is brought up as the girl's brother or sister rather than as her child. It is probable that this practice of familial confusion, once quite common and still not unknown, is usually motivated more by a desire to avoid the social consequences of birth out of wedlock than as any fraud on the law, but, if persisted in, it may have that effect. Maternity may also be in doubt in immigration cases.[30] If there is any doubt as to maternity, an action of declarator of parentage or non-parentage can now be brought either in the Court of Session or in the sheriff court under section 7 of the Law Reform (Parent and Child) (Scotland) Act

---

[27] Craig, *Jus Feudale*, III, vii, 4; *Fenton* v. *Livingstone* (1859) 21 D.(H.L.) 10; *Murray* v. *Earl of Rothes* (1836) 14 S. 1049; Anton and Beaumont, *Private International Law* (2nd ed.) at p. 676.

[28] *Fenton* v. *Livingstone, supra*, described by Anton and Beaumont (at p. 676) as the "high water mark" of the general international private law rule.

[29] Human Fertilisation and Embryology Act 1990, s. 29(1).

[30] Rankin, "DNA Fingerprinting" (1988) 33 J.L.S. 124 at p. 125, describes a case in which a Ghanaian boy born in the U.K. was refused entry into Britain to rejoin his mother because immigration officers suspected that a substitution had occurred and he was not really the child of the woman (the father was unknown). On obtaining the results of scientific tests (to be discussed later) the Home Office conceded the boy the right of entry.

1986.[31] Maternity has to be proved as a fact. In the absence of scientific proof[32] the best evidence is that of those present at the birth, but reputation or the evidence of the entry in the register of births will also be relevant. By statute[33] an extract or abbreviated certificate of birth, duly authenticated,[34] will be sufficient evidence of the facts of the birth, though other evidence, normally oral, will also be required to identify the persons named in the record as the mother and child.[35] The lack of reported cases in which maternity has been doubted suggests that this is not a matter that creates many practical problems.[36]

Adoption

A relationship of mother and child can be created, again in the absence of any genetic link, through the legal process of adoption. This matter is dealt with fully in Chapters 19 and 20 of this book.

Surrogacy

A relationship of mother and child can be created, once more in the absence of any genetic link, by means of a court order in her favour following a surrogacy arrangement.[37] This matter is dealt with fully later in this chapter.[38]

ESTABLISHING PATERNITY

Introduction

Establishing paternity is necessarily less certain and often more problematic than establishing maternity. In the nature of the case there is no equivalent of gestation or birth from which a conclusion of paternity can be drawn. Nor did the common law find any place for deemed paternity except in the strong but rebuttable presumption that the husband of a married woman was the father of her child. In questions of paternity the quest was always for the genetic link, identifying the male parent to whom procreation was attributable, as both the rules for proof in actions of affiliation of illegitimate children and the rules for rebuttal of the presumption *pater est quem nuptiae demonstrant* show. Subject to some statutory modifications and exceptions, that is still so. Proof of the genetic link has until recently had to rely largely on inference. Previously it was impossible to establish by scientific means that, with certainty, a particular man was the father of a particular child though, on the other hand, an exclusion of paternity

---

[31] See further, *post* at pp. 145–147.
[32] See *post* at pp. 151–152.
[33] Registration of Births, Deaths and Marriages (Scotland) Act 1965, s. 41(3).
[34] *Ibid.*, s. 41(1).
[35] See Wilkinson, *The Scottish Law of Evidence* (1986), at p. 172. For births abroad, see the Evidence (Foreign, Dominion and Colonial Documents) Act 1933, and for births at sea, the Merchant Shipping (Returns of Births and Deaths) Regulations 1972, made under the Merchant Shipping Act 1970, s. 75.
[36] One of the few Commonwealth cases in which the issue arose was that of *R.* v. *Jenkins, ex p. Morrison* [1949] V.L.R. 277, decided by the Supreme Court of Victoria. The question arose, though obliquely, in the Scottish case of *Grant* v. *Countess of Seafield*, 1926 S.C. 274, in which the pursuer sought to prove that he was the son of the Earl of Seafield, and also of the Earl's wife. See also *Douglas* v. *Duke of Hamilton* (1769) 2 Pat. 143 (H.L.).
[37] Human Fertilisation and Embryology Act 1990, s. 30.
[38] *Post*, at pp. 142–145.

could sometimes be established beyond any doubt. A positive conclusion could therefore be reached only with the help of inferential evidence such as length of gestation, the alleged father's opportunity for sexual access to the mother, and parental acknowledgment, if any.[39]

Although there has been little occasion for the matter to be considered, the corollary of common law principles placing paternity for legal purposes on a factual and genetic basis is that the fact that procreation was achieved other than by normal sexual intercourse was irrelevant. So, in relation to children conceived as a result of fecundation *ab extra*, their legitimacy depended upon whether or not fecundation was attributable to sperm of the husband of the mother.[40] The same principles, it is submitted, apply at common law in relation to children conceived by artificial insemination, whether to determine their legitimacy or to determine paternity. The technique of AID,[41] whereby a (usually anonymous) donor would provide sperm to a woman for the fertilisation of her egg, is not new,[42] and though in theory the donor was in law the father (and therefore subject to parental obligations) the practice of anonymity for donors made proof virtually impossible. Proof became somewhat easier after the development of more accurate means of identification, particularly through DNA profiling[43]; and this, combined with the growing movement to allow AID (or DI) children (and others born as a result of infertility techniques) access to information concerning their genetic origins,[44] led to fears that donations of sperm would cease, because potential donors would not wish to be subject to parental obligations. In the true donation situation statute therefore now expressly provides[45] that if a person gives his gametes for the purposes of treatment services of others (*i.e.* if he donates his sperm for the treatment of someone other than himself or for the treatment of persons other than himself and another together[46]) and he gives effective consent to them so being used,[47] then he is not to be treated as the father of any child born as a result of his sperm being so used.[48] The genetic link between the sperm donor and the resultant child is therefore in these circumstances irrelevant in determining paternity. In other words, this provision elides all parent-child links between the donor and the child except when the donation is used for the treatment of the donor himself and of his partner.

---

[39] For proof of paternity, see *post*, pp. 147–157.

[40] See *ante* at p. 11.

[41] Now more usually referred to as DI, donor insemination, to avoid confusion with the very similar acronym AIDS.

[42] It was discussed by the Court of Session in the case of *MacLennan* v. *MacLennan*, 1958 S.C. 105, in which the claim was made (unsuccessfully) that a woman undergoing AID was committing adultery. AID has been practised by medical practitioners since at least the beginning of the 20th century: see Cusine, *op. cit.* at pp. 12 *et seq.* The same question as in *MacLennan* arose (and the opposite conclusion reached) in an Ontario decision in 1921: *Orford* v. *Orford* (1921) 58 D.L.R. 251. See Smith, "Adultery and AID," 1957 S.L.T. (News) 69.

[43] See *post* at pp. 151–157.

[44] Recognised and accepted by the Warnock Committee, at para. 4.21 (so long as the information given was non-identifying): see now s.31 of the Human Fertilisation and Embryology Act 1990.

[45] Human Fertilisation and Embryology Act 1990, s. 28(6) and Sched. 3, para. 5.

[46] *Ibid.*, Sched. 3, para. 5(3).

[47] *Ibid.*, Sched 3, para. 5(1).

[48] *Ibid.*, s. 28(6)(*a*).

128   CONSTITUTION OF THE PARENT-CHILD RELATIONSHIP

Paternity is today still primarily, and in the vast majority of cases, established by proving a genetic link between the child and the putative father. This proof can be achieved by leading extrinsic evidence, such as the results of scientific tests,[49] or it can be achieved by relying on a number of presumptions that the law provides. In unusual cases, involving artificially assisted conception, paternity is deemed by the law from certain facts. It is to be noted that merely establishing paternity will be sufficient to impose certain parental responsibilities (such as the obligation to aliment the child) and to confer certain rights (such as succession rights), but it will not be sufficient to confer certain other rights (such as the "parental rights" of guardianship, custody and access), the conferring of which demands satisfaction of rather different criteria.[50]

Proving paternity by evidence will be considered later.[51] The presumptions and deeming provisions are as follows.

Marriage to the Mother

Section 5(1)(*a*) of the Law Reform (Parent and Child) (Scotland) Act 1986[52] provides that a man shall be presumed to be the father of a child if he was married to the mother of the child at any time in the period beginning with the conception and ending with the birth of the child. This is the statutory re-enactment, with important modifications, of the common law principle *pater est quem nuptiae demonstrant*,[53] which was in truth a presumption of paternity rather than a presumption of legitimacy (though it was frequently regarded as the latter, since in many instances that was the legally significant issue). This was a *praesumptio juris* to which, on proof of the basic facts, a court was accordingly bound by law to give effect unless there was evidence sufficiently strong for rebuttal. In the statute the presumption "shall" apply in the relevant circumstances, subject to rebuttal according to the principles shortly to be discussed. The presumption at common law was based on common experience (the majority of children born of married women are procreated by their husbands). The identity of the mother, the marriage at the appropriate date, and the conception and birth of the child at the relevant time are the basic facts that require to be proved before the presumption operates.

The Nature of the Marriage

The couple may end the marriage by divorce before the child is born, or one party may die, or they may marry before conception or before birth: but so long as there is a marriage at some point between the moment of conception and the moment of birth[54] the presumption will take effect. This applies whether the

---

[49] Discussed *post*, at pp. 151–157.
[50] *Post* at pp. 167–168. This will no longer be the case if the proposals of the Scottish Law Commission in their *Report on Family Law* (1992) are enacted, for then paternity alone will confer parental responsibilities and rights just as maternity does.
[51] *Post* at pp. 147–157.
[52] See Thomson, "The Law Reform (Parent and Child) (Scotland) Act 1986," 1987 S.L.T. (News) 129.
[53] Stair, III, iii, 42; Erskine, I, vi, 49; Fraser, p. 1.
[54] The statutory formulation also takes into account the previously existing presumption—of fact, not of law (*Kerrs* v. *Lindsay* (1890) 18 R. 365)—that where a man marries a pregnant woman he

marriage is valid, void, voidable, regular or irregular.[55] At first sight it may seem a little odd to recognise legal consequences of a marriage that is not in law a marriage, but the law previously did this in recognising that a child of a putative marriage was a legitimate child. This provision in fact does no more than presume the relationship between a child and a man, reflecting the fact that the presumption is one of paternity rather than of legitimacy (which is more closely linked to the married status of the parents), and the rule can be justified on the ground that the marriage's invalidity does not affect the presumption that if people go through a ceremony of marriage and thereafter have the opportunity for sexual intercourse they will take that opportunity.[56] In other words a marriage ceremony, whether it leads to a valid marriage or not, is strong presumptive evidence of sexual intercourse.

The Time of Conception

The reference in the statute to the period "beginning with the conception" can lead to difficulties, particularly if the marriage has ended, whether through death or divorce, before birth, and a child is later born. If the child has been conceived before the end of the marriage then the husband is its father, but the date of conception can rarely, if ever, be fixed with precision. At common law, where the *pater est* presumption applied only when there was a marriage at the date of conception, similar difficulties were at one time resolved by reference to fixed periods of time which were held to constitute the minimum and the maximum periods of gestation respectively. The minimum period was six lunar months.[57] There was some divergence of opinion about whether the maximum period should be set at 10 lunar or 10 calendar months.[58] These periods came

---

is presumed to be father of the child. The *locus classicus* of this presumption of fact is the opinion of Lord Gifford in *Gardner* v. *Gardner* (1876) 3 R. 695 at p. 723: "wherever an avowed and open courtship has taken place, there have been opportunities of access, and thereafter the man marries the woman in an advanced state of pregnancy, knowing that she is so...in such a case the presumption is quite as strong as the mere presumption which arises when a child is conceived during marriage that the husband is the father. Indeed in some aspects it seems to be even stronger, for it has in it the element of express or actual confession or avowal, which does not always arise, or arises with less force, from the mere subsistence of a nuptial tie." (And see (1877) 4 R.(H.L.) 56, *per* Lord Cairns L.C. Lord Blackburn at 68 and Lord Gordon at 75). There was no presumption at common law that a man was father when he married the mother of a child conceived and born before the marriage: *James* v. *McLennan*, 1971 S.C.(H.L.) 77. Nor was (or is) there any presumption that a child born to a woman is her cohabitant's child: *A.* v. *G.* 1984 S.L.T. (Sh.Ct.) 65; it will, however, in these circumstances often be easy to draw inferences of fact.

[55] Law Reform (Parent and Child) (Scotland) Act 1986, s. 5(2). There was some authority for the view that at common law the presumption had no application in the case of irregular marriages: Craig, II, xviii, 21; *Swinton* v. *Swinton* (1862) 24 D. 833, *per* Lord Deas at p. 838; *Baptie* v. *Barclay* (1665) Mor. 8413; but Stair, III, iii, 42 and IV, xlv, 20 is explicitly to the contrary. The matter is put beyond doubt by the express terms of the statute. If the proposals of the Scottish Law Commission (*supra*) are enacted the references to voidable and to irregular marriages would disappear, as it is proposed that these concepts be abolished.

[56] *Per* Lord Neaves in *Ross* v. *Fraser* (1863) 1 M. 783.

[57] Erskine, I, vi, 50. The corresponding period in Roman law was six solar months, but Scots law from favour of legitimacy put it at six lunar months.

[58] *Sandy* v. *Sandy* (1823) 2 S. 453, *per* Lord Gillies and Lord Meadowbank. Calculation by calendar months would accord with the favour of legitimacy shown in the calculation of the minimum period. Stair, III, iii, 42 allowed as much as 11 months, subject to the qualification that "in these cases, the probability of the circumstances may make the mother's testimony alone sufficient to instruct the bastardy of the child"; but by the time of Erskine it was settled at 10.

from the civil and the canon law, which in turn depended on the observations of Hippocrates[59] and they did no more than reflect the medical opinion of the times: they must now give way to advances in medical science. Medical practice today is to count pregnancy from the date of the woman's last menstrual period. But that date is clearly not the date of "conception," which occurs not on fertilisation but on the implantation of the fertilised egg into the woman's uterus.[60] If the marriage has ended before the child's birth, therefore, it is conception that must be proved to have occurred at the date before the ending of the marriage, and the common law cases on possible length of gestation remain relevant. The question was widely canvassed, both in relation to proof of legitimacy and in relation to proof of adultery[61]; and although decisions on questions of fact in individual cases constitute neither precedent nor the material of judicial knowledge, it can probably be said that the fact that gestation of more than 10 months is possible, although highly unusual, is now sufficiently notorious to bring it within judicial knowledge. The maximum period of the older law is therefore superseded even in the absence of medical evidence. In cases involving proof of adultery for the purposes of divorce it has been said that where the period of gestation necessary to maintain consistency with the wife's innocence greatly exceeds the normal period the presumption is inverted and the onus is on the wife to prove that the husband is the father of the child.[62] If that were right the onus would similarly pass, where paternity was directly in issue, to the party asserting paternity and for this purpose anything in excess of 10 months might still be taken as greatly exceeding the normal. The better view, however, is probably that the presumption continues to apply, although with weakened effect, where the period of gestation is abnormally long provided that it is within what is known to be possible.[63] Where the limits of possibility are reached is undecided. In an English case the House of Lords declined to hold that 360 days was an impossible period.[64] That view can be supported by extreme cases known to medical science, but it is submitted that, in the absence of medical evidence pointing to an extremely long period of gestation, such extremes should be taken into account only exceptionally, and that the most which a Scottish court should ordinarily entertain as possible is 11 months. That would accord with the furthest extension warranted by Scottish judicial decision[65] and with institutional authority.[66] The whole matter may, however, be ripe for reconsideration in the light of changed attitudes to the standard of proof.

---

[59] *De Septimestri Partu.*

[60] See *ante*, at pp. 84–85.

[61] *Currie* v. *Currie*, 1950 S.C. 10 (336 days not impossible, but improbable and went a long way, together with other facts and circumstances, to justify an inference of adultery); *Jamieson* v. *Dobie*, 1935 S.C. 415 (306 days not impossible—*cf. Williamson* v. *McClelland*, 1913 S.C. 678); *Doherty* v. *Doherty*, 1922 S.L.T. 245 (348 days described in medical evidence as "abnormal and extraordinary"—decree of divorce on ground of adultery granted in the circumstances); *Preston-Jones* v. *Preston-Jones* [1951] A.C. 391 (360 days not impossible); *M.-T.* v. *M.-T.* [1949] P. 331 (340 days not impossible); *Hadlum* v. *Hadlum* [1949] P. 197 (349 days not impossible).

[62] *Gray* v. *Gray* 1919 1 S.L.T. 163, followed in *McIntosh* v. *McIntosh* 1947 S.N. 23.

[63] *Currie* v. *Currie, supra.*

[64] *Preston-Jones* v. *Preston-Jones, supra.* Lord Morton, however, thought than 320 days should be regarded as the maximum.

[65] *Currie* v. *Currie, supra.*

[66] Stair, III, iii, 42.

Questions of the application and the rebuttal of the presumption are at this point closely related and the relaxation in the standard of proof for rebuttal (which is now on the balance of probabilities[67]) carries with it occasion for a reconsideration of the attitude which the court should adopt to questions of the maximum period of gestation. Such a reconsideration may well have shifted the emphasis from what is possible to what is probable and may, in any event, lead to the conclusion that 11 or even 10 months is too long a period to be ordinarily entertained. The result would be that if a child were to be born, say, 10 months after the ending of a marriage, the party claiming that the ex-husband was the father of the child could not rely on the presumption and would have to lead evidence of circumstances tending to support his paternity. Similar considerations apply to the application of the presumption to a child conceived before marriage.

Conflicting Presumptions

One reason why a marriage is void is because one of the parties thereto is a party to a prior subsisting marriage.[68] The inclusion of a provision to the effect that the presumption in section 5(1)(*a*) applies in the case of void marriages[69] appears to mean that, if the mother is party to a prior subsisting marriage and has undergone a later ceremony of marriage, then any child she bears will be presumed to be the child of both of her "husbands." The same problem would arise in the (less likely) scenario of a woman being *validly* married twice during the possible gestational period of the child. This is a problem which because of the common law presumption that demanded marriage at the date of conception, (although there was also a certain presumption of fact where marriage intervened between conception and birth) much concerned some of the older writers in the case of a child born of a woman who remarried so soon after the death of her first husband that the child could have been conceived in marriage either by the first or by the second husband. Stair, in an untypical passage which has justly been described as obscure,[70] appears to favour the view that if the child is born within nine months of the dissolution of the first marriage by death, it will be presumed to be the child of the first husband unless it shows signs of immaturity at birth. Conversely, if it be born more than nine months after the death of the first husband it will be deemed to be the child of the second husband. Probability of paternity is not the issue under section 5(1)(*a*) since the presumption applies for any marriage within the whole gestational period, and will arise simply on proof of the fact of marriage at the relevant time. Probability of paternity is, however, relevant to rebuttal. Where there are two possible fathers it will usually be possible to rebut the presumption in the case of one of them as less likely. In any event it is clearly legally incompetent to presume that a child has more than one father, and such a conclusion can be avoided by holding that when the presumption applies with equal force twice (or even more times) over,

---

[67] Law Reform (Parent and Child) (Scotland) Act 1986, s. 5(4). This is also now the standard of proof of adultery: Divorce (Scotland) Act 1976, s. 1(6). Adultery was the issue in many of the cases cited above.

[68] Marriage (Scotland) Act 1977, s. 5(4)(*b*). See Clive, (3rd ed.) at pp. 76–77.

[69] Law Reform (Parent and Child) (Scotland) Act 1986, s. 5(2).

[70] III, iii, 42, More's annotations.

it cancels itself out. The result would be that the person asserting paternity (or indeed denying paternity) has no presumption to assist him either way and must lead positive and sufficient evidence to prove his own case.

Rebutting the Presumption

The presumption contained in section 5(1)(*a*) is to the effect that a man is the father of a child, that is to say that the relevant genetic link exists between the two. It is however only a presumption, and as such it can be rebutted by showing that the presumed fact is not true. This may be done by leading evidence to the effect that the mother's husband is not (or, which amounts to the same thing, that another man is) genetically related to the child as its father. The presumption can be rebutted by proof on a balance of probabilities.[71] How that balance will be struck must, however, depend upon the facts of each particular case. Scientific proof, such as DNA profiling,[72] will in most cases be available, but if it is not, extrinsic evidence of a number of factors may be led.

The view was at one time held, and is adopted by Fraser,[73] that the common law presumption could be rebutted only by proof of impotence[74] or non-access. The institutional writers[75] do not go as far as that and it is doubtful if it ever was settled law. In *Mackay* v. *Mackay*[76] the child had undoubtedly been conceived during marriage and had, moreover, been accepted as a member of the family by her mother's husband in whose house she had continued to live even after her mother's death. *Prima facie* it was a strong case for giving effect to the presumption. Non-access was out of the question and impotence was not suggested. Yet the presumption was held to be rebutted on evidence of parental declarations that the child was illegitimate, of the mother's loose character and of general reputation of illegitimacy. The Lord Ordinary's opinion that "if there be such clear evidence as completely satisfies the tribunal which has to decide the question, that *de facto* a husband is not the father of his wife's child, that child will be held to be illegitimate, although neither impotency nor the utter impossibility of access be established by that evidence" was adopted and approved

---

[71] Law Reform (Parent and Child) (Scotland) Act 1986, s. 5(4). This alters the common law rule that proof had to be beyond reasonable doubt to rebut the *pater est* presumption: see *Docherty* v. *McGlynn*, 1983 S.L.T. 645, *Ramsay* v. *Ramsay's Curator*, 1987 S.L.T. 799. There was previously some doubt as to the full extent of the common law onus (see *Ballantyne* v. *Douglas*, 1953 S.L.T. (Notes) 10, *per* Lord Justice-Clerk Thomson at p. 11; *Brown* v. *Brown*, 1972 S.L.T. 143, *per* Lord Emslie (Ordinary) at p. 145; *Imre* v. *Mitchell*, 1958 S.C. 439, *per* Lord President Clyde at p. 462), though that seems to have been resolved by *Docherty* and *Ramsay*. The question is now otiose in the light of s. 5(4) of the 1986 Act. In an action of paternity in which the presumption did not operate, the burden of proof has always been on the balance of probabilities: *A.* v. *G.*, 1984 S.L.T. (Sh.Ct.) 65.

[72] See *post* at pp. 151–152.

[73] Fraser (3rd ed.) at p. 5.

[74] As in, for example, *Dundas* v. *Dundas* (1705) Mor. 4083 and *Sandy* v. *Sandy* (1823) 2 S. 453. Even then the presumption would not automatically be rebutted if fecundation *ab extra* or artificial insemination by the husband was a possibility. Proof of sterility rather than impotence would have a much more certain effect.

[75] Stair, III, iii, 42 adds a further ground, being the testimony of both the mother and the husband that the child is not the husband's. Erskine, I, vi, 50, describes impotence and non-access as merely "the two principal grounds."

[76] (1855) 17 D. 494.

by the Inner House.[77] When the later case of *Gardner* v. *Gardner*[78] reached the House of Lords, Lord Gordon, following Lord Gifford in the Court of Session, could say of the common law presumption that "it must yield to evidence, and I think the law of Scotland has always been that the presumption may be overcome, not only by evidence that it was physically impossible that the husband of the mother could be the father of the child, but by every species of moral evidence sufficient to satisfy a reasonable mind that the child was begotten by someone else than the husband".[79] Whatever the historic position may have been, it is now clear in relation to the statutory presumption that not only impotence and non-access (though they remain strong evidence against paternity) but all other facts and circumstances relevant to infer non-parentage may be invoked to rebut the presumption in section 5(1)(*a*). In an action for declarator of parentage or non-parentage in which it is sought to rebut the presumption, the court is looking for the truth and is not to be limited within artificial bounds of evidence. Other relevant circumstances tending to assist the search for the truth may include, for example, evidence of loose moral character or adultery of the mother,[80] reputation of paternity,[81] declarations of non-parentage by the presumptive parents[82] and, in cases free of the risks of fanciful speculation, physical resemblances and family likenesses.[83] None of these elements is conclusive on its own, and the weight to be given to any of them varies with the circumstances, but all are relevant and admissible as tending to establish the probability that a man other than the woman's husband is the father of the child. Scientific evidence will, if available, constitute the best evidence.

Acknowledgment and Registration

Section 5(1)(*b*) of the Law Reform (Parent and Child) (Scotland) Act 1986 provides that a man who is not married to the mother of the child at the relevant time shall be presumed to be the father of the child if *both* he and the mother of the child have acknowledged that he is the father of the child *and* he has been re-

---

[77] *Per* Lord President McNeill at p. 500 and Lords Ivory and Deas at p. 505.

[78] (1877) 4 R.(H.L.) 56.

[79] *Ibid.* at p. 74. *Cf. Montgomery* v. *Montgomery* (1881) 8 R. 403; *Steedman* v. *Steedman* (1887) 14 R. 1066; *Coles* v. *Homer & Tulloh* (1895) 22 R. 716.

[80] Craig, II, xviii, 20; Stair, III, iii, 42; Erskine, I, vi, 49. *Cf. Francis* v. *Francis* [1960] P. 17; *Cotton* v. *Cotton* [1954] 2 All E.R 105.

[81] Balfour, 240, Craig, II, xviii, 20; Stair, III, iii, 42; Bankton, I, v, 62 and III, iii, 101; Spottiswood, *Practicks*, 28; *Roxburghe* v. *Ker* (1822) 6 Paton 820; *Hamilton* v. *Hamilton* (1839) 2 D. 89; *Walker* v. *Walker* (1857) 19 D. 290; *Campbell* v. *Campbell* (1866) 4 M. 867, (1867) 5 M.(H.L.) 115; *Hirpet* v. *Scot* (1618) Mor. 2197; *Crawfurd* v. *Purcels* (1642) Mor. 12636; *Brooke's Exr.* v. *James*, 1971 S.C.(H.L.) 77; *Tennent* v. *Tennent* (1890) 17 R. 1205; *Smith* v. *Dick* (1869) 8 M. 31 (in which reputation was divided but since reputation of illegitimacy was supported by other factors it was that reputation which prevailed).

[82] Craig, II, xviii, 20; Stair, III, iii, 42; Erskine, I, vi, 49.

[83] Though this evidence must be treated with the greatest of care, and, indeed, will normally be excluded: *Rutledge* v. *Carruthers* Jan. 20, 1810, F.C. 528; *Grant* v. *Countess of Seafield*, 1926 S.C. 274; *Slingsby* v. *A.-G.* (1916) 33 T.L.R. 120 (H.L.), *per* Lord Shaw of Dunfermline at p. 122; *H.M.A.* v. *Stewart* (1848) Ark. 471 (in which it was held competent to inquire, in a trial for child-murder of a child found to have six toes on each foot, whether this was a family characteristic shared by other members of its family). See also *S.* v. *S.* 1977 S.L.T. (Notes) 65 in which an allegation that the child was "dark-skinned" and that the mother had had a liaison with a man believed to be an Arab was insufficient to discharge the onus on the husband seeking to bastardise the child.

gistered in the appropriate register as the father. This presumption, like that contained in section 5(1)(*a*), has common law antecedents. Craig, Stair and Erskine[84] took over from the canon law[85] the rule that once a child's legitimacy had been acknowledged by its parents the parents could not by a subsequent oath deprive the child of the status of legitimacy so acquired. The parents were personally barred not only from tendering their own evidence in contradiction of the acknowledgment but also altogether from disputing legitimacy. Under the current statute, there must be both acknowledgment and registration.

Acknowledgment

Both the mother and the man must acknowledge that he is the father of the child. At common law sworn declarations by both parents were sufficient to establish illegitimacy,[86] and unsworn statements were relevant evidence and admissible subject to their competency under the rules relating to hearsay.[87] Under the statute, an "acknowledgment" clearly does not have to be sworn, but it does have to be proved. Statements to friends or acquaintances of the relevant facts will probably be sufficient. The declarations required before the man can be registered as father (see the following paragraph) will suffice.

Registration

Previously, to show that a man was entered as father of a child in the Register of Births was merely one of the elements of evidence used to establish paternity and even now acknowledgment without registration will have no other effect than this. A man cannot be registered as father of a child except (a) at the joint request of the mother and the person acknowledging himself to be the father of the child (in which case the register must be signed by both the mother and the man), or (b) at the request of the mother on the production of both a declaration in the prescribed form made by the mother that that person is the father of the child and a statutory declaration made by that person acknowledging himself to be the father of the child, or on production of a decree by a competent court finding or declaring that person to be the father of the child, or (c) at the request of the man on production of a declaration by him in the prescribed form acknowledging himself to be the father of the child and a statutory declaration made by the mother stating that he is the father of the child.[88]

The registration must be in either a register kept under section 13 (the Register of Births and Still-births) or section 44 (the Register of Corrections, etc.) of the Registration of Births, Deaths and Marriages (Scotland) Act 1965, or in any corresponding register kept under statutory authority in any part of the UK other than Scotland. Registration in a foreign register will not give rise to the presumption, but will be an element in the proof tending to establish paternity, the precise weight to be given to such evidence depending upon the nature of the foreign register, and the appropriate rules of registration.

---

[84] Craig, II, xviii, 20; Stair, IV, xlv, 20: Erskine, I, vi, 49.

[85] Decr. IV, xvii, 3; II, xix, 10.

[86] Craig, II, xviii, 20; Stair, III, iii, 42; Erskine, I, vi, 49.

[87] *Mackay* v. *Mackay* (1855) 17 D. 494.

[88] Registration of Births, Deaths and Marriages (Scotland) Act 1965, s. 18, as amended by Sched. 1, para. 8 to the Law Reform (Parent and Child) (Scotland) Act 1986.

Circumstances in which the Presumption Applies

The presumption in section 5(1)(*b*) was designed to deal with the cohabiting couple who both acknowledge the man as the father of the child. But it is a good deal wider than that. For one thing, there is no requirement that the couple be co-habiting: the only requirements are acknowledgment and registration. It is how-ever unclear whether other situations are covered. In particular there are difficulties if the mother is married but she claims that the father is a man other than her husband, and both she and the other man acknowledge this and register the child as such. The difficulty revolves around the opening words of section 5(1)(*b*): "where paragraph (*a*) above does not apply..." Paragraph (*a*) deals with the situation of the husband of the mother being presumed father, but it is not clear when it "does not apply." Clearly it "does not apply" when the woman is unmarried; but does it also not apply when the presumption has been rebutted, say, because of undisputed non-access by the husband? If a married woman has a child then the husband is presumed father, even although the mother and an-other man acknowledge the child as the other man's, and that presumption applies until it is rebutted. But it could be argued that a presumption that is re-butted is a presumption that nevertheless applies, because the facts giving rise to it exist: it applies, but in the event is rebutted. On this interpretation, section 5(1)(*b*) would be restricted to the situation of a mother who is not married to anyone, and would not be applicable whenever the woman was married. This approach is adopted by the *Current Law Annotator*, and indeed on a literal reading of the section it seems to follow: paragraph (*b*) is stated to come into effect "where paragraph (*a*) above does not apply," and paragraph (*a*) merely contains the condition "if he was married to the mother" at the relevant time. The presump-tion itself is not contained in paragraph (*a*), but in the words of the subsection immediately preceding paragraph (*a*). However, it is suggested that this is too literal an approach, and leads to the absurdity that paragraph (*b*) cannot apply in cases in which the paragraph (*a*) presumption has been rebutted. Rather, the bet-ter approach would be to read section 5(1) as a whole. That subsection sets out two presumptions, the second to take effect, it is submitted, whenever the first does not (for whatever reason). It follows that paragraph (*b*) will apply either where the woman is unmarried, or where the woman is married but the pre-sumption of paternity relating to her husband has been rebutted.[89] Acknowledg-ment by both the mother and the other man that the other man is the father, and registration to this effect, may well be sufficient in themselves to rebut the pre-sumption that the husband is the father; they will certainly be sufficient if com-bined with other factors such as non-access by the husband, so activating section 5(1)(*b*). Again it should be noted that scientific proof can usually resolve cases of dispute, but this form of acknowledgment and registration will, like the previous presumption, obviate the expense of commissioning scientific tests.

Rebutting the Presumption

As with section 5(1)(*a*), section 5(1)(*b*) raises only a presumption that can be

---

[89] We may compare the position under s. 28 of the Human Fertilisation and Embryology Act 1990, discussed *infra*, because alternative provisions there, involving men who are treated as father because of their marriage and men not so treated (s. 28(2) and s. 28(3) respectively) make it quite

rebutted by proof on a balance of probabilities.[90] Such proof will take the form of proof that the man registered as the father is not (or, which amounts to the same thing, that another man is) genetically related to the child as its father. The comments made in relation to rebutting the section 5(1)(a) presumption[91] apply equally here, and reference should be made to them.

Marriage and Assisted Reproduction

Section 28(2) of the Human Fertilisation and Embryology Act 1990 provides that where a woman has become pregnant as a result of the placing in her of an embryo or of sperm and eggs or of her artificial[92] insemination, and at that time she was a party to a marriage, then the other party to the marriage shall be treated as the father of the child. This means that he will be treated in law as the father "for all purposes,"[93] and "references to any relationship between two people in any enactment, deed, or other instrument or document (whenever passed or made) are to be read accordingly."[94] This is not a presumption of paternity and still less is it a presumption of a genetic link (indeed it will only apply when there exists no genetic link[95]). It is, rather, the wholly artificial creation of a father-child relationship, deemed by the law from the husband's consent to the relevant infertility treatment.[96] The donor of the sperm (*i.e.* the genetic father) is not to be treated in law as being the father of the child for any purpose[97] (unless he is otherwise constituted the legal father of the child by an order of the court to that effect under section 30[98]). Unlike the presumption contained in section 5(1)(a) of the Law Reform (Parent and Child) (Scotland) Act 1986, this provision deeming a man to be father cannot be overcome by showing the absence of a genetic link, because this provision deems paternity only in the absence of such a link. Indeed it can only be overcome in the manner later described. Likewise it is not open to another man to claim paternity by showing the existence of the relevant genetic link.[99]

---

clear that the rules in s. 28(3) apply whenever the rules in s. 28(2) do not.

[90] Law Reform (Parent and Child) (Scotland) Act 1986, s. 5(4).

[91] *Supra*, pp. 132–133.

[92] s. 28(2)(a) actually talks only of the woman's "insemination," which is to be compared with s. 28(3)(a) which talks of the woman's "artificial insemination." This might suggest that s. 28(2)(a) would also apply when a woman is inseminated naturally, *e.g.* by having sexual intercourse with a man not her husband; but this interpretation is excluded by s. 28(1) which provides as follows: "This section [which includes s. 28(2)] applies in the case of a child who is being or has been carried by a woman as the result of the placing in her of an embryo or of sperm and eggs or of her *artificial* insemination." The omission of the word "artificial" from s. 28(2)(a), or its addition in s. 28(3)(a), is simply the result of lax draftsmanship.

[93] Human Fertilisation and Embryology Act 1990, s. 29(1).

[94] *Ibid.*, s. 29(3). As with maternity (see *ante*, pp. 120–126), it is open to the person executing a deed to express a different conclusion.

[95] *Ibid.* s. 28(2)(b).

[96] English law has contained a similar provision, though only in relation to artificial insemination, since the passing of s. 27 of the Family Law Reform Act 1987. This is now superseded by s. 28 of the 1990 Act.

[97] s. 28(6)(a) Sched. 3, para. 5, and s. 29(2).

[98] See *post*, at pp. 143–145.

[99] s. 28(4).

Nature of the Marriage

The marriage must be subsisting at the time of the placing in the woman of the embryo or the sperm and eggs, or at the time of her insemination.[1] The provision does not apply if the marriage was dissolved or annulled at that time, or a judicial separation was in force at that time[2] but includes all valid marriages, including those contracted abroad and entitled to be recognised as valid in this country: an actually or potentially polygamous marriage can be a valid "subsisting" marriage.[3] This provision also applies, though this is not stated,[4] to irregular as well as regular marriages: since irregular marriages are as much valid marriages in Scots law as regular marriages,[5] the normal canons of construction will mean that they are to be regarded as "subsisting marriages."[6]

The provision also applies to void marriages if either or both of the parties reasonably believed at the time of the infertility treatment that the marriage was valid.[7] It will be presumed until the contrary is shown that one of the parties to the marriage did reasonably believe at the time of the infertility treatment that the marriage was valid. This form of words follows previous English legislation which preserved the legitimacy of children born of invalid marriages where one or both of the parties reasonably believed that the marriage was valid.[8] It was subsequently made clear in the English legislation that the English rule applied when the belief that the marriage was valid was due to a mistake in law as well as a mistake in fact.[9] The equivalent Scottish rule concerned putative marriages, which preserved the legitimacy of children born of invalid marriages when one or both parties had a *bona fide* belief that the marriage was valid. Now, *bona fide* belief is not the same as reasonable belief, and there was some doubt in Scotland as to whether a mistake in law amounted to an error concerning the validity of a marriage that could be excused and thus save the legitimacy of children.

---

[1] s. 28(7)(a).

[2] s. 28(7)(a), this including a legal separation obtained in a country outside the British Islands and recognised in the United Kingdom under the terms of Pt. II of the Family Law Act 1986: s. 28(9).

[3] See Anton and Beaumont (2nd ed.) at pp. 444–450; Matrimonial Proceedings (Polygamous Marriages) Act 1972. A marriage that is voidable "subsists" until it is annulled, though this is no longer of importance in Scotland.

[4] Law Reform (Parent and Child) (Scotland) Act 1986, s. 5(2), makes this clear in relation to the presumptions contained there. But that was a purely Scottish statue, while the 1990 Act is UK-wide.

[5] Clive at p. 62, Thomson at p. 16.

[6] This will be of diminishing importance if marriages by cohabitation with habit and repute are abolished: Scot. Law Com. No. 135, *Report on Family Law*, May 1992 at para. 7.9 and draft Bill, cl. 22.

[7] Human Fertilisation and Embryology Act 1990, s. 28(7). The problem of having more than one "husband" who can be presumed father that may potentially arise with the similar provision in s. 5(1)(a) of the Law Reform (Parent and Child) (Scotland) Act 1986 (see *ante* at pp. 131–132) would not arise here, because only one of the competing "husbands" would consent to the treatment of the woman.

[8] Legitimacy Act 1976, s. 1 (and before that the Legitimacy Act 1959, s. 2).

[9] Family Law Reform Act 1987, s. 28(2), which adds a new s. 1(3) to the Legitimacy Act 1976 to this effect, expressly "for the avoidance of doubt." The matter had not been unequivocally decided in *Hawkins* v. *A.-G.* [1966] 1 All E.R. 392, for, while it appeared to be accepted in that case that an error of law could sometimes found a reasonable belief, it was held that the particular error of law involved in that case did not. The 1987 Act also added the provision (a new s. 1(4) of the Legitimacy Act 1976) presuming that one or both parties reasonably believed the marriage to be valid, this to obviate certain difficulties of proof that had been encountered.

Fraser[10] said that only an error of fact could found a putative marriage, and he was followed by Clive[11] and Thomson.[12] However it may be doubted whether this is so. The belief that saved legitimacy in Scotland had to be *bona fide* rather than reasonable and a *bona fide* belief may be founded on an error of law, at least where there is a question of *dubium jus*.[13] Reasonable belief, which is here in issue, is not, however, the same as *bona fide* belief. In the context of the previous English legislation "reasonable belief" has been held to import an objective test[14] and since this is the formulation used in the present context of the Human Fertilisation and Embryology Act 1990, it is likely that the English approach will be followed in the interpretation of these words in this UK statute. There is no declaration "for the avoidance of doubt" in the 1990 Act (as there now is in the English Legitimacy Act 1976) that error of law as well as error of fact can found a "reasonable belief," but it is thought that in interpreting this UK statute the English courts will do as they do for the 1976 Act, and accept errors of law as founding a reasonable belief in appropriate cases. The Scottish courts should, it is submitted, do likewise.

Exceptions

The four exceptions to the provisions of the 1990 Act deeming maternity are also applicable, *mutatis mutandis*, to this provision, and the comments made above[15] should be referred to.

In addition to these exceptions there is a further provision applicable only to the paternity provisions in section 28. If a man's sperm, or an embryo the creation of which was brought about with his sperm, was "used after his death," then he is not to be treated as the father of the child.[16] To "use" means, in relation to sperm, to use for the purposes of fertilising a woman's egg, and in relation to an embryo, to use for the purposes of implantation into a woman for its gestation. This provision is designed to avoid any potential succession problems that some other jurisdictions have faced when a child is created a very long time after the death of the man who was its genetic father.[17] The provision is wide enough to deny any other consequence of the father-child relationship arising in these circumstances. A child whose conception is brought about after the death of its father will not, therefore, have any claim for damages for the negligently caused death of its father under the Damages (Scotland) Act 1976,[18] and will not have a claim against its father's estate for aliment *jure representationis*.

Avoiding Paternity—Lack of Consent

Unlike a presumption, a deeming provision cannot be rebutted. Section 28 of

---

[10] 3rd ed. at p. 34.

[11] *Husband and Wife*, (3rd ed.) at p. 75.

[12] *Family Law in Scotland* (2nd ed.) at p. 158.

[13] See *Purves's Trs.* v. *Purves* (1895) 22 R. 513. And see further, *ante* at pp. 12–16.

[14] *Hawkins* v. *A.-G.* [1966] 1 All E.R. 392, commented upon by Samuels, (1966) 29 Mod.L.R. 559.

[15] at pp. 123–125.

[16] Human Fertilisation and Embryology Act 1990, s. 28(6)(*b*), discussed further at pp. 93–94.

[17] On this issue, see Cusine, *op. cit.* at pp. 56–58.

[18] See further, p. 109.

the 1990 Act provides for the wholly artificial creation of the father-child relationship: it does not presume any facts, rather it imposes the responsibilities and rights of paternity *as if* the facts were sufficient to establish the genetic link. This provision can however be avoided, either by showing that it is not applicable in the circumstances (*e.g.* because there is no relevant marriage, or because the husband's sperm was used to bring about the creation of the embryo) or by showing that the husband did not consent to the infertility treatment. This latter means of avoidance is a consequence of section 28(2) which subjects the deeming of paternity to the qualification that it will not apply if "it is shown that [the husband] did not consent to the placing in [the mother] of the embryo or the sperm and eggs or to her insemination (as the case may be)." The result of this provision is that there is a presumption of fact that a husband did consent, and that the onus is on him to show, if he can, that he did not consent to the infertility treatment. The burden of proof that a person claiming no consent is under will, presumably, be on a balance of probabilities. Even when the husband does not in fact consent, this deeming provision will be effective until such time as he rebuts the presumption of consent. So, until that presumption is rebutted, the husband of the woman who receives infertility treatment is treated as father for all purposes of law[19] and can exercise parental rights and is subject to parental responsibilities.

Centres licensed to provide infertility services[20] are obliged by their Code of Practice, issued by the Human Fertilisation and Embryology Authority (which grants the licences) to take all practicable steps to obtain the husband's written consent, or to obtain written evidence that he does not consent.[21] If a husband wishes to deny the validity of his written consent, he must show that it is vitiated for some reason, for example that it was obtained by fraud, or that he did not understand the substance of what he was consenting to. An allegation that he did not understand the legal consequences will not be sufficient if he did understand that his wife might, through the infertility service, become pregnant and give birth to a child.

Effect of Section 5(1)(a) of the Law Reform (Parent and Child) (Scotland) Act 1986

The interplay between section 28(2) of the 1990 Act and the presumption of paternity contained in section 5(1)(*a*) of the Law Reform (Parent and Child) (Scotland) Act 1986 is by no means clear. If the husband rebuts the presumption that he consented to the infertility treatment, then he will not be deemed legal father by section 28(2). Yet he is still married to the mother, which suggests that section 5(1)(*a*) of the 1986 Act will presume that he is genetically (and legally) the father of the child.[22] It would seem to follow that the husband of a woman who gives birth after relevant[23] infertility treatment who wishes to deny paternity must rebut the 1990 presumption of consent *and* the 1986 presumption of

---

[19] Subject to the exceptions discussed *ante* at pp. 123–125 and p. 138.
[20] Under s. 16 of the 1990 Act.
[21] Draft Code of Practice, para. 5.6.
[22] Indeed this presumption seems to be expressly preserved by s. 28(5)(*b*) of the 1990 Act (though the meaning and effect of that provision is opaque in the extreme).
[23] *i.e.* that to which the 1990 Act applies.

(genetic and legal) paternity.[24] However, this two-stage process may not be necessary. If in an action of declarator of non-parentage, raised by a mother's husband, the mother attempted to defend the action by founding upon the 1990 Act, it is implicit in that defence that the presumption in the 1986 Act is false, for the 1990 Act applies *only* when there is no genetic link between husband and child,[25] and the 1986 presumption is a presumption that there is a genetic link. In other words, proof of the facts that make the 1990 Act applicable is proof sufficient to rebut the 1986 presumption. The two provisions should therefore be regarded as alternatives, dealing with quite different sets of facts: the 1990 Act when the absence of a genetic link is accepted or established, and the 1986 Act when there is doubt or it is disputed. There is a true overlap only if the presumption of paternity under the 1986 Act is held to apply to questions of deemed paternity as well as of genetic paternity. It is submitted that it should not be so construed.

Assisted Reproduction Without Marriage

If no man is treated as being the father of a child by virtue of section 28(2) of the Human Fertilisation and Embryology Act 1990 as discussed immediately above, then a man may be treated as being the father of a child for all purposes in law in accordance with the provisions in section 28(3) of the 1990 Act. This provides that where an embryo or sperm and eggs are placed in a woman, or she is artificially inseminated, and this is done "in the course of treatment services provided for her and a man together" by a person licensed to provide these treatment services under the 1990 Act, then the man shall be deemed, for all purposes,[26] father of the child. Again, this deeming provision applies only when there is no genetic link between the man and the child[27] and is not a presumption of the existence of a genetic link: thus it cannot be avoided by proving the lack of any such link. The woman's marital status is irrelevant. No other person is to be treated as the father of the child[28] and it is therefore irrelevant for anyone else to prove a genetic link between the child and any other person. This provision applies in any case where section 28(2) does not, *i.e.* when the woman is not party to a marriage, or when she is party to a marriage but her husband can show that he did not consent to the treatment, or (though this is unlikely) when she is party to a marriage and her husband's sperm was used to bring about the creation of the embryo which is placed in the woman in the course of treatment services provided for her and a man other than her husband.

Treatment must be Provided "Together"

There is no provision presuming that the man consented to the treatment, nor a qualification that the deeming provision will not apply if it can be shown that he did not consent. The reason for this is that this provision only applies when the treatment is given "for" a woman and a man "together," which presupposes

---

[24] On rebutting the 1986 presumption, see *ante* at pp. 132–133.
[25] s. 28(2)(*b*).
[26] Human Fertilisation and Embryology Act 1990, s. 29(1).
[27] *Ibid.*, s. 28(3)(*b*).
[28] *Ibid.*, s. 28(4).

the consent of them both. If consent had not been given, the treatment would not have been provided "for" a woman and a man "together," and this subsection would therefore not apply. In other words, this subsection, like the previous provision, can indeed be avoided by showing that the man did not consent, because doing so would show that the treatment was not provided for the woman and the man "together."[29] In the unlikely situation of a man showing that he had not consented to the treatment but he and the mother nevertheless had acknowledged the child as his and had registered it as such, the presumption in section 5(1)(b) of the 1986 Act would come into play; but since that presumption can be rebutted on proof of a lack of genetic link, and this provision of the 1990 Act only applies when there is no genetic link,[30] the rebuttal of the 1986 presumption should be easy to establish once it is shown that the conception came about by artificial means involving sperm not coming from the woman's partner.

"For All Purposes"

If section 28(3) is applicable, a man who is not married to the mother will be treated in law as the father of the child "for all purposes"[31] (subject to the stated exceptions[32]). This means, for example, that he will have the same succession rights and the same alimentary and child support obligations as the father of a naturally conceived child. In relation to parental responsibilities and rights, "for all purposes" means for all purposes applicable to a man not married to the mother of the child. Sections 28 and 29 do not confer parental responsibilities and rights: they merely deem paternity.

Exceptions

The exceptions to section 28(3) are the same as those to section 28(2), including those discussed in relation to establishing maternity, and the comments made above in both these connections should be referred to.[33]

Adoption

A relationship of father and child can be created, again in the absence of any genetic link, through the legal process of adoption. This matter is dealt with fully in Chapters 19 and 20 of this book.

Surrogacy

A relationship of father and child can be created, once more in the absence of any genetic link, by means of a court order in his favour following a surrogacy arrangement.[34] This matter is dealt with more fully in the next section of this chapter.

---

[29] For the same reason the use of a man's sperm after his death will not impose paternity upon him by this provision: after he is dead, the treatment could hardly be provided for him and the woman together: *ibid.*, s. 28(6)(b).

[30] *Ibid.*, s. 28(3)(b).

[31] *Ibid.*, s. 29.

[32] See below.

[33] *Ante*, at pp. 123–125 and p. 138.

[34] Human Fertilisation and Embryology Act 1990, s. 30.

SURROGATE PARENTHOOD

Introduction

Cusine states,

> "it is important to define the term 'surrogacy' as covering any situation in which one woman agrees to carry a child for another. This includes a case where a couple decide to hand over their child to another couple; also an arrangement whereby a woman is artificially inseminated with semen by a man who, with his wife or partner, will be the child's 'parents'; and finally a situation in which a woman has another couple's embryo implanted in her, on the understanding that she will surrender the child to the couple who produced the embryo, or possibly to someone else".[35]

He goes on to list 19 different permutations of the surrogacy arrangement.[36] At common law, a surrogacy arrangement that involved the woman who gives birth to a child surrendering that child to another would not be criminal, but nor would the agreement be enforceable. It had been held in England that an agreement to surrender a child would not be enforced against a mother who changed her mind,[37] and almost certainly if the agreement were carried out the law would not pay any regard to it (with the result that the carrying mother remained mother for the purposes of the law[38]). In Scotland, although fostering of children has a much longer history than in England, the law is to similar effect. The person who receives the child can be compelled to return it to the mother; but the agreement itself is legally recognised in the sense that its incidents may receive effect in so far as they do not encroach on parental rights.[39] Redelivery of the child would not be ordered at common law if this would involve serious danger to its health or morals[40] and such questions must now be decided on the test of the child's welfare as the paramount consideration. Such an agreement, even where redelivery is not sought or is refused, cannot, however, create a complete parent-child relationship, affecting, for example, succession rights. Adoption is needed to effect such a radical shift in relationships.[41] In the typical surrogacy arrangement it is the intent of the parties that such a parent-child relationship be established. But of course intent does not make law.

Statutory Control of Surrogacy

When the Warnock Committee examined the issue of surrogacy, it could not reach a unanimous conclusion. The majority wanted to criminalise the setting

---

[35] Cusine, *New Reproductive Techniques: A Legal Perspective* (1988), at p. 143.

[36] at p. 209.

[37] See *Humphrys* v. *Polak* [1901] 2 K.B. 385; *A.* v. *C.* (1978) 8 Fam.L. 170, (1984) 14 Fam.L. 241.

[38] In *Humphrys* v. *Polak, supra,* it was held that a mother could not give up her right of custody, because that right was conferred only to allow her to fulfil her parental duties.

[39] See *Kerrigan* v. *Hall* (1901) 4 F. 10; *Macpherson* v. *Leishman* (1887) 14 R. 780, in which Lord President Inglis expressed regret that the arrangement was being brought to an end (this on the basis of the welfare of the child).

[40] *Sutherland* v. *Taylor* (1887) 15 R. 224; *Mackenzie* v. *Keillor* (1892) 19 R. 963; *Campbell* v. *Croall* (1895) 22 R. 869.

[41] See *Re Adoption Application (Surrogacy)* [1987] 2 All E.R. 826.

up or operating of surrogacy agencies whether they were profit-making or not,[42] while a minority saw some place for state-controlled surrogacy.[43] Due to intense public disquiet on the issue,[44] the Government felt that it could not give the time for the consultation and consideration afforded to the other issues raised in the Warnock Committee Report, and shortly after that Report was published, it rushed through Parliament the Surrogacy Arrangements Act 1985. This renders criminal any act designed to establish a surrogacy arrangement if that arrangement is made on a commercial basis, by which is meant if money or money's worth is passed as a consequence.[45] A person or an organisation can be guilty of this offence. Advertising in connection with surrogacy, commercial or otherwise, is also a criminal offence.[46]

The 1985 Act has only limited application. It is expressly designed to catch the agencies who operate for profit by bringing together infertile couples with women willing to act as surrogate mothers. Merely to enter into a surrogacy arrangement is not *per se* a criminal act. The infertile couple and the surrogate mother herself do not commit any offence if they enter into a private arrangement, even when money passes. It is only organisations who attempt for profit to bring them together, or who advertise, that can be caught. In particular, the 1985 Act says nothing about the legal status of the child, which, until the passing of the Human Fertilisation and Embryology Act 1990, depended on the genetic link that existed between the child and its parents.

The issue of enforceability of the contract was expressly avoided, with section 1(9), as orginally passed in 1985, weakly providing that the offence was committed "whether or not" the arrangement itself was enforceable. The Human Fertilisation and Embryology Act 1990 amends this by repealing these words,[47] and adding a new section 1A, to the effect that "no surrogacy arrangement is enforceable by or against any of the persons making it.[48]

Parental Orders in Favour of Gamete Donors

The Human Fertilisation and Embryology Act 1990 also makes provision for the parentage of children born as a result of surrogacy arrangements. The general position is that parentage will be determined, as usual, by the genetic connection, or by utilising one of the presumptions or deeming provisions discussed earlier in this chapter. In addition, the court[49] is given an extraordinary power to make an order providing for a child born as a result of a surrogacy arrangement to be treated in law as the child of the couple who commissioned the surrogate mother to carry the child.[50] An order can only be made in favour of

---

[42] *Report of the Committee of Inquiry into Human Fertilisation and Embryology*, Cmnd. 9314 (1984) (the "Warnock Committee Report"), at para. 8.18.

[43] Expression of Dissent "A."

[44] Described in more detail by Norrie, "Legal Regulation of Human Reproduction in Great Britain", Chap. 7 in McLean (ed.), *Law Reform and Human Reproduction*, (1992).

[45] Surrogacy Arrangements Act 1985, ss. 1(8) and 2(3).

[46] *Ibid.*, s. 3.

[47] Human Fertilisation and Embryology Act 1990, s. 36(2)(*b*).

[48] *Ibid.*, s. 36(1).

[49] By which is meant the Court of Session or the sheriff court of the sheriffdom within which the child is: s. 30(8)(*b*).

[50] *Ibid.*, s. 30(1). This section was added to the legislation at a late stage.

the parties to a marriage, and not, for example, in favour of a cohabiting couple, nor of a married or a single person on his or her own. The child must have been carried by a woman other than the wife of the marriage, as a result of the placing in her of an embryo or sperm and eggs or her artificial[51] insemination[52]; and either the sperm of the husband or the egg of the wife, or both, must have been used to bring about the creation of the embryo[53] (*i.e.* at least one of the parties to the marriage must be the genetic parent). The order must have been applied for (jointly) within six months of the birth of the child, or, in the case of a child born before the coming into force of the Act, within six months of its coming into force.[54] Both at the time of the application and of the making of the order the child's home must be with the married couple,[55] and either one or both of the married couple must be domiciled in a part of the United Kingdom or in the Channel Islands or the Isle of Man.[56] Both husband and wife must have attained the age of 18 at the time of the making of the order.[57] Since the order will provide for the child to be treated in law as the child of the parties to the marriage, and, it may be assumed (though this is not stated), to be treated in law as the child of no other person,[58] the man and woman who would otherwise be father and mother but for the making of such an order (including a man or woman who would be father or mother through the application of any of the other provisions of the 1990 Act) must have freely and with full understanding of what is involved agreed unconditionally to the making of the order.[59] Their legal parenthood is being denied by the order. The agreement of a person who cannot be found or is incapable of giving agreement is not required, and the agreement of a woman who has carried the child is ineffective if given by her less than six weeks after the birth of the child.[60] The court before making the order must be satisfied that no money or other benefit (other than for expenses reasonably incurred) has been given or received by the husband or the wife for or in consideration of (a) the making of the order, (b) any agreement required by the Act, (c) the handing over of the child to the husband and the wife, or (d) the making of any arrangements with a view to the making of the order; it would appear however that the court has the power to authorise any such payment.[61]

Effectively, section 30 provides for a speedy form of adoption, though it should be noted that it contains significantly less control than the adoption legislation.[62] Indeed, this remarkable provision achieves in one section much of what in relation to adoption requires the whole gamut of legislation applicable there-

---

[51] Thus excluding from this provision children conceived naturally but nevertheless as the intended subject of a surrogacy agreement.

[52] s. 30(1)(*a*).

[53] s. 30(1)(*b*).

[54] s. 30(2).

[55] s. 30(3)(*a*).

[56] s. 30(3)(*b*).

[57] s. 30(4).

[58] To hold otherwise would amount to accepting that a person could have more than one mother and more than one father.

[59] s. 30(5).

[60] s. 30(6).

[61] s. 30(7).

[62] See further, Hogg, "Surrogacy—Nobody's Child" [1991] Fam.L. 276; Douglas and Lowe, "Becoming a Parent in English Law" (1992) 108 L.Q.R. 414.

to.[63] This is achieved only by laying down minimal control and protection: for example, while consent of those who would otherwise be parents is required, there is no provision for dispensing with consent if, say, it is unreasonably withheld. Indeed, the effect of a court order under this provision is more dramatic than that achieved by the Adoption (Scotland) Act 1978. It is not stated, but may be assumed, that the child becomes the child of the married couple for all purposes of law, and that there are no exceptions to this.[64] Thus the child subject to an order under section 30 is more completely the child of its legal parents than either the adopted child or the child subject to sections 27–29 of the 1990 Act. The limits to the availability of section 30 must be reiterated: it will be available only to married couples who apply jointly and at least one of whom is the genetic parent of the child. The child must have its home with the couple, and the persons who would otherwise be parents must consent freely and unconditionally to the making of the order. The permissive "may" is used in section 30, which indicates that the making of the order is a discretionary power of the court, and it may be assumed that the power will be exercised only when all the parties are in full agreement, with full knowledge of the consequences, and when in the court's opinion it is in the best interests of the child that the order be made. There is nothing in section 30 to indicate that the child's welfare must be taken into account, but an order under this section is, it is submitted, clearly "an order relating to parental rights" as that phrase is used in section 3 of the Law Reform (Parent and Child) (Scotland) Act 1986, with the result that the welfare test laid down in section 3(2) of that Act must be satisfied, and that the court is barred from making an order under section 30 unless it is satisfied that making the order will be in the interests of the child.[65]

DECLARATORS OF PARENTAGE OR NON-PARENTAGE

In circumstances in which parentage is in issue (e.g. where none of the above presumptions or deeming provisions is applicable, or a pursuer wishes to challenge the result of one of the presumptions), an action for declarator of parentage or of non-parentage can be brought either in the Court of Session or in the sheriff court.[66] The proof that is required is proof on a balance of probabilities, this in relation both to actions in which the result of a presumption contained in the 1986 Act is being challenged[67] and to actions in which no presumption is applicable.[68] A declarator of parentage will have the same effect as the application of the presumptions contained in the 1986 Act, and the effect of a declarator of

---

[63] Regulations to be made under ss. 30 and 45 will, however, apply some of the provisions of the Adoption (Scotland) Act 1978 to these parental orders.

[64] The stated exceptions in the 1990 Act expressly apply only to the deeming provisions in ss. 28 and 29: see, for example, the exceptions contained in s. 29(5) and in Sched. 4, para. 8. The exceptions to the status provisions in the Adoption (Scotland) Act 1978 are not incorporated into the draft Regulations mentioned at n. 63 above.

[65] See Douglas, *Law, Fertility and Reproduction*, (1991) at p. 160.

[66] Law Reform (Parent and Child) (Scotland) Act 1986, s. 7(1).

[67] *Ibid.*, s. 5(4).

[68] Where there is no presumption to rebut, proof has always been on this standard: *A. v. G.*, 1984 S.L.T. (Sh.Ct.) 65.

non- parentage is to displace these presumptions.[69] An action of declarator without any further conclusion is competent.[70]

Jurisdiction

At common law actions of declarator of legitimacy or illegitimacy could be
raised only in the Court of Session, because they were consistorial causes that
fell originally within the exclusive jurisdiction of the Commissaries, before being transferred to the exclusive jurisdiction of the Court of Session when the
consistorial jurisdiction of the Commissaries was abolished by the Court of Session Act 1830.[71] Now, an action of declarator of paternity may be brought either
in the Court of Session or in the sheriff court.[72] The action may be raised in the
Court of Session if and only if[73]:

(1) the child was born in Scotland, or
(2) the alleged or presumed parent or the child was domiciled in Scotland
    on the date the action is brought, or
(3) the alleged or presumed parent or the child has been habitually resid-
    ent in Scotland for not less than one year immediately preceding that
    date, or
(4) the alleged or presumed parent or the child had died before that date
    and he was either domiciled in Scotland at his death or he had been
    habitually resident in Scotland for not less than one year immediately
    preceding his death.

The action may be raised in the sheriff court if and only if[74]:

(1) the child was born in the sheriffdom, or
(2) the action could have been brought in the Court of Session under the
    provisions described above and either the alleged or presumed parent
    or the child was habitually resident in the sheriffdom either on the date
    when the action is brought or on the date of the parent's death.

"The alleged or presumed parent" in the provisions set out above includes a person who claims or is alleged to be or not to be the parent.[75]

Incidental Findings

The court may make in any proceedings an incidental finding as to parentage
or non-parentage for the purposes of these proceedings,[76] as for example in a
declarator of marriage or of divorce as the case may be or in an action for aliment against an alleged father.[77] A conclusion for putting to silence, normally

---

[69] s. 5(3).
[70] Walker, *Civil Remedies*, p. 116; *Magistrates of Ayr* v. *L.A.*, 1950 S.C. 102; *McLay* v. *Farrell*,
1950 S.C. 149; *Fife County Council* v. *L.A.*, 1950 S.C. 314.
[71] s. 33.
[72] Law Reform (Parent and Child) (Scotland) Act 1986, s. 7(1).
[73] *Ibid.*, s. 7(2).
[74] *Ibid.*, s. 7(3).
[75] *Ibid.*, s. 7(6).
[76] *Ibid.*, s. 7(5).
[77] *X.* v. *Y.*, 1921 1 S.L.T. 79; *Brown* v. *Brown*, 1972 S.L.T. 143. See also *Jamieson* v. *Jamieson*,
1969 S.L.T. (Notes) 11.

associated with a declarator of freedom from marriage, is competent against any false claims to personal status and so may be combined with, and follow on, a declarator of non-parentage.[78] It is available against a parent who makes a false claim to a relationship as well as against the child.[79]

Title to Sue

Any person with a legally enforceable interest that turns on the parentage or non-parentage of the child has a title to sue for declarator.[80] That parents and the child have such an interest is self-evident: they have a clear title to sue. A declarator must have at least the possibility of present legal consequences and it will not be granted where the sole interest is in some future or contingent right.[81] Accordingly, while the parents and child are all alive, it will be rarely, if ever, that others have a title to seek a declarator of parentage. On the death of any of them an interest and consequent title may, however, emerge. It was at one time thought that only the Crown or persons whose right was derived from the Crown had a title to sue a declarator of bastardy,[82] probably because the possibility of other interests had not been considered, but such actions have been entertained, not only at the instance of a parent, but of parties with a remoter interest unconnected with the Crown,[83] and it may now be taken as settled that title to sue for declarator of a person's non-parentage depends, as does jurisdiction, on the same principles as those applicable to declarators of parentage.

Proof of Parentage or Non-Parentage

In order to establish parentage or non-parentage where no presumption of law is in point the pursuer must establish, on the balance of probabilities, that there exists, or there does not exist (as the case may be) a genetic link between the alleged parent and the child.[84] In the absence of scientific evidence, those matters already discussed in relation to rebutting the *pater est* presumption[85] will be relevant. Scientific evidence may not be available because, for example one of the parties is dead: in one case the alleged father had, during the mother's pregnancy, placed his hand on her stomach and asked after "his baby", had settled out of court an action for aliment shortly after the child's birth,[86] the mother

---

[78] *Imre* v. *Mitchell*, 1958 S.C. 439.

[79] *Ibid.*

[80] *Shedden* v. *Patrick* (1849) 11 D. 1333, (1853) 15 D. 379; *Benson* v. *Benson* (1854) 16 D. 555; *Grant* v. *Countess of Seafield*, 1926 S.C. 274; *Bosville* v. *Lord Macdonald*, 1910 S.C. 597. See also *Hogg* v. *Dick*, 1987 S.L.T. 716.

[81] Walker, *Civil Remedies*, at pp. 113–114. The rule admits substantial exceptions and where there is a proper contradictor, a future, or even a contingent, legal right can be made the subject of declarator (*Fleming* v. *McLagan* (1879) 6 R. 588, *per* Lord Young at p. 598). It is thought, however, that the scope afforded to such actions cannot extend to the raising of actions by parties whose sole interest is one which may emerge only on the death of a party having a present and primary interest.

[82] Stair, IV, xii, 1, 7 and 8.

[83] *Imre* v. *Mitchell, supra*; *Smith* v. *Dick* (1869) 8 M. 31.

[84] Note that while such evidence will rebut the presumptions in the Law Reform (Parent and Child) (Scotland) Act 1986, it will have no effect on the deeming provisions contained in the Human Fertilisation and Embryology Act 1990.

[85] *Ante*, at pp. 132–133.

[86] See *Antoniewicz* v. *Barty (Wood's Exr.)*, June 27, 1991, in which the alleged father had died four days before he was due to submit to DNA fingerprinting.

had alleged that she had never had sex with any other man and paternity was held to be established. Proof of maternity has already been considered.[87] Proof of paternity is much more difficult and is, in the absence of scientific evidence, necessarily recondite. It is however no longer necessary to provide corroborated evidence[88] (and the doctrine of corroboration by false denial[89] is consequently abolished also[90]), but the court shall not grant decree of declarator unless proof has been established by evidence.[91]

Proof of Intercourse

Proof that sexual intercourse took place at the relevant time will almost always be necessary, and an inference of paternity will ordinarily be drawn where there is such proof and nothing more. This is so notwithstanding that evidence of intercourse, apart from the evidence of the parties, is almost always inferential in character, as, in the highest degree, is the answer to the question whether any given act of intercourse led to conception. Moreover, the facts from which the inferences may be drawn are often, in the nature of things, difficult to prove. The specialities of proof flow in the main from the paucity of testimony usually available. In *Jamieson* v. *Dobie*, Lord President Clyde said: "What was laid down in *Williamson's* case[92] was that, if the pursuer proves connexion at a date such that it is not impossible, according to experience, for the subsequent birth to be connected with it, then the pursuer has done all the pursuer can do to discharge the onus resting on her."[93]

The effect of proof of intercourse with the defender, at a date with which it is not impossible for the subsequent birth to be connected, is, in the absence of any evidence to suggest that another man is the father, to raise a presumption of fact which the defender, if he is to escape liability, must displace. Paternity will not, however, be attributed to the defender where acts of intercourse with other men are proved, or seem likely to have occurred, at about the same time as the proved or admitted act of intercourse with the defender, unless there be some special feature pointing to the likelihood that the defender is the father[94]; and *a fortiori* that will be so where the act of intercourse with another man is consistent with resultant conception followed by a normal period of gestation, whereas the act of intercourse with the defender would be consistent with his paternity only if an abnormal period of gestation were postulated. The question of the maximum possible period of gestation is the same in principle as in cases of rebuttal of the presumption of paternity,[95] but, where the presumption does not apply, the onus

---

[87] *Ante*, at pp. 125–126.
[88] Civil Evidence (Scotland) Act 1988, s. 1(1).
[89] A doctrine applicable to consistorial and affiliation cases: *Hall* v. *Hall*, 1958 S.C. 206; *McInnes* v. *McInnes*, 1954 S.C. 396; *Davies* v. *Hunter*, 1934 S.C. 10.
[90] Civil Evidence Act 1988, s. 1(2).
[91] *Ibid.*, s. 8(1).
[92] *Williamson* v. *McClelland*, 1913 S.C. 678.
[93] 1935 S.C. 415 at p. 418. Averments of intercourse at specified intervals over a period of time within which conception occurred are relevant: *Farrell* v. *Brannan* (1921) 37 Sh.Ct.Rep. 75.
[94] *Robertson* v. *Hutchison*, 1935 S.C. 708; *Sinclair* v. *Rankine*, 1921 S.C. 933; *Hannan* v. *Anderson* (1935) 51 Sh.Ct.Rep. 300. The pursuer cannot "choose her victim" (*Robertson* v. *Hutchison*; *Butter* v. *McLaren*, 1909 S.C. 786), but may show reasons for holding the defender rather than another man to be the father.
[95] *Ante*, at pp. 129–131.

rests on the pursuer to prove that the period of gestation required for consistency with paternity on the part of the defender is not impossible and it is submitted that for that reason, if for no other, the court should be less astute than it was in cases of legitimacy to accept periods of gestation that verge on the fanciful. That will, however, be so only where there is no question of intercourse after the last date admitted or proved. If intercourse at a date too remote to be the occasion of conception is admitted or proved and there has been opportunity thereafter at a time consistent with conception, the onus is on the defender, at least if the pursuer speaks to connection then and is credible, to prove that there was not intercourse when opportunity afforded. This principle was applied in a series of cases in which the requirements of *semiplena probatio* were held to be satisfied so as to admit the pursuer's oath in supplement, although the interval between the last act of intercourse admitted or proved and the birth of the child far exceeded the normal period of gestation.[96] The equivalent in modern practice is that the remote act of intercourse should be taken to give rise to a presumption of continuance which, together with the pursuer's evidence of intercourse at a time appropriate for conception, will often be sufficient to establish the pursuer's case. If the evidence is so regarded, there is no real departure from the normal period of gestation as the proper measure. Similar considerations apply where the minimum period of gestation is in issue[97] and in relation to both the minimum and maximum periods regard must be had to the particular facts of the case including the character of the pursuer. Where there is no question of promiscuity, indulgence may more readily be allowed in considering whether the probable limits have been exceeded.

Other Acts of Intercourse

Evidence that the mother had sexual intercourse with other men within the possible period of gestation is admissible because it is directly relevant to the question of whether the defender is the father.[98] Evidence of specific acts of intercourse between the pursuer and men other than the defender is however, in accordance with the general principle which excludes similar fact evidence, inadmissible if the acts fall outwith that period, although it is thought that, on analogy with cases of rape, evidence of the general loose sexual character of the pursuer may be led.[99] Acts of intercourse between the defender and women other than the pursuer and the defender's loose sexual character are not apt to instruct, except in the most general way, the likelihood of his being the father of the pursuer's child and so evidence of these matters is inadmissible.[1] The rule

---

[96] *Brown* v. *Smith* (1799) Hume 32 (14 months); *Wightman* v. *Tomlinson* (1807) Mor.App. 1 Proof No. 5 (11 months and three weeks); *Leckie* v. *Lindsay* (1810) Hume 33; *Hunter, Petr.*, May 26, 1814, F.C. 614 (one year 14 days); *Kerr* v. *Hamilton* (1852) 4 D. 624 (11 months, 15 days). See Fraser, (3rd ed.) at p. 168. *Cf. Jamieson* v. *Dobie*, 1935 S.C. 415 (306 days); *Gaw* v. *McNab* (1933) 49 Sh.Ct.Rep. 55 (320 days); *Gorman* v. *Smith, ibid.* (315 days).

[97] *Elliot* v. *Scott* (1800) Hume 33 (seven months and four days). *Cf. Watson* v. *Caine* (1936) 52 Sh.Ct.Rep. 213.

[98] *Butter* v. *McLaren*, 1909 S.C. 786. *Cf. Barr* v. *Bain* (1896) 23 R. 1090. When such acts are founded upon, times, places and names should be specified in the pleadings.

[99] See Walker and Walker, *The Law of Evidence in Scotland*, p. 20. But the analogy with rape may now lead to a different conclusion (Criminal Procedure (Scotland) Act 1975 ss. 141 A and B and 346 A and B).

[1] *McDougall* v. *Balonieri* (1916) 32 Sh.Ct.Rep. 186. See, however, *Whyte* v. *Whyte* (1884) 11 R. 710, *per* Lord Mure at p. 711.

excluding similar fact evidence finds, however, an exception in the case of intercourse between the pursuer and defender falling outwith the possible period of gestation. Evidence of such acts is admitted because the pursuer's allegations must be viewed in the light of the whole circumstances of the relationship between the parties and intercourse on occasions other than that which is alleged to have led to conception may be relevant to the character of that relationship.[2] At one time little distinction was made for this purpose between intercourse before and intercourse after the possible time of conception, but it is now recognised that evidence of intercourse before conception has greater evidential force than subsequent intercourse.[3] Where an act of intercourse prior to conception is admitted or proved very little further is required to establish the case; but the contrary is true where the admitted or proved act is subsequent to conception. Once intercourse has taken place, the likelihood, according to ordinary human experience, is that it continues to occur within a continuing relationship.[4] Evidence of an act of intercourse between the parties has accordingly been admitted although it occurred as much as six years before the alleged date of conception.[5] There is not the same strong inferential connection between subsequent intercourse and the probability of intercourse at the time of conception, but it may nonetheless, especially if close in time, cast a light on the relationship of the parties and give a likelihood to the pursuer's evidence which it would not otherwise have.[6]

The Defender as Witness

In actions for declarator of parentage the pursuer may sometimes call the defender as a witness. It is her right to do so; the practice is unobjectionable, at any rate where the defender is adduced immediately before the close of the pursuer's proof, and there is no inference that in doing so the pursuer puts the defender forward as a witness of credit.[7] The problematic case arises where the defender is called as the pursuer's first witness. That is also within the pursuer's rights and it may have tactical advantages, but doubts have been expressed about its propriety and expediency. These doubts have not, however, been uniform. Criticisms in *McArthur* v. *McQueen*[8] were disapproved in *Darroch* v. *Kerr*,[9] but repeated in *McWhirter* v. *Lynch*[10]; and in *Fraser* v. *Smith*[11] the hope

---

[2] *Lawson* v. *Eddie* (1861) 23 D. 876; *Ross* v. *Fraser* (1863) 1 M. 783; *McDonald* v. *Glass* (1883) 11 R. 57; *Scott* v. *Dawson* (1884) 11 R. 518; *Buchanan* v. *Finlayson* (1900) 3 F. 245; *Havery* v. *Brownlee*, 1908 S.C. 424; *Florence* v. *Smith*, 1913 S.C. 978; *Roy* v. *Pairman*, 1958 S.C. 334.

[3] *Florence* v. *Smith, supra*; *Havery* v. *Brownlee, supra*.

[4] *Buchanan* v. *Finlayson, per* Lord Trayner at p. 251 and Lord Justice-Clerk Macdonald at p. 249; *Havery* v. *Brownlee, per* Lord Justice-Clerk Macdonald at p. 425; *Reid* v. *Storry* (1912) 28 Sh.Ct.Rep. 326.

[5] *Macpherson* v. *Beaton*, 1935 S.C. 100.

[6] *Ross* v. *Fraser, per* Lord Justice-Clerk Inglis at p. 785 and Lord Neaves at p. 786; *Florence* v. *Smith, per* Lord Dundas at pp. 985–986; *Buchanan* v. *Finlayson, per* Lord Justice-Clerk Macdonald at p. 249 and Lord Trayner at p. 251. See also *Lawson* v. *Eddie, per* Lord Benholme at p. 880; *McDonald* v. *Glass, per* Lord Justice-Clerk Moncrieff at p. 58 and Lord Young at p. 59.

[7] *Faddes* v. *McNeish*, 1923 S.C. 443, *per* Lord Ormidale at p. 448; *Darroch* v. *Kerr* (1901) 4 F. 396; *sed contra McArthur* v. *McQueen* (1901) 3 F. 1010.

[8] (1901) 3 F. 1010.

[9] (1901) 4 F. 396.

[10] 1909 S.C. 112.

[11] 1937 S.N. 67. See also *Finnegan* v. *Maan*, 1966 S.L.T. (Notes) 47.

was expressed that this method of conducting cases would hereafter be avoided. It has been said, apparently on the view that to call the defender as the pursuer's first witness is unfair to him, that if the practice is followed the defender should be warned of the importance and possible effect of his answers to material questions[12]; but neither the unfairness nor the necessity for warning is clear. The defender has notice of the case against him on the pleadings and that should protect him from improper surprise. He is bound by his oath to tell the truth and it is difficult to understand the need for any special warning that he should do so. A higher degree of fairness to both parties may be obtained if the defender gives his evidence before he has had an opportunity of measuring the full strength of the pursuer's case as disclosed in the evidence than if he does so at a later stage. The only significant element of unfairness to the defender is that he may not have an opportunity of dealing in his evidence with incidental points that may emerge unexpectedly at later stages of the pursuer's proof; but any prejudice caused by that can be remedied by allowing the defender's recall. If the pursuer remains in court during the defender's evidence, the court may find difficulty in assessing the credibility of her subsequent testimony, but that objection can be elided by the pursuer's voluntary absence during the defender's evidence. Both *McWhirter* v. *Lynch* and *Fraser* v. *Smith* show an inadequate appreciation of the cogent considerations advanced by a distinguished bench in *Darroch* v. *Kerr*, but the weight of adverse judicial opinion is now such that it is probably imprudent to adduce the defender as the pursuer's first witness unless there are special reasons for doing so.

Scientific Tests: DNA Profiling

The doubts expressed in *Imre* v. *Mitchell*[13] about the value of scientific evidence of blood tests in rebutting the presumption of paternity must be read in the context of the facts of that case[14] and if intended to have a wider application have, in any event, been superseded by the advance of scientific knowledge. The value of such tests is now undoubted,[15] and indeed in the normal case will now be the best evidence available. Until relatively recently, the ABO blood grouping system was the main scientific test available, and though it could in the vast majority of cases be used only in an exclusionary manner,[16] the test itself was accepted as being "pretty cast iron" by Lord Cullen in *Russell* v. *Wood*.[17] In that case the court found a child to be illegitimate after being satisfied beyond all reasonable doubt[18] that the mother's husband was not the father: the evidence consisted of the mother's assertion of when she last had sex with her husband, and the result of the ABO blood grouping test.

A much more accurate scientific test is now widely available, whereby a per-

---

[12] *McWhirter* v. *Lynch*, 1909 S.C. 112, *per* Lord President Dunedin at p 113.

[13] 1958 S.C. 439.

[14] The case involved a mother attempting to have her own child declared illegitimate, and this clearly did not elicit much sympathy from the court.

[15] *S.* v. *S.*, *W.* v. *Official Solicitor* [1972] A.C. 24, *per* Lord Reid at p. 41, *Docherty* v. *McGlynn*, 1983 S.L.T. 645, *per* Lord President Emslie at p. 648 and Lord Cameron at p. 650.

[16] See Dodd and Lincoln: "An Analysis of 1556 Cases of Doubtful Paternity Submitted for Blood Group Investigation" (1978) 18 Med.Sci.L. 185.

[17] 1987 S.C.L.R. 207 at p. 209.

[18] *i.e.* to a standard higher than was necessary.

son's DNA structure is identified. This test, known as DNA profiling or DNA fingerprinting, can positively identify the parents of a child, to a probability far in excess of what the courts would accept as proof on the balance of probabilities.[19] DNA (deoxyribonucleic acid) is the material from which chromosomes are made. Every (genetically normal) person inherits 23 chromosomes from his mother, and 23 from his father. The DNA is formed in bands which can be measured and X-rayed. In a dispute concerning, say, paternity, a child's DNA bands can be matched with those of his mother. Those bands that do not match with his mother must have come from his father and these bands can then be matched with the putative father (or *vice versa*), giving a positive or a negative result of great accuracy. If this evidence is available, it will clearly be the best evidence of parentage.

Ordering Scientific Tests

As a general principle, a party to litigation is not obliged to assist his opponent by providing that opponent with the evidence upon which to build a case.[20] At common law the Scottish court took the view that it could not direct parties in civil proceedings to undergo medical examinations such as blood tests, this on the ground that any such order would be an unwarranted invasion of a person's private right and would be inconsistent with the principles upon which litigation is carried out in Scotland. Nor could the court order or authorise tests to be carried out upon children, even to prove their legitimacy.[21] However, this approach was increasingly regarded as unwarranted and indeed counter-productive for a number of reasons. First, it was developed at a time when a finding of illegitimacy had profound and unfortunate effects on a child's legal status. This is no longer so. Secondly, it was developed at a time when the tests could not positively identify a child's parents, with the result that the person claiming paternity had nothing to gain and everything to lose, while the person denying it had possibly everything to gain and nothing to lose. This too is no longer so, and DNA profiling gives mutual benefits and drawbacks to both sides. Thirdly, the taking of blood samples involves an invasion of a person's bodily integrity, minor it is to be admitted yet far more than would be required for a DNA test, which can be done using skin scrapings, or hair roots or semen. And finally, a principle that was appropriate for litigious proceedings is not necessarily apt in proceedings relating to a child's welfare: there are few situations indeed in which a child's welfare will not best be served by finding out the truth (particularly since that

---

[19] Rankin, "DNA Fingerprinting" (1988) 33 J.L.S. 124 reports that the chances of error are something in the region of 30,000 million to one, though such accuracy has been challenged: see Macdonald, "DNA Profiling—Less than the Whole Truth?" 1990 S.L.T. (News) 285. In *Torrie* v. *Turner*, 1990 S.L.T. 718 an Extra Division of the Inner House was told that DNA profiling could establish paternity positively "beyond statistical doubt." In the criminal case of *Welsh* v. *H.M.A.*, 1992 S.L.T. 193 it was held that it was for the jury to determine when the criminal standard had been achieved and that the statistical evidence of the chances of someone other than the accused having blood with the same DNA structure as the accused being 1 in 88 million was sufficient evidence to found a conviction.

[20] *Per* Lord Justice-Clerk Thomson in *Whitehall* v. *Whitehall*, 1958 S.C. 252 at pp. 258–259.

[21] *Whitehall* v. *Whitehall, supra*; *Imre* v. *Mitchell*, 1958 S.C. 439; *Torrie* v. *Turner*, 1990 S.L.T. 718.

truth cannot now affect its own legal status). However, the precedents preventing the Scottish court from ordering tests were clear and the Court of Session was not inclined to accept arguments such as those given above to change
its rule.[22] In England the courts were given the power to order scientific tests by
the Family Law Reform Act 1987, which by section 23 amended the Family
Law Reform Act 1969.[23] In Scotland similar (but not identical) powers were
given to the court by section 70 of the Law Reform (Miscellaneous Provisions)
(Scotland) Act 1990.

This provision was passed as a result of the recommendations of the Scottish
Law Commission,[24] who had argued that, if the courts were given the power to
order DNA testing, "the number of cases of disputed paternity which proceed to
a full court hearing would, we suspect, fall dramatically, thus reducing the
courts' overall workload. Spurious cases would be prevented and the courts
would be able to deal more speedily with those that do proceed."[25]

Section 70 provides that the court[26] may, in any civil proceedings,[27] request a
party to the proceedings: (a) to provide a sample of blood or other body fluid or
of body tissue for the purpose of laboratory analysis; or (b) to consent to the taking of such a sample from a child in relation to whom the party has power to give
such consent. Such a request can be made in any civil proceedings brought on or
after the date of commencement of section 70, or brought before that date so
long as the proof has not yet begun.[28] The court is entitled to make such a request
ex proprio motu and it does not need to wait for an application by one of the parties.[29] The court has no right to request that a person who is not a party to the proceedings provide a sample. So a pursuer in an action for declarator of
non-parentage who alleges that someone else not a party to the proceedings is in
truth the parent cannot force that person to provide a sample. Since today testing
can provide a positive or a negative identification conclusively, there will generally be no need to involve a third party in this sort of situation. Allegations that
a third party is the parent are sometimes made as an element of proof that the
pursuer was not the parent; but proof of, or an allegation of, parentage is not required to found an action of non-parentage.

While such a request can be made, it cannot be enforced, for this would involve a person being subjected to a surgical interference, however slight, without his consent: this is perceived to go against an individual's right to physical
integrity. A civil case raises different considerations from a criminal case, because the former is clearly more concerned with a balancing of private inter-

---

[22] See *Torrie* v. *Turner, supra.*
[23] On the extent of the English court's powers at common law, there was some disagreement: See *S.* v. *S., W.* v. *Official Solicitor*, 1972 A.C. 24, *per* Lord Reid at p. 43, Lord Hodson at p. 57 and Lord McDermott at pp. 46–47.
[24] Discussion Paper 80, *Evidence: Blood Group Tests, DNA Tests, and Related Matters*; S.L.C. Report No. 120.
[25] *Ibid.* at para. 3.9.
[26] By which is meant the Court of Session or the sheriff court: Law Reform (Miscellaneous Provisions) (Scotland) Act 1990, s. 70(4).
[27] This is rather wider than the equivalent English provisions, now contained in s. 20(1) of the Family Law Reform Act 1969, for there the court has a similar power only in actions in which a child's parentage falls to be determined.
[28] Law Reform (Miscellaneous Provisions) (Scotland) Act 1990, s. 70(4).
[29] *Ibid.*, s. 70(1).

est.[30] However, if a request has been made, but the person refuses or fails to give consent to the taking of a sample of blood or other body fluid or of body tissue, then "the court may draw from the refusal or failure such adverse inference, if any, in relation to the subject-matter of the proceedings as seems to it to be appropriate."[31] In *Docherty* v. *McGlynn*[32] Lord Cameron thought, even before this statute was passed, that a refusal to consent to scientific tests upon oneself could be sanctioned by "the consequential inference to be drawn adverse to the interest of the party in disobedience"[33]; and although he cited no authority for this proposition, a parallel might have been found in the requirement which may be made of a pursuer in a personal injuries action to submit to medical examination. The authority to draw an adverse inference now lies in section 70 of the Law Reform (Miscellaneous Provisions) (Scotland) Act 1990. The court does not need to draw any adverse inference (*e.g.* if the refusal is based on a sincerely-held religious belief), but it is likely that in most cases of unexplained failure or refusal an adverse inference will appropriately be drawn.

Consent on Behalf of Children

DNA profiling to establish parentage or non-parentage requires, of course, samples of blood or other body fluid or of other body tissue being taken not only from the putative parents but also from the child concerned. If a child is, in the opinion of a qualified medical practitioner, capable of understanding the nature and possible consequences of consenting to the medical procedure of removing a sample, then he or she may provide personal consent thereto.[34] However, if the child is unable to understand, someone else will have to consent on the child's behalf. Now, the general principle is that a parent or guardian or person with custody of the child can consent to its medical treatment so long as that is in the best interests of the child.[35] But if the purpose of the taking of blood or body sample from the child is to establish its non-relationship with a person (and therefore to deny it, *e.g.* the right of aliment or of succession from that person) it is not clear that in all cases this will be in the child's best interests. It was to obviate such doubts that section 6 of the Law Reform (Parent and Child) (Scotland) Act 1986 was passed.[36] This section originally referred only to the taking of blood samples from pupil children, but it has now been extended to cover the taking of other body fluids or of body tissues,[37] and also to apply to children under 16.[38] Section 6 provides that where the sample is sought from a child under 16, consent may be given by his guardian or any person having custody or care and control over him. There is no requirement that the consent be given only if it

---

[30] Scot. Law Com., Discussion Paper No. 80, at paras. 3.20–3.25.

[31] Law Reform (Miscellaneous Provisions) (Scotland) Act 1990, s. 70(2).

[32] 1983 S.L.T. 645.

[33] *Ibid.* at p. 650.

[34] Age of Legal Capacity (Scotland) Act 1991, s. 2(4) This applies to "any surgical, medical or dental procedure or treatment" and as such is amply wide enough to cover the taking of a sample.

[35] See *post*, at pp. 182–189.

[36] Discussed by Thomson in "Law Reform (Parent and Child) (Scotland) Act 1986," 1987 S.L.T. (News) 129 at p. 130.

[37] Law Reform (Miscellaneous Provisions) (Scotland) Act 1990, s. 70(3).

[38] Age of Legal Capacity (Scotland) Act 1991, Sched. 1, para. 42.

furthers the child's best interests, and it is for the person empowered to consent on behalf of the child to decide whether the establishing of the truth will outweigh any financial detriment to the child (*e.g.* by losing a right to aliment from a particular man, or by losing a right to a valuable succession from a particular person's estate[39]). A child's best interests (where relevant) are not to be calculated on a purely financial basis, and the resolving of doubt about its parentage, which DNA profiling now conclusively allows, ought generally to weigh more heavily than the protection of rights that may be falsely based.

The court[40] may request a party to any civil proceedings, who has the power to give consent on behalf of a child, to give that consent to the taking of a sample of blood or other body fluid or of body tissue.[41] If that party refuses or fails to give the consent, or to take any step necessary for the provision or taking of such a sample, the court may draw from the refusal or failure such adverse inference, if any, in relation to the subject-matter of the proceedings as seems to it to be appropriate.[42] Again, there is no need to draw any inference, but it is likely that in most cases of unexplained failure or refusal an adverse inference will appropriately be drawn.

Consent by Presumptive Father

When section 6 of the 1986 Act refers to the guardian or person having custody of the child being able to consent on the child's behalf, this will include men who are presumed fathers as a result of section 5(1) of the same Act. This may lead to conceptual problems when the man's paternity is the very fact at issue. In *Docherty* v. *McGlynn*[43] a presumptive father was held entitled to consent to the taking of blood samples from the child, in an action in which the paramour of the wife[44] sought declarator that the child was his rather than the husband's and presumptive father's. The Lord Ordinary, Lord Wylie, held that since the *de quo* in the action was which of the pursuer or defender was in fact (and in law) the father, the presumptive father had no power to consent on behalf of the child. This was overruled by the First Division on the ground that the defender (the presumptive father) enjoyed the benefit of the presumption until it was overturned, and part of that benefit was the right to custody of the child and the right to exercise in relation to the child the *patria potestas* (from which the right to consent flowed). In Lord President Emslie's words: "The presumption and all the rights which flow from it in favour of the first-named defender in this case cannot be defeated unless and until the pursuer has established that he is, and that the first-named defender could not be, the child's father."[45]

However, the limits of this decision must be recognised. The presumptive father was asserting his right to consent, in order to uphold his claim to be father. The case is no authority for the proposition that the presumptive father

---

[39] *Cf. Russell* v. *Wood*, 1987 S.C.L.R. 207.
[40] By which is meant the Court or Session or the sheriff court: Law Reform (Miscellaneous Provisions) (Scotland) Act 1990, s. 70(4).
[41] *Ibid.*, s. 70(1)(*b*).
[42] *Ibid.*, s. 70(2).
[43] 1983 S.L.T. 645.
[44] Now deceased: this was why she was not able to provide the requisite consent.
[45] *Ibid.* at p. 647.

has the right to consent on behalf of the child in order to *deny* that he is the father (and therefore to deny that he has the right to consent). In *Imre* v. *Mitchell*[46] a married woman was attempting to bastardise her child, and it was held that she could not rely on her husband's consent to blood tests[47] for the child when the purpose was to establish that the husband was not the father. This decision was cited with apparent approval by Lord Emslie in *Docherty* v. *McGlynn*, who described the result as follows: "The pursuer in *Imre's* case, who sought to establish that Mitchell was not the child's father, could not at the same time be heard to assert that Mitchell, as the child's father, was entitled to consent to the sampling and testing of the child's blood."[48] This would suggest that a presumptive father who raises an action of declarator of non-parentage cannot use his presumptive rights in order to acquire evidence to back up his case. Thomson disagrees with this conclusion,[49] and submits that until the presumption of paternity is rebutted, all the rights that flow from that presumption can be exercised by the presumptive father. Though not addressing themselves to this particular point, all three judges in *Docherty* do emphasise that the powers and responsibilities flowing from the presumption apply unless and until it is displaced.[50] *Imre* was not a case in which the presumptive father's capacity to consent was directly in issue, but rather involved the competency of leading evidence already obtained through that consent; and it is suggested that to analyse the issue in terms of the competency of evidence is not the correct approach. Rather, it should be accepted that the whole point of the presumption of paternity is to allow parental rights to be exercised even when the truth is not unequivocally established: no one would deny that, even during the course of an action to deny his paternity, a presumptive father who raised the action could nevertheless consent to necessary medical treatment of the child. There is a logical consistency in holding that one man may consent until it is proved that another man has that right. Even if the issue is correctly one of the competency of evidence, to hold a presumptive father personally barred from leading evidence derived from consent to the testing of the child could have the effect of denying to the court evidence that is now conclusive. If the action were decided in the absence of such evidence, there might remain a doubt in the parties' minds: the judges of the First Division in *Docherty* were strongly of the view that it would not be in the best interests of the child for such a doubt to remain.[51] It is therefore submitted that the parental right to consent on behalf of a child can be exercised by a presumptive father even in the course of an action he raises to establish that he is not, in fact, the father. This conclusion is, however, difficult to reconcile with *Imre* and the *dicta* approving it in *Docherty*. It should be noted that in most cases the mother's consent will be competent and available (in *Docherty* the mother had died).

---

[46] 1958 S.C. 439.
[47] At that time she herself had no right to consent.
[48] 1983 S.L.T. 645 at p. 648.
[49] at p. 155.
[50] *Per* Lord President Emslie at p. 647, Lord Cameron at p. 650, and Lord Grieve at p. 651.
[51] *Per* Lord President Emslie at p. 649, and Lord Cameron at p. 650.

Consent of the Court

Section 6(3) gives the court the power to consent to the taking of a sample of blood or other body fluid or of body tissue from a person who is incapable of giving consent, this in two situations: (a) where there is no person who is entitled to give consent, and (b) there is a person entitled to give consent but it is not reasonably practicable to obtain his consent in the circumstances, or he is unwilling to accept the responsibility of giving or withholding consent. Paragraph (*a*) will cover the situation where either there is no one able to consent on behalf of the child under 16, or the child over 16 is mentally disabled and thus unable to give personal consent: no one could give consent on the basis of parental rights in the latter since these will have disappeared by that age. Paragraph (*b*) will cover the situation where the person entitled to consent on behalf of the child cannot reasonably be contacted, or that person is unwilling for the purpose stated to give consent. In any of these cases the court itself[52] may consent to the taking of the sample; but it will not do so unless it is satisfied that the taking of the sample would not be detrimental to the health of the person from whom the sample is taken.[53] It is unlikely that there will be many cases in which the taking of a sample for DNA analysis will prove detrimental to the health of the person from whom it is taken; but the wording of the section suggests that the court cannot simply assume no harm, but must rather be positively persuaded that no harm will be suffered. The test is *not* the best interests or welfare of the person on whose behalf consent is being given, for that might potentially bring in economic considerations, such as rights to succession and aliment. Rather the test relates solely to the person's health (and this will presumably include mental health as well as physical health). There may be a potential clash of principles if the action of declarator is raised in order to allow a person to exercise parental responsibilities or rights. Section 3(2) of the Law Reform (Parent and Child) (Scotland) Act 1986 provides that in any proceedings relating to parental rights the court shall regard the welfare of the child as the paramount consideration and shall not make any order relating to parental rights unless it is satisfied that to do so will be in the interests of the child. It may be argued that, in deciding whether to consent to the taking of blood or other body sample, the court must also have regard to the principle in section 3(2), at least when the issue arises in an action relating to parental rights.[54] It is suggested that this is not so. In deciding to consent to the taking of blood or other bodily sample, the court is not making any order relating to parental rights, nor itself exercising any parental rights. It is providing consent on the authority of section 6(3) and subject to the condition stated in section 6(4). Having obtained evidence by doing so, the court may then make an order under section 3(1) relating to parental rights, and it is at this point that the court must have regard to the "welfare test" stated in section 3(2).

---

[52] Which means the Court of Session or the sheriff court: Law Reform (Parent and Child) (Scotland) Act 1986, s. 8.

[53] Law Reform (Parent and Child) (Scotland) Act 1986, s. 6(4).

[54] See, *e.g.* the *Current Law Annotator*, Law Reform (Miscellaneous Provisions) (Scotland) Act 1990 (c. 40), s. 70.

INTERNATIONAL ISSUES

Introduction

Until recently international private law issues in relation to parentage (as opposed to legitimacy and illegitimacy) could hardly arise. There was no differentiation between legal systems as to the definition of "mother" or "father," for none other than those universally accepted was conceived possible.[55] International private law issues might of course, and still may, arise in relation to the consequences of the parent-child relationship and, in so far as they do, such issues are dealt with elsewhere in this work. Legal systems might differ as to the methods of establishing the fact of parentage, but such conflicts affected only questions of proof which were peculiarly within the province of the *lex fori*. That too is still the law, and so Scottish rules of evidence apply to any action of declarator of parentage or non-parentage raised in the Scottish court under section 7 of the Law Reform (Parent and Child) (Scotland) Act 1986[56] and the pursuer must comply with the Scottish requirements for proof and can rely upon the Scottish presumptions contained in section 5 of that Act, notwithstanding that both the child and the alleged parent are domiciled and habitually resident elsewhere and nationals of a foreign country.

Since the development of the reproductive technologies with which the Human Fertilisation and Embryology Act 1990 is concerned, it is now possible for true international private law issues to arise in relation to the determination of parentage, for different legal systems may define the parents of a child born as a result of such techniques differently from the definitions given in the 1990 Act. For example, section 27 of that Act deems the woman who carries and gives birth to a child to be that child's mother, rather than, if different, the woman whose egg was used to bring about the pregnancy.[57] Similarly, section 28 provides that where a woman's husband consents to her artificial insemination with the sperm of a donor, that man rather than the donor of the sperm will be deemed to be the father of the child.[58] Another legal system may define "mother" and "father" in all circumstances as the providers of the genetic material. If the child or its parent is domiciled in, habitually resident in, or a national of such other country, the question arises as to which law determines parentage.

The issue is not directly dealt with in the Human Fertilisation and Embryology Act 1990, except to provide[59] that the rules determining parentage apply whether the infertility treatment is given in the United Kingdom or elsewhere. There is, of course, no common law authority directly in point one way or the other. What follows is therefore based on principle and analogous authorities and is necessarily somewhat tentative in character.

A Question of Status

Although at common law "an action of affiliation and aliment is essentially,

---

[55] Except in relation to the artificial creation of a parent and child relationship through the process of adoption: see *post* at chap. 19.
[56] The jurisdictional requirements are described *ante* at p. 146.
[57] *Ante*, at p. 122.
[58] *Ante*, at pp. 136–140.
[59] ss. 27(3) and 28(8).

under the affiliation head, of a declaratory nature,"[60] it was, unlike a declarator of legitimacy or illegitimacy, not determinative of status[61]—the declaratory crave if used (and it was not necessary[62]) being merely a preliminary to the pecuniary crave for a debt due in respect of a confessedly illegitimate child. It has nonetheless some of the elements of an action to determine status.[63] At common law occasion could scarcely arise for a bare declarator of parentage or non-parentage; for such a declarator, cases of affiliation of illegitimate children apart, must necessarily have raised and been inextricably identified with questions of legitimacy and illegitimacy. There is some attraction in likening the modern declarators of parentage and non-parentage introduced by the Law Reform (Parent and Child) (Scotland) Act 1986[64] to the declaratory crave of an action of affiliation and aliment and so divorcing it from questions of status. If status is "the legal standing or position of a person determined by his membership of some class of persons legally enjoying certain rights or subject to certain limitations,"[65] the relationship of parent and child cannot readily be treated as a status in that sense. If one speaks of the "status" of "child of a particular person" in this context it is merely to use a relative term fixing a relationship between two parties and not to use "status" in the sense of fixing the child in a particular legal category.[66] The scheme of the 1986 Act is, however, to assimilate declarators of parentage and non-parentage to declarators of legitimacy, legitimation and illegitimacy.[67] It is difficult to read the Act in a sense which would admit of the latter being, as is indisputable, concerned with status while the former are not. A similar conclusion is indicated by the relevant provisions of the Civil Evidence (Scotland) Act 1988.[68] And the relevant sections of the Human Fertilisation and Embryology Act 1990 (that is, sections 27 to 30) appear under the headnote "Status". The policy of modern statute is, it is submitted, to regard parentage as an aspect of status. That consists with the common law under which, as already noticed, parentage is, except in questions of aliment for a confessedly illegitimate child, inextricably connected with status. Moreover, both custody[69] and adoption[70] of children have been said on high authority to affect status. If that is so, then questions of parentage, which by their nature are of a more fundamental character than custody and no less so than adoption, must also affect status.

Status Determined by Domicile

A consequence of the view that parentage is a matter of status is that it is to be determined by the law of the domicile of the person whose status is in question

---

[60] Walker, *Civil Remedies*, p. 121.
[61] *McDonald* v. *Ross*, 1929 S.C. 240; *Silver* v. *Walker*, 1938 S.C. 595.
[62] *Silver* v. *Walker, cit. sup.*
[63] *Hepburn* v. *Tait* (1874) 1 R. 875, *per* Lord Neaves at p. 878; *McDonald* v. Ross, 1929 S.C. 240 per Lord Sands at p. 248.
[64] s. 7.
[65] *Shorter Oxford English Dictionary.*
[66] *McDonald* v. *Ross*, 1929 S.C. 240, *per* Lord Sands at p. 248.
[67] See s. 7.
[68] s. 8.
[69] *Kitson* v. *Kitson*, 1945 S.C. 434, *per* Lord Justice-Clerk Cooper at p. 439.
[70] *J and J* v. *C's Tutor*, 1948 S.C. 636, *per* Lord President Cooper at p. 642.

as his personal law. In matters of parentage the appropriate time for ascertainment of that domicile must be the birth of the child. That raises the problem that in any case of parentage the status of several persons, *e.g.* the genetic mother, the gestational mother, and the child, may be in issue and their domiciles may not coincide. The solution to that problem, it is submitted, is to treat the status of the child as the matter of primary concern and apply the law of his domicile. If, however, the domicile of the child turns on the disputed question of parentage, a further problem emerges of how the child's domicile is to be ascertained.

A practical solution may be achieved by applying the law of Scotland where one of the putative parents is a person to whom the law of Scotland would ascribe parentage, that person was domiciled in Scotland at the time of the child's birth, and the child's domicile would, if parentage were so ascribed, also be Scottish. That can be justified on the ground that the *lex fori* is to be preferred unless a sufficient cause is shown for displacing it. But the problem remains of what is to be done where the law of Scotland is not a potentially applicable system in the sense just considered. It is submitted that in that situation, and perhaps in others, the appropriate course is to apply the potentially applicable system with which the child has the closest connection. A "closest connection" test has been suggested in connection with proposals for reform of the law on domicile of origin.[71] While reform of the law of domicile on these lines may be a matter for legislation rather than judicial decision, there is no bar to developing by judicial decision a closest connection test, in a hitherto uncharted field, where a person's domicile cannot be ascertained. Such a test is attended with some uncertainties, and presumptions which could in some contexts be used to resolve these uncertainties may not be available in this, but it is better to address these uncertainties case by case than to adopt an arbitrary solution to an otherwise insoluble problem.

Parentage as an Incidental Question

The peculiar difficulties of choice of law in questions of parentage need arise only when parentage has to be considered independently of any other issue. Where a question of parentage arises incidentally to another issue, these difficulties are elided by determining parentage according to the law governing the main issue.

The problem whether "the incidental question" is to be determined by the same law as governs the main qustion, or by the law indicated by the conflicts rule governing the question as if it had arisen independently, is a well-known dilemma in international private law.[72] However that dilemma is to be resolved in other contexts, it is suggested that in this context the proper approach is to regard the *lex causae* as determinative of parentage arising as an incidental question. This produces some anomalies, perhaps more apparent than real—for example, that a person can be a parent for some purposes but not for others, or that a person can have different parents according to the issue which arises—but can be justified on the grounds that parentage will most commonly arise as an

---

[71] Law Commissions' *Report on Domicile*, at paras. 4.14–4.20.
[72] See Anton and Beaumont at pp. 85–89; Morris, *The Conflict of Law* (3rd ed.) at pp. 489–492; Cheshire and North, *Private International Law* (11th ed.) at pp. 53–56.

incidental question rather than independently, that this will normally satisfy the expectations of the parties, and that, as Anton and Beaumont put it,[73] the rules of the *lex causae* derive from the system with which the facts as a whole are likely to be most closely connected.

Practical Examples

There are at least two areas in which parentage can readily be envisaged to arise as incidental questions. The first relates to succession. Consider the situation of a man dying intestate, domiciled in a state in the USA which *ex hypothesi* retains the rule that paternity is determined purely genetically.[74] He was the identified donor of sperm which, through artificial insemination, led to the conception and birth of a child now living in Scotland; there is moveable property in the estate in Scotland. The child claims a right of succession. At first the child may be met with the argument that by section 28(1) his mother's husband is to be treated as his father "for all purposes,"[75] and that "no other person is to be treated as the father of the child,"[76] this "for any purpose."[77] Additionally it may be argued against the child's claim that section 28(8) provides that "this section applies whether the woman was in the United Kingdom or elsewhere at the time of" the infertility treatment. However, such reasoning is predicated upon the false assumption that the 1990 Act applies to all questions within its ambit which come before a Scottish court, no matter how these questions arise. This, it is suggested, is not so. The 1990 Act is applicable only when Scots law or Northern Irish law or English law governs the issue before the court. When an issue of intestate succession to moveable property is before the court, that issue is determined by the law of the deceased's last domicile and that legal system, rather than the law of the forum, should govern the issue of paternity.[78] It would follow in the example postulated that the child would have a right of succession even in the estate of a person who, by our law, is not his father (and would have a further right of succession in the estate of the person who is, by our law, his father if Scots law governed that man's succession).[79]

A second example relates to the law of marriage. If X wishes to marry Y, he cannot do so in Scotland if Y is the daughter of his sister (*i.e.* if Y is his niece).[80] However, if X and Y are both domiciled in a state in the USA which follows the rule in *Calvert* v. *Johnstone*[81] to the effect that the genetic mother rather than the gestative mother is for legal purposes a child's "mother," and Y was borne of X's sister as a result of the process of embryo transfer to the sister, then X and Y may well have capacity to marry each other within the jurisdiction of their domicile. If they do so, then the marriage will be recognised in Scotland notwithstanding that, applying the Scots law of maternity contained in section 27

---

[73] *Op. cit.* at p. 89.

[74] The rule which, of course, applied in Scotland before the coming into force of the Human Fertilisation and Embryology Act 1990.

[75] s. 29(1).

[76] s. 28(4).

[77] s. 29(2).

[78] *Cf. ante* at p. 9.

[79] A further example, relating to succession to immoveable property, is given *ante* at pp. 124–125.

[80] Marriage (Scotland) Act 1977, s. 2(1) and Sched. 1.

[81] (1991) 60 U.S.L.W. 1069. See *ante* at p. 122. The state involved was California.

of the Human Fertilisation and Embryology Act 1990, X has married his niece. That is nothing to the point, because Scots law does not govern the question of essential validity of that marriage. The international private law rule on recognition of marriage is applied, rather than a domestic rule relating to parentage.

Recognition of Foreign Decrees

Scots law allows a party to ask the court for a declarator of parentage or non-parentage,[82] but this is not, it is submitted, the only means by which the Scottish court will recognise parentage. If the relationship has been established or recognised by judicial decree from a foreign country, recognition in this country must be governed by the common law principles for the recognition of decrees affecting status, there being no statutory rules in point. These principles would indicate recognition of decrees of foreign courts which would have jurisdiction on grounds similar to those on which Scottish courts assert jurisdiction whether or not the foreign court actually exercised jurisdiction on these grounds[83]—*i.e.* that the child was born within the territorial jurisdiction of the forum, or the alleged or presumed parent or the child was domiciled there when the action was brought or had been habitually resident there for not less than a year immediately preceding the bringing of the action, or, in the case of a parent or child dying before the bringing of the action, had been so domiciled or resident at the date of death.[84] A case can also be made for recognising the decrees of courts with whose jurisdiction the child or putative parent had a close connection.[85] Recognition of a relationship of parent and child said to exist in the absence of a judicial decree is in reality a question of determining status, which is considered above.[86]

---

[82] Law Reform (Parent and Child) (Scotland) Act 1986, s. 7.
[83] *Cf. post* at pp. 581–583.
[84] Law Reform (Parent and Child) (Scotland) Act 1986, s. 7.
[85] See *ante* at pp. 160–161.
[86] *Ante* at pp. 158–160.

Chapter 5

PARENTAL RESPONSIBILITIES AND RIGHTS: GENERAL

INTRODUCTORY

Scope of this Chapter

Parental responsibilities and rights concern the obligations that parents and those *in loco parentis* have towards their children and the powers they possess in order to fulfil these obligations. The immediately following chapter will examine the nature of a number of particular parental responsibilities and rights and how they are to be exercised; this chapter will be limited to an examination of the concept of parental responsibilities and rights, together with the questions of who may exercise these responsibilities and rights and how they are terminated. Other consequences of the parent-child relationship, which may validly though misleadingly be described as parental rights, such as the right to succeed on death, fall quite outwith the scope of this work.

Judicial Character of Parental Responsibilities and Rights

"That there are natural obligations betwixt parents and children, not proceeding from the consent of either party, or from the constitution of any human law, but from the obedience man oweth to his Maker, who hath written this law in the hearts of parents and children, as to their interests and duties, with capital letters, is evident by the common consent of all the nations of the world, how barbarous soever."[1] For Stair, these obligations were "placed in the common nature that man hath with other animals, and so are given as an evident instance of the law of nature."[2] The power of parents over their children which went with this nexus of interest and obligation was "the only natural authority and government" from which all authority, public and private, civil and criminal, was derived.[3]

It is, then, in the context of obligation inherent in the natural relation that parental power is to be seen. The matter is put succinctly by Erskine. "Parents lie under the strongest obligations, from nature itself, to take care of their issue during their imperfect age, in consequence of which they are vested with all the powers over them which are necessary for the proper discharge of their duty."[4] It is of interest that the institutional writers speak of parental, not paternal, power and that they should do so was consistent with the interrelation of power and obligation. If it was from parents' duties to their children that all powers over them were truly derived, the mother, no less than the father, might enjoy powers correlative to her duties. But it was in the father that parental power or authority

---

[1] Stair, I, v, 1.
[2] *Ibid.*
[3] I, v, 6.
[4] I, vi, 53.

was "chiefly discovered."[5] He had, in effect, the *patria potestas* taken over, though in modified form, from the Romans even if it was seen as originating in the parental relation which both parents shared with the child. In relation to legitimate children, for most purposes of legal consequence, that power vested solely in him and from it he had the right of custody of the child, together with the right to be the child's tutor or curator. By the Guardianship Act 1973, however, the mother of a legitimate child was given the same rights and authority as the law allowed to the father,[6] and so the participation of both parents in parental power acquired a reality which it previously lacked. The illegitimate child was treated quite differently, and the father had no power over the child but was regarded, rather, as a stranger to the child except in so far as he was the subject of certain burdens and restrictions.[7] "A bastard has in law no father; and the person so-called is he who, from contact with the mother, is liable in the burdens of paternity without any of the privileges."[8] The mother of the illegitimate child had the right of custody,[9] and her rights as custodian were little different in relation to the child's person and upbringing from the parental powers over a legitimate child. She did not, however, have the right to be tutor or curator, and any right referable solely to guardianship did not, therefore, vest in her.

The governing statute today is the Law Reform (Parent and Child) (Scotland) Act 1986, which provides[10] that the fact that the child's parents are not or have not been married to one another shall be left out of account in establishing the legal relationship between the child and any other person; and accordingly such relationship shall have effect as if the parents were or had been married to one another. The child's illegitimacy is therefore irrelevant for the purpose of being subject to parental responsibilities and rights, though whether the parents are married or not will have significant effect on who can exercise these rights.[11] Parental rights can be vested in both parents, as we will see, and if they are then the rights and authority of mother and father are equal and exercisable by either without the other.[12] So each enjoys parental power severally. Some advantage is thereby given to the parent who takes the initiative. His or her acts are effective regardless of the attitude of the other parent. In the event of disagreement, however, application may be made to the court for an order relating to parental rights and the court may make such order relating to parental rights as it thinks fit,[13] though it cannot make any such order unless it is satisfied that to do so will be in the interests of the child.[14]

It remains the case, however, that parental responsibilities and parental rights

---

[5] *Ibid.*

[6] s. 10, repealed by Sched. 2 to the Law Reform (Parent and Child) (Scotland) Act 1986.

[7] *Clarke* v. *Carfin Coal Co.* (1891) 18 R.(H.L.) 63. The burden was that of aliment; the restrictions related to the law of marriage (see now the Marriage (Scotland) Act 1977, s. 2 and Sched. 1, as amended by the Marriage (Prohibited Degrees of Relationship) Act 1986, Sched. 2) and the law of incest (see now the Sexual Offences (Scotland) Act 1976, s. 2A(2)(*b*), as amended by the Incest and Related Offences (Scotland) Act 1986, s. 1).

[8] *Weepers* v. *Heritors and Kirk Session of Kennoway* (1844) 6 D. 1166, *per* Lord Jeffrey at p. 1173.

[9] See *ante* at pp. 70–71.

[10] s. 1(1).

[11] *Post* at pp. 167–168.

[12] Law Reform (Parent and Child) (Scotland) Act 1986, s. 2(4).

[13] *Ibid.*, s. 3(1).

[14] *Ibid.*, s. 3(2).

can be seen as different aspects of the same principle, which is that parents are to protect and nurture their children and have the power to do so. "[Parental rights] exist for the benefit of the child and they are justified only in so far as they enable the parent to perform his duties towards the child."[15] "Parental rights are derived from parental duty and exist only so long as they are needed for the protection of the person and property of the child."[16] It follows that a parent is not entitled to exercise his rights, or perform his duties, in such a way as would be positively detrimental to the child: his or her responsibilities would not be fulfilled by doing so. Though the term "parental rights" is commonly used, and has statutory sanction,[17] the term parental power or privilege is jurisprudentially more accurate. The rights of parents are not absolute, nor are they such that if inhibited the parent has a right to claim damages.[18] Rather, parental power is more in the nature of entitlement or privilege, whereby the law will recognise the parent's abilities competently to perform certain acts in relation to and on behalf of the child, and will give legal force to these acts. Parental power is also limited by the requirement that its exercise must satisfy the welfare test: the law of parent and child is moving clearly away from a rights-based system to a welfare-based system.[19] The decision in a case like *Macpherson* v. *Leishman*[20] would not be reached today. There, the mother of an illegitimate child raised an action for delivery of her child against the defender whom she had previously allowed to care for the child. The court ordered delivery of the child, on the ground that the mother had the "right" of custody; but it expressed regret at having to do so, on the ground that the child's welfare would be better served by leaving the child where it was. Today, this matter would be determined by the welfare test embodied in section 3(2) of the Law Reform (Parent and Child) (Scotland) Act 1986. It would however be wrong to say that parents have power only to do that which is *best* for their children, for in truth they have rather more discretion than that.[21] In exercising their rights and powers parents may do things that are neutral or even mildly disadvantageous,[22] so long as their actions are not clearly

---

[15] *Gillick* v. *West Norfolk and Wisbech Area Health Authority* [1985] 3 W.L.R. 830, at p. 841, *per* Lord Fraser of Tullybelton.

[16] *Ibid.* at p. 853, *per* Lord Scarman.

[17] See for example the Social Work (Scotland) Act 1968, s. 16, which talks of parental rights and powers; the Adoption (Scotland) Act 1978, s. 12 and s. 18, which talks of parental rights and duties, and the Law Reform (Parent and Child) (Scotland) Act 1986, ss. 2, 3 and 8, which talks of parental rights. The draft Bill attached to the Scottish Law Commission *Report on Family Law*, Scot. Law Com. No. 135, May 1992, continues to talk of parental rights, while adding the notion of parental responsibilities.

[18] *F.* v. *Wirral Metropolitan Borough Council* [1991] 2 All E.R. 648 (damages denied in an action for breach of the parent's right to be asked to consent to child's adoption).

[19] Though this is not universally welcomed: see Eekelaar, "The Wardship Jurisdiction, Children's Welfare, and Parents' Rights" (1991) 107 L.Q.R. 386. For an earlier analysis, see Eekelaar, "What Are Parental Rights?" (1973) 89 L.Q.R. 210.

[20] (1887) 14 R. 780.

[21] See the interesting discussion by McCall Smith, "Is Anything Left of Parental Rights?" in *Family Rights, Family Law, and Medical Advance* (eds. Sutherland and McCall Smith) (1990). He argues that while parental rights are usually presented as designed to benefit the child, in practice their *rationale* lies more often in the protection of an interest of the parent. The examples he gives are the right to the child's society and the right to determine the child's religious upbringing.

[22] For example piercing the ears of baby girls, circumcising baby boys for non-therapeutic reasons, subjecting the child to an unhealthy (but not seriously detrimental) diet, exposing it to unpopular

against the interests of the child. So for example while it may be best for a child to be vaccinated, the law will permit the parent to refuse consent thereto, for whatever reason, because that refusal does not positively harm the child; but a refusal of a blood transfusion that is necessary to prevent injury to the child is not permitted by the law.[23]

Inalienability of Parental Responsibilities and Rights

The *patria potestas* of the common law was usually said to be inalienable,[24] but that proposition always required some qualification. In its fullness the *patria potestas* belonged only to the father and could be transferred to no one else; it could not be surrendered although its exercise could be delegated.[25] So, it was incapable of voluntary alienation. But in its major aspects, it might be alienated by judicial order. If custody of the child was taken away from the father and given to another, direction of the child's education left in the hands of the custodian or separately regulated by the court, and the father superseded in the management of the child's estate by a judicial factor—all courses of action which, however rare, were competent long before modern statute intervened—the father was left with little but a shadow of the *patria potestas*. If, in the modern law, one is still to speak of parental responsibilities and rights as inalienable, considerably greater qualification must be made. Adoption and procedures for vesting parental rights and powers in local authorities or voluntary organisations effect a transfer of parental power which is virtually complete and the scope for custody orders and for the supersession of parents in the management of a child's estate has been much enlarged. It remains the case, however, that parental responsibilities and rights cannot irrevocably be alienated, during the life of the parent who has them, by voluntary act unsupported by judicial order.[26] Any agreement to transfer parental rights may, in principle, be revoked although whether the consequences of revocation should receive effect is now a question to be determined with regard to the welfare of the child as the paramount consideration.[27] Parental responsibilities cannot, short of adoption, competently be transferred. It is possible for a parent to arrange for his or her parental responsibilities to be met by other persons acting on the parent's behalf, but that does not affect any legal liability of the parent except, where the care of a child has been delegated, in respect of the immediate duties incumbent

---

religious beliefs, giving it a ridiculous name and, generally, acting in a way which may not be best for the child or may result in some unhappiness provided it stops short of cruelty or neglect.

[23] *Finlayson, Applicant*, 1989 S.C.L.R. 601. *Cf. Re B. (A Minor) (Wardship: Medical Treatment)* [1981] 1 W.L.R. 1412; *Re D. (A Minor) (Wardship: Sterilisation)* [1976] 1 All E.R. 326.

[24] *J. and J.* v. *C's Tutor*, 1948 S.C. 636, *per* Lord President Cooper at p. 642.

[25] *Kerrigan* v. *Hall* (1901) 4 F. 10; *Craig* v. *Greig and Macdonald* (1863) 1 M. 1172 at p. 1179. This rule now has a statutory basis in England: Children Act 1989, ss. 2(9)–(11).

[26] The provision in s. 10(2) of the Guardianship Act 1973 to this effect was repealed by Sched. 2 to the Law Reform (Parent and Child) (Scotland) Act 1986 and was there not re-enacted, since this is the position at common law in any case: according to the Scottish Law Commission "parental rights are *extra commercium* and cannot be validly renounced or transferred by mere private agreement": Scot. Law Com. No. 82, *Report on Illegitimacy*, at p. 131. In their *Report on Family Law*, Scot. Law Com. No. 135, May 1992, however, the Scottish Law Commission considered that it would be a helpful restatement to have the matter put on a statutory basis: see draft Family Law Bill, cl. 3(4)–(6).

[27] Law Reform (Parent and Child) (Scotland) Act 1986, s. 3(2).

on a person having care of a child; and that only to the extent that the delegation was reasonable when regard is had to the character and competence of the delegate and any circumstances affecting risk of harm to the child, for ultimate responsibility cannot be delegated.

WHO MAY EXERCISE PARENTAL RESPONSIBILITIES AND RIGHTS

Vesting of Parental Responsibilities and Rights

It may be that more than one person possesses parental responsibilities and rights at any one time. Whoever possesses a particular parental right or power may exercise that right or power without the consent of any other person who has the same right or power, unless the deed or decree conferring the right otherwise provides.[28]

Natural Parents

While the existence of the unborn child can give rise to certain legal consequences, these are not, for the reasons discussed elsewhere,[29] to be classified as parental responsibilities or rights. Parental responsibilities and rights inhere in the nature of the parental relationship and can, therefore, vest in the parent as soon as that natural relationship is created, that is, on birth. While this will always be so in relation to the mother,[30] it will be the case in relation to the father only if he is married to the mother or was married to the mother at the time of the child's conception or subsequently.[31] If the father marries the mother after the birth of the child then parental rights vest in him on the date of that marriage. The marriage may be voidable, or void so long as the father believed in good faith at the time of the marriage that it was valid, this whether the belief was due to an error of fact or an error of law.[32] If a father is never married to the mother at a time after the conception of the child then he has no parental rights until such time as these are conferred upon him by order of the court under section 3(1) of the Law Reform (Parent and Child) (Scotland) Act 1986.[33] In that event parental rights will vest in him on the date of the decree, or on any other date the court may determine.[34]

When a mother or a father has parental rights in a child this means that all the parental rights recognised by the law as such vest in the mother or the father (or both). "Parental rights" is defined to mean: "guardianship, custody or access, as the case may require, and any right or authority relating to the welfare or upbringing of a child conferred on a parent by any rule of law."[35] In substance

---

[28] Law Reform (Parent and Child) (Scotland) Act 1986, s. 2(4).

[29] *Ante* at pp. 111–114.

[30] Law Reform (Parent and Child) (Scotland) Act 1986, s. 2(1)(*a*).

[31] s. 2(1)(*b*).

[32] s. 2(2).

[33] *Montgomery* v. *Lockwood*, 1987 S.C.L.R. 525 (a claim for access by an unmarried father). *Cf. Re C. and Anr. (Minors)* [1992] 2 All E.R. 86.

[34] This difference in the position of the father from that of the mother is to be compared with the principle laid down in Art. 18(1) of the UN Convention on the Rights of the Child (28 *International Legal Materials* 1448, ratified by the UK, December 16, 1991), which provides as follows: "State parties shall use their best efforts to ensure recognition of the principle that both parents have common responsibilities for the upbringing and development of the child."

[35] s. 8, as amended by the Age of Legal Capacity (Scotland) Act 1991.

however all parental rights can be subsumed under either the heading of custody or of guardianship. It follows that a parent with parental rights has rights *qua* parent over both the person of the child (this flowing from the right of custody) and over the property of the child (this flowing from the right of guardianship), and in any other respect that is necessary to fulfil the parental responsibilities of nurture and protection of the child. The granting or withdrawing to or from one parent of one of these rights does not affect the position of the other parent, nor does it affect the other right in relation to either parent.

Custodians

The control and care of the child's person and of his upbringing vest in the custodian of the child, that is, the person who has the right to have the child living with him or her or otherwise to regulate the child's residence. The powers flowing from the day-to-day care of the child vest, therefore, in a custodian who is not a parent[36] just as they would in a parent. It is otherwise with those aspects of parental rights that relate to a child's property and the management of his business affairs. These do not fall within the ambit of custody and so are unaffected by the making of a custody order.[37] It may be debated, as an abstract question, whether control of education and religious upbringing properly pertains to a custodian, but as a practical matter the custodian will have effective control unless it is otherwise regulated by the court. Consent to medical treatment of children under the age of 16 raises similar doubts. Medical treatment can scarcely be dissociated from control and care of the person which is of the essence of custody, and in many cases practical necessity would seem to dictate that the custodian should have power to consent. On the other hand, the providing of consent to medical treatment is the denial to the patient of a right of action against the doctor for assault, and the giving of consent can therefore be analysed as a legal act in relation to which the parent represents the child, so making consent an aspect of legal representation or guardianship. Questions remain therefore of whether (a) where a child is in the custody of someone other than a parental guardian, the consent of a parent should be obtained if there is opportunity to do so and the decision entails long-term consequences for the child, and (b) whether a parent who does not have custody retains power, through guardianship, to consent in the event of the failure to do so of the custodian, be he the other parent or a third party. In both cases the question is one of the effect of a custody order on parental responsibilities and rights. In the absence of a custody order either parent may consent, but there are dangers in allowing a parent who has been divested of custody to interfere in the medical treatment of his child which do not apply where he shares custody with the other parent. A non-custodial parent, though he remains the child's guardian, probably does not have the responsibility to provide day-to-day medical care for the child, and it may follow from that that he has no right to do so. But the better view, it is submitted, is that the right to consent to medical treatment inheres in both the custodian and the guardian, and that each can act independently of the other. If either

---

[36] *i.e.* a person in whose favour a custody order, or an order vesting parental rights, has been made.
[37] *Kirk* v. *Scottish Gas Board*, 1968 S.C. 328.

believes that the consent of the other puts the child's welfare at risk, he is able to seek the intervention of the court.[38]

Custody carries with it the obligation to care for the child both in protecting him from harm, and, more positively, attending to his nurture and wellbeing. In a certain, if limited, sense[39] the custodian has, therefore, a duty to aliment the child. He must at least see that what is immediately necessary for the child's physical support is supplied, whether the need be for food, clothing, medicine and medical treatment or shelter. But, although certain immediate responsibilities for aliment may rest on him, to the extent that if the child should be neglected as a result of his failure he cannot plead in defence that he was not given the means by those on whom the alimentary obligation ultimately lay, that does not derogate from the obligation of those ultimately responsible. A custodian is, therefore, entitled to relief from the parent or other person on whom the alimentary obligation properly lies for necessary expenditure by him in respect of the child's aliment.[40] He may also sue on behalf of the child for an award of aliment to cover future expenditure.[41]

Guardians

Unless the guardian has custody of his ward, his powers and obligations are virtually confined to the management of the ward's estate. The education of a pupil child whose father had died was, however, at common law, subject to the direction of the tutor even if the tutor did not have custody. Accordingly, the mother's custody of the child might be disturbed in so far as was necessary to give effect to the tutor's scheme of education, although, in the event of dispute, the court could adjudicate between mother and tutor and determine the preferable course of education.[42] The law on these matters is, however, now obsolete. On the death of either parent the surviving parent acts alone, or along with any guardian nominated by the deceased parent or appointed by the court.[43] Each can act independently of the other,[44] and disputes are to be resolved in accordance with the welfare principle embodied in section 3 of the Law Reform (Parent and Child) (Scotland) Act 1986. The position is, it is thought, little different on the death or other failure of both parents. If a custodian has been appointed

---

[38] These problems will disappear if the proposal of the Scottish Law Commission in their *Report on Family Law*, draft Bill, cl. 5 that persons with no parental responsibilities or rights but with care and control of the child may give consent to medical or dental treatment, is accepted.

[39] *i.e.* a sense other than that of the Family Law (Scotland) Act 1985 (discussed *post* at chap. 11).

[40] Under the Family Law (Scotland) Act 1985 an action for aliment for a child may be brought by the child himself or on his behalf if he is under 18 by (1) his father or mother; or (2) a person who is entitled to, or is seeking, or has, custody or care of the child (s. 2(4), as amended by the Age of Legal Capacity (Scotland) Act 1991, Sched. 2) and an award of aliment may be backdated to the date of commencement of the proceedings or on special cause shown to an earlier date (s. 3(1)(c)). It is therefore open to a custodian to obtain relief for past expenditure by means of a backdated award in an action for aliment, and that remedy will be available in an action at the instance of a parent custodian against the other parent. The requirement that special cause be shown may, however, present an obstacle in many cases. In such cases a custodian who is not a parent will have a remedy by way of an action for payment founded on the obligation of relief against the parent or other person properly liable for aliment.

[41] *Ibid.*

[42] Fraser (3rd ed.) at p. 295 and cases cited there.

[43] See *post* at pp. 384–390.

[44] Law Reform (Parent and Child) (Scotland) Act 1986, s. 2(4).

by the court, he will have the direction of the child's education unless the court directs otherwise. In that case, however, the guardian retains a certain negative power in that, subject to control by the court, he may decline to employ his ward's estate for a scheme of education of which he does not approve. Even that power is, however, liable to be elusory. The guardian is under a duty to employ the estate under his charge for the education and aliment of the child so far as it is required for that purpose[45] and, in the event of dispute between custodian and guardian, the matter must be resolved by the court with regard to the welfare of the child as the paramount consideration.[46] The principles on which the ward's estate is to be applied to his education and aliment pertain to the management of that estate and are considered later.[47] A guardian who on the death or other failure of both parents has custody of the child or who is given custody by order of the court, has, of course, the same powers as any other custodian.

Persons with Children in their Care

The responsibilities and rights of persons, other than parents and those legally entitled to custody, who have children in their care will vary considerably according to circumstances. In this category may be included foster parents, persons who have actual custody or day-to-day control without any custody order or other legal title, persons to whose care parents have temporarily entrusted their children, child-minders, persons in whose charge children are for purposes of medical care, school teachers, leaders of organised groups of children, and generally anyone into whose care a child, in fact, passes. The general duty is to care for the child. It is the content of that duty that will vary with circumstances. Often it will be enough to take reasonable measures to protect the child from harm. But a person in whose care a child is must see that while in his care, the child does not suffer from neglect and, where care is continuous and extended over a period so as to approximate to custody, there may be a more positive duty of nurture and promotion of welfare such as a custodian has. A person who has the actual custody of a child has the same duties to secure the child's education as are laid on a parent by the Education (Scotland) Act 1980.[48]

The powers of a person with children in his care are those that are necessary for the exercise of his duties towards the children. Thus, the person who has the care of the child may restrain and control him and exercise discipline to the extent that is necessary for that purpose. He stands, if but temporarily and for limited purposes, *in loco parentis* and has the powers of a parent so far as reasonably required for the discharge of his duties and the achievement of the legitimate purposes for which the child is in his care. Where the child has been entrusted to him by a parent, the parent may, by delegation, enlarge his duties and his powers but cannot thereby absolve him from the duty of care for the child or the powers necessary for the exercise of that duty because these arise, independently of delegation, from the *in loco parentis* relationship. Questions

---

[45] Stair, I, vi, 3; Bankton, I, vii, 28; Erskine, I, vii, 7 and 24.
[46] Law Reform (Parent and Child) (Scotland) Act 1986, s. 3(2).
[47] *Post* at pp. 366–367.
[48] s. 30 as applied to a person who has the actual custody of a child by s. 135(1).

may again be posed about choice of education and consent to medical treatment. Clearly, a person in whose temporary care a child is has, in general, no powers in relation to either education or medical treatment; but he may have a duty to secure that such medical treatment is made available as is practicable and the occasion demands. If the child does not have the legal capacity to provide consent himself,[49] the treatment may nevertheless be provided without consent, so long as there exists an emergency, that is, an immediate necessity to act in order to save the life, or avoid serious permanent impairment of the health, of a child.[50] Where there is no emergency, and the child cannot give personal consent, reference should normally be made to the parent or person with equivalent powers. Cases may, however, be posited in which consent is required from someone other than the child and the parent is incapable of consenting, or is, for some other reason, not available to give consent and likely to remain so for a considerable time. In such cases, it is thought that the person who has actual custody of the child has the same powers as a person who has legal custody under a decree of the court and so may consent to treatment necessary for the child's welfare.[51] There is, however, an overlap here with cases of emergency, in which no consent at all is required. The difference lies, it is submitted, in the immediacy of the necessity which is inherent in emergency and not otherwise. Similar situations may arise to which an actual custodian, or person who has similar long-term care of a child, may, by default of others, require to take decisions concerning a child's education and must, therefore, have the power to do so; and certainly an actual custodian must have such power in relation to a child's education as is necessary to enable him to fulfil the duty laid upon him by the Education (Scotland) Act 1980.[52]

Other Persons

Parental responsibilities and rights may vest in other persons as a result of various statutory provisions. In relation to adoption, "parental rights and duties" are vested in the adoptive parent or parents when the adoption order is made.[53] When a child is freed for adoption, vesting in the adoption agency takes place on the making of the freeing order.[54] A local authority resolution under the Social Work (Scotland) Act 1968 has the effect of vesting "parental rights and powers" in the local authority or voluntary organisation when the resolution is passed.[55] "Any person claiming interest" can make an application for "an order relating to parental rights"[56] and the court can confer parental rights, or one such right,

---

[49] *i.e.* is not, in the opinion of a qualified medical practitioner, capable of understanding the nature and possible consequences of the procedure or treatment: Age of Legal Capacity (Scotland) Act 1991, s. 2(4).

[50] See further, *post* at pp. 182–189.

[51] See Scot. Law Com. *Report on Family Law*, draft Bill, cl. 5, in which a person (over 16) with care and control of a child may do what is reasonable in the circumstances of the case for the purpose of safeguarding the child's health, development or welfare, and may in particular consent to medical or dental treatment.

[52] s. 30, as applied to a person who has the actual custody of a child by s. 135(1).

[53] Adoption (Scotland) Act 1978, s. 12.

[54] *Ibid.*, s. 18(5).

[55] Social Work (Scotland) Act 1968, s. 16.

[56] Law Reform (Parent and Child) (Scotland) Act 1986, s. 3(1).

upon the applicant or any other person. Title to raise the action is not limited by artificial restraints,[57] though it is unlikely that the court will confer full parental rights on a stranger to the child. Theoretically, however, this is possible, so long as the applicant can persuade the court that to do so will be in the interests of the child.[58] Any rights conferred will vest on the making of the order, or at any other time determined by the court. The phrases "parental rights," "rights and duties," "rights and powers" and "responsibilities and rights" all mean substantially the same thing and include the parental rights defined in the Law Reform (Parent and Child) (Scotland) Act 1986[59] together with the parental responsibilities for the fulfilment of which these rights are conferred.

Termination of Parental Responsibilities and Rights

Natural Termination

Parental responsibilities and rights are extinguished naturally by death of either parent or the child. The rights of guardianship, custody and access are terminated by the child's attaining the age of 16.[60] Parental rights other than guardianship, custody and access are terminated by the child's attaining the age of 18[61]: it is unclear what rights are intended to be covered by this provision. Other statutory rights will terminate according to the rules in the statutes that create them.[62] It is unlikely that there are any responsibilities and rights existing independently of statute that do not fall within the content of either guardianship, custody or access and which do not therefore end when the child reaches the age of 16 years.[63]

Legal Termination

Parental responsibilities and rights can be terminated by court order or local authority resolution. Most obviously the making of an adoption order has this effect,[64] as does the making of an order freeing a child for adoption.[65] A local authority resolution vesting in themselves or in a voluntary organisation parental rights and powers[66] shall act to divest the parent who had these rights and powers (though it does not relieve any person from liability to maintain or contribute to the maintenance of the child[67]). More generally the Court of Session or the

---

[57] *Syme* v. *Cunningham*, 1973 S.L.T. (Notes) 40; *Whyte* v. *Hardie*, 1990 S.C.L.R. 23; *F.* v. *F.* 1991 S.L.T. 357, and see *post* at pp. 202–204.

[58] Law Reform (Parent and Child) (Scotland) Act 1986, s. 3(2).

[59] s. 8: "guardianship, custody and access and any right and authority relating to the welfare or upbringing of the child conferred on a parent by any rule of law."

[60] Law Reform (Parent and Child) (Scotland) Act 1986, s. 8: the position could perhaps have been put more clearly, but the proposition given in the text must, it is submitted, follow from this interpretation section, which defines "child" to mean "in relation to guardianship, custody and access a child under the age of 16 years."

[61] *Ibid.*, with the same comment.

[62] See for example, Access to Health Records Act, s. 4.

[63] The *Report on Family Law*, Scot. Law Com. No. 135, May 1992, reminds us that the definition in s. 8 of "parental rights" was given merely as a holding measure (para. 2. 18).

[64] Adoption (Scotland) Act 1978, s. 12(3).

[65] *Ibid.*, s. 18(5).

[66] Social Work (Scotland) Act 1968, s. 16.

[67] *Ibid.*, s. 17(6).

sheriff court has the power to make such order relating to parental rights as it thinks fit[68] and it can therefore divest a parent of parental responsibilities and rights when it is satisfied that to do so will be in the interests of the child.[69] The granting of custody to one parent by the court is taken to be the denial of that right to the other parent.

Renunciation and Forfeiture

In addition to the circumstances already discussed, release from parental power may be obtained by express renunciation by the parent or by conduct on the parent's part amounting to forfeiture. Renunciation may be inferred as from "an apparent intention to abandon" the parental power and leave the child to its own guidance.[70] Forfeiture may be by "atrocity" or otherwise dealing unnaturally with the child or showing an unwillingness to discharge parental obligations.[71] Here again, the interrelation of power and obligation can be seen and renunciation today would not relieve the parent of his or her legal liabilities. There is no reason that there should not be renunciation or forfeiture by one parent while the parental power of the other remains intact. In the modern context, renunciation and forfeiture are likely to arise only as elements in a welfare decision.

---

[68] Law Reform (Parent and Child) (Scotland) Act 1986, s. 3(1).

[69] *Ibid.*, s. 3(2).

[70] Fraser (3rd ed.) at p. 88; *Harvey* v. *Harvey* (1860) 22 D. 1198, *per* Lord Justice-Clerk Inglis at p. 1208; *Fraser* v. *Robertson* (1867) 5 M. 819.

[71] Stair, I, v, 13.

CHAPTER 6

PARTICULAR PARENTAL RESPONSIBILITIES AND RIGHTS

Custody, or the Right of Residence

Parental power over a child's person is typified by the concept of custody and the power of physical control which that implies. Custody is more the source of a number of different parental responsibilities and rights over the person of the child than one such parental right in itself, but as the law moves towards regarding the right as one of determining residence, collateral rights will less readily be inferred.[1] Custody as hitherto understood in Scotland, though it has never been defined with any precision, is assumed to include the right to determine how the child is to be brought up, as well as where. It is "the right to determine, generally, the place and manner in which the child's time is spent".[2] The right of custody therefore carries with it many, if not all, of the rights discussed in this chapter. The concept of custody itself, and the making of custody orders, will be examined in detail in Chapter 7.

Custody at common law was a right exercisable only over the pupil child, and even when custody was extended to all children under the age of 16,[3] which is still the case today,[4] it remained a right far more apt for the pupil child than the minor child. In relation to the latter there was no right of dominion and so the power had not the comprehensive, and, within the welfare principle, absolute character that it had in the case of a pupil. Although there continued to be some right of control, the emphasis was not on control but on counsel and aid. The extension of the capacity, or rather lack of it, of the pupil child to all children under the age of 16[5] might be taken to extend the dominion custody gave over pupil children to all children under 16; but it is submitted that this would misinterpret the statutory provision, which extends the child's lack of capacity rather than a parent's dominion. Parental power diminishes as the child grows older. The right of custody has been described as "a dwindling right which the courts will hesitate to enforce against the wishes of the child, the older he is. It starts with a right of control and ends with little more than advice."[6] This was true for Scots, no less than for English, law, at least in the case of children over pupillarity. Today, the right to counsel and aid the child which characterised the custodial right over the minor child before 1991 may be all that remains of the custodial right over a particular child who has acquired the mental maturity and practical abil-

---

[1] *Report on Family Law*, Scot. Law Com. No. 135, May 1992, paras. 2.28–2.30.
[2] Thomson (2nd ed.) at p. 177.
[3] Custody of Children (Scotland) Act 1939, s. 1.
[4] Law Reform (Parent and Child) (Scotland) Act 1986, s. 8.
[5] Age of Legal Capacity (Scotland) Act 1991, s. 1(2).
[6] *Per* Lord Denning M.R. in *Hewer* v. *Bryant* [1969] 3 All E.R. 578 at p. 582, approved in *Gillick* v. *West Norfolk and Wisbech Area Health Authority* [1985] 3 W.L.R. 830, *per* Lord Fraser at p. 843.

ity to determine his or her own lifestyle. This can be illustrated for example in relation to religious upbringing: in the early years of childhood a parent has the right to direct the religious observances of the child, but in later years (the commencement of which cannot be subject to legal rule) the religious beliefs of the child are a matter for the child him or herself. This is similarly the case with medical treatment: the parent can decide, subject to the child's welfare, when the child cannot decide himself, but when the child does acquire legal capacity to give personal consent to medical treatment the parent's right becomes little more than one to advise,[7] and may indeed disappear completely.[8] Custody is, therefore, a diminishing right whose content dwindles as the child grows older and acquires personal beliefs and philosophies and the practical ability to put them into effect. Scots law no longer adopts, if it ever, in truth, did, a strict dichotomy between full dominion before and minimal control after puberty. In the case of real dispute between the parent and the child, concerning some aspect of its upbringing, either may apply to the court for an order relating to parental rights, but in that case, as we will see,[9] the matter is not determined by analysing whose "right" is greater, but rather by the court's obligation to give priority to the interests of the child as the paramount consideration.[10]

Control of Residence

Control of a child's residence is inherent in custody. Therefore the residence of a child may, subject to proper consideration for his welfare, be determined by his parents as custodians. A child who is not subject to custody is free to determine his own residence subject only to such constraints as may be put upon him by lack of capacity to enter into transactions to give his intention effect, to statutory provisions for the protection of children, and to the practical necessities of his situation. Therefore at common law (which contemplated a custodial régime for all pupil children although some, in the absence of judicial decree, might not in fact be subject to custody) it could be said that a pupil child could not choose his residence. A minor, on the other hand, whose parents were dead could, if he were not the subject of a custody order, determine his own place of residence.[11] With the passing of the Age of Legal Capacity (Scotland) Act 1991 the position of the common law pupil has become in many respects that of the child under 16: this might suggest that the pupil's inability to determine his own residence has been extended, but it is submitted that this is not so for reasons already advanced in connection with the extent of the parental power of custody. That inability rested on practical as well as legal considerations; today it may in some cases be practicable for a child below 16 to live away from his parents, and the 1991 Act may be open to the interpretation that, in some circumstances, he has

---

[7] The right to advise does *not* include the right to be consulted in all cases: see Norrie, *Family Planning Practice and the Law* (1991), at pp. 102–105; *contra*, Thomson, "The *Gillick* Case and Parental Rights in Scots Law: Another View," 1985 S.L.T. (News) 223.

[8] See *post* at p. 185.

[9] *Post* at pp. 206–208.

[10] Law Reform (Parent and Child) (Scotland) Act 1986, s. 3(2).

[11] *Graham* v. *Graham* (1780) Mor. 8934.

the legal capacity to enter into transactions for that purpose.[12] Any conflict between the child's wishes and the parent's right has to be resolved with regard to the welfare of the child as the paramount consideration but the question of the extent of the parent's right is to some extent an economic and practical one measured in the light of the parent's obligations. In considering the child's welfare, the parent must have regard to his reasonable requirements in the way of education or of following his occupation or employment, but he is not in all circumstances bound to follow the child's wishes even where he can afford to do so and the child is mentally mature. The parent's obligation of aliment is to provide such support as is reasonable in the circumstances having regard *inter alia* to the needs and resources both of the child and of himself.[13] It is in that context that choice of residence has to be seen. So, often the child will have little real choice. Where he is dependent on his parent he must accept what the parent provides, either in the family home or elsewhere, if that is indicated by his needs and provided it is reasonably adequate in the circumstances. If, on the other hand, the child is able to maintain himself, there is authority for the view that the child above the age of common law pupillarity may even during the parents' lifetime choose his residence if he is of sufficient maturity and understanding to do so.[14] There is nothing in the Age of Legal Capacity (Scotland) Act 1991 which limits this power.[15] It would follow that if a child, even when below 16, has the means to live other than with his parent (or is given the means by others), and has the maturity to understand the consequences of such independence, the parent would not have the right to insist that the child resides where the parent chooses unless he could show that it was in the interests of the child's welfare that the child's choice should, despite this maturity, be overridden.[16] The only remaining problematic case from a legal standpoint would seem to be that of the child below 16 who has the means to maintain himself but lacks the requisite maturity and understanding to choose his own residence. Such a case must fall within the scope of the parental power and the parent may determine

---

[12] Nichols suggests that for a child who is afraid of his parents to enter into a contract with a shelter to live there would be a "reasonable transaction commonly entered into" by someone in his circumstances, and therefore one that the child has legal capacity to undertake: "Can They or Can't They?" 1991 S.L.T. (News) 395 at pp. 397–398.

[13] Family Law (Scotland) Act 1986, ss. 1(2) and 4(1).

[14] Bankton, I, vi, 1, p. 153 thought that a minor was without qualification free to choose his own residence, and that view is followed by More (*Lectures*, p. 87, Notes on Stair, C., pp. xxxi and xxxii), under reference to *Graham* v. *Graham, supra, Marshall* v. *McDowell* (1741) Mor. 8930 and *Anstruther* v. *Murray* (1694) 1 Fountainhall 613, but these are cases in which the father was dead and so the paternal power was extinguished. More's argument for the minor's freedom to marry immediately on the expiry of pupillarity (now on attaining the age of 16) is, however, cogent. Erskine, I, vi, 53, although often cited for the contrary view, is consistent with the minor's freedom to leave home and set up his own residence. Stair, I, v, 4 and 13 takes a larger view of the parental powers than would now be accepted. It is however reasonably clear from *Harvey* v. *Harvey* (1860) 22 D. 1198, *Edgar* v. *Fisher's Trs.* (1894) 21 R. 1076 and *Craig* v. *Greig and McDonald* (1863) 1 M. 1172 that a minor's choice of residence is subject to some parental restraint to be exercised in the light of the minor's maturity and understanding and with regard to his welfare.

[15] See Nichols, *op. cit.* S. 1 (2) of the 1991 Act does not affect the matter because it does no more than provide a rule of statutory interpretation and, unlike other provisions of the Act, has no bearing on the common law position of the child except in so far as that has been modified by the statute.

[16] Law Reform (Parent and Child) (Scotland) Act 1986, s. 3 (2), which applies in any proceedings relating to parental rights.

the child's residence in accordance with what is for his welfare. It would not be "reasonable" for such a child to choose his own residence. Those aspects of custody that can flake away from the parent before the child reaches 16 will do so only when the child has both the mental maturity and the initiative to shake them off.

Discipline

It also belongs to parental power over children to exercise "that degree of discipline and moderate chastisement upon them, which their perverseness of temper or inattention calls for".[17] This aspect of parental power was not easily reconciled with dicta on the nature of that power in relation to minors at common law, but it was never suggested that it ended with pupillarity although, according to the circumstances of the case, the age and maturity of the child were among the factors relevant to the reasonableness of its exercise. If discipline is a power that flows from custody then it now ends when custody ends, that is at age 16; it may also flow, however, from the mere having of a child in care, in which case it lasts, theoretically, for so long as that care lasts, though in all cases its exercise will have to be qualified by practical considerations.[18] The object is the welfare of the child and that object "while it sanctions, also limits the right."[19] So punishment must be moderate and reasonable in relation to its end. If it is, then it constitutes a defence to a charge of cruelty to the child,[20] to a charge of criminal assault,[21] and to a claim for damages for civil assault.[22]

Delegability of Disciplinary Power

It has been argued that because what is at stake is a privilege and not a right, the exercise of a parental power of discipline cannot be delegated.[23] It can be accepted that there is no right to exercise discipline in the strict sense of an enforceable claim in respect of which there is a corresponding duty to satisfy the claim and that, on such an analysis, classification as a privilege is apt. It is also true that the powers of those *in loco parentis* arise from their quasi-parental relationship with the child and not from delegation. As a consequence, where the *in loco parentis* relationship arises independently of contract express or implied, a parent has no right to control the reasonable exercise of disciplinary power such as he would have in the case of a delegate.[24] That does not, however, mean that delegation is excluded. Generally privileges are not delegable, but an analysis on the basis of claims with correlative duties, which leads to the con-

---

[17] Erskine, I, vi, 53.

[18] "A mother, for example, may find difficulty in disciplining her son for refusing to dry the dishes if he is a 15-year-old, 12-stone prop forward": Thomson at p. 186.

[19] Fraser (3rd Ed.) at p. 83.

[20] Children and Young Persons (Scotland) Act 1937, s. 12(7).

[21] *Guest* v. *Annan*, 1988 S.C.C.R. 275; *Stewart* v. *Thain*, 1981 J.C. 13. See Shiels, "Reasonable Chastisement by Parents," 1990 Scolag 115.

[22] See, *e.g. Muckarsie* v. *Dickson* (1848) 11 D. 4; *Ewart* v. *Brown* (1882) 10 R. 163.

[23] Wallington, "Corporal Punishment in Schools," 1972 J.R. 124 at pp. 128–134.

[24] See Wallington, *supra* at pp. 143–144 and, among cases there cited, especially *McShane* v. *Paton*, 1922 J.C. 26 at p. 31 *per* Lord Salvesen. *Cf. Byrd* v. *Wither*, 1991 S.L.T. 206, in which the sole question was whether the force used by the cohabitant of a child's mother was reasonable or not: it seems to have been assumed that the accused, who "acted as a father on a day to day basis to the child," had the power to chastise the child.

clusion that a privilege is involved, is not really appropriate to questions of this kind. It is not a right in the strict sense but parental power or authority that is in issue and there is no reason for excluding delegation of its exercise in this aspect any more than in general nurture or education.[25] A widow or other single mother with an unruly son would, therefore, have the power to authorise, say, the boy's uncle or grandfather to discipline him.

Purpose

The authorities bring out clearly that the power of discipline is related to and limited by the purposes for which a person has a child in his care and the resultant duties. The parental power to discipline a child flows from the duty to further the child's welfare and, importantly, to educate the child. For this reason the power vests in schoolteachers, though only as part of their educative function. "There is no doubt that a school teacher is vested with disciplinary powers to enable him to do his educational work and to maintain proper order in class and in school."[26] "It is clear that a teacher of a public school, being bound to see that the pupils behave correctly, is entitled to administer chastisement when the pupils deserve it."[27] So the power of discipline is often said to rest on the relationship between teacher and pupil.[28] No peculiar significance attaches, however, to that particular relationship, which must now, in any case, be seen in the light of the abolition of the right to administer corporal punishment to pupils in state and other prescribed schools.[29] It is but an instance of the *in loco parentis* relationship which anyone with children in his care enjoys. The schoolteacher's power of discipline is, therefore, the analogue of the parental power and arises from the quasi-parental character of the relationship.[30] Section 48A(1) of the Education (Scotland) Act 1980[31] provides that where in "any proceedings" it is shown that corporal punishment has been given to a pupil by a teacher in a public school, the giving of such punishment cannot be justified on the ground that it was done in pursuance of a right exercisable by the teacher by virtue of his position as such. This does not affect the right to discipline that inheres in anyone *in loco parentis*, otherwise than as a teacher in a public school. Despite the generality of the words "any proceedings" in section 48A(1), this is limited by section 48A (4) to civil proceedings, for it is provided there that anything which previously would have been reasonable chastisement, were it not for section 48A(1), is not an offence. The result of this is that reasonable chastisement remains a defence to a criminal charge of a assault but is no longer a defence to a civil claim for damages. Again, however, the criminal defence remains available to anyone

---

[25] The decision in *Stewart* v. *Thain*, 1981 J.C. 13 can be interpreted as an example either of a teacher acting *in loco parentis* or of a teacher acting as the agent exercising powers delegated from the parents.

[26] *Gray* v. *Hawthorn*, 1964 J.C. 69, *per* Lord Guthrie at p. 75.

[27] *Muckarsie* v. *Dickson, supra, per* Lord President Boyle at p. 5.

[28] *McShane* v. *Paton* 1922 J.C. 26, *per* Lord Salveseon at p. 31; *Brown* v. *Hilsom*, 1924 J.C. 1, *per* Lord Cullen at p. 5.

[29] Education (Scotland) Act 1980, s. 48A, as inserted by Education (No. 2) Act 1986, s. 48. For a discussion, see Phillips, "Teachers, Corporal Punishment, and the Criminal Law: A Retrospect and Prospect," 1992 J.R. 3.

[30] *Stewart* v. *Thain, supra*, at p. 18, *per* Lord Justice-Clerk Wheatley.

[31] See Phillips, *op. cit.* at pp. 14–16.

who can trace their power to the parental power, and it is not a defence limited to teachers alone.

European Convention on Human Rights

The infliction of corporal punishment has raised questions under the European Convention on Human Rights,[32] which, by Article 3, prohibits inhuman and degrading punishment. In no Scottish case has the exercise of disciplinary powers over children been held to contravene that prohibition, but the developing jurisprudence of the European Court of Human Rights, although its decisions are not directly enforceable, may influence views of reasonableness.[33] The Convention also requires respect for the religious and philosphical views of parents and that too may have consequences, if indirect, for the exercise of disciplinary powers by person *in loco parentis*.[34]

Reasonable and Moderate Chastisement

The problematic cases in the exercise of the power of discipline have been cases on the use of corporal punishment. This is because this form of discipline would, without the justification of being a parental right, amount to a civil or criminal wrong, which, for example, imposing extra homework would not.[35] It is only reasonable and moderate chastisement that is permitted, and doubt may now hang over the traditional Scottish methods of corporal punishment within schools. What is today acceptable punishment by parents may well be limited to slaps and the like that do not cause injury, extensive bruising or long lasting pain. Excess constitutes an assault. Standards of reasonableness and moderation are subject to development, and for that reason the older cases may form an imperfect guide. What constitutes excess may, in any event, vary according to the circumstances of the case including the age,[36] sex[37] and any known disabilities

---

[32] See *Campbell and Cosans* v. *United Kingdom* [1982] 4 E.H.R.R. 293; *Costello-Roberts* v. *United Kingdom*, March 25, 1993.

[33] In *Costello-Roberts, supra*, though the majority (five to four) held that corporal punishment by "slippering" a seven-year-old child was not inhuman and degrading punishment when the parents had not indicated any opposition to corporal punishment, they were careful to point out that their judgment was not to be taken to approve in any way the retention of corporal punishment as part of the discipline régime of a school. In the *Report on Family Law* (Scot. Law Com. No. 135), the Scottish Law Commission propose that it should not be regarded as moderate and reasonable chastisement ever to strike a child (i) with a stick, belt or other object of whatever description, or (ii) in such a way as causes injury, or pain or discomfort which lasts for more than a very short time: draft Bill, cl. 4.

[34] The United Kingdom was held in breach of this provision in *Campbell and Cosans* v. *United Kingdom, supra,* and that led directly to the passing of the Education (No. 2) Act 1986. *Cf.* Art. 28 of the UN Convention on the Rights of the Child (28 *International Legal Materials* 1448, ratified by the UK, Dec. 16, 1991) which states that school discipline must be "administered in a manner consistent with the child's human dignity and in conformity with the present Convention" (see also Art. 37 prohibiting cruel, inhuman and degrading treatment or punishment).

[35] Keeping a child locked in a bedroom might, conceivably, amount to wrongful imprisonment, if it were for an unreasonable length of time, or in unreasonable conditions. It has been held in England that a parent with parental rights can be guilty of this wrong: see *R.* v. *Rahman, The Times,* June 5, 1985. If unnecessary suffering or injury to health were likely it would, in any event, be a offence under s. 12 (1) of the Children and Young Persons (Scotland) Act 1937 and if foreseeable harm resulted it would be a civil wrong even if the description "unlawful imprisonment" be thought inappropriate.

[36] *Peebles* v. *MacPhail*, 1990 S.L.T. 245 (two-year-old child).

[37] See *Scorgie* v. *Lawrie* (1883) 10 R. 610, *per* Lord Young at p. 613.

or weaknesses of the child. Factors such as the nature and context of the punishment, the manner and method of its execution, its duration and its physical and mental effects are all to be taken into account.[37a] It has been said that "to slap a child of two years old on the face, knocking him over, is an act as remote from reasonable chastisement as one can possibly imagine".[38] Unforeseen injury does not itself show that there was excess,[39] but punishment which is intended to cause significant physical injury or which is inflicted in disregard of a readily foreseeable risk of such injury is clearly excessive. The fact that the parent is angry when punishing the child does not in itself turn moderate chastisement into an unreasonable punishment inflicted vindictively and with the *mens rea* necessary to constitute an assault.[40] Cases of emotional injury are more difficult to categorise and so less susceptible of proof, but it is thought that punishment that goes beyond the reasonable objects of discipline and is degrading or grossly humiliating is excessive.[41] As in the case of children suffering from physical disability so known cases of serious emotional disturbance or mental defect may give rise to special considerations. Normally the court will not enter into a consideration of whether or not a punishment, not excessive in degree, was justified because in that matter a large discretion is allowed to the parent or teacher.[42] Where, however, a punishment is inflicted without any justification at all, or is entirely out of proportion to the triviality of the offence, it may be wrongful and constitute an assault although the actual physical results would not otherwise have been excessive. Such punishment shows a motive that is inconsistent with the purpose for which the power to discipline exists. The power is abused and so cannot protect the parent or other person with children in his care if the motive is not a disciplinary one but flows from malice, caprice, or rage. So where there had been a succession of punishments by a teacher with little or no just reason for some of them so as to amount to what the sheriff said he could only describe "as a degree of unjust persecution," a conviction for assault was sustained.[43] An objectionable method of punishment may also constitute excess irrespective of whether physical harm results. Thus, in *Ewart* v. *Brown*,[44] although the action failed because a causal connection between the condition from which the pursuer suffered and the assault was not proved, the action of the defender in striking a pupil on the head with a blackboard pointer was clearly considered to amount to a wrong. And in *Ryan* v. *Fildes*[45] Tucker J.

[37a] See note 33, *supra*.

[38] *Peebles* v. *MacPail*, *supra* at p. 246H, *per* Lord Justice-General Emslie and Lords Cowie and Clyde.

[39] *Scorgie* v. *Lawrie*, *supra*; *Mansell* v. *Griffin* [1908] 1 K.B. 160.

[40] *B.* v. *Harris*, 1990 S.L.T. 208; *Guest* v. *Annan*, 1988 S.C.C.R. 275. But see *Kennedy* v. *A.*, March 23, 1993, in which it was held that a father who intended to strike blows which caused extensive bruising on the buttocks of a five-month-old child possessed the necessary *mens rea* for assault "in the absence of justification or other exoneration" (*per* Lords Murray, Osborne and Wylie).

[41] Humiliation that is not degrading may however be part of legitimate punishment, whether the humiliation is public or private: *Stewart* v. *Thain*, 1981 J.C. 13 at p. 18, *per* Lord Justice-Clerk Wheatley. And see the majority judgment of the European Court of Human Rights to like effect in *Costello-Roberts* v. *United Kingdom*, March 25, 1993.

[42] *Gray* v. *Hawthorn*, *supra* at p. 75, *per* Lord Guthrie.

[43] *Ibid.* at p. 76.

[44] (1882) 10 R. 163.

[45] [1938] 3 All E.R. 517 at p. 520.

said of a teacher who had struck a boy on the side of his head with her hand, "the blow struck was moderate in the sense that it was not a very violent blow, but, as punishment, it was not moderate punishment, because I do not think that the proper way of punishing a child is to strike it on the head or the ear." In *Ewart* v. *Brown* the main reason for the condemnation of the punishment seems to have been that the punishment was inherently dangerous.[46] The court will not sanction, as moderate or reasonable, punishment which carries with it an appreciable risk of injury even if that injury does not materialise or is not shown. That consideration may also have played some part in *Ryan* v. *Fildes* but references in that case to what was usual in a school and what "the parent of the child might expect that the child could receive if it did wrong" suggest that the motive for the punishment may also have been in question. In any event it appears that there are certain methods of punishment that are to be regarded as in themselves improper,[47] and that blows to the head, generally, come into that category.

Ambit of Disciplinary Power

It appears that the power of discipline exists as long as the child is in the care of the person exercising it and may be applied, at least in some circumstances, in respect of acts committed outwith that care as well as within it. Thus, it has been held in England that a schoolteacher might inflict punishment on a boy for an offence committed away from school and outwith school hours and that although the boy's father had permitted the conduct in question.[48] It may be that schoolteachers are in a stronger position in this respect than others because of their general responsibility for education in conduct. A person who punishes a child for acts that do not in any way affect the purposes for which he has the child in his care cannot, it is thought, be said to exercise his power of discipline legitimately.

Local Authority Regulations

Local authority regulations sometimes lay down how discipline within schools is to be exercised, or prohibit certain aspects of discipline, such as corporal punishment of foster children by local authority foster parents. Breach of these regulations may give rise to questions between the teacher or foster parent and the authority which employs him, but is *res inter alios acta* and so cannot directly affect the legitimacy of the punishment in a question between the teacher and the child or the child's parents. Similarly, breach of regulations (other than regulations imposing criminal sanctions) or breach of contract cannot, in general, affect criminal liability. There may, however, be circumstances in which such a breach throws some light on questions of motive.

---

[46] See especially Lord Young at p. 169: "The defender, who will thus prevail, is a wrongdoer—in fact, it cannot be reasonably disputed that what he did was a highly imprudent thing, because it never can be known for certain what will be the result of beating a boy on the head with a stick, even when the striker is not in a passion."

[47] See also *McShane* v. *Paton, supra*, where Lord Salvesen refers, at p. 31, to "proper instruments of chastisement," an expression that carries the implication that others may be improper.

[48] *R.* v. *Newport (Salop) Justices, ex p. Wright* [1929] 2 K.B. 416. *Cf. Cleary* v. *Booth* [1893] 1 Q.B. 465. And see *Stewart* v. *Thain, supra*. By contrast, however, punishment for failure to do homework has been held to be wrongful where there was no statutory power to require homework to be done and the child's parents had forbidden it: *Hunter* v. *Johnson* (1884) 13 Q.B.D. 225.

Medical Treatment

The question of the extent of parental power in relation to medical treatment of a child has scarcely arisen in Scotland so far as reported decisions reveal.[49] In England the matter is, in part, determined by the Family Law Reform Act 1969[50] but only in respect of minors who have attained the age of 16, and common law rules remain relevant in the case of younger minors and also, for some purposes, of those who have attained that age.[51] The common law of England, although not free from doubt and controversy, appears to be that the question of the minor's capacity to consent to medical treatment or other medical procedure is a factual one of his ability to understand and to make a decision,[52] and that a parent can consent on behalf of a minor who does not have that ability, at least where the decision can be defended as not detrimental to the minor's welfare. In addition, the Court of Appeal has held (1) that in exercising its wardship jurisdiction the High Court (and the parent[53]) has the power to consent to medical treatment of a minor who is competent to consent but who refuses consent, and (2) that the wardship court or the High Court exercising its inherent protective jurisdiction has an overriding power to refuse consent or forbid treatment to which the minor (below or over 16) has consented but which the court deems not to be in the child's welfare; natural parents do not have this right of veto.[54]

In Scotland at common law the power of dominion, which a parent enjoyed in relation to a pupil child, would seem to have been such that a parent could

---

[49] The issue arose obliquely in *Docherty* v. *McGlynn*, 1983 S.L.T. 645, which involved the question of consent to blood tests of the child in an action of paternity, and rather more relevantly in *Finlayson, Applicant*, 1989 S.C.L.R. 601, where the parental refusal to consent to medical treatment was held to be a ground for referral to a children's hearing.

[50] s. 8.

[51] There has been a burgeoning literature on this topic, particularly since the decision of the House of Lords in *Gillick* v. *West Norfolk and Wisbech Area Health Authority* [1985] 3 W.L.R. 830. As representative but by no means exhaustive of this literature, see Skegg, "Consent to Medical Procedures on Minors" (1973) 36 Mod. L.R. 370; Williams, "The Gillick Saga" (1985) 135 New L.J. 1156, 1179; Drane, "Competency to Give an Informed Consent" (1984) 252 J.A.M.A. 925; Kerr, "Medical Treatment of Children" [1984] 35 N.I.L.Q. 185; Skegg, *Law, Ethics and Medicine* (1984), pp. 58–71; Kennedy and Grubb, *Medical Law: Text and Materials* (1989), pp. 300–330.

[52] *Gillick* v. *West Norfolk and Wisbeck Area Health Authority, supra.* It is unclear from that case whether mental maturity is all that is necessary to confer competence (the approach of Lord Scarman) or whether, in addition, it must be shown that the treatment is in the child's best interests (the approach of Lord Fraser). For a discussion, see Norrie, "Gillick Again: The House of Lords Decides," 1986 S.L.T. (News) 69.

[53] Though this aspect of *Re R., infra* was supported only by Lord Donaldson, M.R.

[54] *Re R. (A Minor) (Medical Treatment)* [1991] 4 All E.R. 177; *Re W. (A Minor) (Medical Treatment)*, [1992] 4 All E.R. 627. For a discussion, see Bainham, "The Judge and the Competent Minor" (1992) 108 L.Q.R. 194; Edwards, "The Right to Consent and the Right to Refuse," 1993 J.R. 52; Bridgeman, "Old Enough to Know Best?" (1993) 13 Leg. Stud. 69. These decisions probably have to be read in the light of their own facts. *Re R.* involved a 15-year-old child who suffered from a psychotic illness and who refused consent to drug treatment of that psychosis during one of her lucid intervals. The Court of Appeal held that her competence was not be judged purely on her state of mind during a lucid interval, which amounts to a holding that the child in that case was incompetent—rendering the comments concerning competent children *obiter*. *Re W.* involved a 16-year-old suffering from anorexia nervosa and it was found that one of the peculiarities of this disease is that the disease itself creates a wish not to be cured: again this raises doubts as to the girl's competence to decide (see particularly the judgment of Balcombe L.J.). See also *Re E (A Minor)*, Sept. 21, 1990, LEXIS, in which Ward J. authorised a transfusion of blood to a 15-year-old boy who, together with his parents, were Jehovah's Witnesses and who refused to consent to the treatment. The boy was a ward of court and for that reason the court could do no other than decide on the basis of the child's best interests.

validly give consent to any medical procedure in respect of such a child, provided the procedure was consistent with the object for which the power existed, *i.e.* the welfare of the child.[55] It was implicit in the power of dominion that it would prevail irrespective of whether or not the child, in fact, had ability to understand and decide although, in a doubtful case, it would be right for the parent to have regard to the wishes of a child capable of forming a rational judgment. The statute that extends pupillarity to all children under the age of 16 years[56] also makes express provision concerning the child's capacity to consent to medical treatment. It is provided that:

> "A person under the age of 16 years shall have legal capacity to consent on his own behalf to any surgical, medical or dental procedure or treatment where, in the opinion of a qualified medical practitioner attending him, he is capable of understanding the nature and possible consequences of the procedure or treatment."[57]

Capacity to consent is therefore a purely factual question of the child's ability to understand, this to be determined by the medical practitioner attending[58] the child. There is no requirement that the proposed procedure or treatment be in the child's best interests or indeed that it in any way enhances his welfare. This is logical: once the child understands, he will understand the risks involved and will be able to determine himself whether or not to take these risks, which the law should allow him the opportunity to do.[59] The words "surgical, medical or dental procedure or treatment" are intended to cover all such procedures or treatments, including examination, diagnosis, treatment, and procedures not amounting to treatment in a strict sense.[60] The words "qualified medical practitioner" are intended to be wider than registered doctors (for which "registered medical practitioner" is the normal statutory wording[61]); it is submitted that it will cover doctors, dentists, anaesthetists, nurses, chiropodists, midwives, and all health professionals qualified to do that which they are doing. The capacity to consent carries with it, it is submitted, capacity to refuse, for the only point in asking a patient to consent to medical treatment is to give the patient the opportunity to refuse. "In logic there can be no difference between an ability to consent to treatment and an ability to refuse treatment."[62]

---

[55] See Norrie, "The *Gillick* Case and Parental Rights in Scots Law," 1985 S.L.T. (News) 157. Thomson has argued that this power flowed from the right of custody rather than the right of tutory, and therefore existed until the child was 16: "The *Gillick* Case and Parental Rights in Scots Law: Another View," 1985 S.L.T. (News) 223.

[56] Age of Legal Capacity (Scotland) Act 1991.

[57] s. 2(4).

[58] Which probably means giving the treatment proposed.

[59] The Scottish Law Commission, in suggesting this legislation, expressly rejected the addition of a welfare test: see Scot. Law Com. No. 110, *Report on the Legal Capacity and Responsibility of Minors and Pupils*, 1987, at para. 3.77, citing Lord Scarman's speech in *Gillick* v. *West Norfolk and Wisbech Area Health Authority, supra,* and Norrie, *op. cit.*

[60] This is to be compared with the situation in England, where s. 8 of the Family Law Reform Act 1969 grants a right to consent to persons above 16 to "surgical, medical and dental treatment": in *Re W. (A Minor) (Medical Treatment), supra,* it was held that this did not cover organ or blood donation since these are not "treatment." They are "procedures" and therefore covered by the Scottish statute.

[61] See for example the Abortion Act 1967, s. 1.

[62] *Per* Balcombe L.J. in *Re W. (A Minor) (Medical Treatment), supra,* at p. 643.

The Mature Child Under 16

The Age of Legal Capacity (Scotland) Act 1991 grants capacity to consent to the child under the age of 16 when the child understands the nature and possible consequences of that treatment. But it also provides that any reference in any rule of law or enactment to tutory of a pupil child is now to be read as a reference to guardianship of a child under 16[63]; custody has for long extended until the child is 16. It follows that, flowing from the parental right of custody or, possibly, from guardianship,[64] the parent of the child below the age of 16 has the right of consent independently of the child's right. The Act does not give any indication as to what happens to the parent's right when the child acquires the right, nor what is to be done, short of an application to the court, if the two disagree. The argument was raised but rejected in *Re R. (A Minor) (Wardship: Medical Treatment)*[65] that once the child acquired the capacity to consent to medical treatment the parent's (and the wardship court's) right to give or to refuse consent was terminated. Lord Scarman's speech in the *Gillick* case was used to support that argument,[66] but the Master of the Rolls distinguished Lord Scarman's comments. The Court of Appeal held, rather, that while parents cannot override the child's consent—that is, cannot veto treatment—they do have the right to consent, which can override the child's refusal. Lord Donaldson saw consent as the "key" to the door to lawful treatment, which must be opened before doctors can provide treatment. Where there are two parents with parental rights there are two "keyholders"; if they disagree then the doctor has an ethical and professional problem, but no legal one since the key of one parent will open the door. All *Gillick* did was to give another key to some children, which could be used without the key of the parent[67]; conversely the parent's key could be used without the key of the child. This approach was followed in *Re W (A Minor) (Medical Treatment)*,[68] in which the court's consent was used to override the wishes of a patient who, under section 8 of the Family Law Reform Act 1969, had the right to consent or refuse (*i.e.* a 16-year-old). Lord Donaldson M.R. modified his comments in *Re R.* only to the extent of changing his "keyholder" analogy into a "flak-jacket" analogy.

At first sight, this English analysis might be fitted neatly into the position in Scots law. When two parents have parental rights each may exercise their right without reference to the other[69]; the Age of Legal Capacity (Scotland) Act 1991 gives the right to consent to some children, which they can exercise without reference to their parent or parents: the doctor can therefore rely on the consent of any of the "keyholders" or providers of "flak-jackets." While the practical result

---

[63] Age of Legal Capacity (Scotland) Act 1991, s. 5(1).
[64] See *post*, at p. 361.
[65] [1991] 4 All E.R. 177.
[66] "Parental right *yields* to the child's right to make his own decisions when he reaches a sufficient understanding and intelligence to be capable of making up his own mind on the matter requiring decision": [1985] 3 All E.R. at p. 422. "Parental right to determine whether or not their minor child below the age of 16 will have medical treatment *terminates* if and when the child achieves a sufficient understanding and intelligence to enable him [to give personal consent]": *ibid.* at p. 423 (emphasis added).
[67] *Per* Lord Donaldson, M.R. at p. 184.
[68] [1992] 4 All E.R. 627.
[69] Law Reform (Parent and Child) (Scotland) Act 1986, s. 2(4).

of this analysis is unobjectionable when the child wishes to consent to the treatment,[70] it is rather less so if the child wishes to refuse consent. If the doctor could rely upon the consent of the parent to override a refusal of the child (using the parent's key or flak-jacket rather than the child's), this could potentially entitle the doctor to force, say, an abortion, or a kidney removal, from a resisting mentally mature child.[71] This would, it is submitted, be quite unacceptable, and can be avoided by one of two ways. First, the Scottish court could accept the argument rejected by Lord Donaldson M.R. in *Re R.* to the effect that the acquisition by the child of capacity to consent is the automatic denial of the parent's right to consent. Authority can be found in the speech of Lord Scarman in the *Gillick* case[72]; and it can further be argued in support that the Age of Legal Capacity (Scotland) Act 1991 follows the logic of that speech rather than any other in that case by relying purely on an "understanding" test.[73] Against that it must be admitted that there is nothing in the terms of the 1991 Act that expressly limits any rights that parents had before its coming into force[74]; and the "key-holder" or "flak- jacket" approach of Lord Donaldson M.R. does have a certain cogency.

A second, but, it is submitted, less persuasive method of avoiding the unacceptable result of allowing parents to override the child's refusal is by relying upon the welfare principle. Parents cannot consent to any treatment they choose: they can only consent to treatment that consists with the child's welfare. Substantial interferences may be permitted if the child is too young to understand; but his or her acquisition of mental maturity is a significant factor in determining his or her welfare. To force a competent child to accept treatment against his or her wishes will in most cases not be in the child's interests, and therefore in most cases the parent would be unable to exercise his or her right to consent if this goes against the wishes of the child.[75] There may be exceptions but these would be highly unusual, though possibly could include the refusal of a child to consent to lifesaving treatment, say, because of peculiar religious be-

---

[70] *Cf. Re P. (A Minor)* (1982) 80 L.G.R. 301, in which the abortion of a 15-year-old girl was permitted when she consented while her parents refused.

[71] See Feenan, "Abortion and Minors" (1992) 37 J.L.S. 111.

[72] Quoted at note 66 *supra*. Lord Donaldson M.R. in *Re R.* held this inapplicable on the ground, unconvincing it is submitted, that Lord Scarman was talking only of the right to consent to medical treatment and not the right to "determine" medical treatment. It is interesting to note that, though agreeing with the result, Staughton L.J. distanced himself from Lord Donaldson M.R.'s difference of opinion from Lord Scarman: [1991] 4 All E.R. at p. 189A. The third judge, Farquharson L.J., expressed no opinion on this point.

[73] See Norrie, "The Age of Legal Capacity (Scotland) Act 1991" 36 J.L.S. 434 at p. 436 and note 55 above. Edwards adopts this approach, with cogent reasoning, in "The Right to Consent and the Right to Refuse," 1993 J.R. 52.

[74] Indeed in one area both child and parent have a statutory right to consent: if a blood sample is to be taken from a child for the purpose of determining parentage (see *ante* at p. 154), the understanding child is given the right to consent by s. 2(4) of the Age of Legal Capacity (Scotland) Act 1991 and the parent is given the right to consent by s. 6(2) of the Law Reform (Parent and Child) (Scotland) Act 1986, as amended by Sched. 1, para. 42 to the 1991 Act. If both have the statutory right to consent in this area it is difficult to argue that the child's acquisition of a right takes away the parent's right in all other circumstances.

[75] *Cf.* the judgment of Balcombe L.J. in *Re. W. (A Minor) (Medical Treatment)* at p. 643, in which this approach receives considerable support.

liefs.[76] However, to resolve the dilemma by relying on the welfare principle sits uneasily with the absence of that principle from the 1991 Act;[77] it also suggests the curious result that capacity to refuse is in some way different from and more difficult to acquire than capacity to consent. The first approach is simpler and, it is submitted, logically more sound.

It might be argued that the dilemma could be resolved in every case by means of an application to the court, but not only might that not be appropriate in all cases, but such a step would itself lead to another dilemma. In any action relating to parental rights the court must regard the welfare of the child as the paramount consideration,[78] which suggests that the court is bound in all cases to determine the matter in that way. But this is not precisely so. The direction to apply the welfare principle applies only in "proceedings relating to parental rights," not to all proceedings involving children.[79] The question therefore becomes whether an application to the court to determine the scope of section 2(4) of the Age of Legal Capacity (Scotland) Act 1991 is one "relating to parental rights." It is submitted that while an application to determine the scope of section 2(4) would certainly *affect* parental rights (since they would be either denied or upheld), this is not sufficient to bring the case within the ambit of section 3(2) of the 1986 Act. The 1991 Act is designed to confer capacity on children, and the very absence of any provision in that Act concerning parents' rights suggests that actions based on that Act are actions relating to children rather than to parents. The express rejection of the welfare principle by the drafters of the 1991 Act[80] encourages the view that in an application to the court to resolve a dispute between the parent and the child, the welfare principle in section 3(2) of the 1986 Act is not determinative.

The Immature Child Under 16

If the child is too young to understand the nature and possible consequences of the proposed treatment then it is within the parental power to determine what medical treatment the child is to receive, subject as always to satisfaction of the welfare test. The transplantation of organs, such as kidneys, gives rise to particularly anxious questions. In such cases, the donor inevitably suffers a significant physical detriment which will be permanent and it is doubtful if parental consent can, in the ordinary case, justify an operation on a mentally immature child as donor. There may, however, be exceptions where the potential recipient is a sibling or other person with whom the child has a strong connection.[81] It

---

[76] See *Re E. (A Minor)* Sept. 21, 1990, in which Ward J. authorised a blood transfusion to save the life of a 15-year-old boy when both he and his parents (Jehovah's Witnesses) refused to consent to the treatment.

[77] See note 59 above.

[78] Law Reform (Parent and Child) (Scotland) Act 1986, s. 3(2).

[79] It is clear that other proceedings relating to children are not proceedings "relating to parental rights," and therefore not subject to s. 3(2), notwithstanding that they affect parental rights. This is so, for example, in relation to adoption where the welfare of the child is the "first" rather than the "paramount" consideration: Adoption (Scotland) Act 1978, s. 6.

[80] Scot. Law Com. No. 110 (1987) at para. 3.77.

[81] In a number of cases from the United States organ transplantation has been approved on the basis that the incapax would receive benefit in the form of the continued existence of the recipient of the donation: see for example *Hart* v. *Brown*, 289 A. 2d 386 (1972) (kidney transplantation between 7-year-old twins); *Strunk* v. *Strunk*, 35 A.L.R. 3d 683 (1969) (kidney transplant from a 27-year-

may be supposed, in such cases, that the child, if adult, would have wished to consent, but that is necessarily a speculative judgment, and in any case this is not the basis upon which the legality of medical treatment of children is normally based.[82] Among the factors to be weighed may be the prospects of success of the transplant, the possibility of alternatives, and, importantly, any indirect benefit that may be supposed to accrue to the child donor, such as, for example, the emotional benefit brought by a sibling restored to health. It is probably not necesssary, in order to justify parental consent, that benefit to the child be shown but merely that what is done is consistent with the child's welfare. If, however, the court should be asked to regulate the matter by way of an order relating to parental rights, the court would require to be satisfied that any order it made would be in the interests of the child. It should perhaps be emphasised that it will only be in highly unusual cases that the test of consistency with the child's welfare, far less positive beneift, could be satisfied by the removal of non-regenerative organs such as kidneys. Regenerative tissues such as skin, bone marrow or blood are on the other hand less problematical and there is therefore, it is submitted, no obstacle to procedures such as the donation of blood for transfusion in which there is no appreciable risk to the child and no permanent detriment.

The Child Over 16

At common law a minor above the age of pupillarity was free from the right of dominion which the law gave to the parent of a pupil child and so would seem, *prima facie* at least, to have been free to consent to medical procedures.[83] The curatorial role of the parent has now been abolished[84] and it would follow that there is no limitation on the 16 and 17-year-old's right to consent or to refuse consent to medical treatment. Such a patient has complete autonomy in the matter of medical treatment, in contradistinction to the position of the 16 or 17-year-old in England.[85] There is no statutory provision analogous to that in England expressly granting the right to consent to those over the age of 16,[86] but

---

old incapax to his brother); and see cases cited in Curran, "A Problem of Consent: Kidney Transplantation in Minors' (1959) 34 N.Y.U.L.R. 891. In *Lausier* v. *Pescinski*, 226 N.W. 2d 180 (1975) authorisation for the transplant was refused from an institutionalised catatonic schizophrenic man for donation to his sister, on the ground that the sister's previous lack of interest in her brother suggested that her survival would not be likely to benefit the donor. See further Norrie, "Human Tissue Transplants" Legal Liability in Different Jurisdictions" (1985) 34 I.C.L.Q. 442.

[82] In US jurisdictions this is known as the "substituted judgment" test, and it was applied in *Re Quinlan*, 70 N.J. 10, 355 A. 2d 647 (1976) in which the Supreme Court of New Jersey held that life-support treatment could be terminated once it was shown that this is what the patient would have wanted had she been competent to make a judgement; and in *Re Grady* 85 N.J. 235, 426 A. 2d 467 (1981) in which the same court permitted the sterilisation of a mentally disabled woman on the same basis. When these issues have been determined by the English courts the treatment is permitted or not permitted not on that basis but on the basis of the best interests of the patient: see for example *F.* v. *West Berkshire Health Authority* [1989] 2 All E.R. 545 (H.L.); *Re B. (A Minor) (Wardship: Medical Treatment)* [1981] 1 W.L.R. 1412 (C.A.); *Airedale N.H.S. Trust* v. *Bland* [1993] 1 All E.R. 821 (H.L.).

[83] For another view, see Thomson, "The *Gillick* Case and Parental Rights in Scots Law: Another View," 1985 S.L.T. (News) 223.

[84] Age of Legal Capacity (Scotland) Act 1991, s. 5(3).

[85] See Balcombe L.J. in *Re W. (A Minor) (Medical Treatment)* [1992] 4 All E.R. 627 at p. 643C.

[86] Family Law Reform Act 1969, s. 8.

the freedom from both custody and guardianship that is now enjoyed by all those over the age of 16 suggests that such a statutory provision, which was merely for the avoidance of doubt in any case, is not necessary in Scotland.

Remedies for Failure to Provide Consent

The parent's power in respect of medical treatment corresponds to his obligation to make that treatment available. Failure to do so when needed may amount to a criminal offence.[87] The sanctions of the criminal law may, however, be inadequate, or come too late, to provide protection for the child. In such cases, the child can be referred to a children's hearing on the ground that lack of parental care is likely to cause him unnecessary suffering or seriously to impair his health or development,[88] but that does not in itself provide a remedy where the difficulty is the parent's refusal, perhaps on religious grounds, to consent to medical treatment in a case in which that consent is required. The making of a supervision requirement by the children's hearing, perhaps with a condition attached, has the effect that the child will be treated as in the care of the local authority for the purposes of the passing of a resolution vesting parental rights and powers in the authority[89] but the grounds for such a resolution may be lacking and it is, in any event, a circuitous and cumbersome procedure in cases of this kind.

In an emergency a doctor is justified in applying treatment that is clearly necessary,[90] even in the absence of parental consent, but he may be denied the opportunity. In England the wardship jurisdiction affords a remedy for such problems unless the child is the subject of a care order,[91] in which case the local authority can apply to the court for leave to make an application for the exercise of the inherent jurisdiction of the High Court.[92] In Scotland the court has an undoubted jurisdiction to control the exercise of parental power, but examples of its use are virtually exhausted by the making of custody orders and the supersession of parents in the management of their children's property. There is, however, no reason that remedies should be restricted to these instances. The control of parental power is based on the *nobile officium* of the Court of Session which acts as *parens patriae* as does the High Court in England in its wardship jurisdiction and is, in principle, no less extensive.[93] It would therefore be open to the Court of Session in exercise of the *nobile officium* to make orders authorising or prohibiting medical treatment. Moreover, both the Court of Session and the sheriff court have a statutory power to make such order relating to par-

---

[87] *Cf. R.* v. *Instan* [1893] 1 Q.B. 450; *R.* v. *Stone* [1977] Q.B. 354.
[88] Social Work (Scotland) Act 1968, s. 32(2)(c), as substituted by Children Act 1975, Sched. 3, para. 54. See *Finlayson, Applicant*, 1989 S.C.L.R. 601.
[89] Social Work (Scotland) Act 1968, s. 44(5).
[90] *Per* Lord Scarman in *Gillick* v. *West Norfolk and Wisbech Area Health Authority* [1985] 3 All E.R. 402 at p. 424; Lord Donaldson M.R. in *Re. R. (A Minor) (Wardship: Medical Treatment)* [1991] 4 All E.R. 177 at p. 184. See also *F.* v. *West Berkshire Health Authority, supra*; *Marshall* v. *Curry* (1933) 3 D.L.R. 260; *Murray* v. *McMurchy* (1949) 2 D.L.R. 442.
[91] *Re. L.* [1968] P. 119; *B.(B.R.)* v. *B.(J.)* [1968] P. 466; *M.(D.K.)* v. *M.(S.V.) & G.* [1969] 1 W.L.R. 843; *Re B. (A Minor) (Wardship: Medical Treatment)* [1981] 1 W.L.R. 1412; *Re R. (A Minor) (Medical Treatment), supra*. See the Children Act 1989, s. 100(2)(c).
[92] Children Act 1989, s.100(3).
[93] See *ante* at p. 182.

ental rights as they think fit.[94] Either of these two procedures seems, therefore, to be amply sufficient to provide remedies in appropriate cases. Where necessary, delivery of the child may be ordered to enforce compliance with the order authorising treatment. This jurisdiction may also be used to resolve some of the other problems of consent discussed above, subject to the qualifications there made.[95] As with all applications under this provision, the court cannot make any order unless it is satisfied that to do so will be in the interests of the child.[96]

Religious Upbringing

The right to determine the religious upbringing of children is part of the parental power. The place of religious considerations in custody disputes, including such disputes after the death of the parents, is considered elsewhere.[97] Although that is the most likely area of conflict, questions may arise in other contexts. As between parent and child the right is virtually absolute during the early years, though this is so more for practical than for legal reasons. The only exception to that would seem to be where the religious upbringing favoured by the parent can be shown to be detrimental to the child. As with other aspects of parental power, the right does, however, progressively diminish as the child matures in mind and comes to be able to make personal judgments. Perhaps in this respect more than in others, the wishes of the child, if based on conviction, are entitled to respect, and in any event are protected by Article 14 of the UN Convention on the Rights of the Child,[98] which obliges the state to "respect the right of the child to freedom of thought, conscience and religion." The same article also protects the "rights and duties of the parents. . .to provide direction to the child in the exercise of his or her rights in a manner consistent with the evolving capacities of the child." The right and duty to provide direction cannot be enlarged into a power of determination. *Religio sequitur patrem* is a maxim grounded in the nature of the *patria potestas* but the father's wishes, with which the mother's must now be put in parity, decline in importance with the weakening of the parental power, and that decline may be more rapid in this matter than in others because of its inseparability from the child's personal convictions. It has been remarked that "in Scotland not a great deal of weight seems to be attached to the question of the father's religion"[99] and in *Kincaid* v. *Quarrier*,[1] a case that arose after the parent's death, the most that Lord Kyllachy was prepared to say was: "It may be—I express no opinion to the contrary—that *prima facie* the father's religion is the religion in which a child should be brought up."[2]

---

[94] Law Reform (Parent and Child) (Scotland) Act 1986, s. 3(1). The Scottish Law Commission have proposed making it plain that the court can grant what it calls "a specific issue order" regulating any specific question which has arisen or may arise in relation to the exercise of parental responsibilities or rights: *Report on Family Law*, Scot. Law Com. No. 135, May 1992, draft Bill, cl. 12(1)(c).

[95] See also Thomson, "Sterilisation of Mentally Handicapped Children," 1988 S.L.T. (News) 1 at pp. 3–4.

[96] Law Reform (Parent and Child) (Scotland) Act 1986, s. 3(2).

[97] *Post* at pp. 221–225.

[98] 28 *International Legal Materials* 1448, adopted Nov. 20, 1989, ratified by the UK Dec. 16, 1991.

[99] Fraser, p. 190.

[1] (1896) 23 R. 676.

[2] *Ibid.* at p. 681.

What was then said of the father must now of course be said equally of the mother. In disputes that reach the court the question is to be decided with regard to the welfare of the child as the paramount consideration,[3] but if the dispute is purely about religious upbringing and no other interests are affected the application of the welfare principle is attended with difficulties which are examined in detail elsewhere.[4] Where the dispute is between parents, no preference can, in principle, be given to either the father or the mother, although the particular facts of the case, such as the greater interest shown by one parent in the child's religious upbringing may, of course, afford a ground of preference. An agreement by a parent to give up his rights in relation to a child's religious upbringing is unenforceable, as is the case with agreements to surrender any aspect of parental responsibility or right, unless the agreement forms part of a separation agreement, and even then it will not be enforced if it will not be for the benefit of the child to give effect to it; but such an agreement may afford evidence of the parent's attitude. Where other aspects of the child's welfare are not in issue a high premium will be put on continuity of religious upbringing and on the wishes of the older child.

Education

Parental Right to Determine Education

There is no doubt that a parent, in the exercise of his parental power, may determine the education of a child under 16. So he may choose whether the child is to be educated within the state system, or, if he has the means to afford it, by other provision amounting to efficient education. As long as his choice meets the requirements of the Education Acts, is consistent with the child's welfare, and is suitable to his needs and position in life, it cannot be challenged. Within these constraints he may choose what kind of education the child is to receive. The older the child is, however, the more the child's own wishes and aspirations are to be taken into account. This is because the more mature he is the greater the weight that is properly to be accorded to his wishes within the context of the welfare principle. Clearly, however, where the child's wishes make demands on the financial support of parents, their reasonableness from that standpoint will be a critical factor in a reconciliation with parental choice; and it is noteworthy that recent legislation on state provision for school education has been concerned to respect parental choice rather than the wishes of the child.[5]

Parental Obligation to Provide Education

The exercise of parental power in determining a child's education is closely related to the question of whether there is a common-law duty to provide education and to the duty of aliment on which that question largely turns. In an early case "it occurred to the court that the *patria potestas* is such, that a peer may breed his son a cobbler, and after putting him in business with a competent stock

---

[3] Law Reform (Parent and Child) (Scotland) Act 1986, s. 3(2).
[4] *Post* at pp. 221–225.
[5] Education (Scotland) Act 1980, s. 28(1).

is relieved from all further aliment."[6] Even that view postulates a certain, if very limited, duty to provide an education in preparation for adult life. Erskine, however, put the parental duty higher and, it is thought, more accurately. Among parental duties he includes giving children "an education suitable to their rank, in their younger years."[7] Despite what occurred to the court in *Scot* v. *Sharp* just quoted, it has not been much disputed that there is a duty such as Erskine asserts. Controversy has centred rather on whether the duty is legally enforceable or merely imperfect.[8] Erskine considered it to be enforceable. Education was part of the obligation of care, protection and aliment, which was not merely natural, "for if they [the parents] refuse to discharge it, they may be compelled to performance by the civil magistrate, according to their station of life and the measure of their fortune."[9] And it is difficult to see why that should not be so. Contrary views turn not on any special feature of the duty to educate rendering it inherently incapable of enforcement, but on the unassailability of the father's discretion in the exercise of the *patria potestas*.[10] Such views are now obsolete. Essentially the question is one of the extent of the parent's duty of aliment, of whether it extends to the maintenance of a child while he is undergoing education and of the provision of the costs of that education. Even at common law the obligation of aliment, although regulated on an economical footing, extended beyond the provision of bare subsistence. It was a question of the relief of want,[11] but want was determined according to the circumstances and condition in life of the claimant.[12] So, Stair juxtaposed the obligation of aliment to the obligation of education. "The main obligations," he says, "are education and provision. The education of children consisteth not only in the care and entertainment of them during infancy, but especially in breeding of them for some calling and employment according to their capacity and condition."[13] Now, under statute, the obligation of aliment is conceived, more broadly than at common law, in terms of reasonableness in the circumstances having regard to the needs, resources and earning capacities of the parties.[14] That it may extend to the provision by a parent of education for his child is borne out by the extension of the obligation beyond majority to the age of 25 where the child is reasonably and appropriately undergoing instruction at an educational establishment or training for employment or for a trade, profession or vocation.[15] So far as children under school leaving age are concerned any general duty of educational provision is, of course, now supplemented and largely superseded by the specific requirements of the Education Acts. For such children, the statutory re-

---

[6] *Scot* v. *Sharp* (1759) Mor. 440.

[7] I, vi, 56.

[8] Hume, *Lectures*, Vol. I, p. 219.

[9] Erskine, *ibid.*

[10] Hume, *ibid.*

[11] *Maule* v. *Maule* (1825) 1 W. & S. 266.

[12] The term necessity "has a relative meaning; relative to the situation of the person who is said to be in want. A person who has received the education of a gentleman. . .would not be placed above the reach of want by getting the relief of a parish pauper": *Thom* v. *Mackenzie* (1864) 3 M. 177, *per* Lord Justice-Clerk Inglis at p. 179.

[13] I, v. 6.

[14] Family Law (Scotland) Act 1985, ss. 1(2) and 4(1).

[15] *Ibid.*, s. 1(5).

quirements will, it is submitted, usually provide the measure of what is required because, within the bounds of reasonableness, the parent is entitled to discharge his duty in an economical fashion and it will be only in an exceptional case, if at all, that education within the state system can be said to be inappropriate to the needs of the child or unreasonable.[16]

Parental Obligation of Care and Nurture

The fundamental parental obligation is to provide for the child's nurture. That is essentially what is meant by the obligation of aliment, although when it comes to questions of enforcement it is nearly always regarded merely in terms of money payment for the child's material support. Aliment in that restricted sense is considered later.[17] The various duties which parents have, although often and conveniently considered separately, are largely subsumed under the heading of nurture and it is from that obligation that the powers of parents, as necessary for its discharge, flow. It is a parent's duty to provide for his children "in bed, board and clothing, and all the necessaries of life,"[18] but the obligation extends beyond the provision of material support to care and nurture in all things that concern the child's welfare in so far as that is required in accordance with the child's age and understanding. In its more intangible aspects, that duty is usually incapable of legal enforcement. It comprehends, however, a duty to "preserve and protect"[19] during nonage which if breached in the case of a child under 16 may amount to the criminal offence of neglect.[20] If such breach results in personal injury to the child, it would seem also to be civilly actionable, but the matter is better illustrated in the case of persons having temporary care *in loco parentis* rather than of parents themselves.

Duty of Care—Liability for Negligence

The duty of care owed by persons who have children in their charge is, apart from criminal neglect, best illustrated by cases on liability for negligence of schoolteachers and authorities responsible for schools. The general principle is that a schoolteacher is bound to take such care of his pupils as a reasonably careful and prudent parent would take of his or her own children.[21] That principle which follows from the *in loco parentis* relationship is, it is conceived, applicable to all cases of persons having children in their care. It requires, however, some elaboration, and even modification, according to circumstances. A parent usually attaches great importance to the safety and wellbeing of his children, although he will also recognise that as they grow up some risks must be run either because, in a practical sense, they are inevitable or because they are to be balanced against the damage inherent in over-protection. The general principle may say no more than that schoolteachers and others with children in their care are expected to be guided by the same fundamental consideration. Beyond that

---

[16] Provision of education is discussed more fully in Chap. 12.

[17] *Post* at chap. 11.

[18] Erskine, I, vi, 56.

[19] *Ibid.*

[20] Children and Young Persons (Scotland) Act 1937, s. 12(1).

[21] *Williams* v. *Eady* (1893) 10 T.L.R. 41, *per* Lord Esher M.R. at p. 42.

it may often be difficult to apply the principle to the particular situations which persons other than parents having children in their care have to face, particularly where a sizeable group of children is concerned. The exigencies of the classroom or the laboratory, even of the gymnasium or the playing field or a children's hostel, may often not be those that a parent ordinarily encounters. The remoteness of the general principle becomes even more marked when the question at issue is not the care required of a person immediately in charge of a child or group of children, but of the care to be shown in the management of a large institution.[22] So, "the standard is that of a reasonably prudent parent judged not in the context of his own home but in that of a school, in other words, a person exhibiting the responsible mental qualities of a prudent parent in the circumstances of school life."[23] If, therefore, it is borne in mind that a person who has the care of children should be animated by the same fundamental considerations as a careful and prudent parent, the test for negligence may often appropriately be put in terms reflecting those applicable to other relationships in which a duty of care arises: whether he took such care as a reasonable person placed in the circumstances in which he was placed would have taken to protect the children in his care from reasonably foreseeable harm.

The ambit of the duty of care is as wide as the circumstances demand but the matters covered usually fall under one or more of three main heads: safety of premises and equipment, organisation of activities, and supervision. In relation to all of them, account has to be taken of the propensities of children, "the ordinary nature of young boys, their tendency to do mischievous acts, and their propensity to meddle with anything that came in their way."[24]

Safety of Premises and Equipment

Because the duty flows from the relationship of care and not merely from the occupation of premises it may be higher in a question of safety of premises than that incumbent on an occupier under the Occupiers Liability (Scotland) Act 1960.[25] As, however, the Act reformulates the duty of reasonable care the difference may not be material provided appropriate weight is given to the relationship between the child and the occupier as among the circumstances affecting the duty. A person with children in his care may, however, have a duty in respect of the safety of premises although he is not the occupier. In the case of schools and other educational establishments under the management of an education authority, there is a further statutory duty to secure that the premises and equipment conform to the standards and requirements laid down in regulations made by the Secretary of State and that they are maintained in such a condition as to conduce to the good health and safety of all persons occupying or frequenting the premises or using the equipment.[26] It has been held on the corresponding words of English legislation that the duty so imposed is absolute and that breach resulting in damage is civilly actionable at the instance of a pupil or other person

---

[22] *Beaumont* v. *Surrey County Council* (1968) 66 L.G.R. 580, *per* Geoffrey Lane J.

[23] *Lyes* v. *Middlesex County Council* (1962) 61 L.G.R. 443, *per* Edmund Davies J. *Cf. Jacques* v. *Oxfordshire County Council* (1968) 66 L.G.R. 440, *per* Waller J.

[24] *Williams* v. *Eady, supra, per* Lord Esher M.R. at p. 42.

[25] See *Lyes* v. *Middlesex County Council, supra.*

[26] Education (Scotland) Act 1980, s. 19(2).

whom the statutory provision is designed to protect.[27] Injuries arising from holes in the floor of a playshed,[28] from glass panels in a door which proved to be too thin[29] and from a swing door which, because of its weight and the strength of the spring, was unsafe for young children,[30] are among those for which damages have been recovered.

Elements of Negligence

What constitutes negligence on the part of those having the care of children is a question of degree which may vary according to the age and personal characteristics of the children. To leave a knife accessible to a child of four would be negligence,[31] but in the case of children of 11 it has been held to be sufficient precaution that knives were kept in an unlocked cupboard.[32] Where the use of articles to which a degree of danger attaches is necessary for some educational purpose, appropriate safeguards should be taken and dangerous substances, when not in use, should be kept in a secure place having in mind the tendency of children to do mischievous acts and their propensity to meddle with anything that comes their way.[33] A distinction is, however, to be made between things dangerous in themselves[34] in which case the greater the danger the higher the standard of diligence the law exacts,[35] and things, in ordinary use, which are not in their essential character dangerous but become a source of danger only on the occurrence of certain circumstances of negligence or mischance.[36] In the latter case there is negligence in not taking safeguards only if an occurrence occasioning danger could reasonably have been foreseen.[37] What is required in the way of supervision is to be measured by what harm may reasonably be anticipated if supervision is not exercised. The standard is, however high. "It is a headmaster's duty, bearing in mind the known propensities of boys and indeed girls between 11 and 17 or 18, to take all reasonable and proper steps to prevent any of the pupils under his care from suffering injury from inanimate objects, from the action of their fellow pupils, or from a combination of the two."[38] A schoolteacher is not, however, expected to exercise such a degree of care that his pupils could never get into mischief.[39] It is reasonable, not constant, supervision that is required.[40] What is reasonable is, of course, a question of circumstances and there may be circumstances in which only constant supervision could meet

---

[27] *Ching* v. *Surrey County Council* [1910] 1 K.B. 736; *Morris* v. *Carnarvon County Council* [1910] 1 K.B. 840; *Lyes* v. *Middlesex County Council, supra*; *Reffell* v. *Surrey County Council* [1964] 1 All E.R. 743.

[28] *Ching* v. *Surrey County Council, supra*.

[29] *Lyes* v. *Middlesex County Council* and *Reffell* v. *Surrey County Council, supra*.

[30] *Morris* v. *Carnarvon County Council, supra*.

[31] *Williams* v. *Eady, supra, per* Cave J.

[32] *Suckling* v. *Essex County Council, The Times* Jan. 27, 1955.

[33] *Williams* v. *Eady, supra*.

[34] *Williams* v. *Eady, supra* (bottles of phosphorus in a conservatory).

[35] *Sullivan* v. *Creed* [1904] 2 I.R. 317, *per* Gibson J, cited with approval in *Wray* v. *Essex County Council* [1936] 3 All E.R. 97.

[36] *Chilvers* v. *London County Council* (1916) 80 J.P. 246; *Dixon* v. *Roper, The Times*, Feb. 3, 1922; *Wray* v. *Essex County Council, supra*.

[37] *Wray* v. *Essex County Council, supra*.

[38] *Beaumont* v. *Surrey County Council, supra*.

[39] *Rickets* v. *Erith Borough Council* [1943] 2 All E.R. 629.

[40] *Clark* v. *Monmouth County Council* (1954) 52 L.G.R. 246.

the test of reasonableness. It has, however, been held not to be necessary to provide continuous supervision for a group of 50 children aged between about six and 10 while in the playground during a school break,[41] and not to be negligence to leave the supervision of well disciplined pupils to prefects.[42] Physical activities that can ordinarily be carried out without serious injury are not to be regarded as dangerous merely because an accident can happen,[43] but there will be negligence where a person in charge of such an activity does not act promptly to avert a danger of which he should be aware.[44] Failure to observe a possibly dangerous happening does not, however, necessarily indicate negligence on the part of a person in charge of a group of children,[45] nor is there negligence in such a person failing to prevent an unexpected and unforseen misfortune.[46] Compliance with a general practice successfully followed over a period of years affords evidence that there was no negligence.[47] Although legislation on safety in factories does not apply to schools, failure to meet the requirements of that legislation may be an indication of negligence in the safety arrangements made by persons responsible for comparable technical processes in schools.[48]

Statutory Parental Rights

In addition to the above rights and powers, there are a number of other rights that adhere to parents (and others) as a result of express statutory provision. These are, in the main, discussed elsewhere in the present text, and are mentioned here only for the sake of completeness. Who may exercise these rights is governed by the statutes controlling them, as is the issue of how long they last. They include the right to agree to adoption,[49] the right to apply for the determination of a resolution vesting parental rights in a local authority,[50] the right to attend at all stages of a children's hearing who are considering the case of the child,[51] the right to appoint a guardian by testamentary deed,[52] the right to register a child's birth,[53] the right to apply for the recording of a change in the child's name,[54] and the right of access to the child's health records.[55] While these rights could be subject to "an action relating to parental rights" under section 3(1) of the Law Reform (Parent and Child) (Scotland) Act 1986, which will therefore be determined according to the welfare test laid out in section 3(2), the rights themselves arise independently of that statute, and vest according to the terms

---

[41] *Ricketts* v. *Erith Borough Council, supra. Cf. Price* v. *Carnarvon County Council, The Times* Feb. 11, 1960.
[42] *Jacques* v. *Oxfordshire County Council* (1968) 66 L.G.R. 440.
[43] *Jones* v. *London County Council* (1932) 96 J.P. 371.
[44] *Gibbs* v. *Barking Corporation* [1936] 1 All E.R. 115.
[45] *Clarke* v. *Bethnall Green Borough Council* (1939) 55 T.L.R. 519.
[46] *Gow* v. *Glasgow Education Authority*, 1922 S.C. 260.
[47] *Wright* v. *Cheshire County Council* [1952] 2 All E.R. 789.
[48] *Butt* v. *Inner London Education Authority* (1968) 66 L.G.R. 379.
[49] Adoption (Scotland) Act 1978, s. 16(1)(*b*).
[50] Social Work (Scotland) Act 1968, s. 18.
[51] *Ibid.*, s. 41.
[52] Law Reform (Parent and Child) (Scotland) Act 1986, s. 4.
[53] Registration of Births, Deaths and Marriages (Scotland) Act 1965, s. 14.
[54] *Ibid.*, s. 43.
[55] Access to Health Records Act 1990, s. 3(1).

of the Act that created them rather than according to the terms of the 1986 Act.[56] Details of these rights can be found in other parts of this book.

---

[56] The parental rights defined as such in s. 8 of the 1986 Act are restricted to guardianship, custody and access, and any other right conferred "by any rule of law." This means that statutory rights are excluded from the terms of the 1986 Act, because, as the Scottish Law Commission point out, "that expression is normally used in statutes in relation to common law rules: if statutory rules are to be included the term normally used is 'any enactment or rule of law'": Discussion Paper No. 88, *Parental Responsibilities and Rights, Guardianship and the Administration of Children's Property*, Oct. 1990, para. 2. 11.

CHAPTER 7

CUSTODY

THE MEANING OF CUSTODY

Custody means keeping or guarding. Speaking of the contract of custody of things, Stair[1] says that it "is most fitly expressed by the duty and obligation thereof, which is to keep or preserve that which is given in custody." The custody of children, as a legal relation, arises not from contract but by operation of law or order of the court and the principles applicable to the custody of things require some refinement if they are to be applied in the case of children. The obligation which the custodian of a child owes is not merely to preserve the child in life and keep him from harm but more positively to care for him and promote his welfare. With that gloss, the stress on keeping and preserving as a matter of obligation is apt. Questions of the custody of children most often arise from claims made by potential custodians and envisage powers to be exercised; and the lawful custodian, of course, has certain powers over the person of the child and the right to exercise these powers to the exclusion of others. But the primary character of custody, in contemplation of the law, is as a source of obligation.[2] He who has the custody of a child has thereby undertaken obligations to which such rights and powers as he has are ancillary.

In English law custody was a term of wide scope and some ambiguity. Although capable of a more restricted meaning, it may have gone so far as to embrace the "whole bundle of rights" and powers vested in a parent or guardian.[3] The amplitude of the concept of parental power, derived from the ancient *patria potestas*, and the institutions of tutory and curatory, obviate the need for such a wide-ranging concept in Scots law. There is no Scottish authority for giving to custody anything other than its ordinary meaning. It is the "cure and keiping" or "keiping and custodie" or simply "keiping" of the person to which the old cases refer.[4] The rights and powers which it confers are, therefore, those of physical control and the regulation of everyday life which goes with that control, and it is not strictly necessary to imply anything further. Exceptionally, however, custody may be given to one party, so that in the event of a change in circumstances he has the right to control the child's upbringing and residence, against his undertaking that as long as circumstances remain unchanged he will allow the child in fact to be in the care of another party.[5] There is in such a case some re-

---

[1] I, xiii, 1.
[2] As are the other parental rights: see *ante* at pp. 163–166.
[3] *Hewer* v. *Bryant* [1969] 3 All E.R. 578, *per* Sachs J. at p. 585, approved by Lord Scarman in *Gillick* v. *West Norfolk and Wisbech Area Health Authority* [1985] 3 W.L.R. 830 at p. 854.
[4] See the cases cited in Balfour, CXXIII to CXXXI, pp. 336–338, *sub nom*, "of keiping of *minoris persounis*."
[5] *Robertson* v. *Robertson*, 1981 S.L.T. (Notes) 7. *Cf.* the English decision of *Dipper* v. *Dipper* [1981] Fam. 31, where the Court of Appeal questioned the general usefulness of this approach.

semblance to the English distinction between custody on the one hand, and care
and control on the other, but in Scotland custody does not carry with it parental
or guardianship powers other than those associated with control of the person.[6]
The change in English law from a concept of custody to a concept of residence[7]
was therefore more fundamental than a similar change would be in Scots law.[8]
The right to keep the child, that is the right to the custody of the child, would become the right to have the child residing with one, and the parental responsibilities would flow not from that right but from the care and control that one has of
the child.

Custody, Education and Upbringing

At one time custody and education were often separated, particularly on the
death of the father,[9] but in modern practice it is taken as a matter of course that
custody carries with it the right to regulate the child's education and upbringing
unless the court specifically orders otherwise.[10] There are obvious convenience
and good sense both in that practice and in a reluctance to make education and
upbringing the subject of separate judicial regulation. In principle it is, however, possible to regulate separately any aspect of a child's upbringing including education, which is not so intimately connected with physical control that its
separate regulation would destroy that control; and there is no doubt that it is
still competent for the court to do so.[11] It is no objection that the rights and powers of the custodian are thereby modified or abridged because that is always
open in the interest of the welfare of the child.[12] There is also no reason, in principle, against giving the child's custody to one person and the regulation of his
education, or some other aspect of his upbringing, to another,[13] but, unless the

---

[6] For the consequences of this rule, see *Kirk* v. *Scottish Gas Board*, 1968 S.C. 328.

[7] Children Act 1989.

[8] As suggested by Scot. Law Com. No. 135, *Report on Family Law*, May 1992, paras. 2.28–2.30.

[9] Thus, on the death of the father, custody and the regulation of the education of his children under
seven were treated as separable, the former vesting in the mother and the latter vesting in the tutor
(*Borthwick* v. *Dundas* (1845) 8 D. 318. *Cf. Campbell* v. *Campbell* (1833) 11 S. 544; *Scot* v. *Scot*
(1759) Mor. 16361). That may be sufficiently explained by the desire to give effect to the wishes
of the father regarding education which the tutor, especially if a tutor nominate, might be supposed to represent and by the fact that the child's estate, which might have to be employed for his
education, was under the management of the tutor.

[10] *e.g. McNaught* v. *McNaught*, 1955 S.L.T. (Sh.Ct.) 9 at p. 10, and *Zamorski* v. *Zamorska*, 1960
S.L.T. (Notes) 26 in which the child's education and religious upbringing were treated as, or
assumed to be, dependent on the decision of custody. Also, in *Robertson* v. *Robertson*, 1981
S.L.T. (Notes) 7, in which the child was allowed to live with the mother although custody was
granted to the father, the judge envisaged that decisions relating to the child's education would be
a matter for the (legal) custodian.

[11] The wording of s. 3(1) of the Law Reform (Parent and Child) (Scotland) Act 1986, allowing the
court to "make such order relating to parental rights as it thinks fit," is clearly wide enough to
allow the court to regulate custody, education and upbringing separately if it thinks fit to do so.
See also s. 20 of the Court of Session Act 1988.

[12] That is implicit in the requirement of s. 3(2) of the Law Reform (Parent and Child) (Scotland) Act
1986 that in any proceedings relating to parental rights the court shall regard the welfare of the
child as the paramount consideration. Moreover, an award of access has always and necessarily
involved some abridgement of the custodian's rights: see *post*, at pp. 226–227.

[13] As in *Robertson* v. *Robertson, supra.* "Custody is a legal right which can be held even if it is not
being physically exercised": *D.* v. *Strathclyde Regional Council*, 1985 S.L.T. 114 at p. 116.

parties are in agreement, that is likely to be productive of conflict.[14] Where, therefore, the education and upbringing of the child are not to be left wholly in the hands of the custodian, it will usually be preferable for the court itself to regulate the excepted matters by specific provision. Where there is no court order dealing with education or upbringing it is submitted that it may now be taken to be the law that the right to regulate both belongs wholly to the custodian. A guardian who is not custodian may not therefore intervene except that, again subject to judicial regulation in the interests of the welfare of the child, he may decline to employ his ward's estate for a course of education or upbringing of which he does not approve.

Custody and Possession

It is sometimes alleged as a defect of the law that by giving children into the custody of adults it allows them to be treated as possessions. Such criticisms may, at first impression, gain added force from the legal ascription to parents of an apparent right of dominion over their children under 16, coming from the common law notion of pupillarity, with a connotation of ownership which, on its face, puts the parental right even higher than possession. The parental right of dominion is, however, qualified by the purpose for which it exists and is very different from rights of ownership which may be exercised over things or which primitive systems may have allowed over persons. In any event custody is to be distinguished from possession. Possession is the holding or detaining of something, either personally or through the instrumentality of others, for one's own use. "To possession there must be an act of the body, which is detention and holding; and an act of the mind, which is the inclination or affection to make use of the thing detained."[15] Custody, although it resembles possession in the material element of detaining or holding, is to be distinguished in the mental element. The custodian holds not for his own use but for behoof of someone else. In the case of custody of children, it is the child himself who is contemplated as the person to be benefited and the exercise of the powers of custody is legitimate only in so far as directed to that end.

Custody in Fact and in Law

The expression "custody" can be used to describe both a factual situation and a legal relation. If we say of someone that "he has the custody" of a child, we may mean either (i) that he has charge of and cares for the child in a way which we associate with custody and usually, therefore, not on a temporary or delegated basis; or (ii) that he is the lawful custodian whether or not he, in fact, exercises the powers and fulfils the obligations to which that gives rise. Although the factual sense may be the primary one on which the legal superstructure has been built, both usages are intelligible and legitimate; custody is not only a factual concept but is capable of definition in legal terms. Because of this ambiguity, expressions such as "actual" or "*de facto*" custody as opposed to "legal" or "*de*

---

[14] For the same reason, the circumstances in which an award of joint custody is appropriate are likely to be rare: *McKechnie* v. *McKechnie*, 1990 S.L.T. (Sh.Ct.) 75 at p. 76 (though competent: *Mackenzie* v. *Hendry*, 1984 S.L.T. 322).

[15] Stair, II, i, 17.

jure" custody are sometimes used. The former describes the factual situation,
the latter the legal relation of the child and lawful custodian. It may be preferable to speak of custody only where it has a legal basis and, in other cases, to use
"charge" or "care"; but even that solution is not completely free from ambiguity
because of the use of care in a legal sense, or at any rate in a sense to which special legal incidents attach, in the case of local authority care and of committals
to care. Usually the sense in which custody is used will be clear from the context; where it is not, the use of qualifying epithets such as "actual" and "legal" or
their equivalents removes any obscurity.[16]

Effect of Welfare Principle on Parental Rights: Residual Rights

Though custody is defined as a parental "right,"[17] because the welfare of the
child is now paramount[18] no one, not even a parent, can have, for the purpose of
judicial proceedings, a right of custody which, if it were to receive effect, would
conflict with the child's welfare.[19] Except where there is, by the standard of the
child's welfare, an even balance among the claimants, all questions of right to
custody, whether parental or otherwise, are altogether excluded. That is true not
only of questions between parents *inter se* but also of questions between parents
and strangers.[20] Moreover, in a question between parents, where both have automatic vested rights,[21] the effect of equating the parents is that there is no priority
attaching to one parent rather than the other from the standpoint of residual
right. There are, however, two, and only two, senses in which it may still be per-
missible to speak of a right inherent in a parent to custody of a child.

First, there is a right to custody which is *prima facie* in the sense that, where
there is no court order regulating custody, the right that arises by operation of
section 2(1)(*a*) (for mothers) or section 2(1)(*b*) (for fathers) of the 1986 Act is
entitled to legal respect and protection unless, and until, there is a court order to
the contrary. Mothers always do and fathers may have such *prima facie* rights
(unless their parental rights and powers have been extinguished by legal process, *e.g.* by an adoption order or by a resolution vesting parental rights and
powers in a local authority) and so do persons in whom parental rights and powers have vested. In a question, however, between parents, or between parents'
nominees, neither party has a higher right than the other pending resolution of
the dispute by judicial decision.

Secondly, in a question between parents and others, parents have a right to be
preferred where there is an even balance from the standpoint of the child's wel-

---

[16] Legislative credence to the separation of the two concepts is given by the Children Act 1975,
where, for the purposes of that Act, "actual custody" is defined to mean "care and control," while
"legal custody" is defined to mean "custody": s. 107(2).

[17] Law Reform (Parent and Child) (Scotland) Act 1986, s. 8.

[18] *Ibid.*, s. 3(2).

[19] Thus the case of *Macpherson* v. *Leishman* (1887) 14 R. 780 is no longer good law. In that case the
"right" of a mother to custody of her illegitimate child was enforced, notwithstanding that the
judges considered this to be against the interests of the child.

[20] *J.* v. *C.* [1970] A.C. 668, which, as a decision on the interpretation of a United Kingdom statute
(the Guardianship of Infants Act 1925) must, it is submitted, be taken as superseding earlier Scottish authorities to the contrary. See also *Cheetham* v. *Glasgow Corporation*, 1972 S.L.T. (Notes)
50.

[21] Under s. 2(1)(*a*) and (*b*).

fare between them and the other claimant or claimants. That is the effect of the common law as amended by the Guardianship Act 1973 and, to that very limited extent, is unaffected by the Law Reform (Parent and Child) (Scotland) Act 1986. On the same principle, after the death of both parents, the nominee of either of them is probably entitled to a preference if the balance from the standpoint of the child's welfare is even as between him and other claimants who are not nominees. In view of the various tragedies which have occurred as a result of a misplaced stress on parental rights it is necessary to emphasise that the rights of parents or their nominees, even in the very limited sense under discussion, are entirely subordinated to a consideration of the welfare of the child. Although the placing of a child in the custody of its parent and so preserving a natural bond, may often be for the child's welfare, it is a question of circumstances of each case whether or not that is so, and there is no rule of law which gives the parent a preference if that does not consist with the welfare of the child. Indeed the law is rather the reverse; the child's welfare must prevail against any consideration which is seriously in conflict with it.

Persons other than Parents

Persons other than parents may sometimes have residual rights to custody. (1) While an application for an adoption order is pending in a case where a parent or guardian of the child has agreed to the making of the order, or (2) while an application made without the consent of each parent or guardian is pending for an order freeing a child for adoption and the child is in the care of the adoption agency, or (3) where a child has been in the care of a local authority for six months or more: in all of these cases parental rights are abridged and the custodial right of the prospective adopters, the adoption agency and the local authority respectively are correspondingly enlarged.[22] Similar protection, enforceable against anyone seeking to disturb it, is given to a person who applies, or gives notice in writing of his intention to apply, for an adoption order and with whom the child whom he proposes to adopt has had his home for five years preceding the application or notice.[23] More generally, persons who do not have a specifically recognised legal right to custody, but into whose actual custody a child has lawfully passed, may, in a question with persons with no better title, be entitled to retain that custody pending judicial determination on the view that they hold under the licence, express or tacit, of the lawful custodian or that, in the absence of sufficient cause to the contrary, the *status quo* should be preserved pending judicial decision. On the latter view, it may be lawful to retain custody even in a question with a person with a better title if there is immediate danger of serious harm to the child should it be removed.

Prima facie rights of the kind under consideration may be of importance in the extrajudicial resolution of disputes, but by their nature can seldom require consideration in judicial proceedings. They may however be relevant where

---

[22] Adoption (Scotland) Act 1978, ss. 27 and 28; Social Work (Scotland) Act 1968, s. 15(3A) (as inserted by the Children Act 1975, s. 73 and amended by the Health and Social Services and Social Security Adjudications Act 1983, Sched. 2, para. 4).

[23] Adoption (Scotland) Act 1978, s. 28, as amended by the Health and Social Services and Social Security Adjudications Act 1983, Sched. 2, para. 43.

plagium is alleged or in other proceedings for the wrongful detention of a child and a person with a right to custody may pursue an action of delivery without the necessity of concluding for custody.

TITLE TO SUE AND AWARD OF CUSTODY

Common Law and Law Reform (Parent and Child)(Scotland) Act 1986

A discussion of rights to custody subsumes the question of title to sue. As has been seen, a consideration of rights is now obsolete except in a limited *prima facie* sense and for certain secondary purposes. Custody decisions have, since 1925,[24] depended entirely on the welfare principle. At first impression, however, that principle appears to be concerned with the question of to whom custody should be given (the award) rather than of who may apply (title to sue) and these questions, although they often coalesce to an extent that they can be separated only with some awkwardness, are in principle, and sometimes in practice, distinct. Section 3(1) of the Law Reform (Parent and Child) (Scotland) Act 1986 provides that "any person claiming interest may make an application to the court for an order relating to parental rights," while section 3(2) directs the court to regard the welfare of the child involved as the paramount consideration "in any proceedings relating to parental rights." It would follow that any person who claims interest will have title to sue, and that the court must determine any application consistently with the welfare test but any conflict inherent in that formulation is removed by a liberal interpretation of what constitutes interest. A trend in the direction of liberality for questions of title to sue had been apprehended by the sheriff-substitute in *Samson* v. *Samson*,[25] when he said: "In this class of cases, *i.e.* for custody of children, the ordinary test of title to sue, viz. a *prima facie* right and an interest, seems subject to modification; some *prima facie* right no doubt there must be, but interest in the pursuer gives place to what is really the true principle—the welfare of the children." More recently Lord Dunpark has said that if the welfare principle

> "was to be applied wherever the custody of an infant was in issue and whoever the parties, it should follow that the court has power not merely to apply that principle to defeat a parent's claim but also to uphold a claim to custody by the opposing party. Unless the section[26] is so construed, it may have the highly undesirable effect of leaving the child in legal limbo with no person having *de jure* custody."[27]

In any event, the common law does not appear to have imposed any close restriction by way of title to sue. Applications have been entertained at the instance of a tutor-at-law,[28] a tutor-nominate,[29] testamentary trustees of the father

---

[24] Guardianship of Infants Act 1925, s. 1.
[25] 1922 S.L.T. (Sh.Ct.) 34.
[26] Guardianship of Infants Act 1925, s. 1, which laid down the welfare principle.
[27] *Cheetham* v. *Glasgow Corporation*, 1972 S.L.T. (Notes) 50 at p. 51.
[28] *Walker* v. *Walker* (1824) 2 S. 788.
[29] *Low, Petr.*, 1920 S.C. 351.

of an illegitimate child,[30] a judicial factor,[31] a stepmother,[32] a great-aunt,[33] and there are numerous instances, both before and after the 1986 Act, of applications by grandparents.[34] These are, however, only illustrations. There is no indication in the authorities of limitation of title to sue to these classes or, indeed, of any other limitation.[35] In *Syme* v. *Cunningham*[36] Lord Keith was relying on the common law rather than statute when he said: "In my opinion, the court has power under the *nobile officium* to entertain and deal with an application for custody of an illegitimate child at the instance of any person who can qualify a proper interest."[37] Although expressed in relation to an illegitimate child, the same principle must today apply to the custody of all children. On this matter there is little or no conflict between the common law and section 3(1) of the Law Reform (Parent and Child) (Scotland) Act 1986 and it can be asserted with some confidence that their combined effect is to free title to sue in custody proceedings from any artificial limitation.[38] There had been conflicting Outer House authority on the question whether the 1986 Act, with its verbal emphasis on "parental rights," limited title to sue to those claiming to be parents,[39] but that conflict has now been resolved by the First Division, Lord President Hope holding that the use of the phrase "parental rights" in the 1986 Act is "merely a convenient way of describing those rights which are defined in section 9 of the 1986 Act. I do not think that it implies any limitation on those persons who may apply

---

[30] *Whitson* v. *Speid* (1825) 4 S. 42.

[31] *A.B.* v. *C.D.* (1837) 9 Sc. Jur. 536; *Paul* (1838) 16 S. 822; *Denny* v. *Mcnish* (1863) 1 M. 268; *Muir* v. *Milligan* (1868) 6 M. 1125; *Gulland* v. *Henderson* (1878) 5 R. 768—all cases at the instance of a judicial factor against the mother of a fatherless legitimate child—*Moncreiff* (1891) 18 R. 1029 (a judicial factor against the father of a legitimate child).

[32] *Stewart* v. *Brodie* (1887) 3 Sh. Ct. Rep. 405 (stepmother against aunt).

[33] *Girvan, Petr.*, 1985 S.L.T. 92.

[34] *e.g. Erskine* v. *Connolly* (1916) 32 Sh. Ct. Rep. 163 (grandmother against father of legitimate child); *Law* v. *Elrick* (1939) 55 Sh. Ct. Rep. 253 (grandmother against stranger for custody of illegitimate child); *Richardson* v. *Burns*, 1963 S.L.T. (Sh. Ct.) 26 (grandmother against father of legitimate child); *Cochrane* v. *Keys*, 1968 S.L.T. (Notes) 64 (maternal grandmother against father of legitimate child); *Klein and Anr., Petrs.*, 1969 S.L.T. (Notes) 53 (paternal grandparents against mother of legitimate child); *Syme* v. *Cunningham*, 1973 S.L.T. (Notes) 40 (grandmother against father of illegitimate child); *F.* v. *F.*, 1991 S.L.T. 357 (grandparents against prospective adopters). See also *MacInnes* v. *Highland Regional Council*, 1982 S.C. 69, in which grandparents sought access, and *M.* v. *Lothian Regional Council*, 1989 S.L.T. 426, in which grandparents sought to be appointed tutors to allow them to make representations to a children's hearing.

[35] In *Hunter's Trs.* v. *Speed*, Dec. 2, 1820, F.C. 211, the court expressed doubt on the petitioners' title to sue when confronted with an argument on their behalf that "it does not seem very material by whom the application is made, provided it be made by a person who, in some shape or other, has some kind of interest in the child," but in subsequent proceedings (*Whitson* v. *Speid (sic)* (1825) 4 S. 42) went on to grant an application at the instance of the same parties (testamentary trustees of the father of an illegitimate child).

[36] 1973 S.L.T. (Notes) 40.

[37] at p. 40. Although reference to the *nobile officium* was made a distinction between the Court of Session and the sheriff court in respect of title to sue would be anomalous in view of the broad terms in which custody jurisdiction has been given to the sheriff court. The reference to the *nobile officium* does not, in this context, confine what is said to the Court of Session because the sheriff court may now exercise the powers of the *nobile officium* in custody matters.

[38] "The apparent purpose of [s. 3 of the 1986 Act] was to remove any restriction or doubt as to title to apply by enacting that it was sufficient that the applicant claimed an interest," *per* Lord Cullen in *M.* v. *Lothian Regional Council*, 1989 S.L.T. 426 at p. 428, approved 1990 S.L.T. 116, and by Lord President Hope in *F.* v. *F.*, 1991 S.L.T. 357 at p. 361H.

[39] In *A.B., Petr.*, 1988 S.L.T. 652, Lord McCluskey held that only persons claiming to be parents had a right to apply for parental rights under s. 3, and consequently that the sister of children adopted had no title to apply for access. In *M.* v. *Lothian Regional Council*, 1989 S.L.T. 426 Lord

for them."[40] It may be added that the fact that custody jurisdiction, although somewhat overlain by statute, is based on the *nobile officium* in itself points to a liberal view of title to sue. It is implicit in other statutory provisions that, in relation to custody at any rate, the application can be made by other than the parents or those claiming to be parents.[41]

"Interest"

Some dicta, however, notably of Lord Keith in *Syme* v. *Cunningham*, stipulate the need for an applicant for custody to qualify a proper interest; and section 3(1) itself appears to limit title to persons "claiming interest." The underlying notion is one of legitimate concern. Usually a prior connection with the child will be necessary to found such concern, but there may be exceptional cases in which the welfare principle requires that a sufficient interest is qualified where, even without prior connection with the child, an applicant can show a *prima facie* case that the custody arrangement which he proposes will be for the child's welfare. In any event, the requisite interest is, it is submitted, possessed by anyone who has lawfully had the child in his or her care for any material length of time. Accordingly, foster parents have title to sue. Indeed, title and interest are probably possessed by practically any *bona fide* applicant. In *Beagley* v. *Beagley*[42] the child's schoolmaster and a close friend of the family are given as examples; but on the same authority it is clear that there are some limitations—it was held in that case that there is no title to sue in a parent on whose account a parental rights resolution has been passed.[43]

Award of Custody to Non-Applicants

Because questions of title to sue, on the one hand, and of the person to whom custody may be awarded, on the other, although closely related are distinct, custody may be awarded to someone other than the applicant. That is a necessary implication from the words of section 3(1) of the 1986 Act, allowing the court to make "such order relating to parental rights as it thinks fit," and it is also, it is submitted, implied in the power given to the court by the Court of Session Act

---

Cullen held that the 1986 Act did not restrict the pre-existing law on title to sue and that consequently the court could entertain applications by any interested third party for the granting of an order relating to rights which were conferred on a parent by a rule of law (Lord Cullen's decision was approved 1990 S.L.T. 116, though the point at issue here was not mentioned by the Inner House). See also *Whyte* v. *Hardie* 1990 S.C.L.R. 23, where the sheriff followed this approach.

[40] *F.* v. *F.*, 1991 S.L.T. 357, *per* Lord President Hope, at p. 361.

[41] The Children Act 1975 provides, by s. 48, that where an application relating to custody of a child is made the person making the application shall, so far as practicable, give notice of that application to each known parent of the child; and by s. 49 that where an application for custody is made by someone not a parent of the child, notice of the application is to be given to the local authority in whose area the applicant resides.

[42] 1984 S.L.T. 202, *per* Lord Fraser of Tullybelton at p. 206.

[43] This limitation can be explained by the need not to undermine the care proceedings with which the case was concerned. Similarly, *A.B., Petr. (supra)* can be explained by the desire of the judge not to undermine the adoption legislation. A supervision requirement under s. 44 of the Social Work (Scotland) Act 1968 does not deprive parents of parental rights, and therefore does not deprive them of title to sue: *D.* v. *Strathclyde Regional Council*, 1985 S.L.T. 114 (though in that case it was held that an application for access was incompetent since it would undermine the scheme of the legislation: an application for custody would not have done so since its effect could be suspended).

1988[44] to make "such order (including an interim order) as it thinks fit relating to parental rights." The effect of these enactments is that there is no restriction on the persons to whose custody a child may be committed except that the committal must be consistent with the welfare of the child regarded as the paramount consideration.

Award of Custody Under the Children Act 1975

The Children Act 1975 contains provisions apparently reformulating the law of Scotland on the persons to whom custody may be awarded. Section 47(2) enacts that, notwithstanding the generality of section 3(1) of the Law Reform (Parent and Child) (Scotland) Act 1986, custody of a child shall not be granted in any proceedings to a person other than a parent or guardian of the child unless that person:

(a) being a relative[45] or step-parent of the child, has the consent of a parent or guardian[46] of the child and has had care and possession of the child for the three months preceding the making of the application for custody; or

(b) has the consent of a parent or guardian of the child and has had care and possession of the child for a period or periods before such application, which amounted to at least 12 months and included the three months preceding such application; or

(c) has had care and possession of the child for a period or periods before such application which amounted to at least three years and included the three months preceding such application; or

(d) while not falling within paragraphs (a), (b) or (c) above, can show cause why an order should be made awarding him custody of the child.

The concluding paragraph (d) deprives the conditions laid down in the preceding paragraphs (a) to (c) of any practical meaning. A custody order cannot be made in favour of a person who satisfies any of the conditions laid down in paragraphs (a) to (c) unless it is also shown that to do so would be consistent with the welfare principle of the 1986 Act. Under paragraph (d), however, it would be sufficient cause for the applicant to show that it is in the interests of the child for custody to be awarded to him, and the wording does no more than emphasise where the onus lies. Section 47(2) is expressly stated to be applicable "notwithstanding the generality of s. 3(1)" of the 1986 Act, which suggests that it is a

---

[44] s. 20, re-enacting s. 9 of the Conjugal Rights (Scotland) Amendment Act 1861, as substituted by the Law Reform (Parent and Child) (Scotland) Act 1986, Sched. 1, para. 2.

[45] For the purposes of these provisions, "relative" means a grandparent, brother, sister, aunt or uncle, whether of the full blood or half blood or by affinity, and includes where the child is illegitimate the father of the child and any person who would be a relative of the child within the meaning of the definition if the child were legitimate: 1975 Act, s. 107(1), referring to the definition given in s. 57(1) of the (now repealed) Adoption Act 1958.

[46] For the purpose of these provisions, "guardian" means (a) a person appointed by a deed or will or by a court of competent jurisdiction to be the guardian of the child and (b) in the case of a child whose father is not married to the mother, includes the father where he has, in relation to the child, guardianship, custody, access, or any other parental right by virtue of an order by a court of competent jurisdiction: 1975 Act, s. 47(5)(a), referring to the definition given in s. 65 of the Adoption Act 1978 (as amended by the Age of Legal Capacity (Scotland) Act 1991, Sched. 1, para. 36).

limitation to that generality, but paragraph (d) has the effect of restoring that very generality, and therefore renders section 47(2) otiose. This was recognised by the First Division in *F*. v. *F*.,[47] where Lord President Hope said: "in my opinion s. 47(2)(*d*) must be read together with s. 3(2) of the 1986 Act, and that sufficient cause is shown if the court is satisfied on balance of probabilities that the welfare of the child requires that the order be made in the child's best interests."[48]

WELFARE OF CHILD AND CRITERIA FOR CUSTODY

The Law Reform (Parent and Child) (Scotland) Act 1986

Section 3(2) of the Law Reform (Parent and Child) (Scotland) Act 1986 requires that the court regard the welfare of the child as the paramount consideration and also that it shall not make any order relating to parental rights unless it is satisfied that to do so will be in the interests of the child. The court is barred from making any order relating to parental rights, which by section 8 includes custody, unless it is satisfied that to do so will be in the interests of the child: the effect of this would appear to be that the onus will always be on the applicant to prove the satisfaction of the welfare test, and that failure to do so will result in the applicant losing the case.[49] The standard of proof that the applicant must satisfy is the normal standard of proof on the balance of probabilities.[50] The section applies, in relation to custody, to all children below the age of 16 years[51] and it applies whether or not the child's parents are married to each other.[52] It is not provided but is, it is submitted, implicit that neither the father's claim nor the mother's claim is to be regarded as stronger: the question is the child's interest, not the strength of the parents' rights. The repealing of section 10 of the Guardianship Act 1973,[53] which granted equality to both parents' rights, is not to be taken to revive the common law preference for the father of the legitimate child, for the 1986 Act treats of parental rights without differentiation between father and mother of a child born in wedlock and in terms which exclude any ground for preference.[54] And the common law preference for the mother of the illegitimate child survives only in the sense that the father of a child born out of wedlock has no parental rights unless he marries the mother or he applies for them and shows that it is in the child's interests that they be granted to him.

---

[47] 1991 S.L.T. 357 at p. 362.

[48] The Scottish Law Commission described these provisions as "a bizarre set of pseudo-restrictions," and, referring to the reasons given by Wilkinson, 1976 S.L.T. (News) 221, has suggested the complete repealing of s. 47: see Scot. Law Com. No. 135, May 1992, recommendation 30 at para. 5.10.

[49] See *Porchetta* v. *Porchetta*, 1986 S.L.T. 105; *Montgomery* v. *Lockwood*, 1987 S.C.L.R. 525; *M*. v. *Lothian Regional Council*, 1989 S.L.T. 426, *per* Lord Cullen at p. 429.

[50] *Per* Lord President Hope in *F*. v. *F*., 1991 S.L.T. 357 at p. 362, approving the sheriff in *Sloss* v. *Taylor*, 1989 S.C.L.R. 407, and disapproving the sheriff in *McEachan* v. *Young*, 1988 S.C.L.R. 98. The House of Lords has held that to prove that there is at least a risk of harm to the child is proof that its welfare is threatened, and that actual harm is not required before the standard of proof is satisfied: *per* Lord Oliver of Aylmerton in *Re K.D. (A Minor) (Ward: Termination of Access)* [1988] 2 W.L.R. 398 at p. 408.

[51] Law Reform (Parent and Child) (Scotland) Act 1986, s. 8.

[52] *Ibid*., s. 1(1).

[53] *Ibid*., Sched. 2.

[54] s. 2(1).

Meaning of "Paramount Consideration"

The court is directed to regard the child's welfare as the paramount consideration.[55] It has been said that paramount does not mean exclusive and so considerations, other than the welfare of the child, may enter into the decision.[56] That is probably still the law but paramountcy is to be understood in a strong sense and the fact that it does not mean exclusive does not detract from the overriding importance of the child's welfare as against any consideration inconsistent with it. The claims of an "unimpeachable parent" or "the essential justice of the case" cannot prevail against it.[57] The course to be followed will be that which is most in the interests of the child's welfare "when all the relevant facts, relationships, claims and wishes of parents, risks, choices and other circumstances are taken into account and weighed." The child's welfare "is the first consideration because it is of first importance and the paramount consideration because it rules upon or determines the course to be followed."[58] If the child's welfare rules upon, or determines, the course to be followed it follows that all the circumstances must be viewed in that context and that no consideration can receive effect in the decision unless it is related to the child's welfare. The only exception to that can be where regard for the child's welfare does not afford a basis of choice because either, or any, of the courses available would serve that interest equally well. Only when, from the welfare standpoint, there is an equal balance can other considerations come into play. That equality of balance should not, however, be regarded in too narrow or closely structured terms. Welfare judgments often embrace a choice among risks, depend on contingencies, and are based upon uncertain opinions. No consideration, however cogent it may otherwise be, can prevail against what is clearly for the child's welfare. Where, however, there is uncertainty there is some scope for giving weight to other considerations always provided that they are not prejudicial to the child's welfare. Since 1925 no intrinsic merit or demerit has attached to the conduct or wishes of one spouse as against the other although a preference may be exercised according to the circumstances of the given case. Beyond that there is no statutory guidance on the considerations other than welfare to be taken into account. It was said in a case under the 1925 Act that where the welfare considerations are equally balanced weight may still be attached to the position of the father as head of the family,[59] but that is difficult to reconcile with the equality of parental authority, created by the Guardianship Act 1973 and implicit in the 1986 Act. Responsibility for the breakdown of the marriage is an aspect of conduct which has frequently been taken into account.[60] The court is not, however,

---

[55] *Ibid.*, s. 3(2).

[56] *Re O. (Infants)* [1962] 1 W.L.R. 724; *Re L. (Infants)* [1962] 1 W.L.R. 886.

[57] *S.* v. *S.* (1975) 5 Fam. L. 148 in which *Re L., supra*, is treated as overruled by *J.* v. *C., supra*. The proposition that paramount does not mean exclusive, if understood in the sense indicated in the text, is not, however, inconsistent with *J.* v. *C. Hume* v. *Hume*, 1926 S.C. 1008 and *M.* v. *M.*, 1926 S.C. 778, in which a larger scope was claimed for considerations other than the child's welfare, must be regarded as overruled by *J.* v. *C.*

[58] *J.* v. *C.* [1970] A.C. 668, *per* Lord MacDermott at p. 711.

[59] *Douglas* v. *Douglas*, 1950 S.C. 453.

[60] *Hume* v. *Hume*, 1926 S.C. 1008 at p. 1010; *Christison* v. *Christison*, 1936 S.C. 381; *Christie* v. *Christie*, 1945 S.L.T. 300; *Spicer* v. *Spicer*, 1946 S.L.T. (Notes) 24; *Douglas* v. *Douglas*, 1950 S.C. 453; *Stevenson* v. *Stevenson*, 1967 S.L.T. (Notes) 7.

concerned, in a question of custody, to penalise spouses for failure in marital duty.[61] In a question between parent and stranger, consideration may have to be given, and weight attached according to circumstances, both to a natural parental desire for the society of a child and the reluctance of persons who have cared for a child over a period of time to see a bond of affection broken. Such matters are, however, always to be entirely subordinated to the regard due to the child's welfare and, in general, it is only in that context that the conduct and claims of parents or others should be taken into account.[62]

Welfare Principle—Meaning and Application

The welfare principle offers an admirable ideal for the regulation of custody disputes, but its protean character gives rise to difficulties in application. Extreme cases are clear. Confronted with squalor, cruelty, neglect or exposure to depravity on the one hand, and a wholesome environment on the other, there is no problem. More often, however, the decision will turn on more subtle and debatable factors on which there may be wide latitude of opinion. It may be objected that the welfare principle leaves matters of the highest importance to child, parent and others in the hands of a virtually unfettered discretion, that such well verified insights into a child's welfare as we have, whether from ordinary lay experience or from scientific knowledge, should be embodied in rules, even if only of a presumptive character, and that, beyond rules so derived, our views of welfare form a dubious basis for decision. Judicial decision has compensated to some extent but unevenly for the fluidity and uncertainty of the welfare principle. On some, but only on some, aspects of welfare a pattern has been set by leading cases into which subsequent decisions fall. Occasionally cases are treated at least as persuasive, if not as binding, authorities,[63] but more often it is a question of a practice developing by way of reaction to broadly similar situations.[64] A decision on welfare is a matter of informed and properly directed discretion. What is for the welfare of the child is essentially a question of fact. Decisions of superior courts may indicate factors to which much or little weight should ordinarily be given, but too much depends on the individuality and variety of circumstances of every case for them to rule subsequent decisions. Rarely do they establish strict precedents or lay down rules of law on what is best for the child.[65] The following discussion of the operation of the welfare principle must be understood in that sense. One rule can, however, be laid down. It is that the child's welfare is to be understood comprehensively, embracing material, physical, intellectual, emotional, moral and, so far as it admits of assessment, spiritual well-being. It has for long been recognised that that is so. In *Re McGrath* in 1892, Lindley L.J. said:

---

[61] *McLean* v. *McLean*, 1947 S.C. 79, *per* Lord Justice-Clerk Cooper at p. 85.

[62] *Christison* v. *Christison, supra; McLean* v. *Mclean, supra.*

[63] *Gray* v. *Gray*, 1961 S.L.T. (Notes) 83, following *McAllister* v. *McAllister*, 1947 S.L.T. (Notes) 9; and *McClements* v. *McClements*, 1958 S.C. 286, following *Mackay* v. *Mackay*, 1957 S.L.T. (Notes) 17.

[64] See *Povey* v. *Povey* [1972] Fam. 40, *per* Sir Jocelyn Simon, P. at p. 49: "Judges exercising a given discretion consistently in order to do justice will tend to react similarly to similar situations; so that a practice will develop."

[65] *Townsend* v. *Townsend* (1973) 4 Fam. L. 127, *per* Davies L.J. at p. 128.

"The welfare of the child is not to be measured by money only, nor by physical comfort only. The word welfare must be taken in its widest sense. The moral and religious welfare of the child must be considered as well as its physical well-being. Nor can the ties of affection be disregarded."[66]

Some of these factors receive separate consideration in the paragraphs that follow. They are, however, to be regarded as interacting with each other so as to constitute a totality. It is error to concentrate on one to the exclusion of the others.[67]

Material Needs

There is a minimum level at which provision for the material needs of a child is fundamental if only because, without it, his physical welfare and probably also his emotional, intellectual and even moral development will be prejudiced. In some of the older cases the inability of an applicant for custody to make such minimum provision was the ground of decision.[68] In modern conditions, however, state social security support should nearly always remove the need to deny the claim of an otherwise suitable custodian on this ground. Beyond such minimum provision, there is little evidence that Scottish courts are influenced in custody decisions by the material wealth or comfort of the potential environment. That, in general, corresponds well with a proper understanding of the welfare principle. Once minimum conditions are satisfied the material advantages or disadvantages of a child's surroundings are likely to be less important from the standpoint of welfare than other less tangible, but nonetheless vital, qualities in the relationship between child and custodian. Moreover, in many cases, and especially in questions between parents, it will be possible, by an appropriate award of aliment, to reduce or remove any disadvantages accruing from giving custody to a party in relatively poor financial circumstances. So, although differences in material wealth should not altogether be excluded from consideration they will usually be of comparatively minor importance. They may, however, attain rather greater importance than would ordinarily be the case if a potential custodian, who, if he is not awarded custody, has no alimentary obligation, can make better material provision for the child than would be afforded on any alternative disposal. That will be particularly so where the potential advantages do not lie solely in immediate material benefits but offer the child the prospect of better opportunities in its future life. Thus, in *Huddart* v. *Huddart*[69] the court entertained, if only peripherally, the somewhat speculative question of the potential advantages of life in Australia as compared with Scotland.[70] Such

---

[66] [1893] 1 Ch. 143 at p. 148.

[67] *Allen* v. *Allen* [1948] 2 All E.R. 413, in which it was held that to stress the supposed moral welfare of the child to the exclusion of other factors was to apply the wrong test. The welfare of the child, both moral and physical, was the paramount consideration. *Cf. Bevan* v. *Bevan* (1973) 3 Fam. L. 126.

[68] *Campbell* v. *Croall* (1895) 22 R. 869; *Alexander* v. *McGarrity* (1903) 5 F. 654; *Mitchell* v. *Wright* (1905) 7 F. 568.

[69] 1961 S.C. 393. See also *Johnson* v. *Francis*, 1982 S.L.T. 285.

[70] *Cf. Re Weston's Settlements* [1968] 3 All E.R. 338, in which, on a question of whether a variation of a trust was for the benefit of a child beneficiary, Lord Denning M.R. pointed out (at p. 342) that

considerations cannot, it is submitted, ever justify disturbing a secure and satisfying relationship but, where other considerations are equal or nearly so, may
play a prominent, or even a decisive, role.

Physical and Emotional Welfare

Physical and emotional welfare are interrelated and the one may strongly affect the other. There is an obvious and extreme sense in which physical welfare
is the more fundamental. A modicum of physical wellbeing is essential for life
and, therefore, a prerequisite of any consideration of life's quality. Beyond such
extreme cases, it is, however, impossible to say whether the physical or the
emotional welfare of the child is the more important. The court should not contemplate a custody placement which seriously endangers either.[71] Because of
the interrelation between physical and emotional welfare, factors which bear on
the one will often bear on the other. Where they are in conflict, stress may sometimes be laid on physical welfare because it is a prerequisite or because it is the
more easily assessed. On the other hand, emotional welfare will often play a
more critical role because physical welfare is relatively easily secured and there
may be little to choose between one placement and another on that account
while the child's emotional welfare depends on the quality of particular relationships which are less likely to be evenly balanced. Some physical risks such
as the risk of communicable disease need seldom determine a custody placement as they can usually be overcome by temporary arrangements.

Defects of character or capacity which put the child's physical welfare in
jeopardy may exist even where there is a warm bond of affection with the child
conducive to its emotional development, and, even in such cases, these defects
can scarcely be ignored. On the other hand, a competent and conscientious person, likely to provide in every way for the child's physical welfare, is not to be
preferred if he or she cannot form a relationship with the child that would satisfy
its emotional needs.

Beyond observations of that kind, perhaps largely self-evident, there is little
that can be said of general application. The circumstances of particular cases are
infinitely variable and what is for the welfare of the child, whether physical or
emotional, requires an assessment of the individual case which will turn very
largely on its peculiar facts. Medical evidence may be of assistance[72] and, if its
intendment is clear, cannot, especially in a question of physical welfare on
which the conclusions of medical science are well established, lightly be disregarded, but it may have to be weighed along with other matters not susceptible of
medical assessment and, in any event, it does not rule the decision.[73] There are,
however, a few considerations of more or less general application which can be

---

the court should not consider merely financial benefit, but also educational and social benefits.
One of the things in life "more worthwhile than money," he said, was "to be brought up in this our
England, which is still 'the envy of less happier lands'."

[71] In relation to physical welfare, this has long been recognised: *Lang* v. *Lang* (1869) 7 M. 445 at p.
447; *Stewart, Petr.* (1870) 8 S.L.R. 279; *Bloe* v. *Bloe* (1882) 9 R. 894.

[72] *Gibson* v. *Gibson* (1894) 2 S.L.T. 71; *Mitchell* v. *Wright* (1905) 7 F. 568; *Pow* v. *Pow*, 1931
S.L.T. 485.

[73] *M*. v. *M*., 1926 S.C. 778.

identified as playing a prominent role in judicial assessment of the child's physical or emotional welfare and these are considered below.

Mother's Custody of Child of Tender Years

There is no settled rule of law that a child, even of tender years, should be in the custody of its mother.[74] Where there have been grounds for withholding custody from the mother, any presumption there may be in favour of her being awarded custody has been treated as not being a major, far less a conclusive, consideration.[75] It is not sufficient ground for disturbing an existing satisfactory relationship with someone else.[76] Nonetheless, some place remains for the view that the mother will often be the person best equipped to have custody and in other cases, where the issues may have been more evenly balanced, a certain preference for her on that ground may be detected.[77] In England too it is recognised that there is no rule of law in favour of the mother but it is the practice to give the custody of very young children, and particularly of young girls, to her unless there are reasons to the contrary. To do so has been said to be a dictate of nature[78] or "one of the facts of nature which always weighed heavily in considering what was in the welfare of children."[79] Some criticisms have been made of the English decisions on the view that they represent role expectations based on an idealised view of motherhood. It has been said that a legal presumption in favour of the father has been turned into a moral presumption in favour of the mother.[80] In the absence of a full survey, it is impossible to say whether Scottish decisions show, with any consistency, a similar pattern and whether they might be open to a similar criticism. In the case of very young children a certain preference for the mother, although one which must yield to any weighty consideration to the contrary is, it is submitted, in any event defensible. Children of either sex may benefit from the presence of parents or parent substitutes of both sexes at all stages of their development, but in the early years the need for the mother, or mother substitute, is almost certainly the stronger. In a ques-

---

[74] *Whitecross* v. *Whitecross*, 1977 S.L.T. 225; *Re B. (An Infant)* [1962] 1 All E.R. 872; *Aldous* v. *Aldous* (1974) Fam. L. 152.

[75] *M.* v. *M.*, 1926 S.C. 778; *Brown* v. *Brown*, 1948 S.C. 5; *Stevenson* v. *Stevenson*, 1967 S.L.T. (Notes) 7; *Whitecross* v. *Whitecross*, *supra*; *Jordan* v. *Jordan*, 1983 S.L.T. 539. *Cf.* before the 1925 Act, *Campbell* v. *Campbell*, 1920 S.C. 31.

[76] *Whitecross* v. *Whitecross, supra.*

[77] *McLean* v. *Hardie*, 1927 S.C. 344; *Christison* v. *Christison*, 1936 S.C. 381; *McLean* v. *McLean*, 1947 S.C. 79; *Nicol* v. *Nicol*, 1953 S.L.T. (Notes) 67. *Cf.* before the 1925 Act: *Reid* v. *Reid* (1901) 3 F. 330; *Robertson, Petr.*, 1911 S.C. 1319. In *Jordan* v. *Jordan*, 1983 S.L.T. 539 Lord Stott in the Inner House quoted, without comment, the Lord Ordinary's view that "*prima facie* a mother is better qualified than a father to bring up two young girls."

[78] *G.* v. *G.* (1975) 6 Fam. L. 43, *per* Stamp L.J. The Inner House of the Court of Session has disapproved of relying on "nature" in support of a mother's claim: "it is not nature but the welfare of the child which is the material matter," *per* Lord Walker in *Hannah* v. *Hannah*, 1971 S.L.T. (Notes) 42 at p. 43.

[79] *P.* v. *P.* (1975) 6 Fam. L. 75, *per* Sir John Pennycuik at p. 76. *Cf. Southgate* v. *Southgate* (1978) 8 Fam. L. 246; *P.* v. *McK (Formerly P.)* (1973) 3 Fam. L. 172.

[80] See Oster, "Custody Proceedings—A Study of Vague and Indefinite Standards" (1965) 5 J. of Fam. L. 21 at pp. 25–26. For an analysis of similar trends in Canada, see Bradbrook: "The Role of Judicial Discretion in Child Custody Adjudication in Ontario" (1971) 21 Univ. Tor.L.J. 402 at p. 405. This, it has been said, amounts to a "maternal bias in custody decisions" (letter in New L.J., Feb. 28, 1980, criticising the decision of the English Court of Appeal in *L.* v. *L.* (1980) 124 Sol.J. 203.

tion between the mother and father it may therefore be better, especially where the mother has until the dispute arose had the child in her care,[81] for the child to be in the mother's custody rather than to embark on the risks inherent in the father's fulfilling a maternal role or in the creating of a new relationship in which there will be a surrogate mother. There are, however, two objections to that view. One is that, once it is allowed, it may be given greater weight that it merits, but that objection is met if there is a sound exercise of judicial discretion. The second objection is that although custody decisions, in contrast with adoption orders, are in principle readily open to review, a custody order once made is, in practice and for good reason, usually very difficult to disturb and that the court should take a long view rather than be influenced by transient considerations applicable only to the early years of a child's life.[82] That is an important objection to which weight should be given where it can be said with confidence that the long-term welfare of the child will be better served by placement with the father. The long view may, however, be speculative and in such cases it may be right to give effect to the general preference for the mother in order to secure the immediate benefits which may be expected to accrue. To do so accords with the solution preferred in the vast majority of divorce actions in which the parties succeed in agreeing about the arrangements for the care of children. That "reflects the fact that the children were usually living with the wife at the raising of the action and that both parties were content that they should continue to do so."[83] It appears that any judicial expectations there may be concerning the maternal role are widely shared throughout society. Even if these expectations are culturally determined they may nonetheless be valid in prevailing social conditions. In the case of older children, however, it is difficult to justify a placement with the mother on the grounds of any *prima facie* preference. Agreed placements with the mother in these cases may be dictated less by any perception of what is for the child's welfare than by the fact that the mother is, more often than the father, willing to undertake the responsibilities of care or that, in an amicable agreement where both parties are willing and other considerations are equal, the father is commonly expected, and may himself expect, to "yield" custody to the mother. The expedient occasionally adopted in the case of older children of giving the custody of boys to the father and of girls to the mother, even to the extent of splitting custody in the case of families of boys and girls,[84] may be justified in the circumstances of a particular case but does not, it is thought, have any justification on general grounds.[85]

---

[81] Thomson, *Family Law in Scotland* (2nd ed.) at pp. 203–204, explains the preference some judges show towards mothers as doing no more than reflecting a preference for the *status quo*, coupled with the fact that on the break-up of most parental relationships, young children tend to go with their mother.

[82] See *M.* v. *M.* 1926 S.C. 778 at p. 786. In *Hastie* v. *Hastie*, 1985 S.L.T. 146 Lord Davidson awarded custody to the mother, after the child had been looked after by the father and the father's mother for four years, this notwithstanding admitted short-term difficulties, on the ground that awarding custody to the father could cause greater, long-term difficulties.

[83] Clive, *Husband and Wife* (2nd ed.) at p. 573.

[84] As in *Symington* v. *Symington* (1874) 1 R. 871, (1875) 2 R.(H.L.) 41 which, although before the 1925 Act, turned on a consideration of welfare.

[85] So prevalent is the preference for wives in custody disputes between husbands and wives that it has been suggested that "since wives will, under most circumstances, be awarded custody regardless of the statutory standard, and since it seems wise to discourage traumatic custody contests

Maintenance of Established Relationships

In *Re Thain, Thain* v. *Taylor*[86] Eve J. said, with reference to the removal of a child from the care of an uncle and aunt by whom she had been brought up for some years,

> "it is said that the little girl will be greatly distressed and upset at parting from Mr and Mrs Jones. I can quite understand it may be so, but, at her tender age, one knows from experience how mercifully transient are the effects of partings and other sorrows, and how soon the novelty of fresh surroundings and new associations effaces the recollection of former days and kind friends, and I cannot attach much weight to this aspect of the case."

A similar attitude was adopted by the Lord Justice-Clerk in *Begbie* v. *Nichol*,[87] in which he described as irrelevant an averment regarding the disturbance caused to a child of seven who had been in the care of foster parents for practically the whole of her life. So too in *Minto* v. *Minto*[88] the effects of disruption were discounted. *Minto* v. *Minto* was decided before the passing of the Guardianship of Infants Act 1925 and in *Begbie* v. *Nichol* only Lord Jamieson referred to the paramountcy of the welfare of the child, the other judges apparently taking the view, in accordance with the indications given in *Hume* v. *Hume*[89] that the 1925 Act applied only to disputes between parents of a legitimate child. That view must now be regarded as mistaken, and in any case is obsolete.[90] Neither case, therefore, offers any sure guidance in a context in which the child's welfare is paramount. They may, however, be taken to reflect a judicial attitude which, because the effects were thought likely to be transient, regarded disruption of relationships as of little enduring significance for the child's welfare. Modern authorities by contrast stress the importance of continuity. In *J.* v. *C.*[91] Lord MacDermott had *Re Thain, Thain* v. *Taylor* in mind when he said:

> "Some of the authorities convey the impression that the upset caused to a child by change of custody is transient and a matter of small importance. For all I know that may have been true in the cases containing dicta to that effect. But I think that a growing experience has shown that it is not always so and that serious harm even to young children may, on occasion, be caused by such a change. I do not suggest that the difficulties of this

---

whenever it is possible to do so, the Act should discourage those few husbands who might wish to contest by establishing a presumption that the wife is entitled to custody. The presumption resolves several value conflicts: it may well be true that because of the presumption some fathers who would be better custodians than their wives will either fail to seek custody or will be denied custody following a contest, but that disadvantage has a lower 'social cost' than the disadvantages of any alternative statutory formulation—more contested cases (with the trauma that contests seem to produce), more risk of a custody award to a father who will be only marginally better than the mother or even much worse": Ellsworth and Levy, (1969) 4 *Law and Society Review* 167, at p. 203.

[86] [1926] Ch. 676 at p. 684.
[87] 1949 S.C. 158 at p. 164.
[88] 1914 2 S.L.T. 381.
[89] 1926 S.C. 1008 at p. 1014.
[90] See *ante*, p. 80.
[91] [1970] A.C. 668 at p. 715.

subject can be resolved by purely theoretical considerations, or that they need to be left entirely to expert opinion. But a child's future happiness and sense of security are always important factors and the effects of a change of custody will often be worthy of the close and anxious attention which they undoubtedly received in this case."

In that case the House of Lords refused to order the return to unimpeachable parents of a child who, for a protracted period, had been in the care of foster parents. Although a number of factors entered into the decision, the dangers of disruption were prominent among them and probably played a determinative part. A similar emphasis in the related field of adoption can be seen in *A. & B., Petrs.*[92] It accords with a widely expressed and increasing recognition of the importance of the continuity of relationships.[93] In some literature, derived in the main from psychoanalytic sources,[94] that has been pressed to the extent of saying that no existing relationship should be disturbed unless there is positive evidence both that the existing relationship is detrimental to the welfare of the child and that an alternative placement would be less detrimental. That may take the matter too far. As was pointed out by the Lord Justice-Clerk in *Begbie* v. *Nicol*, changes may sometimes be inevitable. Most children are capable of adapting to change and damage is not an inevitable result of the adaptation. Sometimes change, even from a favourable environment, may be beneficial. Much, no doubt, depends on the reasons for the change, the child's perception of them and the quality of the new relationship. When every allowance has been made for that, however, disturbance of an existing satisfactory relationship for a new one, whose benefits must always in some degree be speculative, involves risks, including the risk that a trauma which might be expected to be transient may become permanent; and these risks are particularly high when the disturbance comes about in the circumstances of contentious litigation. Despite earlier dicta to the contrary, Scottish decisions, both before and after *J.* v. *C.*, show considerable respect for the continuity of relationships[95]: the courts do not, of course, hestitate to disturb existing arrangements if required by the welfare of the child.[96]

Wishes of the Child

The UN Convention on the Rights of the Child[97] provides that the child's

---

[92] 1971 S.C.(H.L.) 129.

[93] See "Alternatives to 'Parental Rights' in Child Custody Disputes Involving Third Parties" (1964) 73 Yale L.J. 151 at pp. 159 *et seq.*; Michaels, "The Dangers of a Change of Parentage in Custody and Adoption Cases" (1967) 83 L.Q.R. 547 at p. 549.

[94] *e.g.* Goldstein, Freud and Solnit: *Beyond the Best Interests of the Child*, (1973).

[95] *Macallister* v. *Macallister*, 1962 S.C. 406 at p. 413; *Cheetham* v. *Glasgow Corporation*, 1972 S.L.T. (Notes) 50; *Wincentzen* v. *Wincentzen*, 1974 S.L.T. (Notes) 26; *Robertson* v. *Robertson* 1981 S.L.T. (Notes) 7. In the last-named case legal custody was awarded to the father on the understanding that the child was to remain in the care of the mother, with whom the child had been living. In *Sinclair* v. *Sinclair*, 1988 S.L.T. 87 Lord Prosser held, in effect, that the onus of proving that current arrangements should be disturbed lay with the party claiming it: see p. 89I. See also *Breingan* v. *Jamieson*, 1993 S.L.T. 186.

[96] See, *e.g. Hastie* v. *Hastie*, 1985 S.L.T. 146; *Early* v. *Early*, 1990 S.L.T. 221.

[97] 28 *International Legal Materials* 1448, ratified by the UK, Dec. 16, 1991.

views must be taken into account in any decisions affecting him or her.[98] Custody disputes provide the typical example of decisions that affect a child in a fundamental way and it is submitted that the law should be applied in the light of this international obligation. The Law Reform (Parent and Child) (Scotland) Act 1986, in contrast with the provisions relating to adoption,[99] places no obligation on the court adjudicating in a custody dispute to ascertain the wishes and feelings of the child or to give consideration to them.[1] Pupils at common law were probably regarded as too young to have proper views on the matter, but in so far as a minor *pubes* could be the subject of custody at common law it required a strong case to justify an award against his expressed wishes.[2] The common law has, however, been modified in a number of important respects. First, the power of courts to regulate custody which, with some qualifications, applied only to pupil children[3] has been extended to comprehend children under the age of 16,[4] and questions of the custody of all children are now subject to the paramountcy of the child's welfare, even although the child approaching 16 may well be capable of forming an independent and fixed view. Secondly, the welfare principle has been given a role predominant over the parent's rights and also over the child's right: the child's wishes can therefore never be given effect to if this is not consistent with its interests. The question is not so much one of how strong the case to the contrary must be before the child's wishes can be denied, but whether his wishes can be given effect in a manner consistent with regard for his welfare as the paramount consideration. In the event of conflict the course indicated by his welfare must, in the last resort, prevail. But it will be an unusual case in which such a conflict arises. In *Gover* v. *Gover*[5] Lord Thomson said: "When the child is a minor it would be, in my opinion, quite unrealistic, and indeed wrong, for the Court, in an issue of custody or access, to do other than place very great and usually decisive weight on the wishes of the child."[6] The primary matter is not an abstract regard for the legal status of the child, although that is entitled to respect, but the recognition that to enforce a custody placement against the wishes of an adolescent is likely to be detrimental and that a right to a measure of choice between alternative placements is appropriate to the later stages in personal development. The older child's desires are clearly a matter relevant to the determination of where his interests lie.

---

[98] Art. 12 assures to the child "who is capable of forming his or her own views freely in all matters affecting the child, the views of the child being given due weight in accordance with the age and maturity of the child."

[99] Adoption (Scotland) Act 1978, s. 6. See further, *post* at pp. 550–552.

[1] The proposal in Scot. Law Com. No. 135, *Report on Family Law*, May 1992, that a person making a major decision affecting a child should take account of the child's views, and that a child over the age of 12 years is to be presumed to be capable of expressing a reasonable view (draft Bill, cl. 6), does not apply to the decisions of the court.

[2] *Harvey* v. *Harvey* (1860) 22 D. 1198; *Fisher* v. *Edgar* (1894) 21 R. 1076 at p. 1078. *Cf. Flannigan* v. *Inspector of Bothwell* (1892) 19 R. 909, *per* Lord President Robertson at p. 912; *Morrison* v. *Quarrier* (1894) 21 R. 1071 at p. 1075. See *ante* pp. 69–70.

[3] See *ante*, p. 73.

[4] Custody of Children (Scotland) Act 1939, s. 1. In any event the attributes of pupillarity are now extended to children under the age of 16: s. 5(1) of the Age of Legal Capacity (Scotland) Act 1991.

[5] 1969 S.L.T. (Notes) 78 at p. 78.

[6] *Cf. Hannay, Petr.*, 1947 S.L.T. (Notes) 55; *Klein and Anr., Petrs.*, 1969 S.L.T. (Notes) 53; *Johnson* v. *Johnson*, 1972 S.L.T. (Notes) 15.

Different considerations are appropriate in the case of the younger child. The pupil child at common law had no legal right to be heard and that rule may formally have survived subsequent changes in the law and now extend to all children under the age of 16.[7] The older child's wishes are clearly an element relevant to its welfare and it is submitted that to deny a hearing to a child of sufficient understanding, whatever his age, would in almost all circumstances, amount to a failure to observe the duty laid upon the court by section 3(2) of the 1986 Act. A young child should not be disturbed by choices beyond his capacity: he may have a "right not to have to make a decision."[8] Once however, the child is capable of forming and expressing a view his wishes will at least be relevant to, and may be an important element in, determining his welfare. The weight to be given to them will, however, vary not only according to the child's age and understanding but according to the circumstances in which the wishes are expressed. Not only the wishes themselves but the reasons for them, real rather than professed, will, if they can be ascertained, afford important clues to where the child's welfare lies. Moreover, some regard for the child's wishes if they are genuine and do not rest on some adventitious ground is required by the respect due to the child as a person. It will, therefore, usually be right to ascertain the wishes of young children of sufficient age and understanding. The interpretation to be put on these wishes and the effect, if any, to be given to them will, however, vary greatly from case to case.[9]

Relationships with Custodians, Siblings and Others

The welfare of the child is intimately connected with the relationships which he has formed and will form.[10] Probably, once minimum standards of physical care and provision have been met, no aspect of custody is more important than the child's relationship with the prospective custodian. Usually it will be the critical factor on which the case turns. Unfortunately it may be difficult to assess. The child's wishes give an indication but not the only, nor always the most reliable, indication of what the relationship is likely to be. Negative reactions

---

[7] See ss. 1(2) and (3)(*f*)(i) and 5(1) of the Age of Legal Capacity (Scotland) Act 1991. It may be noted that s. 2(3) of that Act amends ss. 12(8) and 18(8) of the Adoption (Scotland) Act 1978 so that they now provide that an adoption order or an order freeing a child for adoption, respectively, shall not be made in relation to a child of or over the age of 12 years unless with the child's consent (though that consent may be dispensed with if the court is satisfied that the child is incapable of giving consent).

[8] *M.* v. *M.* (1973) Fam.L. 17.

[9] See *Pow* v. *Pow*, 1931 S.L.T. 485 (girl of 10, boy of eight); *Hannay, Petr.*, 1947 S.L.T. (Notes) 55 (boy of 12); *Johnson* v. *Johnson*, 1972 S.L.T. (Notes) 15 (children between ages of seven and 14); *Fowler* v. *Fowler*, 1981 S.L.T. (Notes) 9 and 78 (girl of 10). *Cf. Nicol* v. *Nicol*, 1953 S.L.T. (Notes) 67, in which the wishes of children of 11 and 10 were considered but did not receive effect. For a view stressing the risks of undue emphasis on giving effect to the child's wishes, see Plant, "The Psychiatrist Views Children of Divorced Parents" (1944) 10 *Law and Cont. Prob.* 807 at p. 815.

[10] So in *Hill* v. *Hill*, 1991 S.L.T. 189 it was held that a relevant consideration in determining welfare was that the granting of custody to one parent would terminate the child's relationship with the other (since the mother lived in Scotland and the father lived in Canada). The same is true of access: in *Breingan* v. *Jamieson, Herald*, March 3, 1992 Lord Penrose allowed a father access to his seven-year-old daughter so that she could act as a flower girl at his wedding, this because attendance at the wedding would allow her to identify herself as a member of the new family unit being created. Custody was granted to the child's aunt with whom she lived, in a later action: 1993 S.L.T. 186.

such as fear or hostility may, however, be apparent and, where these underlie the child's wishes, they afford, unless there are both a cogent and satisfactory explanation and good grounds for believing that the negative reaction can be overcome, compelling reasons for giving the child's wishes effect. It is, more-over, easier to ascertain the qualities of an existing relationship than to predict the effects of a change. Relationships with others, although less important than the relationship with the custodian, may have a considerable bearing on the child's welfare. It is no doubt generally true that children benefit from the com-panionship of other children,[11] from the "rough and tumble of family life"[12] rather than seclusion and from being in one family unit with their brothers and sisters[13] but these generalities admit of exceptions.[14] In this, as in other matters, an assessment has to be made in relation to the particular child and the particular circumstances of the case. The general social environment will usually be only a minor factor, but it may assume importance if the child is likely to be exposed to hostility in the form of acute social, religious, racial or ethnic prejudice. The drawbacks of appearing to yield to prejudice must be subordinated to the para-mountcy of the child's welfare.[15]

Moral Welfare

The moral welfare of the child has always been an important consideration and has often been associated with moral judgments on a parent's behaviour. At common law immoral conduct on the father's part opened the door to judicial intervention.[16] Sometimes, as in cases of drunkenness or cruelty, the conduct, although reflecting on the father's moral character, was not primarily moral in its effect but bore as much, or more, on the child's physical as on its moral wel-fare. In these cases interference with the father's powers was, in any event, ne-cessary for the protection of the child's health. Danger to the child's moral development was, however, usually an element in such decisions and was an in-dependent and, even where it stood alone, a sufficient ground for removing a child from its father's control.[17] It was in these cases with the effect, or possible effect, and the likelihood of its continuance that the court was primarily con-cerned rather than with the father's conduct as such. So in *Lang* v. *Lang*[18] Lord

---

[11] *Christison* v. *Christison*, 1936 S.C. 381 *per* Lord Anderson at pp. 385–386.

[12] *Begbie* v. *Nichol*, 1949 S.C. 158, *per* Lord Justice-Clerk Thomson at p. 164.

[13] *Steuart* v. *Steuart* (1870) 8 M. 821; *Morrison* v. *Quarrier* (1894) 21 R. 1071; *Mackellar* v. *Mack-ellar* (1898) 25 R. 883; *Nicol* v. *Nicol*, 1953 S.L.T. (Notes) 67; *Douglas* v. *Douglas*, 1950 S.C. 453 at p. 457; *Reynolds* v. *Reynolds* (1974) 4 Fam.L. 193; *Early* v. *Early*, 1989 S.L.T. 114, affirmed 1990 S.L.T. 221.

[14] See *Johnson* v. *Johnson*, *supra*, and *Barr* v. *Barr*, 1950 S.L.T. (Notes) 15, for cases in which the separation of siblings may be accepted.

[15] This question has been considered in the United States of America. See *Fountaine* v. *Fountaine*, 57 A.L.R. 2d 675 (1956), discussed by Clive, *Husband and Wife* (3rd ed.) at p. 543. See also *Early* v. *Early*, 1990 S.L.T. 221.

[16] *Baillie* v. *Agnew* (1775) 5 Mor. Supp. 526; *Craig* v. *Thomson* (1829) 1 Sc.Jur. 201; *Cameron, Petr.* (1847) 9 D. 1401.

[17] See, *e.g. McFarlane* v. *McFarlane* (1847) 9 D. 904, *per* Lord Jeffrey: "Unless the health or morals of the child be affected by allowing its father to have the custody, we must just submit to that general rule which delivers the child to him." Cruelty to the children justified the court's intervention in *Baillie* v. *Agnew*, *supra*, but cruelty to a wife (and mother of the children) was not usually considered enough (*McFarlane* v. *McFarlane*, *supra*).

[18] (1869) 7 M. 445 at p. 447.

Neaves could say: "It is not that he has committed faults, but that he teaches, or is likely to teach, evil to [the children], and to corrupt their morals, that can alone entitle us to interfere." Changes in accepted standards of conduct, particularly in sexual matters, and changes in the law have made the content of much of the older decisions obsolete, but the concentration of attention on actual, or prospective, moral harm arising from the custodians's influence, rather than on past misconduct as such, is even more apt now than it was at common law. A welfare judgment looks to the present and the future although the inferences on which it is based must be drawn from past events. But subtle influences, to which past conduct and its effects can be the only guide, will often be more important than express teaching. The problems of whether past patterns of conduct are likely to repeat themselves and of what effect, if any, they have had or are likely to have on the moral formation of the children are problems for the modern, as they were for the older, law. The older cases, however, were little troubled by questions of what constituted morality. They proceeded on an assumption of moral consensus. The growth, or wider recognition, of moral pluralism raises questions of the meaning of moral welfare. In what does the child's moral welfare consist?

Problems of standards of sexual conduct are, perhaps, particularly acute. The double standard has gone which, under the older practice, looked more leniently, in custody disputes between the parents of legitimate children, on the sexual misdemeanours of the father than of the mother. That double standard, although largely based on the moral notions of the time, could be explained on the view that, according to the law as it then was, more was required to deprive a father of custody which, subject to some qualifications, was his right than to withhold it from a mother to whom custody could be awarded, if at all, only as a matter of discretion.[19] Adultery, by either spouse, is generally no longer an obstacle to an award of custody[20] and, even where it is an element taken into consideration it is often as an aspect of conduct that may influence the decision independently of the child's welfare where the welfare considerations are evenly balanced.[21] Unless it has taken some gross or promiscuous form there seems to be no ground in the modern authorities for regarding adultery by a parent as having a close, or necessary, bearing on the child's moral welfare. Occasionally it may be relevant to the child's emotional welfare if it is associated with or shows instability or indifference to the family. Other aspects of sexual conduct do, however, remain controversial, as reflected in changing attitudes to extramarital sexual relations and to homosexuality, and the proper response from the standpoint of the child's welfare is problematic. The child's moral welfare although always an important, is never an isolated, consideration and re-

---

[19] Cf. Lang v. Lang (1869) 7 M. 445; Symington v. Symington (1875) 2 R. (H.L.) 41; A.B. v. C.D. (1847) 10 D. 229; Bowman v. Graham (1883) 10 R. 1234; Shirer v. Dixon (1885) 12 R. 1013. See also McIver v. McIver (1859) 21 D. 1103.

[20] Christie v. Christie, 1945 S.L.T. 300; Johnston v. Johnston, 1947 S.L.T. (Notes) 26; Nicol v. Nicol, 1953 S.L.T. (Notes) 67; McClements v. McClements, 1958 S.C. 286; Zamorski v. Zamorska, 1960 S.L.T. (Notes) 26. Even before the 1925 Act the importance attached to adultery as a factor adverse to an award of custody had declined—see Stewart v. Stewart, 1914 2 S.L.T. 310; McCurdie v. McCurdie, 1918 2 S.L.T. 250; Allan v. Allan, 1919 2 S.L.T. 88.

[21] See Hume v. Hume, 1926 S.C. 1008.

gard for the child's welfare as a whole may resolve many practical difficulties. Where that is not so, the court must make the best judgment it can according to what are deemed to be the prevailing moral notions in the forum. To expose the child to a sexually promiscuous environment, or to the risk of sexual corruption or exploitation, whether heterosexual or homosexual, would be considered inconsistent with its welfare. There is authority, if controversial, for the view that even at the cost of permanent separation a reasonable parent would not wish his child to be subject to homosexual influences,[22] and, if that is so, such influences would be regarded as contrary to the child's welfare. In *Early* v. *Early*[23] a child was removed from the mother with whom he had lived for some years and custody awarded to the father, after the mother had entered into a lesbian relationship, and set up home with another woman. The court took the view that the environment in which the child lived was unsuitable in that it lacked any male role-models for the child, and might expose him to teasing and other difficulties at school. There was no allegation that the child was exposed to any sexual or moral danger.[24] Homosexuality is not, of course, an automatic bar. In *Hill* v. *Hill*,[25] a child was returned to his homosexual father, who lived openly in a homosexual relationship, this against the wishes of the mother, who had, in breach of the father's custody rights, removed the child from Canada to Scotland.[26] The mother here alleged that the child would be exposed to "harmful influences."

The difficulties which may arise in some controversial areas do not, however, justify a radical moral scepticism. Divergence of view on some issues does not preclude a broad consensus on others. There may be arguments about the importance or desirability of taking the child's moral welfare into consideration,[27]

---

[22] *Re D. (An Infant) (Adoption: Parent's Consent)* [1977] A.C. 602. Though this was an adoption case, where the question was one of the reasonableness of the parent withholding consent to adoption rather than the child's welfare, the views there expressed have obvious application in custody cases, but they do not, and cannot, lay down any rule of law.

[23] 1990 S.L.T. 221.

[24] And in any case there were other factors that pointed to the child's welfare being better served by custody with the father, in particular the fact that the other children of the marriage lived with the father, and the fact that the father had a more balanced and mature view as to what was best for the child.

[25] 1991 S.L.T. 189.

[26] The basis of this decision was that the Canadian court was a more appropriate forum to decide the issue of custody than the Scottish court, but the court accepted (at p. 192C) that homosexuality is not, nor is living openly as such, an automatic bar to an award of custody. It cannot be while the paramount consideration is the welfare of the child. See Bates, "Unravelling the Tangled Web," 1990 S.L.T. (News) 69 for a discussion of *Early* v. *Early* and other cases involving homosexual parents from the Australian and US courts.

[27] Concern with moral welfare may be said to put a premium on conformity and prejudice unfairly the innovative or idiosyncratic (*cf.* the decision in *Early* v. *Early*, 1990 S.L.T. 221, where the risk of a child being teased at school as a result of his unusual family circumstances was held to be a relevant factor). That is a serious objection, in principle, and it has practical force in some cases of conflict between established views and the beliefs and conduct of minority groups. With these exceptions it is, however, in existing conditions of tolerance only a marginal problem. Even where the problem is real, it has to be balanced against society's interest in the reflection, in the moral formation of children, at least of certain minimum standards of conduct and the state's interest to promote that. It can also be argued that virtue is an integral part, or even the highest form, of the child's wellbeing and even if judicial regulation of custody can do little to promote that it can at least contribute to the avoidance of evil.

but there is no doubt that the law does require it to be considered[28] and the difficulties in giving it effective meaning are, outside some areas of controversy, largely academic rather than real. Moral assumptions underlie both the civil and the criminal law and, provided the limitations of the judicial function in judging of moral welfare are kept in mind, afford sufficient guidance. The court's function is essentially protective. The court may prefer one moral regime to another as the more likely to achieve generally acceptable standards or even as the more likely to cultivate them to a higher degree, but it has never been suggested, nor is it practicable, that it should distinguish between them on the positive merits of the goals at which they aim where neither is objectionable by the standards of the forum. Because it is the child's moral welfare and not the moral character of the potential custodian which, as such, is at stake, it is no answer that the custodian has no alternative and is, himself, free from fault if the surroundings into which he would bring the child expose him to risk of moral harm. On the other hand, the culpability of the custodian can, so far as the question of welfare is concerned, be disregarded if there is no consequential risk of moral harm to the child. Thus, little weight need be attached to an isolated conviction for dishonesty.[29] The question always is: what are the risks for the moral welfare of the child and what weight is to be given to these risks when considered in the totality of circumstances affecting welfare? The risks which require to be so considered include that the child may be led into ways of criminality, dishonesty, irresponsibility, violence, deceit, the intentional or reckless harming of others, and the moral abuses associated with the abuse of alcohol and drugs and with sexual promiscuity.[30] Often practical necessity will constrain the inquiry into moral welfare within these negative limits. Occasionally, however, cases may present, in a more positive form, questions of what is the more wholesome custody placement from the standpoint of the promotion of generally accepted moral goals and when that is so, the comprehensive regard for the welfare of the child which the statute envisages requires that that be taken into account.

Education

The promotion of a child's skills and aptitudes, his capacities for work and recreational pursuits, his intellectual and artistic development, forms an integral part of his welfare. No general rule can be laid down on such problems of choice as may arise except that leaving scope for the maximum development of the child's potential is always an important consideration. These elements of welfare will often be associated with the child's emotional and moral development and sometimes with his religious upbringing. All may be comprehended under the heading of education broadly conceived. The need for custody choices to depend on educational considerations is somewhat reduced so far, at least, as provision for formal instruction is concerned, by the power of the court to make orders with respect to education independently of custody.[31] In many cases it

---

[28] *Hume* v. *Hume*, 1926 S.C. 1008.

[29] *A.C.* v. *B.C.* (1902) 5 F. 108. Great weight was however attached to a conviction and long history of drug abuse in *F.* v. *F.*, 1991 S.L.T. 357 at p. 363.

[30] *Hume* v. *Hume, supra*; *Gray* v. *Gray*, 1961 S.L.T. (Notes) 83; Stuart, "Consistorial Actions Involving Criminal Offenders," 1973 J.R. 43 at pp. 56–58.

[31] See *ante*, at pp. 198–199.

has, however, to be accepted that the custody placement will profoundly influence the educational possibilities for the child.

Religious or Spiritual Welfare

In the seventeenth century, when religious controversy and confidence in the rightness of sectional religious opinions ran high, robust views were sometimes entertained of state powers of interference in the religious upbringing of children. In 1665 the Scottish Privy Council, from which the Court of Session's jurisdiction in custody matters is derived, ordered the children of Scott of Raeburn and his wife "being infected with the error of Quakerism" to be taken from them and, later in the same year, the young Marquis of Huntly was taken from the custody of his mother and guardians "they being Popishly inclined" and entrusted to the care of the Protestant Archbishop Sharp of St Andrews under a direction that "no person Popishly inclined have liberty to serve or attend him."[32] By an Act of 1661[33] "All children under Popish tutors or curators" were taken from their care, and by an Act of 1700[34] not only professed Papists but also those suspected of Popery were declared incapable of the offices of tutory or curatory unless they signed a prescribed formula purging themselves of that taint. Roman Catholics were therefore precluded from claiming custody *qua* tutors, and that disability remained until repealed in 1829.[35] Even in the seventeenth century interference with custody on the ground that the custodian's religious beliefs were objectionable seems to have been exceptional and no reported Scottish cases thereafter have been traced. Nor is interference on the ground of lack of religious belief well attested by the older authorities, although Fraser[36] considered that the court would interfere if the government of the father was calculated to engender irreligious or atheistical opinions.

Two modern Scottish cases take substantially the same view as Fraser and apply it in the context of the paramountcy of the child's welfare. In *Mackay* v. *Mackay*[37] custody was given to an atheist father, but only on an understanding which provided for the child's religious instruction. Lord President Clyde said that it would be almost impossible for a court in Scotland to award custody to an atheist with the prospect of the child's being brought up without the solace and guidance of any religious teaching at all "for atheism and the child's welfare are almost necessarily mutually exclusive, according at least to our standards of

---

[32] Fraser at pp. 90–91.

[33] 1661 c. 8.

[34] 1700 c. 3.

[35] Roman Catholic Relief Act 1829, s. 10.

[36] at p. 90. This view has some support in English authority: see *Re Besant* (1878) 11 Ch.D. 508, in which the refusal of the mother to allow the child to receive religious instruction was an element in the decision. See also *Shelly* v. *Westbrooke* (1817) Jac. 266; *Re Agar-Ellis* (1878) 10 Ch.D. 49, *per* Malins V.C. at pp. 56–57. These cases may, however, now require to be understood as instances of religious opinion manifesting itself in conduct which the law regards as vicious and immoral (*Re Carroll* [1931] 1 K.B. 371, *per* Slesser L.J. at p. 354), and in any event the decision in *Re Agar-Ellis* has been characterised in the House of Lords as "so out of line with present-day views that it should no longer be treated as having any authority": *per* Lord Fraser of Tullybelton in *Gillick* v. *West Norfolk and Wisbech Area Health Authority* [1985] 3 All E.R. 402 at p. 412. Lord Scarman at p. 419 described the decision in *Re Agar-Ellis* as "horrendous."

[37] 1957 S.L.T. (Notes) 17.

civilised society."[38] In *McClements* v. *McClements*[39] an atheist father was refused custody and given access only on condition that he did not attempt to influence the child's religious beliefs. The decision can be justified, so far as the
custody award is concerned, on grounds independent of the question of religious beliefs including the expressed preference of the child and the lack of any
sufficient ground for disturbing the interim arrangement under which the child
had been in the custody of the mother. Among the reasons given for the decision
were, however, that the child "ought not to be denied the opportunity of being
brought up in the generally accepted religious beliefs of the society in which he
lives."[40] That view seems to have been expressed on general grounds as there is
no indication that lack of religious belief would have created particular problems in the locality or surroundings in which the child would have lived had he
been entrusted to his father's custody.

The dicta in these cases are surprising. There must be many divorce and separation cases in which custody orders are made in favour of a parent of atheistic
or agnostic opinions if only because, in the absence of dispute on custody, the
issue is never raised. There are also cases of disputed custody in which such
awards are made since both parties are opposed or indifferent to a religious upbringing for the child and neither, therefore, puts it in issue. Nor is it the practice
of the court, in the exercise of its statutory duty to consider the arrangements for
the care of the children of the marriage before granting decree of divorce or
nullity of marriage or separation,[41] to make particular inquiries about religious
upbringing. And there must, of course, be many children whose custody is
never the subject of judicial regulation who are brought up by parents who have
no religious beliefs. If the views expressed in *Mackay* and *McClements* are
sound they merit a wider application than the fairly few cases in which a religious, as opposed to an atheistic or agnostic, upbringing is raised as a matter of
controversy by the parties; yet it is to such cases that it seems they must be confined. However, *Mackay* and *McClements* lay down, it is submitted, no rule of
law. In so far as the preference they indicate is accepted, it can only be as an element in the totality of circumstances affecting welfare.[42] In view of the difficulties in applying it, the part it will play must usually be small. It should too be
seen in the context of tolerance as a widely held moral value affecting religious
belief and one to which the court might properly have regard in connection with
the child's moral welfare.[43] Exposure to narrow and bigoted religious influence
on the one hand, whether Christian or otherwise, or to a militant and uncom-
promising atheism, on the other, may be seen as detrimental to the child's welfare. Regarded as warnings against the latter danger *Mackay* and *McClements*
can be more readily accepted than on any other ground but, even on that view,
they seem to go too far in elevating the matter into a necessarily critical factor in
the custody decision.

---

[38] *Ibid.* at p. 17.
[39] 1958 S.C. 286.
[40] *Ibid.* at p. 289, *per* Lord Justice-Clerk Thomson.
[41] Matrimonial Proceedings (Children) Act 1958, s. 8.
[42] See *ante*, pp. 208–209.
[43] *Re T. (Minors)*, Dec. 10, 1975, unreported, *per* Scarman L.J., quoted in *Re H. (A Minor)* (1980) 10
    Fam.L. 248 at p. 249.

It is submitted that there are at least two assumptions which it is reasonable to make without thereby embarking on an examination of the merits of any given form of religious upbringing. The first is that the child's religious welfare will be best served by respect for his autonomy as an individual.[44] The second is that it will be promoted by allowing progressive development without externally imposed change. From the first it follows that weight should be given to the child's wishes and sentiments even to a degree which would be inappropriate in other contexts. Although much must depend on age and ability for choice, that is a particularly important factor where the child has strongly held convictions.[45] From the second it follows that patterns to which the child has become accustomed should not readily be disturbed. A purely formal religious connection is, however, of little importance.[46] These conclusions indicate, of course, only how the child's religious or spiritual welfare may be determined and not how these aspects of welfare are to be weighed in relation to other aspects. They have, however, the merit that they accord with criteria used in other aspects of welfare and will often tend to promote harmony in a total assessment. Where conflict between the child's religious welfare so considered and other aspects does emerge, it seems that the disposal indicated by the latter must be preferred at least where the arguments in favour of it are strong. The child's physical, emotional or moral well-being can scarcely be jeopardised for the sake of continuity of religious upbringing or even out of respect for the child's own convictions. In such a case the separate regulation of religious upbringing may have to be considered.[47]

The religious upbringing of the child is usually considered as a matter bearing on the custody decision for the understandable reason that the custodian is likely to influence strongly the child's religious and spiritual development. Because of that, and of the risks of conflict which may arise, the courts have been reluctant to make orders regulating religious upbringing as a matter separate from custody.[48] In *Mackay* v. *Mackay*,[49] however, the court imposed what was in effect a condition on custody in order to secure separate provision for the child's religious upbringing. There is no doubt that such regulation by orders specifically dealing with upbringing is competent.[50] That may sometimes be a convenient and appropriate way, especially in the case of older children, of securing the continuity of their religious upbringing or of giving effect to their wishes while at the same time enabling a custody placement with a custodian of different religious persuasion to proceed. That will, however, only be so where

---

[44] Bearing in mind that autonomy is a concept that matures with the child.

[45] See *Re M. (Infants)* [1967] 1 W.L.R. 1479.

[46] *Re C. (M.A.) (An Infant)* [1966] 1 W.L.R. 646.

[47] *Re E. (An Infant)* [1964] 1 W.L.R. 51; *J.* v. *C.* [1970] A.C. 668, in which the order at first instance of Ungoed Thomas J., for the separate regulation of religious upbringing, was not disturbed.

[48] *Barr* v. *Barr*, 1950 S.L.T. (Notes) 15; *McNaught* v. *McNaught*, 1955 S.L.T. (Sh. Ct.) 9. *Cf.* *Zamorski* v. *Zamorska*, 1960 S.L.T. (Notes) 26, in which the child's education and religious upbringing were treated as, or assumed to be, dependent on the decision on custody.

[49] 1957 S.L.T. (Notes) 17.

[50] *Ante*, pp. 198–199. There are a number of English examples of the separate regulation of religious upbringing: *Re E. (An Infant)*; *J.* v. *C.*, *supra*, but the dangers of resultant tension within the family have also been recognised in *B.(M.)* v. *B.(R.)* [1968] 1 W.L.R. 1182.

the risk that tension will thereby be introduced into the relationship with the custodian is small.

Harmful Effects of some Religious Influences

Questions may sometimes be raised about the harmful effect of a particular form of religious upbringing. They are properly questions not of the child's religious or spiritual welfare but of the impact of a particular religious environment on his moral, emotional, educational or even physical welfare. They are therefore to be resolved by a consideration of the seriousness of that impact assessed by the criteria relevant to the aspects of welfare which are endangered in the context of the child's welfare as a whole. There are several English cases illustrative of the problems which arise. In *Hewison* v. *Hewison*[51] a father who was a member of the Exclusive Brethren was deprived of custody and a custody order made in favour of the mother who did not belong to that sect. The judgment turned materially on the harmful influence that an upbringing in the Exclusive Brethren would have had.

> "The mode of life and code of behaviour enforced by the sect upon its members and their children is [it was said] harsh and restrictive. The children are greatly deprived of normal social contacts with the vast majority of other children. They are handicapped in respect of further education, professional qualification and opportunities for academic life and technical skills. They are taught to regard themselves as different and separate from the rest of the children."[52]

Among other matters referred to were that members of the sect were required to associate with other members of the sect and avoid any close friendships outside it, were not permitted to go to the cinema or theatre or visit the homes of families outside the sect or watch television or listen to radio and were controlled to some extent in the books they read and music they listened to. In *T.* v. *T*,[53] in which the mother was said to be obsessed with the Jehovah's Witnesses, Stamp L.J. took notice of the fact that growing up in the narrow world of the Jehovah's Witnesses "would lead the children into isolation from the rest of the world, socially and intellectually and would deprive them of some of the sweet and wholesome joys of life"[54]; but that was only an element in the decision which turned, primarily, on the mother's mental instability. Membership of the Church of Scientology was, however, given greater weight in the case of *Re B. and G. (Minors) (Custody)*.[55] Caution has been sounded against exaggerating, because a sect may be unpopular or some of its practices unusual, the harmful effect on a child's welfare of an upbringing in an unconventional religious environment.

> "We live in a tolerant society. There is no reason at all why the mother should not espouse the beliefs and practice of Jehovah's Witnesses. There

---

[51] (1977) 7 Fam.L. 207.
[52] *Ibid.* at p. 208.
[53] (1974) 4 Fam.L. 190.
[54] *Ibid.* at p. 191.
[55] [1985] F.L.R. 134.

is nothing immoral or socially obnoxious in the beliefs and practice of the sect. There is a great risk, because we are dealing with an unpopular sect, in overplaying the dangers to the welfare of these children inherent in the possibility that they may follow their mother and become Jehovah's Witnesses."[56]

Accordingly custody has been awarded to a Jehovah's Witness mother who was "moderate in her religious attitude," and was prepared to undertake that she would not take the children proselytising with her, that she would allow access to the father so as to enable Christmas, Easter and birthdays to be celebrated and that she would accept and use a certificate signed by the father consenting to a blood transfusion if ever the child needed one.[57] In general, English courts, while recognising that certain aspects of the way of life of Jehovah's Witnesses may seem "somewhat awkward, difficult and not very good for children," treat these matters as of relatively light weight in a custody decision.[58] Similar considerations apply, it is submitted, to other sects or religions that are not immoral or socially obnoxious. The weight to be given may, however, vary according to the other circumstances of the case. The restrictive and inhibiting influences exerted by some forms of religious upbringing may be of little weight against grounds for maintaining a custodial arrangement in which the child is settled and which is otherwise satisfactory, but yet constitute a substantial objection to a placement which would subject a child to these influences for the first time.

---

[56] *Re T. (Minors)*, Dec. 10, 1975, unreported, *per* Scarman L.J., cited in *Re H. (A Minor)* (1980) 10 Fam.L. 248.

[57] *Re H. (A Minor), supra; Jane* v. *Jane* (1983) 13 Fam.L. 209, in which custody was granted to the father so that he could consent to medical treatment, while care and control was given to the Jehovah's Witness mother. *Cf. McKechnie* v. *McKechnie*, 1990 S.L.T. (Sh.Ct.) 75, in which the father was a Jehovah's Witness and custody was awarded to the mother, one of the relevant factors mentioned being the possibility of difficulties in the event of the child requiring a blood transfusion. The issue of blood transfusion arose in another context in *Finlayson, Applicant*, 1989 S.C.L.R. 601, for there both parents refused to consent to blood transfusions for their haemophiliac son, though this was due to fear of the son contracting the HIV infection rather than for religious reasons. Their refusal was held to be a ground establishing that the child was in need of compulsory measures of care under s. 32 of the Social Work (Scotland) Act 1968: on that issue, see Chap. 17.

[58] *Re C. (Minors) (Wardship: Jurisdiction)* [1978] Fam. 105, *per* Ormrod L.J. at p. 119.

CHAPTER 8

ACCESS, OR THE RIGHT OF CONTACT

The Meaning of Access

The definition of access has received little attention. Like custody, it is a concept both of fact and of law and in the latter context it is sometimes convenient, to avoid ambiguity, to speak not simply of access but of a right of access.[1] The ordinary factual meaning, importing "the right to see a child and to spend time with him or her,"[2] or the right to maintain personal relations and direct contact with the child on a regular basis,[3] is the basis of the content of the legal right but it is clear from judicial orders granting access on terms which envisage the child's being taken away by, or even residing for short periods with, the person entitled to access, that a right of access may extend beyond the visiting of the child which the ordinary meaning would suggest. The lack of definition seems to have given rise to little practical difficulty. In a broad sense the meaning of access is well understood and the terms of a court order, or of agreement between the parties, will afford more specific information in the circumstances of a particular case. There remains some vagueness, particularly on the relation of access to custody, but it is clear that access is something much weaker than custody. It is "the lesser and more restricted right" compared with the greater right of custody.[4] It is a burden or restriction on the custodian's right of control over the child.[5] The powers afforded by a right of access are minimal and, in relation to the child's person, virtually non-existent. So the person with the right of access does not acquire thereby powers over the child such as inhere in the custodian: access is too weak a term for that purpose and its use with that weak connotation is, it is submitted, deliberate. If the child passes into the care of the person entitled to access, as frequently happens, that person will have both the responsibilities and rights associated with care but their source is in the relationship of care for which access is the occasion, rather than in access itself. The person entitled to access has, therefore, no power to compel a child to submit thereto. The right of control of the child, its style and manner of living, its education, religion and medical treatment, remains throughout with the custodian except in so far as it is necessarily modified by an actual transfer of care.

Access and Custody

Because the powers over the child remain with the custodian, it is within his

---

[1] Access is one of the "parental rights" listed in s. 8 of the Law Reform (Parent and Child) (Scotland) Act 1986. To what extent it is jurisprudentially appropriate to describe it as a "right" is examined *post*, at pp. 229–231.

[2] Enc. 10, 1293.

[3] Scot. Law Com. No. 135, *Report on Family Law*, May 1992, draft Bill, cl. 2(1)(*c*).

[4] *Stokes* v. *Stokes*, 1965 S.C. 246 at p. 251, *per* Lord President Clyde.

[5] "Access is a modification of a party's legal right to have care and control of a child," *per* the Second Division in *D.* v. *Strathclyde Regional Council*, 1985 S.L.T. 114 at p. 116.

practical power to defeat the exercise of a legal right of access. But the custodian must exercise his right in a way that admits of access and that must often mean that he temporarily yields immediate control. Moreover, he is obliged to persuade and encourage the child to see the person entitled to access and allow access to take place in the way for which the order provides.[6] If he fails to do so and, more seriously, if he seeks to influence the child against access, he may be guilty of contempt of court. He is not, however, obliged physically to force the child to enable access to take place.[7] Conversely, the exercise of the right of access should not unreasonably restrict the custodian's freedom provided he acts consistently with the welfare of the child. In the event of dispute between the person with a right of access and the person with a right of custody, the welfare of the child is, as always, the determining issue.[8] Accordingly, an access order may be varied even to the extent that it is in effect recalled, if a change of residence consistent with the child's welfare means that it is no longer practicable for it to receive effect; and that is so even if, as a result, the child is taken outwith the jurisdiction.[9]

Access at Common Law

The Legitimate Child

At common law the *patria potestas* was such as to give the father not only the custody of his legitimate child but the control in his discretion of access to the child by others. It was not, however, an arbitrary power and its exercise would ordinarily admit of access to a child by its mother. If, as might happen on separation or divorce, such access were denied, the mother might by application to the court enforce her right of reasonable access. The enforcement of the right was at the discretion of the court and to that extent imperfect, but it was the rule to grant reasonable access unless there was something in the mother's conduct, or in the circumstances of the case (such as a matter affecting the interests of the children), to deprive her of the right.[10] Similarly, on the death of the father, the mother, if she did not have custody, had a right of access.[11] When, on the death of the father, the mother had custody, access might be granted to paternal relatives.[12] Indeed, the court's jurisdiction was by virtue of the broad equitable nature of the *nobile officium* free from any artificial limits as to the classes of persons in whose favour an award of access might, in a proper case, be made although the father's right to dictate the manner of upbringing of his children was at common law so strong that during his lifetime it would be rare for access to be awarded in favour of anyone other than the mother.[13]

---

[6] *Brannigan* v. *Brannigan*, 1979 S.L.T. (Notes) 73; *Blance* v. *Blance*, 1978 S.L.T. 74.

[7] *Ibid.*

[8] Law Reform (Parent and Child) (Scotland) Act 1986, s. 3(2).

[9] *Huddart* v. *Huddart*, 1961 S.C. 393. See also *Johnson* v. *Francis*, 1982 S.L.T. 285.

[10] *McIver* v. *McIver* (1859) 21 D. 1103, especially *per* Lord Curriehill at p. 1107; *cf. A.B.* v. *C.D.* (1847) 10 D. 229; *Steuart* v. *Steuart* (1870) 8 M. 821; *Symington* v. *Symington* (1874) 1 R. 871, (1875) 2 R.(H.L.) 41; *Lilley* v. *Lilley* (1877) 4 R. 397.

[11] *Heatlie* v. *Cathcart* (1827) 5 S. 341; *Borthwick* v. *Dundas* (1845) 8 D. 318.

[12] *McCallum* v. *McCallum* (1853) 15 D. 535.

[13] *S.* v. *S.*, 1967 S.C.(H.L.) 46 at p. 51, *per* Lord Reid.

The Illegitimate Child

The question of access to an illegitimate child seems seldom to have arisen for consideration at common law, but was also subject to regulation of the *nobile officium*.

Statutory Modification of the Common Law

Just as with custody the history of legislative intervention shows a gradual movement away from a concentration on parental rights to a concentration on children's welfare, so too this may be seen in relation to access. The Guardianship of Infants Act 1886,[14] whose provisions on custody have already been noticed,[15] provided in the same terms for the regulation of the right of access of either parent. Thus the court could make such order as it thought fit having regard to the welfare of the child and to the conduct of the parents and to the wishes as well of the mother as of the father. These provisions were of less importance in relation to access than they were in relation to custody. On access they did little more than restate the common law. The Guardianship of Infants Act 1925[16] provided for the regulation of the right of access of the surviving father or mother of a child where an order had been made that a testamentary guardian appointed by the deceased parent was to be the sole guardian of the child. The order regulating access could be such as the court thought fit having regard to the welfare of the child. The Illegitimate Children (Scotland) Act 1930 provided for the right of access of either parent of an illegitimate child in the same terms as it did for custody[17] (*i.e.* the court could make such order as it thought fit having regard to the welfare of the child and to the conduct of the parents and to the wishes as well of the mother as of the father). Although the 1930 Act referred only to the right of access of either parent it did not, it is submitted, derogate from the power under the *nobile officium* to make orders for access in favour of other persons. These Acts were all repealed in 1986, with the enactment of the Law Reform (Parent and Child) (Scotland) Act 1986, which defined "parental rights" to include the right of access.[18] It is there provided that the court may make such order relating to parental rights as it thinks fit,[19] and that in any proceedings relating to parental rights the court shall regard the welfare of the child involved as the paramount consideration and shall not make any order relating to parental rights unless it is satisfied that to do so will be in the interests of the child.[20] This does not alter the pre-1986 position. Under section 1 of the Guardianship of Infants Act 1925 access, though not expressly referred to in that section, was embraced by the custody and upbringing provisions and was thus brought within the matters to be decided by having regard to the welfare of

---

[14] s. 5, (repealed by the Law Reform (Parent and Child) (Scotland) Act 1986, Sched. 2).
[15] *Ante*, pp. 76–78.
[16] s. 5 (4) (repealed by the Law Reform (Parent and Child) (Scotland) Act 1986, Sched. 2).
[17] s. 2 (1) (repealed by the Law Reform (Parent and Child) (Scotland) Act 1986, Sched. 2).
[18] Law Reform (Parent and Child) (Scotland) Act 1986, s. 8.
[19] *Ibid.*, s. 3 (1).
[20] *Ibid.*, s. 3 (2).

the child as the first and paramount consideration.[21] As with custody[22] the onus is on the applicant to prove, on a balance of probabilities,[23] that the child's welfare would be served by an award of access.[24] The court may make an access order over a child up to the age of 16. This is the result, it is submitted, of defining "child," in relation to guardianship, custody and access, as a child under the age of 16.[25] By the age of 16, the child will usually be old enough to decide himself who is to have access to him, and for that reason a court order relating to access to a child of that age or older would be worthless and, indeed, inhibiting of the child's personal freedom. Below the age of 16, the matter of access is now determined entirely by a consideration of the welfare of the child, and the common law rules that limited the court's discretion by reference to parental right or to parental conduct are completely superseded.

The Nature of the Right of Access

It is not difficult to find support for the description of access as a "right." It has been said in an English case that access is "no more than the basic right of any parent," and also to be the basic right of the child.[26] Section 8 of the Law Reform (Parent and Child) (Scotland) Act 1986[27] defines for the purposes of that statute "parental rights" to mean, *inter alia*, guardianship, custody and access.[28] However, notwithstanding the wording of that section, the nature of the rights of guardianship and custody is very different from the nature of the right of access. Guardianship and custody are parental rights which the mother of the child always has, and can always exercise, whether or not she is or has been married to the child's father[29] and which the father of the child always has, and can always exercise, if he is married to the child's mother or was married to her at the time of the child's conception or subsequently.[30] Access is not like that and, though it is defined as a parental right in exactly the same way as guardianship and custody are and will therefore vest in the mother and, subject to the qualification given, the father, it cannot be exercised automatically in the way the other two are. Access is in its nature a limitation on the right of custody, and is subsumed

---

[21] It was never doubted that under the Conjugal Rights (Scotland) Amendment Act 1861, s. 9, which did not, as originally enacted, expressly deal with access but with "custody, maintenance and education of any pupil child of the marriage," the court had jurisdiction to deal with access and that was the statutory warrant under which, in actions of separation or divorce, the jurisdiction of the Outer House of the Court of Session was consistently exercised before 1986 in questions of access as well as custody (see *S.* v. *S.*, 1967 S.C.(H.L.) 46 at p. 51, *per* Lord Reid). S. 9 was amended by the Law Reform (Parent and Child) (Scotland) Act 1986, Sched. 1, defining the parental rights with which it deals by referring to the definition of "parental rights" contained in s. 8 of the 1986 Act: this provision is now embodied in the Court of Session Act 1988, s. 20.

[22] See ante., p. 206.

[23] *Armstrong* v. *Gibson*, 1991 S.L.T. 193. See also, in relation to custody, *F.* v. *F.*, 1991 S.L.T. 357.

[24] *Porchetta* v. *Porchetta*, 1986 S.L.T. 105; *Montgomery* v. *Lockwood*, 1987 S.C.L.R. 525. See also, in relation to custody, *Potter* v. *Potter*, 1992 S.C.L.R. 788.

[25] Law Reform (Parent and Child) (Scotland) Act 1986, s. 8, as amended by the Age of Legal Capacity (Scotland) Act 1991, Sched. 1, para. 43 and Sched. 2.

[26] *S.* v. *S.* [1962] 1 W.L.R. 445 at p. 448, *per* Willmer L.J.

[27] As amended by the Age of Legal Capacity (Scotland) Act 1991, Sched. 1, para. 43 and Sched. 2.

[28] See also s. 20 of the Court of Session Act 1988, which imports the 1986 Act's definition of parental rights. S. 5 of the (now repealed) Guardianship of Infants Act 1886 mentioned the "right of access," as did s. 85 of the Children Act 1975 (an English provision).

[29] Law Reform (Parent and Child) (Scotland) Act 1986, s. 2 (1) (*a*).

[30] *Ibid.*, s. 2 (1) (*b*).

into custody. "Access is something which is physically operable at the instant time, whereas custody is a legal right which can be held even if it is not being physically exercised."[31] So the parent with the right of custody has automatically the right of access, the exercise of the latter being naturally subsumed into the former, greater right. But where a parent loses custody (or *a fortiori* has never had the right of custody) it is wrong to talk in terms of a right of access because the losing of custody (certainly legal custody and probably also *de facto* custody[32]) means the loss of the legal right of access.[33] Access can only be restored (or granted) in these circumstances by order of the court, and the court will not determine the issue on a rights-based analysis, but rather according to the welfare of the child. It follows that both the parent who has parental rights but has lost custody, and the parent who does not have parental rights, must apply to the court under section 3(1) of the 1986 Act for an order relating to parental rights in order to obtain access. A right of access in any meaningful sense comes into being only when the court so orders.[34] The court will only grant a right of access when it has been persuaded that to do so will be in the interests of the child: it will not recognise and enforce the "right" of access simply from parenthood, notwithstanding section 2(1) of the 1986 Act.[35] Ormrod L.J. put it thus[36]: "So far as access to a child is concerned, there are no rights in the sense in which lawyers understand the word. It is a matter to be decided always entirely on the footing of the best interests of the child, either by agreement between the parties or by the court if there is no agreement." This was quoted with approval in the House of Lords by Lord Oliver of Aylmerton,[37] who added:

> "Whatever the position of the parent may be as a matter of law—and it matters not whether he or she is described as having a 'right' in law or a 'claim' by the law of nature or as a matter of common sense—it is perfectly clear that any 'right' vested in him or her must yield to the dictates of the welfare of the child. If the child's welfare dictates that there be access, it adds nothing to say that the parent has also a right to have it subject to considerations of the child's welfare. If the child's welfare dictates that there should be no access, then it is equally fruitless to ask whether that is

---

[31] *Per* the Second Division in *D.* v. *Strathclyde Regional Council*, 1985 S.L.T. 114 at p. 116.

[32] On the difference between the two, see *ante*, pp. 199–200.

[33] The sheriff in *Girvan* v. *Girvan*, 1988 S.L.T. 866 at p. 869I said: "In my opinion, if there is no award of access [in a divorce action] to the non-custodial parent, his or her legal rights as a parent are excluded." In other words, losing custody involves losing the legal right of access. Thomson, "Whither the 'Right' of Access?" 1989 S.L.T. (News) 109 at p. 111, considers this analysis "unsound," but it was accepted in *Hamilton* v. *Mooney*, 1990 S.L.T. (Sh. Ct.) 105, in which it was held competent to charge the father of a legitimate child with plagium, he having lost the right of custody (and not been awarded access) by an award of custody in favour of the child's mother.

[34] In *Montgomery* v. *Lockwood*, 1987 S.C.L.R. 525, the sheriff principal said of a father who did not have parental rights by operation of s. 2 of the 1986 Act, "the pursuer had no right of access to the child unless the court granted it." For the reasons given in the text this is also the case for the parent who does have parental rights by operation of s. 2.

[35] *Porchetta* v. *Porchetta*, 1986 S.L.T. 105; *Russell* v. *Russell*, 1991 S.C.L.R. 429. See also the English case of *Re K.D. (A Minor) (Ward: Termination of Access)* [1988] 2 W.L.R. 398.

[36] *A.* v. *C.* [1985] F.L.R. 445 at p. 455.

[37] *Re K.D.* [1988] 2 W.L.R. 398 at p. 413.

because there is no right to access or because the right is overborne by considerations of the child's welfare."[38]

Thomson[39] criticises this approach and argues that Lord Oliver is wrong in not accepting that the starting point in every case should be that a parent's right of access ought to be given effect to unless persuaded that to do so would be against the child's interests.[40] This is simply a plea for a presumption that access is good for the child, with the onus then being on those denying it.[41] The House of Lords in *Re K.D.* effectively held that there is no such presumption one way or the other, and that the person claiming the right must prove that he is entitled to exercise it, by proving that it is in the interests of the child.[42] In this sense Thomson is correct to conclude[43] that to characterise the parental right of access as a "right" is no longer jurisprudentially tenable.[44] However, once the court grants such a right, under section 3(1) of the Law Reform (Parent and Child) (Scotland) Act 1986, the use of the word "right" is more correct, because the holder's position is recognised, and may be enforced, by the law.

Title to Sue and Enforceability

Who May Apply for Access

The typical applicant is a parent but there is no artificial restriction on who may apply.[45] Nor is there any restriction, other than that indicated by regard for the welfare of the child, excluding any person or class of persons from those in whose favour an order may be made. In a divorce action, or other action to which the Matrimonial Proceedings (Children) Act 1958 applies, an order may be made on a parent's application for access in favour of a third party such as a grandparent and, in any event, the award of access in a proper case to a person other than a parent is within the scope of the *nobile officium*.[46] More generally, section 3(1) of the Law Reform (Parent and Child) (Scotland) Act 1986 allows "any person claiming interest" to make an application for an order relating to parental rights, one of which is in that Act stated to be access.[47] As with cus-

---

[38] *Ibid.*, at p. 414.

[39] *Op. cit.* at p. 112.

[40] For support, see Eekelaar, "What Are Parental Rights?" (1973) 89 L.Q.R. 210 at pp. 218–219.

[41] This was described by the sheriff in *Russell* v. *Russell*, 1991 S.C.L.R. 429 at p. 430, as "the traditional approach," but he agreed with the decision in *Porchetta, supra*, that this approach has now been superseded by s. 3 of the Law Reform (Parent and Child) (Scotland) Act 1986, which requires access to be refused unless the court is satisfied that it would be in the best interests of the child to award it.

[42] That this is also so in other Commonwealth jurisdictions is clear from cases discussed in Kodilinye, "Access to Children in Commonwealth Law" (1992) 41 I.C.L.Q. 190.

[43] *Op. cit.* at p. 113.

[44] The current English legislation talks of "parental responsibility" rather than "parental rights": s. 2, Children Act 1989, though that is defined (s. 3 (1)) to mean "all the rights, duties, powers, responsibilities and authority which by law a parent of a child has in relation to the child and his property." The Scottish Law Commission, in their *Report on Family Law* No. 135, May 1992, have suggested that statute lists parental responsibilities as well as parental rights. Such a change will be little more than in terminology.

[45] In *MacInnes* v. *Highland Regional Council*, 1982 S.C. 69 Lord Grieve (Ordinary) rejected an argument to the effect that only parents and persons *in loco parentis* could apply for access.

[46] *S.* v. *S.* 1967 S.C.(H.L.) 46.

[47] Law Reform (Parent and Child) (Scotland) Act 1986, s. 8.

tody,[48] this has the effect of freeing questions of title from artificial limitation, and also of tying them in with the question of the merits of the case. It has been held not appropriate to award access to a sibling after a child has been adopted,[49] and though the reasoning in that decision has subsequently been disapproved,[50] it is probable that the result is correct. The proper approach, it is submitted, is to make access by a sibling a condition of the adoption.[51] Where parental rights and powers have vested in a local authority or voluntary organisation by way of a parental rights resolution[52] the parent whose rights and powers have been assumed do not have title to sue for custody[53] but they may, nonetheless, request that arrangements for access be made and, if the request is refused or arrangements which have been made are terminated, may apply to the sheriff court for an access order.[54] On the other hand, a parent with parental rights may not seek access to a child concerning whom there is a residential supervision requirement[55]: access, being operable at the instant time, cannot be suspended by the supervision requirement in the way that custody can be,[56] with the result that ordering access would interfere with the discretion granted to the local authority under the supervision requirement.[57] The removal of the child from the parents is often the removal of the child from the source of danger which justifies its being found in need of compulsory measures of care in the first place.

Decisions on Access

Applications for access are applications for orders relating to parental rights within the meaning of section 3(1) of the 1986 Act, and it follows that the court is to be guided by the welfare principle set out in section 3(2). To a large extent the considerations relevant to determining welfare in relation to custody will be relevant here also, and reference should be made to the discussion of that issue in the previous chapter.[58] But the purpose of access is different from the purpose of custody, and the determination of welfare must reflect that fact. The natural wish of a parent to maintain contact with a child from whom he or she is separated, and the interest which a child may normally have in maintaining familial ties on the one hand, and his aversion from access and, particularly, the preference independently formed of an older child on the other hand, are all important

---

[48] *Ante*, pp. 202–204.
[49] *A.B., Petr.*, 1988 S.L.T. 652.
[50] *F.* v. *F.*, 1991 S.L.T. 357.
[51] As happened in *Re C. (A Minor) (Adoption: Conditions)* [1989] A.C. 1. See further, *post* at pp. 552–553. For another view, see Enc. 10, 1303.
[52] Under s. 16 of the Social Work (Scotland) Act 1968.
[53] *Beagley* v. *Beagley*, 1984 S.C.(H.L.) 69. See *ante*, p. 204 and *post* at p. 433.
[54] Social Work (Scotland) Act 1968, ss. 17A and 17B, as inserted by the Health and Social Services and Social Security Adjudications Act 1983, s. 7 (2). These provisions apply only to parents and guardians, but it was held in *MacInnes* v. *Highland Regional Council*, 1982 S.L.T. 288 that it was not incompetent for grandparents to seek access (at common law, and now, it may be assumed, under s. 3 (1) of the Law Reform (Parent and Child (Scotland) Act 1986) to children subject to a parental rights resolution. In the House of Lords case of *Beagley* v. *Beagley, supra*, Lord Fraser of Tullybelton could see "no reason to suppose that that decision was not correct" (1984 S.C.(H.L.) at p. 89).
[55] Under s. 44 of the Social Work (Scotland) Act 1968.
[56] *Aitken* v. *Aitken*, 1978 S.C. 297.
[57] *D.* v. *Strathclyde Regional Council*, 1985 S.L.T. 114.
[58] *Ante*, at pp. 206–225.

considerations, but it is submitted that nothing is gained by elevating any of them to the status of a right: to do so is to run the risk of depriving the welfare principle of its primacy, and to go against the nature of the "right" of access as described above. The interests of persons other than the child can more readily be reconciled with the child's welfare in questions of access than they can in questions of custody, but it is perhaps too readily assumed that maintenance of contact with a person who does not have custody is nearly always in the interests of the child as well as of the parent.[59] That will often be so but the possibility of enforced access, especially if frequent, having a disturbing effect on the child has also to be considered.[60] Family circumstances are so diverse that it is probably wrong for the court ever to start off with an assumption that one thing or another is in the interests of a particular child. The prohibition on the court from making any order relating to parental rights unless it is *satisfied* that to do so will be in the interests of the child[61] suggests, it is submitted, that the court in each case requires proof of where the child's welfare lies. Access may, therefore, be refused to a parent who, over a considerable period of time, has shown little interest in the child[62] or who entertains vindictive feelings towards the parent with custody.[63] It is also against access that it will bring the child into undesirable associations.[64]

The Wishes of the Child

The best interests of the child are to be determined by the court rather than the child himself,[65] but the wishes and disposition of the child are entitled to respect, and they raise questions of peculiar delicacy. It is, as has been submitted,

---

[59] *Cf.* for example, Mitchell, "Children's Experience of Divorce" (1988) 18 Fam.L. 460; Thomson, *Family Law in Scotland* (2nd ed.) at p. 185; "Whither the 'Right' of Access?" 1989 S.L.T. (News) 109. In the last-mentioned article, Thomson bases his criticism of the approach of certain judges in relation to access on the proposition that there should be an "assumption" that access by a non-custodial parent will be in the child's interests, and that "it is *prima facie* always in the child's best interests to retain contact with his or her parents." For support, see Eekelaar, "The Wardship Jurisdiction, Children's Welfare and Parents' Rights" (1991) 107 L.Q.R. 386. For the reasons given in the text, it is suggested that there is no such assumption.

[60] Goldstein, Freud and Solnit: *Beyond the Best Interests of the Child* put the possible detrimental effects so high that they recommend that access should always be on a purely voluntary basis. That, however, is clearly not the present law. For a case in which access was refused because of the disturbing effect on the children and the importance of the children's having a sense of security in a settled home free from a conflict of loyalties, see *M.* v. *M.* [1954] C.L.Y. 959. Similar reasons were adduced to deny a mother access in *Re K.D. (A Minor) (Ward: Termination of Access)* [1988] 2 W.L.R. 398.

[61] Law Reform (Parent and Child) (Scotland) Act 1986, s. 3(2).

[62] *Urquhart* v. *Urquhart*, 1961 S.L.T. (Notes) 56; *Porchetta* v. *Porchetta*, 1986 S.L.T. 105. *Cf. Gray* v. *Gray*, 1961 S.L.T. (Notes) 83 and *McAllister* v. *McAllister*, 1947 S.L.T. (Notes) 9.

[63] *C.D.* v. *A.B.*, 1908 S.C. 737. In *Porchetta* v. *Porchetta*, 1986 S.L.T. 105 the hostility came from the custodial parent: access was refused on the ground that "any attempt at access at the present time will only sustain this hostility, and the child will sooner or later sense it and suffer thereby": *per* Lord Dunpark.

[64] *Gray* v. *Gray, supra; McClements* v. *McClements*, 1958 S.C. 286. See also Stewart: "Consistorial Actions Involving Criminal Offenders," 1973 J.R. 43 at pp. 58–60. The father claiming access in *Montgomery* v. *Lockwood*, 1987 S.C.L.R. 525 was awarded interim access on showing that the mother had had a conviction for growing cannabis. The sheriff principal overturned the decision on the ground that there was not enough material for the court to decide where the interests of the child lay.

[65] *Gover* v. *Gover*, 1969 S.L.T. (Notes) 78.

doubtful if an access order can be enforced against children in any way other than through the intermediacy of the custodian. It was within the custodian's powers to compel at least a pupil child[66] to comply with an access order, and that power must now be taken to extend to custodians of all children under the age of 16,[67] but it is recognised that the court will normally not require the custodian to exert compulsion if the child's resistance is genuine and free from external pressure.[68] It has been said that the child's resistance must also be reasonable[69] and that, no doubt, usually affords a good indication of whether the child's views are genuine and independent, but if they are, and are strongly held, it is unattractive to compel a child to act against them merely because to the adult mind they appear irrational.[70] A custodian must not, however, use the child's alleged resistance as a pretext for obstructing access for reasons of his own and even if the child's resistance is genuine he should, once an access order has been made, use every effort, short of physical compulsion, to ensure that the child complies with it.[71] "The child should be persuaded, encouraged, and instructed, but not physically forced to go with the person to whom access has been granted."[72] Even apart from problems of enforcement, however, the wishes of a child are entitled to respect. They should be taken into account before an access order is made, notwithstanding the lack of domestic statutory obligation to do so.[73] Much will depend on the age and capacity for independent judgment of the child. The strongly-held genuine wishes of the older child will have great and usually decisive weight in questions of access as they do in questions of custody.[74]

Effect of Agreement

Although access is often, and conveniently, arranged by agreement between parties, it is, as explained above, only by an order of the court that a legal right of access, in an enforceable sense, arises. Such an order will not be made unless the court is satisfied that making it will be in the interests of the child. Accordingly any agreement about access cannot be enforced unless it satisfies that test. Moreover, just as, at common law, any agreement by a parent (or, it is submitted, by any other lawful custodian) to surrender custody is revocable, so any agreement to burden custody by a right of access is, by parity of reasoning,

---

[66] The extent of custodial powers over a minor *pubes* was uncertain at common law but were clearly much less than in the case of a pupil child. See *ante* at pp. 68–70.

[67] s. 5(1), Age of Legal Capacity (Scotland) Act 1991.

[68] *Blance* v. *Blance*, 1978 S.L.T. 74; *Cosh* v. *Cosh*, 1979 S.L.T. (Notes) 72; *Brannigan* v. *Brannigan*, 1979 S.L.T. (Notes) 73.

[69] *Cosh* v. *Cosh*, *supra*.

[70] In *Russell* v. *Russell*, 1991 S.C.L.R. 429, a five-year-old child exhibited "signs of extreme distress" at the thought of her father having access to her. The sheriff regarded this as highly significant in determining the child's interests, "however unfairly" the child had acquired the negative feelings.

[71] Indeed it has been said that custodians have an "unqualified obligation" to avoid prejudicing in any way the relationship between the child and the parent with access: *per* Lord Penrose in *Breingan* v. *Jamieson*, *Herald*, March 3, 1992.

[72] *Blance* v. *Blance*, *supra*, *per* Lord Stewart at p. 75.

[73] Though it is to be noted that Art. 12 of the UN Convention on the Rights of the Child (28 *International Legal Materials* 1448, ratified by the UK, Dec. 16, 1991) provides that the child's views should be taken into account in any decision that affects him or her.

[74] *Gover* v. *Gover*, 1969 S.L.T. (Notes) 78.

revocable. Although, therefore, agreement may be relevant background it can never in itself be a sufficient basis for an enforceable right of access.

CHAPTER 9

JURISDICTIONAL AND PROCEDURAL ASPECTS OF CUSTODY AND ACCESS

Scope of this Chapter

The preceding two chapters examined the development of, content of, and decision-making in relation to, respectively, custody and access. This chapter will deal with a number of loosely related issues involving these two parental rights.

JURISDICTION

Jurisdiction before 1986

The Court of Session

Common law jurisdiction in custody and related questions, including access, rested entirely on the *nobile officium*[1] and as such was exercised by the Inner House. The court acted as *parens patriae* and its jurisdiction could be compared with the wardship jurisdiction exercised at one time by the Court of Chancery in England and later by the Chancery, and now the Family, Division of the High Court.[2] Although its incidents were less well developed in detail it was, in principle, as extensive as the English wardship jurisdiction. The various statutes regulating the rules of custody were sometimes referred to as if they were separate sources of jurisdiction, but the better view is probably that all jurisdiction in custody before 1986, although extended and regulated by statute, flowed from the *nobile officium*. In cases outwith the Conjugal Rights (Scotland) Amendment Act 1861[3] procedure in the Court of Session was by petition to the Inner House, except that in vacation it was at one time competent for the Lord Ordinary on the Bills to exercise all the powers and prerogatives of the court.[4] It was later provided that petitions for the custody of children brought under any Act of Parliament or at common law could be presented in the Outer House.[5]

The Sheriff Court

No order for custody is truly permanent. It may be recalled or varied by the court for sufficient cause. A distinction may, however, be made between, on the one hand, an order that is permanent in the sense of having in its contemplation

---

[1] *S.* v. *S.*, 1967 S.C.(H.L.) 46.

[2] *McLean* v. *McLean*, 1947 S.C. 79 at p. 84, *per* Lord Justice-Clerk Cooper; *Stuart* v. *Stuart* (1861) 4 Macq. 1 at p. 60, *per* Lord Campbell L.C. and at p. 66, *per* Lord Cranworth.

[3] Repealed in relevant part by the Court of Session Act 1988, Sched. 2.

[4] *Edgar* v. *Fisher's Trs.* (1893) 21 R. 59; *Buchan* v. *Cardross* (1842) 4 D. 1268; Fraser (3rd ed.), at p. 294.

[5] Rule of Court 189(*a*)(XX), as inserted by Act of Sederunt of January 30, 1970 (S.I. 1970 No. 134). See *Syme* v. *Cunningham*, 1973 S.L.T. (Notes) 40.

the regulation of the child's custody unless occasion for recall or variation emerges or until, by operation of the law, the child ceases to be subject to it and, on the other hand, an interim or temporary order that has as its purpose the regulation of custody in an emergency, or during the dependence of an action or for like reasons of a temporary kind until a permanent order is made. Because the regulation of custody involved the exercise of the *nobile officium* the sheriff court had, with one possible exception, no jurisdiction at common law to regulate custody on a permanent basis. As judge ordinary of the bounds the sheriff might, however, make temporary orders in an emergency so as to regulate custody until the matter could be decided by the supreme court.[6] There is also some authority—the exception just referred to—for the view that the sheriff could make a permanent order if its sole effect was to support a legal right to custody[7]; there was in such a case no appeal to the *nobile officium* which was exercised only when custody rights were curtailed.

In 1886 the sheriff court jurisdiction was extended to applications by a mother of a legitimate child[8] and in 1907, more generally, to actions regulating the custody of children.[9] The jurisdiction thereby given to the sheriff court was not limited to cases under statute but extended to those in which direct appeal was made to the *nobile officium*.[10] The custody jurisdiction of the sheriff court therefore became co-extensive with that of the Court of Session and so the sheriff could deal with disputes to which persons other than parents were parties, including disputes between parents (or a parent) and a third party, as well as with disputes between parents *inter se*.[11]

Grounds for Jurisdiction Today: Family Law Act 1986

Part I of the Family Law Act 1986, passed as a consequence of the recommendations of the Law Commission and the Scottish Law Commission in their joint report *Custody of Children—Jurisdiction and Enforcement Within the UK*,[12] entirely supersedes the previously existing rules of jurisdiction,[13] not only in relation to custody but also in relation to access.[14] It had long been felt unsatisfactory that the jurisdictional rules in Scotland were different from those in England, not least because of the potential conflicts this might give rise to in questions of recognition and enforcement.[15] As early as 1959 there had been re-

---

[6] *Gillan* v. *Barony Parish Council* (1898) 1 F. 183; *Hood* v. *Hood* (1871) 9 M. 449; *Brand* v. *Shaws* (1888) 15 R. 449; *Mackenzie* v. *Keillor* (1892) 19 R. 963; *Speid* v. *Webster* (1821) 1 S. 221.

[7] *Murray* v. *Forsyth*, 1917 S.C. 721 at p. 724, *per* Lord Skerrington; *Brand* v. *Shaws* (1888) 15 R. 449, 16 R. 315. See, however, the reservations expressed in *Harvey* v. *Harvey* (1860) 22 D. 1198, *per* Lord Justice-Clerk Inglis at p. 1209, and in *Hood* v. *Hood* (1871) 9 M. 449 at p. 455. See also Fraser, p. 94, note 2, citing *Herd* v. *Ellis* (1864) 3 Scot. Law Mag. (NS) 143.

[8] Guardianship of Infants Act 1886, ss. 5 and 9 (repealed by the Law Reform (Parent and Child) (Scotland) Act 1986, Sched. 2).

[9] Sheriff Court (Scotland) Act 1907, s. 5(2) (as originally enacted).

[10] *Murray* v. *Forsyth, supra.*

[11] *Ibid.*

[12] Law Com. No. 138, Scot. Law Com. No. 91, Cmnd. 9419 (1985).

[13] s. 8.

[14] s. 1(1)(*b*) of the Family Law Act 1986 (as amended by the Children Act 1989, Sched. 13, para. 62) defines "Part I order," for which the jurisdictional rules are laid down, as "an order made by a court of civil jurisdiction in Scotland under any enactment or rule of law with respect to the custody, care or control of a child, access to a child, or the education or upbringing of a child."

[15] See *post*, at pp. 267–270

commendations to harmonise the jurisdictional rules in relation to custody for all the parts of the United Kingdom,[16] but it was not until proposals from the Council of Europe and the Hague Conference, aimed at dealing with the problems of recognition and enforcement of foreign custody decrees, and the return of children taken abroad in breach of custody rights,[17] were nearing enactment into United Kingdom domestic law that the Law Commissions recommended the changes in the law that were *inter alia* incorporated into the Family Law Act 1986. The purpose of Part I of that Act is twofold: first, to lay down a uniform system of jurisdiction throughout the United Kingdom, which aims to ensure, so far as possible, that there is only one court at any one time with jurisdiction to deal with custody of and access to a child, these jurisdictional rules being, so far as possible, the same throughout the United Kingdom; and secondly to provide for the automatic recognition and speedy enforcement of the custody and access orders made in one part of the United Kingdom throughout the other parts of the United Kingdom. Recognition and enforcement will be dealt with later[18]; this part of the chapter will consider the grounds of jurisdiction of the Scottish courts.[19]

Existence of Matrimonial Proceedings

The pre-eminent ground of jurisdiction in questions of custody and access is the existence of matrimonial proceedings to which orders for custody or access are ancillary. This is the result of section 11 of the Family Law Act 1986, which excludes the other, subsidiary grounds for jurisdiction (except the emergency ground under section 12) when, on the date of an application for a custody or access order, there are continuing in a court in any part of the United Kingdom matrimonial proceedings in respect of the marriage of the parents of the child.[20] "Matrimonial proceedings" are defined[21] to mean "proceedings for divorce, nullity of marriage or judicial separation." It is therefore to the rules of jurisdiction in relation to matrimonial proceedings that we must turn to determine the pre-eminent ground of jurisdiction in relation to custody and access.[22]

The Scottish court may make such order as it thinks fit relating to parental rights (including custody and access) in any action for divorce, judicial separation or declarator of nullity of marriage,[23] and it has the necessary jurisdiction to do so.[24] Its jurisdiction to entertain the action for divorce, separation or nullity

---

[16] Report of the Committee on Conflicts of Jurisdiction Affecting Children, Cmnd. 842 (1959) (the Hodson Committee).

[17] See *post*, at pp. 270–277.

[18] *Post*, at chap. 10.

[19] See further, Enc. 10, 1314–1318; Balfour, "Family Law—Cross-Border Child Abduction" (1989) 34 J.L.S. 96; Jamieson, "Custody of Children and the Family Law Act 1986," 1991 S.L.T. (News) 438.

[20] Family Law Act 1986, s. 11(1).

[21] *Ibid.*, s. 18(1).

[22] For a discussion of jurisdiction in matrimonial proceedings more detailed than is necessary here, see Clive, *Husband and Wife*, (3rd ed.) at pp. 610–618.

[23] Court of Session Act 1988, s. 20, re-enacting the Conjugal Rights (Scotland) Amendment Act 1861, s. 9 (as substituted by the Law Reform (Parent and Child) (Scotland) Act 1986, Sched. 1, para. 2).

[24] Domicile and Matrimonial Proceedings Act 1973, s. 10.

itself comes from the same source.[25] The Court of Session has jurisdiction to entertain an action for divorce or separation if (and only if) either of the parties to the marriage in question (a) is domiciled in Scotland on the date when the action is begun; or (b) was habitually resident in Scotland throughout the period of one year ending with that date.[26] It has jurisdiction to entertain an action for declarator of nullity of marriage if (and only if) either of the parties to the marriage (a) is domiciled in Scotland on the date when the action is begun; or (b) was habitually resident in Scotland throughout the period of one year ending with that date; or (c) died before that date and was either domiciled in Scotland at death or had been habitually resident in Scotland throughout the period of one year ending with the date of death.[27] The sheriff court has jurisdiction to entertain an action for divorce or separation[28] if (and only if) (a) either party to the marriage in question is domiciled in Scotland at the date when the action is begun, or was habitually resident there throughout the period of one year ending with that date, and (b) either party to the marriage was resident in the sheriffdom for a period of 40 days ending with that date, or had been habitually resident in the sheriffdom for a period of not less than 40 days ending not more than 40 days before the said date and has no known residence in Scotland at that date.[29]

If matrimonial proceedings are continuing on the basis of the jurisdictional grounds described above, then the court in which the proceedings are continuing also has jurisdiction to determine applications in respect of custody of or access to the children of that marriage. Proceedings, once commenced, are deemed to be "continuing" in a court in Scotland until the child reaches the age of 16, or until the proceedings have been dismissed or decree of absolvitor granted before then (whichever is sooner).[30] The court will not however have jurisdiction in relation to custody or access if it has made an order declining jurisdiction under section 13(6).[31]

"Child of the Marriage"

The power of the court in an action of divorce, nullity of marriage or separation to make orders relating to custody or access extends only to any child of the marriage to which the action relates, that is the child of both parties to the marriage (whether natural or by adoption), and the child of one party to the marriage who has been accepted as one of the family by the other party.[32] Whether the child of one spouse has been accepted as one of the family by the other is a question of fact, the answer to which is usually to be inferred from the circumstances. A typical situation is where a man marries and "sets up home with his

---

[25] *Ibid.*, ss. 7 and 8.

[26] *Ibid.*, s. 7(2).

[27] *Ibid.*, s. 7(3).

[28] The sheriff court has no jurisdiction to nullify a marriage.

[29] Domicile and Matrimonial Proceedings Act 1973, s. 8(2) (as amended by the Divorce Jurisdiction, Court Fees and Legal Aid (Scotland) Act 1983, Sched. 1, para. 18).

[30] Family Law Act 1986, s. 42(3). Proceedings are deemed to be "continuing" in a court in England and Wales or Northern Ireland until the child reaches the age of 18, or the proceedings are dismissed or decree of absolvitor granted before then: s. 42(2).

[31] See *post*, at p. 244

[32] Family Law Act 1986, s. 42(4)(*b*). The same formula is used in the Court of Session Act 1988, s. 20.

wife, the children [of the wife] come to live there, he treats them as his own and does his best to make them not only members of the family, but to feel that they are members of the family."[33] There is no reported Scottish case that shows that any difficulty has been experienced in deciding whether acceptance as one of the family has taken place. When the same test was used in England, however, it gave rise to a substantial amount of judicial interpretation.[34] By requiring acceptance and relating it only to children of the other spouse, Parliament was taken to have intended something narrower than children "who were living in family with the spouses," which the Royal Commission on Marriage and Divorce[35] had contemplated. This follows from the clear words of the statute and so it has been held that a child who is the child of neither party to the marriage does not come within the custody jurisdiction exercisable in divorce actions because he has been "accepted into the family of the parties".[36] In the English cases, attention has been concentrated on the acceptor's knowledge of all material facts and on consent of both spouses to the acceptance of the child.[37] The consent must have been unequivocal but might be inferred from conduct. On that view acceptance was essentially a question of contract. A narrowly contractual approach has, however, been criticised[38] and it is submitted that the criticism is sound. Acceptance as one of the family is apt to describe the formation of a relationship rather than a contract. The relationship is formed when acceptance takes place, even if that acceptance be based on defective knowledge. Lack of knowledge on the part of the accepting spouse may affect the order which the court should make but does not nullify acceptance and so does not strike at jurisdiction.

Whatever may be the arguments for a wider definition in other contexts, it seems clear that, when the Act speaks of acceptance into the family, family is to be understood as based on marriage. Acceptance can be given at any time before, at, or after marriage,[39] so long as the family subsists, but if given before marriage, it is proleptic in that it has in contemplation the family to be constituted by marriage. Acceptance before marriage is probably, therefore, ineffect-

---

[33] *Bowlas* v. *Bowlas* [1965] P. 450, *per* Salmon L.J. at p. 461; but *cf. Holmes* v. *Holmes* [1966] 1 W.L.R. 187 and *R.* v. *R.* [1971] C.L.Y. 3364. There may be acceptance of one partner although the parties never cohabit (*R.* v. *R.*), but the mere fact of marriage is not sufficient to give rise to the inference that one partner has accepted into the family the children of the other (*Bowlas* v. *Bowlas*).

[34] See for example *Holmes* v. *Holmes* [1966] 1 W.L.R. 187; *R.* v. *R.* [1968] P. 414; *Dixon* v. *Dixon* [1968] 1 W.L.R. 167; *B.* v. *B. and F.* [1969] P. 37; *P.* v. *P.* [1969] 1 W.L.R. 898. The English test is now whether the child has been "treated by both...parties as a child of their family": Family Law Act 1986, s. 42(4)(*a*); Children Act 1989, s. 105(1).

[35] Cmnd. 9678 (1956), para. 393 (which led to the formula being introduced into Scots law with the now repealed ss. 1 and 14 of the Matrimonial Proceedings (Children) Act 1958).

[36] *Bradley* v. *Bradley*, 1987 S.C.L.R. 62 (Sh.Ct.).

[37] *Dixon* v. *Dixon, supra; G.* v. *G.* (1965) 109 Sol.J. 831. The possessive attitude of the parent spouse and the fact that the non-parent spouse is not asked to assume any significant financial liability are relevant but not conclusive factors (*Dixon* v. *Dixon, per* Wrangham J., *supra.*, at p. 171).

[38] *Snow* v. *Snow* [1972] Fam. 74, *per* Davies L.J. at p. 114.

[39] *Bowlas* v. *Bowlas, supra; Snow* v. *Snow, supra.* In the former case it was said by Salmon L.J. (at p. 461) that acceptance must be before or at the time of the marriage. It is, no doubt, unlikely that non-acceptance at the time of the marriage will be superseded by acceptance later, but there is nothing in the wording of the Act to exclude it.

ive if it has lapsed or been withdrawn by the time the marriage takes place.[40] With that exception, the duration of the relationship constituted by acceptance is irrelevant. A relationship may be destroyed if acceptance on which it depends lapses or is withdrawn, but it cannot on that account be said never to have existed. A personal relationship, as a fact that exists independently of legal concepts, is in that respect in contrast with a contract which can rightly be said never to have existed if the consent, which is its essence, can be shown to have been vitiated *ab initio* by essential error. It has been held that a child *in utero* can be accepted as one of the family, even if the spouses separate before the child is born.[41] It is doubtful if the Act had such cases primarily, or at all, in contemplation, but the reasoning is clear and should be followed, in appropriate cases, in Scotland.[42]

Habitual Residence

If matrimonial proceedings are not continuing in a court in any part of the United Kingdom in respect of the marriage of the parents of the child, then an independent application for a custody or access order may be entertained (a) by the Court of Session if, on the date of the application, the child concerned is habitually resident in Scotland or (b) by the sheriff if, on the date of the application, the child concerned is habitually resident in the sheriffdom.[43] Habitual residence has the meaning ascribed to it in other areas of international private law.[44] If the child is removed from or retained outside or himself leaves or remains outside a part of the United Kingdom in which he was habitually resident before his change of residence, and this is done (a) without the agreement of the person or all persons having the right to determine where he is to reside or (b) in contravention of an order made by a court in any part of the United Kingdom, then he shall be treated as continuing to be habitually resident in that part of the United Kingdom for a period of one year after his removal, etc.,[45] or until he reaches the age of 16, if sooner, or until the person or persons whose agreement was not obtained subsequently agrees, if sooner.[46] This is to prevent the purpose of the Act being frustrated simply by moving the child to another jurisdiction.

Presence

If matrimonial proceedings are not continuing in a court in any part of the United Kingdom in respect of the marriage of the parents of the child, then an independent application for a custody or access order may be entertained (a) by the Court of Session if, on the date of the application the child concerned is present in Scotland and is not habitually resident in any part of the United Kingdom,[47] or (b) by the sheriff if, on the date of the application, the child is present

---

[40] *Snow* v. *Snow, supra.*
[41] *Caller* v. *Caller* [1966] 2 All E.R. 754.
[42] See further *ante*, at pp. 95–96.
[43] Family Law Act 1986, s. 9.
[44] For a discussion, see Anton and Beaumont (2nd ed.) at pp. 146–152 and 514; Enc. 17, 190. And see the Inner House discussion of habitual residence in *Dickson* v. *Dickson*, 1990 S.C.L.R. 692. See also *Scullion* v. *Scullion*, 1990 S.C.L.R. 577 (Sh. Ct.); *Rellis* v. *Hart*, 1993 S.L.T. 738.
[45] Family Law Act 1986, s. 41(1) and (2).
[46] *Ibid.*, s. 41(3).
[47] *Ibid.*, s. 10(*a*).

in Scotland and the child is not habitually resident in any part of the United Kingdom and either the pursuer or the defender in the application is habitually resident in the sheriffdom.[48] This section is intended to act as a safety net to ensure that jurisdiction exists over children physically present in Scotland and over whom it is felt that there should be jurisdiction, even though there is no emergency facing the child.[49] It will allow the Scottish court to determine custody and access over a child brought from abroad as soon as it enters Scotland.[50] This jurisdiction is limited to cases in which the child is not habitually resident in any part of the United Kingdom (including Scotland), and thus there is no overlap with the previous ground of jurisdiction. Nevertheless it may well be correct that, given the emergency jurisdiction about to be discussed, this ground based on mere presence "smacks of exorbitancy."[51]

Emergency

Notwithstanding that any other court, whether within or outside Scotland, has jurisdiction to entertain an application for a custody or access order, the Court of Session or the sheriff has jurisdiction to entertain such an application if (a) the child concerned is present in Scotland or, as the case may be, in the sheriffdom on the date of the application; and (b) the Court of Session or the sheriff considers that, for the protection of the child, it is necessary to make such an order immediately. This emergency jurisdiction supersedes all other grounds, including jurisdiction based upon the existence of matrimonial proceedings, and it was enacted to take account of the Law Commissions' recommendation[52] that "the ability to invoke the jurisdiction of the court on this basis should [never] be excluded by reason of the fact that some other basis of jurisdiction may be available." It is not specified what nature of necessity has to exist before the section is operable, and it is a matter to be decided by the court in each particular case. The sorts of emergency that, at common law, justified the Court of Session in exercising jurisdiction included threats of the child being abducted from its parents[53] and threats of "injury, physical or moral, to the child."[54] At common law the basis of the emergency jurisdiction was the welfare of the child[55] and that, doubtless, remains the basis of the exercise of the jurisdiction under the statutory provisions. It is difficult to see how this ground of jurisdiction could be appropriately invoked in relation to an application for access.

Further Modification of the Rules

The jurisdictional rules are further modified by section 13 of the Family Law Act 1986 in the following ways:

---

[48] *Ibid.*, s. 10(*b*).

[49] This was the case at common law in Scotland: *Kelly* v. *Marks*, 1974 S.L.T. 118. See also *Babington* v. *Babington*, 1955 S.C. 115 at pp. 121 and 124; *Calder* v. *Calder*, 1960 S.L.T. (Notes) 52.

[50] See for example *Hill* v. *Hill*, 1991 S.L.T. 189.

[51] Anton and Beaumont (2nd ed.) at p. 515.

[52] Law Com. No. 138, Scot. Law Com. No 91, Cmnd. 9419 (1985) at para. 4.99.

[53] *Murray* v. *Forsyth*, 1917 S.C. 721.

[54] *Westergaard* v. *Westergaard*, 1914 S.C. 977, *per* Lord Justice-Clerk Macdonald at p. 981. See also *Oludimu* v. *Oludimu*, 1967 S.L.T. 105; *McShane* v. *McShane*, 1962 S.L.T. 221.

[55] *Stuart* v. *Moore* (1861) 23 D. 902, *per* Lord Campbell L.C. at p. 908.

(1) Under section 9 of the Matrimonial Proceedings (Children) Act 1958 the court could make provision relating to parental rights, which includes custody and access,[56] within a reasonable time after an action for divorce, nullity or separation had been dismissed, or decree of absolvitor granted. This would be inconsistent with the scheme under the Family Law Act 1986, where the court in which matrimonial proceedings take place has jurisdiction only until the child reaches 16 or the action is dismissed. Consequently, section 9 of the 1958 Act has been amended and is now subject to section 13(2) of the 1986 Act, with the result that the court shall not have jurisdiction under section 9 after the dismissal of matrimonial proceedings, or after decree of absolvitor is granted therein, to entertain an application for a custody order unless the application was made on or before the dismissal or the granting of the decree of absolvitor.

(2) If a decree of separation has been granted by one court then that court will normally have jurisdiction to entertain an application for a custody or access order until the child reaches the age of 16.[57] However, if after the granting of the decree of separation an action for divorce or nullity of marriage is raised in another court, both courts would theoretically have jurisdiction under the 1986 Act: the separation court under section 42(3) and the divorce or nullity court under section 11. It was considered that in that situation the divorce or nullity court should have precedence, and section 13(3) gives effect to this by depriving the Scottish court that granted the decree of separation of jurisdiction to entertain an application for a custody or access order if, on the date of the application, proceedings for divorce or nullity of marriage in respect of the marriage concerned are continuing in another court in the United Kingdom.[58] This however is qualified if the court in which matrimonial proceedings are continuing has waived its jurisdiction in favour of the court that granted the decree of separation[59]: in that case the separation court will have jurisdiction.

(3) The Scottish court that makes a custody or access order under section 9(1) of the Matrimonial Proceedings (Children) Act 1958 does not have jurisdiction to entertain an application for the variation of that order if, on the date of the application, matrimonial proceedings in respect of the marriage concerned are continuing in another court in the United Kingdom.[60] This however is qualified if the court in which matrimonial proceedings are continuing has waived its jurisdiction in favour of the court that made the original order[61]: in that case the original court will have jurisdiction to vary the order.

---

[56] Law Reform (Parent and Child) (Scotland) Act 1986, s. 8.

[57] Family Law Act 1986, s. 42(3).

[58] *Ibid.*, s. 13(3). (The other court could be in Scotland, or in another part of the United Kingdom.)

[59] *Ibid.*, s. 13(5).

[60] *Ibid.*, s. 13(4). This supersedes the normal rule (s. 15(2)) that the court that had jurisdiction to make a Pt. I order will have jurisdiction to vary and recall the original order, notwithstanding that it would no longer have jurisdiction to make the original order.

[61] *Ibid.*, s. 13(5).

(4) The Scottish court that has jurisdiction on the basis of the continuation of matrimonial proceedings to entertain an application for a custody or access order may make an order declining jurisdiction if both the following conditions are satisfied: (a) it appears to the court that, but for the existence of matrimonial proceedings, another court in Scotland or elsewhere in the United Kingdom would have jurisdiction; and (b) the court considers that it would be more appropriate for matters relating to custody[62] of that child to be determined in that other court.[63] The court may recall an order made under this provision.[64]

Refusal of Application and Sisting of Proceedings

Notwithstanding that the court has jurisdiction to entertain an application for a custody or access order, it may refuse the application in any case where the matter in question has already been determined in other proceedings.[65] The other proceedings may be in Scotland, elsewhere in the United Kingdom, or in a foreign country. Also, the court to which application has been made may sist the proceedings at any stage if it appears to the court that proceedings in relation to matters to which the application relates are continuing outside Scotland or in another court in Scotland[66] or where it appears to the court that it would be more appropriate[67] for those matters to be determined in proceedings outside Scotland or in another court in Scotland, and that such proceedings are likely to be taken there.[68] This provision was enacted to clear up doubt as to whether the court could decline its essentially protective jurisdiction in custody cases; but in any case in deciding whether to sist the proceedings before the Scottish court, the welfare of the child is the paramount consideration.[69] The exercise of the power to sist proceedings is a matter of judicial discretion, which cannot be interfered with on appeal just because the appellate court would have decided otherwise.[70]

Remission from Sheriff Court to Court of Session

The sheriff has a discretion, exercisable at any stage in any custody action, to remit the cause to the Court of Session.[71] Although parties may no doubt invite the sheriff to exercise his discretion, it is essentially a power to be exercised *ex proprio motu* and neither its exercise nor the failure or refusal to exercise it is

---

[62] Or, though it is not stated, access. Pt. I of the 1986 Act originally talked of "custody orders," which it defined to include access orders. Since the Children Act 1989 it has talked of "Part I Orders," which is defined to include custody and access orders. The use of the word "custody" in s. 13, reflecting the wide meaning of "custody order" as it was originally used, should retain a wide meaning including access. In any case, access being a qualification to custody (see *ante* at pp. 229–230), it is a "matter relating to custody."

[63] Family Law Act 1986, s. 13(6).

[64] *Ibid.*, s. 13(7).

[65] *Ibid.*, s. 14(1).

[66] *Ibid.*, s. 14(2)(*a*). See *Hill* v. *Hill*, 1991 S.L.T. 189.

[67] For what is envisaged by this, see Law Com. No. 138, Scot. Law Com. No. 91, at para. 4.97.

[68] Family Law Act 1986, s. 14(2)(*b*).

[69] *Hill* v. *Hill, supra, per* Lord McCluskey at p. 192B.

[70] See *Messenger* v. *Messenger*, 1992 S.L.T. (Sh.Ct.) 29.

[71] Sheriff Courts (Scotland) Act 1971, s. 37(2A), as inserted by Law Reform (Miscellaneous Provisions) (Scotland) Act 1980, s. 16.

subject to review.[72] That is, however, without prejudice to the right of a party to any ordinary cause to move the sheriff to remit the cause to the Court of Session because its importance or difficulty makes it appropriate to do so and a decision to remit or not to remit on such a motion is subject to appeal to the Court of Session.[73] As the matter is entrusted to the discretion and opinion of the sheriff, it would seem that it is only if he has failed to give the matter proper consideration or has proceeded on some improper ground, that an appeal will be successful.

PROCEDURE

Custody proceedings are not consistorial actions[74] but they do concern status[75] and, as the court is under a mandatory duty to regard the welfare of the child as the paramount consideration, proof, or some substitute for proof, is necessary even if the case be undefended.[76] Where the applicant is not a parent, notice must be given to the local authority within whose area the applicant resides or, if he does not reside in Scotland, to a local authority specified by the court.[77] Custody proceedings are excluded from the provisions for summary trial in section 10 of the Administration of Justice (Scotland) Act 1933.[78] When they are raised independently of an action of divorce, separation or nullity of marriage, procedure is by way of petition in the Court of Session and in the sheriff court by initial writ.

The following rules apply to questions of custody and access raised in connection with Court of Session actions for divorce, nullity of marriage, or separation and to all proceedings relating to custody and access in the sheriff court.

(1) Where the action is dismissed at any stage after proof on the merits has been allowed, or if decree of absolvitor is granted, provision for custody may be made by an order pronounced either forthwith or after dismissal or absolvitor, so long as the application was made on or before such dismissal or the granting of the decree of absolvitor.[79] If custody is not regulated at that time an application cannot subsequently be made in the same process.

(2) A custody order may be made, at least in the Court of Session, although there is no conclusion for custody.[80]

(3) In the Court of Session the defender may claim custody of or access to a child by lodging defences containing, in addition to averments and

---

[72] *Ibid.*, s. 37(3), as substituted by the Law Reform (Miscellaneous Provisions) (Scotland) Act 1980, s. 16(*c*).

[73] *Ibid.*, s. 37(1)(*b*) and (3)(*b*), as inserted or substituted by the 1980 Act, s. 16(*a*) and (*c*).

[74] *A.B.* v. *C.B.* (1906) 8 F. 973, *per* Lord McLaren at p. 974.

[75] *Kitson* v. *Kitson* 1945 S.C. 434 at p. 439.

[76] In the sheriff court the Ordinary Cause Rules provide that decree may be granted "after such enquiry as the sheriff thinks necessary" (Sheriff Courts (Scotland) Act 1907, r. 22(2)).

[77] Children Act 1975, s. 49(1); Rule of Court 170B (14); Ordinary Cause Rules (Sheriff Court) no. 130 (8).

[78] s. 10(8); Rule of Court 231 (O)(iv).

[79] Matrimonial Proceedings (Children) Act 1958, s. 9, as amended by the Family Law (Scotland) Act 1985, Sched. 2, Law Reform (Parent and Child) (Scotland) Act 1986, Sched. 1, para. 6, and Family Law Act 1986, Sched. 1, para. 5; Family Law Act 1986, s. 13 (2).

[80] *Symington* v. *Symington* (1874) 1 R. 871, (1875) 2 R.(H.L.) 41.

pleas-in-law, a conclusion for custody of the child.[81] So too, a defender who does not want to claim custody himself, but wishes to oppose the pursuer's claim for custody, may do so by lodging defences.[82] In the sheriff court, procedure, where the defender wishes to claim custody or access, is by counter claim.[83]

(4) The parties may enter into a joint minute agreeing the custody of the child and access and the court may interpone authority to that minute.[84] The court must, however, be satisfied that to do so accords with the child's welfare.

(5) Where the court may make an order in respect of the custody of or access to a child who is (a) in the care of a local authority, (b) a child of one party to the marriage and has been accepted as one of the family by the other party but is liable to be maintained by a third party, or (c) in the *de facto* custody of a third party, intimation of the action must be made to the local authority or third party concerned.[85]

(6) Where the court proposes to commit the care of a child to an individual other than one of the parties to the marriage or to a local authority, or where the court has made an order placing the child under the supervision of a local authority, the court is required to order intimation to be made to the individual or the local authority concerned.[86]

(7) A person to whom intimation has been made under the above provision may apply to be heard in the action by way of minute to which either party to the marriage may lodge answers within such period as the court may allow. Where the child is in the care of a local authority, or is liable to be maintained by a third party, or is in the *de facto* custody of a third party, the minute should include a crave for leave to be sisted as a party to the action as well as any relevant averments in relation to the care and maintenance of the child.[87]

(8) At any stage the court may refer the parties to a specified family conciliation service.[88]

(9) Application for variation or revocation of a custody order is by way of minute lodged in the original process.[89] In the Court of Session, an application for variation or recall of an order for access may, however, be made by motion.[90] Such a motion must include a brief statement of the reason for the variation or revocation and be intimated to the other party, or to a solicitor known to be acting on his behalf, on an *induciae* of 14 days. If the motion is opposed and if, in the opinion of the court, it is desirable to do so, the court may order that application be made by

---

[81] Rule of Court 170B (3).
[82] *Ibid.*, (4).
[83] Ordinary Cause Rules, no. 56.
[84] R.C. 170B (5); cf. O.C.R. 56 (3).
[85] R.C. 170B (6) (a); O.C.R. 130 (4) and (6).
[86] R.C. 170B (6) (b); O.C.R. 130 (7).
[87] R.C. 170B (14); cf. O.C.R. 130 (12).
[88] R.C. 170B (15); O.C.R. 132 F.
[89] R.C. 170B (8); O.C.R. 129 (2) (c).
[90] R.C. 170B (10).

way of a minute and may make such order as to the lodging of answers as it thinks fit. In that event the minute must contain supporting conclusions, averments, and pleas-in-law.

(10) Where an application for variation or revocation of an order for custody or access is competently made in connection with an action for divorce, separation, or declarator of nullity of marriage, the court has jurisdiction to entertain the application even if it would no longer have jurisdiction to entertain the principal action.[91] In addition, application may be made to the sheriff court for variation or recall of a custody or access order made by the Court of Session in any such action.[92] The application may be made although the order to which it relates is itself an order varying a previous order. The sheriff has the like powers in relation to such an application as the Court of Session but is bound to remit it to the Court of Session if requested to do so not later than the first calling of the application in court by any party other than the applicant. The sheriff court has jurisdiction for this purpose if it has jurisdiction over any party on whom the application has to be served on grounds of residence, carrying on business, or prorogation.

The procedure for petitions for custody in the Court of Session and for variation and discharge of orders made in such petitions is set out in section 15 of the Rules of Court.

It should be noted that in any case in which an applicant for custody is not a parent section 49 of the Children Act 1975 requires that notice be given to the local authority of the area in which the applicant resides or, if he does not reside in Scotland to a local authority specified by the court. Where, in such cases, section 47 of that Act requires the consent of a parent or guardian Rule of Court 260D (2) and (3) and, in the sheriff court, Ordinary Cause Rule 3 (10) and (11) regulate procedure as they also regulate procedure for notice to parents or guardians and, in the sheriff court, the convening of them as defenders in all cases where the applicant is not a parent.

JUDICIAL POWERS AND DUTIES ASSOCIATED WITH CUSTODY AND ACCESS

Enforcement

Although a custody order confers on the person in whose favour it is made a right to have the child under his or her control, it is not directly enforceable. But a separate action for delivery is not necessary. If the process in which custody was awarded is still in dependence, the court may, on a motion made in that process, ordain the person with actual possession of the child to deliver him to the lawful custodian.[93] A delivery order may be sought by one parent against the other although its purpose is not to implement a custody or other similar order

---

[91] Domicile and Matrimonial Proceedings Act 1973, s. 10.

[92] Law Reform (Miscellaneous Provisions) (Scotland) Act 1966, s. 8.

[93] *Brown* v. *Brown*, 1948 S.C. 5 at p. 11; *Fowler* v. *Fowler (No. 2)*, 1981 S.L.T. (Notes) 78. It is a contempt of court to fail to comply (*Muir* v. *Milligan* (1868) 6 M. 1125; *Leys* v. *Leys* (1886) 13 R. 1223; *Brown* v. *Brown, supra*).

and jurisdiction to make such an order follows the same rules as jurisdiction to make custody or access orders.[94] In addition warrants may be granted to messengers at arms, or sheriff officers, to search for and seize the child so that he may be delivered to the custodian.[95] Individual sanctions such as sequestration of trust income may also be used and have sometimes proved successful.[96]

An ancillary conclusion for delivery is strictly appropriate in all cases in which the claimant seeks custody with a view to the child's removal from its existing custodian. There is, however, no practical disadvantage in the neglect of such a conclusion where custody is disputed in connection with an action of divorce, separation or declarator of nullity of marriage. In these cases the reservation which must be invoked in the final interlocutor has the effect of continuing the action in dependence so far as it relates to custody,[97] and the process of the principal action can still be used for incidental applications for enforcement. In applications for custody not connected with such actions it is prudent to conclude for delivery as well as for custody; if that is not done and decree passes without reference to delivery, independent proceedings may subsequently be necessary to secure enforcement. Actions or petitions for delivery alone were at one time common at the instance of the person legally entitled to custody—usually the father—against anyone not so entitled in whose control the child was.[98] The enhancement of the mother's rights has made such proceedings inappropriate in disputes between parents when they both have parental rights, unless where a custody order is already in force.[99] The general weakening of rights to custody so that, in the absence of a custody order, they can now be asserted only in a *prima facie* sense,[1] may also have contributed to a decline in actions for delivery unless combined with conclusions for custody. Strictly, however, a conclusion for custody is unnecessary at the instance of a person with a *prima facie* title against a person not so entitled. An application for delivery alone is appropriate in such a case and also where a custody order has already been made

---

[94] Family Law Act 1986, s. 17.

[95] *Muir* v. *Milligan, supra; Nicolson* v. *Nicolson* (1869) 7 M. 1118; *Marchetti* v. *Marchetti* (1901) 3 F. 888; *Low, Petr.*, 1920 S.C. 351 (recommendation to English magistrates to lend their aid). For circumstances in which warrant was refused, see *Robertson, Petr.*, 1911 S.C. 1319. Fraser (3rd ed.) at p. 294, says that the warrant may also cover apprehension of the person violating the order. It has been said that only the Inner House can exercise this power (*Guthrie* v. *Guthrie* (1906) 8 F. 545), but it is submitted that it is no more than an aspect of custody jurisdiction now vested in the Outer House and the sheriff court which "impliedly carries with it all the powers which are necessary for its proper exercise" (*Sanderson* v. *Sanderson*, 1921 S.C. 686, *per* Lord Skerrington at p. 693). The wide scope of the sheriff court jurisdiction (*Murray* v. *Forsyth*, 1917 S.C. 721), and the fact that the Inner House no longer exercises any original jurisdiction in custody matters, afford ground for considering the dicta in *Guthrie* to be obsolete even if they were well founded at the time they were made.

[96] *Ross* v. *Ross* (1885) 12 R. 1351; *Edgar* v. *Fisher's Trs.* (1893) 21 R. 59 and 325; *Fisher* v. *Edgar* (1894) 21 R. 1076.

[97] Rule of Court 170B (8) and (9) and O.C.R. (Sh. Ct.) 90A and Form Z.

[98] *A.* v. *B.* (1870) 42 Sc.Jur. 224; *Ketchen* v. *Ketchen* (1870) 8 M. 952; *Markey* v. *Colston* (1888) 15 R. 921; *Hutchison* v. *Hutchison* (1890) 18 R. 237. If the right to custody were not clear, the claimant would, however, seek an order dealing with custody as well as with delivery (*Reilly* v. *Quarrier* (1895) 22 R. 879) and sometimes even fathers of legitimate children thought it prudent to seek an order for custody in support of their claim for delivery (*Pagan* v. *Pagan* (1883) 10 R. 1072; *Beattie* v. *Beattie* (1883) 11 R. 85).

[99] *Brown* v. *Brown*, 1948 S.C. 5 at p. 11.

[1] See *ante*, at pp. 200–201.

in favour of the applicant but the enforcement procedures of the original process cannot be used because it is no longer in dependence or where the order has been made by a court of pre-eminent jurisdiction outwith Scotland. If the application is defended, the applicant's right to custody is necessarily put in issue and that question must be resolved by having regard to the welfare of the child as the paramount consideration. Where, however, the matter has already been determined by a court of competent jurisdiction, a fresh inquiry may not be necessary.[2]

The Family Law Act 1986 confers on the court the power to order any person who it has reason to believe may have relevant information as to the child's whereabouts to disclose that information to the court in any proceedings for or relating to custody or access.[3] A person cannot be excused from complying with such an order on the ground that to do so may incriminate him or his spouse of an offence, though any statement or admission made in compliance with the order will not be admissible in evidence against either spouse in proceedings for any offence other than perjury.[4]

Interim Orders

In actions of divorce, separation and declarator of nullity of marriage, there is statutory power in the court to make such interim orders as it thinks fit relating to parental rights, including custody and access.[5] That provision, whose purpose is to enable such orders to be made in the process of the actions to which they relate, does not derogate from the general power of the court under the *nobile officium* to make interim orders in custody processes. That power is now exercisable in the sheriff court as well as the Court of Session because the extension of custody jurisdiction to the sheriff court "impliedly carries with it all the powers which are necessary for its proper exercise"[6] and indicates the powers of the *nobile officium*. The form of interim order that may be made is not limited in any way so long as it is in respect of custody or access. Orders for interim custody and for interim interdict designed to prevent disturbance of the existing arrangements for care of the child, or to avoid prejudice to the eventual disposal of the case, are among those most commonly encountered. The general test for interim interdict, *i.e.* the balance of convenience, has to be applied in the context of the welfare of the child as the paramount consideration. The requirement that no order relating to custody or access should be made unless the court is satisfied that it is in the child's interests to do so applies to interim no less than to final orders, but at the stage of an interim order no issue of standard of proof arises. It is a question of whether the court is satisfied on the information before it.[7]

---

[2] *Sargeant* v. *Sargeant*, 1973 S.L.T. (Notes) 27; *Campbell* v. *Campbell*, 1977 S.C. 103; *Lyndon* v. *Lyndon*, 1978 S.L.T. (Notes) 7; *Thomson, Petr.*, 1980 S.L.T. (Notes) 29.

[3] Family Law Act 1986, s. 33(1), and see *Abusaif* v. *Abusaif*, 1984 S.L.T. 90. "Any proceedings" includes those for the enforcement of an order made outside the U.K. which is recognised in Scotland: s. 33(3).

[4] *Ibid.*, s. 33(2).

[5] Court of Session Act 1988, s. 20. Conjugal Rights (Scotland) Amendment Act 1861, s. 9 as amended by Law Reform (Parent and Child) (Scotland) Act 1986, Sched. 1, para. 2.

[6] *Sanderson* v. *Sanderson*, 1921 S.C. 686, *per* Lord Skerrington at p. 693 (talking of the extension of custody jurisdiction from the Inner to the Outer House).

[7] *Armstrong* v. *Gibson* 1991 S.L.T. 193.

The Family Law Act 1986 makes specific provision for interim interdict prohibiting the removal of a child from the United Kingdom or any part of the United Kingdom or out of the control of the person in whose custody the child is.[8] An application for interim interdict can be made (a) at any time after the commencement of proceedings[9] in connection with which the court would have jurisdiction to make a custody order, or (b) in any proceedings in which it would be competent for the court to grant an interdict prohibiting the removal of a child from its jurisdiction.[10] The court can be the Court of Session or the sheriff[11] and the application can be at the instance of any party to the proceedings,[12] the guardian of the child concerned,[13] and any other person who has or wishes to obtain custody or care of the child.[14] The court may grant interim interdict if satisfied that there is a likelihood that the child will be removed.[15] Whether the court, once satisfied of that, should grant interim interdict is a matter of discretion to be determined with regard to the welfare of the child as the paramount consideration. The risk of temporary prejudice to the child's welfare may, however, have to be balanced against the need for interim interdict if conditions are to be preserved that will enable the eventual disposal of the case in accordance with the welfare principle.

The Child Abduction and Custody Act 1985 also provides that, where an application has been made to the Court of Session under the Hague Convention for an order for the return of a child wrongfully removed to Scotland,[16] or under the European Convention for the registration or enforcement of a foreign custody order,[17] the court may give such interim directions as it thinks fit for the purpose of securing the welfare of the child or of preventing changes in the circumstances relevant to the determination of the application.[18]

Although these statutory provisions on interim interdict may, by specification, contribute to clarity, it is doubtful if they add anything to the general powers of the the court seised of custody proceedings.

Committal to Care

The Matrimonial Proceedings (Children) Act 1958 provides that in actions of divorce, separation, and declarator of nullity of marriage, the court may make an order committing the child to the care of an individual other than the parents,

---

[8] Family Law Act 1986, s. 35(3). S. 37 allows the court to require any person to surrender any United Kingdom passport that has been issued to, or contains particulars of, the child.

[9] "Commencement" is defined as meaning, in the Court of Session, when a summons is signeted or a petition is presented and, in the sheriff court, when the warrant of citation is signed: Family Law Act 1986, s. 35(5).

[10] Family Law Act 1986, s. 35(3).

[11] *Ibid.*, s. 35(5).

[12] *Ibid.*, s. 35(4)(*a*).

[13] *Ibid.*, s. 35(4)(*b*).

[14] *Ibid.*, s. 35(4)(*c*).

[15] Interdict *ad interim* was refused in *Woodcock* v. *Woodcock*, 1990 S.L.T. 848 because there was no evidence that the mother was likely to remove the child furth of the United Kingdom: at p. 853A.

[16] See *post* at pp. 274–277.

[17] See *post* at pp. 270–274.

[18] Child Abduction and Custody Act 1985, s. 5 (Hague Convention); s. 19 (European Convention).

or to the care of a local authority.[19] That power may be exercised only where there are exceptional circumstances making it impracticable or undesirable for the child to be entrusted to either of the parties to the marriage. It is exercisable as respects any child for whose custody the court has power to make provision, whether or not there is an application for the custody of that child. The effect of committal to care is not altogether clear, particularly where the committal is to the care of an individual but it appears that it precludes the exercise by parents of custody rights and that, beyond that, parental rights and powers are unaffected by the committal itself[20] although, in the case of a local authority committal, the authority may, in certain circumstances, assume these rights and powers.[21] Before making an order for committal to the care of a local authority, the court must hear any representations from the authority including representations as to the making of an order for payment for the maintenance and education of the child.[22] The provisions of the Social Work (Scotland) Act 1968 on the treatment of children in care apply to a child committed to the care of a local authority as if the child had been received into care under section 15 of that Act, except that (a) so long as the order is in force, the child shall continue in care notwithstanding any claim by a parent or other person[23] (which is not the case where a child is received into care under section 15); (b) the provisions of the Act on arrangements for the emigration of a child do not apply[24]; and (c) the exercise by the authority of certain other powers under the Act are subject to directions given by the court.[25] It is the duty of any parent or guardian of a child committed to the care of a local authority to secure that the authority is informed of his address for the time being. An order committing a child to care may be varied or revoked by a subsequent order of the court made either *ex proprio motu* or on the application of any person concerned. "Child" is defined as meaning a child under 16 years of age.[26] The local authority to whose care a child may be committed is the regional or islands council for the area in which, in the opinion of the court, the child was resident before the order was made.[27]

In the case of applications for custody other than applications to which the Matrimonial Proceedings (Children) Act 1958 applies, that is, in applications for custody made independently from actions for divorce, separation or nullity of marriage, the court again has powers, under by the Guardianship Act 1973, to commit a child to the care of a specified local authority.[28] These powers are virtually identical to the powers discussed immediately above in relation to the 1958 Act. The following points of difference may, however, be noticed:

(1) The power under the 1973 Act is exercisable if it appears to the court

---

[19] Matrimonial Proceedings (Children) Act 1958, s. 10(1) as amended by the Law Reform (Parent and Child) (Scotland) Act 1986, Sched. 2 and the Family Law Act 1986, Sched. 1, para. 6.

[20] See *post* at p. 413.

[21] This power is discussed in detail *post*, at chap. 16.

[22] Matrimonial Proceedings (Children) Act 1958, s. 10(2).

[23] *Ibid.*, s. 10(3).

[24] *Ibid.*, s. 10(4)(*b*).

[25] *Ibid.*, s. 10(4)(*a*).

[26] *Ibid.*, s. 15.

[27] *Ibid.*, s. 10(2).

[28] Guardianship Act 1973, s. 11.

that there are exceptional circumstances making it impracticable or undesirable for the child to be entrusted to either of the parents *or to any other individual*[29]; there is no power to commit to the care of an individual.

(2) The committal is to be to the care of a specified local authority. It must be a regional or islands council, but need not be the authority for the area in which the child was resident before the order was made.

(3) The 1973 Act specifically provides (a) that the court may make a further order requiring the payment by either parent of such weekly or other periodical sum towards the maintenance of the child as the court thinks reasonable having regard to the means of that parent,[30] and (b) that an order for committal shall cease to have effect when the child attains the age of 16.[31] In the Matrimonial Proceedings (Children) Act 1958 contributions to maintenance are, apart from the provision for representation, left to the legislation on children in care,[32] and the time when committal ceases is left to implication.

(4) Some of the local authority powers which in the Matrimonial Proceedings (Children) Act 1958 are declared to be subject to directions given by the court are not included in that category under the Guardianship Act 1973.[33]

The provisions on committal to care in both the Matrimonial Proceedings (Children) Act 1958 and in the Guardianship Act 1973 are supplemented for the proceedings to which they relate by provisions for the making of orders placing a child under the supervision of a local authority. The 1958 Act provides[34] that such an order may be made if it appears to the court that there are exceptional circumstances making it desirable that the child should be under the supervision of an independent person. The order may be in respect of any period during which the child is committed to the custody of any person. The authority may be any regional or islands council selected by the court and specified in the order. The power is not exercisable where the child is committed to the care of a local authority. The corresponding provisions of the Guardianship Act 1973[35] are that if either parent, or any other person (other than a local authority), is given the custody of the child but it appears to the court that there are exceptional circumstances making it desirable that the child should be under the supervision of a local authority the court may order that the child shall be under the supervision of a specified local authority subject to any direction given by the court. In both Acts "child" is again defined as meaning a child under the age of 16, and in the

---

[29] *Ibid.*, s. 11(1)(*a*).

[30] *Ibid.*, s. 11(3).

[31] *Ibid.*, s. 11(1).

[32] *i.e.* the Social Work (Scotland) Act 1968, ss. 78–83.

[33] ss. 5, 20 to 22, 59, and 60 of the Social Work (Scotland) Act 1968 relating to the performance of functions under the general guidance of, and regulations made by, the Secretary of State particularly in relation to the boarding-out of children, the provision of residential and other establishments, the control of such establishments and the treatment and control of persons in them are declared in the Matrimonial Proceedings (Children) Act 1958, s. 10(4)(*a*), but not in the Guardianship Act 1973, to be subject to directions given by the court.

[34] Matrimonial Proceedings (Children) Act 1958, s. 12.

[35] Guardianship Act 1973, s. 11.

Guardianship Act 1973 it is provided that a supervision order shall cease to have effect when the child attains that age.[36]

Arrangements for Care and Upbringing

In actions of divorce, separation and declarator of nullity of marriage, the court is precluded from granting decree unless and until it is satisfied about the arrangements for the care of the children.[37] The duty so laid on the court relates to every child for whose custody the court has power to make provision in that action and applies whether or not custody is in issue. It is therefore independent of the court's duty under section 3(2) of the Law Reform (Parent and Child) (Scotland) Act 1986 to regard the child's welfare as the paramount consideration in any actions relating to parental rights, for matrimonial proceedings are not, in themselves, actions relating to parental rights. The court has to be satisfied either (a) that arrangements have been made for the care and upbringing of the child and that those arrangements are satisfactory or are the best that can be devised in the circumstances, or (b) that it is impracticable for the party or parties appearing before the court to make any such arrangements. Exceptionally the court may, if it thinks fit, proceed to grant decree without observing these requirements, but only if it appears that there are circumstances making it desirable that decree should be granted without delay and a satisfactory undertaking has been obtained from either or both of the parties to bring the question of the arrangements for the children before the court within a specified time.[38] A difficulty about adopting that course is that it may leave the court without effective sanctions. No doubt it is a contempt to fail to comply with the undertaking, and it is probably also a contempt to fail to supply relevant information which the court has required and can reasonably be obtained. But if when the question is brought before it on adequate information the court regards the arrangements as unsatisfactory, it is obscure what steps, if any, are open to it to secure an improvement. If the court concludes that it is impracticable for satisfactory arrangements to be made by the parties, committal to care may have to be considered.[39]

There is no Scottish authority on the consequences of decree being granted where the court, through ignorance of a child's existence, has failed to satisfy itself as to the arrangements for his care. If the parties have knowingly misled the court, that would be a contempt but no positive duty is placed upon the parties and so mere failure to disclose would not appear to attract any sanction. With similar provisions in England, it was at one time held that the decree was void,[40] but the authorities to that effect have been overruled in favour of the view that the decree is voidable.[41] There is, however, no statutory warrant for treating the decree as void or voidable and unless both parties have been guilty of a fraud on

---

[36] *Ibid.*, s. 11(1).

[37] Matrimonial Proceedings (Children) Act 1958, s. 8, as amended by the Law Reform (Parent and Child) (Scotland) Act 1986, Sched. 2 and the Family Law Act 1986, Sched. 1, para. 4.

[38] *Ibid.*, s. 8(2).

[39] *Ibid.*, s. 10; *ante*, at p. 250.

[40] *B.* v. *B.* [1961] 1 W.L.R. 856; *N.* v. *N.* (1964) 108 Sol.J. 99.

[41] *F.* v. *F.* [1971] P. 1; *P.* v. *P. and J.* [1971] P. 217, in which the principle in *F.* v. *F.* is approved and *B.* v. *B.* and *N.* v. *N.* overruled.

the court, it is difficult to see on what principles of Scots law the decree could be reduced.

For the purpose of satisfying itself as to the proposed arrangements for the care and upbringing of a child the court may appoint an appropriate local authority to investigate and report on all the circumstances of the child and on the proposed arrangements.[42] That power is without prejudice to the court's power to appoint any other person not being an officer of the relevant authority. If, on a consideration of the report the court, either *ex proprio motu* or on the application of any person concerned, thinks it expedient to do so it may require the person who furnished the report to appear and to be examined. Court of Session, but not sheriff court, practice requires that he is not otherwise to be cited as a witness.[43] Any expenses incurred in connection with the preparation of the report form part of the expenses of the cause and are to be defrayed by such party to the action as the court may direct.[44] Reports are not, however, the only nor in the ordinary case the primary means by which the court obtains the information necessary to discharge its duty regarding the arrangements for the child's care and upbringing. The pursuer in the action has an interest and a corresponding responsibility to obtain adequate information about the circumstances of the children and that is so even if he or she does not seek custody and avers that satisfactory arrangements have been made by the defender or a third party. It is, therefore, for the pursuer to lead evidence and to take all reasonable steps to ensure that it is adequate for the purpose. In an uncontested case of that kind the court will not normally accede to a motion for a remit to a local authority for reports. Where the reporter is not examined the court may accept the statements of fact made in the report and consider them along with any relevant facts proved in the case.[45]

Proof

In custody disputes, as in other matters, parties are entitled to a proof of their averments. Remits to a reporter have, however, long been in use as a means of informing the court on custody questions and are the only practicable means of making an informed decision on an application for an interim order, except perhaps where there is no substantial conflict of fact in the *ex parte* statements and they afford a clear basis for decision. On the final disposal of the case after proof, a report may be taken into account and considered along with the oral evidence; and, as has been noticed above, there is statutory warrant for requiring the reporter to appear and be examined in the case of a report obtained under the Matrimonial Proceedings (Children) Act 1958. Proof and the contents of reports may be supplemented in the discretion of the court by the judge's inter-

---

[42] Matrimonial Proceedings (Children) Act 1958, s. 11.
[43] Court of Session Practice Note, June 6, 1968.
[44] Matrimonial Proceedings (Children) Act 1958, s. 11(5).
[45] *Wallace* v. *Wallace*, 1963 S.C. 256 at pp. 257–258; *Hunter* v. *Hunter*, 1979 S.L.T. (Notes) 2.

viewing the child,[46] but an interview cannot be substituted for proof[47] and the court should not dispose of the case on an interview without taking account of the evidence as a whole.

CONFLICTS WITH OTHER ORDERS AND STATUTORY REQUIREMENTS

Conflict of Custody Orders Inter Se

A foreign custody order cannot be enforced in Scotland without the intervention of the Scottish courts.[48] There can, therefore, be no conflict between a Scottish and a foreign order. There may, however, be a conflict between one Scottish order and another Scottish order or an order made by a court in another part of the United Kingdom. As no custody order is truly permanent, a subsequent application to the court is not subject to the plea of *res judicata*[49] and so there may be a succession of orders. There is no formal requirement regulating the conditions on which a second or subsequent application will be entertained, but making repeated applications would seem to be an abuse of process in the absence of a material change in circumstances.[50] There is express provision for variation or revocation of an earlier order by a later only in the case of orders made in actions for divorce, judicial separation or nullity of marriage[51] and, as noted below, of the variation or recall by the sheriff court of certain Court of Session orders. Section 3(1) of the Law Reform (Parent and Child) (Scotland) Act 1986, which entitles the court to make any order relating to parental rights as it thinks fit, implicitly includes the right to vary or revoke an earlier order. Further, and explicitly, section 15(2) of the Family Law Act 1986 provides that a custody or access order made by a Scottish court may be varied or recalled by a subsequent order of that court provided the original order has not ceased to have effect and notwithstanding that the court no longer has the jurisdiction on which the original order proceeded. Cases may, however, occur despite those ample provisions, in which a custody order is made without variation or recall of an earlier inconsistent order. In such cases the principle, that a subsequent order has the effect of varying or revoking a prior order inconsistent with it, applies. Accordingly, where it appears that a child has been the subject of more than one custody order, it is the last in point of time that is effective. At any rate where the later order was pronounced by a court of equivalent or superior jurisdiction.

---

[46] *Wallace* v. *Wallace*, 1947 S.L.T. (Notes) 47; *Nicol* v. *Nicol*, 1953 S.L.T. (Notes) 67; *Huddart* v. *Huddart*, 1961 S.C. 393; *Cochrane* v. *Keys*, 1968 S.L.T. (Notes) 64; *Klein and Anr., Petrs.*, 1969 S.L.T. (Notes) 53; *Johnson* v. *Johnson*, 1972 S.L.T. (Notes) 15; *Blance* v. *Blance*, 1978 S.L.T. 74; *Cosh* v. *Cosh*, 1979 S.L.T. (Notes) 72; *Fowler* v. *Fowler*, 1981 S.L.T. (Notes) 9. The Law Commission (Working Paper No. 15—arrangements for the care and upbringing of children, Feb. 6, 1968, p. 10) found a variety of views among English judges about the minimum age at which it was suitable to interview children and the circumstances favouring an interview. In Scotland the practice has been said to be very helpful even with quite young children (*Glasgow Herald*, Dec. 1, 1980, reporting an address by Lord Dunpark to the Scottish Child Law Group).

[47] *Macdonald* v. *Macdonald*, 1985 S.L.T. 245.

[48] See *post* at p. 271.

[49] Though the court does have a discretion under s. 14(1) of the Family Law Act 1986 to refuse to entertain an application for a custody or access order where the matter has already been determined in other proceedings: see *ante* at p. 244.

[50] But see *S.* v. *S.* 1965 S.L.T. 131 at pp. 132–133.

[51] Court of Session Act 1988, s. 20.

That was the rule at common law, and is now statutorily so[52] when the later order is competently made by another court, even of inferior jurisdiction, in any part of the United Kingdom, or is made outside the United Kingdom and is recognised in Scotland according to the rules discussed later.[53] It is also provided by statute[54] that where a custody order has been pronounced by the Court of Session in connection with an action of divorce, separation or declarator of nullity of marriage it may be varied or recalled in the sheriff court as also may an order made under section 20 of the Court of Session Act 1988, under Part II of the Matrimonial Proceedings (Children) Act 1958, or by virtue of Part II of the Guardianship Act 1973. Apart from that provision, it is doubtful if, before the Family Law Act 1986, a Court of Session decree could be superseded by a decree in the sheriff court. That is no longer so but if an application should be presented in the sheriff court which is in conflict with an existing decree of the Court of Session to which the specific statutory exception does not apply, the proper course may still often be removal or remission to the Court of Session.[55]

Conflict of Custody Orders with Statutory Measures

General Principle

An apparent conflict may sometimes arise between a custody or access order and measures taken under certain statutory provisions for the care of children. The measures in question are committals to the care of a local authority or an individual under the Matrimonial Proceedings (Children) Act 1958 or to a local authority under the Guardianship Act 1973, place of safety orders issued under section 37 of the Social Work (Scotland) Act 1968, supervision requirements made by children's hearings, and the vesting of parental rights and powers in a local authority or voluntary organisation. The conflict in such cases is apparent rather than real. The guiding principle is that a custody or access order is subject to such other lawful measures as may be taken in relation to the child.[56] A custody order gives the custodian powers over the child which he may vindicate in a question with others only if they have no lawful authority to interfere. Nearly all children under 16 are in the custody of someone and, in the vast majority of cases, that custody is not regulated by any court order. The position of children in respect of whom custody orders have been made does not, in principle, differ from the position of those whose custody is regulated by operation of law without any court order. In both cases, it is evident that statutory measures may modify the effect of custody. If that were not so, the statutory provisions would be reduced to a nullity. While the statutory provisions may affect custody, and to a lesser extent access, they will not affect other parental rights whose exercise by parents would not be inconsistent with the statutory purposes.[57]

---

[52] Family Law Act 1986, s. 15(1).
[53] *Post*, at pp. 267–277.
[54] Law Reform (Miscellaneous Provisions) (Scotland) Act 1966, s. 8.
[55] See *ante* pp. 244–245.
[56] Thomson, "Parental Rights and Children in Care: A 'Confusing Overview,' " 1991 S.L.T. (News) 379.
[57] Thomson, *op. cit.*.

Conflict with Committals to Care

As committals to care, under both the Matrimonial Proceedings (Children) Act 1958 and the Guardianship Act 1973,[58] are made by order of the court, there is little likelihood of conflict, or even of apparent conflict, with custody orders. The committal order can be made only if there are exceptional circumstances making it impracticable or undesirable for the child to be entrusted to either of the parties to the marriage, in the case of the 1958 Act,[59] or to either of the parents or to any other individual in the case of the 1973 Act.[60] Committal to care is then an alternative to a custody order to be adopted where the latter is inappropriate. A custody order may, however, already be in force at the time of committal to care or may subsequently be made. Where committal is to the care of a local authority, it is provided that, while the committal order is in force, the child is to continue in the care of the local authority notwithstanding any claim by a parent or other person[61]; so any custody order is, in effect, suspended as long as the committal order remains in force. If, however, the committal order is revoked or discharged, the custody order will come again into full effect unless some intervening event, *e.g.* the assumption by the local authority of parental rights and powers, avoids that result. Where committal is to the care of an individual, as it may be under the 1958 Act, the consequences are more obscure, but it is thought that, as in the case of competing custody orders, the later order prevails. The effect of section 15(1) of the Family Law Act 1986 is that a subsequent custody order supersedes committal to the care of a local authority.

Conflict with Supervision Requirements by Children's Hearings

A supervision requirement[62] is a compulsory measure of care under which the child is treated as being, for certain purposes, in the care of a local authority. The child may, nonetheless, often remain at home and custody rights are affected only if a residential requirement, or a requirement with a residential condition, is made. In that event, the effective exercise of custody rights is suspended so long as the residential stipulation remains in force but revives as soon as the requirement, or the residential element in it, comes to an end.[63] It follows that a custody order may have its effect suspended by a supervision requirement, even to the extent that the child is obliged to reside with a person denied custody under the terms of the custody order. Similarly, a custody order made while a supervision requirement is in force receives effect subject to the requirement, and the rights conferred by such an order are inhibited for so long as the requirement subsists.[64] It has however been said that "it would seldom be appropriate for an order for custody to be pronounced in favour of persons who could not in practice exercise those rights for the time being."[65]

---

[58] See *ante*, pp. 432–433.
[59] Matrimonial Proceedings (Children) Act 1958, s. 10(1).
[60] Guardianship Act 1973, s. 11(1)(*a*).
[61] Matrimonial Proceedings (Children) Act 1958, s. 10(3); Guardianship Act 1973, s. 11(2).
[62] *Post*, pp. 229–230.
[63] *Aitken* v. *Aitken*, 1978 S.C. 297.
[64] *Ibid.* at p. 302, *per* Lord President Emslie.
[65] *F.* v. *F.* 1991 S.L.T. 357, *per* Lord President Hope at p. 363.

Conflict with Place of Safety Orders

A place of safety order can be issued under the Social Work (Scotland) Act 1968[66] authorising a constable or any person to take a child to a place of safety, and to detain him there, on the satisfaction of certain conditions.[67] The children's hearing can grant warrants for detention, subject to certain time limits.[68] Such detention will clearly suspend the exercise of the parent's right of custody, but, as in the case of a supervision requirement, the right of custody revives as soon as the detention ends, either because the appropriate time has elapsed, or the warrant has been recalled by the children's hearing or the court. Thomson has argued,[69] and the principle is sound, that parental rights—even, one assumes, those that flow from custody—can be exercised in so far as they are not inconsistent with the child's detention in a place of safety. So while the parent or other custodian is not entitled to have the child living with him, he retains the right, for example, to consent to medical treatment.

Conflict with Vesting of Parental Rights and Powers

The vesting of parental rights and powers in a local authority or a voluntary organisation does not abrogate the custody jurisdiction of the court.[70] The parent or guardian on whose account the parental rights resolution has been passed, has, however, no title to sue for custody,[71] or, at the most, only such title as any other stranger to the child has.[72] His remedies are restricted to reduction, if grounds for that exist, and to applying to the sheriff for determination of the resolution.[73] But a parent or guardian unaffected by the resolution may apply for custody and, as he stands *in pari casu* with the local authority or voluntary organisation in relation to the child, the dispute is to be resolved on ordinary principles. Applications by third parties are also competent[74] and are also to be determined with regard to the welfare of the child as the paramount consideration, but, unless there is evident abuse, the court will, it is thought, be slow in such a case to go against the judgment of the child's welfare formed by the authority or organisation in which the parental rights and powers have vested and to which it may be supposed that Parliament has entrusted such decisions in a question with those who do not have equivalent rights.[75] If a custody order is already in force in favour of the parent whose parental rights and powers are assumed, the custody order is superseded by the vesting resolution because custody is among the rights and powers which are transferred; but if the resolu-

---

[66] s. 37(2).

[67] See *post* at pp. 457–459.

[68] See *post* at pp. 460–462.

[69] *Op. cit.* at p. 380.

[70] *Aitken* v. *Aitken, supra; Beagley* v. *Beagley,* 1984 S.L.T. 202.

[71] *Beagley* v. *Beagley, supra.*

[72] The Law Reform (Parent and Child) (Scotland) Act 1986 gives title to "any person claiming interest," and the decision in *Beagley* must now be read in that light. The 1986 Act must, however, be read along with the Social Work (Scotland) Act 1968 and it is submitted that it would be contrary to the legislative intention embodied in ss. 16 and 17 of that Act to entertain an application for custody at the instance of a parent in respect of whom parental rights and powers had been assumed.

[73] *Ibid.* at pp. 205–206.

[74] See *ante* at pp. 202–204.

[75] *Beagley* v. *Beagley, supra* at p. 206.

tion lapses or ceases to have effect, the order will revive. If, however, when a vesting resolution is passed, a child is already the subject of a custody order in favour of a person other than the parent or guardian in respect of whom parental rights and powers have been assumed, the custody order is unaffected by the vesting resolution. The result, in that case, is that the custodian under the custody order continues to have the sole right to custody because, *ex hypothesi* of the existence of a custody order in his favour, the parent in respect of whom parental rights and powers have been assumed had, at the material time, no custodial rights and no right can vest in the local authority or voluntary organisation other than that possessed by the parent or guardian whose rights and powers have been assumed.[76]

Conflict with Reception into Care

No question of conflict arises when a child, in respect of whom a custody order is in force, is received into care under section 15 of the Social Work (Scotland) Act 1968. Such reception is voluntary and custody rights are unaffected. The return of the child may be requested at any time. If, however, the child has been in the care of the local authority for six months or more, 28 days' notice is required if the child is to be removed without the consent of the authority.[77] To that extent there is a limited suspension of custody rights. There is no objection to the making of a custody order while a child is in care under section 15.

Conflicts Concerning Access Orders

Much the same principles apply to access as to custody but access orders may, in their nature, be more amenable than custody orders to reconciliation with the purposes of statutory measures. Rights of access may continue to be exercised in so far, but only in so far, as that exercise is consistent with the statutory measure in question. Thus, rights of access will not be affected by a supervision requirement made by a children's hearing unless, as in the case of a residential requirement or a requirement with a residential condition, there is conflict with the terms of the requirement or the consequent powers and duties of the local authority. Where there is potential for such conflict it has been held that, while a custody order can be granted, although with suspended effect, during the currency of a supervision requirement, an access order cannot be so granted, because access, being a right instantly operable, cannot have its effects suspended in the way that custody can.[78] Nor was it deemed appropriate to grant access against a local authority which would only be exercisable once the local authority care came to an end.[79]

Usually, rights of access are granted in a question with the custodian, and they are a qualification of the custodian's rights.[80] It follows that they are not exigible against third parties into whose care the child lawfully passes. It is for the custodian in such a case to see that access is enabled; but the custodian can-

---

[76] See further, *post* at pp. 432–433.
[77] Social Work (Scotland) Act 1968, s. 15(3A).
[78] *D.* v. *Strathclyde Regional Council*, 1985 S.L.T. 114.
[79] *Ibid.* at p. 116.
[80] See *ante* at pp. 229–230.

not do that where by a statutory measure he has been deprived of control. So where a child is the subject of a residential supervision requirement, or a requirement with a residential condition, an access order granted in a question with the person who, apart from the requirement, is the child's custodian is of no avail against any other person, with whom the child must reside under the requirement. Similarly, access orders in ordinary form granted before the statutory intervention will create no rights against the person or authority to whom the child's care has been committed under the Matrimonial Proceedings (Children) Act 1958 or the Guardianship Act 1973 or an authority which has received the child into care. In these cases it may, however, be competent to seek an order for access against the person or authority in question.[81] Such applications have no specialties and are to be determined with regard to the paramountcy of the welfare of the child. Where, on the other hand, a child's residence is regulated by a supervision requirement it is primarily for the children's hearing to assess what the child's welfare demands and, as already noted, the court cannot competently make an award of access that might conflict with the exercise by the hearing of its statutory function.[82] If persons have a legal right to access, "that legal right is inhibited by and during the currency of the supervision requirement in that the local authority can decide that it is not in the child's interest that the legal right should be exercised."[83]

Likewise, where parental rights and powers have been assumed they should not be hindered by an award of access in conflict with their proper exercise by the authority or organisation in which they have vested and to whose care the child is by statute entrusted. It is, however, consistent with that principle that where the rights and powers of only one parent have been assumed an award of access should be made in favour of the other parent and such awards are also competent in favour of third parties, particularly where they represent deceased parents or where access would serve to maintain a family connection.[84] It is now provided that a local authority or voluntary organisation may not terminate arrangements for access by a parent or guardian to a child in respect of whom parental rights have been assumed or refuse to make such arrangements unless they have first given notice to that effect.[85] In the event of such notice being given, the parent or guardian may then apply to the sheriff, by way of summary application, for an access order. Apart from that provision, a parent or guardian on whose account a parental rights resolution has been passed has no title to apply for access.[86]

---

[81] See *Browne* v. *Browne*, 1969 S.L.T. (Notes) 15, and *Aitken* v. *Aitken*, 1978 S.C. 297 at p. 303.

[82] *D.* v. *Strathclyde Regional Council, supra.* The Second Division in that case speculated upon, but refused to decide the competence of, the possibility of access being regulated by the court on an appeal from the decision of the children's hearing under s. 49 of the 1968 Act.

[83] *Ibid.* at p. 116, *per* Lord Justice-Clerk Wheatley and Lords Brand and Wylie.

[84] *Beagley* v. *Beagley, supra; MacInnes* v. *Highland Regional Council*, 1982 S.C. 69.

[85] Social Work (Scotland) Act 1968, s. 17A, inserted by the Health and Social Services and Social Security Adjudications Act 1983, s. 7(2). See also ss. 17B to 17E.

[86] *D.* v. *Strathclyde Regional Council, supra; Beagley* v. *Beagley, supra.*

OFFENCES IN CONNECTION WITH CUSTODY

Children Act 1975

Where an application for custody of a child is pending in any court and the child has been in the care and possession of the applicant for a period or periods, before the making of the application, which amount to at least three years, it is an offence to remove the child from the custody of the applicant against the applicant's will.[87] Exceptions are provided for removal with the authority of a court, or under authority conferred by any enactment, or on the arrest of the child. The prohibition applies to removal by a local authority even if the child was in the care of the local authority before he began to have his home with the applicant and remains in its care. In such a case, however, the Act provides for removal with the authority of a Justice of the Peace or a children's hearing in terms of Part III of the Social Work (Scotland) Act 1968.[88] The primary purpose of the legislation creating this offence was to give long term foster parents security in pursuing applications for custody without risk of disturbance whether from the natural parents or from the placing authority,[89] but it is capable of wider application, including disputes between parents. The penal provisions are reinforced by power given to the court (1) to order the person who has removed the child to return the child to the applicant, and (2) to interdict removal of the child from the applicant's custody on the application of any person who has reasonable grounds for believing that such removal is intended.[90] "Child" means a person who has not attained the age of 18 years.[91]

Child Abduction Act 1984

Under the Child Abduction Act 1984 it is an offence for "a person connected with a child under the age of 16 years" to take or send the child out of the United Kingdom: (a) "without the appropriate consent" if there is, in respect of the child either (i) an order of a court in the United Kingdom awarding custody to any person, or (ii) an order of a court in England, Wales, or Northern Ireland making the child a ward of court; or (b) if there is any order of a court in the United Kingdom prohibiting the removal of the child from the United Kingdom or any part of it.[92] A person connected with a child means (i) a parent or guardian, (ii) a person to whom custody has been awarded (whether solely or jointly) by an order currently in force of a court in the United Kingdom, or (iii) in the case of a child whose parents are not and have never been married to one another, a person believed, on reasonable grounds, to be the father of the child.[93] Appropriate consent in relation to the crime under (a) means either (i) the consent of each person who is a parent or guardian or is the custodian of the child under an order of a court in the United Kingdom, or (ii) the leave of the court

---

[87] Children Act 1975, s. 51.

[88] *Ibid.*, s. 51(2)(*b*).

[89] See *Report of the Departmental Committee on the Adoption of Children*, Cmnd. 5107 (1972), recommendation No. 36, para. 126.

[90] Children Act 1975, s. 52.

[91] *Ibid.*, s. 107.

[92] Child Abduction Act 1984, s. 6(1).

[93] *Ibid.*, s. 6(2) (as amended by the Law Reform (Parent and Child) (Scotland) Act 1986, Sched. 1, para. 20).

which made the custody order or made the child a ward of court.[94] Alternative (i) is not, however, available where a wardship order is in force.[95] Consent is no defence to the crime under (b) above.[96] Where more than one custody or wardship order is in force in relation to a child, the leave of any court which has made such an order suffices.[97] Taking, or sending, a child out of the United Kingdom means (a) causing or inducing the child to accompany the person charged with the offence or any other person, and (b) causing the child to be taken or sent.[98] "Guardian" means a person appointed by deed or will or by order of a court of competent jurisdiction to be the child's guardian.[99]

It is a defence for the accused person to show that, at the time of the alleged offence, he had no reason to believe that a custody or wardship order was in existence in relation to the child.[1] Except where the child is a ward of court, an offence is not committed if the person taking or sending the child (a) did so in the belief that each person who is a parent or guardian or custodian of the child either had consented, or would have consented if he was aware of all the relevant circumstances, or (b) has taken all reasonable steps to communicate with each such person but has been unable to do so.[2]

Put briefly, the effect of the above provisions of the Child Abduction Act 1984 is to apply a criminal sanction, where a custody or wardship order or an interdict against removal is in force, in order to prevent the removal of the child outside the United Kingdom at the instance of a parent, guardian, or custodian unless the other interested persons have consented or the court has granted leave. The Act, therefore, strikes at acts by persons with an established connection with the child that are in defiance of, or would circumvent the purpose of, a court order. A typical situation is where a parent who does not have custody takes the child abroad with a view to defeating the rights under a custody order in favour of the other parent; but it is to be noted that the custodian parent is also subject to the Act and may commit an offence if, for example, he takes the child abroad in order to defeat the other parent's right to access. Although it will usually be prudent to obtain all relevant consents, the temporary removal of a child for a short period, without such consent, for a holiday or for educational or medical purposes may often be justified on the ground that it was done in the belief that the person whose consent was required would have consented if he was aware of all the relevant circumstances. That justification would not, however, be available where the child is a ward of the English, or Northern Irish, courts.

Plagium and Abduction

The provisions of the Child Abduction Act 1984 applicable to England and Wales are, in a number of respects, different from their Scottish counterparts.

---

[94] *Ibid.*, s. 6(3).
[95] *Ibid.*
[96] See *Deans* v. *Deans*, 1988 S.C.L.R. 192 (Sh. Ct.).
[97] Child Abduction Act 1984, s. 6(3).
[98] *Ibid.*, s. 6(6).
[99] *Ibid.*, s. 6(7) (as amended by the Age of Legal Capacity (Scotland) Act 1991, Sched. 2—restoring the subsection to its original wording).
[1] *Ibid.*, s. 6(5).
[2] *Ibid.*, s. 6(4).

There is no Scottish equivalent at all for the English provision under which anyone not connected with the child commits an offence if, without lawful authority or reasonable excuse, he takes or detains a child under 16 so as to deprive anyone entitled thereto of lawful control.[3] The reason may be that such acts were thought to be criminal in Scotland at common law. The relevant common law crimes, plagium and abduction, are, however, inexact counterparts.[4]

It is the crime of plagium to take a pupil child[5] away from the custody of his parents or those to whom his parents have entrusted him, whether or not the child is willing to go.[6] A parent can be guilty of this crime.[7] To take someone of any age away against his will or, probably, by obtaining his consent through deception, is to commit the crime of abduction unless it is done with lawful authority.[8] These crimes leave, however, three areas of possible doubt so far as children are concerned. First, if a child below the age of common law pupillarity is in the custody of someone other than his parent or the person to whom his parent has entrusted him, is it criminal to remove the child from the control of his custodian? It is submitted that the answer is plainly affirmative although there may be some doubt whether the crime is plagium or abduction. It is perhaps better treated as abduction because a custodian, other than a parent, does not have the rights of *dominium* which, if on rather outmoded reasoning, underlie plagium.[9] Although abduction normally involves overcoming the will of the person abducted, it is entirely consistent with the legal understanding of pupillarity, at least at common law, that the pupil child's will should be regarded as irrelevant to a question of his abduction and that the will of the custodian should be the relevant consideration.[10] Secondly, where a child above the age of common law pupillarity has a custodian, is it criminal to remove the child against his will but with the consent of his custodian? It is implicit in the concept of custody that the custodian has authority to move the child from place to place, and, although the extent of that authority was at common law, and still may be, subject to substantial qualification in the case of a minor *pubes*, it is difficult to envisage that the custodian could be guilty of abduction. If that is correct, it must follow that those who act on his authority or with his consent are in a like position. Thirdly, is it abduction to take a child above the age of common law

---

[3] Child Abduction Act 1984, s. 2.

[4] The Scottish Law Commission have recommended that plagium be abolished, but that abduction be retained: Scot. Law Com. No. 102, *Report on Child Abduction* (1987). And see Kelly, "Child Abduction," 1991 S.L.T. (News) 53.

[5] *i.e.* a boy below 14 or a girl below 12. This remains the case although for many purposes pupillarity is now in effect extended to 16 (Age of Legal Capacity (Scotland) Act 1991), for s. 1(3)(*c*) of that Act provides that nothing in it shall affect the criminal responsibility of any person: it cannot therefore be taken to have extended the crime of plagium to all children under 16.

[6] Hume, I, 84; Alison, I. 280; Macdonald, 21; *H.M. A.* v. *Cairney or Cook and Anr.* (1897) 2 Adam 471; *H.M. A* v. *Mary Millar or Oates* (1861) 4 Irv. 74; *H.M. A.* v. *Helen Wade* (1844) 2 Broun 288; *H.M. A.* v. *Rachel Wright* (1809) 1 Hume 84; *H.M. A.* v. *Janet Douglas* (1817) 1 Hume 85; *H.M. A* v. *Marion Rosmond or Skeoch* (1855) 2 Irv. 234.

[7] *Downie* v. *H.M. A.*, 1984 S.C.C.R. 365; *Hamilton* v. *Mooney*, 1990 S.L.T. (Sh. Ct.) 105; and see John M. Fotheringham; "Plagium: the Sins of the Father *v.* the Rights of the Parent" (1990) 35 J.L.S. 506.

[8] Macdonald at p. 124.

[9] It is because parental rights over a pupil child were characterised at common law as a right of *dominium* that plagium can be regarded as a species of theft.

[10] *Cf.* plagium, to which the pupil's will is clearly irrelevant.

pupillarity away, with his consent freely given, if that is against the will of his custodian? The relative freedom of a minor *pubes* at common law was, it is submitted, such that his consent validated his being taken away without the necessity of obtaining his custodian's prior approval. Today it may be argued that the *dominium* exercised over pupils at common law has been extended to age 16,[11] *i.e.* is now conterminous with rights of custody, and that the custodian's consent is therefore always required for the child's removal.

The Age of Legal Capacity (Scotland) Act 1991 cannot, however, be invoked in support of that argument as it does not affect the previously existing criminal law in any way [12] and it is submitted that the definition in section 8 of the Law Reform (Parent and Child) (Scotland) Act 1986, which defines child in relation to custody as a child under the age of 16 years, does not affect the content of custodial powers and, in any event, applies only for the purposes of that Act and does not affect criminal liability.

A child above the age of pupillarity was free, in a way in which a pupil was not, to form purposes of his own and assume responsibility for his actions. Whatever other remedies may be available, he commits no offence if, in pursuit of these purposes, he moves out of the control of his custodian. In that situation it is difficult to see how someone who merely co-operates with the child over the age of common law pupillarity but below the age of 16, or who facilitates his movements, is guilty of abduction and there is no authority for the view that, in the absence of fraud, any common law offence is thereby committed.

It is, however, an offence to take an unmarried girl under 18 out of the possession of her father or mother or any other person having lawful care and charge of her with intent that she should have unlawful sexual intercourse.[13] It is essential to the commission of the offence that the taking away should have been against the will of the person having care and charge. There must be an actual taking, or causing to be taken, and it is not an offence merely to consent to the girl's leaving or to fail to return her if she leaves.[14] Nor, as unlawful sexual intercourse means intercourse outwith marriage,[15] is it an offence to take a girl away with a view to marriage.[16] The consent of the girl is no defence if she is actually taken rather than leaves without active involvement by the accused amounting to taking.[17] But it is a defence that the accused had reasonable cause to believe that the girl was of or above the age of 18[18] or that he did not know that the girl was in the possession of her parents or in anyone's care and charge.[19] It is obscure to what extent a child over 16, and thus free from the constraints of custody, can be said to be in the possession of anyone.

---

[11] See *ante* at p. 174.
[12] s. 1(3)(*c*).
[13] Sexual Offences (Scotland) Act 1976, s. 8.
[14] *R.* v. *Jarvis* (1903) 20 Cox. C.C. 249; *R.* v. *Olifier* (1866) 10 Cox C.C. 402.
[15] *Mohamed* v. *Knott* [1969] 1 Q.B. 1.
[16] *R.* v. *Chapman* [1959] 1 Q.B. 100.
[17] *R.* v. *Manktlow* (1853) 6 Cox C.C. 143; *R.* v. *Jones* [1973] Crim. L.R. 621.
[18] For the meaning of "reasonable cause", see *H.M. A.* v. *Hoggan* (1893) 1 Adam 1, *per* Lord Justice-Clerk Macdonald at pp. 3–4; and *H.M. A.* v. *Macdonald* (1900) 3 Adam 180, *per* Lord Mclaren at p. 182.
[19] *R.* v. *Hibbert* (1869) L.R. 1 C.C.R. 184.

CHAPTER 10

INTERNATIONAL ASPECTS OF CUSTODY AND ACCESS

Choice of Law

In custody and access cases there is little room for choice of law questions in the pure sense of choosing a legal system to govern the issue before the court. Section 3(2) of the Law Reform (Parent and Child) (Scotland) Act 1986 applies to "any proceedings relating to parental rights," which includes issues of custody and access,[1] and so whatever the provisions of any potentially applicable foreign legal system may be, the case has to be decided with regard to the welfare of the child as the paramount consideration. Usually, therefore, the rules of foreign legal systems will require to be considered only in so far as they bear on the child's future welfare. Once the welfare test has been satisfied, account should, in principle, be taken of any preferences which the law of the child's domicile or habitual residence may indicate but, except in questions of recognition of foreign custody or access orders, the matter has been little considered and can seldom arise. It is in the recognition and enforcement of foreign custody and access orders, a question closely associated with conflicts of jurisdiction, that the main problems have been experienced, and the main statutory regulation exists.

Recognition of Foreign Orders: Common Law

At common law the Scottish court would recognise foreign custody decrees if granted by the court of the child's domicile.[2] That was justified on the view that custody affects status[3] in which the grand rule is that it "is governed universally by one single principle," namely that of domicile.[4] A status, when created by the law of the domicile, "is, or ought to be, judicially recognised as being the case everywhere, all the world over."[5] So judgments of the courts of the domicile, and only those judgments, had the character of judgments *in rem*.[6] While the strength of that conclusion in purity of principle can be acknowledged, a rigid adherence to it, particularly if it meant that judgments of courts other than those of the domicile were disregarded, could have unfortunate consequences in some cases. The use of domicile as the jurisdictional test, though logical, could lead to anomalies. Domicile is more easily applied retrospectively to the situation of the *propositus* at a fixed time in the past than in the fluid context of an

---

[1] Law Reform (Parent and Child) (Scotland) Act 1986, s. 8.
[2] Anton and Beaumont, p. 521, suggest, and the principle seems sound, that the common law rules apply to recognition of foreign custody rights arising by operation of law as well as those arising from a court decree.
[3] *Kitson* v. *Kitson*, 1945 S.C. 434, *per* Lord Justice-Clerk Cooper at p. 439.
[4] *Udny* v. *Udny* (1869) 7 M.(H.L.) 89, *per* Lord Westbury at p. 99.
[5] *Re Luck* [1940] Ch. 864 at p. 891, *per* Scott L.J.
[6] *Kitson* v. *Kitson*, *supra* at p. 439; *Radoyevitch* v. *Radoyevitch*, 1930 S.C. 619 at p. 624; *Ponder* v. *Ponder*, 1932 S.C. 233 at p. 236.

ongoing dispute. It could also be uncertain and require elaborate proof when expedition and concentration on other issues were important. Sometimes, especially when a domicile of origin was revived after having been lost, it could be
an artificial concept lacking any real connection with the child. The concept of
habitual residence was increasingly perceived as more appropriate than domicile for custody cases, and, indeed, in the context of family law in general.[7] In
1986 the common law rule was altered so that, where domicile of the child was
previously the ground for recognising custody orders made outside Scotland,
habitual residence of the child is now to be the ground for recognising custody
orders made outside the United Kingdom.[7a]

However, foreign judgments, even from courts of competent jurisdiction,
will not be recognised or enforced automatically, for the question of recognition
is secondary to the question of the welfare of the child. Since 1925 the child's
welfare has by statute been the paramount consideration in any proceedings before the court in which the custody or upbringing (*inter alia*) of the child was in
question.[8] It has consequently been held that an order of a foreign court of competent jurisdiction is entitled to "grave consideration" but not to automatic enforcement[9]; that a foreign order cannot inhibit the Scottish court from reaching
an independent conclusion on the merits where the child's welfare so requires[10];
and that there is no presumption that the order of the court of the domicile (now
habitual residence) should be followed.[11] The Scottish court will give effect to
an order of a foreign court of competent jurisdiction, provided (a) it is shown
that that can be done without injury to the interests of the child, and (b) the party
to whom custody is granted is in a position to make suitable arrangements for
the child's welfare. An inquiry into welfare is not always necessary. It is entirely a question of the circumstances of each case but it will often be evident,
especially where the foreign order is recent and supported by documents showing that it was based on a full consideration of the child's welfare, that the child
could be entrusted to the custodian under the foreign order without further
inquiry.[12]

Statutory Recognition and Enforcement: Introduction

Today, custody and access rights and orders emanating from jurisdictions
outwith Scotland are statutorily subject to three distinct régimes of recognition
rules, depending upon the country of origin, and upon whether and to what extent that country is party to certain international conventions and agreements. In

---

[7] See Anton and Beaumont (2nd ed.) at pp. 150–152.

[7a] Family Law Act 1986, s. 26.

[8] Guardianship of Infants Act 1925, s. 1. See now Law Reform (Parent and Child) (Scotland) Act
1986, s. 3(2).

[9] *McKee* v. *McKee* [1951] A.C. 352 (P.C.), *per* Lord Simonds at p. 365. *Cf. Radoyevitch* v. *Radoyevitch, supra; McLean* v. *McLean*, 1947 S.C. 79; *Girvan, Petr.* 1985 S.L.T. 92, *per* Lord Stewart at
pp. 93–94; *Sinclair* v. *Sinclair*, 1988 S.L.T. 87, *per* Lord Prosser at p. 89C.

[10] *Campins* v. *Campins*, 1979 S.L.T. (Notes) 41; *Radoyevitch* v. *Radoyevitch, supra; McKee* v.
McKee, supra; Sinclair v. *Sinclair, supra.*

[11] *Sinclair* v. *Sinclair, supra*, at p. 89, *per* Lord Prosser.

[12] *Sargeant* v. *Sargeant*, 1973 S.L.T. (Notes) 27; *Campbell* v. *Campbell*, 1977 S.C. 103; *Lyndon* v.
Lyndon, 1978 S.L.T (Notes) 7; *Thomson, Petr.* 1980 S.L.T. (Notes) 29.

relation to custody orders from courts in other parts of the United Kingdom, the courts in Scotland will recognise and give effect to them according to the rules laid down in Part I, Chapter V of the Family Law Act 1986. In relation to custody orders and rights emanating from countries outside the United Kingdom that are party to the European Convention on the Recognition and Enforcement of Decisions Concerning Custody of Children, or the Hague Convention on the Civil Aspects of International Child Abduction, the court in Scotland will recognise and give effect to them according to the rules in these conventions, insofar as they are brought into United Kingdom law by the Child Abduction and Custody Act 1985. In relation to custody orders and rights emanating from countries outside the United Kingdom that are not party to either the European Convention or the Hague Convention, or which are not in the circumstances covered by the conventions,[13] the court in Scotland will recognise and give effect to them according to the common law rules described above.

Recognition and Enforcement of Custody and Access Orders within the United Kingdom

The Family Law Act 1986 laid down, as we have already seen,[14] the rules governing the jurisdiction of the Scottish courts in relation to custody and access. Comparable rules, similarly based on matrimonial proceedings, habitual residence, presence and emergency, are laid down in that Act for England and Wales[15] and for Northern Ireland.[16] Not only does the Act lay down uniform rules for jurisdiction in custody and access cases throughout the United Kingdom, but it also provides the basis for recognition and enforcement in one part of the United Kingdom of the custody and access orders from courts in any other part of the United Kingdom. The harmonisation of the rules on jurisdiction has allowed for the general principle to be enacted that the custody and access orders made by a court in one part of the United Kingdom will be entitled to recognition in all other parts without anything further. If the order is to be enforced in a part other than the part whose courts granted the order, then a certain, though minimal, procedure has to be gone through. Because of the new jurisdictional rules it will generally not be possible, once custody is granted in one part of the United Kingdom, to seek a fresh custody order in another part instead of applying for recognition and enforcement.

Recognition

Section 25(1) of the Family Law Act 1986 provides that where a Part I order made by a court in any part of the United Kingdom is in force with respect to a child, then the order shall be recognised in any other part of the United Kingdom as having the same effect in that other part as if it had been made by the appropriate court in that other part and as if that court had had jurisdiction to make it.

---

[13] See for example *Hill* v. *Hill*, 1991 S.L.T. 189, in which, though the child had been brought from Ontario, where both Conventions apply, the European Convention was inapplicable since the removal had taken place before the making of a custody order. (It seems not to have been realised in that case that the Hague Convention would not be inapplicable for this reason alone.)

[14] *Ante*, at pp. 237–245.

[15] Family Law Act 1986, ss. 2–7.

[16] *Ibid.*, ss. 19–24.

A "Part I order" includes orders of the court regulating custody and access (or either).[17] The "appropriate court" in relation to Scotland means the Court of Session.[18] "Child" means a child under the age of 16 years. It follows that a residence (custody) order or a contact (access) order granted by, for example, an English court which had jurisdiction to do so according to the English jurisdictional rules in the 1986 Act will be recognised in Scotland automatically, and it will have the same effect in Scotland as if a custody order or access order had been made by the Court of Session. Scottish orders will be recognised in England and Wales, and in Northern Ireland, according to the same rules. If the order includes provision as to the means by which the rights conferred by the order are to be enforced, then that provision of the order is to be ignored[19]: the Act itself lays down the enforcement procedure that must be followed.

While enforcement of a custody or access order is another issue (shortly to be discussed), its recognition alone will give the person in whose favour the order is made certain rights. So, for example, a custodian can consent to the medical treatment of the child, and a person with residence rights granted by an English court can give consent to medical treatment in Scotland, and that consent will be legally effective. If, however, the exercise of the rights of custody is challenged, or the holder of the rights wishes to enforce them, the procedure described in the next paragraph has to be adopted.

Enforcement

A court in a part of the United Kingdom in which a custody or access order from another part is recognised in accordance with the provision described above cannot enforce the order unless it has been registered in that part of the United Kingdom under section 27 of the Family Law Act 1986 and proceedings for enforcement are taken in accordance with section 29.[20] If a custody or access order is to be enforced in a part of the United Kingdom other than the part in which it was granted, then the person on whom rights are conferred by the order may apply to the court that made the order to have it registered in another part of the United Kingdom.[21] On receiving an application to have its order registered in another part of the United Kingdom, the court has no discretion and must grant the application, unless it appears that the order is no longer in force[22] (for example, because the child subject to the order has since it was granted attained the age of 16 years). On receiving the application the court that made the order must cause to be sent to the appropriate court (a) a certified copy of the order, (b) where the order has been varied, prescribed particulars of any variation that is in force, and (c) a copy of the application and of any accompanying documents. The appropriate court is, if the order is to be enforced in Scotland, the Court of Session or, if the order is to be enforced in England and Wales or Northern Ireland, the High Court.[23] When the prescribed officer of the appropriate court re-

---

[17] *Ibid.*, s. 1(1)(*b*).
[18] *Ibid.*, s. 32(1).
[19] *Ibid.* s. 25(2).
[20] *Ibid.*, s. 25(3).
[21] *Ibid.*, s. 27(1).
[22] *Ibid.*, s. 27(3).
[23] *Ibid.*, s. 32(1).

ceives the certified copy of the order he must forthwith cause the order, together with particulars of any variation, to be registered in that court.[24] Registration cannot be refused, unless the order is in respect of a child who has attained the age of 16,[25] and the registration of an order shall cease to have effect when the child attains that age.[26] Registration can be cancelled where the order ceases to have effect in the part of the United Kingdom in which it was made, cancellation being on the court's own motion or on the application of any person who appears to the court to have an interest.[27]

The effect of registration is that the court in which the order is registered has the same powers in relation to enforcement of the order as if it had itself made the order and had jurisdiction to make it.[28] Accordingly, an English residence order registered in the Court of Session can be enforced in Scotland by following the procedures appropriate for the enforcement of a custody order made by the Court of Session.[29] Where the order ceases to have effect in the part of the United Kingdom in which it was made, or it has ceased to have effect in Scotland as a result of the making of an order in proceedings outside the United Kingdom, then, if enforcement proceedings are brought in Scotland in accordance with section 29, any person who appears to the court to have an interest in the matter may apply for the proceedings to be dismissed.[30] If in either case the court is satisfied that the registered order has ceased to have effect then it shall (*i.e.* must) dismiss the proceedings for enforcement.[31]

Notwithstanding that the procedure laid down by the 1986 Act has been followed, an ultimate discretion in relation to enforcement lies with the Court of Session, because the Act "has not elided the limited protective jurisdiction of the Court of Session to refuse to give effect to the custody order of a foreign court...which the Court of Session may always exercise if it is satisfied that enforcement of the foreign decree would result in physical or moral injury to the child."[32] It is submitted that it is only in exceptional circumstances that this limited protective jurisdiction could be invoked; otherwise the whole basis of this part of the 1986 Act would be placed in jeopardy.[33]

Interim Directions and Sisting of Enforcement Proceedings

Where an application for the enforcement of an order registered under section 27 is made the court may, at any time before the application is determined, give such interim directions as it thinks fit for the purpose of securing the welfare of the child concerned and of preventing changes in the circumstances rel-

---

[24] *Ibid.*, s. 27(4).
[25] *Ibid.*, s. 27(5). It is competent for the courts in England and Wales and in Northern Ireland to grant residence (custody) orders over children until the age of 18.
[26] *Ibid.*
[27] *Ibid.*, s. 28.
[28] *Ibid.*, s. 29(1).
[29] For which see *ante*, at pp. 247–249.
[30] *Ibid.*, s. 31(1) and (2).
[31] *Ibid.*, s. 31(3).
[32] *Woodcock* v. *Woodcock*, 1990 S.L.T. 848, *per* Lord President Hope, Lords Dunpark and Milligan at p. 853B: this opinion was expressed "for future guidance."
[33] See Edwards, "A Domestic Muddle: Custody Orders in the United Kingdom" (1992) 41 I.C.L.Q. 444.

evant to the determination of the application.[34] Where proceedings for enforcement are taken, any person who appears to the court to have an interest may apply for the proceedings to be sisted on the ground that he has taken or intends to take other proceedings the result of which may be that the order will cease to have effect, or have a different effect, in the part of the United Kingdom in which it is registered.[35] So, for example, in *Woodcock* v. *Woodcock*[36] a father obtained from the Family Division in England an order against the mother for the delivery of a child to him. This order (which was a Part I order as defined in section 1(1)(*a*) of the 1986 Act) was registered in the Court of Session in accordance with section 27(1) and the father petitioned the court for an order for delivery of the child in accordance with section 29. The mother successfully moved the court to sist the proceedings on the ground that in a divorce action in England the delivery order against her might be lifted. If, having granted a sist, it appears to the court that there has been unreasonable delay in the taking of the other proceedings, or that the other proceedings are concluded and the registered order is still in force, the court may recall the sist.[37]

Recognition and Enforcement of Custody Orders from outwith the United Kingdom

In relation to those countries that have ratified the Hague Convention on the Civil Aspects of International Child Abduction or the European Convention on Recognition and Enforcement of Decisions Concerning Custody of Children,[38] and in circumstances in which the conventions are applicable, custody and access orders will be recognised and enforced in Scotland in accordance with the terms of the Child Abduction and Custody Act 1985. In Schedule 1 and Schedule 2 to that Act these conventions are respectively reproduced, in so far as they are adopted into United Kingdom law.[39]

Recognition and Enforcement under the European Convention

The European Convention provides for the mutual recognition between contracting states of decisions relating to custody, which are defined to mean decisions "of an authority in so far as it relates to the care of the person of the child, including the right to decide on the place of his residence, or to the right of ac-

---

[34] Family Law Act 1986, s. 29(2): this requires some inquiry by the court into whether it would be in the child's best interests to give directions: *Woodcock* v. *Woodcock, supra* at p. 852F.

[35] *Ibid.*, s. 30(1).

[36] *Supra.*

[37] *Ibid.*, s. 30(3). This provision is without prejudice to any other power of the court to recall a sist: s. 30(4).

[38] For countries not party to these Conventions, the common law rules apply: see *ante* at pp. 265–266.

[39] The provisions set out in the schedule have the force of law (ss. 1(2) and 12(2)). For a description of the terms of the full Conventions, see respectively Anton, "The Hague Convention on International Child Abduction" (1981) 30 I.C.L.Q. 537, and Jones, "Council of Europe Convention on Recognition and Enforcement of Decisions Relating to the Custody of Children" (1981) 30 I.C.L.Q. 467. The full text of the Hague Convention may be found in (1981) 15 Fam.L.Q. 149. See also Eekelaar, "International Child Abduction by Parents" (1982) 32 Univ.Tor.L.J. 281; Sachs, "Child Abduction" (1988) 18 Fam.L. 81; Crawford, "International Child Abduction" (1990) 35 J.L.S. 277.

cess[40] to him."[41] "Child" means a person of any nationality, so long as he is under 16 years of age and has not the right to decide on his own place of residence under the law of his habitual residence, the law of his nationality, or the internal law of the state addressed. The fundamental principle in the European Convention is contained in Article 7, which provides that "a decision relating to custody given in a contracting state shall be recognised and, where it is enforceable in the state of origin, made enforceable in every other contracting state." The courts of contracting states must therefore recognise and enforce the custody decisions of courts and administrative bodies in other contracting states, subject only to the exceptions shortly to be discussed. The provisions of the convention apply to decisions made before the child was removed to another country, and to decisions made afterwards if they contain a declaration that the removal was unlawful.[42] The Scottish court has the power to make such a declaration in relation to children taken out of the United Kingdom.[43]

The procedure for recognition and enforcement by the Scottish courts of custody decisions covered by the European Convention is laid down in the body of the Child Abduction and Custody Act 1985.[44] Recognition, as the convention itself demands, is automatic unless refused on an application made to the court.[45] To be enforced, the custody decision must be registered in the appropriate court, which in Scotland is the Court of Session.[46] This is done by the person on whom rights are conferred by the custody decision making an application to the court.[47] The application must be granted by the court (subject to what is said below) and the decision can then be enforced as if it were a decree of the Court of Session, the court having the same powers for the purpose of enforcing the decision as if it had been made by that court.[48] If one of the grounds for refusing recognition (shortly to be discussed) exists, the court must refuse to register the decision,[49] as it must do if the decision is not, in the opinion of the court, covered by the convention,[50] or if an application under the Hague Convention, discussed later, is pending.[51] If the decision is varied or revoked in the country in which it was made, the person on whose behalf it was registered in Scotland must notify the Court of Session,[52] which will then vary or cancel the registration accordingly.[53] The court may also do this on the application of any person appearing to the court to have an interest in the matter.[54]

Any person who has obtained in a contracting state a decision relating to the

---

[40] It is further provided in Art. 11 that decisions on rights of access shall be recognised and enforced subject to the same conditions as other decisions relating to custody.

[41] Art. 1(c).

[42] Art. 12.

[43] Child Abduction and Custody Act 1985, s. 23(2).

[44] *Ibid.*, ss. 12–24.

[45] *Ibid.*, s. 15.

[46] *Ibid.*, s. 27(2).

[47] *Ibid.*, s. 16(1).

[48] *Ibid.*, s. 18.

[49] *Ibid.*, s. 16(4)(a).

[50] *Ibid.*, s. 16(4)(b).

[51] *Ibid.*, s. 16(4)(c).

[52] *Ibid.*, s. 17(1).

[53] *Ibid.*, s. 17(2) and (3).

[54] *Ibid.*, s. 17(4).

custody of a child and who wishes to have that decision recognised or enforced in another contracting state may, if he needs help in so doing, submit an application to the central authority of any contracting state.[55] In Scotland the central authority is the Secretary of State,[56] and in England and Wales and in Northern Ireland it is the Lord Chancellor.[57] Applications can be made to any central authority (or to none) and if an application is made to an authority in a country different from that in which the applicant seeks to have the order recognised or enforced, the authority addressed must directly and without delay send the documents to that other central authority.[58] The purpose of the central authorities is to provide such assistance as is required to the person in whose favour the custody order was made, in tracing the child if necessary, taking action to have the custody order recognised and enforced, and in arranging for the return of the child.[59]

Grounds for Refusing Recognition and Enforcement

The general principle is that recognition of the custody order will be automatic, and it is provided expressly that "in no circumstances may the foreign decision be reviewed as to its substance."[60] However the convention, as enacted in the 1985 Act, requires the courts in the state addressed to refuse recognition of custody or access orders on grounds laid down by Articles 9 and 10.[61] These Articles provide that recognition and enforcement may be refused:

(1) In the case of a decision given in the absence of the defendant or his legal representative, if the defendant was not duly served with the document that instituted the proceedings in sufficient time to enable him to arrange his defence. This ground cannot, however, be used if the failure to effect service was a result of the defendant having concealed his whereabouts from the person who instituted the proceedings.[62]

(2) In the case of a decision given in the absence of the defendant or his legal representative, if the competence of the authority giving the decision was not founded (i) on the habitual residence of the defendant, (ii) on the last common habitual residence of the child's parents, at least one parent still being habitually resident there, or (iii) on the habitual residence of the child.[63]

(3) If the custody decision is incompatible with a decision relating to custody which became enforceable in the state addressed before the re-

---

[55] Art. 4.
[56] On whose behalf the functions are performed by Scottish Courts Administration.
[57] *Ibid.*, s. 14(1).
[58] Art. 4(3).
[59] Art. 5.
[60] Art. 9(3).
[61] Child Abduction and Custody Act 1985, s. 16(4)(*a*). The Convention itself allowed the Art. 9 grounds to be applied only when the application was made within six months of a removal of the child from the jurisdiction in which the order was made to another. The Convention as enacted by the 1985 Act makes no distinction between the grounds under Art. 9 and Art. 10: *i.e.* they apply whenever the application is made.
[62] Art. 9(1)(*a*).
[63] Art. 9(1)(*b*).

moval of the child, unless the child has had his habitual residence in the territory of the requesting state for one year before his removal.[64]

(4) If it is found that the effects of the decision are manifestly incompatible with the fundamental principles of the law relating to the family and children in the state addressed.[65] In Scotland this would entitle the court to refuse to recognise or enforce a custody decision that is contrary to the interests of the child, the welfare principle being fundamental in child law in Scotland. However, it has been suggested that this ground is not satisfied just because a Scottish court would have reached a different conclusion from that of a foreign court as to where the child's welfare lies.[66] This must be so, otherwise the court would be breaching the injunction not to review the foreign decision as to its substance.[67]

(5) If it is found that by reason of a change in the circumstances including the passage of time but not including a mere change in the residence of the child after an improper removal, the effects of the original decision are manifestly no longer in accordance with the welfare of the child.[68] This is not simply the welfare test, for the standard of proof to be met by a party founding on this provision is "a very high one."[69] In making a decision under this head the court is obliged to ascertain the child's views unless this is impracticable having regard in particular to his age and understanding.[70]

(6) If at the time when the proceedings were instituted in the state of origin (i) the child was a national of the state addressed or was habitually resident there and no such connection existed with the state of origin or (ii) the child was a national both of the state of origin and of the state addressed and was habitually resident in the state addressed.[71] This ground justifies refusal of recognition and enforcement when stronger connections exist between the child and the state asked to recognise the order than between the child and the state in which the order was originally made.

(7) If the decision is incompatible with a decision given in the state addressed or enforceable in that state after being given in a third state, pursuant to proceedings begun before the submission of the request for

---

[64] Art. 9(1)(c).
[65] Art. 10(1)(a).
[66] Enc. 10, 1329.
[67] Art. 9(3).
[68] Art. 10(1)(b).
[69] *Campins-Coll, Petr.*, 1989 S.L.T. 33 at p. 36L, *per* Lord Kirkwood. In this case, that standard was satisfied, particularly due to the fact that the child, a boy of 15½, whom the judge described as an "intelligent and level-headed boy who knows that he wants to do with his life," expressed an adamant refusal to return to Spain. It was held that it would be manifestly contrary to his welfare to force him to return against his will and thereby separate him from his brother (who was 17) and also thereby further disrupt his education. In *F. v. F. (Minors) (Custody: Foreign Order)* [1989] Fam. 1, the passage of 21 months, together with the father's changed attitude towards access, was held to constitute a change of circumstances in the lives of children aged five and three at the time of the hearing, and thus recognition and enforcement was refused under this ground.
[70] Art. 15(1).
[71] Art. 10(1)(c).

recognition or enforcement, and if the refusal is in accordance with the welfare of the child.[72] Both conditions must be satisfied before this ground can be used to refuse recognition and enforcement.

Return of the Child under the Hague Convention

The Hague Convention is in many respects rather wider than the European Convention, and not just in its geographical extent. Most significantly, it is not restricted in its terms to custody and access decisions, but includes custody and access rights, whether these rights arise from an order of a court or administrative body or a legally effective agreement or by operation of law.[73] The aim of the Hague Convention is to ensure the "immediate and summary return"[74] of children who have been taken across international borders[75] in breach of custody rights. If a child is wrongfully removed to or retained in a country other than that in which he was habitually resident[76] then a court or authority in the state in which the child is present is directed to order the return of the child[77] forthwith, when a period of less than one year has elapsed from the date of the wrongful removal or retention, and, when a longer period has elapsed, to order the return of the child forthwith unless it is demonstrated that the child is now settled in its new environment.[78] "Forthwith," means without delay[79] and the courts are directed by the convention to "act expeditiously."[80] The convention applies to children under 16 who were habitually resident in a contracting state immediately before the breach of custody or access rights.[81] "Rights of custody" include rights relating to the care of the person of the child, and in particular the right to determine the child's place of residence; and "rights of access" include the right to take the child for a limited period of time to a place other than the child's habitual residence.[82]

---

[72] Art. 10(1)(d). See Campins-Coll, Petr., supra, in which a Spanish decree in favour of the father, granted in 1982, was not enforced as it was incompatible with a Scottish decree in favour of the mother, dated 1977.

[73] Art. 3. See Kilgour v. Kilgour, 1987 S.L.T. 568; Viola v. Viola, 1988 S.L.T. 7; MacMillan v. MacMillan, 1989 S.L.T. 350. In C. v. S. (Minor: Abduction: Illegitimate Child) [1990] 2 All E.R. 449, 961 it was held that "custody rights" meant those recognised by law and did not include de facto custody that a parent might be exercising without legal authority.

[74] MacMillan v. MacMillan, supra at p. 355A.

[75] To remove a child in breach of custody rights from, say, Dumfries to Thurso would not activate the Hague Convention, and domestic enforcement measures would have to be adopted. The Hague Convention is concerned only with international abduction, i.e. that in which the child is taken across borders.

[76] See Crawford, " 'Habitual Residence of the Child' as the Connecting Factor in Child Abduction Cases: A Consideration of Recent Cases," 1992 J.R. 177.

[77] Return is ordered back to the country of the child's habitual residence and not necessarily back to the person holding the custody rights that had been breached: Re A (Minor) (Abduction) (1988) 18 Fam.L. 54.

[78] Art. 12.

[79] In Viola v. Viola, supra, it was held that "forthwith" meant so soon as practicable and not necessarily immediately on the conclusion of the court proceedings. The court in that case also decided that the requirement in Art. 13 to consider social background reports could not be used to delay the proceedings until such reports were available. See also MacMillan v. MacMillan, supra, in which the Lord Ordinary was criticised by the Inner House for delaying his decision to see if arrangements could be made to avoid the risk to the child that would have justified refusal of return.

[80] Art. 11.

[81] Art. 4.

[82] Art. 5.

The convention applies only when there has been a "wrongful removal or retention" of the child, and removal or retention is considered to be wrongful where (a) it is in breach of rights of custody attributed to a person, an institution or any other body, either jointly or alone, under the law of the state in which the child was habitually resident immediately before the removal or retention,[83] and (b) at the time of the removal or retention those rights were actually being exercised, either jointly or alone, or would have been so exercised but for the removal or retention. Under condition (a) there is some conflict of opinion as to whether removal by one parent against the wishes of the other is wrongful when both enjoy custody rights. In *H* v. *N*[84] the English High Court held that there was a wrongful removal by a mother who had custody of the child when the father also had custody and had not agreed to the removal. Anton and Beaumont[85] state that "where the law concedes, or the court grants, joint custody rights, the removal of a child by one parent without the consent of the other would clearly be a wrongful removal in the sense of article 3." On the other hand, in *Taylor* v. *Ford*,[86] it was held in the Outer House that a father who had removed a child from Canada was not guilty of a "wrongful removal" when both he and the mother had custody rights and the removal was against the wishes of the mother: the right of custody carried with it the right to determine the residence of the child and the exercise of that right could not amount to "wrongful removal." Now, it is true that in the domestic law when two or more parties have parental rights each may exercise them independently of the other[87] and that for one party to exercise such a right against the wishes of the other is not in itself a breach of the other's rights, but it may be a breach of the other party's rights if the effect of the removal, as by taking the child outwith the jurisdiction, is to prevent the exercise of his rights. The true question in relation to wrongful removal is whether there has been a breach of a right recognised by the Hague Convention. An act that prevents a person exercising a right is, it is submitted, a breach within the meaning of the Hague Convention, with the result that *Taylor* v. *Ford* was wrongly decided.

Condition (b) is designed to prevent people relying on the convention when, while they have rights legally, they have not been exercising them in fact, such as for example a Scottish father who is married to the mother (and thus has custody rights) but who does not have *de facto* custody of the child, because he lives apart from the mother and the child. "Retention," like "removal," is an event (being the initial retention) rather than a continuing state of affairs, otherwise there would be no point from which the one year mentioned in Article 12 could be measured.[88] Consequently, a child removed before the convention comes into force in a particular country is not wrongfully retained if he or she is

---

[83] The wrongfulness lying in the removal of the child from the jurisdiction rather than from its parent: *per* Lord Brandon of Oakbrook in *Re H. and Anr. (Minors) (Abduction: Custody Rights)* [1991] 3 All E.R. 230 at p. 240.

[84] [1990] 2 F.L.R. 439.

[85] *Private International Law (2nd ed.) at p. 531, citing H. v. N.*

[86] 1993 S.L.T. 654.

[87] Law Reform (Parent and Child) (Scotland) Act 1986, s. 2(4).

[88] *Per* Lord Brandon of Oakbrook in *Re H. and Anr. (Minors), supra,* at p. 240.

retained after its coming into force.[89] Because of the different nature of access, however,[90] a retention after a removal from a particular country, before the convention comes into force there, may breach current access rights.[91] "Removal" and "retention" are mutually exclusive events, removal occurring when a child which has previously been in the state of its habitual residence is taken across the frontier of that state, retention occurring where a child which has previously been for a limited period of time outside the state of its habitual residence is not returned to that state on the expiry of such limited period.[92]

Like the European Convention, the Hague Convention establishes central authorities[93] (being the same as those established under the European Convention) which can be approached for assistance by the person whose rights have been breached, and which have various duties in relation to discovering the whereabouts of the child, to prevent harm to the child, to ensure its safe return, for the raising of proceedings with a view to securing the return of the child and in cooperating with other central authorities.[94]

Grounds for Refusing to Order Return

The grounds upon which a Scottish court asked to order the return of the child under the Hague Convention can refuse to do so are a good deal narrower than the grounds under the European Convention for the refusal of recognition or enforcement of custody orders. It is provided under the Hague Convention that the judicial or administrative authority of the state to which the child has been taken is not bound to order the return of the child if the person who opposes the return establishes one of the following situations:

(1) That the person, institution or other body having the care of the person of the child was not actually exercising the custody rights at the time of the removal or retention, or had consented to or subsequently acquiesced in the removal or retention.[95] This reflects the definition of wrongful removal, which, as seen above, requires that the rights were being exercised at the time of the removal or retention.

(2) That there is a grave risk that his or her return would expose the child to physical or psychological harm or otherwise place the child in an intolerable situation.[96] It is not enough to establish this ground of refusal that it would be against the best interests of the child to be sent back:

---

[89] *Kilgour* v. *Kilgour*, 1987 S.L.T 568, followed by the House of Lords in *Re H. and Anr. (Minors) (Abduction: Custody Rights), supra.*

[90] See *ante,* pp. 229–231.

[91] *B.* v. *B. (Minors: Enforcement of Access Abroad)* [1988] 1 All E.R. 652 (though the applicant in this case was ultimately unsuccessful since it had not been established that the child was habitually resident in a contracting state before its removal and the result is that access will be treated in the same way as custody in respect to the retroactivity of the Convention).

[92] *Per* Lord Brandon of Oakbrook in *Re H. and Anr. (Minors), supra,* at p. 240.

[93] Child Abduction and Custody Act 1985, s. 3(1).

[94] Art. 7.

[95] Art. 13(*a*). Acquiescence can be either (i) acceptance of the removal or retention, signified by express words of consent or by conduct inconsistent with an intention to insist on legal rights, or (ii) passive acquiescence inferred from silence and inactivity for a sufficient period in circumstances where different conduct was to be expected on the part of the aggrieved parent: *Re A. and Anr. (Minors) (Abduction: Acquiescence)* [1992] 1 All E.R. 929.

[96] Art. 13(*b*). And see Enc. 10, 1339.

the matter before the court is restricted to determining whether or not the party opposing the return has established the existence of a grave risk of the kind specified.[97] Were it otherwise, the whole convention would be nullified and the matter dealt with according to the domestic law of Scotland. "Grave" risk means a "weighty" risk, of "substantial and not trivial" harm.[98]

(3) That the child objects to being returned and has attained an age and degree of maturity at which it is appropriate to take account of its views.[99] This is a matter that can be determined only on a case-by-case basis. Maturity refers to mental maturity.

(4) In a case in which a period of more than one year has elapsed from the date of the wrongful removal or retention, that the child is now settled in its new environment.[1] The whole purpose of the convention is to minimise disruption in the life of the child, and this exception is based on the assumption that to unsettle the child more than is necessary will be against its welfare—as always, the parent's "right" to custody or access takes second place to the welfare of the child.

Access

The right of access is expressly covered in Article 21, which obliges the central authorities to promote the peaceful enjoyment of access rights and the fulfilment of any conditions to which the exercise of those rights may be subject. An application to make arrangements for organising or securing the effective exercise of rights of access may be presented to the central authorities in the same way as an application for the return of the child.

---

[97] *Viola* v. *Viola*, 1988 S.LT. 7 at p. 10, *per* Lord McCluskey, holding that this ground of refusal was not satisfied by allegations that the child, if returned, would be looked after by an elderly grandfather who spoke no English. In *MacMillan* v. *MacMillan*, 1989 S.L.T. 350, the Inner House held that this ground of refusal was satisfied because the father, from whom the mother had wrongfully removed the child, had a long history of alcoholism and depression. The ground was held not satisfied in *C*. v. *C*. *(Abduction: Right of Custody)* [1989] 1 W.L.R. 654 when the mother refused to accompany the child back from England to Australia, even although the mother's presence in the child's life was deemed necessary for its welfare. An intolerable situation for the child does not necessarily exist when the situation is intolerable to the other parent: *Whitley* v. *Whitley*, April 29, 1992 (2nd Division) *(LEXIS)*.

[98] *Re A. (A Minor) (Abduction)* (1988) 18 Fam.L. 54, *per* Nourse L.J. See also *Whitley* v. *Whitley*, *supra*.

[99] Art. 13.

[1] Art. 12.

CHAPTER 11

ALIMENT

THE OBLIGATION TO ALIMENT

Nature of the Alimentary Obligation

"The main obligation of a parent is to aliment the child."[1] When questions of enforcement arise the obligation is seen nearly always in terms of payment of money, but the money payment is but a substitute for, or a means of effecting, provision in kind. Aliment is that part of the general duty of nurture which can be met by material provision. It is a parent's duty to provide his children "in bed, board, and clothing, and all the necessaries of life"[2] and that duty will often be fulfilled, at least in large part, by entertainment of the child in the family home without any question of money payment. So to provide for the child is the characteristic performance of the duty and, unless need for other provision arises, its sufficient discharge.

The obligation of aliment is not based on implied contract and so cannot be irrevocably discharged[3] nor is it based on the parental power as such because it subsists although parental power be lost,[4] and might at common law devolve on those who did not have that power. It is rather an "evident instance of the law of nature"[5] based on the parental relationship in lines of descent and ascent. So at common law the duty was enforceable *ex debito naturali* not only against parents but on their failure against descendants and remoter ascendants. The natural tie giving rise to the obligation was not, however, seen as embracing collaterals although persons who did not have a natural obligation to provide aliment, including collaterals, might fall under an obligation *ex jure representationis* as successors to the estate of a person bound *ex debito naturali*.[6]

The Family Law (Scotland) Act 1985

The common law has now been superseded in virtually all its aspects by the Family Law (Scotland) Act 1985.[7] In relation to alimentary claims from the executors of a deceased person or from any person enriched by the succession to a deceased person's estate (that is to say the liability *ex jure representationis*) the common law rules have, however, been expressly preserved[8] and in some other

---

[1] Hume, *Lectures*, Vol. I, p. 206.

[2] Erskine, I, vi, 56.

[3] Fraser, pp. 99 and 121; Stair, I, v, 1.

[4] This was certainly the case at common law, and is given statutory effect by the Child Support Act 1991, s. 1(1) of which provides "each parent of a qualifying child is responsible for maintaining him"; s. 3 defines "qualifying child" to be one whose parent or parents does or do not live in the same household as the child.

[5] Stair, *ibid.*

[6] Fraser, pp. 102 and 103, and see *post* at pp. 286–290.

[7] ss. 1–7. See Nichols, *The Family Law (Scotland) Act 1985* (2nd ed., 1991), Chap. 2.

[8] Family Law (Scotland) Act 1985, s. 1(4).

respects reference may still have to be made to the common law principles for assistance in the interpretation of the Act or for the solution of questions that are left open. Most of the previous statute law on the substance of the alimentary obligation is repealed and the law is now contained in the 1985 Act. Before the repeal of the Guardianship of Infants Act 1925[9] the welfare of the child, at least when a pupil, was the first and paramount consideration in questions of aliment as in other questions relating to the upbringing of the child. Welfare is now the paramount consideration only in actions relating to parental rights,[10] which do not cover the parental obligation of aliment. However, the terms of the 1985 Act are sufficiently wide to enable the court to observe the spirit of the welfare principle, though its application would not justify the court awarding a child aliment when the child is not otherwise entitled thereto.[11] Statutory rules for enforcement are largely unaffected by the 1985 Act.

The following are the main features of the new legislation:

Obligants

Liability for aliment now attaches only to (a) the spouse of the person to be alimented, (b) the father or mother of the person to be alimented, or (c) a person who has accepted the child to be alimented as a child of his family.[12] In the last case, the obligation does not, however, apply where the child has been boarded out with the acceptor. A grandparent or other ascendant therefore has no obligation now unless he has accepted the grandchild as a child of his own (immediate) family, and the rule under which liability might attach to children and remoter descendants has also been abolished. The alimentary obligation of spouses lies outwith the scope of this book and is considered here only in so far as it impinges on the parental obligations. Categories (a) and (b) are questions of fact and will seldom lead to difficulties. Category (c) is more problematic, and will depend on a number of circumstances that may differ in each case. The concept of "child of his family" is not restricted, as it is in relation to jurisdiction in custody,[13] to the child of one spouse being accepted as one of the family by the other spouse,[14] and it can therefore include a child who is the child of neither spouse.[15] There is indeed no need for the family into which the child is accepted to be based on marriage, or to consist of two adults. "Family," as used in the Act, includes a one-parent family.[16] Acceptance as a child of the family probably re-

---

[9] By Sched. 2 to the Law Reform (Parent and Child) (Scotland) Act 1986.

[10] Law Reform (Parent and Child) (Scotland) Act 1986, s. 3(2).

[11] *Cf.* s. 2 of the Child Support Act 1991, which provides that the Secretary of State or a child support officer "shall have regard to the welfare" of the child in exercising any discretionary power under that Act. There is no requirement to further welfare, nor to regard it as paramount, and the section does no more than oblige the Secretary of State or the child support officer to take account of the child's welfare.

[12] Family Law (Scotland) Act 1985, s. 1(1).

[13] See *ante* at pp. 239–240.

[14] Though this will be the typical example of its application, and, indeed was the intendment of the now repealed s. 7 of the Matrimonial Proceedings (Children) Act 1958, under which the court in divorce proceedings could order aliment to be paid by a spouse to his or her stepchildren.

[15] *Bradley* v. *Bradley*, 1987 S.C.L.R. 62 (Sh. Ct.) was decided on different statutory words, which required the child of one spouse to be accepted by the other: the case related to jurisdiction in custody.

[16] Family Law (Scotland) Act 1985, s. 27.

quires an intention for the arrangement to be permanent, or at least indefinite, and the temporary looking after of a child, even if the child is treated in all respects alike with the natural children of a family, will be insufficient to impose the alimentary obligation.[17] Some interpretative help may be obtained from the cases decided on similar provisions relating to jurisdiction in custody.[18] The acceptance must be after the coming into force of the Act[19] before the obligation in the Act can be founded upon,[20] but acceptance is, it is submitted, a continuing concept so that a family that is established before the relevant date and continues after that date could found acceptance and thus an obligation under the Act.

Status Irrelevant

No distinction is now made for the purposes of aliment between legitimate and illegitimate children. It is paternity or maternity[21] that imposes the obligation, and a child can be an obligee in relation to aliment whether or not his or her parents have ever been married to one another.[22] This alters the common law and consists with section 1 of the Law Reform (Parent and Child) (Scotland) Act 1986, under which the fact that a person's parents are not or have not been married to one another is to be left out of account in establishing the legal relationship between two persons. An adopted child is for this, as for other, purposes in the same position as a child born of the obligant.[23] The biological parent of an adopted child is not subject to the obligation of aliment.

How Amount of Aliment is to be Determined

Aliment is such support as is reasonable in the circumstances having regard to the needs and resources of the parties, their earning capacities and, generally, all the circumstances of the case.[24] Both present and foreseeable needs and resources are to be taken into account[25] and a consideration of earning capacity clearly entitles the court to have regard not only to present earned income and opportunities in present employment but, more generally, to the potential income which it may be within a party's capacity to earn. Reasonable choices of employment are, however, it is submitted, to be respected and although unemployment, where it is voluntary and avoidable, no doubt needs to be justified

---

[17] See *Inglis* v. *Inglis*, 1987 S.C.L.R. 608.

[18] *Bowlas* v. *Bowlas* [1965] P. 450; *Holmes* v. *Holmes* [1966] 1 W.L.R. 187; *R.* v *R.* [1968] P. 414; *Dixon* v. *Dixon* [1968] 1 W.L.R. 167. The English legislation upon which these cases were based has now been changed, but the Scottish wording remains the same as that upon which these cases were decided.

[19] On September 1, 1986.

[20] *Forbes* v. *Forbes*, 1991 S.C.L.R. 389.

[21] On the establishment of which, see *ante*, Chap. 4. This often has to be proved before aliment can be claimed: see *Torrie* v. *Turner*, 1990 S.L.T. 718.

[22] Family Law (Scotland) Act 1985, s. 27, as amended by the Law Reform (Parent and Child) (Scotland) Act 1986, Sched. 1, para. 21.

[23] Adoption (Scotland) Act 1978, s. 39(1).

[24] Family Law (Scotland) Act 1985, ss. 1(2) and 4(1). This can include awards previously made under other provisions: *Jowett* v. *Jowett*, 1990 S.C.L.R. 348, and the conduct of the defender in attempting to conceal his financial position: *Walker* v. *Walker*, 1991 S.L.T. 649. S. 4(3)(*b*) provides that the court shall not take account of the conduct of any party in determining the amount due unless it would be "manifestly inequitable to leave it out of account."

[25] *Ibid.*, s. 27(1).

there may be cases, as of a student obligee, or a retired obligant, where it is, in the circumstances, right to have regard to present earnings rather than those of which the party may be capable.

Plurality of Obligants

Where there are two or more obligants there is no order of liability.[26] In deciding how much, if any, aliment to award against any one obligant the court is, however, to have regard, among the other circumstances of the case, to the obligation of aliment owed by any other person.[27] And in an action brought by or on behalf of a child under the age of 16 years, the court in assessing the amount may award such provision as it considers to be in all the circumstances reasonable in respect of the expenses incurred wholly or partly by the person having care of the child for the purposes of caring for the child[28] (e.g. that if the child is being cared for by one parent only, the other parent's liability to the child may be increased to reflect the expenses of the caring parent).[29] A consequence would seem to be that liability for aliment is not joint and several and that a claimant should, therefore, direct his claim against all parties subject to the obligation and that the court will make, not an apportionment inter se but a separate award against each obligant.[30] A further consequence of there being no order of liability is the abrogation of the rules that the obligation of aliment rested primarily on the child's father, that as long as the father's means were sufficient to enable him adequately to aliment the child no decree for aliment could be pronounced against any other person and that it was unnecessary and incompetent to consider the ability of any other person, including the child's mother, to provide aliment.[31] The mother now stands in like position to the father and, in determining the amount of aliment to be paid by each parent, the court is to have regard to both parents' respective needs, resources and earning capacities and all the circumstances of the case.[32] Yet another consequence, perhaps more surprising, of the complete abolition of any order of liability is that the parental obligation to aliment a married child is no longer, as a matter of law, postponed to the obligation of a spouse.[33] The scheme of the Act is such that questions of amount of aliment and extent of liability are interrelated[34] and it would seem that it opens up a comparison at large between the needs and means of the child to be supported, of his or her spouse, and of his or her parents in determining both the appropriate amount of aliment and the extent, if any, to which the spouse or the parents should contribute. A parent whose means are greater than a spouse's may, therefore, be called upon to make the greater or even the sole contribution; but it is of the nature of marriage that spouses should look to each

---

[26] Ibid., s. 4(2).
[27] Inglis v. Inglis, 1987 S.C.L.R. 608.
[28] Family Law (Scotland) Act, s. 4(4), as inserted by the Child Support Act 1991, Sched. 5, para. 5.
[29] This provision is, it is submitted, somewhat illogical, particularly because the award of aliment goes to the child and not to the caring parent who suffers the expenses that increase the obligant's liability.
[30] See Nichols, op. cit., at pp. 11–12.
[31] Dickinson v. Dickinson, 1952 S.C. 27.
[32] Scully v. Scully, 1989 S.C.L.R. 757.
[33] Fraser (3rd ed.) at p. 124 and cases cited therein (notes 2 and 3).
[34] Family Law (Scotland) Act 1985, ss. 1 and 4.

other rather than to a parent for support and it is submitted that in the circumstances of most cases that consideration should place a restraint on the extent of parental liability.

Duration of Obligation

The parental obligation to aliment a child subsists only until the child reaches the age of 18 years or, where he is reasonably and appropriately undergoing instruction at an educational establishment or training for employment or for a trade, profession or vocation, until he reaches the age of 25 years.[35] Doubts about the obligation to aliment a child who was able to earn a livelihood but was instead undergoing education or training are thus removed and a limit put on the duration of the obligation; but doubts may yet remain, though of a different nature, of whether education or training is undertaken "reasonably and appropriately."[36] At the same time, the common law rule disappears that the obligation to aliment a child unable to earn his livelihood or otherwise support himself subsisted throughout his incapacity even if that incapacity were lifelong.[37] Except where he is under 25 and undergoing education or training, a person who is over the age of majority and unable to earn a livelihood must look to his or her spouse or to State schemes of assistance and not to his parents so far as any legally enforceable claim for support is concerned; and that is so even if his inability is due to physical or mental incapacity. The death of either obligant or obligee ends the obligation of aliment; the ending of the parental relationship by adoption terminates the obligation[38]; the assumption of parental rights and powers by local authority resolution does not.[39]

Common Law Principles

The common law rules on the nature and purpose of aliment are now entirely replaced by the statutory definition of the alimentary obligation.[40] That definition is, however, so wide that an outline of the common law rules may serve to give it content although they cannot detract from its generality or from the freedom of comparison and evaluation which the statute gives. A number of principles evolved at common law that are not inconsistent with the Family Law (Scotland) Act 1985.

Economy of Provision and Relevance of Obligant's Means

In *Maule* v. *Maule*[41] it was held by the House of Lords that aliment extended to no more than "support beyond want; and all that is beyond that, is left to paternal affection." That decision, made in the early nineteenth century had, however, to be interpreted in the light of changing social perspectives. The court was not bound by ancient concepts. The rules of law relating to aliment were

---

[35] *Ibid.*, s. 1(1)(c) and (d) and (5). See *Jowett* v. *Jowett*, 1990 S.C.L.R. 348.
[36] See Nichols at p. 6.
[37] Erskine, I, vi, 56.
[38] Adoption (Scotland) Act 1978, s. 39(1).
[39] Social Work (Scotland) Act 1968, s. 17(6).
[40] Family Law (Scotland) Act 1985, s. 1(2).
[41] (1825) 1 W. & S. 266.

fluid and varied with social conditions.[42] In any event, "want" was a relative term. It did not mean bare subsistence but was relative to the situation of the party who made the claim. So "a person who has received the education of a gentleman...would not be placed above the reach of want by getting the relief of a parish pauper."[43] Such comments required adaptation to modern conditions but indicated an award which was a reasonable but economical provision for the applicant in the light of his condition and circumstances. Provided the applicant's needs so measured could be met by the obligant without depriving him of proper support for himself or others for whom he had a prior responsibility, the means of the obligant were, it had been said, irrelevant.[44] In most cases the statutory test will now point to a similar result but the scope for taking account of the obligant's needs and means is wider while, on the other hand, it is no longer necessary, within the bounds of what is reasonable, to have special regard to economy of provision.[45]

Obligee's Means

Because the common law was that the need of the person to be alimented must be established before the obligation to aliment him became exigible, it was a bar to any claim that the claimant already had the means of his own aliment.[46] These principles are consistent with the Family Law (Scotland) Act 1985 and, in particular, with the reference to needs as among the matters to which the court is to have regard.[47] The Act gives wider discretion according to circumstances and comparative means and needs of parties, but in general it will remain the case that there can be no valid claim for aliment where the claimant's income whether earned or derived from his property would be sufficient to provide his aliment, and the possession of capital capable of sale will usually bar a claim where the proceeds of sale would provide sufficient aliment. At one time, the father's position in relation to the aliment of his children constituted an exception. He might not encroach on the child's capital nor it seems use the child's income for the purpose of the child's aliment, so long at least as the child was not major and not forisfamiliated and the father had sufficient means to provide aliment. In *Fairgrieves* v. *Hendersons* Lord President Inglis said: "the father's obligation to aliment his children is absolute and unconditional; he is not in a position to say that the children shall maintain themselves out of any money they may have before he is called upon."[48] It was, however, settled before the 1985 Act that a child's estate might be applied to his aliment in relief of the father's obligation even where the father was of sufficient means and that, at least in some circumstances, the father might be justified in encroaching on the child's

---

[42] *Polland* v. *Sturrock's Exrs.*, 1952 S.C. 535, *per* Lord Justice-Clerk Thomson at pp. 544–545.

[43] *Thom* v. *Mackenzie* (1864) 3 M. 177, *per* Lord Justice-Clerk Inglis at p. 179.

[44] *Ibid.*; Erskine, I, vi, 56; Stair, I, v, 7; Fraser, pp. 109 and 110.

[45] In determining the extent of the obligant's liability, his or her income is to be assessed net of tax: *Begg* v. *Begg*, 1987 S.C.L.R. 704; *Wiseman* v. *Wiseman*, 1989 S.C.L.R. 757; *Pryde* v. *Pryde*, 1991 S.L.T. (Sh. Ct.) 26.

[46] Erskine, I, vi, 53; Stair I, v, 7.

[47] s. 4(1)(*a*).

[48] (1885) 13 R. 98 at pp. 99–100, *sed contra Hutcheson* v. *Hoggan's Trs.* (1904) 6 F. 594; *Polland* v. *Sturrock's Exrs.*, *supra.*

capital for that purpose.[49] That view can readily be reconciled with the Act and the freedom with which it can be applied is enlarged, but it may still be the law that encroachment on a child's capital by a father, or now by a mother, for the purpose of alimenting the child is to be regarded as exceptional, and will not be justified where the parent's means are ample and the child's resources are small.

Effect of Establishment in Trade, Business or Profession

Again, at common law, no aliment was due where a child had been established in a business, trade, profession or other way of life and had as a result means sufficient to support himself.[50] But the mere attainment by a child of a qualification which could, given the opportunity, be applied in the earning of a livelihood did not relieve the parent of his liability. If the child was unemployed and could not with reasonable diligence secure employment the parent remained liable and if the child, having been gainfully employed, fell into unemployment or if his business failed so that he was no longer able to support himself, the parental liability revived.[51] The extent to which a parent was required to go in setting up his child in a business, trade or profession was not well settled. Stair speaks of "breeding of them for some calling and employment according to their capacity and condition"[52] and in *Polland* v. *Sturrock's Exrs.*,[53] Lord Justice-Clerk Thomson referred to "the obligations and duties of a father under modern conditions, especially in regard to a daughter's education and training for earning her own living."[54] Much depended on circumstances, including the parents' means and assistance available from State and other sources, but where the parents' means so considered were sufficient it seems to be clear that the duty extended to providing for an education and training reasonably suited to the child's abilities and aptitudes. If the child's needs, including his need for education and training, so required, liability to provide aliment continued after the child attained majority and, in the case of a child incapable of earning a living because of physical or mental infirmity or other insuperable cause, subsisted throughout the child's life.[55] But where a child had once been established in a suitable way of earning his livelihood he could not make further demands for aliment unless he had fallen into necessitous circumstances from which he had no means of retrieving himself.[56] The obligation was, therefore, perpetual in the sense that it was never fully discharged and might at any time become exigible in the event of necessity. The Act has now put a term on the duration of the parental obligation, but, within that term, it contains nothing that affects the principle that an alimentary obligation that has lapsed may revive. So a child who at 16 became self–supporting may, if need arises, again call upon his parents for aliment at any time before his majority or, if he is reasonably and

---

[49] *Polland* v. *Sturrock's Exrs.*, *supra.*

[50] Erskine, I, vi, 53; Stair, I, v, 7; Fraser, p. 121.

[51] *Ibid.*

[52] I, v, 6.

[53] 1952 S.C. 535.

[54] at p. 544.

[55] See Hume, *Lectures*, Vol. 1, pp. 214 and 215 and cases discussed therein and in the editorial footnotes.

[56] *A.B.* v. *C.D.* (1848) 10 D. 895; *Hunter's Trs.* v. *Macan* (1839) 1 D. 817; *Maule* v. *Maule* (1825) 1 W. & S. 266.

appropriately undergoing education or training, before attaining the age of 25. And the law does not now require that in order to make such a claim he must have fallen into necessitous circumstances from which he cannot extricate himself. So a child who has been established in a way of livelihood may give it up and call upon his parents to support him until the age of 25 in education or training which he has reasonably and appropriately undertaken. Whether parents are obliged to meet such a claim is a question of what is reasonable in the circumstances having regard to the factors which the Act lays down.

Obligant's Discretion in Discharge of Obligation

Subject to the constraints imposed by the obligee's need, the obligant had at common law a wide discretion in the provision of aliment.[57] So he might implement his obligation in the way he considered most economical for himself provided the legitimate needs of the person to be alimented were not thereby jeopardised. So, a parent might insist on his children living in family with him as the most economical way of alimenting them.[58] On the other hand a child could not complain if a parent chose to discharge his obligation by providing separate accommodation, provided that that was consistent with relief of the child's needs.[59] But in the case of a child who had not been established in a way of earning a livelihood, a parent could be required to provide aliment such as to enable the child to live in separate accommodation if that were necessary for the purpose of his education or training or for the early stages of his employment before he was in a position to earn sufficient to maintain himself. Under a long line of authority of considerable antiquity, a parent who had ill-treated his children could not, whatever their age, require them as a condition of aliment to live in family with him; in such cases aliment would be decreed sufficient to enable separate provision to be made.[60]

In the circumstances of many cases a parent will still be entitled to implement his alimentary obligation in the way he considers most economical because it is reasonable to allow him to do so, but it is now a question of reasonableness rather than of right. The stress of the common law on economical discharge is lessened. The Act does, however, make specific provision which, although still invoking the test of reasonableness, goes some way to protect the parent's position. It is a defence to an action for aliment by or on behalf of a person other than a child under the age of 16 that the defender is making an offer, which it is reasonable to expect the person concerned to accept, to receive that person into his household and to fulfil the obligation of aliment.[61] For that purpose, however, the court is to have regard to any conduct, decree or other circumstances which appear to be relevant.[62] The rule is, therefore, in effect preserved that a parent

---

[57] *Bell* v. *Bell* (1890) 17 R. 549.
[58] Erskine, I, vi, 56.
[59] In *Kirklands* v. *Kirklands* (1685) Mor. 403 it had, however, been found that a mother was bound *jure naturali* to aliment the younger children *in familia* and the modern law even before the 1985 Act would undoubtedly have considered the aliment of minor children in separate accommodation from the standpoint of the welfare of the child.
[60] Erskine I, vi, 56; Bankton I, vi, 14; and cases cited in Erskine.
[61] Family Law (Scotland) Act 1985, s. 2(8).
[62] *Ibid.*, s. 2(9).

may by ill-treatment forfeit any right to require his children, as a condition of aliment, to live in family with him. No provision is required in relation to children under 16 because questions of their residence will be determined under the custody jurisdiction by having regard to their welfare as the paramount consideration.[63]

Plurality of Obligees

If a parent had means sufficient to aliment some but not all with a claim upon him, those children who had remained under the parental protection were, at common law, to be preferred to those who had been forisfamiliated.[64] There is now no fixed rule that children who stay in the parental home are to be preferred in this way.

Agreements on Aliment

It followed from the perpetual character of the common law alimentary obligation that no conventional discharge, however conclusive and comprehensive in its terms, could bar a later demand in the event of need reviving. Agreements to exclude future liability for aliment or to restrict the right to sue for aliment are, however, now subject to specific statutory regulation under which they are of no effect unless fair and reasonable in all the circumstances of the agreement at the time it was entered into.[65] Courts may be reluctant to interfere with arrangements between parties of full age in so far as they affect themselves but may be expected to look critically at any exclusion of children's future aliment."[66] An agreement on aliment will not prevent any party from applying for a maintenance assessment under the Child Support Act 1991, and any provision purporting to restrict that right is void.[67] Agreements to pay aliment may be varied at the instance of the obligant or of the person to whom the obligation is owed on the occurrence of a material change of circumstances.[68]

Representational Liability

The General Principle

Erskine says that "a father is not barely bound to maintain his children during his own life; he ought so to provide for all of them, that they may be able to live comfortably after his death."[69] The obligation so stated is moral rather than legal and so "is left entirely upon the conscience, without being enforced by any civil sanction." The law, however, goes further and provides that where on the death of a parent a child is left with insufficient means to support himself he may claim aliment from his parent's estate.[70] The claim is prestable against exec-

---

[63] Law Reform (Parent and Child) (Scotland) Act 1986, s. 3(2).

[64] Stair, I, v, 9.

[65] Family Law (Scotland) Act 1985, s. 7(1).

[66] See Nichols at p. 19.

[67] Child Support Act 1991, s. 9.

[68] Family Law (Scotland) Act 1985, s. 7(2); see Nichols at p. 20. And see *Mackenzie* v. *Mackenzie*, 1987 S.C.L.R. 671.

[69] I, vi, 58; *cf.* Stair, I, v, 7.

[70] Erskine, *ibid.*; *Beaton* v. *Beaton's Trs.*, 1935 S.C. 187. The Scottish Law Commission have, however, recommended that aliment *jure representationis* be abolished: see *Report on Succes-*

utors but, as executors and trustees are not bound to retain funds sufficient to meet it on a continuing basis, it is good against them only prior to the period of distribution. The right to claim aliment transmits thereafter against those who have succeeded to the parent's estate. The liability thus incurred arises purely *ex jure representationis* and so is subject to rather different principles from those applicable to direct liability.[71]

Preservation by the Act of Representational Liability

This common law representational liability is preserved by the Family Law (Scotland) Act 1985, which provides that

> "nothing in this section shall affect...any rule of law by which a person who is owed an obligation of aliment may claim aliment from the executor of a deceased person or from any person enriched by the succession to the estate of a deceased person."[72]

The provision is unhappily expressed. Section 4, which governs the amount of aliment, applies to representational liability but section 1(2), which defines the obligation of aliment and is to be read along with section 4, is excluded. The statutory definitions of the persons to and by whom the obligation of aliment is owed (which occur in section 1) are also excluded: with the result, it would seem, that these persons are to be ascertained by the common law rules. The apparent difficulties and anomalies which might ensue are, however, largely elided if the representational character of liability is kept in view. The representative can be liable only for a debt for which the deceased would have been liable had he been alive and liability is limited to the extent of the estate falling under the succession or, in the case of a person who has been enriched by the succession, to the extent of his enrichment. Despite the preservation of common law definitions of the person to whom the obligation is owed, there cannot therefore be liability to the ascendants of the deceased or to his grandchildren because, although there could, at least on some authorities and in some circumstances, have been such liability at common law, the result of the Act is that the deceased himself would not have been liable to them. Nor, although for a different reason, can there be liability to a child accepted into his family by the deceased: under the Act the deceased might have had a liability to such a child but his representative has none because he has no liability at common law and the Act, while preserving the common law rule, creates no new representational liability.

Extent of Representational Liability

The statutory rules on determining the amount of aliment[73] apply, but the manner of their application is obscured by the omission of the reference to what is "reasonable in the circumstances"[74] as the basis on which the criteria are to be applied. In any event common law rules inherent in the nature of representa-

---

sion, Scot. Law Com. No. 124 (1990) at para. 9.5; this on the ground that the proposed new rules of succession will obviate the need for such alimentary liability.

[71] Fraser, p. 128.

[72] Family Law (Scotland) Act 1985, s. 1(4).

[73] *Ibid.*, s. 4.

[74] *Ibid.*, s. 1(2).

tional liability may still play a controlling role. Not only is the liability of the successor restricted to the extent of his enrichment by the succession but, within that restriction, equity in the distribution of the estate may limit the extent of his liability at least where the successor stands in the same relationship to the deceased as do the claimants. Representational liability has been seen as designed to compensate as far as necessary to meet alimentary need for the inequitable distribution of the estate—e.g. where the heritable part of the estate is large and has not passed to the deceased's children or has been distributed unequally among them, while the moveable estate is small.[75] Accordingly, it has been held that a successor is under no liability to aliment a brother or sister who has taken a corresponding benefit from the same succession.[76] The equity of that view may be questioned if it is strictly applied in all cases and the Act may open the way for reconsideration. If the estate has been divided equally among the children but the share of one of them, perhaps much younger than the others, is insufficient when taken along with his other resources to meet his alimentary needs, the priority of the alimentary claim over rights of succession would suggest that he should be entitled to pursue a claim against his brothers and sisters *qua* successors to the extent that they have been enriched by the succession and have a surplus over their own alimentary needs. It is also doubtful whether considerations of equity of distribution have any necessary limiting role in a claim against a successor who is not a brother or sister of the claimant. There can, however, be no question but that full account must always be taken of anything received from the deceased's estate whether by way of legitim or of succession before a claim to aliment can arise against the deceased's representatives.

Classes of Representative Liable

Erskine discusses liability *ex jure representationis* as attaching only to heirs in heritage,[77] but it is settled that it attaches also to those who have succeeded to the moveable estate of the deceased.[78] The alimentary interests of the children disadvantaged by the division of the moveable estate—and children are now the sole class of claimants—will often, however, be sufficiently protected by their claims for *legitim*. The claim for aliment is competent both where the estate has passed by the testamentary conveyance of the parent and where succession is on intestacy,[79] but in the latter event questions are unlikely now to arise in view of the equitable division of both heritable and moveable estate among children affected by the modern law of intestate succession.[80] The cases have been mainly concerned with claims by one or more of the deceased parent's children against

---

[75] If the moveable estate is large the children's claim to *legitim* will usually be sufficient provision for their aliment.

[76] *Mackintosh* v. *Taylor* (1868) 7 M. 67.

[77] I, vi, 58.

[78] *Scot* v. *Sharp* (1759) Mor. 440; *Thomson* v. *Wilkie* (1678) Mor. 419; *Stokers* v. *Moubray* (1632) 1 Mor. Supp. 332. See also Ivory's note to Erskine, *ibid.*

[79] *Spalding* v. *Spalding's Trs.* (1874) 2 R. 237; *Ormiston* v. *Ormiston's Trs.* (1838) 11 Sc. Jur. 232; *Drummond* v. *Swayne* (1834) 12 S. 342; *Fenton* v. *Scott* (1832) 4 Sc. Jur. 457; *Riddell* v. *Riddell* (1802) Mor. App. 1 Aliment 4; *Scot* v. *Sharp, supra; Hastie and Ker* v. *Hastie* (1671) Mor. 416 and 5922.

[80] See Succession (Scotland) Act 1964.

relatives, but neither principle nor authority support Fraser's view[81] that the doctrine cannot be applied where property is left to a stranger.

Duration of Representational Liability

Unlike common law liability *ex debito naturali*, liability *ex jure representationis* subsists only until the majority of the child to be alimented[82] and in some cases an earlier period has been fixed on the view that by then the child should be able to earn a livelihood.[83] The reason appears to be that there are insufficient grounds for extending liability further where it is based on positive rather than natural law. Where, however, there is a mental or physical incapacity to earn a livelihood aliment may be continued beyond majority.[84] But even in these cases liability will now normally come to end at majority because the representative's liability cannot be more extensive than the parent's, *i.e.* it will extend beyond majority only if the child is undergoing reasonable and appropriate education or training and in that event it will end at 25.[85] The cases are obsolete in which it was held that the obligation to aliment ladies of rank might extend beyond majority until their marriage—"for the daughters of gentlemen can do as little for themselves after as before majority, 'til they get a husband to provide for them."[86] Marriage before majority cuts off the claim.[87] If the claimant is also a beneficiary of the deceased's estate, the vesting of payment of whose share has been postponed, aliment is due only until the term of payment[88] and if in the interval he is entitled to interest, that must be applied to his aliment and any aliment due by the heir as representative reduced accordingly.[89]

Order of Liability Between Representatives and Others

The statutory provision that there shall be no order of liability[90] applies in a question with representatives of deceased parents. Accordingly, in determining the amount of aliment which he should pay a representative is to be considered along with other obligants and, subject to the limitation that his liability cannot exceed the amount by which he has been enriched by the succession, his other resources, his earning capacity and his needs are to be taken into account. There

---

[81] p. 132. The cases Fraser cites (*Riddell* v. *Riddell, supra*, and *Scot* v. *Sharp, supra*) do not vouch his proposition.

[82] Erskine, I, vi, 58; Bankton, I, vi, 16; *Hunter's Trs.* v. *Macan* (1839) 1 D. 817, *per* Lord Ordinary; *Strathmore* v. *Strathmore* (1825) 1 W. & S. 402; *Douglasses* v. *Douglass* (1739) Mor. 425.

[83] *Seatons* v. *The Heir* (1764) Mor. 431; *Don* v. *Don* (1697) Mor. 420; *Hastie and Ker* v. *Hastie* (1671) Mor. 416.

[84] *Thomson* v. *Wilkie* (1678) Mor. 419.

[85] Family Law (Scotland) Act 1985, s. 1(5).

[86] *Douglasses* v. *Douglass, supra. Cf.* Erskine, I, vi, 58; *Dalziel* v. *Dalziel* (1788) Mor. 450; *Bissets* v. *Bisset* (1748) Mor. 413.

[87] *Maxwell* v. *Maxwell* (1711) Mor. 423. This is settled only in the case of the marriage of daughters, but it is thought that the same view would be taken of the marriage of the son of the deceased. Although at common law as now under statute a parent might in certain circumstances be liable for the aliment of a married son (or of a married daughter) the marriage of a son or daughter is in a question with the heir an assertion of independence which frees the latter from liability.

[88] *MacNeil* v. *MacNeil* (1749) Mor. 426; *Straitons* v. *Lauriston* (1679) Mor. 418. *Children of Lawriston* v. *Lawriston* (1677) Mor. 418; *Stuart and Innes* v. *Rosyth* (1668) Mor. 415; *Frazer* v. *Frazer* (1663) Mor. 415; *Otter* v. *Otter* (1663) Mor. 414.

[89] *Dudgeon* v. *Arnot* (1830) 9 S. 36; *Gordon* v. *Maitland* (1757) Mor. 11161.

[90] Family Law (Scotland) Act 1985, s. 4(2).

may be cases, although they are likely to be rare, in which the whole liability will fall on the representative of a deceased parent to the exclusion of the surviving parent.[91] In such a case the surviving parent's obligation may become prestable on the expiry of the representative's liability, as on the majority of a child not mentally or physically incapable who is continuing to undergo education or training.

Posthumous Children and Aliment Ex Jure Representationis

The obligation to aliment a child is a debt that becomes a debt "so soon as the child was begotten."[92] It follows that a child born after the death of his parent can claim aliment from the deceased's estate or his representatives in the same way as surviving children can. This issue is discussed more fully in Chapter three of this book.[93]

Reimbursement of Aliment Paid

Reimbursement by Child

Where a child is living in family with a parent or other person, he will usually be alimented as part of the family provision even if he himself is of sufficient means. In that and other cases in which a person is alimented in kind or expenditure is incurred for his aliment, questions of reimbursement may arise. Whether a parent or other person under alimentary obligation can be compelled to provide aliment without looking for reimbursement is now a question of what is reasonable in the circumstances, having regard to the respective means and resources of the parties. At common law a parent might contract for payment of board with a child living at home who was earning a sufficient livelihood,[94] and that is probably still the law.[95] Anyone not under an alimentary obligation who provides aliment may, of course, freely contract with the recipient for reimbursement provided the recipient has contractual capacity; and if notice is given that reimbursement is expected a contract will be inferred from the continued acceptance of the provision. We are, however, here concerned with cases in which there is no contract. Stair lays down the principle:

> "in all cases aliment or entertainment, given to any person without paction, is presumed a donation, if the person was major, and capable to make agreement. But entertainment to minors or weak persons doth ever infer recompense according to the true value of the benefit received. And

---

[91] The mother's heirs have a representational liability at common law (Bankton I, vi, 16; *Scot* v. *Sharp*, *supra*; *Thomson* v. *Wilkie*, *supra*). In a question between the heir to the father's estate and the mother, the mother's liability was postponed to the heirs (Erskine, I, vi, 58; *Douglasses* v. *Douglass*, *supra*) and was activated only if the heir's estate did not afford a sufficient aliment for himself as well as for the other children (Ivory's Note on Erskine, *ibid.*; *Bissets* v. *Bisset*, *supra*).

[92] *Spalding* v. *Spalding's Trs.* (1874) 2 R. 237, *per* Lord Deas at p. 251.

[93] *Ante* at pp. 94–96.

[94] Erskine, I, vi, 53.

[95] The child would have contractual capacity to enter into such a contract under ss. 1(1)(*b*) and 2(1) of the Age of Legal Capacity (Scotland) Act 1991.

in the case of those, who are in use to furnish provision for money, the presumption ceaseth, and recompense is due."[96]

That aliment to minors (*i.e.* in this context all persons below the age of 18) "doth ever infer recompense" admits, however, of exceptions where the aliment is provided by a relative, as examples given by Stair show. In such cases there may be a question of some delicacy whether aliment was given *ex pietate* or on conditions of reimbursement. It has been held that in the absence of contract the ordinary presumption against donation does not always apply and that, on the contrary, there may be a certain presumption in favour of gift *ex pietate*.[97] Where, however, the person alimented is in receipt of income the relative providing aliment is entitled to reimbursement from any income the recipient had during the period he was alimented unless it appears that the provision was made with a contrary intention.[98] Moreover it is doubtful if, except in the case of aliment by parents, a presumption in favour of gift *ex pietate* survives the abolition of the alimentary obligation of relatives other than parents. Similarly, authorities in which it was held that a relative could not insist on repayment from a child out of the child's capital, at least where the property was small, unless a contract had been made with the child or his administrators-at-law,[99] are now obsolete because they proceed on a view of the relative's obligations which can now be applied only to parents or persons who have accepted a child as a child of their family. In *Polland and Anr.* v. *Sturrock's Exrs.*[1] it was held that in a proper case a father, although of ample means, might be entitled to be recompensed out of the capital of his children's estate, and that must apply *a fortiori* to persons not under an alimentary obligation. A contention that aliment was given *ex pietate*, and thus that no recompense is due, is strongest where the provision was made by a parent because he has an obligation to aliment, but a brother or sister, or even a more distant relative, may be held on a consideration of all the facts to have acted *ex pietate*.[2]

Reimbursement by Obligant for Expenditure by Others

Questions of reimbursement may also arise where a relative or a stranger aliments a child in place of a parent or other person with an alimentary obligation, as where a grandparent keeps a child in his home while the child's parents are alive and have sufficient means to provide aliment. Where in such a case a child has been brought up by a person other than a parent and the parent seeks to regain his custody, the court could previously, in its discretion, if it ordered the child to be given up to the parent, further order that the parent pay to the person

---

[96] Stair, I, viii, 2.

[97] Stair, I, viii, 2; *Gordon* v. *Lesly* (1680) Mor. 11426; *Guthrie* v. *Mackerston* (1672) Mor. 10137; *Hamilton* v. *Symington* (1667) Mor. 382; *Ludquharn* v. *Gight* (1665) Mor. 11425; Bankton, I, ix, 22.

[98] *Steven* v. *Simpson* (1791) Mor. 11458; *Hutcheson* v. *Hoggan's Trs.* (1904) 6 F. 594; *Webb* v. *Cleland's Trs.* (1904) 6 F. 274; *Duke of Sutherland, Petr.* (1901) 3 F. 761; *Seddon, Petr.* (1893) 20 R. 675; *Muir* v. *Muir's Trs.* (1887) 15 R. 170.

[99] *Galt and Ors.* (1830) 8 S. 332.

[1] 1952 S.C. 535.

[2] *Drummond* v. *Swayne* (1834) 12 S. 342; *Cuningham* v. *McGachan* (1831) 9 S. 472; *Rig* v. *Rig* (1676) Mor. 11426. *Cf. McGaws* v. *Galloway* (1882) 10 R. 157 and *Chisholm* v. *Steedman* (1703) Mor. 11428.

who had brought up the child the whole of the costs properly incurred in bringing him up, or such portion of them as seemed to the court to be just and reasonable having regard to all the circumstances of the case.[3] The court no longer has this power, and the general rule in a claim at the instance of a relative is that, as the parties were free to make a contract and had not done so, there is in the absence of contract or of necessity no claim for recompense.[4] The general rule admits, however, of an exception. Where a parent has, whether expressly or by clear implication, been called upon to fulfil his alimentary obligation and has refused or neglected to do so, as where a grandparent requires that a parent take a child home and the parent does not do so, the presumption of donation *ex pietate* is in these circumstances rebutted, with the result that recompense may be claimed.[5] It seems, moreover, that if a relative aliments a child for whom the primary liability rests on someone else *ex jure representationis*, there is a good claim for reimbursement without the necessity of contract. *Pietas* has, it has been said, no weight where the question is with extraneous heirs.[6] Nor does *pietas* have any place where the aliment has been provided, whether by accommodation in his home or in money or in kind, by a stranger and the claim for recompense is at his instance. The having of a child in a person's care is sufficient to impose obligations upon the carer.[7] The presumption against donation will then apply but, except where he acts from necessity, the circumstances may often be such as to rebut the presumption. Recompense for relief of necessity is best illustrated where tradesmen supply food, clothing or other necessaries to a child in need whose parent has failed to provide them. In such a case the parent is liable to the tradesmen.[8] "Necessaries to a person's wife or child are necessaries to himself."[9] The doctrine applies as long as the child has no property or means of earning a livelihood. It is for the tradesman to satisfy himself that the child is in need, and he will have no remedy where the parent has in fact provided a competent allowance or otherwise arranged for the child's necessaries to be supplied.[10] *Ex hypothesi* of the case, the tradesman looks to the parent for payment and has no action against the child unless perhaps where the child has misrepresented his true situation.[11] As the action lies for relief of necessity, nothing extravagant will be allowed, but necessity will be related to what is suitable to the child's station in life.[12] An action on this ground is to be distinguished, although the distinction is not always attended, from an action on the ground of the parent's implied mandate. In the latter case, which may arise from a course of dealings between the child and the tradesman in which the par-

---

[3] Custody of Children Act 1891, s. 2, repealed by the Children Act 1989, Sched. 15.

[4] Fraser, p. 120; *Ludquharn* v. *Gight* (1665) Mor. 11425; *Barclay* v. *Berry* (1700) 4 Mor. Supp. 491.

[5] *Gordon* v. *Lesly* (1680) Mor. 11426.

[6] *Gourlay* v. *Urquart* (1697) Mor. 11438; *Wilkie* v. *Morison* (1675) Mor. 5923; *Stirling* v. *Ottar* (1663) Mor. 11432.

[7] See *post* at pp. 407–408.

[8] Erskine, I, vi, 57.

[9] Fraser, p. 111, quoting Evans' Pothier, II, p. 29.

[10] Erskine, I, vi, 57.

[11] *Hamilton* v. *Forrester* (1825) 3 S. 572; *Gray* v. *Purves* (1816) Hume 411; *Crichton* v. *Kilmarnock* (1744), Elchies, *Minor*, No. 11; *Lamb* v. *Tweedie* (1623) Mor. 13424; *Anderson* v. *Craig, ibid.*

[12] Erskine, I, vi, 57.

ent has accepted responsibility for the child's transaction, but not in the former, the parent's liability will cease on his giving notice to the tradesman to that effect.[13] On the other hand, a case based on relief of necessity will always be confined to necessaries, whereas a case on implied mandate, although normally similarly confined, may extend beyond that if the circumstances justify the implication.

Parent's Right to Child's Earnings

Stair and Erskine lay it down that as long as children are living in family with their parents and alimented by them the children may be obliged to employ themselves for the common benefit of the family and that profit or earnings arising therefrom belong not to the children but to the parents.[14] It seems that they held, as did Bankton, that the parental right to the fruits of the childrens' labour subsisted until forisfamiliated even if the child was major. Stair attributed this right to the parental power, but Bankton says that the father "has right to their service for their entertainment, if they are not able otherwise to recompense him."[15] The parent's right to insist that his child work for him must now be regarded as obsolete, but it is no doubt still the law that if called upon, a child must, in so far as is reasonably within his power, recompense a parent by whom he is being alimented. The child's obligation is limited to what is required for recompense, and in that respect Bankton accurately reflects the modern principle. So, when a child earning a wage or salary is living in family with his parents, the parents are entitled to payment for board and accommodation provided[16] but not to any surplus of his earnings. The child may, however, have no liability for recompense in respect of aliment before the demand for payment was intimated, on the view that aliment prior thereto is taken to have been provided *ex pietate*.[17]

Child Support

A concept closely related to aliment which may usefully be dealt with at this point is that of child support, which is governed by the Child Support Act 1991.[18] This scheme was designed to improve the position of children who are not receiving proper (financial) support from their parents, to make the assessment and enforcement of that support easier and quicker, and to take the issue out of the province of the courts.[19] It applies only to "qualifying children," that is those with an "absent parent" or parents, *i.e.* parents who do not live in the

---

[13] Fraser, pp. 114–115; *Knox* v. *Hay* (1813) Hume 351; *Samson* v. *Goldie* (1808) Hume 425; *Barclay* v. *Douglas* (1758) Mor. 9624; Stair, I, v. 7.

[14] Stair, I, v, 6 and 8; Erskine, I, vi, 53.

[15] I, vi, 1, p. 153.

[16] Erskine, I, vi, 53.

[17] *Ante* at p. 292.

[18] For a useful discussion, see Eekelaar, "Child Support—An Evaluation" [1991] Fam. Law 511; "The Child Support Act 1991" (1993) 38 J.L.S. 44 and 93. A description of the Act is in Burrows, *The Child Support Act 1991: A Practitioner's Guide*, Butterworths, 1993

[19] *Cf.* Art. 27(4) of the UN Convention on the Rights of the Child (28 *International Legal Materials* 1448, ratified by the UK, Dec. 16, 1991), which provides that "state Parties shall take all appropriate measures to secure the recovery of maintenance for the child from the parents or other person having financial responsibility for the child."

same household[20] as the child while the child has his home with another person (normally the other parent) with care of him.[21] In relation to such children, the person with care of the child or the absent parent, or the child himself if over 12,[22] may apply to the Secretary of State for a maintenance assessment to be made,[23] and the Secretary of State may arrange for the collection and enforcement of the child support maintenance payable in accordance with the assessment.[24] If a parent (*i.e.* the parent who is caring for the child) claims income support, family credit or any other benefit of a kind to be prescribed, the Secretary of State may require him or her to authorise the recovery of child support maintenance from the other parent.[25] On receipt of the application to make a maintenance assessment, the Secretary of State shall refer the application to a child support officer, whose duty it is to assess the amount payable.[26] There is no discretion such as lies with the court in assessing aliment: rather the child support officer must apply a mechanical formula set out in Schedule 1 to the Act, using various prescribed figures. There is provision for periodic reviews of circumstances and for reviews of the decisions of the child support officers.[27] Appeal may be had to a child support appeal tribunal,[28] then, on a question of law, to a Child Support Commissioner,[29] and finally, on a question of law, to the English Court of Appeal unless the Child Support Commissioner directs that, having regard to the circumstances of the case and in particular the convenience of the persons who may be parties to the appeal, the appropriate court is the Court of Session.[30] Thereafter, though this does not appear in the Act, appeal may be had to the House of Lords.[31]

Collection and enforcement of child support maintenance is also provided for in the Act. The main method envisaged is through a "deduction from earnings order," which the Secretary of State is empowered to make in relation to anyone liable to make payments of child support maintenance under the assessment.[32] This will be directed to the employer of the person liable and shall operate as an instruction to the employer to make deductions from the liable person's earnings and to pay the amount deducted to the Secretary of State. If it is inappropriate to make a deduction from earnings order, for example because the person liable is not in employment, the Secretary of State may apply to the sheriff for a liability order,[33] which the sheriff must make, without questioning the assess-

---

[20] On the meaning of "household" (in different contexts), see *Santos* v. *Santos* [1972] Fam. 247; *McGregor* v. *H.*, 1983 S.L.T. 626; *Kennedy* v. *R's Curator ad litem* 1993 S.L.T. 295.

[21] Child Support Act 1991, s. 3.

[22] *Ibid.*, s. 7.

[23] *Ibid.*, s. 4(1).

[24] *Ibid.*, s. 4(2).

[25] *Ibid.*, s. 6.

[26] *Ibid.*, s. 11.

[27] *Ibid.*, ss. 16–19.

[28] *Ibid.*, s. 20.

[29] *Ibid.*, s. 24.

[30] *Ibid.*, s. 25. The constitutionality of this bizarre jurisdictional rule is questioned by Jamieson, in "The Child Support Act 1991 and the Act of Union 1707" (1992) 37 J.L.S. 484.

[31] (1993) 38 J.L.S. at pp. 95–96.

[32] Child Support Act 1991, s. 31.

[33] *Ibid.*, s. 33(1) and (2).

ment,[34] if satisfied that the payments are payable by the liable persons and have not been paid.[35] Diligence may be done upon such an order.[36] Imprisonment may follow wilful refusal or culpable neglect in complying with the liability order.[37]

These provisions will not be available to provide maintenance or support for all children. The limitations are discussed later in this chapter.[38]

JURISDICTION AND PROCEDURE

Jurisdiction: Introduction

Actions for aliment of a child are personal actions for payment. The ordinary jurisdictional rules for such actions are, however, supplemented by a number of specialties. The Civil Jurisdiction and Judgments Act 1982[39] is now the primary context for consideration of these matters.

The jurisdictional provisions of the Civil Jurisdiction and Judgments Act 1982 fall into three categories, which may be broadly described as (1) jurisdiction in the United Kingdom where the person sued is domiciled in a "Contracting State," that is a state (including in some cases certain dependent territories) which was a party to or subsequently acceded to the Brussels Convention on Jurisdiction and the Enforcement of Judgments in Civil and Commercial Matters 1968 (the "1968 Convention"), *i.e.* a member of the European Community; (2) allocation of jurisdiction among the several parts of the United Kingdom; and (3) the enactment of a new and comprehensive code of civil jurisdiction in Scotland. The effect of the Act on questions of aliment requires consideration under each of these hearings.

Jurisdiction as between Contracting States

One of the effects of the Civil Jurisdiction and Judgments Act 1982 is to make the 1968 convention part of the law of Scotland.[40] As the jurisdictional provisions of the convention apply solely to cases where the person sued is domiciled in a contracting state, the rules here under consideration have no application where the defender is domiciled in a country outwith the European Community. The meaning of domicile is, however, different from that usually attributed to it in Scottish rules of international private law.[41] The fundamental

---

[34] *Ibid.*, s. 33(4).

[35] *Ibid.*, s. 33(3).

[36] *Ibid.*, s. 38.

[37] *Ibid.*, s. 40.

[38] *Post*, at pp. 298–300.

[39] The reader is referred to Anton, *Civil Jurisdiction in Scotland*, (1984), for a full discussion of the Act. Only the special provisions on aliment and such other matters as are necessary to put those provisions in context are considered here.

[40] Civil Jurisdiction and Judgments Act 1982, s. 2(1). For ease of reference the 1968 Convention and the amendments thereto occasioned by later accessions are set out in Scheds. 1–3B to the Act, as substituted and added by Civil Jurisdiction and Judgments Act (Amendment) Order 1990 (S.I. 1990 No. 2591).

[41] *Ibid.*, s. 41(2) provides that an individual is domiciled in the United Kingdom if, and only if (a) he is resident in the United Kingdom and (b) the nature and circumstances of his residence indicate that he has a substantial connection with the United Kingdom. Art. 52 provides that in order to determine whether a person is domiciled in another Contracting State the court is to apply the law of that state. S. 41(7) provides that an individual is domiciled in a state other than a Contracting

jurisdictional principle of the convention is that persons domiciled in a contracting state are, irrespective of nationality, to be sued in the courts of that state and not of any other contracting state.[42] Jurisdiction, in other words, follows the domicile of the defender. This applies to alimentary actions as it does to others. So, a person domiciled in Scotland may be sued for aliment in the Scottish courts and, generally speaking, a person domiciled in a contracting state other than the United Kingdom may not be so sued. However, to the general rule there are a number of exceptions, one of the most important of which concerns aliment, in relation to which the pursuer's as well as the defender's position may be used to found jurisdiction. It is provided that in matters relating to aliment there is jurisdiction in the courts of the place where the alimentary creditor is domiciled or habitually resident, or, if the matter is ancillary to proceedings concerning status, in the courts which, according to its own law, has jurisdiction to entertain those proceedings.[43] So, although the defender is domiciled in another contracting state, an action for aliment may be raised in the Scottish courts if the pursuer is domiciled or habitually resident in Scotland; and where a question of aliment arises as an ancillary matter in a Scottish action of divorce, separation, nullity of marriage or custody the Scottish court has jurisdiction to determine it despite the domicile in another contracting state of the person against whom the claim for aliment is directed. In an action for aliment, as in other actions, there may also be jurisdiction by prorogation.[44]

Neither the Act nor the convention contains specific provision for jurisdiction in the revocation or variation of alimentary decrees. In all the contracting states it would be accepted that a court has power to vary or revoke its own decrees as long as it retains jurisdiction to pronounce the decree in question. However, in contrast with the general understanding in the United Kingdom, the law of most of the contracting states seems to be that if jurisdiction to pronounce a decree is lost the power to vary or revoke it is lost at the same time, and the convention is probably to be interpreted to that effect.[45] For the alimentary creditor there is little problem; if he seeks to vary the decree he merely follows the jurisdictional rules which the convention supplies and which he can readily invoke. The position of the alimentary debtor seeking variation or revocation is more problematic. It has been suggested that if the court which pronounced the decree is no longer seised of jurisdiction the only courts to which he can go are those of the domicile of the alimentary creditor.[46] The habitual residence of the alimentary creditor is, it is submitted, available as an alternative, provided always he is domiciled in a contracting state, but, with that exception, the alimentary debtor is driven back to the general principle that jurisdiction rests on the domicile of the person sued in the application under consideration.[47] He cannot rely on his

---

State if, and only if, (a) he is resident in that state and (b) the nature and circumstances of his residence indicate that he has a substantial connection with that State.

[42] *Ibid.*, Sched. 1, art. 2.

[43] *Ibid.*, Sched. 1, art. 5(2).

[44] *Ibid.*, Sched. 1, arts. 17 and 18.

[45] Anton, *Civil Jurisdiction in Scotland*, at pp. 76–77.

[46] *Ibid.*

[47] Civil Jurisdiction and Judgments Act 1982, Sched. 1, art. 2.

own domicile, or habitual residence, as a source of jurisdiction in the way in which the alimentary creditor can. The absence from the convention of any uniform scheme for variation and revocation and the potential jurisdictional conflict which that absence entails are major weaknesses of the convention and so of the Act.

The convention contains a saving provision for any other conventions to which the contracting states are, or will be, parties and which, in relation to particular matters, govern jurisdiction or the recognition or enforcement of judgments.[48] So far as jurisdiction is concerned there are at present no applicable conventions to which the United Kingdom is a party.[49] It should also be noted as applicable to alimentary, as well as to other, proceedings that under the 1968 convention application may be made to the courts of a contracting state for such provisional, including protective, measures as may be available under the law of that state, even if under the convention, the courts of another contracting state have jurisdiction as to the substance of the matter.[50]

Jurisdiction as between Parts of the United Kingdom

In relation to jurisdiction in the United Kingdom the Act follows the general provisions for the allocation of jurisdiction discussed above in relation to the European Community. The 1968 Convention is modified for application within the United Kingdom and is enacted in this modified form in Schedule 4 to the Civil Jurisdiction and Judgments Act 1982. Again the general rule refers to the domicile of the defender (with the special definition of domicile[51] being applied). So it is provided that persons domiciled in a part of the United Kingdom are to be sued in the courts of that part; this applies to proceedings for aliment of children as it does to other civil proceedings.[52] To the general rule there are again a number of exceptions, including one relating to aliment, and it is provided that there is to be jurisdiction in the court for the place where the alimentary creditor (*i.e.* the pursuer) is domiciled or habitually resident, or, if the matter is ancillary to proceedings concerning status, in the court which, according to its own law, has jurisdiction to entertain those proceedings.[53] The rules on allocation of jurisdiction do not, however, apply (a) to proceedings under section 80 of the Social Work (Scotland) Act 1968 (contributions in respect of children in care) or section 81 of that Act (applications for or for variation of affiliation orders in respect of children in care)[54] nor (b) to proceedings brought in pursuance of any statutory provision which either implements an international convention protected by Article 57 of the 1968 Convention, or makes provision with respect to jurisdiction in any field to which such a convention relates, nor to any rule of law so far as it has the effect of implementing any such convention.[55]

---

[48] *Ibid.*, Sched. 1, art. 5(2).
[49] For other conventions that are affected, see Anton and Beaumont, *Private International Law* (2nd ed.), at p. 248.
[50] Civil Jurisdiction and Judgments Act 1982, Sched. 1, art. 24.
[51] See *ante*, at p. 295, note 41.
[52] Civil Jurisdiction and Judgments Act 1982, Sched. 4, art. 2.
[53] *Ibid.*, Sched. 4, art. 5(2).
[54] *Ibid.*, s. 17 and Sched. 5, para. 5(*a*) and (*b*).
[55] *Ibid.*, s. 17 and Sched. 5, para. 6.

There is also a general exception for "any enactment which confers jurisdiction on a Scottish court in respect of a specific subject-matter on specific grounds."[56] The effect of these words is not free from doubt, but it would seem that jurisdictional rules specifically laid down by statute or statutory instrument for actions of aliment remain in force. Some of the jurisdictional provisions of the Maintenance Orders Act 1950 are, however, repealed.[57]

General Rules on Jurisdiction in Scotland

Subject to the rule concerning the allocation of jurisdiction as between the contracting states and also as between the several parts of the United Kingdom the new jurisdictional code for Scotland determines "in what circumstances a person may be sued in civil proceedings in the Court of Session or in the sheriff court."[58] This code applies to persons not otherwise governed by the provisions described above, though the rules in each situation are closely similar. The general rule of the code is that a person is to be sued in the courts for the place where he is domiciled, or, where he has no fixed residence, in a court within whose jurisdiction he has been personally cited, and this applies to alimentary actions as to others.[59] In addition, there is a special rule which, in matters relating to aliment, vests a concurrent[60] jurisdiction in the courts for the place where the alimentary creditor (*i.e.* the pursuer) is domiciled or habitually resident or, if the matter is ancillary to proceedings concerning the status of a person, in the court which has jurisdiction to entertain those proceedings.[61] It is, however, provided that an action for affiliation and aliment is not to be treated as a matter ancillary to proceedings concerning the status of a person.[62] Jurisdiction may be prorogated.[63] Existing rules on variation and recall are preserved[64] with the result that, where this code applies, a court retains power to vary or revoke its own decrees even if it no longer has jurisdiction in respect of the original decree.[65]

The code supersedes previous rules on jurisdiction where questions of aliment were ancillary to actions of divorce, separation or nullity of marriage or to custody orders.[66]

Denial of Jurisdiction under the Child Support Act 1991

A Scottish court that would otherwise have jurisdiction in an action for aliment may have that jurisdiction denied by the provisions of the Child Support

---

[56] *Ibid.*, s. 17(1).

[57] *Ibid.*, Sched. 14.

[58] *Ibid.*, s. 20(1).

[59] *Ibid.*, Sched. 8, paras. 1 and 2(1).

[60] Sched. 8, r. 2 is clearly to the effect that the special jurisdictions are concurrent with that conferred by the general rule, because it states that a person may "also" be sued in certain courts in the special circumstances. *Cf.* the wording in Sched. 1, art. 5 and Sched. 4, art. 5, which, though less clear, also confer a concurrent rather than an exclusive jurisdiction: Anton and Beaumont at p. 547.

[61] *Ibid.*, Sched. 8, para. 2(5).

[62] *Ibid.*, Sched. 8, para. 2(5).

[63] *Ibid.*, Sched. 8, para. 5. And see *British Steel Corporation* v. *Allivane International Ltd.*, 1989 S.L.T. (Sh. Ct.) 57.

[64] *Ibid.*, s. 23(1)(*a*).

[65] *Ante*, p. 297.

[66] For these rules, see *ante* at pp. 236–245.

Act 1991. The main purpose of that Act, as has already been described,[67] is to allow assessments of child support to be made and enforced by a child support officer. Section 8 of the Act provides that whenever a child support officer would have jurisdiction to make a maintenance assessment (which includes circumstances in which the child support officer would not make an assessment[68]), no court shall exercise any power that it would otherwise have to make, vary or revive any maintenance order in relation to the child and the parent concerned.[69] Jurisdiction lies with the child support officer (and thus is denied the court) only when the child or the absent parent or the person with care of the child is habitually resident in Scotland,[70] and only when the child is a "qualifying child."[71]

The purpose of the Act is to ensure that assessment and enforcement of maintenance payments in relation to children of "absent parents" are entirely in the hands of the Child Support Agency set up by the Act and its officers, rather than in the hands of the courts, but its limitations should be recognised. Section 8 does not deny the court jurisdiction in a number of circumstances. First, the court retains jurisdiction whenever the child is not a "qualifying child." This covers the situation when both parents live in the same household with the child. More importantly, when a child has been accepted by a person as a member of his family it can never be a qualifying child in relation to that person.[72] It also covers the situation of the child or young person who is neither under 16 years of age, nor under 19 and receiving full-time education at a recognised educational establishment.[73] Secondly, the Lord Advocate is given the power to provide by order that the court shall not be prevented from exercising any power which it has to make a maintenance order in relation to a child if (a) a written agreement (whether or not enforceable) provides for the making, or securing, by an absent parent of the child of periodic payments to or for the benefit of the child, and (b) the maintenance order which the court makes is, in all material respects, in the same terms as that agreement.[74] If the Lord Advocate exercises this power, it will allow the court to give its imprimatur to alimentary agreements. Thirdly, the court retains jurisdiction if it is satisfied that the circumstances of the case make it appropriate for the absent parent to make a periodical payment under a court order in addition to those payable by him in accordance with the maintenance assessment[75]: this only applies when a maintenance assessment is in force and the alternative formula for assessment under Schedule 1 has been used. Effectively, it allows a top-up to the assessment. Fourthly, the court retains power to make orders requiring a person to meet some or all of the

---

[67] *Ante*, at pp. 293–295.

[68] Child Support Act 1991, s. 8(2).

[69] *Ibid.*, s. 8(1) and (3).

[70] *Ibid.*, s. 44.

[71] *i.e.* if one or both of his parents is or are, in relation to him, an "absent parent": s. 3(1). A parent is an "absent parent" if that parent is not living in the same household with the child and the child has his home with a person who is a person with care: s. 3(2).

[72] Child Support Act 1991, s. 8(10) preserves the court's right to make a maintenance order against a person with care of the child: in Scotland such a person only has an obligation of aliment if he has accepted the child as a member of his family. See *ante* at pp. 279–280.

[73] *Ibid.*, s. 55.

[74] *Ibid.*, s. 8(5).

[75] *Ibid.*, s. 8(6).

educational expenses of a child,[76] or the expenses attributable to a child's disability.[77]

Procedure and Remedies

Actions for aliment present some procedural specialties in addition to those associated with enforcement which are noted later. In the Court of Session when questions of aliment arise in connection with a consistorial action the same procedural rules apply as those already considered with regard to access[78] with the addition that, in the case of a motion relating to the variation or recall of an order for aliment, intimation is to be made by means of recorded delivery and the party making intimation is to lodge in process a copy of the letter of intimation, the post-office receipt of posting, and written evidence of the party's earnings, or, if he or she is not employed, written evidence to that effect. The provisions on variation and recall are, by a separate rule,[79] applied to alimentary decrees generally and not merely to those granted in consistorial causes. An order for aliment made in the Court of Session may be varied or recalled on application to the sheriff court within whose jurisdiction any party on whom the application has to be served resides or has a place of business or whose jurisdiction he has prorogated.[80]

In any sheriff court action of separation or affiliation and aliment or for the custody of a child, a defender who intends only to dispute the amount of aliment claimed may, instead of lodging a notice of intention to defend, lodge a minute condescending on the facts relevant to the amount of aliment.[81] The same procedure is available in actions of divorce and may be used to dispute liability as well as amount and to put in issue any other matter relating to aliment.[82] Moreover in an action of divorce or separation a defender who himself seeks an order for aliment, including aliment sought on behalf of a child, may proceed by way of minute. In that case the minute should include a crave for the order sought.[83] Applications to vary or recall an award of aliment follow the same procedure as already considered in relation to sheriff court processes for custody and access.[84]

An application to the Court of Session for variation or termination of an agreement on aliment is made by summons and it is open to a party to apply for interim variation pending determination of the action.[85] In any sheriff court action in which an alimentary crave is competent (whether or not it is made) a party who seeks an order for the variation or termination of an alimentary agreement may do so either in the initial writ or by separate minute.[86] In any other cir-

---

[76] *Ibid.*, s. 8(7).

[77] *Ibid.*, s. 8(8).

[78] See Chap. 9, *ante*.

[79] Rule of Court 170.

[80] Law Reform (Miscellaneous Provisions) (Scotland) Act 1966, s. 8. See *McGuire* v. *McGuire*, 1987 S.C.L.R. 378 (in relation to access).

[81] O.C.R. 34(1).

[82] *Ibid.*, 34(2).

[83] *Ibid.*, 34(3).

[84] O.C.R. 129, *ante* at pp. 246–247.

[85] R.C. 170R.

[86] O.C.R. 132 A(1).

cumstances procedure for variation or termination of such an agreement is by way of summary application.[87] There is, in contrast with the Court of Session, no express provision for interim variation.

A claim for aliment only (whether or not expenses are also sought) may be made in the Court of Session or the sheriff court.[88] Summary cause procedure may be used where the amount of aliment sought for a child does not exceed £35 per week.[89] Otherwise procedure in the sheriff court is ordinary cause. Unless the court considers it inappropriate in any particular case a claim for aliment may also be made in proceedings:

(a) for divorce, separation, declarator of marriage, or declarator of nullity of marriage,
(b) relating to orders for financial provision,
(c) concerning rights and obligations in relation to children,
(d) concerning parentage or legitimacy;
(e) of any other kind where the court considers it appropriate to include a claim for aliment.[90]

An action for aliment of a child may be brought (a) by the child himself, (b) by the curator *bonis* of an incapax child,[91] (c) on behalf of a child under 18 by the parent or guardian of the child or by a person entitled to, seeking, or having custody or care of the child.[92] A woman, whether married or not, may bring an action for aliment on behalf of her unborn child as if the child had been born, but no such action can be heard or disposed of before the birth of the child.[93] Any person qualified to bring an action for aliment of a child may give a good receipt for aliment paid under the decree in the action.[94]

Where a person for, or on behalf of, whom aliment is claimed is living in the same household as the defender it is a defence to the action that the defender is fulfilling the obligation of aliment and intends to continue doing so.[95] And, as already noticed, it is a defence to an action for aliment by, or on behalf of, a person other than a child under the age of 16 years that the defender is making an offer which it is reasonable to expect the person concerned to accept to receive that person into his household and to fulfil the obligation of aliment.[96] In considering whether it is reasonable to expect a person to accept such an offer the court is, however, to have regard among other things to any conduct, decree or other circumstances which appear to the court to be relevant.[97]

---

[87] *Ibid.*, 132 A(2).
[88] Family Law (Scotland) Act 1985, s. 2(1).
[89] Sheriff Courts (Civil Jurisdiction and Procedure) (Scotland) Act 1963, s. 3. Applications for variation or recall must, it seems, be by summons (Summary Cause Rule 79) but Macphail suggests (*Sheriff Court Practice*, paras. 25–32) that procedure by minute may also be open. Interim orders may be granted (Rule 79(2)).
[90] *Ibid.*, s. 2(2).
[91] On curators *bonis* of children, see *ante* at pp. 404–406.
[92] *Ibid.*, s. 2(4), as amended by the Age of Legal Capacity (Scotland) Act 1991, Sched. 1, para. 40 and Sched. 2.
[93] *Ibid.*, s. 2(5). And see *ante* at pp. 94–95.
[94] *Ibid.*, s. 2(10).
[95] *Ibid.*, s. 2(6) and (7).
[96] *Ibid.*, s. 2(8).
[97] *Ibid.*, s. 2(9). See also *ante*, at pp. 285–286.

The powers of the court in granting decree in an action for aliment extend to (a) ordering the making of periodical payments whether for a definite or indefinite period or until the happening of a specified event, (b) ordering the making of alimentary payments of an occasional or special nature, including payments in respect of inlying, funeral or educational expenses, (c) the backdating of an award of aliment to the date of the bringing of the action or to such later date as the court thinks fit, or on special cause shown to a date prior to the bringing of the action, and (d) the award of an amount less than that claimed even if the claim is undisputed.[98] There is also provision for awards of interim aliment payable until disposal of the action or until such earlier date as the court specifies, and for the variation or recall, but not the backdating, of such awards.[99]

A decree granted in an action for aliment may, on an application by or on behalf of either party to the action, be varied or recalled if, since the date of the decree, there has been a material change of circumstances. Pending the determination of any such application, the court may make such interim order as it thinks fit and where it backdates an order for variation or recall it may order any sums paid under the decree to be repaid.[1]

INTERNATIONAL ISSUES

Choice of Law

In *Macdonald* v. *Macdonald*[2] it was held that the law of the mother's domicile governed her liability to aliment her son, and in *Rosses* v. *Sinhjee*[3] that a claim for aliment for an illegitimate child depended on the law of England which was the law of the mother's domicile and also, following that, of the child's. The correct principle would seem to be that liability for aliment should be dependent on its being exigible by the proper law of the debt. That will be the law with which the relationship has the closest and most substantial connection. The law of the child's domicile will have a strong, but not a conclusive, claim and the domicile of the person against whom the claim is directed will also be relevant. Where the child himself is not the claimant, the domicile of the parent or other person who seeks payment in respect of the child's aliment is, as such, an adventitious factor which will normally be of no account. There would, however, be a good deal of convenience and probably little risk of injustice in a rule which, without consideration of domicile or other connecting factors, allowed choice of law to follow jurisdiction and so applied Scots law where the Scottish court was competently seised of the case. That consideration has particular force where aliment is ancillary to an action of divorce, separation or nullity of marriage and is followed in the comparable field of financial relief between spouses.[4] The Scottish Law Commission has suggested[5] that this position be put on a statutory basis.

---

[98] *Ibid.*, s. 3.
[99] *Ibid.*, s.6.
[1] s. 5. See further, Nichols at pp. 17–19.
[2] (1846) 8 D. 830.
[3] (1891) 19 R 31.
[4] Divorce (Scotland) Act 1976, s. 5.
[5] Scot. Law Com. No. 135, *Report on Family Law*, May 1992, at para. 18.5 and draft Bill, cl. 43.

Recognition and Enforcement: General

Decrees for payment of aliment for children are, in principle, enforceable in the same way as other decrees for the payment of a debt. Enforcement at common law of foreign decrees (including English and Northern Irish decrees) was, however, obstructed by the rule that only final decrees could be the subject of a decree conform.[6] As alimentary decrees are usually subject to variation or recall, they did not meet that test and so could not be enforced except for arrears and even arrears could not be recovered if they were subject to variation or recall under the foreign decree.[7] The same difficulty did not arise on the face of the Judgments Extension Act 1868 or the Inferior Courts Judgments Extension Act 1882,[8] which provided an improved means of enforcement of judgments for debt within the United Kingdom but these Acts were not much used for the enforcement of alimentary decrees, perhaps because it was thought that a restriction as to finality should be implied, and it was not until 1950 that, by the Maintenance Orders Act of that year, procedures were supplied specifically adapted to the enforcement of alimentary decrees within the United Kingdom. Today, alimentary decrees from outwith the United Kingdom are recognised and enforced here, and Scottish alimentary decrees are recognised and enforced outside the United Kingdom, in accordance with a number of different régimes, depending upon whether the other country is (i) a member state of the European Community, i.e. a "contracting state" for the purposes of the Civil Jurisdiction and Judgments Act 1982, (ii) one of a number of Commonwealth and ex-Commonwealth states and thus a "reciprocating country" for the purposes of Part I of the Maintenance Orders (Reciprocal Enforcement) Act 1972, (iii) one of a number of foreign and Commonwealth countries that is a "convention country" for the purposes of Part II of the 1972 Act, or (iv) another country with which the United Kingdom has entered into a bilateral agreement under Part III of the 1972 Act. In relation to countries subject to none of these régimes, the common law or the procedures under the Administration of Justice Act 1920 or the Foreign Courts (Reciprocal Enforcement) Act 1933 remain.[9] Before looking at each of these different statutory régimes, the position within the United Kingdom, governed by the Maintenance Orders Act 1950, will be examined.

Enforcement as between Different Parts of the United Kingdom

The normal means for the enforcement, in one part of the United Kingdom, of judgments of the courts of another part are contained in the Civil Jurisdiction and Judgments Act 1982, but the provisions of that Act do not apply to an order to which section 16 of the Maintenance Orders Act 1950 applies.[10] The result is that the 1950 Act continues to regulate the enforcement, within the United Kingdom, of maintenance orders made by Scottish, English or Northern Irish courts. Also, where an alimentary judgment of a foreign court has been regis-

---

[6] Anton, *Private International Law*, (1st ed.), pp. 586–587; Morris, *Conflict of Laws* (3rd ed.) at p. 224.

[7] Morris, *ibid.*

[8] Both of these statutes were repealed by the Civil Jurisdiction and Judgments Act 1982, Sched. 14.

[9] For a full discussion thereof, see Anton and Beaumont, *Private International Law*, (2nd ed.) at pp. 219–247.

[10] Civil Jurisdiction and Judgments Act 1982, s. 18(5)(a).

tered in the United Kingdom and falls to be treated for the purposes of enforcement as a judgment of a court of law in the United Kingdom, the rules for its enforcement remain those contained in the legislation providing for its registration whether under Part II of the Administration of Justice Act 1920, or Part I of the Foreign Judgments (Reciprocal Enforcement) Act 1933, or Part I of the Maintenance Orders (Reciprocal Enforcement) Act 1972, or section 5 of the 1982 Act itself.[11]

Part II of the Maintenance Orders Act 1950 provides for the enforcement, in parts of the United Kingdom other than that in which the order was made, of maintenance orders made by courts in England and Wales, Scotland, and Northern Ireland.[12] Maintenance order is defined so as to include any decree for payment of aliment for children and similar orders, of an alimentary nature, for payment of weekly or periodic sums, including orders under the Social Work (Scotland) Act 1968 and the Social Security Act 1986 as well as the corresponding English or Northern Irish orders.[13] Procedure is by registration. A maintenance order made in one part of the United Kingdom may be registered in another if it appears that the person liable to make payments under the order resides there and it is convenient that the order should be enforceable there.[14] The decision as to residence and convenience rests with the court that made the order or its prescribed officer and not with the court in which the order was registered.[15] Orders have to be registered with the court of corresponding jurisdiction within which the defender appears to be.[16] There is no discretion to refuse registration.[17] Once registered, the order is enforceable in all respects as if it had been made by the court in which it is registered and as if that court had had jurisdiction to make it.[18] The application for registration should be made to the court by which the order was made.[19] Arrears which have accrued before registration may be recovered if supported by a statutory declaration or an affidavit or by certificate of an officer of the court to, or through whom, payments were required to be made.[20] Variation or discharge of the order remains a matter for the court which made it and not for the court in which it is registered, except that an order registered in the sheriff court or in a magistrate's court may be varied as the court thinks fit in respect of the rate of payments under the order, provided the liability thereby imposed does not exceed any maximum authorised by law in the part of the United Kingdom in which the order was made.[21] Registration may be cancelled on application by, or on behalf of, the person entitled to payment, to the prescribed officer of the court in which the order is registered provided no proceedings for variation are pending; and the person liable to make

---

[11] *Ibid.*, s. 18(7).
[12] Maintenance Orders Act 1950, s. 16(1).
[13] *Ibid.*, s. 16(2), as frequently amended. See also *Tayside Regional Council* v. *Thaw*, 1987 S.L.T. 69.
[14] *Ibid.*, s. 17(2).
[15] *Ibid.*, s. 17(1).
[16] *Ibid.*, s. 17(3).
[17] *Ibid.*, s. 17(4).
[18] *Ibid.*, s. 18.
[19] *Ibid.*, s. 17(1).
[20] *Ibid.*, s. 20.
[21] *Ibid.*, ss. 21 and 22.

payments under the order may apply to the court by which the order was made to have registration cancelled on the ground that he has ceased to reside in the part of the United Kingdom in which the order is registered, and if it appears to that court, or its prescribed officer, that that is so, registration will be cancelled on the sending of a notice to that effect to the registering court.[22] A registered order cannot be enforced otherwise than under the provisions of Part II of the Act and so is unenforceable so long as the registration remains in force in that part of the United Kingdom in which the order was made.[23]

Enforcement as between European Community States

The rules of the Civil Jurisdiction and Judgments Act 1982 on recognition and enforcement within one European Community state of the alimentary judgments of the courts of another[24] afford only a few points of distinction from those applicable to civil judgments generally.[25] An application for enforcement, instead of being, as in the case of other civil judgments, submitted directly to the Court of Session is, in Scotland, to be submitted to the sheriff court on transmission by the Secretary of State.[26] The relevant sheriff court is to be determined by reference to the place of domicile of the person against whom enforcement is sought, or, if he is not domiciled in Scotland, by reference to the place of enforcement.[27] The application is to be determined in the first instance by the sheriff clerk, from whose decision there is an appeal to the court.[28] Where enforcement is authorised to any extent, the order is to that extent to be registered in that court.[29] An order so registered is for the purposes of its enforcement of the same force and effect, the registering court has in relation to its enforcement the same powers, and proceedings with respect to its enforcement may be taken, as if it had been originally made by the registering court.[30] Corresponding procedures are available for the enforcement of Scottish alimentary decrees in other contracting states.[31]

The 1982 Act applies only to recognition and enforcement in the United Kingdom of the judgments of the courts of contracting states.[32] In such cases it supersedes all rules of law inconsistent with it except where Article 57 has the effect of permitting their continued application. Article 57 provides that the convention shall not affect any other convention to which the contracting states are parties and which, in relation to a particular matter, governs jurisdiction or the recognition or enforcement of judgments. It is of more consequence in questions of recognition and enforcement than it is in jurisdiction. Accordingly,

---

[22] *Ibid.*, s. 24.

[23] *Ibid.*, s. 18(6).

[24] Civil Jurisdiction and Judgments Act 1982, s. 5.

[25] *Ibid.*, s. 4, and 1968 Convention, as set out in Sched. 1.

[26] *Ibid.*, s. 5(1) and art. 32 of the Convention.

[27] *Ibid.*

[28] *Ibid.*, s. 5(2) and Arts. 37 and 40. There is a single further appeal to the Inner House of the Court of Session on a point of law (s. 6(3)).

[29] *Ibid.*, s. 5(3).

[30] *Ibid.*, s. 5(4).

[31] Title III of the Convention (set out in Sched. 1). This raises no question of Scots Law as the procedure is governed by the law of the State in which enforcement is sought (Art. 33).

[32] *Ibid.*, s. 2(1) and Arts. 25, 26 and 31.

where means of recognition and enforcement of alimentary judgments is afforded by United Kingdom legislation referable to an international convention, these means remain available in addition to those provided by the 1982 Act and the 1968 Convention. Procedures under the Reciprocal Enforcement of Maintenance Orders (Hague Convention Countries) Order 1993[33] and under the Reciprocal Enforcement of Maintenance Orders (Republic of Ireland) Order 1993[34] are therefore available in cases to which they apply as alternatives at the option of the party seeking enforcement.[35]

Enforcement as between "Reciprocating Countries"

Part I of the Maintenance Orders (Reciprocal Enforcement) Act 1972[36] provides, on a reciprocal basis, for the enforcement in the United Kingdom of maintenance orders made by courts in foreign or Commonwealth countries,[37] and for the enforcement in these countries of orders made by courts in the United Kingdom. It is the main means for such enforcement except that for the enforcement in the United Kingdom of judgments of courts of Member States of the European Community it is largely superseded by the Civil Jurisdiction and Judgments Act 1982, and procedures available under the 1968 Convention will be the usual vehicle for enforcement of Scottish decrees in these countries.[38] Procedures under the Administration of Justice Act 1920 or the Foreign Judgments (Reciprocal Enforcement) Act 1933 or at common law remain as alternatives to the extent that they are applicable to alimentary decrees but will seldom be appropriate where the 1972 Act applies.

For the purposes of the Act, a maintenance order is an order that provides for the periodic payment of sums of money towards the maintenance of anyone whom the payer (the person liable to make payments under the order) is liable to maintain according to the law of the place where the order was made.[39] It therefore comprehends all decrees for payment of aliment for children. In the case of affiliation orders it includes an order for the payment, by the father, of expenses incidental to the child's birth, or, where the child has died, of his funeral expenses.[40] The procedures which the Act provides are available only between the United Kingdom and reciprocating countries or territories as designated by Or-

---

[33] *Post* at pp. 319–321.

[34] *Post* at pp. 318–319.

[35] On the relative priorities between the provisions contained in the 1982 Act and those contained in the other provisions, see Anton and Beaumont, *Private International Law* (2nd ed.), at pp. 562–563.

[36] An outline of the Act is given in the following pages. For a more detailed discussion the reader is referred to Clive, *Husband and Wife*, (3rd ed.) at pp. 191–221, and Anton and Beaumont at pp. 551–555. See also *Enc.* 8, 578–581.

[37] For a list of the countries covered, see *Enc.* 8, 578. All are either Commonwealth or ex-Commonwealth countries.

[38] No Member State of the European Community is, in fact, a reciprocating country for the purposes of the Act, but some (France, Ireland, Italy, Luxembourg, the Netherlands and Portugal) participate in reciprocal arrangements to which a modified version of the Act applies under the Reciprocal Enforcement of Maintenance Orders (Republic of Ireland) Order 1974 and the Reciprocal Enforcement of Maintenance Orders (Hague Convention Countries) Order 1979. See *post* at pp. 318–321.

[39] Maintenance Orders (Reciprocal Enforcement) Act 1972, s. 21.

[40] *Ibid.*

der in Council.[41] A country may be designated either as regards maintenance orders generally or as regards a specified class or classes of orders and is to be regarded as a reciprocating country only as regards orders of the class to which the designation extends.[42]

Two forms of procedure are laid down by the Act. The first is for the transmission for the purposes of enforcement in a reciprocating country of a maintenance order made by a court in the United Kingdom and for registration in the United Kingdom of such orders made by courts in reciprocating countries. The second form provides for the making of provisional orders in the United Kingdom with a view to their confirmation and enforcement in reciprocating countries and for the confirmation and registration in the United Kingdom of provisional orders made in reciprocating countries. It will be convenient to consider the operation of these procedures in relation to (1) the enforcement in reciprocating countries of Scottish decrees, and (2) the enforcement in this country of orders made in reciprocating countries.

Transmission of Scottish Maintenance Orders

Where the person liable for payment under a Scottish alimentary decree or other maintenance order is residing in a reciprocating country, the payee may apply for the order to be sent to that country for enforcement.[43] This procedure does not apply in relation to a provisional order or to an order made under Part II of the Act.[44] The application is to be made to the Deputy Principal Clerk of Session in the case of a Court of Session order, or, in the case of a sheriff court order, to the sheriff clerk of the court which made the order who, if satisfied that the payer is residing in a reciprocating country, is to send to the Secretary of State (a) a certified copy of the order, (b) a certificate that the order is enforceable in the United Kingdom, (c) a certificate of arrears, (d) a statement giving information as to the whereabouts of the payer, (e) a statement for facilitating the identification of the payer, and (f) where available, a photograph of the payer.[45] The Secretary of State is then to transmit these documents to the responsible authority in the reciprocating country if he is satisfied that the statement relating to the whereabouts of the payer gives sufficient information to justify that being done. It should then be possible for the order to be enforced in the reciprocating country under provisions of its laws similar to those under which corresponding orders of its courts are enforceable in this country.

Transmission of Scottish Provisional Orders

The direct method of transmission just described enables a Scottish decree to be enforced abroad without further judicial process. Procedure by way of provisional order, on the other hand, contemplates a judicial act of confirmation in the foreign jurisdiction. If, in any action, (a) the sheriff has jurisdiction by virtue of the domicile or habitual residence of the maintenance creditor in the sher-

---

[41] *Ibid.*, s. 1(1). For a list of reciprocating countries, see *Enc.* 8, 578.

[42] *Ibid.*, s. 1(2).

[43] *Ibid.*, s. 2(1).

[44] For which, see *post* at pp. 315–317.

[45] Act of Sederunt (Maintenance Orders (Reciprocal Enforcement) Act 1972 Rules) 1974 (S.I. 1974 No. 939).

iffdom or because the question of maintenance is ancillary to proceedings concerning status, and (b) the defender resides in a reciprocating country, any maintenance order granted by the sheriff is a provisional order.[46] There is no corresponding provision for Court of Session alimentary decrees. Where the sheriff has no power to make an order for aliment, unless he also makes an order for custody, the pursuer is to be deemed, for the purpose of enabling the sheriff to make the order for aliment, to be a person to whom the custody of the child has been committed by a decree of the sheriff which is, for the time being, in force.[47] An action in which a provisional order is sought may commence and proceed without the necessity of citation of any person and so without notice to the payer.[48] No decree can, however, be granted unless the grounds of action have been substantiated by sufficient evidence and the evidence is to be recorded even if the action is a summary cause.[49] The sheriff's power of remit to the Court of Session is excluded.[50]

Where a provisional order is made, the sheriff clerk must send to the Secretary of State (a) a certified copy of the order, (b) a document setting out, or summarising, the evidence given in the proceedings, (c) a certificate of the grounds on which the making of the order might have been opposed by the payer, (d) a statement of such information as was available to the court as to the whereabouts of the payer, (e) a statement of such information as the sheriff clerk possesses for facilitating the identification of the payer, and (f) where available, a photograph of the payer.[51] The Secretary of State is then to transmit these documents to the responsible authority in the reciprocating country in which the payer is residing if he is satisfied that the statement relating to the payer's whereabouts gives sufficient information to justify that being done.[52] The order will then be subject to confirmation procedure in the reciprocating country and, if confirmed by a competent court, is to be treated for all purposes as if it had never been provisional and had been made by the sheriff in the form in which it is confirmed.[53]

Enforcement, Variation and Revocation of Scottish Orders

So far as the Scottish courts' power of enforcement, variation or revocation of Scottish orders is concerned, it is immaterial whether the order sent to the reciprocating country is a plenary or a provisional order. Whichever procedure has been used, transmission of any subsequent process to the reciprocating country does not affect the powers of United Kingdom courts to enforce or revoke or vary the order.[54] As long, however, as the payer is residing in a reciprocating country, a provisional order is the only means by which the court can, on the application of the payee, vary the order by increasing the rate of the pay-

---

[46] Maintenance Orders (Reciprocal Enforcement) Act 1972, s. 4(1) as substituted by the Civil Jurisdiction and Judgments Act 1982, Sched. 12, Pt. II, para. 3(1).

[47] *Ibid.*, s. 4(3).

[48] *Ibid.*, s. 4(4)(*a*).

[49] *Ibid.*, s. 4(4)(*b*).

[50] *Ibid.*, s. 4(5).

[51] *Ibid.*, ss. 3(5) and 4(6) and S.I. 1974 No. 939.

[52] *Ibid.*

[53] *Ibid.*, s. 3(6).

[54] *Ibid.*, ss. 2(5) and 3(6).

ments thereunder. The Act also envisages extensive scope for the use of provisional orders by a court in a reciprocating country for varying or revoking Scottish maintenance orders. Indeed it is to be anticipated that, except in certain prescribed and very limited circumstances[55] revocation or variation of a Scottish maintenance order by a foreign court will always be by means of a provisional order. Where a certified copy of such provisional order, together with a document setting out or summarising the evidence given in the proceedings in which the provisional order was made, is received by the Scottish court which made the maintenance order, that court may confirm or refuse to confirm the provisional order.[56] If the provisional order relates to variation the Scottish court may confirm it with such alterations as it thinks reasonable. Confirmation must be preceded by intimation to the payee that the provisional order has been received and that unless appearance is entered within the prescribed period it will be confirmed.[57] Variation, whether by a foreign or a United Kingdom court, is effective from the date on which the varying order is made and, where the varying order is a provisional order which has been confirmed, it has effect as if it had been made in the form in which it was confirmed and had never been a provisional order.[58] It seems that the confirmed order takes effect retroactively from the date on which the provisional order was made.

The provisions on the effect of revocation are similar to those on variation. The maintenance order is deemed to have ceased to have effect as from the date on which the revoking order was made, but this is subject to the exception that arrears due under the maintenance order at the date of revocation remain exigible.[59] Where revocation is by means of a provisional order made by a foreign court and confirmed by a court in the United Kingdom, it seems that revocation takes effect from the date on which the provisional order was made.

A provisional order is not appropriate to the revocation by a United Kingdom court of a Scottish maintenance order. A United Kingdom court which has power to vary a Scottish maintenance order may, however, do so by provisional order and is required to do so where the rate of payment under the maintenance order is increased.[60] Where a United Kingdom court makes a provisional order varying a maintenance order the prescribed officer of the court must send to the court in a reciprocating country having power to confirm the provisional order, a certified copy of that order, together with a document setting out or summarising the evidence given in the proceedings.[61] It is not necessary for the payee to intimate to any person the making by him of an application for such a provisional order varying the maintenance order by increasing the rate of payments[62] and, *a fortiori* of that, intimation must be unnecessary where the rate of payment is not to be increased.

---

[55] Such as apply under s. 9(2) and (3) to the variation or revocation by a Scottish court of a maintenance order made by a court in a reciprocating country.

[56] *Ibid.*, s. 5(5).

[57] *Ibid.*, s. 5(6).

[58] *Ibid.*, s. 5(7).

[59] *Ibid.*, s. 5(8).

[60] *Ibid.*, s. 5(2) and (3).

[61] *Ibid.*, s. 5(4).

[62] *Ibid.*, s. 5(3A).

Registration of Foreign Orders

Enforcement in Scotland of maintenance orders made in reciprocating countries depends on registration. Where a certified copy of the foreign order is received by the Secretary of State and it appears to him that the payer under the order is residing or has assets in Scotland, he is to send the copy of the order to the sheriff clerk of the court within whose jurisdiction the payer is residing.[63] The sheriff clerk is then to take such steps as he thinks fit for the purpose of ascertaining whether the payer is residing or has assets within the court's jurisdiction.[64] If after taking these steps he is satisfied that the payer is not so residing and has no assets within the jurisdiction of the court, he is to return the certified copy of the order to the Secretary of State with a statement giving such information as he possesses as to the whereabouts of the payer. In any other case he must register the order.[65] A maintenance order for the purpose of these provisions includes a provisional order which has been confirmed by a court in another reciprocating country, but not an unconfirmed provisional order.[66]

Confirmation and Registration of Foreign Provisional Orders

Where the Secretary of State receives a certified copy of a provisional order made by a court in a reciprocating country together with (a) a document setting out or summarising the evidence given in the proceedings in which the order was made and (b) a statement of the grounds on which the making of the order might have been opposed by the payer, he is, if it appears to him that the payer is residing in Scotland, to send the copy of the order and accompanying documents to the sheriff clerk of the court within whose jurisdiction the payer is residing.[67] The sheriff clerk must then intimate to the payer that the order has been received and will be confirmed unless appearance is entered within the prescribed period.[68] If such intimation cannot be given, the sheriff clerk is to return the copy order and accompanying documents to the Secretary of State with a statement giving such information as he possesses as to the whereabouts of the payer.[69] If the case proceeds the sheriff is to apply with respect to sufficiency of evidence the law in force in the country in which the order was made[70] and the statement received from the foreign court of the grounds on which the making of the order might have been opposed by the payer is to be conclusive evidence

---

[63] *Ibid.*, s. 6(2), as amended by the Civil Jurisdiction and Judgments Act 1982, Sched. 11, para. 10.
[64] *Ibid.*, s. 6(4), as similarly amended.
[65] *Ibid.*, s. 6(3).
[66] *Ibid.*, s. 6(1).
[67] *Ibid.*, s. 7(1) and (2).
[68] *Ibid.*, s. 7(4) (as applied to Scotland by s. 7(7)).
[69] *Ibid.*, s. 7(6).
[70] *Ibid.*, s. 7(7). The Act is silent on how the foreign law on sufficiency of evidence is to be ascertained. A remit under s. 14(5) to the foreign court may be competent but otherwise the foreign law must be proved by evidence. Either expedient seems unnecessarily burdensome but if the presumption that the foreign law is the same as Scots law is applied, the statutory provision is deprived of much of its force. In any event it is extremely unlikely that the foreign law makes the requirement of corroboration previously made by Scots law and, indeed, the contrary may, with safety, be presumed. In *Killen* v. *Killen*, 1981 S.L.T. (Sh. Ct.) 77 Sheriff Macphail took judicial notice (at p. 82) that "a general rule of law requiring corroboration in civil actions is peculiar to the laws of Scotland and, perhaps, Portugal," and it is submitted that that was a sound course. On the other hand, foreign systems may have requirements for proof unknown to Scots law and the statute clearly envisages that they should be ascertained and applied.

that the payer might have raised a defence on any of these grounds.[71] If the payer appears and establishes any such defence as he might have raised in proceedings in which the order was made, the court must refuse to confirm the order.[72] In any other case it must confirm the order either without alteration or with such alterations as it thinks reasonable. If the order is confirmed the sheriff clerk is to register the order in the Maintenance Orders (Reciprocal Enforcement) Act 1972 Register kept by him for that purpose.[73] If the court refuses to confirm the order he is to return the certified copy order and the accompanying documents to the Secretary of State.

Enforcement of Foreign Registered Orders

A foreign order registered under the Act may be enforced in the United Kingdom as if it had been made by the registering court and as if that court had had jurisdiction to make it; and proceedings for or with respect to the enforcement of the order may be taken accordingly.[74] In any enforcement proceedings a certificate of arrears sent to the sheriff clerk is sufficient evidence of the facts stated therein.[75] Sums payable under the order are payable from the date on which the order was made, except that the court confirming a provisional order may direct that the sums payable under it shall be deemed to have been payable from such date, being a date later than the date on which the order was made, as it may specify.[76] Subject to any such direction, a provisional order which has been confirmed shall be treated as if it had been made in the form in which it was confirmed and as if it had never been a provisional order.

Variation or Revocation of Foreign Registered Orders

The registering court has like power to vary or revoke a registered order as if it had itself made and had had jurisdiction to make the order.[77] It may do so on the application of the payer or payee. Variation must be by a provisional order unless:

    (a) Both the payer and the payee are for the time being resident in the United Kingdom, or

    (b) the application is made by the payee, or

    (c) the courts in the country in which the order was made do not have power according to their own law to confirm provisional orders varying maintenance orders and the variation (i) consists in a reduction of the rate of payment and (ii) is made solely on the grounds that there has been a change in the financial circumstances of the payer since the order was made or, in the case of a provisional order, since it was confirmed.[78]

---

[71] *Ibid.*, s. 7(3).

[72] *Ibid.*, s. 7(2).

[73] *Ibid.*, s. 7(5); S.I. 1974 No. 939, Act of Sederunt (Maintenance Orders (Reciprocal Enforcement) Act 1972 Rules 1974, para. 13.

[74] *Ibid.*, s. 8(1).

[75] *Ibid.*, s. 8(6).

[76] *Ibid.*, s. 8(7) and (8).

[77] *Ibid.*, s. 9(1).

[78] *Ibid.*, s. 9(2).

Revocation must be by provisional order unless both the payer and the payee are for the time being residing in the United Kingdom.[79] The registering court cannot vary or revoke a registered order if neither the payer nor the payee is resident in the United Kingdom.[80]

It is unnecessary for the payer to intimate to anyone the making by him of an application for a provisional order varying or revoking a registered order.[81] Intimation would seem to be necessary in the limited classes of case in which variation or revocation can be otherwise than by a provisional order. The law to be applied to the revocation of a registered order is the law applied by the reciprocating country in which the order was made (which may not necessarily be the law of that country[82]). That law need not, however, be applied where both the payer and the payee are for the time being residing in the United Kingdom and in such a case it would seem that Scots law can be applied if the order is registered in a Scottish court. Where a foreign law has to be applied the court may make a provisional order if it has reason to believe that the ground on which the application is made is a ground on which the order could be revoked according to the law applied by the reciprocating country, notwithstanding that it has not been established that it is such a ground.[83] The Act is silent on the law to be applied to an application for variation. The law applied by the reciprocating country would seem to be the appropriate law, but Scots law may be applied on the view that if it differs from that law, the necessary adjustment can, in the case of a provisional order, be made by the foreign court in deciding on confirmation.[84] Where the registering court makes a provisional order varying or revoking a registered order the sheriff clerk must send to the court that made the registered order a certified copy of the provisional order together with the document setting out or summarising the evidence given in the proceedings.[85]

The initiative in the variation or revocation of the registered order need not always be taken in the country in which the order is registered. It may often be taken, particularly at the instance of the payee, in the courts of the country in which the order was made.[86] In some cases of variation the foreign court will proceed by way of a provisional order, a certified copy of which will be transmitted to the registering court together with a document setting out or summarising the evidence given in the proceedings in which the provisional order was made.[87] On receipt of the certified copy the sheriff clerk must intimate to the payer that the provisional order has been received and will be confirmed unless appearance is entered within the prescribed period. The court may thereafter (i)

---

[79] *Ibid.*, s. 9(3).

[80] *Ibid.*, s. 9(1B).

[81] *Ibid.*, s. 9(4A).

[82] *Ibid.*, s. 9(4). By virtue of the international private law rules of the reciprocating country the law applied by the courts for that country may be a system other than the domestic law of the forum.

[83] *Ibid.*

[84] In the limited circumstances in which a registered order can be varied otherwise than by a provisional order, it seems that the law of Scotland should be applied.

[85] *Ibid.*, s. 9(5).

[86] *Ibid.*, s. 9(6).

[87] *Ibid.*, s. 9(7).

confirm the order either without alteration or with such alterations as it thinks reasonable, or (ii) refuse to confirm the order.[88]

Where a registered order has been varied by an order (including a provisional order which has been confirmed) made by a Scottish court or by a competent court in a reciprocating country, the registered order is to have effect as varied from the date on which the varying order was made.[89] Where the varying order was a provisional order it is to have effect as if that order had been made in the form in which it was confirmed and as if it had never been a provisional order. Where a registered order has been revoked (a) by an order made by a Scottish court (including a provisional order which has been confirmed by a competent court in a reciprocating country), or (b) by an order made by a competent court in a reciprocating country, the registered order is deemed to have ceased to have effect as from the date on which the revoking order was made with the exception that any arrears due under the registered order at that date remain exigible.[90] The sheriff clerk is to register any order varying a registered order other than a provisional order which is not confirmed.[91]

Cancellation of Registration of Foreign Order

The registration of an order registered in a Scottish court is to be cancelled if (1) the order is revoked by the order of a competent court, or (2) the payer ceases to reside or have assets in Scotland. These two grounds of cancellation require separate consideration.

(1) A registered order is to be cancelled where it is revoked by (a) an order made by the registering court, or (b) a provisional order made by the registering court and confirmed by a court in a reciprocating country, or (c) an order made by a court in a reciprocating country.[92] In the case of (b) and (c) cancellation is effected on receipt by the registering court of notice of confirmation or revocation respectively. Any arrears due at the date of cancellation are effected on receipt by the registering court of notice of confirmation or revocation, respectively. Any arrears due at the date of cancellation continue to be recoverable as if the registration had not been cancelled.

(2) Where the sheriff clerk of the registering court is of the opinion that the payer under a registered order is not residing within the jurisdiction of that court and has no assets within that jurisdiction against which the order can be effectively enforced he is to cancel the registration and send the certified copy of the order to the Secretary of State along with a certificate of arrears signed by him, a statement giving such information as he possesses as to the whereabouts of the payer, and the nature and location of his assets, and any other relevant documents in his possession.[93] If it appears to the Secretary of State on receipt of the certified copy order that the payer is residing or has assets in the United Kingdom he is to transfer the order to the appropriate court by sending the certified copy and related documents to the prescribed officer of that court (in Scotland

---

[88] *Ibid.*, s. 9(6).
[89] *Ibid.*, s. 9(8).
[90] *Ibid.*, s. 9(9).
[91] *Ibid.*, s. 9(10).
[92] *Ibid.*, s. 10(1).
[93] *Ibid.*, s. 10(2) and (7).

the sheriff clerk).[94] The prescribed officer is then to take such steps as he thinks fit for the purpose of ascertaining whether the payer is residing or has assets within the jurisdiction of the court.[95] If he is then satisfied that the payer is not so residing and has no assets within the jurisdiction of the court, he is to return the certified copy order and relevant documents to the Secretary of State, along with a statement giving such information as he possesses as to the whereabouts of the payer.[96] In any other event he must register the order. Where it appears to the Secretary of State on receipt by him of the certified copy of the order, whether from the court in which it was registered or on its being returned from another court to which it was sent by him, that the payer has ceased to reside and has no assets in the United Kingdom, he is to send to the responsible authority in the reciprocating country from which the order was received (a) a certified copy of the order and of any order varying it, (b) a certificate of arrears signed by the prescribed officer, (c) a statement giving such information as the Secretary of State possesses as to the whereabouts of the payer and the nature and location of his assets, and (d) any other relevant documents in his possession.[97] Alternatively, if having regard to all the circumstances he thinks it proper to do so, he may send the certified copy of the order and the other documents to the responsible authority in another reciprocating country. Where the certified copy order and documents are sent to the responsible authority in a country other than that in which the order was made, the Secretary of State is to inform the responsible authority in the country in which the order was made of what he has done.[98]

Appeals

No appeal lies from a provisional order made by a Scottish court,[99] but where a Scottish court confirms or refuses to confirm a provisional order made by a court in a reciprocating country, whether the provisional order was a maintenance order or an order varying or revoking a maintenance order, the payer or payee has the like right of appeal from confirmation or refusal to confirm as he would have if the order were not a provisional order.[1] Where a Scottish court makes or refuses to make an order varying or revoking a maintenance order made by a court of a reciprocating country then, provided the varying or revoking order is not a provisional order, the payer or payee has the right of appeal from the varying or revoking order or from the refusal to make it as he would have if the maintenance order had been made by a Scottish court.[2] These provisions do not affect any right of appeal conferred by any other enactment.[3]

Enforcement after Provisional Revocation

Where the sheriff has made a provisional order revoking a registered main-

---

[94] *Ibid.*, s. 10(5).
[95] *Ibid.*, s. 10(6).
[96] *Ibid.*
[97] *Ibid.*, s. 11(1).
[98] *Ibid.*, s. 11(2).
[99] *Ibid.*, s. 12(1).
[1] *Ibid.*, s. 12(2).
[2] *Ibid.*, s. 12(3).
[3] *Ibid.*, s. 12(4).

tenance order, it is incompetent except with the leave of the sheriff to enforce, whether by diligence or otherwise, the payment of any arrears which accrue after the making of the provisional order.[4] On an application for leave the sheriff may refuse leave or grant it subject to such restrictions and conditions (including conditions as to the allowing of time for payment or the making of payment by instalments) as he thinks appropriate, or remit the payment of the arrears or of any part thereof.[5]

Enforcement as between "Convention Countries"

Part II of the Maintenance Orders (Reciprocal Enforcement) Act 1972 is not concerned with the enforcement of judgments as such but is a method of facilitating the pursuit of actions of aliment where the pursuer is in one country and the defender is in another. It gives effect to the United Nations Convention on the Recovery Abroad of Maintenance Orders 1956[6] and applies as between countries or territories ("convention countries") specified by Order in Council to which that convention extends.[7]

Transmission of Claims to Foreign Countries

An applicant in the United Kingdom who claims to be entitled to recover aliment from a person who is subject to the jurisdiction of a convention country may apply to the Secretary of State to have his claim for recovery of aliment transmitted to that country.[8] Likewise, if he seeks to vary any provision made in a convention country for payment of aliment to him by a person for the time being subject to the jurisdiction of that country, he may apply to the Secretary of State to have his application for variation transmitted to that country.[9] In either case the application is made through the sheriff clerk or sheriff clerk depute of the sheriff court within whose jurisdiction the applicant is residing and he is to assist the applicant in completing an application which will comply with the law applied by the convention country.[10] The application is then sent to the Secretary of State together with such other documents as are required by the law of the convention country and on receipt of the application and documents the Secretary of State is to transmit them to the appropriate authority in the convention country unless he is satisfied that the application is not made in good faith or that it does not comply with the requirements of the law applied by that country.[11] The Secretary of State may in that connection request the sheriff clerk to obtain from the court which he serves specified information relating to the application, and it is the duty of the court to furnish the Secretary of State with that informa-

---

[4] *Ibid.*, s. 20.
[5] *Ibid.*
[6] New York, June 20, 1956 (Cmnd. 6084).
[7] Maintenance Orders (Reciprocal Enforcement) Act 1972, s. 25. For a list of the countries specified by Order in Council, see *Enc.* 8, 582. Pt. II of the Act is applied with a minor procedural modification to many of the states of the United States of America by the Recovery of Maintenance (United States of America) Order 1979 (S.I. 1979 No. 1314) (the states not covered are listed in *Enc.* 8, 583).
[8] *Ibid.*, s. 26(1).
[9] *Ibid.*, s. 26(2).
[10] *Ibid.*, s. 26(3).
[11] *Ibid.*, s. 26(4).

tion.[12] If the application is transmitted to a convention country, it will follow procedures similar to those applicable in this country to applications received from convention countries.

Receipt of Foreign Claims and Registration of Consequent Forms

On receipt from the appropriate authority in a convention country, of an application by a person in that country for the recovery of aliment from another person for the time being resident in Scotland, the Secretary of State is to send the application together with any accompanying documents to the Secretary of the Law Society of Scotland, who is in turn to send the application and documents to a solicitor practising in the sheriff court of the jurisdiction within which the person against whom the claim is directed is residing, or to such other solicitor practising in Scotland as appears to the Secretary to be appropriate, this for the purpose of enabling the solicitor to take such steps on behalf of the applicant as appear to him appropriate.[13] These steps would seem normally to include proceedings for the recovery of aliment, and any order made by the sheriff in such proceedings containing a provision requiring the payment of aliment is to be registered in the Maintenance Orders (Reciprocal Enforcement) Act 1972 Register.[14]

Transfer and Cancellation of Registration

Where the sheriff clerk or sheriff clerk depute of the registering court is of the opinion that the payer under a registered order has ceased to reside in Scotland, he is to send a certified copy of the order and related documents to the Secretary of State unless he is of the opinion that the payer has ceased to reside in the United Kingdom, in which case he is instead to send a notice to that effect to the Secretary of State.[15] On receipt of a certified copy of the order the Secretary of State, if it appears to him that the payer is still residing in the United Kingdom, is to transfer the order to the appropriate court by sending the copy order and related documents to the prescribed officer of that court.[16] The prescribed officer is then to take such steps as he thinks fit for the purpose of ascertaining whether the payer is residing within the jurisdiction of the court.[17] If after taking those steps he is satisfied that the payer is not so residing he is to return the certified copy order and related documents to the Secretary of State, together with a statement giving such information as he possesses as to the whereabouts of the payer.[18] In any other case he must register the order and give notice of registration to the prescribed officer of the court in which immediately before that it was registered and to the Secretary of State.[19] The previous registration is then to be cancelled,[20] and the Secretary of State is to send a copy of the registered order

---

[12] *Ibid.*, s. 26(5).
[13] *Ibid.*, s. 31(1), as amended by the Legal Aid (Scotland) Act 1986, Sched. 3, para. 1.
[14] s. 31(2).
[15] *Ibid.*, s. 32(1).
[16] *Ibid.*, s. 32(3).
[17] *Ibid.*, s. 32(4).
[18] *Ibid.*
[19] *Ibid.*, s. 32(3) and (6).
[20] *Ibid.*, s. 32(7).

and related documents to the Secretary of the Law Society of Scotland for transmission to a solicitor practising in the registering court or to such other solicitor practising in Scotland as appears to the Secretary to be appropriate, this with a view to his taking, on behalf of the person entitled to the payments for which the order provides, such steps as appears to him appropriate to enforce the order.[21]

Enforcement of Registered Order

An order registered in a court other than that by which it was made may be enforced as if it had been made by the registering court and as if that court had had jurisdiction to make it.[22] For the purpose of enforcement a certificate of arrears signed by the prescribed officer of the court in which the order was previously registered is sufficient evidence of the facts stated therein.[23] So long as the order is registered in a Scottish court any provision is of no effect by which payments are required to be made through or to any officer or person on behalf of the person entitled to the payments.[24] Part II of the Maintenance Orders Act 1950 does not apply to an order registered under these provisions.[25]

Variation and Revocation of Registered Order

An order registered in a court other than that by which it was made may be varied or revoked by the registering court as if it had been made by it and as if that court had had jurisdiction to make it; and no other court shall have power to vary or revoke the order.[26] There is a like right of appeal against variation or revocation of a registered order or refusal to vary or revoke as there would be in respect of an order made by the registering court.[27] On revocation the registration is to be cancelled.[28]

On receipt from the appropriate authority in a convention country of an application by a person in that country for variation of a registered order, the Secretary of State is to send the application and accompanying documents to the Secretary of the Law Society of Scotland for transmission to a solicitor practising in the registering court or to such other solicitor practising in Scotland as appears to the Secretary to be appropriate, this with a view to the solicitor's taking on behalf of the applicant such steps as appear to him appropriate.[29]

Arrangements with the Republic of Ireland and Hague Convention Countries

Part III of the Maintenance Orders (Reciprocal Enforcement) Act 1972 envisages the United Kingdom entering into bilateral agreements with other countries not otherwise covered, for the reciprocal recognition and enforcement of maintenance orders.[30] In pursuance of this, such agreements have been entered

---

[21] *Ibid.*, s. 32(7A), as inserted by the Legal Aid (Scotland) Act 1986, Sched. 3, para. 1(2).
[22] *Ibid.*, s. 33(1).
[23] *Ibid.*, s. 33(5).
[24] *Ibid.*, s. 32(7B), as inserted by the Legal Aid (Scotland) Act 1986, Sched. 3, para. 1(2).
[25] *Ibid.*, s. 33(6).
[26] *Ibid.*, s. 34(1).
[27] *Ibid.*, s. 34(4).
[28] *Ibid.*, s. 34(2).
[29] *Ibid.*, s. 34(3), as substituted by the Legal Aid (Scotland) Act 1986, Sched. 3, para. 1(3).
[30] *Ibid.*, s. 40.

into with the Republic of Ireland and with the countries to which the Hague Convention on the Recognition and Enforcement of Decisions Relating to Maintenance Obligations 1973 is in force.[31] In relation to both, a modified version of Part I of the Maintenance Orders (Reciprocal Enforcement) Act 1972 is adopted.[32] There is a certain overlap between the modified provisions and those already discussed, at least in relation to some countries, and parties would seem to be free to choose whichever provisions they prefer to rely upon.

The modifications to Part I of the Act follow a similar pattern in both orders. A central common feature is the absence of any provisional order procedure,[33] with the result that all alimentary decrees to which the orders apply are directly enforceable in the country to which they are transmitted without the necessity of confirmation, or, subject to certain safeguards, other judicial process. Despite these similarities it will be convenient to treat the procedures under each order separately. The orders should be read in conjunction with the provisions of Part I of the 1972 Act as described above, since they are both, as already stated, modifications thereof.

Republic of Ireland

The modifications to Part I of the 1972 Act contained in the reciprocal enforcement arrangements with the Republic of Ireland, all of which are related to the absence of provisional order procedure, can be considered under four main headings—(1) jurisdiction, (2) registration, (3) restrictions on enforcement, and (4) variation and revocation. Heading (1) is relevant to the making of orders in Scotland and their transmission to Ireland, while headings (2) and (3) relate to making Irish orders effective in Scotland. Heading (4) is relevant to both Scottish and Irish orders.

(1) *Jurisdiction and Restriction on Granting Decree*

Because of the changes in grounds of jurisdiction introduced by the Civil Jurisdiction and Judgments Act 1982 the extension of sheriff court jurisdiction, for which the 1974 Order provided, is no longer necessary. If, however, it appears that the defender is residing in the Republic of Ireland and the judgment is to be enforceable there, decree cannot be granted unless (a) a copy initial writ and warrant for citation has been sent to the appropriate authority in the Republic of Ireland for service on the defender, (b) a copy initial writ has been served in accordance with the requirements of Irish law in sufficient time to enable the defender to arrange his defence, and (c) the grounds of action have been substantiated by sufficient evidence. The purpose of these provisions and of those noted in heading (2) below is to protect the defender from prejudice as a

---

[31] The relevant countries (as at April 5, 1993) are Germany, Finland, France, Italy, Luxembourg, the Netherlands, Netherlands Antilles, Norway, Portugal, Slovakia, Sweden, Switzerland, the Czech Republic, and Turkey. Agreement has also been entered into with the United States of America, and a modified version of Pt. II of the 1972 Act is in force in relation to most of the states there: see *ante* at p. 315.

[32] See Reciprocal Enforcement of Maintenance Orders (Republic of Ireland) Order 1993 (S.I. 1993 No. 594), and Reciprocal Enforcement of Maintenance Orders (Hague Convention Countries) Order 1993, (S.I. 1993 No. 593).

[33] S.I. 1993 No. 594, Sched. 1, contains references to provisional orders (paras. 2 and 3) but these do not apply to Scotland (para. 19).

result of the absence of any need for the order to be confirmed in the Republic of
Ireland.[34]

(2) *Registration*

Special provisions apply to the registration of an Irish maintenance order in
this country. The order will not be registered (i) if registration is contrary to public policy, (ii) if the payer did not appear in the proceedings in the Republic of
Ireland and was not served in accordance with the law of his place of residence
with notice of the institution of the proceedings in sufficient time to enable him
to arrange for his defence, or (iii) if the order is irreconcilable with a judgment
given in the United Kingdom in proceedings between the same parties. Otherwise the order must be registered. Notice must be given to payer and payee if the
order is registered, and to the payee if it is not registered. If the order is registered the payer may, within one month, apply to the court in which it was registered to set the registration aside. The grounds of challenge of registration are
limited to the three grounds on which registration might have been refused. If
the order is not registered, the payee may within one month apply to the sheriff
to set aside the decision not to register it.[35]

(3) *Restriction on Enforcement*

A registered Irish order is unenforceable for the one month period during
which the payer can apply for registration to be set aside. If an application to set
the order aside is made, the only measures of enforcement that can be taken
against the property of the payer pending a decision on the application are such
as are designed "to protect the interests of the payee."[36] Poinding and arrestment
are, therefore, competent during that time but not sale or furthcoming.

(4) *Variation and Revocation*

The powers of revocation and variation of an order remain exclusively with
the courts of the country in which the order was made. A Scottish order, although transmitted to Ireland, can therefore be varied or revoked by a Scottish
court and proceedings for variation or revocation will not be entertained by an
Irish court. A Scottish court will, however, vary or revoke an order on the application of the pursuer only if the defender has been given notice of the proceedings and had an opportunity to defend.[37] No application for variation or
revocation of an Irish order will be entertained by the Scottish courts.[38]

Hague Convention Countries

The scheme of the Hague Convention Order (S.I. 1993 No. 593) is similar to
that of the Republic of Ireland Order (S.I. 1993 No. 594). The main points of
distinction relate to (1) restrictions on the recognition of certain types of orders,
(2) conditions of registration, and (3) variation and revocation. Under the

---

[34] S.I. 1993 No. 594, Sched. 1, para. 4(4) and Sched. 2, para. 4(4).

[35] *Ibid.*, Sched. 1, para. 6 and Sched. 2, para. 6.

[36] *Ibid.*, Sched. 1, para. 8 and Sched. 2, para. 8.

[37] *Ibid.*, Sched. 1, para. 4(2) and (4) and Sched. 2, para. 4(2) and (4).

[38] *Ibid.*, Sched. 1, para. 9 and Sched. 2, para. 9 provide the sole means of revocation or variation of
Irish orders.

Hague Convention a country which is party to the convention may nonetheless reserve the right not to recognise or enforce a maintenance order (i) in so far as it relates to a period of time after a maintenance creditor attains the age of 21 years or marries (except where he is the spouse of the maintenance debtor), (ii) in favour of collaterals of the payer or persons related by affinity to him, and (iii) not providing for the periodical payment of maintenance. The United Kingdom has reserved the right not to recognise or enforce orders in category (iii) and also orders in category (ii) other than those in favour of a child of the family (for the purposes of the law of England and Wales and Northern Ireland) or of a child of the payee who has been accepted as a child of the family by the maintenance debtor (for the purposes of the law of Scotland). Where a maintenance order made in a Hague Convention country is of a description which that country or the United Kingdom has reserved the right not to recognise or enforce it is not a maintenance order for the purposes of the Hague Convention Order.[39] Accordingly, it cannot be enforced in the United Kingdom under the provisions of the order.

Variation and Revocation

Scottish courts retain power to vary or revoke Scottish alimentary decrees although transmitted to a Hague Convention country. Whether or not the decree can be varied or revoked by a court in that country is a matter for the foreign law but the Hague Convention Order, in contrast with the Republic of Ireland Order, envisages that that can be done.[40] If a Scottish alimentary decree transmitted to a Hague Convention country is varied or revoked by a competent court there it will have an effect in Scotland subject to the variation or, if revoked, will cease to have effect except in relation to arrears.[41]

If an order made in a Hague Convention country, but transmitted to Scotland, is varied or revoked by a court in the country in which it is made the variation order will, on transmission, be registered in Scotland and the original order will have effect subject to the variation. Equally, however, the Scottish court may vary or revoke the order and it has like power to do so on application by either payer or payee as if the order had been made by a Scottish court with jurisdiction to make it. That power can be exercised, however, only if (i) the payer had his habitual residence in the United Kingdom at the time when the proceedings for variation were instituted or (ii) the party against whom the application for variation is directed has prorogated the court's jurisdiction.[42]

Registration

The conditions on which registration of an order made in a Hague Convention country may or must be refused resemble those applicable to Irish orders, but the provisions are more extensive and even where there is a resemblance the resemblance is not exact. Registration may be refused by the sheriff clerk in the following circumstances:

---

[39] S.I. 1993 No. 593, Sched. 2, para. 21(2) and Sched. 3, para. 21(1).
[40] *Ibid.*, Sched. 2, paras. 5(9), (10) and (11) and Sched. 3, paras. 5(9), (10) and (11).
[41] *Ibid.*, paras. 5(9) and (10), *supra.*
[42] *Ibid.*, Sched. 2, para. 9 and Sched. 3, para. 9.

(i) if the court in the Hague Convention country did not have jurisdiction to make the order on any of the prescribed grounds of jurisdiction,

(ii) if registration is manifestly contrary to public policy,

(iii) if the order was obtained by fraud in connection with a matter of procedure,

(iv) if proceedings between the same parties, and having the same purpose, are pending before a court in Scotland and those proceedings were the first to be instituted, or

(v) if the order is incompatible with an order made in proceedings between the same parties and having the same purpose either in the United Kingdom or another country provided that the latter order itself fulfills the conditions necessary for its registration and enforcement under Part I of the 1972 Act.

In addition the prescribed officer must refuse to register unless (i) the payer appeared in the proceedings in the Hague Convention country in which the order was made or (ii) notice of the institution of the proceedings, including notice of the substance of the claim, was served on him in accordance with the law of that country and having regard to the circumstances he had sufficient time to enable him to defend the proceedings.[43]

Application to Set Registration Aside

The payer has, as under the Republic of Ireland Order, one month in which to apply for registration to be set aside but, in contrast with the Republic of Ireland Order, the payee's application to have refusal to register set aside is subject to the same time limit.[44]

---

[43] *Ibid.*, Sched. 2 para. 6 and Sched. 3 para. 6.
[44] *Ibid.*

CHAPTER 12

EDUCATION OF CHILDREN

Scope of this Chapter

It has long been held to be part of a parent's duty towards a child to provide it with education. Originally, as with other aspects of the parental duty, this attached to the father alone, but now of course it attaches to both parents. At first, this was seen as an aspect of the obligation to maintain the child, for that included an obligation to make the child able to take its place in society and to earn its own living;[1] but today the obligation to educate the child is better seen as an independent parental duty, arising from the common law but governed by statute.[2] The discussion in this chapter is limited to the duty of parents to educate their children, their right to determine the form of the child's education, and the subsidiary duties of local authorities to make provision to allow parents to fulfil their duty and exercise their right. This book is not the place for a comprehensive description of the governance and control of schools, public or private, nor their funding, and these issues are not dealt with except peripherally in so far as they affect the parental obligation.

THE OBLIGATION TO EDUCATE CHILDREN

Statutory Duty of Parents

Under the Education (Scotland) Act 1980,[3] it is the duty of the parent of every child of school age to provide efficient education for him suitable to his age, ability and aptitude, either by causing him to attend a public school regularly or by other means. Subject to certain adjustments by reference to school commencement dates and school leaving dates,[4] a child is of school age if he has at-

---

[1] See Erskine, I, vi, 56. See *ante* at pp. 190–191.

[2] Education (Scotland) Act 1980, to which references in this chapter relate, unless otherwise stated.

[3] s. 30.

[4] s. 31. A child who does not attain the age of five years on a school commencement date is deemed not to have attained that age until the school commencement date next following his fifth birthday (s. 32(3)). A child whose 16th birthday is on or after March 1, but before October 1, in any year is deemed to have attained the age of 16 on the summer leaving date (May 31) in that year, and a child whose 16th birthday is on or after October 1 in any year, but before March 1 in the following year is deemed to have attained the age of 16 on the intervening winter leaving date (the first day of the Christmas holiday period for a pupil in attendance at school and December 21 in any other case) (s. 33). School commencement dates are fixed by the local authority (s. 32(1) and (2)) which must also fix an appropriate latest date on or before which a child must attain the age of five years in order to come within the category of children whom the authority consider of sufficient age to commence attendance at a public primary school (s. 32(4)). Children who are under five at the commencement date but have attained that age by the appropriate latest date may, therefore, be enrolled in a public primary school but will not be subject to the compulsory provisions of the Act until the arrival of the commencement date next following. The period between an appropriate latest date and the next following school commencement date applicable to the same school must not be more than six months and seven days (s. 32(7)).

tained the age of five years and has not attained the age of 16 years. An exemption from the obligation to attend school, so as to enable him to give assistance at home, may however be granted in respect of a child over 14 years of age if, after due inquiry, the education authority are satisfied that by reason of any circumstances existing at his home it would cause exceptional hardship to require him to attend school.[5] The exemption may be on such conditions, if any, as to the amount and manner of further attendance at school until the child reaches the upper limit of the school age as the authority think fit. The exemption is not to extend beyond the date for commencing school attendance next following the date upon which the exemption was granted but it may be renewed. When an exemption is in force the parent of the child cannot be prosecuted or be the subject of any other proceeding under the Act for neglecting to provide for the child's education.[6]

The parent's duty to provide efficient education for his or her child is the primary principle of the Act. The duty laid on the education authority to secure adequate and efficient school education[7] is merely an ancillary means by which the parent's duty can be carried into effect. "Parent" is defined to include guardian and any person who is liable to maintain, or has the actual custody of a child or young person.[8] "Guardian" is not defined but must, it is submitted, mean in this context a person entitled to custody. The duty, it seems, may rest on a person who has accepted his spouse's child as one of the family and is thus "liable to maintain" the child by virtue of the Family Law (Scotland) Act 1985.[9] The duty rests on both parents and it is no defence in the event of failure that the child was in the care of a third party.[10] Equally it would seem to be no defence for either parent that the child was effectively in the care of the other.[11] But the parent's duty is, it is submitted, elided if a custody order is made in favour of someone else, whether the other parent or a third party, because such an order, unless made on special terms, in effect deprives a parent who does not have custody of control of the child's education. A fortiori of that, the parent's duty, of course, lapses in the event of adoption or of the vesting of parental rights and powers in a local authority or voluntary organisation.

Alternatives to State Education

Instead of securing the regular attendance of his child at a public school, a parent is free to perform his duty by "other means."[12] There is no requirement as

---

[5] s. 34.

[6] s. 34(3).

[7] s. 1(1).

[8] s. 135(1).

[9] An obligation to aliment the child is a liability to maintain that child.

[10] *London School Board* v. *Jackson* (1881) 7 Q.B.D. 502. The case was one of failure to comply with an attendance order and may turn on the fact that the parent was the person against whom the order was made, but the principle that liability is not elided by the fact that the child is in the care or actual custody of someone else is capable of wider application.

[11] The view that the mother was not included in the term "parent" where father, mother and child were living together, with the result that liability attached solely to the father (*London County Council* v. *Stansell* (1936) 154 L.T. 241) has been doubted (*Plunkett* v. *Alker* [1954] 1 Q.B. 421) and in any event is difficult to reconcile with the equality of parental rights and powers created by the Guardianship Act 1973 and now the Law Reform (Parent and Child) (Scotland) Act 1986. It does not today represent the law.

[12] s. 30.

to what these means should be. It is enough that they enable the parent to perform his duty. The parent may, therefore, choose to send the child to an independent school or have him attend, or take by correspondence, a variety of courses, or provide tuition for him at home, or indeed proceed in any way he thinks right provided an efficient education suitable to the child's age and aptitude is thereby attained. The generality of these words leaves much to parental discretion. "Efficient instruction in some other manner" (the words used in the Elementary Education Act 1874) was interpreted as meaning "efficient instruction in the subjects of the curriculum approved for elementary schools,"[13] but the standard of state schools, although it may afford a guide, does not determine the matter.[14] For a mother who has no educational qualifications to have her children at home, encouraging them to follow any subject which interests them but without any lessons and without any prescribed course of study, probably does not meet the test,[15] but the lack of structure or formal instruction should not in itself be an objection if it can be shown that it is, in the result, efficient in affording an education suitable to the age, ability and aptitude of the child concerned.

Enforcement of Parental Duty

The method of enforcing the parental duty varies according to whether or not the child has attended a school, called in the Act "public school,"[16] within the state system. Such attendance is the mark of the parent's election to use the state system rather than other means as the way of performing his duty. Beyond that, there is no formal requirement that the parent give notice of his election. Where a child has once attended a public school the child's parent can fail in his duty to provide efficient education suitable to the child's age, ability and aptitude only if thereafter the child does not attend regularly.[17] In such a case the method of enforcement of the parental duty is by proceedings in respect of the parent's failure to secure the child's regular attendance at school.[18] The parent's election to use the state system is not, however, irrevocable. A child may, with the consent of the education authority, be withdrawn from a public school which he has attended and, in that event, the sanctions for failure to secure his regular attendance cease to apply.[19] Moreover, the education authority's consent is not to be withheld unreasonably. In view of the primacy of the parental duty to provide efficient education and the corresponding parental right of choice, it would seem that the authority's withholding of consent would be unreasonable wherever means of providing efficient education outwith the state system were available and the reason for withdrawal was the parent's wish to make use of these

---

[13] *Osborne* v. *Martin* (1927) 138 L.T. 268, *per* Avory J. at p. 269.

[14] *Osborne* v. *Martin, supra*; *Bevan* v. *Shears* [1911] 2 K.B. 936.

[15] *Baker* v. *Earl* [1960] Crim. L.R. 363.

[16] "Public school" is defined as meaning "any school under the management of an education authority": s. 135(1).

[17] This is implicit in s. 37 under which the education authority's powers where they are not satisfied that a parent is providing efficient education arise only where a child of school age has not attended a public school or has attended such a school and has been withdrawn or excluded. In other cases s. 36 applies.

[18] s. 36.

[19] s. 35(1).

means. Where a parent has elected to use such means, but has failed thereby to provide an efficient education, or where a parent has altogether neglected his duty to provide an efficient education, the method of enforcement, whether the child has never attended a public school or has attended such a school and been withdrawn with the consent of the authority, is by attendance order.[20]

Enforcement in Relation to Children at Public Schools

Where a child of school age who has attended a public school on one or more occasions fails, without reasonable excuse, to attend regularly at that school, then, unless the education authority has consented to the withdrawal of the child from the school, the child's parent is guilty of an offence.[21] Where a child has attended more than one public school the school in question would seem to be that which he last attended. Regular attendance connotes attendance in accordance with arrangements lawfully made by the education authority and for the whole time for which these arrangements provide. "A parent is not obliged to avail himself of the free education provided by the state, if he prefers to provide privately for his child's education; but if he does avail himself of it, he must take it as a whole."[22] So a parent is guilty of an offence if his child attends a public school for only part of the time stipulated even if the parent provides education by other means and at other times and the education so provided, when considered along with the child's part-time attendance at a public school or even by itself, is sufficient to amount to efficient education suitable to the child's age, ability and aptitude. Thus, a child may not, unless with the consent of the education authority, be withdrawn for a period during school hours so as to obtain independent instruction in a particular subject.[23] Similarly lateness, at least if more than *de minimis*, may amount to non-attendance and, if persistent, to failure to attend school regularly.[24] A child does not attend school if he is refused admission after being sent in a condition in which it is known that he will not be admitted.[25]

Meaning of Reasonable Excuse

There is deemed to be a reasonable excuse for non-attendance if:

> (a) there is within two miles of the child's home, in the case of a child under eight, and within three miles in the case of any other child, measured in both cases by the nearest available route, no public or other school the

---

[20] s. 37(2). Attendance orders may, however, also be used in the event of a failure of a child to attend a public school regularly (s. 36(2)).

[21] s. 35(1).

[22] *Osborne* v. *Martin, supra, per* Slater J.

[23] *Ibid.*

[24] *Hinchley* v. *Rankin* [1961] 1 All E.R. 692.

[25] *Spiers* v. *Warrington Corporation* [1954] 1 Q.B. 61; *Saunders* v. *Richardson* (1881) 7 Q.B.D. 338; *Fox* v. *Burgess* [1922] 1 K.B. 623. In contrast with the law of England as laid down in *Spiers* v. *Warrington Corporation* it is open to a Scottish court to take account of any circumstances which in its opinion afford a reasonable excuse (s. 42(1)). So, while a child does not attend school if he is refused admission after being sent in a condition in which it is known that he will not be admitted, there may be a reasonable excuse for his non-attendance if it can be shown that for some reason pertaining to the child it was reasonable that he should be sent to school in the condition in which he was sent.

managers of which are willing to receive the child and to provide him with free education, and either (i) no arrangements have been made by the education authority for enabling the child to attend an appropriate school, or for the provision of transport or the payment of travelling expenses, or (ii) any arrangements so made are such as to require the child to walk more than two miles or three miles as the case may be in the course of any journey between his home and school, or

(b) the child is being prevented by sickness from attending school or receiving education,[26] or

(c) there are other circumstances which in the opinion of the education authority or the court afford a reasonable excuse.[27]

Where, however, a child has, in consequence of a placing request,[28] been placed in a school other than a school in which the education authority proposed to place him in accordance with their arrangements, the provisions of the Act relating to walking distance between the child's home and school do not apply—provided that, where the school in which the authority proposed to place the child is more than walking distance from the child's home, the authority offered to make suitable arrangements under which the child would not require to walk more than walking distance to that school.[29]

Apart from the above, the parent will not be guilty of an offence if there are "other circumstances which in the opinion of the education authority or the court afford a reasonable excuse." A wide range of matters may be considered here, but the excuse must be one that affects the child and is reasonable in relation to him. Thus, it has been held to be no defence to a prosecution that an invalid parent reasonably required the services of a child at home.[30] Where, however, an exemption from attendance at school has been granted in respect of a child over 14, to enable the child to give assistance at home, the parent is, in that event, immune from prosecution.[31] Similarly, a *bona fide* and reasonable belief on the part of the parent that the child was attending school when, in fact, he was not, affords no defence.[32] And it has been held that a child's illness, due to his addiction to "glue-sniffing," does not provide a reasonable excuse, notwithstanding that the child rather than the parent was thereby responsible for the

---

[26] This does not include "sickness" which is self-induced as a result of a deliberate course of conduct on the part of the child. "Sickness" as used in the statute means something unavoidable: *Kiely* v. *Lunn*, 1983 S.L.T. 207.

[27] s. 42(1).

[28] See *post* at pp. 337–338.

[29] s. 42(1A), as inserted by the Education (Scotland) Act 1981, s. 2(1).

[30] *Jenkins* v. *Howells* [1949] 2 K.B. 218. The words there under construction were "unavoidable cause" and in *Spiers* v. *Warrington Corporation, supra,* Lord Goddard C.J. who had been a party to the decision in *Jenkins,* said, at p. 68, that it was "a very hard case, but we felt that the statute was too strong; we could not go into the question of reasonableness." The *ratio* of *Jenkins* appears however to be that "unavoidable cause" must be construed in relation to the child and affect the child. The reason for non-attendance given in that case affected, it was held, the mother and not the child. On that reasoning it seems that reasonable excuse too must affect the child and there may be sound policy for that. To open up a consideration of family excuses might by its breadth and uncertainty defeat the purposes of the Act. Certain cases of exceptional hardship are covered by s. 34.

[31] s. 34(3).

[32] *Crump* v. *Gilmore* (1969) 113 Sol.J. 998.

failure to attend.[33] So the offence is treated as one of strict liability in relation to the parent. That view may, however, take too little account of the reservations on the creation of offences of strict liability expressed by the House of Lords in *Sweet* v. *Parsley*[34] in which Lord Diplock said that it was

> "a general principle of construction...that even where the words used...would not in any other context connote the necessity of any particular mental element, they are nevertheless to be read as subject to the implication that a necessary element of the offence is the absence of a belief, held honestly and upon reasonable grounds, in the existence of facts which, if true, would make the act innocent."[35]

There may also be some room for the maxim *impotentia excusat legem* where it is physically impossible for the parent to secure the child's attendance, as in the case of a parent in hospital in a condition in which he is incapable of giving directions for the child's care. But it may be argued against the application of that maxim, and of the doctrine in *Sweet* v. *Parsley*, that criminal liability does not, on the wording of the Act, arise from any act or omission of the parent and so it is irrelevant whether he was incapable of acting or whether his failure to act was based on honest and reasonable belief. On that view liability attaches to the parent on the occurrence of an event, *i.e.* the child's failure to attend school regularly without reasonable excuse, and no connection between the parent and the event need exist. To say that is, however, to ignore the substance of the matter which is that the parent should secure the child's regular attendance. A duty to secure readily falls within the *ratio* of *Sweet* v. *Parsley* and, it is submitted, should not be so construed as to give rise to liability where through no fault of the parent performance by him was impossible.

Effect of Exclusion on Reasonable Excuse

Where a child has been required to discontinue for any period his attendance at a school on account of his parent's refusal or failure to comply with the rules, regulations or disciplinary requirements of the school, he is, unless the court otherwise determines, deemed to have failed without reasonable excuse to attend regularly.[36] The power of the court to determine otherwise appears to open the way to a consideration of the reasonableness of the exclusion and of the rules, regulations or disciplinary requirements in question. Where a child believed to be infested with vermin or in a foul condition has been excluded until examination or cleansing can be carried out,[37] his exclusion constitutes a defence to any proceedings in respect of his failure to attend school on any day on which he is excluded unless it is proved that the issue of the exclusion direction was necessitated by the wilful default of his parent.[38]

---

[33] *Kiely* v. *Lunn*, 1983 S.L.T. 207.
[34] [1970] A.C. 132.
[35] *Ibid.* at p. 163.
[36] s. 35(2).
[37] See *post* at pp. 344–345.
[38] s. 58(6).

Prosecution of Parent

An education authority which considers that a parent has committed an offence in respect of a child's failure to attend school regularly is not, on that account, empowered to take steps forthwith to institute prosecution of the parent. A notice must be served on the parent requiring him, within a specified time, not less than 48 hours nor more than seven days from the service of the notice, to appear with or without the child before the authority and explain the reason for the absence of the child from school.[39] If the parent fails to satisfy the authority that he had a reasonable excuse, the authority may then instruct that he be prosecuted forthwith or may warn the parent and postpone, for a period not exceeding six weeks, a decision on whether to prosecute. In the latter event the authority may make an attendance order requiring the parent to cause the child to attend the public school which he has been attending or, if the child has changed his residence, a school attended by children residing in the same neighbourhood.[40] It is not clear what is gained by the making of an attendance order in these circumstances except that if the child's non-attendance should recur during the period of postponement the parent may be prosecuted for failure to comply with the attendance order as well as for the child's original failure to attend school regularly. The Act is silent about the basis on which a decision as to whether to prosecute is to be taken at the end of the period of postponement: it is however to be supposed that if the child has, in the interval, attended regularly no further proceedings will be taken while if his non-attendance without reasonable excuse has recurred a prosecution will be instituted. Whether or not a prosecution is instituted or a decision thereon postponed the education authority may refer the child to the reporter of the appropriate local authority with a view to the child's referral to a children's hearing.[41] If a prosecution is brought and the court is satisfied that the child has failed without reasonable excuse to attend school regularly, the court may then direct that the case be referred to the reporter.[42] Such a direction may be made whether or not the parent is convicted and, in making the direction, the court must certify the failure as a ground established for the purposes of Part III of the Social Work (Scotland) Act 1968 (i.e. a ground upon which compulsory measures of care may be taken[43]). Alternatively, the court may make an attendance order requiring the parent to cause the child to attend the public school which he has been attending, or, if the child has changed his residence, a school attended by children residing in the same neighbourhood.[44] The onus is on the parent to satisfy the court that there was a reasonable excuse for the child's non-attendance.[45]

Exclusion of Pupil

Regulations provide that an education authority shall not exclude a pupil

---

[39] s. 36(1).
[40] s. 36(2).
[41] s. 36(3).
[42] s. 44(1).
[43] See *post*, Chap. 17.
[44] s. 44(2).
[45] *Buchanan* v. *Price*, 1982 S.C.C.R. 534. See also *Lanarkshire County Clerk* v. *Vincent*, 1976 J.C. 5.

from a school to which he has once been admitted unless they consider that, having regard to the general principle, so far as it is compatible with the provision of suitable instruction and training and the avoidance of unreasonable public expenditure, that pupils are to be educated in accordance with the wishes of their parents:

> (a) the continued attendance of the pupil at the school would be inconsistent with arrangements made by the authority in the exercise of their functions under the Act, or
>
> (b) the parent of the pupil refuses or fails to comply or to allow the pupil to comply with the rules, regulations or disciplinary requirements of the school, or
>
> (c) they cannot otherwise than by exclusion of the pupil ensure the provision of adequate and efficient school education.[46]

The last ground of exclusion does not, it is thought, refer only to the provision of adequate and efficient school education for the pupil in question but comprehends provision of such education for other pupils at the school. It may therefore be used where the presence of a child would cause a hazard to others. The regulations merely prescribe that exclusion is unlawful unless one of the grounds for exclusion is satisfied. They do not lay down that satisfaction of one of these grounds necessarily justifies exclusion. Accordingly, questions of the reasonableness of the authority's actings may remain. There is a further specific statutory ground of exclusion where a medical officer, authorised by the education authority, or a person authorised by him, has reason to believe that the body or clothing of any pupil is infested with vermin or in a foul condition but action for examination or cleansing cannot immediately be taken.[47] In such a case the medical officer, or authorised person, is to advise the authority which may, if they consider it necessary to do so in the interests either of the pupil or of other children in attendance at the school, direct that the pupil be excluded from the school until the examination or cleansing can be carried out.

Review of Exclusion

Where by decision of the education authority a child is excluded from a school under the authority's management which he attends, the child's parent may refer the authority's decision to an appeal committee which may confirm or annul the decision and, if it confirms a decision excluding a child until certain conditions are complied with, may modify the conditions.[48] The decision of the appeal committee and the reasons for it must be notified in writing to the parent and to the education authority. The authority must comply with the decision of the appeal committee. The parent has a right of appeal to the sheriff having jurisdiction where the school is situated. There is no corresponding right of appeal for the education authority against a decision of the appeal committee annulling the authority's decision. The sheriff's powers on hearing and disposing of the

---

[46] Schools General (Scotland) Regulations 1975 (S.I. 1975 No. 1135), reg. 4.

[47] s. 58(6).

[48] s. 28H, as inserted by the Education (Scotland) Act 1981, s. 1(1). Where the pupil is over school age but under 18 he may himself refer the decision to the appeal committee.

appeal are similar to those of the appeal committee. The provisions on the form of application, the time within which it must be lodged, hearing in chambers, expenses and finality of the sheriff's judgment apply to appeals in relation to the exclusion of a child from a school as they apply to appeals to the sheriff in relation to decisions on placing requests.[49] In contrast, however, with cases arising from decisions on placing requests, no criteria are prescribed for deciding appeals whether by the appeal committee or by the sheriff and the matter would seem to be at large for them. Among the matters to be considered, however, must be whether there were grounds for exclusion in terms of the regulations and whether the decision to exclude was reasonable in the circumstances.

Enforcement in Relation to Children outwith the State System

Where a child is not attending a public school the education authority have certain powers and duties designed to ensure that the child receives an efficient education. These powers and duties arise if a child of school age (a) has not attended a public school, or (b) has attended such a school and has been withdrawn with the consent of the education authority, or (c) has attended such a school and has been excluded by the education authority, and in any of these cases the authority are not satisfied that the child's parent is providing efficient education for him suitable to his age, ability and aptitude.[50] The authority must then serve a notice on the parent requiring him, within a specified time not less than seven nor more than 14 days from the service of the notice, either (a) to appear (with or without the child) before the authority and to give such information as the authority may require regarding the means, if any, he has adopted for providing education, or, in the parent's option, (b) to give such information to the authority in writing. If the parent fails to satisfy the authority, either that he is providing efficient education, or that there is a reasonable excuse for his failure to do so, the authority must make an attendance order.[51]

Attendance Orders—General

An attendance order is an order in writing requiring the parent of a child to cause the child to attend the school named in the order.[52] The school need not be a public school but may be any school the managers of which are willing to receive the child. A school at which the parent will be required to pay fees must not, however, be named except at the parent's request and a special school must not be named unless the child has been recorded in the Record of Needs as having pronounced specific or complex special educational needs.[53] Before making an attendance order, the authority must consider any views expressed by the parent as to the school which he desires his child to attend.[54] At that stage the authority is not required to do any more than consider these views and, provided

---

[49] *Post* at p. 338.
[50] s. 37(1).
[51] s. 37(2).
[52] s. 38(1).
[53] s. 38(2). See *post* at pp. 345–351.
[54] s. 38(3).

such consideration is given, does not, it seems, require to justify failure to give them effect. The parent may, however, at any time while the attendance order is in force, apply to the authority requesting that another school be substituted for that named in the order and the authority must amend the order in compliance with that request unless it is of the opinion that the proposed change of school is unreasonable or inexpedient in the interests of the child.[55] It seems also that notwithstanding that an attendance order is in force, a parent may make a placing request.[56] The authority must cause a copy of the attendance order to be served upon the parent and it then becomes the duty of the parent, subject to an appeal to the sheriff, to cause the child to attend regularly at the school named in the order.[57] An appeal to the sheriff may be taken within 14 days and the sheriff, whose decision is final, may confirm, vary or annul the order.[58]

Amendment of Attendance Order by Education Authority

At any time while an attendance order is in force the education authority which made the order may amend it by substituting the name of another school for that named in the order and where a child, in respect of whom an attendance order is in force, moves his residence the education authority of the area to which the child has moved may amend the order by substituting for the name of the school appearing in the order the name of a school attended by children residing in the same neighbourhood as the child.[59] Amendment is effected by a decision of the authority to that effect following service upon the parent of a notice of intention to amend. The parent may, within 14 days of service of the notice, intimate in writing to the authority objections to the proposed amendment and the amendment cannot be made until after the expiry of that period and consideration by the authority of any objections the parent has made.[60] The same restriction as to schools that can be named apply to the amendment of an order as apply to its making. As in the case of the original order, a copy of the amended order must be served on the parent and, thereafter, the parent has a duty to comply with the amended order. The parent has the same right of appeal against the amendment of an order as against its making.

Revocation of Attendance Orders

At any time while an attendance order is in force a parent may apply to the authority by whom the order was made or amended requesting that the order be revoked on the ground that arrangements have been made for the child to receive efficient education suitable to his age, ability and aptitude at a school other than that named in the order, or elsewhere than at a school.[61] On such an application the authority must revoke the order unless they are of the opinion that the arrangements made for the education of the child are not satisfactory. A parent aggrieved by a failure of the authority to reach a decision upon his application

---

[55] s. 39(4).
[56] See *post* at pp. 337–338.
[57] s. 38(4).
[58] s. 38(5).
[59] s. 39(1) and (2).
[60] s. 39(3).
[61] s. 39(4).

within one month, or by the authority's refusal to comply with his request, whether for amendment or revocation, may appeal to the sheriff. The sheriff, on an appeal being made, is to give such direction as he thinks fit.[62]

Duration

An attendance order, unless revoked or annulled, continues in force as long as the child is of school age.[63] If, however, a Record of Needs of a child who had pronounced specific or complex special educational needs falls to be discontinued by virtue of any enactment, any attendance order requiring the attendance of that child at a special school is deemed to be annulled.[63]

Non-Compliance

If an attendance order is in force and is not complied with after a copy has been served on the parent, the parent is guilty of an offence unless he satisfies the court that he has a reasonable excuse.[65] The parent's duty is "to cause the child to attend" the school named in the order.[66] In the event of non-compliance the parent's acts and omissions are, therefore, directly in issue. The question of whether this is an offence of strict liability, noticed earlier in connection with the failure of a child to attend a public school regularly,[67] is again raised and perhaps in sharper form. Reasonable excuse appears in this context to include reasons personal to the parent as well as those directly affecting the child.[68] The fact that an application has been made to the education authority to amend or revoke the attendance order, or that an appeal to the sheriff is pending, is not to be deemed to be a reasonable excuse.[69] Subject to these qualifications, the statutory provisions on reasonable excuse are the same in relation to non-compliance with attendance orders as to failure to attend a public school regularly. Where a public school has been named in the order, the offences of non-compliance with the order and of the child's failure to attend regularly at the school may both arise from the same facts. A prosecution cannot, however, be brought for both offences without contravening the prohibition against double jeopardy. But if the court, before which a prosecution is brought for non-compliance with an attendance order, is satisfied that the child has failed without reasonable excuse to attend regularly at the school named in the order (whether or not a public school) the court may direct that the case be referred to the reporter of the appropriate local authority with a view to the child's being brought before a children's hearing.[70] If the case is so referred, the court is to certify the child's failure as a ground established for the purposes of Part III of the Social Work (Scotland) Act 1968 (*i.e.* a ground upon which compulsory measures of care

---

[62] *Ibid.*
[63] s. 40.
[64] *Ibid.*
[65] s. 41.
[66] s. 38(1).
[67] *Ante*, at p. 327.
[68] What is in issue is whether there is reasonable excuse for the parent's failure to cause the child to attend.
[69] s. 42(2).
[70] s. 44(1).

may be taken[71]). The reference may be made whether or not the parent is convicted.

EDUCATION AUTHORITY'S DUTY

Provision of Education

The UN Convention on the Rights of the Child[72] recognises "the right of the child to education." The United Kingdom fulfils its obligations under this provision by imposing duties to provide education on local authorities. Under the Education (Scotland) Act 1980 it is the duty of every education authority (*i.e.* Regional or Islands Council[73]) to secure that there is made for their area adequate and efficient provision of school education and further education.[74] By school education is meant progressive education appropriate to the requirements of pupils in attendance at institutions for the provision of primary and/or secondary education whether that institution be a public school (*i.e.* a school managed by the education authority) or a self-governing school (*i.e.* a school managed by a board of management incorporated under the Self-Governing Schools Etc. (Scotland) Act 1989), or an independent school (*i.e.* a school which is not a public school, self-governing school or grant-aided school and at which full-time education is provided for five or more pupils of school age) regard being had to the age, ability and aptitude of such pupils. It includes education by special methods appropriate to the requirements of pupils whose physical, intellectual, emotional or social development cannot be adequately promoted by ordinary methods of education ("special education"). It also includes the teaching of Gaelic in Gaelic-speaking areas and nursery education for pupils who are under school age, but although there is a power, there is no duty to provide nursery schools or classes. Further education includes voluntary part-time or full-time courses of instruction for persons over school age, and also various forms of social, cultural and recreative activities and physical training for persons over school age. The word "pupil" where used in the Act means a person of any age for whom education is, or is required to be, provided under the Act[75] and does not, therefore, carry the special meaning previously associated with it in the general law of Scotland.[76] In addition to providing school and further education, every education authority is obliged to provide, for their area, a regional or island authority psychological service in clinics whose function includes (a) the study of children with special educational needs, (b) the giving of advice to parents and teachers as to the appropriate methods of education for such children, (c) in suitable cases the provision of special education for such

---

[71] See *post*, Chap. 17.
[72] (1989) 28 *International Legal Materials* 1448, ratified by the UK, Dec. 16, 1991.
[73] s. 135.
[74] s. 1(1). S. 70 of the Act (as amended by the Self-Governing Schools Etc. (Scotland) Act 1989, Sched. 4, para. 6) provides for complaint to the Secretary of State if a person considers that the education authority or managers of the school or other educational establishment have failed in their duties to provide adequate and efficient education. This provision does not exclude the court's right to hear an application for judicial review of the carrying out of these duties: *Walker* v. *Strathclyde Regional Council (No. 1)*, 1986 S.L.T. 523.
[75] s. 135.
[76] See *ante*, at pp. 52–58.

children in clinics, and (d) the giving of advice regarding the assessment of the needs of any child for the purposes of the Social Work (Scotland) Act 1968 or any other legislation.[77]

It is the duty of an education authority, in the performance of the above functions, to provide for their area sufficient accommodation in public schools, and other educational establishments under their management to enable them to perform these functions.[78] Subject to certain exceptions, school education provided by an education authority is to be provided without payment of fees,[79] and books, writing material, stationery, mathematical instruments, and other articles necessary to enable the pupils to take full advantage of the education provided are to be made available free of charge.[80]

Self-Governing Schools

The existence of self-governing schools in the education authority's area, the boards of management of which have a duty to provide "suitable and efficient school education,"[81] does not detract from the authority's obligation to provide "adequate and efficient school education" in their area, although their duty to maintain the self-governing school is superseded on the incorporation of the board of management by an equivalent duty of the Secretary of State.[82] In carrying out those obligations under the Education (Scotland) Act 1980 owed to all children, whether at a public school or a self-governing school, the education authority are not to distinguish, as regards the benefits or services provided or as regards the terms on which they are provided, between the pupils in the different categories of school.[83]

Religious Observance

It is unlawful for an education authority or the board of management of a self-governing school to discontinue religious observance or the provision of instruction in religion in a public school unless in pursuit of a resolution duly passed by the authority and approved by a majority of the local government electors for the area of the authority voting at a poll taken for that purpose.[84] Every public school, every grant-aided school, and every self-governing school must, however, be open to pupils of all religious denominations.[85] Any pupil may be withdrawn by his parent from any instruction in religious subjects and from any religious observance, and no pupil is to be placed at any disadvantage

---

[77] s. 4.

[78] The functions of the authority are to be carried out in accordance with schemes approved by the Secretary of State (s. 7) and accommodation is to be provided in accordance with such schemes (s. 17).

[79] s. 3.

[80] s. 11(1). The same rule applies for self-governing schools, who must provide the stated items free of charge: Self-Governing Schools Etc. (Scotland) Act 1989, s. 11(3)(a). A self-governing school may, however, charge for articles of clothing provided which are suitable for physical exercise or for any activities of the school for which special clothing is desirable: s. 11(3)(b).

[81] Self-Governing Schools Etc. (Scotland) Act 1989, s. 7(1).

[82] Ibid., s. 1.

[83] Ibid., s. 25(1).

[84] Education (Scotland) Act 1980, s. 8(2).

[85] s. 9.

with respect to secular instruction by reason of the denomination to which the pupil or his parents belong or by reason of his being withdrawn from instruction in religious subjects.[86] An education authority must, if requested to do so by the parent of any pupil who is a boarder at any public school or other educational establishment under the management of the authority or board of management of a self-governing school, make arrangements for affording to the pupil reasonable opportunities for attending worship on Sundays or other days exclusively set apart for religious observance by the religious body to which his parent belongs or for receiving religious instruction or practising religious observance outside the working hours of the school or other establishment.[87] Where a denominational school has been transferred to an education authority, the time set apart for religious instruction or observance must be not less than that set apart according to the use and wont of the former management of the school, and all teachers appointed to the staff must be approved as regards their religious belief and character by representatives of the church or denominational body in whose interest the school has been conducted.[88]

Duty to Have Regard to Parental Wishes

The Education (Scotland) Act 1980 requires the Secretary of State and education authorities, as had previous legislation, to have regard to the general principle that, so far as is compatible with the provision of suitable instruction and training and the avoidance of unreasonable public expenditure, pupils are to be educated in accordance with the wishes of their parents.[89] The provision does not, by itself, oblige either the Secretary of State or an education authority to give parents an opportunity of making representations regarding any proposed exercise of the Secretary of State's or the authority's powers and functions under the Act, but if representations come to their notice they are bound to consider them. It has been said that the corresponding legislation in England and Wales refers, on its true construction, to the wishes of particular parents in respect of their own particular children and not to the wishes of parents generally,[90] but it is submitted that that should not be understood as meaning that where a decision may affect all the school children in a locality, or any large number of school children, it may on account of its generality be made without regard to the wishes of the parents of the children affected. There is no authority in the section for any such restriction nor for restricting its application to questions of curricula, the provision of religious instruction, and whether or not a school should be coeducational.[91] The section bears rather to apply, without qualification, to the exercise and performance by the Secretary of State and the education authorities of their powers and functions under the Act and would seem, therefore, to comprehend all such powers and functions to which the wishes of parents may be relevant. The section does not, however, require that the wishes of parents should receive effect. It only lays down a general principle

---

[86] *Ibid.*
[87] s. 10.
[88] s. 21(2C).
[89] s. 28.
[90] *Wood* v. *Ealing London Borough Council* [1967] Ch. 364, *per* Goff J.
[91] *Ibid.*

to which the Secretary of State and the education authority must have regard,[92] and if they do so, the fact that the education authority comes to a view different from that of the parents does not raise a presumption that the authority disregarded the parent's views.[93] Unless it can be shown that parental wishes were wholly disregarded, or were overborne by some improper consideration, or that the authority paid to the parents' wishes a degree of regard less than any reasonable authority would have paid, it would seem to have little enforceable content. The general principle is to be taken into account so far as is compatible with the provision of suitable instruction and training and the avoidance of unreasonable public expenditure, and there had been some conflict of sheriff court authority on whether these considerations exhausted the matters which it was competent for an education authority to balance against parental wishes.[94] The preponderance of recent decision, supported by English authority, was that a duty to have regard to the general principle admitted of considerations other than those specified being taken into account.[95] The matter was put beyond doubt in *Harvey* v. *Strathclyde Regional Council*,[96] in which the House of Lords affirmed the decision of the First Division[97] which proceeded, *inter alia*, on the view that an education authority would be entitled to have regard to relevant considerations other than those expressly mentioned, and indeed that there might be exceptions to the general principle.

Parental Choice of School

In relation to choice of school, the duty under section 28 to have regard to parental wishes was subsequently supplemented by sections 28A to 28H (introduced by the Education (Scotland) Act 1981). These sections greatly enhance parental rights in choosing a particular school to which a parent can send his or her child. The provisions about to be described refer to public schools; analogous provisions contained in the Self-Governing Schools Etc. (Scotland) Act 1989[98] deal with self-governing schools.

Information

Every education authority must publish, or otherwise make available, information as to their arrangements for the placing of children in schools under their management.[99] Where a child falls in accordance with those arrangements to be placed in a school under the authority's management, the authority must,

---

[92] *Watt* v. *Kesteven County Council* [1955] 1 Q.B. 408; *Keeney* v. *Strathclyde Regional Council*, 1986 S.L.T. 490.

[93] *Harvey* v. *Strathclyde Regional Council*, 1989 S.L.T. 612 (H.L.).

[94] That the specified conditions are exhaustive is supported by *Huckstep* v. *Dunfermline District Education Sub-Committee*, 1954 S.L.T. (Sh. Ct.) 109 and *Kidd* v. *New Kilpatrick School Council*, 1978 S.L.T. (Sh. Ct.) 56. See also *Brown* v. *Lothian Regional Council*, 1980 S.L.T. (Sh. Ct.) 14.

[95] *Edwards* v. *Lothian Regional Council*, 1980 S.L.T. (Sh. Ct.) 107; *Sinclair* v. *Lothian Regional Council*, 1981 S.L.T. (Sh. Ct.) 13; *Watt* v. *Kesteven County Council, supra*; *Cumings* v. *Birkenhead Corporation* [1972] Ch. 12. See also *Parlane* v. *Perth and Kinross J.C.C.*, 1954 S.L.T. (Sh. Ct.) 95; *Grieve* v. *Lothian Regional Council*, 1978 S.L.T. (Sh. Ct.) 24; and *Keeney* v. *Strathclyde Regional Council*, 1986 S.L.T. 490.

[96] 1989 S.L.T. 612.

[97] 1989 S.L.T. 25.

[98] s. 10 and Sched. 2.

[99] s. 28B.

where they propose to place the child in a particular school, inform the child's parent of that school and in every case must inform the parent of the general effect of section 28A and of the parent's right to make a placing request.[1] The duty to inform of the general effect of section 28A and of the right to make a placing request applies, however, only where the existence of the child and the fact that he falls to be placed in a school under the authority's management is known to the authority.[2] The authority must, in addition, in making arrangements for the performance of their functions under the Act, formulate guidelines to be followed by them as respects placings in schools generally or, if they think it necessary, in any particular school. The authority must also, on request, supply a parent with certain prescribed information about any school under their management.

Placing Request

Where a parent makes a written request to an education authority to place his child in a school specified in the request, being a school under the authority's management, it is the duty of the authority to place the child accordingly.[3] If two or more schools managed by the authority are specified, the duty applies in relation to the first-mentioned such school.[4] The specification of a school outwith Scotland is not an effective request.[5] The duty does not apply:

(a) if placing the child in a specified school would (i) make it necessary for the authority to take an additional teacher into employment, (ii) give rise to significant expenditure on extending, or otherwise altering, the accommodation at, or facilities provided in connection with, the school, (iii) be seriously detrimental to the continuity of the child's education, or (iv) be likely to be seriously detrimental to order and discipline in the school or the educational wellbeing of the pupils there;

(b) if the education normally provided at the specified school is not suited to the age, ability or aptitude of the child;

(c) if the education authority have already required the child to discontinue his attendance at the specified school;

(d) if, where the specified school is a special school, the child does not have special educational needs requiring the education or special facilities normally provided at that school; or

(e) if the specified school is a single-sex school and the child is not of the appropriate sex.[6]

These exceptions qualify the duty but do not restrict the powers of the education authority. Accordingly, the authority may place a child in the specified school notwithstanding that one or more of the exceptions to the duty applies. The authority must inform the parent, in writing, of their decision on the placing re-

---

[1] s. 28B(1).
[2] s. 28B(4).
[3] s. 28A(1).
[4] s. 28A(2).
[5] *Lamont* v. *Strathclyde Regional Council*, 1988 S.L.T. (Sh. Ct.) 9.
[6] s. 28A(3). For self-governing schools, see Self-Governing Schools Etc. (Scotland) Act 1989, Sched. 2, para. 2.

quest and where they decide to refuse the request must give the parent written reasons for the decision and inform him of his right to refer it to an appeal committee.[7] If the parent is not informed in writing of the authority's decision within a prescribed period the placing request is deemed to have been refused.[8]

Appeal

Except where the authority's refusal was in respect of the placing of a child in a nursery school or nursery class, a parent whose placing request has been refused may refer the authority's decision to an appeal committee.[9] If a reference has previously been made in respect of the same child no further reference is competent during the period of 12 months beginning with the day in which the immediately preceding reference was lodged.[10] The reference must be lodged within 28 days of the receipt by the parent of the decision of the education authority but the committee may, on good cause being shown, hear a reference notwithstanding that it was not lodged within that time.[11]

The appeal committee may confirm the education authority's decision only if it is satisfied both (a) that one or more of the grounds of refusal specified in the Act exist and (b) that in all the circumstances it is appropriate to do so.[12] Otherwise it must refuse to confirm the authority's decision and require the authority to place the child in the specified school. Where the authority's decision is not confirmed and the specified school is a special school, the appeal committee may, if the authority has decided not to record the child as having pronounced specific or complex special educational needs, require the education authority to reconsider their decision.[13] The appeal committee's decision must be notified in writing together with the reasons for it to the parent who made the reference, and to the education authority, and where the authority's decision is confirmed the parent must be informed of his right to appeal to the sheriff.[14] Where the appeal committee refuses to confirm the authority's decision, the authority must give effect to the placing request.[15] Where the appeal committee's decision is inconsistent with any decision of the authority refusing a placing request in respect of another child, the authority must review their decision so to refuse and must inform the parent of the other child, in writing, of their decision upon that and the reasons for it.[16] If, upon such a review, the authority decide not to reverse their decision, the parent of the other child may refer that decision to an appeal committee and the appeal procedure follows thereon as if the decision on the review were a decision refusing a placing request.[17]

---

[7] s. 28A(4).

[8] s. 28A(5), and Education (Placing in Schools—Deemed Decisions) (Scotland) Regulations 1981 (S.I. 1981 No. 1561), reg. 3.

[9] s. 28C. For self-governing schools, see Self-Governing Schools Etc. (Scotland) Act 1989, Sched. 2, paras. 3–7.

[10] s. 28C(3).

[11] s. 28C(4).

[12] s. 28E(1).

[13] s. 28E(2).

[14] s. 28E(3).

[15] s. 28E(4).

[16] s. 28E(5).

[17] s. 28E(6).

A parent who has referred an education authority's decision to an appeal committee is entitled to a hearing before the committee at which he may be accompanied by up to three friends, including someone representing him.[18] As an alternative he may lodge written representations and choose not to appear before the committee. The hearing of two or more references concerning different children and parents may be combined if they concern decisions in relation to placing requests all of which relate to the same stage of education at the same school and, in the committee's opinion, have been refused for substantially the same reasons. The parties may call evidence and question persons giving evidence and there is provision for the submission of information relevant to the decision by either party and for the inspection, by a party, of documents submitted in evidence by the other party.

A parent who has referred the refusal of a placing request to an appeal committee may appeal to the sheriff having jurisdiction where the specified school is situated against the decision of the appeal committee.[19] There is no corresponding right of appeal for the education authority. The education authority may be, and the appeal committee shall not be, a party to the appeal.[20] The appeal, which is by way of summary application, must be lodged within 28 days from the date of receipt of the decision of the appeal committee[21] but on good cause being shown the sheriff may hear an appeal notwithstanding that it was not lodged within that time.[22] The appeal is to be heard in chambers and the sheriff's powers in deciding the appeal are governed by similar provisions to those applying to the appeal committee's decision.[23] There are also similar provisions relating to the review by the authority of a decision, whether confirmed by the appeal committee or not, refusing a placing request in respect of another child which is inconsistent with the sheriff's judgment on the appeal and for the consequences of refusal to reverse that decision.[24] The sheriff's judgment on the appeal is final,[25] unless the challenge is to competency.[26] The sheriff may make such order regarding expenses as he thinks proper.[27]

Choice of School by Young Person

The provisions of the Education (Scotland) Act 1980 on choice of school have so far been considered in relation to children not over school age and their parents. They apply, however, equally to any young person over school age but under 18 who is a pupil (i.e. a person for whom education is, or is required to be, provided under the Act) with the difference only that in their application to him

---

[18] Education (Appeal Committee Procedures) (Scotland) Regulations 1981 (S.I. 1981 No. 1560).
[19] s. 28F(1).
[20] s. 28F(2).
[21] s. 28F(3).
[22] s. 28F(4).
[23] s. 28F(3)(c) and (5).
[24] s. 28F (6) and (7).
[25] s. 28F(9).
[26] Lamont v. Strathclyde Regional Council, 1988 S.L.T. (Sh. Ct.) 9.
[27] s. 28F(8).

reference to the parent of a child as well as references to the child himself are to be construed as references to the young person.[28]

Assistance in Taking Advantage of Educational Facilities

Education authorities have a number of powers and duties designed to assist persons to take advantage of educational facilities. Some of these powers and duties apply specifically to school education but others have a wider or different application. The beneficiaries may, unless it is otherwise stated or the context so requires, be of any age. Where the reference is to a "pupil" it means a person of any age for whom education is, or is required to be, provided under the Act,[29] and therefore comprehends anyone who is receiving education provided by the education authority.

Allowances, Bursaries and Scholarships

An education authority has power for the purpose of enabling persons to take advantage, without hardship to themselves or their parents, of the facilities for school education available to them, and to pay allowances for the purpose of defraying in whole or in part,

(a) such expenses of a person's attending any school as may be expedient to enable him to take full part in the activities of the school;

(b) the fees and expenses payable in respect of persons attending schools at which fees are payable; and

(c) the maintenance expenses of persons over school age who are attending schools.[30]

The authority also has power to make payment of bursaries, scholarships or other allowances to persons over school age attending courses of full-time or part-time education whether held in Scotland or elsewhere which are not courses of school education, or, in the case of courses outside Scotland, are not courses of education comparable to school education in Scotland.[31]

Arrangements for Exceptional Circumstances

Where, in the opinion of an education authority,

(a) any pupil is, owing to the remoteness of his home or the conditions under which he is living or other exceptional circumstances, unable to receive the full benefit of school education unless special arrangements are made for him, or

(b) school education suitable to the age, ability and aptitude of any pupil can best be provided for him at any particular school,

---

[28] s. 28G. For self-governing schools, see Self-Governing Schools Etc. (Scotland) Act 1989, Sched. 2, para. 8.

[29] s. 135(1).

[30] s. 49(2). References to attending school are to attending schools in Scotland and in other parts of the United Kingdom (s. 49(2A), as inserted by the Self-Governing Schools Etc. (Scotland) Act 1989, Sched. 10, para. 8).

[31] s. 49(1).

the authority shall, after consultation with the parent, make such arrangements of either a temporary or a permanent character as they think best suited to the purpose of enabling that pupil to attend an appropriate school. These arrangements may include (a) the provision of travelling facilities or the payment of travelling expenses, (b) the accommodation of the pupil at a boarding school or in a hostel, home, or other institution, (c) other provision of board and lodging provided that, so far as practicable, effect is given to the wishes of the parent with respect to the religious denomination of the person with whom the pupil is to reside, or (d) provision for travelling, board and lodging of teachers.[32]

Transport and other Facilities

Such arrangements, as the education authority consider necessary, are to be made for the provision of the following facilities in respect of pupils attending schools or other educational establishments:[33]

(a) for the conveyance of pupils, without charge, for the whole or part of the journey between their homes and the schools or other educational establishments which they are attending. If after the requirements of these pupils have been met, there are vacant places in a vehicle used for their conveyance it is the duty of the authority to allow such places to be used without charge by other pupils to be selected by them.

(b) for making bicycles, or other suitable means of transport, available to pupils, or to their parents for the use of pupils, upon such terms and conditions as may be arranged, or for paying money allowances in lieu thereof.

(c) for paying the whole or any part, as the authority think fit, of reasonable travelling expenses.

Any arrangement made in respect of any pupil may make provision for more than one of these facilities. The authority may moreover pay the whole or part of the expenses of attendance for examination or interview where these are necessarily incurred by anyone whose attendance is required as a condition of admission to any educational institution.

Board and Lodging

Where board and lodging are provided by the authority under section 50 of the Act[34] no sum is recoverable from the parent or young person in respect of that provision.[35] In any other case, however, an education authority, who have provided a pupil with board and lodging whether at a school, hostel, or elsewhere, may, in their discretion, require the parent to pay such sum not exceeding the cost of such board and lodging as, in the opinion of the authority, he is able without financial hardship to pay.[36] Where the board and lodging have been provided for a young person in an educational establishment in connection

---

[32] s. 50(2).
[33] s. 51, as amended by the Self-Governing Schools Etc. (Scotland) Act 1989, Sched. 6, para. 1.
[34] *Ante*, at pp. 340–341.
[35] s. 52.
[36] *Ibid.*

with which the authority have provided a hostel the authority, if satisfied that the young person is in a financial position to pay, may instead recover from him the whole or any part of the sum recoverable from his parent.[37]

School Meals

An education authority may provide milk, meals or refreshment for pupils in attendance at public schools and other educational establishments under their management, either on the premises or elsewhere, and such facilities as the authority considers appropriate are to be provided for the consumption of any meals or other refreshments brought to the school or other educational establishment by pupils.[38] The authority must, subject to what is said in the next sentence, charge for anything provided by them in the way of milk, meals and other refreshment and must charge every pupil the same price for the same quantity of the same item.[39] In relation to a pupil whose parents are in receipt of income support or who is himself in receipt of it, an authority shall exercise the power to provide milk, meals and other refreshment in a way that ensures that such provision is made to the pupil in the middle of the day as appears to the authority to be requisite and shall make that provision for him free of charge.[40] These provisions apply in relation to pupils in attendance at a self-governing school and the board of management of that school as they apply in relation to pupils in attendance at a public school and the education authority that manages it.[41] Where special arrangements have been made for a pupil to receive education elsewhere than at an educational establishment he may, at the discretion of the authority, be deemed to be in attendance at a public school under their management for the purpose of these provisions.[42]

Clothing

When it is brought to the notice of an education authority that a pupil attending either a school under its management or a self-governing school is unable, by reason of the inadequacy or unsuitability of his clothing, to take full advantage of the education provided, the authority are to make such provision for the pupil as they deem necessary, for the purpose of ensuring that he is sufficiently and suitably clad.[43] That provision is to be made during such period while the pupil is attending school, including days when the school does not meet, as the authority may determine. The expense thereby incurred may be recovered from the parent of the pupil in whole or in such part as the parent is, in the opinion of the authority, able without financial hardship to pay.[44] Without prejudice, however, to their other powers, an education authority may provide clothing free of charge for any pupil who is a boarder at a school or for any pupil

---

[37] *Ibid.*

[38] s. 53(1).

[39] s. 53(2), as amended by s. 77 of the Social Security Act 1986.

[40] s. 53(3), as amended by s. 77 of the Social Security Act 1986.

[41] s. 53(3A), as inserted by the Self-Governing Schools Etc. (Scotland) Act 1989, Sched. 10, para. 8.

[42] s. 53(4).

[43] s. 54, as amended by the Self-Governing Schools Etc. (Scotland) Act 1989, Sched. 6, para. 1. See *Shaw* v. *Strathclyde Regional Council*, 1987 S.C.L.R. 439.

[44] s. 54(2).

in attendance at a nursery school or nursery class under the management of the authority, or for any pupil who is a boarder at a self-governing school.[45] For all purposes connected with the provision of clothing, a pupil on attaining the age of five years is, pending his admission to school, deemed to be attending a school under the management of the authority in whose area he is ordinarily resident and a pupil for whom it is the duty of an education authority to provide special education is deemed to be attending a school under the management of that authority.[46]

Meals and Clothing at Independent Schools

An education authority may, with the consent of the managers of any school in their area which is not a public school and upon such financial and other terms, if any, as may be agreed, make arrangements for securing the provision for pupils in attendance at the school of milk, meals and other refreshment; and, except in relation to self-governing schools, where any such pupil is unable, by reason of the inadequacy or unsuitability of his clothing, to take full advantage of the education including physical exercise provided by the school, the authority may provide such clothing as is necessary for the purpose of ensuring that he is sufficiently and suitably clad while he remains a pupil at the school.[47]

Rights in Relation to Clothing Provided

Provision of clothing by an education authority under any of their powers conferred by the Act may be made so as to confer, at the option of the authority, either a right of property in the clothing or a right of use only.[48]

Assisted Places at Independent Schools

For the purpose of enabling pupils, who might otherwise not be able to do so, to attend and receive education at independent schools, the Secretary of State is to establish and operate a scheme whereby participating schools remit fees that would otherwise be chargeable in respect of pupils admitted to assisted places under the scheme and the Secretary of State reimburses the schools for the fees that are remitted.[49] The Secretary of State is to determine which schools are to be participating schools for this purpose and in doing so is to have regard to the desirability of securing an equitable distribution of assisted places throughout Scotland and between boys and girls.[50] The fees covered by the scheme are (a) tuition and other fees the payment of which is a condition of attendance at a participating school, but excluding boarding fees, and (b) entrance fees for public examinations paid by a participating school in respect of candidates from the school.[51] The remission is to the extent provided for in a family income scale

---

[45] s. 54(3), as amended by the Self-Governing Schools Etc. (Scotland) Act 1989, Sched. 6, para. 1.
[46] s. 54(4).
[47] s. 55, as amended by the Self-Governing Schools Etc. (Scotland) Act 1989, Sched. 6, para. 1.
[48] s. 56.
[49] s. 75A(1), as inserted by the Education (Scotland) Act 1981, s. 5(1).
[50] s. 75A(2).
[51] s. 75A(7).

laid down by regulations.[52] Provision is also made for requiring or enabling participating schools to make grants in respect of expenses including travelling expenses, to remit specified charges, to make provision of meals or other refreshments, or of facilities for their consumption and to make provision of appropriate clothing, provided the expenses, charges, or provision in question are in respect of matters incidental to, or arising out of, the attendance at the school of pupils holding assisted places under the scheme.[53]

Grants by Secretary of State and Industrial Scholarships

The Secretary of State may, in accordance with regulations made by him, apply such sums as he thinks necessary or expedient for the purpose *inter alia* of the payment of allowances to or in respect of persons attending courses of education.[54] He may also award industrial scholarships or make payments in respect of the award of such scholarships by other persons.[55] An industrial scholarship is a scholarship tenable by persons undertaking full-time courses of higher education provided by a university, college, or other institution in the United Kingdom which are relevant to a career in industry. A course is full-time for this purpose although full-time study alternates with associated industrial, professional or commercial experience.

Health and Cleanliness

Medical and Dental Inspection

An education authority or board of management of a self-governing school may require the parent of any pupil in attendance at any school under their management to submit the pupil for medical or dental inspection in accordance with arrangements made by the appropriate health board in agreement with the authority or board of management.[56] The authority or board of management may similarly require any young person in attendance at any educational establishment under its management to submit himself for medical or dental inspection.[57] Anyone who fails without a reasonable excuse to comply with a requirement so made may be guilty of an offence.[58]

Examination for Cleanliness

An education authority or board of management of a self-governing school may, by directions in writing, issued with respect to all schools and other educational establishments under their management or any of them, authorise a medical officer to cause examination to be made of the bodies and clothing of all, or any, of the pupils whenever, in the medical officer's opinion, such examinations are necessary in the interest of cleanliness.[59] Any such examination is to be

---

[52] s. 75A(9); Education (Allowances for Assisted Places in Secondary Schools) (Scotland) Regulations 1981 (S.I. 1981 No. 488).
[53] s. 75B(1).
[54] s. 73(f).
[55] s. 76.
[56] s. 57(2), as amended by the Self-Governing Schools Etc. (Scotland) Act 1989, Sched. 6, para. 1.
[57] *Ibid.*
[58] s. 57(3).
[59] s. 58(1).

made by the medical officer, or by a person authorised in writing by him, and no female is to be examined or cleansed except by a registered medical practitioner or by a woman authorised for that purpose.[60] If the body or clothing of any pupil is then found to be infested with vermin or in a foul condition, the authority or board of management may serve a notice upon the parent or, in the case of a young person, upon the young person himself. The notice must inform the person on whom it is served that cleansing will be carried out under arrangements made by the education authority or board of management unless, within the period limited by the notice and not more than 24 hours after its service, the body and clothing of the pupil are cleansed to the satisfaction of the medical officer or authorised person specified in the notice.[61] If the medical officer or authorised person is not then satisfied that the body and clothing of the pupil have been properly cleansed an order may be issued which will be sufficient authority for compulsory cleansing and which carries with it powers to convey and detain for that purpose. It is an offence if, after cleansing has been carried out in compliance with a notice or compulsorily, the body or clothing of the pupil is again found to be infested with vermin or in a foul condition at any time while he is in attendance at a school or other educational establishment; provided it is proved that the condition of his body or clothing is due to neglect on the part of the parent, or of the young person, as the case may be.[62]

SPECIAL EDUCATIONAL NEEDS

Introduction
It is the duty of an education authority,

(a) to disseminate in their area information as to the importance of the early discovery of special educational needs and the opportunity for assessment available;

(b) to establish which of those children in their area, who are (i) of school age or (ii) under school age but being at least two years of age have come to the attention of the authority as having special educational needs, have pronounced specific or complex special educational needs such as require continuing review; and

(c) to keep a Record of Needs of each such child.[63]

---

[60] s. 58(2) and (7).

[61] s. 58(3), as amended by the Self-Governing Schools Etc. (Scotland) Act 1989.

[62] s. 58(5).

[63] s. 60(1) and (2) as substituted by the Education (Scotland) Act 1981, s. 4(1), and as amended by the Self-Governing Schools Etc. (Scotland) Act 1989, s. 72(1). Special educational needs are needs caused by a learning difficulty which calls for special provision, *i.e.* where (a) a child or young person has significantly greater difficulty in learning than the majority of children or young persons of his age, or (b) suffers from a disability which either prevents or hinders him from making use of educational facilities of a kind generally provided for children or young persons of his age, or (c) in the case of a child under the age of five, he is or would be if provision for special educational needs were not made for him, likely to be in such need if over the age of five (s. 1(5) (*d*) as added by the Education (Scotland) Act 1981, s. 3(1)). A child or young person is not, however, to be taken as having a learning difficulty solely because the language in which he is or will be taught is different from a language, including a form of the teaching language, spoken in his home (*ibid.*).

The authority also have a power but not a duty to establish which children in their area under school age (not otherwise covered), and which young persons (over school age but under 18) who are receiving school education, have such needs; and to open and keep a Record of Needs in respect of each of them. In relation to a young person, the power is exercisable only on a request by the young person or his parent.[64]

The Record is to include four parts containing respectively (a) a summary of the child's or young person's impairments, (b) a statement of the special educational needs arising from those impairments, (c) a statement of the measures proposed by the education authority to meet those needs, and (d) where appropriate, the nomination of a school to be attended by the person recorded.[65]

Examination and Assessment

It is not lawful to establish and record a child's needs unless the child has undergone a process of assessment, including a medical and a psychological examination and a report by any teacher in the authority's employment who has been concerned in his education.[66] The authority must, by notice in writing, invite the child's parent to submit the child for examination and if a parent of a child to whom the authority owe a duty in terms of section 60(2) fails, without reasonable excuse, to comply the authority may, by notice in writing, require him to do so.[67] Failure of the parent to comply with the latter notice absolves the authority from its duty to establish and record the child's needs,[68] and if the failure is without reasonable excuse the parent is guilty of an offence.[69] If the parent of any child requests the education authority, for the area to which the child belongs, to make arrangements for the child to undergo assessment the authority must comply with that request unless in its opinion the request is unreasonable.[70]

It is not lawful for an education authority to establish that a young person has pronounced specific or complex special educational needs and to record him unless the young person has undergone a process of assessment and he or, where the education authority is satisfied that he is not capable of expressing his views, his parent has been invited by the authority to express his views as regards these needs and the measures required to meet them.[71]

Decision to Record

In deciding whether or not to record a child or young person, an education authority must take into consideration the advice given to them in consequence of the process of assessment, any views expressed by the parent or by the young person, any reports or other information with respect to the child or young per-

---

[64] s. 60(5).
[65] s. 65D(2).
[66] s. 61(1).
[67] *Ibid.*, as amended by the Self-Governing Schools Etc. (Scotland) Act 1989, s. 72(2).
[68] s. 61(5).
[69] s. 61(4).
[70] s. 61(6).
[71] s. 61(7).

son obtained from the managers or teachers of any school which he has attended, and any other reports or information relevant to his educational needs which the authority are able to obtain.[72] The decision of the authority, the reasons for the decision and the terms in which the authority propose to record the child or young person, must be intimated forthwith by a notice in writing to the parent, or, in the case of a young person capable of expressing his view, to the young person.[73] Within 14 days of that notice, the parent or young person may express to the authority his views on the terms on which the record should be made and, in recording the child or young person, the authority must have regard to these views. Thereafter, the authority must notify the parent or young person of (a) their decision as to the terms, (b) the parent's or young person's right of appeal, and (c) the name and address of the person to whom application may be made for advice and information about the child's or young person's special educational needs. The authority must then ensure that the provision made by them for the recorded child or young person includes provision for his special educational needs.[74]

Appeals

Reference to Appeal Committee

The parent of a recorded child may refer to an appeal committee any of the following decisions by an education authority:[75]

(a) A decision to record the child, or, following a review, to continue to record him.

(b) A decision as to the terms on which a summary of the child's impairments or a statement of his special educational needs arising from those impairments are recorded; and any such decision following a review.

(c) A decision as to nomination of a school to be attended by the child or young person or any such decision following a review. A reference to the appeal committee is competent under this heading, however, only if a placing request has been made and no other such reference has been made in respect of the child within the previous 12 months.

(d) A decision refusing a placing request in respect of the child provided no reference under this heading, or under heading (c) above, has been made within the previous 12 months.

A young person, or, where the authority were satisfied that the young person was not capable of expressing his view, his parent, may refer to an appeal committee decisions of the education authority corresponding to the decisions (b), (c) and (d) above.[76]

Any reference to an appeal committee must be lodged within 28 days of re-

---

[72] s. 62(1).
[73] s. 62(2).
[74] s. 62(3), as amended by the Self-Governing Schools Etc. (Scotland) Act 1989, s. 72(3).
[75] s. 63(1).
[76] s. 63(2).

ceipt of the notification of the decision of the education authority as to the terms in which they recorded the child or young person but the appeal committee has power, on good cause being shown, to hear a reference notwithstanding that it was not lodged within that time.[77] Regulations may make provision (a) requiring the authority to make information relevant to a decision available to the appeal committee and to the parent or young person, and (b) for deeming an appeal committee to have confirmed the decision of the education authority if the committee's decision has not been notified within a prescribed time.[78]

Reference to the Secretary of State

Where the reference relates (a) to a decision to record, or to continue to record, a child or (b) to the terms in which the summary of a child's or young person's impairment, and a statement of the special educational needs arising from those impairments, are to be recorded, the appeal committee must refer the reference to the Secretary of State.[79] Also, where an appeal committee considers that it cannot deal with a reference which relates to the education authority's decision as to the nomination of a school, without having the decision of the Secretary of State on the question of whether or not a child should be recorded or the terms in which the summary of impairments and statement of special educational needs should be recorded, it must refer that question, or so much of the reference as relates to those terms, to the Secretary of State. When any of these matters has been referred to him, the Secretary of State shall then (a) confirm or refuse to confirm the education authority's decision to record or continue to record the child, (b) confirm with or without modification the terms in which the summary of impairments and statement of special educational needs are recorded.[80] Where, however, the reference has been made to the Secretary of State because the appeal committee considered that without having his decision it could not deal with the reference to it of an education authority's decision as to the nomination of a school to be attended by a child or young person, the Secretary of State is not to make his decision unless he has first obtained and taken into consideration the views of the parent or young person who made the reference to the appeal committee.[81] Where the Secretary of State refuses to confirm an education authority's decision to record or to continue to record a child, he shall direct the authority to discontinue the record of the child and the authority must comply with that direction.[82] Where the Secretary of State confirms an education authority's decision with modifications as to the terms in which the summary of impairments and statement of special educational needs are to be recorded, he is to direct the authority to modify the record accordingly and the authority must comply with that direction.[83] The Secretary of State's decision is

---

[77] s. 63(5).

[78] s. 63(6). See Education (Appeal Committee Procedures) (Scotland) Regulations 1982 (S.I. 1982 No. 1736).

[79] s. 64(1).

[80] s. 64(4).

[81] s. 64(7).

[82] s. 64(5).

[83] s. 64(6).

to be notified to the appeal committee, the person who made the reference to the appeal committee, and the education authority.[84]

Decision of Appeal Committee

The effect of the above provisions is that references of decisions to record, or to continue to record, a child and of decisions as to the terms in which the summary of impairments and statement of special educational needs are to be recorded, are, in effect, references to the Secretary of State and also that questions relating to these matters, which arise in connection with the reference of other decisions, are to be decided by the Secretary of State. The references which remain for decision by the appeal committee are those relating to the nomination of a school to be attended by the child or young person and decisions refusing a placing request. As a decision on the nomination of a school can be referred only if there has been a placing request,[85] all the decisions taken by the appeal committee are essentially decisions on placing requests. The appeal committee may confirm the education authority's decision as to nomination of a school or refusing a placing request only if it is satisfied that (a) in relation to the placing request one or more of the specified grounds of refusal, as they apply to recorded children or young persons, exist, and (b) it is, in all the circumstances, appropriate to do so.[86] Otherwise the appeal committee must refuse to confirm the authority's decision and require it to place the child or young person in the school specified in the placing request. If the specified school is an independent school, the appeal committee is to require the authority to meet the fees and other necessary costs of the child's or young persons's attendance at that school and the authority must comply with that requirement.[87] Where the appeal committee has referred the reference, or any part of it, to the Secretary of State, they are not to dispose of so much of the reference as relates to the school to be attended by the child or young person until the Secretary of State's decision upon the matter referred to him is notified to the appeal committee; and the appeal committee is to reach its decision as respects the child or young person in the light of the Secretary of State's decision.[88]

The appeal committee's decision and the reasons for it are to be notified in writing to the person who made the reference and to the education authority, and where the authority's decision as to the nomination of a school, or refusing a placing request, has been confirmed, the person who made the reference is to be informed of his right of appeal to the sheriff.[89] Where the authority's decision is not confirmed, the authority must place the child or young person in the specified school and amend accordingly any nomination in his record of a school to be attended by him.[90]

---

[84] s. 64(8).
[85] s. 63(3).
[86] s. 64(2).
[87] s. 64(3).
[88] s. 64(9).
[89] s. 64(10).
[90] s. 64(11).

Appeal to Sheriff

There is an appeal to the sheriff against a decision of an appeal committee on references relating to an education authority's decision on the nomination of a school or refusing a placing request in respect of a recorded child or young person.[91] The decision is at the instance of the person who made the reference. The education authority has no corresponding right of appeal. The provisions of the Act on parties to appeals, the form of appeal, the time within which it must be lodged, hearings in chambers, and expenses, apply to these appeals as they do to appeals in respect of placing requests.[92] Where the sheriff considers that he cannot deal with the appeal without having the decision of the Secretary of State on the question of whether or not the child should be recorded, or on the terms in which the summary of impairments and statement of special education needs should be recorded, he may refer that question or those matters to the Secretary of State.[93] He can, however, perhaps surprisingly, do so only on the motion of a party to the appeal, and he is not to refer to the Secretary of State if there has already been a reference to him by the appeal committee.[94] The sheriff's powers and the grounds on which he is to confirm, or refuse to confirm, the decision of the education authority, are the same as those of the appeal committee.[95] Where there has been a reference to the Secretary of State, either by himself or by the appeal committee, the sheriff is to dispose of the appeal in the light of the Secretary of State's decision.[96]

Review and Reports

It is the duty of an education authority to keep under consideration the cases of all recorded children and young persons belonging to their area and to review the decision to record whenever they think it expedient or when requested to do so by notice in writing given by the parent of the child or by the young person, or by the parent of a young person who in the opinion of the authority is not capable of expressing his views.[97] The parent of a recorded child, the recorded young person, or, as the case may be, the parent of a recorded young person, is not, however, entitled to request a review of the decision to record at an interval of less than 12 months from the date of that decision, or its most recent review, whichever is the later, nor of the information entered in the record at an interval of less than 12 months from the date of the commencement of the record or the most recent review of the information, whichever is the later.[98] It is also the duty of an education authority to consider, during the period beginning two years before a recorded child ceases to be of school age and ending nine months before then, what provision would benefit the child after he ceases to be of school age and to make a report thereon.[99] That consideration may be carried out in con-

---

[91] s. 65(1).

[92] s. 65(2). See *ante*, at pp. 338–339.

[93] s. 65(3).

[94] s. 65(5).

[95] s. 65(6).

[96] s. 65(8).

[97] s. 65A(1).

[98] s. 65A(2).

[99] s. 65B(1) and (2).

junction with a review in relation to the child.[1] The report is to include the authority's recommendation as to whether the child would benefit from school education after he ceases to be of school age and, if it does so recommend, whether or not his record should be discontinued.[2] A copy of the report is to be sent to the child's parent, who is to be informed of his right to have the record discontinued. In any case where they consider it appropriate to do so, the education authority is also to send a copy of the report to the local authority falling to perform functions in relation to the child under the Social Work (Scotland) Act 1968, the health board for the area in which the child resides and, with the consent of the child's parent, any other body making provision from which the child might benefit.[3] A copy of the report sent for this purpose is, where possible, to be sent not later than six months before the child or young person to whom the report relates is expected to cease receiving school education.[4]

Discontinuance of Record

An education authority are to discontinue the record of a young person if requested to do so by him, or, where he is incapable of expressing a request, by his parent.[5] Subject thereto the record of a child who ceases to be of school age, but as a young person receives school education, is to be continued for so long as he receives such education.[6]

Provision of Special Educational Needs outwith the United Kingdom

Without prejudice to the powers described above, an education authority also have the power to make such arrangements as they think fit to enable a child or young person to attend an establishment outwith the United Kingdom if that establishment makes provision wholly or mainly for persons with pronounced, specific or complex special educational needs.[7] It is not necessary that there be a record of needs in relation to the child.[8] The arrangement may include defraying, wholly or partly (a) the fees payable for the child's or young person's attendance and his travelling, maintenance and other expenses in respect of that attendance; and (b) the expenses of the child's or young person's parent, parents or other person where in the opinion of the authority it would be to the advantage of the child or young person to be accompanied by such parent or other person.[9]

---

[1] s. 65B(4).
[2] s. 65B(5).
[3] s. 65B(6).
[4] s. 65B(7).
[5] s. 65C(3).
[6] s. 65C(1).
[7] s. 65G(1), as inserted by the Self-Governing Schools Etc. (Scotland) Act 1989, s. 71.
[8] s. 65G(2).
[9] s. 65G(3).

CHAPTER 13

CAPACITY AND LEGAL REPRESENTATION OF CHILDREN

Introduction

Legal capacity is the ability to perform on one's own behalf juridical acts such as entering contracts and raising or defending actions. For long Scots law, following the Roman law, adopted a gradualist approach to the acquiring of legal capacity which reflected, if somewhat crudely, the fact that children's physical and mental capacities increase with age and experience.[1] There was, as explained more fully earlier, a radical difference between the capacity of pupils (boys below 14 and girls below 12) and that of minors (children above pupillarity but below majority[2]), the former having, generally speaking, no legal capacity and the latter having full legal capacity subject, for most acts, to the need, if they had curators, for the curators' concurrence. The old rules were replaced in respect of transactions occurring on or after September 25, 1991 by a whole new framework, contained in the Age of Legal Capacity (Scotland) Act 1991. That Act lays down, in general, that persons under the age of 16 years have no legal capacity while persons of or above that age do have legal capacity. It also provides[3] that "any reference in any enactment to a pupil (other than in the context of education or training) or to a person under legal disability or incapacity by reason of nonage shall, insofar as it relates to any time after the commencement of this Act, be construed as a reference to a person under the age of 16 years." The statutory rules governing the legal capacity of pupils before the commencement of the 1991 Act apply after that date, in so far as they are capable of being reconciled with the Act, to all persons under the age of 16. A full description of the legal capacity of pupil children before the 1991 Act is given in Chapter 2, to which reference should be made. Unlike the statutory rules, the common law rules relating to pupils (with the exception of some rules relating to civil proceedings) are not expressly preserved, but are largely replaced by the provisions of the 1991 Act and applied to persons under the age of 16. This chapter will examine the details of the 1991 Act; it will then examine the law of guardianship, through which legal acts can be performed on behalf of those persons under 16 who do not, for that reason, have legal capacity; and finally it will consider a number of other issues of legal capacity and incapacity for children and young persons.

---

[1] See *ante* at pp. 52–53.
[2] Originally 21, now 18: Age of Majority (Scotland) Act 1969.
[3] s. 1(2).

CAPACITY UNDER THE AGE OF LEGAL CAPACITY (SCOTLAND) ACT 1991

Capacity of Persons below 16

Section 1(1)(*a*) of the Age of Legal Capacity (Scotland) Act 1991 provides that, as from the commencement of the Act, a person under the age of 16 years shall, subject to certain stated exceptions, have no legal capacity to enter into any transaction. "Transaction" is defined to mean "a transaction having legal effect, and includes:

> (*a*) any unilateral transaction;
> (*b*) the exercise of testamentary capacity;
> (*c*) the exercise of any power of appointment;
> (*d*) the giving by a person of any consent having legal effect;
> (*e*) the bringing or defending of, or the taking of any step in, civil proceedings;
> (*f*) acting as arbiter or trustee;
> (*g*) acting as an instrumentary witness."[4]

A transaction entered into by a person under 16 which he has no legal capacity to enter into is void,[5] and such a transaction has to be undertaken by the person entitled to act on the child's behalf. Legal representation of the child is examined in some detail below.[6] If a person under 16 purports to perform a legal transaction, such as entering into a contract, then any remedy accruing to the other party will be determined by the general law. If the person under 16 has committed a fraud, for example in misrepresenting his age, then delictual remedies will be available to the person injured thereby.[7] In other cases the principle of unjust enrichment may afford a remedy.[8]

Exceptions

While the general rule is that a person under 16 has no legal capacity, this is qualified by the enactment of a number of specific exceptions, and one general exception. The specific exceptions are as follows:

> (1) A person of or over the age of 12 years has testamentary capacity.[9] This matter is considered more fully later in this chapter.[10]
> (2) A person of or over the age of 12 years has legal capacity to consent to the making of an adoption order over him or an order freeing him for adoption.[11] The adoption legislation[12] had previously provided that the consent of minor children was necessary for their own adoption, and

---

[4] Age of Legal Capacity (Scotland) Act 1991, s. 9.
[5] *Ibid.*, s. 2(5).
[6] *Post* at pp. 357–375.
[7] The child's capacity for delict is considered *post* at pp. 375–377.
[8] Stair, I, viii, 6.
[9] Age of Legal Capacity (Scotland) Act 1991, s. 2(2).
[10] *Post* at pp. 378–379.
[11] *Ibid.*, s. 2(3).
[12] Adoption (Scotland) Act 1978, ss. 12 and 18.

this provision preserves that position while equalising the age of consent for boys and girls.

(3) A person under the age of 16 years has legal capacity to consent on his own behalf to any surgical, medical or dental procedure or treatment where, in the opinion of a qualified medical practitioner attending him, he is capable of understanding the nature and possible consequences of the procedure or treatment.[13] This provision is widely drawn and is intended to cover all forms of health care provision. The determination of capacity is in the hands of the appropriate qualified medical practitioner.[14]

The general exception laid down in the 1991 Act is that a person under the age of 16 years shall have legal capacity to enter into a transaction (a) of a kind commonly entered into by persons of his age and circumstances and (b) on terms that are not unreasonable.[15] Condition (a) builds in a recognition that there are different levels of understanding at different ages, and it is designed to allow even very young children to enter into some minor transactions, such as purchasing sweets or comics, while at the same time prohibiting them from entering into more major transactions. A five-year-old might validly buy a packet of sweets, a ten-year-old might purchase a cinema ticket, and a 15-year-old might, perhaps, purchase an expensive computer programme. The condition is capable of covering any type of transaction, whether a unilateral transaction, or a contract of purchase or of lease or of employment, or any other transaction having legal effect. It is designed to be tailored to the individual child's particular circumstances and in that respect is a subjective test. The words "transaction of a kind commonly entered into" are, however, attended by difficulties. Transaction is defined for the purposes of the Act as "a transaction having legal effect". As a transaction cannot have legal effect unless the parties have capacity to enter into it, condition (a), if strictly construed, is reduced to a meaningless tautology. That result can be avoided only at the cost of some violence to the language of the statute. It is, however, submitted that condition (a) can, and should, be read, on a liberal construction, to the effect that a person under 16 "shall have legal capacity to enter into a transaction *so as to give it legal effect* if that transaction (read in its ordinary sense and without any necessary legal connotation) is of a kind ...". That construction gives the condition an intelligible meaning and has the further advantage of leaving open the possibility of development according to changing circumstances in the kind of transactions which may satisfy the condition. Parliament no doubt intended that persons under 16 should have capacity to transact in circumstances in which one would ordinarily expect them to have such capacity but unless some such device as is here suggested is adopted that intention must fail. Condition (b) makes plain that the person under 16 does not have capacity to enter into a transaction whose terms are unreasonable: an unreasonable transaction will be void.[16] An unreasonable

---

[13] Age of Legal Capacity (Scotland) Act 1991, s. 2(4).
[14] This provision is discussed more fully *ante* at pp. 182–187.
[15] *Ibid.*, s. 2(1).
[16] *Ibid.*, s. 2(5).

transaction is, it is submitted, one which an adult, exercising reasonable prudence, would not have entered into in the circumstances of the child; it does not need to have caused the child prejudice before it can be termed unreasonable.

Persons above 16 and below 18

Section 1(1)(*b*) of the Age of Legal Capacity (Scotland) Act 1991 provides that, as from the commencement of the Act, a person of or over the age of 16 years shall have legal capacity to enter into any transaction.[17] Such a person does not need a legal representative to undertake any legal transaction on his behalf nor to consent thereto, and accordingly curatory on the ground of age is abolished.[18] Transactions by persons in this age group are therefore valid and binding. The law however still recognises that a person aged 16 or 17 may be inexperienced and might in some circumstances require some legal protection. It is therefore provided[19] that a person who entered into a transaction while he was of or over the age of 16 years but under the age of 18 years may make an application to the court to set aside the transaction on the ground that it is a prejudicial transaction. This right of challenge has to be exercised by the person before attaining the age of 21 years,[20] and there is no requirement that he be over 18 before doing so: indeed his general capacity after the age of 16 to raise and defend legal proceedings gives him the right to apply for the setting aside of his own transactions any time after they are undertaken.

A "prejudicial transaction" is defined to mean a transaction which "(a) an adult, exercising reasonable prudence, would not have entered into in the circumstances of the applicant at the time of entering into the transaction, and (b) has caused or is likely to cause substantial prejudice to the applicant."[21] Both conditions must be satisfied. "Substantial prejudice" has much affinity with the notion of enorm lesion, which provided a similar ground for challenge at common law[22] and reference should be made to the discussion of minority and lesion given in Chapter 2. However, substantial prejudice cannot be taken to be the statutory equivalent of enorm lesion, for the 1991 Act is designed to provide a whole new statutory régime: in particular the difference is that challenge under the 1991 Act is challenge to transactions undertaken by the young person on his own behalf without concurrence of any adult person while challenge on the ground of minority and lesion was frequently challenge to transactions which tutors had undertaken or curators had consented to. There were some situations in which lesion would be irrebuttably presumed and others in which there was a rebuttable presumption.[23] In the absence of statutory provision to that effect it is submitted that it will not be possible for the court to presume substantial prejudice for the purposes of the 1991 Act. Having said which, however, there will

---

[17] "Transaction" being defined in the same way as in relation to persons below the age of 16: s. 9.
[18] *Ibid.*, s. 5(3).
[19] *Ibid.*, s. 3(1).
[20] *Ibid.*
[21] *Ibid.*, s. 3(2).
[22] See *ante*, at pp. 63–68.
[23] See *ante*, at pp. 64–66.

clearly be situations (gift of a large portion of the person's estate would seem a typical example) in which the court might readily hold that there has been substantial prejudice.

Where an application to set aside a transaction can be made or could have been made under this provision by a person below the age of 21, such an application can be made instead by that person's executor, trustee in bankruptcy, trustee acting under a trust deed for creditors or curator *bonis* so long as the challenge is made at any time prior to the date on which that person would have attained or does attain the age of 21 years.[24] The application can be made in the Court of Session or in the sheriff court, either as a separate action or as an incidental application in other proceedings in these courts.[25] The court may set aside the transaction and make such further order, if any, as seems appropriate to the court in order to give effect to the rights of the parties.[26]

Unchallengeable Transactions

The Act sets out a number of transactions and legal acts that cannot be challenged by the young person on the ground that they are prejudicial transactions[27] (though they may, of course, be challenged for other reasons permitted by other legal rules). These are as follows:

(a) the exercise of testamentary capacity;

(b) the exercise by testamentary writing of any power of appointment;

(c) the giving of consent to the making of an adoption order;

(d) the bringing or defending of, or the taking of any step in, civil proceedings;

(e) the giving of consent to any surgical, medical or dental procedure or treatment;

(f) a transaction in the course of the applicant's trade, business or profession;

(g) a transaction into which any other party was induced to enter by virtue of any fraudulent misrepresentation by the applicant as to age or other material fact;

(h) a transaction ratified by the applicant after he attained the age of 18 years and in the knowledge that it could be the subject of an application to the court to set it aside;

(j) a transaction ratified by the court under section 4 of the 1991 Act.

Ratification of Transactions by the Court

Any transaction that is liable to be set aside under the provisions described above can be ratified by the court before it is entered into, if a joint application by all the parties to the proposed transaction is made to the court to do so.[28]

---

[24] *Ibid.*, s. 3(4).
[25] *Ibid.*, s. 3(5).
[26] *Ibid.*
[27] *Ibid.*, s. 3(3).
[28] *Ibid.*, s. 4(1).

Transactions cannot be ratified by the court retrospectively and there is no obligation on the parties to a proposed transaction to seek prior ratification. The aim is to provide a means whereby an adult party who might be unwilling to enter into a transaction because of the potential risk of later reduction can obviate that risk in circumstances in which the proposed transaction is not unreasonable: in other words the provision is designed to avoid people being discouraged from transacting with persons over 16 and below 18.

The procedure is by means of a summary application to the sheriff of the sheriffdom in which any of the parties to the proposed transaction resides, or, where none of the parties resides in Scotland, to the sheriff at Edinburgh; the decision of the sheriff is final and there is no appeal.[29] The sheriff shall not grant the application to ratify the proposed transaction if it appears to the court that an adult, exercising reasonable prudence and in the circumstances of the party to the transaction who is over 16 years but under 18 years of age would not enter into the transaction.[30] If the application is granted by the sheriff, the transaction will then be unchallengeable on the ground that it is a prejudicial transaction.[31]

LEGAL REPRESENTATION OF CHILDREN

Introduction

In the limited circumstances in which a child (*i.e.* a person under 16 years of age) has legal capacity to enter into a transaction then there is no need for a parent or guardian to represent the child in that transaction. However, where, as will be the usual case, a child does not have legal capacity to enter into a particular transaction, then that child's parent or guardian must exercise the parental right of guardianship, or legal representation, and by that means perform the particular act on behalf of the child. The decision whether to enter into, and how to conduct, any transaction lies with the child's legal representative, but that decision is governed by the requirement that a parent or guardian acts in the interests of the child or ward.

The Representative Role of Guardians

Guardianship entitles a person to represent a child who lacks legal capacity in transactions and other juridical acts, to undertake on the child's behalf acts with legal effect, and to administer the child's property. It is one of the parental rights listed as such in the Law Reform (Parent and Child) (Scotland) Act 1986,[32] and as a result it inheres in all parents who have parental rights under that statute.[33] It inheres also in persons who are appointed guardians, the position of whom will be examined in detail later.[34] Until recently, "guardianship" was not a term of

---

[29] *Ibid.*, s. 4(3).
[30] *Ibid.*, s. 4(2).
[31] *Ibid.*, s. 3(3)(*j*).
[32] s. 8.
[33] See s. 2.
[34] *Post* at pp. 381–394.

art in Scots law, but the word is now to be understood, as we will see, in the sense of tutory at common law. In so far as the right of guardianship inheres in parents it serves merely to indicate that aspect of parental power concerned with legal representation and the administration of property. The Scottish Law Commission have proposed legislation to make this clear, by enacting, without reference to guardianship, that parents have the responsibility and the right of legal representation by virtue of their parenthood, and restricting guardianship *per se* to parent-substitutes appointed as "guardians" with all the responsibilities and rights that parents have in relation to their children.[35] Such a change would be a terminological improvement. Although parents can be described as guardians of their children in the exercise of the whole range of parental powers and duties, it is anomalous to designate one aspect by that title. "Guardian" is more aptly reserved for those who come in the place of parents, as, in common usage, the expression "parent or guardian" suggests. In neither respect would there be, however, a substantive change in the law. No new right would be given to parents nor any existing right taken away. Nor would the position of guardians as parent-substitutes be affected to any significant degree. They presently have the same powers and duties as did tutors.

At common law there were two distinct forms of guardianship over children: tutory (for pupil children) and curatory (for minor children).[36] The powers of a tutor were far greater than those of a curator, this in two major respects. First, the pupil child was not *sui juris* and therefore could not perform any juridical act: this had to be done on his behalf by his tutor. The minor child on the other hand was *sui juris* and could perform on his own behalf juridical acts, though if he had a curator he (usually) had to obtain the curator's consent before the act was valid. Secondly, the tutor had power over the person of the child as well as over the child's property. This allowed the tutor, at common law, to retain custody of the child, to determine where he was to live, to determine who was to have access to the child, and to decide what medical treatment the child was to receive.[37] The curator had no such power over the person of the child, and so could not, for example, provide valid consent to the medical treatment of the child.[38] The law underwent fundamental change in 1991 when curatory of children was abolished and tutory was, effectively, extended to age 16 for both sexes. Section 5(1) of the Age of Legal Capacity (Scotland) Act 1991 provides:

> "any reference in any rule of law, enactment or document to the tutor or tutory of a pupil child shall be construed as a reference to the guardian or, as the case may be, guardianship of a person under the age of 16 years; and accordingly the guardian of such a person shall have in relation to him and his estate the powers and duties which. . .a tutor had in relation to his pupil."

It is therefore to the law of tutory that we must look to determine the position of

---

[35] Scot. Law Com. No. 135, *Report on Family Law* (May 1992), paras. 2.27 and 3.01–3.16.

[36] For a full examination of tutory and curatory prior to 1991, see *ante*, pp. 37–51.

[37] All these were, after the Guardianship of Infants Act 1925, subject to the powers being exercised for the child's welfare.

[38] See Norrie, "The *Gillick* Case and Parental Rights in Scots Law," 1985 S.L.T. (News) 157.

guardians today, because the right of tutory has become the right of guardianship and that right now applies until the child reaches the age of 16.[39]

There was a certain ambiguity, already alluded to, inherent in the concept of tutory. It was a term used to describe the representational role of a person who acted on behalf of a pupil in legal transactions and in administration of his estate because of the child's lack of legal capacity; it was in that sense that a father was, in the exercise of the representational aspect of the parental power, designated tutor of his pupil child. It was also, however, the term used to describe the office of those who acted in place of the father with, as has been seen, wider powers which were not purely representational. That ambiguity persists in the modern concept of guardianship but when modern statute speaks of guardianship as a parental right it is, it is conceived, the representational role which is in contemplation. It is with that representational role, whether exercised by parents or others, that the discussion of guardianship in this chapter is concerned. The office of guardians as parent substitutes and their wider role in that connection are discussed later.[40] It should, however, be noted that the representative function of guardianship, although primarily associated with the protection and administration of the child's estate, is wider than that and can involve acts that affect the child's person as well as his property. So, the guardian as legal representative will represent the child in civil proceedings which may concern the child's personal wellbeing as well as his proprietorial interests.

Source and Rationale

Although, in the case of tutory, there were feudal antecedents, the Roman law was the primary source of both tutory and curatory in their modern form.[41] The underlying consideration was the necessity, reflected in practically all legal systems, to provide for the protection of the person and the management of the affairs of those who have not reached an age and discretion at which they can be expected to take full responsibility for the protection of their own interests and act with the independence attributed to adults. That is a function that is usually thought to belong naturally to parents, in default of whom some substitute must be found. So, for Stair, tutory had its roots in natural or divine law:

> "If there were not positive law, the natural infirmity of pupilage would not want its natural remedies, provided by him, who is the father of the fatherless and layeth his obediential obligations upon those whom, by the law written in their hearts, he hath bound to the performance of these duties."[42]

That reasoning, as Stair recognised, did not apply to curatory for the minor was, in contemplation of the law, much more capable of responsible independent action than was the pupil. Although a minor who had no parents was the subject of a degree of legal protection, his acts might have received legal effect without the

---

[39] Law Reform (Parent and Child) (Scotland) Act 1986, s. 8, as amended by the Age of Legal Capacity (Scotland) Act 1991, Sched. 1, para. 43.
[40] See *post*, Chapter 14.
[41] See Montgomery, "Guardian and Ward," in *Scottish Legal History* (Stair Society, Vol. 20), at pp. 125–129.
[42] I, vi, 1.

necessity of the appointment of curators. It is the protective element indicated by Stair in relation to tutory that provides the main *rationale* for guardianship today.

Parents as Guardians

In formal deeds and in legal proceedings the father of a child used commonly to be designed a tutor and administrator-at-law,[43] or as curator, according to whether the child was a pupil or minor. After the Guardianship Act 1973 a similar designation was appropriate to the mother. The usage was ancient and was entirely apt as a description of the exercise of parental power. It was, however, misleading if it is taken to suggest that a distinct office of tutory or curatory rested in the parent, or that parents were subject to all the rules applicable to tutors and curators. In relation to the management of a child's estate and to acts connected therewith, such as the granting of deeds and the taking of legal proceedings, a parent could be and still can be superseded in the exercise of his powers by an order of the court, but there is no office from which he can be removed. So in *Robertson, Petrs.*[44] Lord Justice-Clerk Inglis said of a father,

> "There appears to me to be no room for removing him from the office of administrator-in-law to his son, for there is no such office in the proper sense of the term. It is a position inseparable from the relation of parent and child, and recognised by the municipal law of the country, and all, therefore, that the Court can do is to supersede him in the exercise of his powers derived from that relation, but not to deprive him of any office."[45]

In other words, a parent who acted as tutor and administrator-at-law, or as curator, acted properly *qua* parent and not by virtue of any separate authority. This remains the case today in relation to the parent's responsibility and right of legal representation. One of the parental rights conferred on all mothers and on fathers who are or were married to the mother at or after the conception of the child[46] is the right of guardianship[47]; but a parent who has parental rights can act as the child's legal representative because he is a parent and not because he holds a separate office. The father of a child who is not and has not been married to the mother does not have the parental right of guardianship unless and until appointed to that office by the court[48]: such a father will hold an office separate from his parenthood and he takes his authority from the court rather than from his paternity.[49] If without appointment to that office he performs the functions of a guardian, he thereby takes on the character of what at common law was known as a pro-tutor, and it would seem appropriate that he should now be described as a pro-guardian.[50]

---

[43] The phrase appeared in s. 1(2) of the Trusts (Scotland) Act 1961 until these words (*inter alia*) were removed by Sched. 2 to the Age of Legal Capacity (Scotland) Act 1991.

[44] (1865) 3 M. 1077.

[45] *Ibid.*, at p. 1079.

[46] Law Reform (Parent and Child) (Scotland) Act 1986, s. 2.

[47] *Ibid.*, s. 8.

[48] Under s. 3(1) of the Law Reform (Parent and Child) (Scotland) Act 1986.

[49] See, in a different context, the same conclusion reached in *C.* v. *Kennedy*, 1991 S.L.T. 755.

[50] See *post* at pp. 399–402.

The Extent of the Guardianship Role

Fraser says[51] that "the office of tutory is strictly one of administration." This was not at common law wholly accurate, for, as has been seen, the tutor did have a number of rights over the person of the child, such as the right to custody, including the right to determine the child's place of residence and the various powers flowing from custody. In so far as they are inherent in custody these rights over the child's person may be exercised exclusively by the custodian if different from the guardian, except to the extent that they require the consent of the guardian for the application of funds under his control. A question remains, however, of the extent to which the residual powers of a guardian who is not a custodian, particularly in respect of legal representation, may be so exercised as to impinge on matters directly affecting the child's person and wellbeing. Is the guardian entitled, for example, to consent to the child's medical treatment, because the giving of consent is an act with the legal effect of providing a doctor with a defence to an action for assault and is therefore an aspect of legal representation of the child, notwithstanding that this amounts to an exercise of rights over the child's person? Or can that be done only by the custodian as the person with control over and responsibility for the child's person? The question is undecided.[52] However, there is no doubt that the main content of the right of guardianship is in relation to the child's affairs and his estate, and the major role of the guardian is to represent the child in transactions which, because he lacks legal capacity,[53] he cannot enter into or perform himself. The office of guardian is, therefore, primarily but not entirely one of administration and representation. It includes also the right to enter into contracts, to conduct litigation on behalf of the child, and to perform other juristic acts that are necessary for the protection of the child or his estate. The right of guardianship lasts until the child is 16 years of age.[54]

Acts of representation performed by guardians, or parents exercising the parental right of guardianship, are no longer challengeable on the ground of minority and lesion.[55] It might be perceived that the position of the child has thereby become less secure than it was at common law, where transactions undertaken on behalf of the child could be challenged by the child.[56] The policy of the law today, however, is to give protection to persons under 16 by ensuring that transactions are performed on their behalf by their legal representatives and allowing, where appropriate, a right of personal action against the representative if harm is caused.[57]

---

[51] at p. 307 (3rd ed.).
[52] See further, *ante* at pp. 168–169.
[53] See Age of Legal Capacity (Scotland) Act 1991.
[54] Law Reform (Parent and Child) (Scotland) Act 1986, s. 8.
[55] Age of Legal Capacity (Scotland) Act 1991, s. 1(5).
[56] *Ante*, at pp. 63–64.
[57] The Scottish Law Commission have suggested putting this position on to a statutory basis. So in their *Report on Family Law*, Scot. Law Com. No. 135 (May 1992), they propose (draft Bill, cl. 10(3)) that the child's legal representative should be entitled to do anything in relation to the child's property that the child could do if of full age and capacity, and (cl. 10(1)) that the legal representative should be liable to account to the child for his or her intromissions with the child's property.

The Guardian's Rights and Powers

The similarity between the guardian and the trustee has already been noted.[58] A guardian is indeed brought within the definition of "trustee" for the purposes of the Trusts (Scotland) Act 1921,[59] the Trusts (Scotland) Act 1961[60] and the Trustee Investments Act 1961[61]; and that definition expressly includes the parents acting as guardian of a child under the age of 16 years,[62] even although, as explained above, parents do not really hold a separate "office" of guardian.[63] There is a certain awkwardness in defining a trustee to include a guardian,[64] in particular because guardians do not have any property rights in the estate with which they are entitled to deal while such property rights are of the essence of trusteeship[65]: a guardian represents his ward and manages the ward's estate for him, but the ward himself remains properly the proprietor and titles to property are taken in the name of the ward and not of the guardian.[66] Although guardians are not judicial factors, the same rule is generally applicable to judicial factories where there is a living ward.[67] The assimilation of guardians to trustees has, however, the advantage that the rights and responsibilities of trustees (and thus of guardians) are set out in some detail in statutory form. It is therefore to the law of trusts that we must turn in determining the guardian's rights and powers in the management of the child's property. It should be noted, however, as we will see, that not all the rules contained in the Trusts Acts can appropriately be applied to the situation of the guardian.

Management of the Child's Property

The Trusts (Scotland) Act 1921 provides many of the basic rules for the administration of trust (and children's) estates. Certain powers are provided to all trustees (and guardians) by section 3, "unless the contrary be expressed," which words might have relevance to guardians appointed as parent-substitutes[68] but which are meaningless for parents who have guardianship

---

[58] *Ante* at pp. 47, 49 and 50.

[59] s. 2, as amended by the Age of Legal Capacity (Scotland) Act 1991, Sched. 1, para. 25.

[60] s. 6(1), importing the definition in the 1921 Act.

[61] s. 17(5), importing the definition in the 1921 Act.

[62] This was put beyond doubt by s. 10 of the Guardianship of Infants Act 1925.

[63] Even before 1921, tutors were included in the trust legislation for the purposes of conferring upon them (and others in a fiduciary capacity) the same powers and privileges as trustees: see Trusts (Scotland) Act 1867. In addition to the trust legislation, common law tutors had been subject to specific statutory regulation and were, for most purposes, judicial factors within the meaning of the Judicial Factors Act 1849, but none of these provisions apply to the modern guardian (see the Law Reform (Parent and Child) (Scotland) Act 1986 and the Age of Legal Capacity (Scotland) Act 1991). See formerly the Tutors and Curators Act 1696, Judicial Factors Act 1849 and the Guardianship of Infants Act 1886.

[64] It has been suggested (Scot. Law Com. No. 135, *supra*, para. 4.21 and draft Bill, Sched. 2) that a parent or guardian acting as a child's legal representative in relation to a child's property should no longer be regarded as a trustee for the purposes of the Trusts Acts.

[65] *Linton* v. *Inland Revenue*, 1928 S.C. 209, at p. 214, *per* Lord President Clyde. See also Norrie and Scobbie, *Trusts*, at p. 2.

[66] *Duff* v. *Gorrie* (1849) 11 D. 1054; *Scott, Petr.* (1865) 18 D. 624; *Maconochie* (1857) 19 D. 366; *Taylor* v. *Duff* (1894) 2 S.L.T. 366 (p. 353).

[67] Fraser (3rd ed.), p. 205, note 1. Walker, *Judicial Factors*, p. 83.

[68] See *post* at chap. 14.

rights without being appointed to any office. However most of the section 3 powers are inapplicable to parents exercising guardianship rights. Section 3(*a*) provides the power to resign: while appointed guardians may have this power,[69] parents cannot resign from their parenthood. Section 3(*b*) provides the power to assume new trustees (or guardians): this has been superseded in relation to guardians by section 5(2) of the Age of Legal Capacity (Scotland) Act 1991, which provides that no guardian can be appointed to a child except under s. 3 (orders relating to parental rights) or s. 4 (power of parents to appoint guardians in their wills) of the Law Reform (Parent and Child) (Scotland) Act 1986. Appointed guardians can therefore no longer rely on s. 3(*b*) of the 1921 Act for authority to assume new guardians. Section 3(*c*) provides that a majority of trustees (or guardians) shall be a quorum: this is superseded in relation to guardians by section 2(4) of the Law Reform (Parent and Child) (Scotland) Act 1986, which provides that where two or more persons have any parental right, each of them may exercise that right without the consent of the other person unless any decree or deed conferring the right otherwise provides (that proviso being inapplicable, of course, to parents). Section 3(*d*) provides that each trustee (or guardian) shall be liable only for his own acts and intromissions and shall not be liable for the acts and intromissions of co-trustees and shall not be liable for omissions. This is the only section 3 power that is applicable to parental guardians and its limitations are discussed later.[70]

Section 4 of the Trusts (Scotland) Act 1921 lays down powers which trustees in all trusts, and therefore guardians, possess where the exercise of such power is not at variance with the terms or purposes of the trust (or guardianship). In relation to appointed guardians these powers must be read subject to the terms of their appointment; no such question arises in the case of parents. Both appointed guardians and parents exercising the right of guardianship must, however, act in confirmity with the purposes of guardianship, which are to protect the child, administer his estate fairly and to represent the child to his advantage in any legal transaction. When the exercise of any of these powers would be at variance with the purposes of guardianship then their exercise will be without legal authority.[71] The powers listed are as follows[72]:

(a) To sell the child's estate or any part thereof, heritable as well as moveable.
(b) To grant feus of the heritable estate or any part thereof.
(c) To grant leases of any duration (including mineral leases) of the heritable estate or any part thereof and to remove tenants.
(d) To borrow money on the security of the child's estate or any part thereof, heritable or moveable.
(e) To excamb any part of the child's estate which is heritable.

---

[69] See *post* at p. 395.
[70] *Post* at p. 372.
[71] If the Scottish Law Commission's proposals (*supra*, note 57) are accepted, the powers of guardians and legal representatives would be rather broader for they would have the legal authority to do anything in relation to the child's property that the child, if of full age, could have done.
[72] Except those that are not appropriate in relation to guardians. For the full list, see the Trusts (Scotland) Act 1921, s. 4(1)(*a*) to (*p*).

(f) To acquire with funds from the child's estate any interest in residential accommodation (whether in Scotland or elsewhere) reasonably required to enable the guardian to provide a suitable residence for the child.

(g) To appoint factors and law agents and to pay them suitable remuneration.[73]

(h) To uplift, discharge, or assign debts due to the child's estate.

(i) To compromise or to submit and refer all claims connected with the child's estate.

(j) To grant all deeds necessary for carrying into effect the powers vested in the guardian.

(k) To pay debts due by the child's estate without requiring the creditors to constitute such debts where the guardian is satisfied that the debts are proper debts of the child.

(l) To make abatement or reduction, either temporary or permanent, of the rent, lordship, royalty or other consideration stipulated in any lease of land, houses, tenements, minerals, metals, or other subjects, and to accept renunciation of leases of any such subjects.

(m) To apply the whole or part of the child's estate which the guardian is empowered by his appointment[74] to invest in the purchase of heritable property in the repayment or redemption of any debt or burden affecting the heritable property.

(n) To concur, in respect of any securities of a company held by the child in any scheme or arrangement for certain listed matters.[75]

(o) To exercise any conditional or preferential right to subscribe for any securities in a company held by the child, and various other rights in relation to such securities.[76]

While this list is exhaustive of the powers of trustees in relation to the management of a trust estate[77] it is submitted that it is not exhaustive of the powers of guardians in relation to the management of the child's property. The primary rule for trustees is that their powers are derived, either expressly or by implication, from the terms of the trust deed. The function of section 4 is to confer on trustees additional powers provided these powers are not at variance with the terms and purposes of the trust. The list is necessarily exhaustive in the case of trustees because there is no source from which further powers can be drawn unless these are conferred by the trust deed itself. These considerations have no application to powers of guardians. Their powers rest not on any deed but on the law. The effect of section 4 is no more to supplant a guardian's common law powers than it is to supplant the powers conferred on a trustee by the trust deed.

---

[73] This power existed at common law: see Stair, I, vi, 36; Erskine, I, vii, 16; Fraser (3rd ed.), at pp. 361–362. While a guardian can appoint a factor or other suitable agent to perform acts of administration on his behalf, he cannot do so in such a way as will effectively delegate the rights and obligations of guardianship to another: *Scott* v. *Occidental Petroleum (Caledonia) Ltd.*, 1990 S.L.T. 882.

[74] Thus this only applies to non-parental guardians.

[75] See Trusts (Scotland) Act 1921, s. 4(1)(*o*).

[76] See Trusts (Scotland) Act 1921, s. 4(1)(*p*).

[77] Apart from those in the trust deed itself.

The guardian's common law powers therefore remain entire. These have never been as limited as those of trustees because, not being owner of the property involved, guardians have less opportunity to abuse their office. So, for example, while trustees have no general right to purchase heritable property[78] there is no reason to impose this limitation on guardians, bearing in mind that the predominant consideration of the guardians must at all times be prudent investment for the welfare of the child. They have such a power at common law.[79] The section 4 powers should be seen as being in addition to those that the guardians would otherwise have, or as being specified merely for the avoidance of doubt.

Investment

It is a necessary part of the administration of an estate held for more than a minimal period of time, and the only means of protecting it against inflation and other economic dangers, that it be invested properly.[80] After mentioning the tutor's duty of care of the child's person and the duty "to aliment them out of the pupil's own means, according to the condition thereof; and to educate them for a station in the commonwealth according to their quality and capacity," Stair lists among the natural obligations of tutors the management of their wards' affairs "with such diligence as provident men use in their own affairs, that nothing may be lost but everything improven to the best advantage; in all which they are not to exerce voluntary acts of dominion at their choice, as disposing of what is secure, but only necessary acts for the preservation and recovery of what will or may perish, and for improving the profits of it."[81] Fraser interpreted that passage and other passages from the institutional writers as meaning that the object of tutory, with regard to property, was "rather to preserve than to acquire; to keep the pupil's estate in the same condition as the tutor found it, so far as consistent with its nature, rather than to attempt by speculations to improve it, because it can never be improved without risk."[82] The warning against speculation is apt in the case of a tutor or guardian as of other trustees,[83] but all improvement is in a sense speculative and Fraser's interpretation of the authorities does not consist with their terms. In any event, it is inapplicable to modern conditions in which the risk of detriment from a guardian's keeping the child's estate in the same condition as he found it might well be considerably greater than those of pru-

---

[78] s. 4(ee) and (n) of the 1921 Act (paragraphs (f) and (m) in the text above) grants the power to purchase heritage only for the limited specified purpose.

[79] Stair, I, vi, 36 states that tutors cannot purchase land with the pupil's money, but that rule must be seen in the light of the generally inalienable nature of land at the time he wrote, and in any case the rule has been departed from: *Graham* v. *Hopeton* (1798) Mor. 5599; *Kennedy* v. *Innes* (1823) 2 S. 375. Erskine (I, vii, 25) regards Stair's doctrine as "suited better with those times than with the present". Fraser accepts (3rd ed. pp. 322–323) that there is a general power to purchase heritage but, citing *Lambe* v. *Chapman* (1834) 12 S. 775, excepts purchase of house property. It is submitted that the exception is anomalous and, in modern conditions, obsolete. See also *Gilray* (1876) 3 R. 619; *Campbell* (1881) 8 R. 543 and *Wardlaw's Trs.* (1902) 10 S.L.T. 229 (p. 349).

[80] It is to be noted, however, that there is no absolute rule that the child's estate must be preserved: see *Polland and Anr.* v. *Sturrock's Exrs.*, 1952 S.C. 535, in which it was held that a father could use part of the child's estate to pay for the child's education, even although he was able to do so from his own estate. See also *Steele's Trs.* v. *Cooper* (1830) 8 S. 926.

[81] I, vi, 3.

[82] 3rd ed. at p. 307.

[83] In relation to trustees, see for example *Henderson* v. *Henderson's Trs.* (1900) 2 F. 1295; *Bartlett* v. *Barclay's Bank Trust Co. (No. 1)* [1980] 1 All E.R. 139.

dent improvement and reinvestment. As the modern guardian is a trustee, within the meaning of the Trusts Acts, his duties and powers in this respect, as in others, such as protecting and defending the estate, do not differ from those of other trustees. Investment must be suitable to the size of the estate and for most children their estates will be small. The estates of children with rather more patrimony are likely today to be held under deed of trust, in which case the right and duty of investment will fall on the trustees rather than the guardian. In any event the guardian's powers of investment are delimited by the Trustee Investments Act 1961, for the purposes of which a guardian is a trustee.[84] Under that Act guardians must invest the child's funds only in those investments expressly listed in Schedule 1, which is in three parts, each of which lists different types of investment. The investments listed in Part I may be made at the guardian's absolute discretion and without his first having obtained financial advice; for small estates Part I investments may often suffice. Part II investments may be made only after taking financial advice on the question of whether the investment is satisfactory having regard to the need for diversification and the suitability of the proposed investment; such advice must be obtained from a person who is reasonably believed by the guardian to be qualified by his ability in and practical experience of financial matters, and it may be given by a person notwithstanding that he gives it in the course of his employment as an officer or servant.[85] Part III investments may be made only with not more than one half of the original estate and only after financial advice of the same nature as that required for Part II investments has been taken.[86]

Aliment from the Estate

A guardian must see that in so far as it is required proper provision is made for the aliment of his ward from the estate under his charge.[87] This duty may sometimes seem to conflict with the guardian's duty to preserve the ward's estate and so not to encroach on capital. On some old authorities, it was held that the ward must be alimented only out of the income of the estate and, "except in very singular cases," no more could be given.[88] That doctrine must, however, yield to necessity and if the aliment of the ward cannot otherwise be arranged the guardian may encroach upon capital and that may extend, with the authority of the court, to the sale of heritage if aliment "cannot be afforded otherwise."[89] And trust funds in which the child has an interest may be drawn upon for his aliment. In *Hamilton*[90] authority was granted for the repayment, out of the capital of the

---

[84] Trustee Investments Act 1961, s. 17(5).

[85] *Ibid.*, s. 6.

[86] For a more detailed description of the terms of the Trustee Investments Act 1961, in relation to trust law, see Norrie and Scobbie, *Trusts*, Chap. 8.

[87] Erskine, I, vii, 24.

[88] Fraser (3rd ed.), p. 295; *Pearson* v. *Belshes* (1678) Mor. 16296; *Sandilands* v. *Tailfer* (1684) Mor. 16300; *Duncanson* v. *Duncanson* (1715) Mor. 16336; *Kennedy* v. *Rutherglen* (1860) 22 D. 567.

[89] Stair, I, vi, 18; *Gordon* v. *H.M.A.* (1755) Mor. 16356. See also *Polland* v. *Sturrock's Exc.*, 1952 S.C. 535.

[90] (1859) 21 D. 1379.

trust estate under a marriage contract, of sums advanced by a mother for the education of her children where she was entitled to the liferent of the whole fund and the children's sole interest was in the capital of the estate. Payment, out of capital, for the aliment and education of the children for a further year was also authorised and leave was reserved to make further applications thereafter. At common law such advances were authorised under the *nobile officium* and could be made only if the interest of the children had vested. By the Trusts (Scotland) Act 1921, however, re-enacting, with some modification, similar provisions of the Trusts (Scotland) Act 1867, the court is empowered to author-ise trustees to make advances from capital for the maintenance or education of beneficiaries who are not of full age and to whom the capital of the fund out of which payment is made is destined either absolutely or contingently.[91] It is ne-cessary before such advance can be authorised that it should appear that the in-come of the fund is insufficient for, or not applicable to, the maintenance or education of the beneficiaries and that the advance is necessary for that purpose. The advance must not be especially prohibited by the trust deed and the rights of the beneficiaries, if contingent, must be contingent only on their survivance.

The child's estate should be applied to his aliment only to the extent that his alimentary needs are not met from other sources. The amount in which a parent or other person under an alimentary obligation is liable to contribute to the ali-ment of a child is now determined by what is reasonable in the circumstances having regard to the respective needs, resources and earning capacities of the obligants and the child and, generally, to all the circumstances of the case.[92] The extent to which a guardian should apply the child's estate to his aliment will therefore depend, *inter alia*, on whether any alimentary liabilities, so deter-mined, are exigible.

Contracts

A child under the age of 16 years has, generally speaking, no contractual ca-pacity[93] (a contract being a "transaction having legal effect") and as a result any contract has to be entered into on his behalf by his guardian. At common law the power to enter into contracts belonged to the tutor, but the powers of tutory are now the powers of guardianship.[94] The contracts that tutors could and guardians can enter into on behalf of the child are limited in nature to those that are re-quired properly to administer the child's estate and to fulfil the guardian's gen-eral duty of protection. A guardian who enters into an entirely unnecessary contract on behalf of the child will doubtless in doing so create a valid and en-forceable contract, just as the guardian does who enters into one on disadvant-ageous terms, though he may well, by doing so, open himself to personal liability to the child.[95]

---

[91] Trusts (Scotland) Act 1921, s. 16.
[92] Family Law (Scotland) Act 1985, s. 1(2) and s. 4.
[93] Age of Legal Capacity (Scotland) Act 1991, s. 1(1). See *ante*, at pp. 353–355.
[94] *Ibid.*, s. 5(1). On the powers of tutors, see *ante* at pp. 37–41.
[95] See *post* at pp. 371–372.

There are certain contracts that a child under the age of 16 will have capacity to enter into, being those that are both (a) of a kind commonly entered into by persons of his age and circumstances and (b) on terms that are not unreasonable.[96] It is not stated in the Act whether if the child does have the capacity to enter into a particular contract, the guardian's power to act on behalf of the child is affected. The question is, in other words, whether or not the guardian's power to enter into a contract survives the acquisition by the child (before the age of 16) of capacity to enter into that contract. Section 5(1) of the 1991 Act provides that the powers of guardians are to be what at common law the powers of tutors were, and tutors had the power to enter into any contract on behalf of the child. Guardians' powers are not expressly limited by the provision granting capacity to the child and, it is submitted, they are not impliedly limited either. Some parents continue to act on behalf of their inexperienced children even in circumstances in which the child could act for himself, and it would be consistent with the parent's protective role if the law were to recognise their continued ability to do so. Thus the parent of a 15-year-old who uses the child's money and on the child's behalf purchases an item of clothing for the child is validly exercising a guardianship power, notwithstanding that the child himself had the capacity to enter into that particular contract.[97]

Litigation

The pupil child at common law was not *sui juris*[98] and this proposition now applies to children under the age of 16. One of the consequences of a person being in nonage is that, subject to important qualifications,[99] he has no *persona standi in judico* and he is therefore generally unable to raise or defend actions in his own name. The guardian's right of legal representation finds its most typical expression here, and actions can and should be raised in the name of the guardian on behalf of the child, or against the guardian as representing the child. It is indeed incorrect to libel the child as pursuer (except in circumstances in which the child has no guardian or for other reason, such as contrary interest of the guardian or the guardian's disqualification, the jurisdiction of the court has to be invoked independently of the guardian[1]) and the correct practice is to name the guardian and designate him as guardian of the child.[2] If the child is the defender he should be named, with the guardian named as the second defender. The guardian is entitled to use his discretion in deciding how the action is to be conducted, but he must, of course, bear in mind at all times that his paramount consideration is the welfare of the child. He may validly decide not to pursue an

---

[96] Age of Legal Capacity (Scotland) Act 1991, s. 2(1). See *ante*, at pp. 353–355.

[97] Different considerations are brought into play in relation to a child's capacity to consent to medical treatment, and that issue is considered elsewhere: see *ante* at pp. 182–183.

[98] Fraser (3rd ed.) at p. 204; *ante* at p. 52.

[99] See *ante* at pp. 56–57.

[1] See further, *ante* at pp. 56–57.

[2] Fraser at pp. 270–271. In *Bell* v. *Trotter's Trs.* (1841) 3 D. 380 it was held that "the trustees of A.B." without the trustees being named individually was not a *nomen juris* under which parties can sue or defend an action or use diligence. The trustees or guardians must be named.

action because the chances of success are low, or to settle, but he may not refuse to raise an action for ulterior motives or if the chances are good;[3] nor is he entitled to waive any legal defences open to the child if he is being sued.[4] Losing in litigation does not in itself suggest that the guardian has acted wrongly in raising an action, for that might inhibit guardians from pursuing potentially successful claims. A guardian will not be liable to the child for the expenses of an unsuccessful action unless his decision to pursue the case was one that no reasonable guardian acting with ordinary care and diligence would have made.[5]

Other Aspects of Legal Representation

Administration of the child's estate, entering into contracts, and conducting litigation on behalf of the child are the major elements of the representative role of the guardian, but there are others, and the protective aspect of the guardian's role justifies the wider proposition that the guardian may represent the child in any situation in which the child needs protection but is unable legally to act for himself. A guardian is entitled to grant discharges on behalf of the child, for example to executors or trustees of estates of which the child is a beneficiary.[6] The guardian is not bound to find caution unless the court so directs.[7] The right to appoint factors and agents is another aspect of legal representation, and has already been mentioned.[8]

Extension of Guardian's Powers

If the guardian wishes to exercise a power that he does not have, or if he is unsure whether what he proposes to do is a proper exercise of his power, he has a number of possible options. Of the three considered here, the last will nearly always be the preferred course, but the others are mentioned for completeness and any merits they may have in particular circumstances. First, he may raise an action under section 5 of the Trusts (Scotland) Act 1921 for the granting of any power listed under section 4 of that Act which he does not have. By the terms of section 5 the power is available to the court to grant trustees authority to exercise any of the section 4 powers that they do not otherwise possess. All trusts,

---

[3] If he does so refuse, the court can appoint a curator *ad litem* on the child raising the action in his own name, and the case would then be pursued in the name of the curator: *McConochie* v. *Bennie* (1847) 9 D. 791; see *post* at p. 403. The rule that a child may raise or defend an action in his own name when his guardian refuses to do so even when he is not yet 16 years of age, is preserved by s. 1(3)(*f*)(i) of the Age of Legal Capacity (Scotland) Act 1991, and the court's power to appoint a curator *ad litem* to a child in any civil proceedings is preserved by s. 1(3)(*f*)(ii).

[4] *Hunter and his Tutor, Petrs.* (1739) Mor. 16341.

[5] In *Cunningham's Tutrix*, 1949 S.C. 275 a guardian was awarded expenses out of the ward's estate having raised an action for the extension of her powers notwithstanding that the petition was dismissed as unnecessary.

[6] *Govan* v. *Richardson* (1633) Mor. 16263; *Dumbreck* v. *Stevenson* (1861) 4 Macq. 86; *Murray's Trs.* v. *Bloxsom's Trs.* (1887) 15 R. 233.

[7] Judicial Factors Act 1849, s. 25(2), as inserted by the Law Reform (Parent and Child) (Scotland) Act 1986, and Sched. 1, para. 1.

[8] *Ante* at p. 364.

however, possess the section 4 powers unless they are at variance with either the terms or the purposes of the trust. Authority will be granted under section 5 so long as the exercise of the requested power is "in all the circumstances expedient for the execution of the trust." Applying this to guardianship, all the section 4 powers would inhere in guardians unless they are at variance with the purposes of the guardianship, and section 5 could only be utilised when the exercise of the section 4 power was in all the circumstances expedient for the execution of the guardianship. It is difficult to imagine a situation in which the exercise of a power would be expedient for and at the same time at variance with the purposes of the guardianship. In *Cunningham's Tutrix*[9] a petition under section 5 was dismissed as unnecessary when a mother, as tutrix of her pupil son, asked for authority to sell two heritable properties to which the son had succeeded on his father's death. As the properties required considerable capital expenditure and a good offer had been received for them it was not at variance with the purposes of the guardianship.[10] The guardian's second option is to petition the Court of Session under section 1 of the Trusts (Scotland) Act 1961 to approve an arrangement enlarging the powers of the guardian of managing or administering the child's estate. This is a good deal wider than an application under section 5 of the 1921 Act since it allows the court to grant any power, including that of investment (otherwise regulated by statute,[11]) and the test applied is simply that the exercise of the power must not be prejudicial. However, the application of this provision to guardians can be achieved only with some awkwardness, even although guardians are expressly included in the definition of trusts and trustees for the purposes of the Act. Section 1 is designed to provide a consent to the alteration of a trustee's powers when that consent cannot otherwise be obtained. In relation to guardianship the court would not be providing a consent otherwise necessary, because there is never any question of the child consenting to the enlargement, or indeed the exercise, of the guardian's powers: this provision is therefore probably best avoided.

The third and most plausible option for the guardian wishing to increase his powers (indeed the one that will invariably be used) is to apply to the Court of Session or the sheriff court under section 3(1) of the Law Reform (Parent and Child) (Scotland) Act 1986 for an order relating to parental rights. The availability of this option renders reliance on the previous two provisions redundant. An application under section 3(1) might be made whenever the guardian is unsure whether or not he possesses a power that he wants to exercise, or when he knows that he does not possess the power but believes that it would be in the interests of the child for him to be granted and to exercise the power, or when he is unsure whether or not its exercise would be in the interests of the child. As an application relating to parental rights the court will regard the welfare of the child involved as the paramount consideration and will not make an order increasing the guardian's powers unless it is satisfied that to do so will be in the

---

[9] 1949 S.C. 275.

[10] See also *Dempster*, 1926 S.L.T. 157; *Brunton, Petr.*, 1928 S.N. 112.

[11] Trustee Investments Act 1961. The court in applying s. 1 of the Trusts (Scotland) Act 1961 to investments is not limited by the terms of the Trustee Investments Act 1961: *Henderson, Petr.*, 1981 S.L.T. (Notes) 40; *University of Glasgow, Petrs.*, 1991 S.L.T. 604.

interests of the child.[12] The guardian's role is limited by the representative character of his office, and for that reason the court could not grant the guardian power to do anything that the child, if of full age and capacity, could not do himself.

Liabilities of Guardians

Guardianship, like custodianship, is a right that confers not only powers but also responsibilities that necessarily carry duties and liabilities. The protective aspect of the guardian's duty has already been mentioned. The exercise of the right of guardianship is proper only if it does no harm to the interests of the child, and acting against these interests may potentially open the guardian to personal liability. It is probably wrong today to suggest[13] that there are different standards of care required of guardians depending on how they are appointed. The welfare of the child is the determining principle and anyone exercising guardianship rights, however appointed, must bear that in mind.[14] Though the Trusts Acts do not spell out the nature of a trustee's liabilities to the beneficiaries of a trust, the common law liabilities of trustees do, it is submitted, provide an apt analogy with the situation of the guardian and child, for both trustee and guardian stand in an essentially fiduciary position in relation to their charges. The test for a breach of trust can easily be adapted to the guardian acting wrongfully. In relation to trustees it has been said that the true test for establishing whether there has been a breach of trust is to ask—"has it. . .been shewn that the trustee failed to exercise that degree of diligence which a man of ordinary prudence would exercise in the management of his own affairs?"[15] A guardian will be liable to account to the child for any loss that he occasions the child's estate by his failure to exercise that degree of diligence which a man of ordinary prudence would have exercised in the management of his own affairs. The extent of the guardian's liability will be the extent of the loss to the estate and, like a trustee, the guardian cannot set off his generally beneficial administration against a loss caused by a single wrongful act.[16] The remedy is for the child to seek damages, or to raise an action for count, reckoning and payment, this latter as a consequence of the guardian's duty to account and to restore and to refund.[17] The practical effect of both remedies is the same since the level of damages is the extent of the loss, but there are procedural differences, as well as different limitation periods.[18] The remedy will be available to the child when he attains the age

---

[12] Law Reform (Parent and Child) (Scotland) Act 1986, s. 3(2). Any residual common law power of the Court of Session to increase the guardian's powers as an exercise of the *nobile officium* is probably subsumed into this provision.

[13] See Fraser (3rd ed.) at pp. 390–393.

[14] It has been proposed (Scot. Law Com. No. 135, *Report on Family Law*, May 1992, para. 4.23 and draft Bill, cl. 10) that the sole standard of care to be demanded of persons acting as the child's legal representative should be the standard of the reasonable and prudent person acting on his or her own behalf.

[15] *Per* Lord Herschell in *Raes* v. *Meek* (1889) 16 R.(H.L.) 31 at p. 34. See also Lord Watson in *Learoyd* v. *Whiteley* (1887) 12 App.Cas. 727 at p. 733; and Lord Atkinson in *Buchanan* v. *Eaton* 1911 S.C.(H.L.) 40 at p. 45.

[16] *Clarke* v. *Clarke's Trs.*, 1925 S.C. 693; Walker, *Civil Remedies*, at p. 1072; Norrie and Scobbie, *Trusts*, at p. 144.

[17] Stair, I, vi, 21.

[18] See *Hobday* v. *Kirkpatrick's Trs.*, 1985 S.L.T. 197.

of 16 years, and to any co-guardian or any curator *ad litem* appointed by the court before then. Indeed any interested party, which would include anyone with care and control of the child, would be able to call the guardian to account for his intromissions with the child's estate.[19] The remedy might be granted if, for example, the guardian enters into a contract on behalf of the child that proves to be detrimental to his interest, or if he conducts litigation in a prejudicial manner, or fails to enforce the child's legal rights. The legal transactions themselves will not be challengeable if the guardian is acting within his authority as legal representative of the child, but he will be personally liable to the child if the valid transaction causes loss and his actions satisfy the test for liability given above. As trustees, guardians are liable only for their own acts and intromissions, and not for their omissions or the acts and intromissions of co-guardians unless, in the case of guardians appointed by a parent or by the court, the deed of appointment or decree of the court expressly provides to the contrary.[20] A failure to do something, however, may properly be regarded as an act rather than as an omission, such as the failure to exercise reasonable care, or even the failure to call in a debt timeously,[21] and the provision exempting trustees and guardians from liability for omissions probably has little substantive content. A guardian may, of course, be liable for the acts of co-guardians which he has adopted or ratified or in which he has acquiesced.

Auctor in Rem Suam

Even before trustees were defined by statute so as to include guardians, it was recognised that the office of guardian had a fiduciary character which required that the guardian should not allow himself to become *auctor in rem suam*,[22] and the rule against such actings applies to guardians on the same principles as it applies to trustees. A guardian therefore must not place himself in a situation in which his interest as an individual may conflict with his duty as a guardian. Even the mere possibility of such conflict must be avoided and questions of fairness or whether an actual advantage was obtained are irrelevant. "The criterion...is not what was done, but what might be done."[23] The consequence of breaching this duty is that if a personal advantage is gained by the guardian then the guardian will hold that benefit on a constructive trust for the benefit of the child.[24] The transaction itself is open to reduction at the instance of the child or at the instance of any other guardian, though not at the instance of the other

---

[19] Fraser (3rd ed.), at p. 421.

[20] Trusts (Scotland) Act 1921, s. 3(*d*). This changes the common law, under which tutors were liable for omissions as well as acts: see Stair, I, vi, 21. Fathers were not liable for omissions and in the case of tutors nominate liability for omissions and liability *in solidum* might be waived in the deed of appointment (Erskine, I, vi, 55 and I, vii, 26).

[21] See Norrie and Scobbie at p. 147; *Forman* v. *Burns* (1853) 15 D. 362.

[22] Stair, I, vi, 17; Erskine, I, vii, 19; Fraser (3rd ed.) at pp. 372–389 (and cases cited therein).

[23] *Per* Viscount Dunedin in *Wright* v. *Morgan* [1926] A.C. 788 at p. 798.

[24] *Cherry's Trs.* v. *Patrick*, 1911 2 S.L.T. 313.

party in the transaction.[25] The child's right to reduce such a transaction is not lost by prescription.[26]

The principle will prevent the guardian from transacting with the child's estate on his own behalf.[27] Thus for example the guardian cannot purchase for himself items from the child's estate,[28] nor sell his own property to the child, nor lend to or borrow from the estate.[29] The clash of interests in that situation is obvious. Nor may the guardian exercise any discretionary right that he may be entitled to exercise in relation to the child's estate for his own benefit.[30] The principle will also prevent the guardian from claiming remuneration for acting as such. This of course would be inappropriate in any case in relation to parental guardians, but it may be that an appointed guardian wishes remuneration for the time and trouble that acting as such will cause him: in that case he must be given authority to charge remuneration to the child's estate from the deed or decree that appoints him and in the absence of such authority he will be in the same, non-remunerative, position as a parental guardian.

If the guardian finds himself in a position in which he wishes to transact with the child, then he may in exceptional circumstances receive authority to do so from the court. This is the only way in which the principle could be avoided. Thus he could raise an action under section 3(1) of the Law Reform (Parent and Child) (Scotland) Act 1986 for an order relating to parental rights: the order could authorise him, for example, to purchase an item of property from the child, or to sell to the child something that he owns. The court of course will regard the welfare of the child as paramount and will not make any order unless it is satisfied that to do so will be in the interests of the child.[31]

Relief from Liability

A guardian or legal representative who is liable to the child for a breach of his or her duty of care may be relieved wholly or partly therefrom by an order of the court under section 3 of the Law Reform (Parent and Child) (Scotland) Act 1986. The court in doing so would be bound to regard the welfare of the child involved as the paramount consideration and would not relieve the guardian from any liability unless satisfied that to do so would be in the interests of the child.[32]

---

[25] *Hall's Trs.* v. *McArthur*, 1918 S.C. 646, *per* Lord Johnston at p. 651. Lord Johnston was talking about the situation with trustees, but the principle seems sound and should, it is submitted, be applied equally to guardians. The point of this rule is to protect the beneficiaries or the child, not the other party to the transaction.

[26] *Magistrates of Aberdeen* v. *University of Aberdeen* (1877) 4 R.(H.L.) 48, *per* Lord O'Hagan at p. 54, affirming (1876) 3 R. 1087.

[27] If the proposals of the Scottish Law Commission are accepted (*supra*, note 57) and guardians acquire the power to enter into any transaction the child could if of full age and capacity, this might suggest that the guardian will be able to transact with him or herself. It is, however, submitted that the principle *auctor in rem suam* will act as an implicit qualification to the guardian's power, even in the face of the words of a statute.

[28] Dig. xviii, 1, 34, 7.

[29] *Tennant* v. *Tennant* (1673) Mor. 16288.

[30] *Inglis* v. *Inglis*, 1983 S.L.T. 437.

[31] Law Reform (Parent and Child) (Scotland) Act 1986, s. 3(2). *Cf.* the circumstances in *Coat's Trs.*, 1914 S.C. 723.

[32] *Ibid.*

There will be few situations in which it would be in the interests of the child to deprive him of a right of recompense from a guardian who acted wrongfully, but since welfare must be given a wide scope and will include more than merely economic considerations, relief might exceptionally be considered appropriate for parental guardians if that protects family harmony.

Powers that Guardians Lack

While the *raison d'être* of guardianship is to furnish the child with a person *sui juris* who can represent him and undertake on his behalf legal transactions, a guardian is not entitled to perform every sort of legal act on behalf of the child that a capax adult could perform on his own behalf.[33] There are a number of acts with legal effect that a guardian is unable to perform on behalf of the child, and any purported performance of such an act will be void and of no effect.

First, a guardian cannot make a will on behalf of the child. The age for testamentary capacity in modern Scots law is 12 years for both males and females and over both heritable and moveable property,[34] and it follows that any child who dies before attaining that age will die intestate. The making of a will is the exercise of a most personal discretion and it is something that cannot be delegated to another,[35] and which cannot be performed on one's behalf by another.[36] Secondly, a guardian cannot consent on behalf of a child who is a beneficiary under a private trust to a variation of its terms or purposes. All persons under the age of 18 are deemed by the Trusts (Scotland) Act 1961 to be incapable of assenting to any proposed variation: this is expressly provided for in relation to persons aged 16 and 17 years, whether or not they act with the concurrence of any curator or guardian they may have;[37] and it is implicitly understood in relation to children under the age of 16 years (because they are in nonage). The result is that in all cases in which the consent of a person under the age of 18 years is required, the court must be asked to grant that consent on that person's behalf under section 1(1) of the 1961 Act. Thirdly, a guardian has no right to consent to the adoption of his ward's child or to an order freeing the ward's child for adoption, unless he is the guardian of that child also. The adoption legislation provides[38] that the court shall not make an adoption order unless satisfied that the parent or guardian has freely and with full understanding of what is involved agreed unconditionally to the making of the order.[39] There is no age limit on the parent's rights and, if the parent is a child his or her capacity to consent to adoption, being a consent with legal effect, is determined by the Age of Legal Capacity (Scotland) Act 1991.[40] If the under-16-year-old parent is so young as to be

---

[33] This will be qualified to a certain extent when Parliament enacts the proposal of the Scottish Law Commission that a child's legal representative should be entitled to do anything in relation to the administration of the child's property that the child could do if of full age and capacity: see Scot. Law Com. No. 135, *Report on Family Law*, May 1992, para. 4.19 and draft Bill, cl. 10(3)(*b*).

[34] Age of Legal Capacity (Scotland) Act 1991, s. 2(2): see further, *post* at pp. 378–379.

[35] *Rintoul's Trs.* v. *Rintoul*, 1949 S.C. 297 at p. 299, *per* Lord Justice-Clerk Thomson.

[36] Erskine, I, vii, 18; Fraser (3rd ed.) at p. 351.

[37] S.1(2), as amended by the Age of Legal Capacity (Scotland) Act 1991, Sched. 1, para 27.

[38] Adoption (Scotland) Act 1978, s. 16(1).

[39] See further, *post* at pp. 530–534.

[40] See *ante* at pp. 353–357.

incapable of understanding, or does not satisfy the conditions for capacity to consent in the 1991 Act, this justifies the court dispensing with the parent's agreement[41] rather than giving the parent's guardian the right to consent on his or her behalf. Fourthly, guardians who are not parents cannot appoint or assume new guardians for the child. This is a consequence of section 5(2) of the Age of Legal Capacity (Scotland) Act 1991, which provides that guardians can only be appointed by the court or by a parent, and is in contrast with the English provisions which give non-parental guardians rights equal to those of parents to appoint new guardians.[42] Fifthly, guardians cannot dispose of the child's property by way of gift.[43] This would breach the duty of the guardian to preserve the child's estate. Donations can be made only by adult capax persons. Guardians can, of course, make valid donations to their wards.[44] Sixthly, guardians cannot transfer assets belonging to the child to a trust, even although the trust is set up solely for the benefit of the child, because this would amount to an unlawful delegation of the rights and duties in relation to administration from the guardian to the trustees. It is an important principle of law "that the right which is given to a child's mother or father to act as that child's [guardian] is not capable of being transferred to others. This principle is analogous to that by which it is recognised that a trustee cannot delegate his trust."[45] Nor would it make any difference that the guardian was one of the trustees, because section 3(a) of the Trusts (Scotland) Act entitles trustees to resign.[46] It is similarly incompetent for the court itself to create a trust over money it awards the child as damages in such a way as completely to supersede the guardian.[47]

OTHER ASPECTS OF THE CAPACITY OF CHILDREN

Capacity in Delict

The institutional writers do not distinctly treat of the capacity of pupils and minors to incur delictual liability. Erskine, however, states the general principle of delictual liability to be that "every one who has the exercise of reason, and so can distinguish between right and wrong, is naturally obliged to make up the damage befalling his neighbour from a wrong committed by himself."[48] The developed Roman law was that the *infans* (*i.e.* child under the age of seven years)

---

[41] Adoption (Scotland) Act 1978, s. 16(2)(a).

[42] Children Act 1989, s. 5(4). The Scottish Law Commission have proposed legislation bringing Scots law into line with English law on this matter: Scot. Law Com. No. 135, *Report on Family Law*, May 1992, draft Bill, cl. 7(2).

[43] Fraser at p. 335. This rule would be abolished if Parliament accepts the proposals of the Scottish Law Commission, *supra*, at para. 4.19, that the legal representative could do anything with the child's property that the child could have done if of full age and capacity.

[44] See, *e.g. Linton* v. *Commissioners of Inland Revenue*, 1928 S.C. 209.

[45] *Scott* v. *Occidental Petroleum (Caledonia) Ltd.*, 1990 S.L.T. 882, *per* Lord President Hope at p. 885K.

[46] *Ibid.*, at p. 886G. *Quaere* whether the position would be different if the trust deed expressly withheld the right to resign from the guardian. It is submitted that this would not make a difference, because guardianship is essentially a different office from trusteeship.

[47] *Boylan* v. *Hunter*, 1992 S.C. 80. Rules of Court (Rules of Court 131–134 (Court of Session); Sheriff Courts (Scotland) Act 1907, Sched. 1, r. 128 (sheriff court)) now provide for the appointment by the court of a judicial factor when the court is satisfied that the administration of damages cannot otherwise be reasonably secured.

[48] III, i, 13.

was not *doli capax*,[49] and that is followed in the Roman-Dutch tradition by the law of South Africa which holds that children under the age of seven are capable neither of intentional delict nor of negligence.[50] There is no Scottish authority unequivocally laying down a rule for intentional delict,[51] but in view of the affinities of such delict to crime a minimum of seven or now of eight could be justified by comparison with criminal responsibility. With that possible exception the maxim applicable appears to be *neminem in delictis aetas excusat* in the sense that liability depends on rational capacity for discrimination rather than on age. In relation to negligence, that view is supported by authority. In *Campbell* v. *Ord and Maddison* Lord Justice-Clerk Moncrieff said:

> "Negligence implies a capacity to apprehend intelligently the duty, obligation, or precaution neglected, and that depends to a large degree on the nature of that which is neglected, as well as on the intelligence and maturity of the person said to have neglected it. The capacity to neglect is a question of fact in the individual case, as much so as negligence itself, which is always a question of fact."[52]

It is evident from that passage that the test of capacity for negligence is the subjective one of the mental condition of the person alleged to be negligent. A distinction, perhaps difficult to maintain, is however to be made between whether a person had capacity for negligence and whether he was actually negligent ("negligence itself"). To apply the same test as that for capacity to negligence itself would be to displace the objective test of the conduct of the reasonable man. The view that capacity for delict is a question of fact has been followed in a number of cases in which the court has, if with some reluctance, allowed issues of contributory negligence by very young children to be considered.[53] This position is unaffected by the Age of Legal Capacity (Scotland) Act 1991.[54]

Delictual Liability of Parents

A parent is not as such liable for the delict of his children. It seems, however, to be implicit in *Lewis* v. *Carmarthen County Council*[55] and *Home Office* v. *Dorset Yacht Co.*[56] that parents or others who have actual custody or care of

---

[49] Donaldson, *Minors in Roman Law*, p. 86, s. 177.

[50] Donaldson, *op. cit.*, p. 96, s. 186; McKerron, *The Law of Delict* (3rd ed.), p. 113.

[51] See *Somerville* v. *Hamilton* (1541) Mor. 8905 in which a six-year-old child was apparently found liable in spuilzie. Stewart however analyses the case as more nearly a claim for unjust enrichment: see Stewart, "Liability for Pupils in Delict," 1989 S.L.T. (News) 404. *Cf. Bryson* v. *Sommervill* (1565) Mor. 8906 in which a defence to an action of spuilzie was upheld that the defender was 10 and not 14.

[52] (1873) 1 R. 149 at p. 153.

[53] *Campbell* v. *Ord and Maddison, supra* (four-year-old); *Frasers* v. *Edinburgh Street Tramways Co.* (1882) 10 R. 264 (six-year-old); *Plantza* v. *Glasgow Corporation*, 1910 S.C. 786 (five-year-old); *Banner's Trs.* v. *Kennedy's Trs.*, 1978 S.L.T. (Notes) 83 (five-year-old); *Harvey* v. *Cairns*, 1989 S.L.T. 107 (six-year-old).

[54] Age of Legal Capacity (Scotland) Act 1991, s. 1(3)(*c*): "Nothing in this Act shall. . .affect the delictual. . .responsibility of any person."

[55] [1953] 2 All E.R. 1403.

[56] [1970] A.C. 1004.

children may be liable for failure to take reasonable care that those under their charge do not become the occasion of danger to others or cause injury or damage. The limitations are not clear, but it would seem to be necessary both that the injury should have been foreseeable and that the precaution desiderated should have been one that a reasonable person in charge of children or young persons would have taken in the circumstances.[57]

Criminal Responsibility

At one time the minimum age of criminal responsibility was attended with some uncertainty but it is now fixed by statute at eight.[58] The seeming harshness of such an early age is mitigated by the consideration that children under the age of 16 will not normally be prosecuted but will be subject to proceedings before a children's hearing or otherwise dealt with by the reporter.[59] The minimum age applies to all crimes and therefore includes those of strict liability. This position is unaffected by the Age of Legal Capacity (Scotland) Act 1991.[60]

Capacity to Marry

The common law rule was that children attained capacity to marry on the attaining of legal puberty, that is 12 for girls and 14 for boys: pupils could not marry because they were incapable of giving consent.[61] The law was altered in 1929[62] when the age was raised, for both sexes, to 16 at which age it remains. The law is now contained in the Marriage (Scotland) Act 1977, which provides[63] that no person domiciled in Scotland may marry before he attains the age of 16. This rule applies no matter where the marriage takes place, and there is an identical rule to govern all marriages that take place in Scotland, no matter the domicile of the parties.[64] Capacity to marry is a personal capacity and does not depend on the capacity of the other party. It follows that while a person domiciled in Scotland cannot marry anywhere before attaining the age of 16, after attaining that age a person domiciled in Scotland may marry someone below that age if the ceremony takes place in a country that allows such a marriage and the other person has personal capacity to enter into such a marriage.[65]

It has been suggested that an under-age marriage could, at common law, be validated by continued cohabitation after both parties had attained the appropriate age,[66] but Clive doubts whether, even if this were correct, such a rule would have survived the enactment of modern statutory provisions.[67] It is clear from the Marriage (Scotland) Act 1977 that an under-age marriage is void[68] with the

---

[57] Cf. Muir v. Wood and Anr., 1970 S.L.T. (Notes) 12.

[58] Criminal Procedure (Scotland) Act 1975, ss. 101 and 331A.

[59] See post at pp. 446–447.

[60] Age of Legal Capacity (Scotland) Act 1991, s. 1(3)(c): "Nothing in this Act shall...affect the...criminal responsibility of any person."

[61] Stair, I, iv, 6; Erskine, I, vi, 2.

[62] Age of Marriage Act 1929.

[63] Marriage (Scotland) Act 1977, s. 1(1).

[64] Ibid., s. 1(2).

[65] Anton and Beaumont, Private International Law (2nd ed.) at p. 437.

[66] Johnston v. Ferrier (1770) Mor. 8931; Erskine, I, vi, 2.

[67] Clive (3rd ed.) at p. 78.

[68] s. 1(2).

result that there is nothing to validate, and the better view today is that continued cohabitation after both parties attain the age of 16 might found a new marriage by cohabitation with habit and repute rather than validating an already existing marriage.[69]

Affinitive Marriages

There is one exception to the rule that a person has capacity to marry on attaining the age of 16. While the general rule is that a person may not marry those to whom he is related within one of the degrees specified in Schedule 1 to the Marriage (Scotland) Act 1977,[70] there are exceptions[71] to the prohibitions on affinitive marriages. A person may marry a person who used to be a step-child or a step-parent of his so long as (a) both parties are over the age of 21 years and (b) the younger of the two had not at any time before attaining the age of 18 lived in the same household as the other party and been treated by the other party as a child of his family.[72] A person may marry a person who used to be a child-in-law or a parent-in-law so long as (a) both parties are over the age of 21 years and (b) both the ex-spouse and the ex-spouse's other parent are now dead.[73]

Testamentary Capacity

At common law testamentary capacity, like many other capacities, was acquired when the child became minor *pubes*. Indeed the capacity of minors was not limited in any way by the existence of curators, with the result that minors could test even without the consent of their curators.[74] This capacity was, however, restricted to wills over moveables: "for in order to alter the legal succession of heritage, there must be a deliberate *animus* in the granter of the deed, which cannot be presumed in a minor; and it would be most dangerous to allow the consent of curators to supply that defect."[75]

By section 28 of the Succession (Scotland) Act 1964, a minor was given the like capacity to test on heritable property as he had on moveable property, which meant an unlimited right to do so with no requirement that the curator's concurrence be obtained. Though this section was repealed in 1991[76] the old law

---

[69] *A.B.* v. *C.D.*, 1957 S.C. 415; Clive (3rd ed.), p. 79.
[70] Relationships of consanguinity, affinity or adoption, as there defined. See Clive (3rd ed.), pp. 21–23, 79–80.
[71] Introduced into the law by the Marriage (Prohibited Degrees of Relationship) Act 1986, amending the Marriage (Scotland) Act 1977. For a history of this legislation, see Nichols, "Step-Daughters and Mothers-in-Law," 1986 S.L.T. (News) 229.
[72] Marriage (Scotland) Act 1977, s. 2(1A) and Sched. 1.
[73] *Ibid.*, s. 2(1B) and Sched. 1. See further, Norrie, "Incest and the Forbidden Degrees of Marriage in Scots Law" (1992) 37 J.L.S. 216. The Scottish Law Commission have proposed (Scot. Law Com. No. 135, *Report on Family Law*, May 1992, at para. 8.13 and draft Bill, cl. 20) scrapping the rules prohibiting marriages between ex-relations-in-law.
[74] Erskine, III, ix, 15; McLaren, *Wills and Succession* (3rd ed.), pp. 262–263.
[75] Erskine, I, vii, 33.
[76] Age of Legal Capacity (Scotland) Act 1991, Sched. 2.

cannot be taken to have revived. The position is now governed by section 2(2) of the Age of Legal Capacity (Scotland) Act 1991, which provides "A person of or over the age of 12 years shall have testamentary capacity, including legal capacity to exercise by testamentary writing any power of appointment." No difference is made between heritable and moveable property, and no role is given to the guardian of the child under 16.

Calculation of Age

At common law a person aged *de momento in momentum* and so attained an age at the precise moment on the relevant anniversary of his birth.[77] This remains the rule for anniversaries occurring before September 25, 1991. Since that date,[78] a person attains a particular age at the beginning of the relevant anniversary of his date of birth.[79] When a person has been born on 29th February the relevant anniversary in any year other than a leap year shall be taken to be 1st March.[80]

---

[77] Stair, I, vi, 33; Erskine, I, vii, 36.
[78] When the Age of Legal Capacity (Scotland) Act 1991 came into force.
[79] Age of Legal Capacity (Scotland) Act 1991, s.6.
[80] *Ibid.*, s. 6(2).

CHAPTER 14

GUARDIANS AS PARENT-SUBSTITUTES

INTRODUCTORY

When a child is left without parents the most pressing need is usually to provide him or her with custodians, that is persons with whom the child can reside. The right of custody of course carries with it the right and duty to control and protect the child's person.[1] While the custodian may well also have the right of guardianship this is not invariably so; and at common law tutory did not follow custody—rather it was more the other way around. It may therefore happen that a child who is left without parents or other person having parental rights by virtue of the Law Reform (Parent and Child) (Scotland) Act 1986[2] requires a guardian as well as a custodian, because he needs someone who can fulfil the role of legal representative of the child and exercise the rights and powers flowing therefrom. Where provision is not otherwise made for custody, the guardian will have custody of the child.

Decline in Importance

A number of factors have combined to reduce the significance of guardianship as the law's response to the need for parent-substitutes.[3] At common law, occasion to provide for the guardianship of a legitimate child arose on the death or incapacity of his father or where the father was deprived by the court of the exercise of his paternal powers. For on the failure of the father, guardianship did not devolve on the mother. She was not automatically entitled even to the custody of her pupil children, although that might in some circumstances be given to her. There was therefore a gap in provision for the child which tutory and curatory supplied. That has all been changed by legislation. The process began with the Guardianship of Infants Act 1886[4] under which, on the death of the father, the mother became tutor of her pupil children either alone or jointly with any tutor appointed by the father. The Guardianship Act 1973[5] gave the mother full equality of parental power; and the Law Reform (Parent and Child) (Scotland) Act 1986 now confers parental rights on all mothers, and on fathers who are married to the mother or were married to her at the time of the child's conception or subsequently.[6] Accordingly, when both parents have parental rights over the child, it is only on the death or other failure of both that any need to con-

---

[1] See *ante*, at pp. 197–200.
[2] ss.2 and 3.
[3] The Scottish Law Commission has concluded that, "It seems probable. . .that guardianship is not very widespread in modern conditions": S.L.C. Discussion Paper 88 (Oct. 1990) at para. 3.2.
[4] Repealed by the Law Reform (Parent and Child) (Scotland) Act 1986, Sched. 2.
[5] Repealed in relevant part by the Law Reform (Parent and Child) (Scotland) Act 1986, Sched. 2.
[6] Law Reform (Parent and Child) (Scotland) Act 1986, s. 2(1).

sider questions of guardianship will ordinarily arise. Even in that event, guardianship will often be of importance only if deceased parents have made testamentary provision for them. The protection of the child's person may be the subject of separate arrangements for custody. Guardians will still have a role in relation to the management of property, but there too, in modern conditions the appointment of a judicial factor or of a curator *bonis*, who have rather clearer delimitations of powers, might sometimes be preferred. If children succeed to substantial sums of money, it is likely that the estate will be subject to a trust rather than be left to the administration of guardians. Adoption, local authority care, and provision for the vesting in local authorities and voluntary organisations of parental rights and powers have also contributed to the declining importance of guardianship. Nonetheless, the Scottish Law Commission are of the view "that there is still a need for the law to provide for private guardianship, if only because it will often be a reassurance to parents to know that there is a way in which they can make some provision for the care of their children if they should die while the children are still young."[7]

Scope of this Chapter

The treatment in this chapter is confined to guardianship as a distinct office succeeded in the place of (or in addition to) parents and not, except incidentally, as an aspect of parental responsibilities and rights (which are considered in detail elsewhere[8]). It is further confined to a consideration of the circumstances affecting the appointment of guardians, of persons who may be so appointed, and of the duration of their office and its termination.

APPOINTMENT OF GUARDIANS

Introduction

Section 5(2) of the Age of Legal Capacity (Scotland) Act 1991 provides as follows:

> "Subject to section 1(3)(*f*) above, as from the commencement of this Act no guardian of a person under the age of 16 years shall be appointed as such except under section 3 (orders as to parental rights) or section 4 (power of parent to appoint guardian) of the Law Reform (Parent and Child) (Scotland) Act 1986."

Section 1(3)(*f*) preserves the court's power to appoint a curator *ad litem* or a *curator bonis* to persons under the age of 16. Apart from these relatively unusual situations, the two basic methods by which a person can become guardian are appointment by the parent, and appointment by the court. Before considering the two methods of appointment themselves, however, the question of disability from the office of guardian will be treated, for the principles involved apply however the appointment to the office is made.

---

[7] Scot. Law Com. Discussion Paper 88 (Oct. 1990) at para. 3.2.
[8] *Ante* at pp. 357–375.

Disqualification from Office

The general rule is that every person *sui juris* and of sane mind is eligible for appointment to the office of guardian.[9] That general rule admits, however, of a few exceptions.

Age

Under the Roman law no-one under the age of 25, the Roman age of majority, could hold the office of tutor. In Scotland that rule was applied to tutors-legitim[10] by statute[11] until the Age of Majority (Scotland) Act 1969 substituted the age of 18.[12] Erskine[13] says that tutors-nominate[14] and tutors-dative[15] could be received at 21 but, in saying that, he had the age of majority in mind. Bankton[16] refers to 21 years in the context of majority and More[17] expressly refers to the years of majority. Eighteen, the modern age of majority, might, therefore, be taken to be the qualifying age for guardians today. However, the terms of the Age of Legal Capacity (Scotland) Act 1991 throw considerable doubt on this, and an argument can be sustained that the qualifying age is now 16. Section 1(1)(*b*) of the 1991 Act confers legal capacity upon persons of or over the age of 16 years to enter into any transaction. "Transaction" is given a wide meaning[18] and includes the bringing or defending of, or taking any step in, civil proceedings, as well as acting as trustee. If a 16-year-old has this capacity to act on his own behalf it is difficult to see why he should not have that capacity to act on behalf of someone else. The age of majority was adopted because it was the age at which a person left the curatory of another and became fully *sui juris*. That *rationale* no longer exists in relation to the age of 18 and can be applied now to the age of 16. It is further provided[19] that nothing in the 1991 Act shall prevent any person under the age of 16 years from (i) being appointed as guardian to any child of his or (ii) exercising parental rights in relation to any child of his. The result of these provisions is, it is submitted, that there is no age limit on a person being or being appointed[20] guardian to his own child (subject only to the appointment made being in the child's best interests[21]), and that the age limit on a person being appointed guardian to other than his own child is now 16.[22] It remains obscure how a person under 16, who has no legal capacity, can exercise

---

[9] Fraser (3rd ed.) at p. 449; Erskine, I, vii, 12; Bankton, I, vii, 18.

[10] See *ante* at p. 39.

[11] Tutors Act 1474, c. 6 (repealed by the Age of Legal Capacity (Scotland) Act 1991, Sched. 2).

[12] s. 1.

[13] I, vii, 5.

[14] See *ante*, at pp. 38–39.

[15] See *ante*, at p. 40.

[16] I, vii, 18.

[17] Notes on Stair, p. xxxv, note D, para. 1.

[18] Age of Legal Capacity (Scotland) Act 1991, s. 9.

[19] *Ibid.*, s. 1(3)(*g*).

[20] Under s. 3(1) of the Law Reform (Parent and Child) (Scotland) Act 1986.

[21] *Ibid.*, s. 3(2).

[22] s. 2(1) of the 1991 Act confers legal capacity on persons under the age of 16 to enter into transactions "of a kind commonly entered into by persons of his age and circumstances." It is unlikely to be considered common for a person under 16 to be appointed guardian to anyone other than his own child.

such capacity in relation to his child, and it may be doubted whether the legislature intended to grant that capacity.

Sex and Marriage

Under the Roman law, which accounted tutory an *officium virile*, no woman, with the exception of certain classes of mother of the child, could be appointed tutor. That doctrine was accepted by the institutional writers only in the case of tutors- legitim and women could be appointed tutors-nominate or tutors- dative. Married women were, however, absolutely excluded on the view that it was illogical to give guardianship of others to persons who were themselves under guardianship (*i.e.* the curatory of their husbands). That reflects the requirement that tutors be persons who are themselves *sui juris*.[23] The theoretical basis for the rule was, therefore, abrogated by the abolition of the husband's curatory[24] and with its abolition the exclusion of married women is obnoxious to the Sex Disqualification Removal Act 1919 which provides that a person shall not be disqualified by sex or marriage from being appointed to, or holding, any civil office. This today will certainly include guardianship, for which sex or marriage is therefore no longer a disqualification.

Other Disabilities

There is old authority that aliens are incapable of being tutors.[25] Fraser gives as the reasons for this disability that it attaches to the alien on account of his connection with a foreign country and his incapacity to hold heritable property within the United Kingdom.[26] The former reason seems insubstantial and the latter no longer corresponds with the law[27]: the prohibition may therefore be taken to be obsolete. Residence in a foreign country is no objection.[28] It has been held that a partnership may not be appointed tutors,[29] and the same reasoning would apply to corporations.[30] It has been suggested[31] that legislation provide that only individuals and not corporate bodies may be appointed as guardian. Such legislation would not, it is submitted, effect any change in the law. Under the law of Justinian, although not of the older Roman law, creditors and debtors

---

[23] Erskine, I, vii, 12.

[24] Married Women's Property (Scotland) Act 1920, s. 2; Law Reform (Husband and Wife) (Scotland) Act 1984, s. 3.

[25] *Donaldson* v. *Brown* (1627) Mor. 4647; *Miller* v. *Allen* (1792) Mor. 4651. The objection is not merely on the ground of residence outwith the jurisdiction, because someone resident in England may be appointed (*Sim* v. *Robertson* (1901) 3 F. 1027, but *cf. Fergusson* v. *Dormer* (1870) 8 M. 426; *Fenwick* v. *Hannah's Trs.* (1893) 20 R. 848; *Napier, Petr.* (1902) 9 S.L.T. 375, p. 439).

[26] (3rd ed.) p. 236.

[27] This disability was abolished by the Naturalisation Act 1870, s. 2.

[28] *Sim* v. *Robertson, supra; Fenwick* v. *Hannah's Trs, supra; Rob* v. *Rob*, Dec. 22, 1814 F.C. 117; *Bell* v. *Henderson* (1784) Mor. 16374; More's Notes on Stair, p. xxxv. Appointment may, however, be refused or annulled where residence outwith the jurisdiction makes the appointment inexpedient (More, *ibid.*).

[29] Fraser, p. 236. The only authority Fraser gives is *De Mazar* v. *Pybus* (1799) 4 Ves. Jun. 644 and there is no Scottish authority in point, but the exclusion of partnerships seems consistent with the personal character of guardianship.

[30] *Cf.* the court's dislike of appointing corporate trustees to private trusts which involve the exercise of discretion in personal matters: *Ommanney, Petr.*, 1966 S.L.T. (Notes) 13. It is otherwise in England: see Norrie and Scobbie, *Trusts*, at pp. 62–63.

[31] Scot. Law Com. No 135, *Report on Family Law*, May 1992, para. 3.2 and draft Bill, cl. 7.

of the child were incapable of the office of guardian,[32] but Erskine says that that is not the law of Scotland.[33] Disabilities on the ground of religious profession should be regarded as obsolete.[34]

Effect of Disqualification

If persons disqualified from the office of guardian are nominated in a parent's testamentary deed their purported appointment is null and the deed will be read under deletion of their names so that the nomination of other persons properly qualified can take effect.[35] It had previously been suggested that the only exception to that was where a minor had been nominated, in which event his appointment was merely suspended until majority.[36] If the above proposition relating to age is correct,[37] then this exception is qualified so that appointments of those under 16 are suspended until that age is reached.

Testamentary Appointment of Guardian by Parent

The parent of a child may appoint any person (subject to the disqualifications discussed above[38]) to be guardian of the child after his or her death.[39] In order to be effective, the appointment must be in writing and be signed by the parent,[40] and the parent at the time of his death must have been guardian of the child or would have been such guardian if he had survived until after the birth of the child.[41] So a father who does not have parental rights over the child at the time of his death (e.g. because he has never had them or because he has been deprived of them by due process, such as adoption of the child or the passing by a local authority of a resolution vesting parental rights in the authority or a voluntary organisation) cannot appoint a guardian. The appointment comes into force immediately on the death of the appointing parent and it is not (unless the appointment so provides) postponed, as it is in England,[42] until the other parent dies or loses parental responsibilities.[43] Before the coming into force of the 1986 Act there was detailed provision to deal with the situation of the appointed guardian acting along with a surviving parent who remained tutor or curator of the

---

[32] Nov. 94, cl.

[33] I, vii, 12. This was also the pre-Justinian Roman law.

[34] Stair does not treat of the matter and the only religious disability of which Erskine takes notice is the statutory disability attaching to professed or suspected papists and abolished by the Roman Catholic Relief Act 1829. More, Notes on Stair, D 24, points out that apart from a doubt expressed in *Burnet* v. *Burnet* (1670) 2 Mor. Supp. 462 there is no authority for Bankton's doctrine excluding pagans and persons of reprobated religions.

[35] Erskine I, vii, 3; *Baird* (1711) Mor. 7431.

[36] More, Notes on Stair, DD4; Fraser at p. 235.

[37] *Ante*, p. 382.

[38] *Ante*, pp. 382–384.

[39] Law Reform (Parent and Child) (Scotland) Act 1986, s. 4.

[40] At common law tutors-nominate could be appointed by any writing, formal or informal, that sufficiently indicated the parent's wishes. This remains the case under the statute and the only requirement is that the deed be signed by the parent.

[41] Law Reform (Parent and Child) (Scotland) Act 1986, s. 4.

[42] Children Act 1989, s. 5(8).

[43] The Scottish Law Commission have suggested that this remain the position in Scots law: Scot. Law Com. No. 135, *supra* at para. 3.12.

child.[44] These provisions have now been abrogated in favour of the simpler rule that both the surviving parent with parental rights and the appointed guardian have guardianship rights, which each may exercise without the consent of the other; if more than one guardian is appointed, each may act without the other.[45] This reflects the rule, supported by the same authority, that two parents, both of whom have parental rights, can individually exercise their rights without the consent of the other.

Being of a testamentary nature, the appointment is ambulatory and can be revoked in the same way as a will can before the parent's death.[46] The appointment can come into effect posthumously, so that it remains effective even if the parent making the appointment dies before the child to whom it is made is born.[47]

Delegation of Appointment

Because the nomination of guardians belongs personally to the parents and is part of the parental power, it is not delegable nor, on the death or incapacity of the parents, can it be exercised by anyone in their place. So where a testator conferred on the trustees, under his testamentary settlement, power to assume new trustees and appointed the trustees "named or to be named or assumed" tutors of his pupil children, the appointment of assumed trustees as tutors was held to be invalid.[48] The matter is put beyond doubt by section 5(2) of the Age of Legal Capacity (Scotland) Act 1991, which provides that a guardian may be appointed only by the court or by a parent. This means that, at the moment, a guardian, however appointed, is unable to appoint a new guardian (in the way that, for example, trustees can assume new trustees[49]). Legislation has however been proposed to allow Scottish guardians a similar right to that already held by English guardians[50] to appoint another individual to take his or her place as the child's guardian in the event of his or her death.[51] As with parental appointments, such an appointment would be testamentary and could not be used simply to delegate the responsibility of the existing guardian during life.

Nomination of Plurality of Guardians

Section 4 of the Law Reform (Parent and Child) (Scotland) Act 1986 provides that a parent may appoint "any person" to be guardian. In accordance with general principles of statutory interpretation, where the singular is taken to include the plural,[52] there would seem to be nothing in this provision preventing a

---

[44] ss. 4 and 5 of the Guardianship of Infants Act 1925. Under these provisions parents could act independently of each other, but where there was a guardian appointed and a surviving parent, and where there were more than one guardian appointed, they had to act jointly.

[45] Law Reform (Parent and Child) (Scotland) Act 1986, s. 2(4).

[46] Stair, I, vi, 6; Erskine, I, vii, 2. Cf., in England, the Children Act 1989, s. 6, which lays down statutory rules for revocation of appointment in England. These are suggested for adoption in Scotland: Scot. Law Com. No. 135, supra at para. 3.7 and draft Bill, cl. 8(1)–(4).

[47] Murray v. Merschall (1555) Mor. 16226.

[48] Walker v. Stronach (1874) 2 R. 120.

[49] Trusts (Scotland) Act 1921, s. 3(b).

[50] Children Act 1989, s. 5(4).

[51] Scot. Law Com. No. 135, supra, para. 3.4 and draft Bill, cl. 7(2).

[52] Interpretation Act 1978, s. 6(c): "Words in the singular include the plural and words in the plural include the singular."

parent appointing more than one person to the office of guardian. This was clearly competent at common law, and section 2(4) of the 1986 Act indeed supposes that there might be a situation in which there is more than one person appointed.[53]

Where a parent names more than one person as guardian, the effect will vary according to the exact terms of the nomination. The normal construction, in the absence of indication to the contrary, is that the appointment subsists in the acceptors and the survivors of them.[54] So the appointment is not construed as joint in the strict sense under which non-acceptance or other failure of one would render ineffective the appointment of all. The reason is the respect accorded to the will of the parent and his or her *delectus personae*.[55]

> "The ultimate decision and choice by the father is to be preferred in all cases where any portion of it remains, and where even one part of it remains, though the other part is taken away. Though you may say, *non constat*, that he should have appointed one, if the other had not been added, yet it was for him to state the difference—it was for him to state the jointure—it was for him to say *sine quo non* or *sine quibis non*; and as he has not said so, the Court will assume that he preferred even one of those, if all could not be had, to any other person whom the law might appoint, or whom the Court might appoint."[56]

So express words are required for a joint appointment under which each guardian is *sine quo non*.[57] Where such words are used, the result is that if one of the nominees fails the whole appointment falls.[58] The general rule is that that will be so whether the failure is due to death after acceptance or to non-acceptance. There is, however, authority for the view that if one of the nominees predeceases the parent making the joint nomination, the appointment nonetheless subsists in the others.[59] The general rule may, of course, be modified by the terms of the particular appointment. The words "whom failing" will, if unqualified, be construed as referring to failure on any ground; and where one group is nominated whom failing another, the substitution will not be effected until all those in the first group have failed.

Where a number of guardians are appointed each may act without the consent of the others unless the decree or deed appointing them directs otherwise.[60] If the deed provides for a quorum, any act of the guardians requires the consent of a number sufficient to satisfy the quorum and is valid only if that consent is obtained. Similarly, one or more of a number of guardians may be appointed *sine quibis non* with the result that his or their consent is essential to any act of

---

[53] It makes provision for when "two *or more*" persons have parental rights. There can only ever be more than two such persons if either the court or the parent appoints more than one person to hold a particular parental right.

[54] Stair, I, vi, 14; Bankton I, vii, 20.

[55] *Scot* v. *Stewart* (1834) 7 W. & S. 211, *per* Lord Brougham at pp. 236–237.

[56] *Ibid.* at p. 241.

[57] The Scottish Law Commission, *supra* at para. 3.9 and draft Bill, cl. 7(4) suggest that, for the avoidance of doubt, this rule be put on a statutory basis.

[58] Erskine I, vii, 30; *Drummond* v *Feuars of Bothkennel* (1671) Mor. 14694.

[59] *Scott* v. *Scott* (1775) Mor. 16371.

[60] Law Reform (Parent and Child) (Scotland) Act 1986, s. 2(4).

administration. In the event of a failure of a quorum, or of a guardian *sine quo non*, through death, non-acceptance or resignation, the whole appointment falls.[61] That result has been doubted in the case of the failure of a quorum[62] but its logic seems clear and is authoritatively affirmed in *Drumore* v. *Somervil*.[63] Equally, the whole appointment falls if all the guardians, except those appointed *sine quibis non*, fail, because an appointment *sine quo non* implies the existence of other guardians with less powers.[64] Again, where there has been a joint appointment of guardians, the whole appointment falls on the failure of one[65]:

> "The reason in all these cases is the same, that the father seems to have put no trust in the rest without the quorum or without the *sine quo non*, or in any one or more of tutors named jointly without the whole."[66]

The appointment does not, of course, fall if express provision to the contrary has been made, as by a declaration that the guardian should subsist after the failure of a guardian *sine quo non*, or of a quorum or of a joint guardian.[67] The ultimate test is the parent's intention as disclosed in the deed. In the case of joint guardians in the strict sense unanimity is essential for any administrative act, but, if they are unable to agree on any question affecting the welfare of the child, any of them may apply to the court for an order relating to parental rights and the court may make such order as it thinks fit.[68]

Appointment of Guardian by the Court

Development of the Law

As was seen earlier,[69] the Court of Session in the exercise of the *nobile officium* had at common law the power to appoint tutors-dative to pupil children. This power was enlarged in some respects by various statutes before 1986. Under the Guardianship of Infants Act 1925[70] if one parent of a pupil child died, survived by the other parent, without nominating tutors, or if the tutors nominated by the deceased parent were dead or refused to act, the court could, if it thought fit, appoint a tutor to act jointly with the surviving parent. Under the same Act as later amended,[71] where a pupil child had no parent, no guardian of the person and no other person having parental rights with respect to him, the court, on the application of any person, could, if it thought fit, appoint the applicant to be the child's tutor. That provision added nothing to the substantive

---

[61] Erskine, I, vii, 29; *Montrose* v. *Tutors* (1688) Mor. 14697.

[62] More's Notes on Stair, D. 5 and cases cited therein.

[63] (1742) Mor. 14703.

[64] *Primrose* v. *Roseberry* (1715) Mor. 16335; *Blair* v. *Ramsay* (1735) Mor. 14702, 5 Mor. Supp. 633.

[65] *Drumore* v. *Somervil* (1742) Mor. 14703.

[66] *Ibid*.

[67] *Drumore* v. *Somervil, supra; Scott* v. *Scott* (1775) Mor. 16371; *Aikenheads* v. *Durham* (1703) Mor. 14701.

[68] Law Reform (Parent and Child) (Scotland) Act 1986, s. 3(1).

[69] *Ante*, at p. 40.

[70] s. 4(1) and (2) (repealed by the Law Reform (Parent and Child) (Scotland) Act 1986, Sched. 2).

[71] s. 4(2A), added by the Children Act 1948, s. 50 (repealed as above).

law as it stood before it was passed, except that, where a tutor-legitim had not served, it could enable a tutor-dative to be appointed in preference to a tutor-legitim and without the necessity of waiting for the expiry of a year and a day from the death of the latter of the two parents to die. Jurisdiction was, however, enlarged in that under the Guardianship of Infants Act an appointment could be made in the sheriff court. Under the Agricultural Holdings (Scotland) Act 1949[72] where a landlord or tenant was a pupil or a minor who did not have a tutor, curator or other guardian, the sheriff, on the application of any person interested, could appoint to him a tutor or curator for the purposes of the Act and could recall the appointment and appoint another as the occasion required. Under the Merchant Shipping Act 1894[73] where, by reason of nonage, any person interested in any ship or any share therein is incapable of making any declaration or doing anything required or permitted by the Act to be made or done in connection with the registry of the ship or share, any court having jurisdiction in respect of the property of incapable persons may appoint a person to make such declaration and do such act or thing in the name and on behalf of the incapable person. This last is limited to the performing on behalf of the child of a specific act and though it does contemplate a representative power it does not amount to the appointing of a guardian for the child. The other statutes mentioned above are now repealed in so far as they allow the appointment of a guardian to a child (but no further). In 1986 the court was given the power to make such order relating to parental rights as it thinks fit,[74] though it is not to make any order unless satisfied that to do so will be in the interests of the child.[75] This power was originally in addition to any other power that the court might have, but in 1991 it was provided[76] that the only means by which the court could appoint a guardian was by way of petition under section 3 of the 1986 Act. There is therefore no longer any room for the Court of Session to appoint guardians in the exercise of its *nobile officium*.

The court can grant the right of guardianship under section 3 until the child reaches the age of 16 years, and the right that is so granted will last until that age.[77] The "court" means the Court of Session or the sheriff.[78] The court can at any time vary or recall any order made under section 3,[79] and its power to do so is subject to the welfare test in section 3(2), for a variation or recall is clearly proceedings "relating" to parental rights.

Title and Appointment

Title to raise an action under section 3 attaches to "any person claiming inter-

---

[72] s. 84 (repealed in so far as it related to children by the Age of Legal Capacity (Scotland) Act 1991, Sched. 2).

[73] s. 55(1), as amended by the Age of Legal Capacity (Scotland) Act 1991, Sched. 1, para. 24.

[74] Law Reform (Parent and Child) (Scotland) Act 1986, s. 3(1). Jurisdiction depends upon the habitual residence of the child within Scotland on the date of the application (for the Court of Session) or within the sheriffdom (for the sheriff court): Family Law Act 1986, s. 16(1).

[75] Law Reform (Parent and Child) (Scotland) Act 1986, s. 3(2).

[76] Age of Legal Capacity (Scotland) Act 1991, s. 5(2).

[77] Law Reform (Parent and Child) (Scotland) Act 1986, s. 8.

[78] *Ibid.* For the jurisdictional criteria, see note 74 above.

[79] s. 9(2).

est." As with applications for custody,[80] which are raised under the same section, questions of title coalesce to a large extent with questions relating to the merits of the case, and it is likely that the courts will be slow in placing artificial limitations on who can raise the action.[81] Anyone who can make out a *prima facie* case that the guardianship arrangements he proposes will be for the child's welfare will, it is submitted, possess title to raise an action under section 3. In response to the application the court may make "such order relating to parental rights as it thinks fit." It is not therefore limited to granting or denying guardianship rights to the applicant, but may award these rights to a non-applicant. So for example in a petition raised by the child's maternal grandparents for guardianship rights (say, after the death of the unmarried mother) the court may award guardianship rights to the child's father who does not otherwise have parental rights, if this is held to be in the child's best interests. Nor is there any limitation on the number of guardians appointed, nor on whether they take office only on the death of the remaining parent. The court may make such order as it thinks fit, and it is therefore competent for the court to appoint any number of guardians, consistent with the child's welfare and, if that welfare so demands, these guardians can take office even when there remains a parent with parental rights. Any one guardian (or parent with parental rights if such remains) can exercise parental rights without the consent of the other,[82] and for that reason, together with general administrative convenience, it will seldom be in the child's interests for provision to be made for more than two guardians to be in office at any one time. The court may make the appointment joint, in which case the considerations discussed above in relation to joint appointments by parents will be relevant, but in the absence of express provision in the decree, the appointment will not be joint, either in a question with other appointees or with a remaining parent who has parental rights.

The Father as Guardian

A father who is married to the mother of the child or was married to her at the time of the child's conception or subsequently shall have parental rights, including the right of guardianship.[83] In that situation his authority to exercise the right of guardianship comes from his paternity rather than from his holding any separate office.[84] If he is not and never has been married to the mother of the child he will not be automatically entitled to exercise the right of guardianship and would have to apply to the court under section 3 of the 1986 Act to be appointed to that office[85]: in that case his authority flows from the office rather than from his paternity. A father who does not have parental rights has no better claim (in law) to be appointed guardian than a stranger to the child, for any applicant un-

---

[80] See *ante*, at pp. 202–204.

[81] See *F.* v. *F.*, 1991 S.L.T. 357, which though a custody decision, was decided under s. 3 and lays down principles applicable to all actions under that section.

[82] Law Reform (Parent and Child) (Scotland) Act 1986, s. 2(4).

[83] *Ibid.*, ss. 2 and 8.

[84] See *ante*, at p. 360.

[85] This will no longer be so on the enactment of the proposals contained in Scot. Law Com. No. 135, *Report on Family Law*, May 1992, at para. 2.50, under which both parents will have parental responsibilities and rights, including that of legal representation (guardianship) simply through paternity and will not be dependent upon marriage.

der section 3(1) must satisfy the court that it will be in the interests of the child that he be so appointed and paternity on its own will not enhance that claim.[86]

Welfare

The only limitation to the court's discretion is that the court may not make any order relating to parental rights unless it is satisfied that to do so will be in the interests of the child.[87] While many of the factors relating to welfare previously discussed when dealing with custody[88] will be relevant here also, it is to be remembered that welfare is inherently connected to the purposes for which the order is made. The objective in awarding guardianship rights is to protect the child by satisfactory guardianship arrangements, that is by providing the child with someone who can act as his or her representative in transactions having legal effect, and welfare is to be looked at and assessed in these terms. The wishes of the older child, which will have a significant influence on determining where its welfare lies in relation to custody and access, may be less significant in determining his welfare in relation to guardianship. Guardianship is designed to protect the child, and particularly his estate, from his own inexperience and his wishes, formed through inexperience, can more easily harm his welfare than can his wishes in relation to custody which will seldom be satisfactorily settled if decided against the express and genuine wishes, however formed, of the child. This is by no means to say that in guardianship cases the child's wishes can be ignored, for whenever the child is of an age and maturity to be capable of forming sensible views on the matter at issue, these views will always, it is submitted, be entitled to respect. The common law age of puberty provides a satisfactory benchmark, but cannot now be taken to lay down any absolute rule about when to consult a child. Consultation is inherent in the child's welfare, and its age is necessarily a relevant factor in the determination.[89]

Entry into Office

Acceptance

In Roman law, tutory was a *munus publicum* with the result that persons appointed might be compelled to act unless they were in some exempt category. Scots law, however, has not followed the Roman model in that respect. Acceptance of the office of guardian by the nominee or appointee is, in every case, required before the duties of the office attach.[90] Problems of whether or not there

---

[86] *Porchetta* v. *Porchetta*, 1986 S.L.T. 105, though an access case, was decided on the same section and applied the same principle.

[87] Law Reform (Parent and Child) (Scotland) Act 1986, s. 3(2).

[88] *Ante*, at pp. 208–225.

[89] The Scottish Law Commission, *supra*, note 85, propose that legislation provide that before a person reaches a major decision concerning the child, the child's views be taken into account, and that a child aged 12 or more be presumed capable of expressing a reasonable view (draft Bill, cl. 6). This does not bind the court, but gives an indication that the court should, where appropriate, pay regard to the child's views.

[90] Erskine, I, vii, 20; *Scrimgeour* v. *Kingheny* (1675) Mor. 6357. It is otherwise in England where, under s. 6(5) of the Children Act 1989 appointment is automatic unless it is expressly disclaimed in formal writing. The Scottish Law Commission recommend (draft Bill, cl. 7(3)) that the Scottish position be retained.

has been acceptance arise mainly in the case of guardians nominated by parents, because the court is unlikely to appoint a person guardian unless it is satisfied that that person is willing and able to act. Acceptance may be inferred from actings that are not consistent with any intention other than acceptance; because the consequences of acceptance may be onerous, it will not be implied unless the actings are unequivocal.[91] A guardian appointed by a parent cannot, of course, be held to have accepted by implication if he had no knowledge of his appointment. So if, in ignorance of his appointment, he acts in a way suggestive of management of the child's affairs, he will not be held, on that ground, to have impliedly accepted office although he may, by his actings, incur certain liabilities in respect of the acts themselves. Where the acts are weighty and such as would ordinarily be undertaken only by an accepting guardian, the onus, however, will be on the guardian to show his lack of knowledge.[92] But even after he knows of his appointment, not every act relating to the child's affairs will infer acceptance. There will be no such inference from anything which can be fairly attributed to friendship or to a humane concern for the child's unprotected condition.[93] Acceptance will, however, be inferred from actings which can only be referable to guardianship management such as giving up inventories *habile modo*,[94] or taking the oath *de fideli administratione*,[95] or signing deeds, or taking receipts in which he is designated as guardian, or authorising legal proceedings at his instance *qua* guardian.[96] Ordinarily, of course, there should be no need to have resort to implication. Express acceptance is affixed by any writing signed by the guardian which is to that effect or necessarily bears that construction.[97] The usual form is by a minute or declaration endorsed on the deed by which the guardian is nominated. Where a guardian, who is also a trustee under the parent's testamentary settlement, has intromitted with the child's property, it is a question of circumstances whether acceptance of the office of guardian, as well as that of trustee or executor, will be inferred. In *Mollison* v. *Murray*[98] Lord Gillies said:

> "The same deed which named them trustees also named them tutors. They accepted and acted under that deed. They did not limit their acceptance to the one character of trustee, and express their repudiation of the other character of tutor. They acted generally under the deed, and this, in all the circumstances, I hold to infer their acceptance generally of the deed. I consider therefore that they cannot now repudiate the character of tutors."

Where, however, there is appointment as trustee or executor and guardian, ac-

---

[91] Erskine, *ibid*. He says: "Acceptance, as it may draw severe consequences after it, is not to be inferred by implication," but it is clear from the discussion that follows that he means that only of persons who handle the ward's affairs in ignorance that they have been nominated as tutors.

[92] *Beatson* v. *Beatson* (1678) Mor. 16298.

[93] Erskine, *ibid.; Beatson, supra.*

[94] *Watson* v. *Watson* (1714) Mor. 3244.

[95] *Kirktoun* v. *Hunthill* (1662) Mor. 16268; *Napier* v. *Wood* (1669) Mor. 16280.

[96] Erskine, *ibid.*; Stair, I, vi, 6; *Seton* v. *Seton* (1668) Mor. 2185 and 12767; *Cunningham* (1684) Mor. 16305; *Murrays* v. *Murray* (1832) 10 S. 276.

[97] Erskine, *ibid.*

[98] (1833) 12 S. 237 at p. 240.

ceptance of the former will not necessarily infer acceptance of the latter,[99] and effect will be given to a clause in the deed that acceptance of the office of trustee is not to imply acceptance of the office of guardian.[1]

Refusal, if not express, will be inferred only from very clear circumstances.[2] Mere delay in acceptance does not have any effect on the guardian's right. Accordingly he may accept office and enter into the management of the child's affairs even if his acceptance has been delayed for a period of years.[3] As the freedom of the guardian to delay is obviously productive of abuse, an action may be raised by anyone having an interest, which will certainly include the ward, to put him to his election as between acceptance and refusal.

In the case of a guardian appointed by the court, his having consented to his name being put forward will be sufficient evidence of his acceptance as will, *a fortiori*, his having expressly solicited the office by raising the action himself. It is only where he has not allowed his name to be put forward or has not himself been the petitioner that it will be necessary to have recourse to express or implied acceptance much as in the case of a guardian appointed by a parent. As in that case, any act by a guardian subsequent to his appointment by the court that impinges on the management of the child's affairs may be taken to be referable to the appointment.

Caution

Tutors-dative were required to find caution before they were vested in their office and could lawfully intromit with the pupil's affairs. The 1986 Act does not lay this down as a requirement to the appointment of a guardian either by a parent or by the court, but since the court may make any order it thinks fit, it remains competent for the court to require that its appointee finds caution. If the order does so require, then the principles evolved before 1986 in relation to caution remain applicable.

Although there is some authority to the contrary, Erskine states,[4] and it seems to be a sound principle, that omission to find caution when required cannot put the tutor (now guardian) in a better case than if he had obeyed the law and from that it follows that although bereft of the privileges he is subject to all the liabilities which would have attached to him if caution had been found and the office had duly vested in him. On the same principle, failure to take the declaration *de fideli administratione*, which was required of a tutor-dative but not of a tutor-nominate or a tutor-legitim,[5] and may now be required if the court so orders, cannot excuse the guardian from his liabilities. In the case of a tutor-nominate,

---

[99] *Paterson* v. *Moncrieff* (1866) 4 M. 706; *Hill* v. *City of Glasgow Bank* (1879) 7 R. 68, *per* Lord President Inglis at p. 76.

[1] *Hunter* v *Matthew* (1844) 16 Sc.Jur. 337.

[2] *Ramsay* v. *Dalhousie* (1699) Mor. 16313.

[3] *Auchterlony* v. *Oliphant* (1631) Mor. 16258; Erskine, I, vii, 3.

[4] I, vii, 20. See also *Cass* v. *Ellis* (1671) Mor. 3504 and 16285, but see *Commissaries of Dunkeld* v. *Abercromby* (1628) Mor. 16248.

[5] Fraser (at p. 256) corrects by reference to MacKenzie, I, vii, 5 and Bankton, I, vii, 8 Erskine's statement (I, vii, 7) that a tutor-legitim ought to make oath *de fideli*. Both Stair (I, vi, 11) and Bankton (I, vii, 15) affirm that the oath *de fideli administratione* was required of a tutor-dative, although Erskine (I, vii, 9) is to the contrary. All are agreed (Stair, I, vi, 6; Bankton, I, vii, 5 and Erskine, I, vii, 3) that tutors-nominate were exempt from the oath (now declaration).

on the other hand, due appointment and acceptance were in themselves sufficient warrant to enter into the exercise of his office and he did not require to find
caution,[6] unless the court on the application of anyone having an interest so directed.[7] A similar rule will now apply in relation to parental appointment under
section 4 of the 1986 Act, for the court may make any order it thinks fit if an application is made under section 3. Failure to comply with such a direction would
afford ground for removal, but it does not appear that the guardian's authority to
act is suspended until caution is found.

Formerly a long delay in finding caution for a tutor-legitim did not constitute
any objection to its eventual reception unless, in the meantime, the appointment
of a tutor-dative had intervened or prejudice to the pupil could be shown,[8] but
now all guardians from whom caution is required must find caution within one
calendar month of the interlocutor appointing them unless that interlocutor
otherwise provides. On a motion enrolled at any time before the expiry of that
period, the court may, however, on cause shewn, prorogate the time.[9] The Accountant of Court must be satisfied as to the sufficiency of the cautioner.[10] Under the Judicial Factors Act 1849[11] the court may, on cause shown, limit the
caution to be found to a specified amount, but that power is now modified by
provisions of the Rules of Court[12] which require (a) that, where such limitation
is proposed, caution be found to the satisfaction of the Accountant of Court to
the extent of not less than two-thirds of the value of the moveable and other easily realisable estate and (b) that the Accountant shall not report thereon to the
court except in the event of his requiring larger caution and then only if the
guardian requires him, in writing, so to report. The court on considering the report is to instruct the amount of caution to be found being for not less than two-
thirds of the value of the moveable and other realisable estate. The effect appears to be that if any limitation on the amount of caution is proposed, the
caution found must be for at least two thirds of the value of the moveable and
other realisable estate and must be for a larger amount if the Accountant of
Court so requires unless the guardian asks for the amount to be fixed by the
court on a report from the Accountant.

Inventories

Under the Tutors and Curators Act 1672 no tutor had authority to exercise his
office or to meddle with the writs and estate of the pupil until he had first made
up an inventory with the consent of the pupil's nearest of kin on both his father's

---

[6] Stair, I, vi, 6; Bankton I, vii, 5; Erskine I, vii, 3.
[7] Guardianship of Infants Act 1886, s. 12 (repealed by the Law Reform (Parent and Child) (Scotland) Act 1986, Sched. 2). At common law the Court of Session could ordain tutors-nominate to
give security and under the Tutors and Curators Act 1696 (repealed by the Age of Legal Capacity
(Scotland) Act 1991, Sched. 2) the court could ordain a tutor-nominate who came under the protection of that act and whose condition had "changed" to find good and sufficient caution for his
administration.
[8] *Irvine* v. *Elsick* (1632) Mor. 16260; *A.* v. *B.* (1632) Mor. 16261; but see *Riddell* v. *Riddell* (1669)
Mor. 16281.
[9] Rules of Court. r. 200(*c*).
[10] Rules of Court, r. 200(*e*)(i).
[11] s. 27 (as amended by the Age of Legal Capacity (Scotland) Act 1991, Sched. 1, para. 10).
[12] r. 200(*e*)(ii).

and his mother's side who were major and within the kingdom at the time. That Act was repealed in so far as was necessary to give effect to the provisions of the Judicial Factors Act 1849[13] relating to rentals, lists and inventories.[14] Under the latter Act the concurrence of the nearest of kin is not required and the compilation of an inventory is not a condition precedent to a guardian's exercising his office. Accordingly, although penalties may attach to failure to compile the required rental, list and inventory, and to lodge it with the Accountant of Court within the prescribed time,[15] the validity and lawfulness of a guardian's actings are not in any way thereby affected.

TERMINATION OF GUARDIANSHIP

Termination of guardianship may be brought about in a number of different ways, to be discussed in the following paragraphs. However it occurs, a guardian's powers cease immediately on the termination of his office.[16] Any act of management thereafter exposes him to the liabilities of a pro-guardian.[17] Equally, his duties come to an end and he is not bound to attend to the management of any matter which is incomplete at that time.[18]

Natural Termination

The natural termination of a guardian's office occurs on the ward's reaching the age of 16 years or on the death, before that date, of either the guardian or the ward. The age of 16 years[19] is absolutely fixed and termination of guardianship cannot be postponed even by the direction of a parent purporting to give to guardians powers of guardianship for an extended period.[20] The ward attains the age of 16 years at the moment commencing the 16th anniversary of the date of his birth.[21] If a child is born on February 29, the anniversary falls on March 1 if the year is not a leap year and on February 29, if the year is a leap year.[22] On the death of a guardian, the office did not, even under the older law, pass to his heir; and it does not do so today. The proper course in modern practice is for a new guardian to be appointed by the court under section 3 of the 1986 Act, but that will not always be necessary if there remains a guardian in office or a parent with parental rights.

---

[13] s. 3.

[14] And has now been repealed in its entirety: Age of Legal Capacity (Scotland) Act 1991, Sched. 2.

[15] Judicial Factors Act 1849. s. 6. See also *ibid.*, ss. 1(1) and 25(2).

[16] *Lockhart* v. *McKenzie's Trs.* (1826) 5 S. 136, affd. (1829) 3 W. & S. 481. See also *Bruce* v. *Sinclair* (1610) Mor. 16239; *Foster* v. *Foster* (1610) Mor. 16238 and *Forbesses* v. *Forbes* (1683) Mor. 16287.

[17] See *post* at pp. 399–402.

[18] *Cass* v. *Ellis* (1672) Mor. 16285. See also *A.* v. *B.* (1533) Mor. 16218; Balfour, p. 121, No. 135.

[19] Law Reform (Parent and Child) (Scotland) Act 1986, s. 8. See Scot. Law Com. No. 135, draft Bill, cl. 8(5), under which guardianship will last until age 18.

[20] *Graham* v. *Graham* (1780) Mor. 8934, *per* Lord Braxfield (referring to the attainment of the age of puberty bringing tutory to an end).

[21] Age of Legal Capacity (Scotland) Act 1991, s. 6(1), altering the common law position that a person aged from moment to moment: see Stair, I, vi, 33.

[22] *Ibid.*, s. 6(2).

Satisfaction of Condition

The satisfaction of a condition on which the guardian's appointment is dependent also brings the office to an end. The mere satisfaction of the condition is enough to have that effect by operation of law without the necessity of declarator or other legal proceedings.[23] Examples of this occur when a parent, in appointing a guardian under section 4 of the 1986 Act, has provided that the office should last for a fixed period or until the occurrence of a certain event. Also in this class are appointments of guardians subject to a quorum, of guardians *sine quibus non* and of joint guardians. In the event of the failure of the quorum, or of a guardian *sine quo non* or of any one of two or more joint guardians, the appointment of all the guardians falls and their guardianship is terminated.[24] The same result follows if one or more guardians have been nominated *sine quibis non* and all the other guardians fail, because an appointment *sine quo non* implies the existence of other guardians with lesser powers.[25] These results will, however, be avoided if express provision has been made for the continuance in office of the remaining guardians. Where several guardians have been appointed, the appointment will be held to be joint only if express words so provide. Accordingly, when one of several guardians, not expressly stated to be joint guardians, fails, the office of the remainder continues. That view is taken, with appointments by parents, out of respect for the wishes of the nominating parent which, it is held, should prevail to the extent that is possible, even if they have failed in part, unless, of course, the parent has provided to the contrary. It was at one time otherwise in the case of tutors-dative.[26] Where two or more tutors-dative were appointed, the appointment was held to be joint, although there was no declaration to that effect. The tutory was deemed, by its nature, to be joint whether words of jointure were used or not. By statute, however, a majority of guardians accepting and surviving (whether appointed by a parent or by the court) constitute a quorum, unless the contrary is expressed in the deed or decree by which they are appointed.[27] Accordingly in the case of all guardians, whoever appoints them, express words are now required to bring about a joint appointment. The provisions in the Guardianship of Infants Act 1925[28] concerning when an appointed guardian will have to act jointly with a surviving parent have now been repealed,[29] and in the absence of anything to the contrary in the decree or deed appointing the guardian, the appointment is not joint, either with a surviving parent or with other appointed guardians.

Resignation

Under the older law, the tutor of a pupil child might resign if he had accepted office but had not entered on the management of the estate. But any intromission with the estate deprived him of that liberty and he could, thereafter, resign only

---

[23] *Et sic quidem etiam ipso jure sine facto hominis finitur tutela*: Inst, I, xxii 2 and 5; D. xxvi, 1, 14 (3 and 5).

[24] See *ante*, pp. 385–387.

[25] *Ibid.*

[26] *Scot* v. *Stewart* (1834) 7 W. & S. 211; *Stewart* v. *Baikie* (1829) 7 S. 330.

[27] Trusts (Scotland) Act 1921, s. 3(c) (guardians being trustees for the purposes of that Act: s. 2).

[28] ss. 4 and 5.

[29] Law Reform (Parent and Child) (Scotland) Act 1986, Sched. 2.

with leave of the court.[30] By the Trusts (Scotland) Act 1921,[31] under which guardians are, for the purposes of that Act, assimilated to trustees, power is given to any trustee to resign office unless the contrary has been expressed in the deed or decree from which his powers are derived.[32] It is however further provided in that Act that a sole trustee may not resign unless either (1) he has assumed new trustees and they have declared their acceptance of office, or (2) the court has appointed new trustees or a judicial factor.[33] The first limb is not applicable to guardians since guardians cannot be assumed by existing guardians,[34] and so a sole guardian can resign only when the court has appointed a new guardian[35] under section 3 of the Law Reform (Parent and Child) (Scotland) Act 1986, or a judicial factor. Apart from that provision, the liberty to resign does not apply to a guardian who has accepted any legacy or bequest or annuity expressly given on condition that he accept the office of guardian, nor to any guardian appointed on the footing of receiving a remuneration for his services. In these cases, a guardian is free to resign only if the deed by which he was appointed expressly so provides. The court may, however, on the petition of such a guardian, grant authority to resign on such conditions (if any) with respect to repayment or otherwise of any legacy received as the court may think just.[36] As this would be "proceedings relating to parental rights" within the meaning of section 3(2) of the 1986 Act, the welfare of the child must be the paramount consideration for the court in determining whether and on what conditions to allow the guardian to resign.[37]

Although the liberty of a sole guardian to resign is limited by the 1921 Act, the Act is silent so far as regards the position of guardians *sine quibus non* and joint guardians. It seems that they are free to resign even if, by doing so, they bring the tenure of other guardians to an end. Similarly, it seems that guardians may resign, although the effect of their doing so will be to terminate the tenure of others by reducing the number below a quorum, or by leaving no guardians other than guardians *sine quibus non*. It has been held that resignation of a body of trustees is competent, but such conduct was stigmatised as "extremely improper."[38] Wilson and Duncan[39] are of the view that a body of trustees can resign on the authority of section 3 of the 1921 Act only on satisfaction of the proviso requiring the assumption or appointment of new trustees. This is so, with added

---

[30] Fraser at pp. 408–410 and authorities cited therein.

[31] As amended by the Age of Legal Capacity (Scotland) Act 1991, Sched. 1, para. 25.

[32] s. 3(*a*). See also the Judicial Factors Act 1849, s. 31, under which the court has a general power to accept the resignation of any guardian coming under the provisions of the Act, but only "on cause shown."

[33] s. 3, proviso (1).

[34] Age of Legal Capacity (Scotland) Act 1991, s. 5(2): see *ante*, at p. 375.

[35] The 1921 Act uses the plural "trustees," which suggests that the court must appoint more than one trustee (or guardian) in these circumstances. It has however been held that the plural here includes the singular: *Kennedy, Petr.*, 1983 S.L.T. (Sh.Ct.) 10. See further, Norrie and Scobbie, *Trusts* (1991), at pp. 69–70.

[36] Trusts (Scotland) Act 1921, s. 3, proviso (2).

[37] The Scottish Law Commission has suggested that the law should be amended so that once a guardian has accepted office then, unless the appointment provides otherwise, the guardian can resign only with authority of the court: see Scot. Law Com. No. 135, para. 3.16 and draft Bill, cl. 8(5).

[38] *Maxwell's Trs.* v. *Maxwell* (1874) 2 R. 71 at p. 74, *per* Lord President Inglis.

[39] *Trusts, Trustees, and Executors* at p. 256.

force, in the case of guardians, who must act, as parents must, for the welfare of the child: it would seldom, if ever, be in the interests of the child to be left without anyone who could represent him or her in transactions having legal effect. This is the case also when a guardian *sine quo non* wishes to resign. Where such a course is contemplated, the appropriate action is to petition the court under section 3 of the Law Reform (Parent and Child) (Scotland) Act 1986, prior to resignation, for the appointment of a new guardian or new guardians.

Removal

Superintendence of guardians belongs to the Court of Session as *parens patriae* in the exercise of its *nobile officium*. By virtue of these powers of superintendence a jurisdiction to remove guardians, where that was necessary for the protection of the ward's estate, has been in use from early times (at any rate in relation to tutors of pupil children). By an Act of 1555,[40] jurisdiction to remove was extended to any judge ordinary and in the seventeenth century it was held that tutors-dative might be removed by the Court of Exchequer[41] on whose authority the Crown gift of tutory proceeded to them and so might be recalled. Long before the abolition of the Court of Exchequer as a separate court, it had, however, come to be accepted that jurisdiction to remove tutors pertained exclusively to the Court of Session.[42] The grounds for removal were always wide, embracing neglect as well as positive acts of maladministration or fraud, but the court sometimes showed a reluctance to go as far as removal and instead appointed a curator to act along with the tutor and control his administration.[43]

Authority for Removal

Section 3(1) of the Law Reform (Parent and Child) (Scotland) Act 1986 allows the court to make such order relating to parental rights as it thinks fit on application of any person claiming interest to the court for an order relating to parental rights. An application for removal of the guardian can be made under this section. Section 3(2) of the 1986 Act applies to the removal of guardians as it does to any proceeding relating to parental rights. As a result, the welfare of the child is the paramount consideration by which the merits of removal must be decided. Before 1986 a number of other statutes had been superimposed on the common law without greatly modifying or adding to it. By the Judicial Factors Act 1849[44] the court is empowered, on cause shown, to remove any guardian and to appoint a curator *bonis* in his room. By the Trusts (Scotland) Act 1921 a guardian may be removed if he is, or becomes, insane or incapable of acting, by reason of physical or mental disability, or is absent from the United Kingdom or has disappeared for at least six months.[45] Under the 1986 Act, power to remove

---

[40] c. 35.
[41] *Mersington* v. *Fletcher* (1694) 4 Mor. Supp. 272.
[42] Erskine, I, vii, 29.
[43] Erskine, *ibid.; McBrae* v. *McLaine* (1667) Mor. 16278; *McBrair* v. *McBrair* (1667) Mor. 16279; *A.* v. *B.* (1534) Mor. 16219.
[44] s. 31 (as amended by the Age of Legal Capacity (Scotland) Act 1991, Sched. 1, para. 11 and Sched. 2).
[45] Trusts (Scotland) Act 1921, s. 23: see Norrie and Scobbie, *Trusts*, at pp. 71–72.

may be exercised by the Court of Session or the sheriff court;[46] under the 1849 Act and the 1921 Act the power to remove is given to the Court of Session. Procedure under the Trusts (Scotland) Act 1921 is by petition to the Outer House and that is appropriate also to cases under the Judicial Factors Act 1849.[47] Procedure under the common law has been by petition and complaint to the Inner House or ordinary action, but there is no fundamental reason why in these cases too petition to the Outer House should not be adopted.[48] Application under the Trusts (Scotland) Act 1921 may be made by a co-guardian or "other person interested in the trust estate."[49] In other cases application by anyone showing relevant interest is competent, including next-of-kin, other relatives, a co-guardian and the child himself if his action is subsequently authorised by a curator *ad litem.*

In summary, the result of the common law and statute is as follows: (1) any guardian may be removed under the common law or the Judicial Factors Act 1849 or the Law Reform (Parent and Child) (Scotland) Act 1986; (2) any guardian may be removed under the Trusts (Scotland) Act 1921 provided the conditions of insanity, incapacity, absence or disappearance laid down by that Act are satisfied; (3) the welfare test laid down by section 3(2) of the Law Reform (Parent and Child) (Scotland) Act 1986 applies to the decision of all questions of removal but in cases under the Trusts (Scotland) Act 1921 the grounds for removal laid down by that Act must also be satisfied. In view of the wide application of the welfare principle, applications at common law or under the Judicial Factors Act 1849 or the Law Reform (Parent and Child) (Scotland) Act 1986 differ little from one another and it is doubtful if there is any advantage in having resort to the Trusts (Scotland) Act 1921.

Grounds for Removal

Subject to the welfare principle, the common law grounds for removal of a guardian are still of relevance. The general principle is that a guardian is suspect if by act or omission he has given rise to injury or reasonable apprehension of the risk of injury to the child's affairs. Evil intention is not required. The maxim applies *non solum dolus vel lata negligentia suspectum reddit tutorem, verum etiam levior culpa.*[50] Even that maxim is, however, too narrow. Although usu-

---

[46] Law Reform (Parent and Child) (Scotland) Act 1986, s. 8.

[47] Rule of Court 189 (*a*)(iii) and (xxiii) provides for petitions under the Trusts (Scotland) Act 1921. Petitions under the Judicial Factors Act 1849 fall within the general category of r. 189(*a*) for all petitions "not falling within any of the classes mentioned in Rule 190." The Judicial Factors Act 1849 had contemplated (s. 21) that at least in certain circumstances proceedings for removal of a factor (to whom a guardian is assimilated) should be by petition and complaint but procedure by simple petition has been allowed (*Marshall* v. *Chisholm* (1901) 3 F. 642).

[48] The original form of process at common law was by ordinary action but procedure by petition and complaint came to be adopted and seems latterly to have been the prevailing mode (see Fraser at pp. 415–416 and cases cited therein, especially at p. 416, note 2). Petitions and complaints must be presented to the Inner House but a simple petition seems to be as appropriate in modern practice to cases under common law as to the statutory cases for which it is in use. If a procedure is by simple petition rather than petition and complaint, it falls within the category of Outer House petitions by virtue of the general provision of Rule of Court 189(*a*).

[49] s. 23. The section applies to trusts generally. In the case of a child's estate, the child himself would seem to be an "other person interested in the trust estate."

[50] Inst. I, 22, 6; D. xxvi 10, 3, 5; Code v, 43, 9.

ally there will be fault, *culpa* is not always necessary. Failure to perform the duties of the office, or evident ground for fearing that they will not be performed in the future, is the test and it matters not whether the cause is evil intent, negligence, or some entirely innocent circumstance such as disability or incapacity. Failure to make up inventories within the required time justifies removal,[51] as does failure to find caution where that is required.[52] Other particular instances include delay in defending the child's rights,[53] wilful omission to state a valid defence, abandonment of the administration, refusal of necessaries for the child's aliment and education where there are sufficient funds in hand to do it, embezzlement of the child's funds, failure to institute necessary actions,[54] insolvency of the guardian or of his cautioner,[55] wastage or neglect of the child's means,[56] violation of a custody order made by the court, clandestine or unwarrantable removal of the child from the jurisdiction,[57] and employment of the child's means for the guardian's own trade or business.[58]

PRO-GUARDIANS

By pro-guardians "are understood those who act as tutors or curators [now guardians] without having a legal title to the office, whether they sincerely believe themselves tutors, or know that they are not."[59] This is not just a convenient label to describe those who act irregularly in this respect. In a limited, but important, sense pro-guardianship is an office, however irregular, recognised by the law. He who acts as pro-guardian not only renders himself liable for what he has done but thereby subjects himself to all the duties of a guardian and so becomes, if he neglects these duties, liable for omissions as well as for his intromissions. The doctrine goes back to the Roman law and is justified on the view that "he who assumes to himself an office to which he hath no title, ought to be in no better case than one who acts under a proper warrant."[60] At first, however, it was not clear that the Roman law had been received on this matter and in *Swinton* v. *Notman*[61] in 1665 the court held that the defender, who had been nominated as an overseer but had acted, contrary to the testament, under the name of tutor, should be liable only for his intromissions "seeing he had no law or custom regulating the case." At the same time, however, the court enacted by

---

[51] *Austin* v. *Wallace* (1826) 5 S. 177; *Gibson* v. *Sharp*, Dec. 21, 1811, F.C. 454; *Lothian* v. *Somerville* (1724) Mor. 16337; *Turnbull* v. *Bisset* (1698) Mor. 16317; *Brown* v. *Thomson* (1692) 4 Mor. Supp. 72; *Burnet* v. *Johnston* (1685) Mor. 16307; *Gibson* v. *Commissary of Dunkeld* (1680) Mor. 16299, 3 Mor. Supp. 364.

[52] Bankton, I, vii, 34; *Welsh* v. *Welsh* (1778) Mor. 16373; *Witherspoon* (1775) Mor. 7450 and 16372, 5 Mor. Supp. 604.

[53] See generally D. xxvi, 10, 3 (5, 12, 14, 15, and 17); 10, 7 (1); Erskine, I, vii, 29; *Mersington* v. *Fletcher* (1694) 4 Mor. Supp. 272.

[54] *Ibid.*

[55] *McLaurin, Petr.* (1831) 3 Sc.Jur. 550; *Mersington* v. *Fletcher, supra.*

[56] *Heriot* v. *Livverton* (1564) Mor. 16229.

[57] *Stuart* v. *Moore* (1860) 22 D. 1504; *Reoch* v. *Robb*, Nov. 14, 1817, F.C. 388; *Gordonston's Trs.* v. *Gordon* (1708) 4 Mor. Supp. 725. *Cf.*, however, *Edgar* v. *Fisher's Trs.* (1893) 21 R. 325. See also *Harris, Petr.* (1893) 1 S.L.T. 254 at p. 257.

[58] *Dewar* (1853) 16 D. 163 and 489.

[59] Erskine, I, vii, 28.

[60] *Ibid.*

[61] (1665) Mor. 16273.

Act of Sederunt,[62] "that whosoever in time coming meddled with pupils' or minors' means as pro-tutors or pro-curators, should be liable from henceforth as tutors or curators for intromissions and omission." The Act of Sederunt is the foundation of the subsequent law. It has since been provided[63] that "no guardian of a person under the age of 16 years shall be appointed as such except under section 3…or section 4…of the Law Reform (Parent and Child) (Scotland) Act 1986." In so far as pro-guardianship is an office it is distinct from that of guardian with the result that this provision does not prevent its arising; and in any case pro-guardians are not "appointed." Although pro-guardians come in the place of guardians they are not, as guardians are, trustees within the meaning of the Trusts (Scotland) Act 1921[64] and so do not enjoy the protection against liability for omissions that, in the absence of provision to the contrary, that Act gives to trustees.[65]

Commencement

The commencement of pro-guardianship is from the first intromission with the child's property and is not, unless on special grounds, drawn back to an earlier time, usually the death of his parents, when the child first became *indefensus*. Where there is room for doubt, there will be reluctance to imply an early commencement if the office has been assumed from friendship or the necessitous circumstances of the child's affairs. If, however, the first act of intromission is shortly after the parent's death, an accounting may be required from the date of death.[66]

Assumption of Office

Assumption of the office may sometimes be supported by express words as when someone claims to be guardian and acts accordingly. A mere verbal pretension to the office, unaccompanied by acts, probably does not infer liability unless, it is thought, where it amounts to a course of holding out from which prejudice to the child results. Where there is a claim to be guardian, any intromissions with the child's estate can readily be attributed to that character, but where there is no such claim the act must be unequivocally referable to the office before pro-guardianship will be inferred.[67] "It is not every management of the affairs of a pupil that will infer a pro-tutory but only such as is *qua* tutor, that is, where one acts under the character of tutor and he is not."[68] So, when trustees intromitted with the share of the estate of a deceased parent, which had been left in trust for his children, it was held that having acted in the character of trustees they did not thereby become pro-tutors.[69]

---

[62] June 24, 1665 F.

[63] Age of Legal Capacity (Scotland) Act 1991, s. 5(2).

[64] s. 2.

[65] s. 3(d). For the extent of the protection given by that provision, see Norrie and Scobbie, *Trusts*, at p. 147.

[66] Erskine, *ibid.; Muir* v. *Crawfurd* (1697) Mor. 16316.

[67] For cases in which pro-tutory or pro-curatory has been inferred, see *Fowler* v. *Campbell* (1739) Mor. 16343; *Muir* v. *Crawfurd, supra; McDuff* v. *McDuff* (1637) Mor. 514; *Vanllange* v. *Kincaid* (1630) Mor. 513 and *Cass* v. *Ellis* (1671) Mor. 3504.

[68] *Fowler* v. *Campbell, supra, per* Lord Kilkerran, cited in *Fulton* v. *Fulton* (1864) 2 M. 893.

[69] *Fulton* v. *Fulton, supra.*

It is no defence to an allegation of pro-guardianship that lawful guardians were in office and acting. It has been held that that is so, even if the alleged pro-guardian acted along with persons entitled to the office.[70]

Powers, Duties and Liabilities

By usurping office, the pro-guardian brings upon himself all the duties that a lawful holder of the office has. *Qui pro tutore negotia gerit, eandem fidem et diligentiam praestat, quam tutor praestaret.*[71] Indeed, his position is more onerous than that of the lawful office holder. "It is a familiar maxim in the law, that a pro-tutor or pro-curator is liable in even stricter diligence than the tutor or curator with a legal title"[72] and, contrary to what is now the ordinary case with guardians, a pro-guardian will be liable for omissions.[73] The ambiguity of his situation is acute and perilous. He has a duty to act, if that should be necessary to protect or promote the child's interests, but he has no active title and so, where the institution of actions or other legal acts are required, he has no power to carry out that duty.[74] Thus, he will be liable for loss occasioned by failure to pursue a debt due to the child but, if he does sue, he may be met by a plea of "no title to sue."[75] The apparent dilemma of that situation may, however, be circumvented by raising an action in the child's name, and thereafter securing the appointment of a curator *ad litem.*[76] A more intractable problem may be that, while he has a duty to employ the child's estate profitably, he has no title to grant the deeds that may be necessary for that purpose. It is undecided whether the Court of Session, in the exercise of its *nobile officium*, may relieve a pro-guardian who has inadvertently assumed office from the harshness of some of the consequences which that may entail. An application for relief will however constitute "proceedings relating to parental rights," allowing the court to make such order as it thinks fit under section 3(1) of the Law Reform (Parent and Child) (Scotland) Act 1986, though if an application is made relief will be granted on the basis not of the innocence and reasonableness of the pro-guardian's actions but on the basis that to do so is in the interests of the child.[77] If relief means that the child's estate loses a claim against the pro-guardian it is difficult to see how the granting of relief could be in the child's interests.[78] Short of that, it appears that the only escape for the pro-guardian is to take the steps necessary to bring his office to an end. A pro-guardian is liable for all loss to the child's estate resulting from his neglect, including loss of interest or other loss flowing from fail-

---

[70] *Cass* v. *Ellis, supra.*

[71] D. xxvii, 5, 4.

[72] *Fulton* v. *Fulton, supra, per* Lord Kinloch (Ordinary) at p. 896.

[73] Act of Sederunt, June 24, 1665.

[74] Erskine, I, vii, 28.

[75] *Ibid.*; Fraser at p. 564.

[76] See *post*, pp. 403–404.

[77] Law Reform (Parent and Child) (Scotland) Act 1986, s. 3(2).

[78] It might, however, be possible to envisage an unusual situation in which the child is dependent upon the guardian, and to hold the guardian liable would bankrupt him, to the detriment of the child also.

ure to employ the estate profitably.[79] On an accounting, he is, however, entitled to credit for moneys of his own which he has expended for the child's behoof.[80]

Because a pro-guardian has no active title, third parties cannot acquire a good title from him. All alienations of property, by gift or sale or otherwise, are null even if for value and in a question with a *bona fide* purchaser;[81] and a debtor paying to a pro-guardian is not discharged unless he can show that the payment was applied *in rem versum* of the child.[82] Stair, however, allows an exception to that where "the person had been long holden and repute tutor."[83] In that case he says that the deed would be likely to be sustained unless it could be reduced on proof of lesion. It is no longer possible to reduce deeds entered into by guardians on the ground of lesion,[84] so if Stair is correct even deeds prejudicing the child may remain valid in the circumstances postulated.

Termination of Office

There can be no pro-guardian where there could be no guardian. So pro-guardianship ends when the child reaches the age of 16 years,[85] even if the pro-guardian continues to manage the property thereafter.[86] Termination of the office by death is, of course, the same as in guardianship generally. How it is ended, short of these natural terms, is uncertain. The child can call the pro-guardian to account before the natural termination of the office,[87] and unless there are subsequent acts such an accounting probably has the effect of termination. The same effect probably follows where lawful guardians (a) put the pro-guardian on notice, either expressly or by necessary implication from their actings, that they hold office to his exclusion unless, again, there are subsequent acts or (b) take up office subsequent to the act constituting the pro-guardianship. Mere abstention from intromissions after the original act cannot, however, bring the office to an end unless, perhaps, the abstention is for a long period and a change in circumstances intervenes; liability for omissions can scarcely be destroyed by inactivity. Whether an intimation of withdrawal from all acts of management serves to terminate the office would seem to depend on whether or not there are lawful guardians in office. If there are, such intimation is, no doubt, effective at least if accompanied by an accounting. If not, however, a bare intimation probably does not suffice. To hold otherwise would be to give pro-guardians a power to resign which at common law guardians did not possess and, *a fortiori* of their case, he who has assumed an office without authority should not be released from it until he has secured that the office is lawfully fulfilled. That view consists with the liabilities of pro- guardians as noted above.

---

[79] Fraser, *ibid.*

[80] Erskine, *ibid.; Gray* v. *Irving* (1692) Mor. 8927.

[81] Fraser at p. 563; D. xxvii, 5, 2; xxvii, 10, 8.

[82] Erskine, *ibid.; Allan* v. *Hamilton* (1715) Mor. 5654.

[83] I, vi, 12.

[84] Age of Legal Capacity (Scotland) Act 1991, s. 1(5).

[85] *Cass* v. *Ellis, supra*; D. xxvii, 5, 1.

[86] Any liability for actings after the child attains 16 years of age is as a *negotiorum gestor*.

[87] Erskine, *ibid.*

CURATORS AD LITEM AND CURATORS BONIS

Introduction

Curatory is a lesser form of guardianship than was tutory at common law, for it is directed at the ward's estate rather than his person.[88] As we have seen, the Age of Legal Capacity (Scotland) Act 1991 extended tutory (now known as guardianship) to age 16 for both sexes, and abolished curatory on grounds of age alone.[89] It did not, however, abolish curatory as a legal institution, and that may still be used in other circumstances,[90] so while childhood alone is no longer a sufficient ground for placing one person under the curatory of another, there will remain circumstances in which it is appropriate for a person to be appointed curator of a child. Where there are court proceedings involving a child, a curator *ad litem* may be appointed to him. Where the child is mentally incapax and is likely to remain so into adulthood, or on the failure of the child's guardian, or when it is considered necessary to supersede the guardian, the court may appoint, for purely administrative or representative purposes, a curator *bonis*. While curators *ad litem* are not limited to children, this provides the main instance in which the appointment will be made; curators *bonis* are similarly not limited to children, but appointment as such may still in some circumstances be considered appropriate. Consequently a brief discussion of the main features of both offices is not inappropriate here.

Curators ad Litem

The responsibility for instructing the conduct of actions raised on behalf of a child and of defences to actions raised against him normally rests, of course, with the child's parents or guardians. There are however a number of circumstances in which a curator *ad litem* will be appointed to take over the management of the case on the child's behalf and supplant parents or guardians in that function. At one time the expression "*tutor ad litem*" was often employed and can be found in at least one statute,[91] but "curator" is the modern and the better usage. There is no personal connection with the child, nor an overall protective function such as the title "tutor" previously suggested. A curator *ad litem* cannot intermeddle with the management of the child's affairs, nor has he any responsibility for the child's person or estate except to take care that the case is properly conducted on the child's behalf so that his legitimate interests are safeguarded and, so far as may be, promoted.[92] An appointment may be made *ex proprio motu*, or at the request of a party in an appropriate case. There must be a pending *lis* and so an appointment cannot be made before an action is raised, or, in the

---

[88] Stair, I, vi, 35; Erskine, *I*, vii, 1; Bell, *Prin.*, s. 2090.

[89] Age of Legal Capacity (Scotland) Act 1991, ss. 5(1) and (3).

[90] For example, to provide administration and protection of the estates of the mentally incapax. The appointment of a tutor-dative over an incapax remains competent as a means of protecting or controlling the person of the incapax: see *Dick* v. *Douglas*, 1924 S.C. 787, and more recent cases reported by Ward in "Revival of Tutors-Dative," 1987 S.L.T. (News) 69 and in "Tutors to Adults: Developments", 1992 S.L.T. (News) 325.

[91] Entail Amendment Act 1848, s. 31.

[92] A curator *ad litem* cannot even grant a discharge for moneys decerned in favour of a child, and a factor must be appointed for that purpose. See *Pratt* v. *Knox* (1855) 17 D. 1006; *Collins* v. *Eglinton Iron Co.* (1882) 9 R. 500; *Connolly* v. *Bent Colliery Co. Ltd.* (1897) 24 R. 1172.

case of a child defender, before appearance is entered.[93] The following are
among the circumstances in which a curator *ad litem* might be appointed:

(1) where the child's parents are dead and he has no guardians[94]

(2) where an action has been raised in the child's name alone,[95] and a parent or guardian has not subsequently adopted and so validated the instance;[96]

(3) where the action is by, or on behalf of, a child against his parent or guardian or where it is by a parent or guardian against his child or ward;[97]

(4) to protect the interests of the child before a children's hearing at which one or more of the grounds of referral concern the parent's alleged abuse or neglect of the child;[98]

(5) generally where there is a conflict of interest between parent or guardian and the child;[99]

(6) where a parent or guardian is under an incapacity or disability; and

(7) for the purpose of protecting the position of a 16- or 17-year-old child where an application is made to the court under section 1 of the Trusts (Scotland) Act 1961 to provide consent on the child's behalf to a variation of a private trust of which the child is a beneficiary.[1]

The above examples are not exhaustive. An appointment of a curator *ad litem*
may be made wherever, in the opinion of the court, the child's interests so require. A parent or guardian should not, however, be displaced without cause.

A curator *ad litem* makes the declaration *de fideli administratione* and then
enters on the duties of his office. As an officer of the court he may not, it is
thought, resign without leave of the court. His appointment may be recalled by
the court and comes to an end with the completion of the proceedings to which it
relates unless earlier terminated by recall or death.

Curators Bonis

If a child is left without parents and guardians, or without parents and guardians with legal capacity to act as such, or where there are grounds for superseding parents or guardians in the exercise of their administrative and representative powers, the court may appoint a curator *bonis*. This power of ap-

---

[93] *Inglis, Petr.* (1855) 17 D. 1005; *Young, Petrs.* (1828) 7 S. 220; *Baird, Petrs.* (1741) Mor. 16346; *Johnston* v. *Johnston* (1740) Mor. 16346; *Pyper* (1711) Mor. 16330.

[94] *MacNeil* v. *MacNeil* (1798) Mor. 16384.

[95] This is competent if the child has no guardian, or if the guardian is unable (whether by reason of conflict of interest or otherwise) or refuses to bring or defend such proceedings: see Age of Legal Capacity (Scotland) Act 1991, s. 1(3)(*f*)(i).

[96] *McConochie* v. *Binnie* (1847) 9 D. 791.

[97] *MacNeil* v. *MacNeil* (1798) Mor. 16384; *Keith* v. *Archer* (1836) 15 S. 116, *per* Lord Balgray at p. 118; *Paterson* v. *Sandilands* (1617) Mor. 8968; *Donaldson* (1629) Mor. 16253; *Calderhead's Trs.* v. *Fyfe* (1832) 10 S. 582; *Studd* v. *Studd* (1880) 8 R. 249, (1883) 10 R. (H.L.) 53.

[98] *Sloan* v. *B.*, 1991 S.L.T. 530.

[99] *Bogie* v. *Bogie* (1840) 3 D. 309; *Park's Trs.* v. *Park* (1876) 3 R. 850; *Ross* v. *Tennant's Trs.* (1877) 5 R. 182.

[1] The power to appoint a curator *ad litem* in this situation is preserved by the Age of Legal Capacity (Scotland) Act 1991, s. 1(3)(*f*)(iii).

pointment is preserved by section 1(3)(iv) of the Age of Legal Capacity (Scotland) Act 1991.

Before the abolition of curatory on the ground of age alone,[2] there was some doubt as to the effect of the appointment of a curator *bonis* to a minor child. Fraser[3] suggested that the powers of factors *loco tutoris*[4] and curators *bonis* "are the same over the estate as those of tutors and curators, *in loco* of whom they come." While that was vouched by authority in relation to factors *loco tutoris*[5] it was more doubtful in the case of curators *bonis*. As a court appointment he should have had the full powers of a judicial factor rather than the much more limited powers that curators had at common law over minors. Since tutory gave wide powers the problem did not arise with pupil children, and since tutory is now extended to age 16 the problem cannot today arise in relation to children under that age. A curator *bonis* today appointed to a person under the age of 16 will have the full powers of management of the estate, and the responsibilities, that a guardian and a judicial factor has. In view of the full legal capacity now enjoyed by a person over the age of 16, the appointment of a curator *bonis* to a person of that age will be necessary only if he is mentally incapax.

Previously the traditional ground for the appointment of a curator *bonis* was when a minor child was left without parents or guardians, the parents not having nominated by testamentary deed any curators to act after their death. That situation may, of course, still arise today, but in most circumstances the appointment under section 3 of the Law Reform (Parent and Child) (Scotland) Act 1986 of a guardian will probably be considered appropriate. However, it may exceptionally be considered more appropriate to appoint a curator *bonis* because his role is purely administrative and representative while the guardian's role is primarily but not exclusively so: the difference may be increased if legislation provides, as is proposed,[6] that the guardian is to have all the parental responsibilities and rights of a parent. A single transaction may require a person to represent the child as a matter of urgency, without that person being needed (or willing) to take on the quasi-parental role of guardian. As always, the child's welfare is the determining factor. Other considerations that may point to the aptness of a curator *bonis* include the parent's or guardian's bankruptcy, his or her maladministration with the child's estate (while care of the child's person is satisfactory),[7] or a conflict of patrimonial though not personal interests.[8] The appointment may also be appropriate if it is deemed necessary to ensure that the administrative role is subject to the responsibilities, for example, of accounting and supervision contained in the Judicial Factors Act 1849. Likewise there would be advantages if the child were mentally incapax and likely to remain so into adulthood, for in that situation the appointment of a curator *bonis* rather than a guardian would survive the child's attaining majority and thus obviate the need for a fresh appointment.

---

[2] Age of Legal Capacity (Scotland) Act 1991, s. 5(3).
[3] (3rd ed.) at p. 585.
[4] Abolished by the Age of Legal Capacity (Scotland) Act 1991, s. 5(4).
[5] *Robertson* v. *Elphinstone*, May 28, 1814, F.C. 631; *Paul* (1838) 16 S. 822.
[6] Scot. Law Com. No. 135; *Report on Family Law*, May 1992, at para. 3.14 and draft bill cl. 7(5).
[7] *McNab* v. *McNab* (1871) 10 M. 248.
[8] *Earl of Buchan* v. *Harvey* (1839) 2 D. 275; *Cochrane, Petr.* (1891) 18 R. 456.

The tenure of a curator *bonis* of his office comes to an end on his death or the death of his ward, or when the ward, unless mentally incapax, attains the age of 16,[9] or by the resignation of the curator, or when the decree making the appointment otherwise provides. Further court orders may replace the curator or terminate the curatory without replacement. Such court orders are made under section 3(1) of the Law Reform (Parent and Child) (Scotland) Act 1986, and consequently are governed by the welfare of the child.[10]

---

[9] At which age the child can take over the administration of his own estate: Age of Legal Capacity (Scotland) Act 1991, s. 1(1)(*b*).
[10] Law Reform (Parent and Child) (Scotland) Act 1986, s. 3(2).

CHAPTER 15

RELATIONSHIPS OF CARE

Scope of this Chapter

Apart from adoption and the assumption of parental rights and powers, both of which are dealt with in depth later,[1] there are a number of other ways in which a person may come to stand *in loco parentis* to a child and be subject to some of the responsibilities and entitled, in a partial and limited sense, to the rights and powers of a parent. The strongest example is where someone, other than a parent, becomes entitled to the custody of a child as a result of a custody order or becomes entitled by judicial or testamentary appointment to be guardian. Questions of custody and of the guardianship of children have already been considered in detail.[2] For the present, consideration will be confined to the constitution, and the consequences, of a quasi-parental relationship through the assumption, other than by virtue of a custody order or guardianship, of the charge and care of a child.

Personal Relationships of Care

Whenever a child comes into the charge or care of another person, even if only temporarily, a relationship is created which resembles, for the time being, some aspects of the relationship of parent and child.[3] To have a child in one's charge or care is, in some degree, to stand *in loco parentis* to him. The fact of possession and control gives rise to a duty of care; where the child is lawfully in one's care there is a corresponding right of possession and control. Some parallel may be drawn with the situation of an adult who, because he is sick or is infirm through age, is in the care of someone else, as may happen where he has been specifically entrusted to the care of the other person or the assumption of care is imported by relationship or force of circumstances. In that situation too there are duties to which legal sanctions attach.[4] There are, however, material

---

[1] *Post* at Chap. 16 (assumption of parental rights and powers) and Chap. 19 (adoption).

[2] *Ante* at Chap. 7 (custody) and Chap. 14 (guardianship).

[3] Charge and care are not used here in any technical sense, nor are the presumptions of s. 27 of the Children and Young Persons (Scotland) Act 1937 necessarily implied. Whether a child is in the charge and care of another person is a question of fact and the meaning to be given to the words is the ordinary meaning. Once, however, the factual relationship is established, the result in contemplation of the law is that the one term largely denotes the other. He who has charge of a child has a duty to care for him. It is no doubt possible, as an agent of another, to care for a child without having the element of control implied in having charge if the principal for whom one acts is present and able himself to exercise effective control, but when a child is said to be "in the care of" another person, the right to some degree of control arises by necessary implication. While, at the risk of some overlap or redundancy of meaning, both terms are used—"charge" to indicate the element of control regarded as a right or power and "care" to indicate the duty of protection and nurture—no sharp distinction is intended.

[4] *R.* v. *Instan* [1893] 1 Q.B. 450; *R.* v. *Chattaway* (1922) 17 Crim.App.Rep. 7; *R.* v. *Stone* [1977] Q.B. 354; Gordon, *Criminal Law of Scotland* (2nd ed.), p. 88.

points of distinction between this and the situation of a child. While an adult's need for care is exceptional, a child may be presumed to be in need of a degree of care appropriate to his age and maturity and in the case of a very young child the presumption that some degree of care is necessary will be absolute. The circumstances in which a child will be held to be in the care of another person are, therefore, much wider than in the case of an adult and an adult may repudiate the care of another with a freedom that is not open to a child. There is, too, a distinction in respect of rights and powers. He who has the care of another adult acquires thereby no rights and powers in a question with the person in his care unless that person be insane or mentally defective. A person in lawful charge of a child is armed with such rights and powers over the person of the child as are necessary for the discharge of his duties in the circumstances. These rights and powers are treated as arising from the *in loco parentis* relationship and not as instances of delegation.[5] Where, however, the child passes from a parent into the care of another under a voluntary arrangement unregulated by statute, the parent may, it is conceived, control the extent and manner of exercise of the powers thereby conveyed as if they were delegated unless necessity requires otherwise. There is no abridgement of the parent's rights, powers and duties except to the extent that absence makes impossible their personal performance and so, whenever the parent is able to resume charge and care, he may bring the temporary arrangement to an end unless it is protected by judicial order or other legal requirement.[6] The parent's rights may be enforced by an action of delivery, though such would, of course, be an action relating to parental rights[7] and therefore could be enforced only when to do so would be in the interests of the child.[8] However, in the absence of evidence to the contrary, an inference will normally be drawn that a child's interests will be served by its being in the care of its parent, when the parent is willing and able to resume that care.

Statutory Duty to Receive into Care

The reception of a child into care by a local authority is an instance of the transfer of care to which the principles discussed above will in general apply, but which has some statutory specialties. Section 15(1) of the Social Work (Scotland) Act 1968 provides that a local authority has a duty to receive into its care a child appearing to be under the age of 17 if:

---

[5] See also *ante* at pp. 177–178.

[6] *e.g.*custody orders, committals to care under the Matrimonial Proceedings (Children) Act 1958 and the Guardianship Act 1973, supervision requirements under Pt. III of the Social Work (Scotland) Act 1968. A schoolteacher has, however, no right to detain a child in school against a parent's wishes. If a parent removes a child from school he may, as a result, commit an offence but that does not give the schoolteacher, or the managers of the school, or the education authority, power to detain the child.

[7] Law Reform (Parent and Child) (Scotland) Act 1986, s. 3(1); *M.* v. *Dumfries and Galloway Regional Council* 1991 S.C.L.R. 481.

[8] *Ibid.*, s. 3(2). It is jurisprudentially inaccurate, for reasons discussed *ante* at pp. 163–166 to talk of parental "rights" even to obtain possession of the child. In *Macpherson* v. *Leishman* (1887) 14 R. 780, where the court ordered return of the child to its parent, Lord President Inglis expressed regret that he had to decide that way, because in his view the child's interests would be better served by remaining where it was. S. 3(2) effectively overrules this decision.

(a) the child has neither parent nor guardian or has been, and remains, abandoned by his parent or guardian or is lost, *or*

(b) his parent or guardian is, for the time being, or permanently, prevented by reason of illness or mental disorder or bodily disease or infirmity or other incapacity or any other circumstances from providing for his proper accommodation, maintenance and upbringing, *and*

(c) in either case, the intervention of the local authority under section 15 is necessary in the interests of the welfare of the child.

With the possible exception of certain duties of purely temporary care created by situations of emergency, no person or body other than a local authority or the child's parents or guardian has a duty to receive a child into their care unless by virtue of their own undertaking voluntarily given. In large measure, section 15 is designed to provide for cases in which parental care, or the care of guardians, has failed whether permanently or temporarily and there is no one else able and willing to look after the child.[9] In that context the imposition of duty, as distinct from the conferment of power, is to be stressed. Section 15 confers no power to "take", but only a duty to "receive" and to "keep," in care.[10] The choice of words is critical. The duty to receive cannot arise until the child is available for reception and a child in the care of a parent or guardian, or other person lawfully having his care, will not be so available against the will of that parent, guardian or other person. The duty to receive cannot therefore give rise to any corresponding power to bring the child into care. Local authority intervention under section 15 does not extend at the initial stage to compulsory intervention. Means for the taking of compulsory measures of care are provided elsewhere.[11] Once, however, a child has been received, a power to keep him in care, correlative to the duty, is, in a question with persons other than parents or guardians, implied; in a question with parents and guardians it is expressly excluded.[12]

The natural construction of section 15(1), especially in view of the reference in paragraph (c) to "either case," is that paragraphs (a) and (b) constitute strict alternatives. It has been suggested in relation to the similar English provisions (now repealed) that there is a resultant dilemma where one parent comes within paragraph (a) and the other within paragraph (b). The example postulated is that a parent who had been awarded custody in a divorce process might abandon the child (being within paragraph (a)) and that the other parent might be prevented by cogent circumstances from taking over the care of the child (being within paragraph (b)).[13] Such a case, it is said, does not come wholly within either paragraph (a) or paragraph (b) and, as the case must fall within either one paragraph or the other, cases that fall within both are excluded with the result that in such

---

[9] The local authority also has the duty to promote social welfare by making available advice, guidance and assistance where such assistance appears to them likely to diminish the need to receive a child into its care: Social Work (Scotland) Act 1968, s. 12.

[10] *Lewisham London Borough* v. *Lewisham Juvenile Court Justices* [1979] 2 All E.R. 297, *per* Viscount Dilhorne at p. 300, Lord Keith at p. 315, Lord Scarman at p. 318.

[11] Social Work (Scotland) Act 1968, Pt. III. See *post*, Chap. 17.

[12] *Ibid.*, s. 15(3).

[13] Bevan, *Child Law* (1989) at p. 691.

cases the local authority have no duty to act. That result, if correct, flowed, however, from the use of the plural form "parents" in both paragraphs of the English legislation.[14] In section 15, on the other hand, "parent" is used in the singular throughout. In Scotland therefore, the local authority has a duty to receive the child into care if a condition of paragraph (*a*) or paragraph (*b*) is satisfied in respect of either parent, provided, of course, its intervention is necessary in the interests of the welfare of the child (paragraph (*c*)). It is then immaterial whether a condition under paragraphs (*a*) or (*b*) could be satisfied in relation to the other parent except that, usually, paragraph (*c*) will not be satisfied unless that is so. As section 15 gives no compulsory powers against parents, there is no prejudice to their rights.

Review of the Child's Case

When the child has been in the care of a local authority throughout the preceding six months and they have not during that period held a review of his case, the local authority have a duty to review the child's case as soon as is practicable after the expiry of that period; and, if a supervision requirement is in force with respect to him, the local authority must consider in the course of the review whether to refer his case to their reporter for the review of that requirement by a children's hearing.[15] The effect of this is that there must be a review of the case of every child in the care of a local authority at least once every six months.

Enforcement of Duty

Although the question of judicial intervention while a child is in the care of a local authority has been discussed in a number of English cases, there is no authority in Scotland on enforcement of the duty to receive into care. As the duty to receive arises only where "it appears to the local authority" that the conditions stipulated in section 15(1) of the Social Work (Scotland) Act 1968 exist, a *bona fide* decision on whether a child should be received into care cannot be challenged on its merits, but relief will be available by way of judicial review in the Court of Session if, in an appropriate case, the question has not been considered or if failure or refusal is coloured by irregularity or impropriety, or represents a decision which no reasonable authority could in the circumstances have reached. If there is a clear contravention of the statute a convenient remedy is provided by petition to the Court of Session to ordain the authority to perform its statutory duty,[16] and procedure by action for declarator and implement, available in the sheriff court as well as the Court of Session, is probably also competent.[17] The duty under section 15 does not in itself relate to parental rights,[18] with the result that a remedy is not available under section 3(1) of the

---

[14] Children Act 1948, s. 1. The same wording was used in the Child Care Act 1980, s. 2(1), but a quite different statutory formulation now appears in the Children Act 1989, s. 20, which in this aspect as in others is in much broader terms.

[15] s. 20A, inserted by the Children Act 1975, s. 80.

[16] Court of Session Act 1868, s. 91, as amended by the Court of Session Act 1988, Sched. 2, Pt. II.

[17] *Hardie* v. *Walker*, 1948 S.C. 674.

[18] Though it has been held in the sheriff court that an action of delivery by parents against a local authority who had fulfilled their duty under s. 15 but were retaining the child against the parent's wishes was "an action relating to parental rights," and so could be resisted if the return of the child was not shown by the parents to be in the interests of the child: *M.* v. *Dumfries and Galloway Re-*

Law Reform (Parent and Child) (Scotland) Act 1986, and that the statutory direction in section 3(2) of that Act to regard the welfare of the child as the paramount consideration does not apply. The welfare of the child is, however, a question which is raised by the terms of section 15(1) itself.

The Appropriate Local Authority

The duty under section 15 to receive into care extends only to children within the area of the authority to whom the duty attaches. Mere physical presence at the time the need to receive arises is sufficient irrespective of domicile, nationality or residence but, if the child is ordinarily resident in another area the authority for that area may take over the care of the child.[19] It may do so at any time with the concurrence of the authority into whose care the child has been received, but in the absence of such concurrence must act within three months after the determination of the ordinary residence of the child.[20] Before exercising its right to take over the care of the child the authority concerned must be satisfied that to do so would not be detrimental to the child's welfare but no right is given to the authority which first took the child into care to resist the taking-over on welfare grounds. Apart from these specific provisions regarding children ordinarily resident in another area, one local authority may arrange to hand a child in its care over to another with the result that, when the child is brought into the area of the authority to which it has been handed over, that authority has a duty to receive the child into care.[21] That will be competent, however, only where it appears to the first authority that the welfare of the child no longer requires that the child be in its care.[22] In the event of dispute, questions of ordinary residence are to be determined by the Secretary of State.[23] Where a child, ordinarily resident in the area of one local authority, is received into care by another local authority, expenditure incurred by the latter is recoverable from the former.[24]

Duration and Termination of Duty

Once a child is received into care there is a duty to keep him in care so long as his welfare requires it and he is under the age of 18.[25] Welfare is to be understood here, as in other similar contexts, in a wide sense.[26] The duty to keep in care carries with it corresponding rights but the local authority is not thereby au-

---

gional Council, 1991 S.C.L.R. 481.

[19] Social Work (Scotland) Act 1968, s. 15(4).

[20] Whether by agreement between the local authorities or by the Secretary of State under the statutory provisions to that end: ss. 15(4) and 86.

[21] Barker v. Westmoreland County Council (1958) 56 L.G.R. 267; Halvorsen v. Hertforshire County Council (1974) 5 Fam.L. 79. The disapproval of Halvorsen in B. v. B. (1975) 6 Fam.L. 79 and Bawden v. Bawden [1978] 3 W.L.R. 798 does not extend to this point.

[22] Social Work (Scotland) Act 1968, s. 15(2).

[23] Ibid., ss. 15(4) and 86(2).

[24] Ibid., s. 86(1). The provisions are extended to local authorities in England and Wales.

[25] Ibid., s. 15(2).

[26] See Re McGrath (Infants) [1893] 1 Ch. 143, per Lindley L.J.: "The welfare of the child is not to be measured by money only, nor by physical comfort only. The word welfare must be taken in its widest sense. The moral and religious welfare of the child must be considered as well as his physical wellbeing. Nor can the ties of affection be disregarded." As the matter is left to the judgment of the local authority (s. 15(2)), judicial review will be open only on principles similar to those discussed above in relation to the reception of the child into care.

thorised to keep a child in their care if any parent or guardian desires to take over care.[27] Such authorisation may, however, be gleaned from other provisions[28]: thus the duty is not terminated merely by an expression of parental wish to resume or take over care, for the fulfilment of that wish must not conflict with the child's welfare. It has also been held that where a parent or guardian wishes to take over care there is not a positive duty to secure that the child is handed over.[29] As a consequence, it seems that, if the local authority considers that the return of the child would not consist with the consideration it is bound to give to the welfare of the child and the child's wishes and feelings,[30] it need take no action unless ordered to do so by the court and, in particular, need not take proceedings to recover the child from third parties, such as foster parents, who have actual control of the child at the time of the parental request.[31] Indeed, because an action by the parents against the local authority for delivery of the child would be an action "relating to parental rights" within the meaning of section 3(1) of the Law Reform (Parent and Child) (Scotland) Act 1986, it would seem that the local authority has a residual discretion to refuse the return of the child, even without statutory authority, because the court will not grant an application for delivery unless it is satisfied that to do so will be in the interests of the child.[32] In all cases, however, where it appears to be consistent with the welfare of the child so to do, the local authority must endeavour to secure that the care of the child is taken over either by a parent or guardian or by a relative or friend.[33] The relative or friend should, if possible, be of the same religious persuasion as the child or should give an undertaking that the child will be brought up in that religious persuasion[34] but it is thought that if that requirement conflicts with the duty to give first consideration to the need to safeguard and promote the welfare of the child throughout his childhood the latter must prevail.

Criminal Sanctions

Consistently with the voluntary character of reception into care and in contrast with cases in which parental rights and powers have been assumed, the general rule is that no special criminal sanctions apply to the removal of a child from care or to assisting or inducing him to run away or to harbouring or concealing him. If, however, a child has been in the care of a local authority for six months the same sanctions apply as in the case of a child in relation to whom parental rights and powers have been assumed and a parent or guardian is deemed not to have lawful authority to take the child away unless with the con-

---

[27] Social Work (Scotland) Act 1968, s. 15(3).

[28] *Central Regional Council v. B*, 1985 S.L.T. 413; *M v. Dumfries and Galloway Regional Council*, 1991 S.C.L.R. 481; see the discussion of these cases, *post* at pp. 424–425.

[29] *Krishnan v. London Borough Council of Sutton* [1970] Ch. 181. See also the discussion of this question in relation to the assumption of parental rights and powers, *post* at pp. 421–425.

[30] Social Work (Scotland) Act 1968, ss. 15(2) and 20(1).

[31] See comments on *Krishnan* in *London Borough of Lewisham v. Lewisham Juvenile Court Justices* [1979] 2 All E.R. 297.

[32] Law Reform (Parent and Child) (Scotland) Act 1986, s. 3(2); *M v. Dumfries and Galloway Regional Council, supra.*

[33] Social Work (Scotland) Act 1968, s. 15(3).

[34] *Ibid.* Such an undertaking is not enforceable. A very young child cannot, it is submitted, properly have a religious "persuasion," for that word presupposes the ability to be persuaded. Perhaps, however, that is not quite what is meant.

sent of the local authority or on giving 28 day's notice of his intention to do so.[35] Similar provisions apply where a child is in the care of a voluntary organisation. For this purpose a child is in the organisation's care if it is providing accommodation for the child in a residential establishment or has boarded the child out.[36]

Committal to Care

If in any action for divorce, nullity of marriage, or separation it appears to the court that there are exceptional circumstances making it impracticable or undesirable for a child for whose custody it has power to make provision to be entrusted to either of the parties of the marriage, the court may, if it thinks fit, make an order committing the care of the child to any other individual or to a local authority.[37] The appropriate local authority is the Regional or Islands Council in which the child was, in the opinion of the court, resident before the order was made and the court must, before making the order, hear representations from the authority including representations as to the making of an order for payment for the maintenance and education of the child.[38] A child so committed is treated as if he had been received into care under section 15 except that he shall continue in the care of the local authority notwithstanding any claim by a parent or other person[39] and that the exercise by the local authority of certain of their powers is subject to direction by the court and the power to arrange emigration of the child does not apply.[40] Any parent or guardian of a child committed to the care of a local authority under these provisions must see that the local authority are informed of his address for the time being.[41] The court has similar powers, to which similar provisions apply, in the case of applications for the custody of a child.[42] Orders committing children to the care of local authorities may be varied or revoked by subsequent orders.[43]

Children subject to Supervision Requirement

For certain purposes a child who is the subject of a supervision requirement under Part III of the Social Work (Scotland) Act 1968[44] is treated as being in the care of the local authority.[45] These purposes are the assumption of parental

---

[35] s. 15(3A), as inserted by the Children Act 1975, s. 73, and as amended by the Health and Social Services and Social Security Adjudications Act 1983, Sched. 2, para. 4.

[36] Social Work (Scotland) Act 1968, s. 25A, as inserted by the Children Act 1975, s. 81.

[37] Matrimonial Proceedings (Children) Act 1958, s. 10(1), as amended by the Law Reform (Parent and Child) (Scotland) Act 1986, Sched. 2 and the Family Law Act 1986, Sched. 1, para. 6. For further details on this power, see *ante*, at pp. 250–251.

[38] *Ibid.*, s. 10(2).

[39] *Ibid.*, s. 10(3).

[40] *Ibid.*, s. 10(4).

[41] *Ibid.*, s. 10(6).

[42] Guardianship Act 1973, s. 11, as amended by the Children Act 1975, ss. 17(4) and 48(3). On the differences between this and the Matrimonial Proceedings (Scotland) Act 1958, see *ante* at pp. 251–253.

[43] Guardianship Act 1973, s. 12(1), under which the order can be made only on the application of a parent or (after the death of either parent) any guardian or the local authority having the care of the child.

[44] Discussed in detail, *post* at chap. 17.

[45] Social Work (Scotland) Act 1968, s. 44(5), as amended by the Law Reform (Miscellaneous Provisions) (Scotland) Act 1985, s. 28.

rights and powers; the obligation imposed on local authorities to give first consideration, in any decision relating to the child, to the need to safeguard and promote his welfare and give due consideration to his wishes and feelings; the
obligation to review the child's case; the obligation to provide financial assistance towards his expenses of maintenance, education or training of persons
over school age, or the guaranteeing of indentures and other deeds of apprenticeship; after care; burial and cremation of the dead and payment of visiting expenses of parents and others, and of expenses of attendance at funerals; and the
freeing of the child for adoption.[46] Under the Children and Young Persons
(Scotland) Act 1937 a local authority qualified as a fit person to whose care a
child might be committed and, if that were done, had, under that legislation, the
same rights, powers and liabilities as a parent.[47] The effects of a supervision requirement under the 1968 Act are, therefore, less far-reaching in relation to
local authority rights, powers and duties than committal to the care of a local authority as a fit person had been. On the other hand, supervision requirements are
now made in many cases in which measures other than committal to care would
have been adopted under the previous legislation and in these cases the local authority is given a new role.

Discretion to Receive into Care

In the instances so far considered a local authority is obliged to receive or
have children in its care whether because the circumstances giving rise to a duty
under section 15 exist or because of an order of the court or a supervision requirement. In addition to these obligatory cases a local authority has, however, a
discretion to receive into care a protected child[48] or a foster child who has, by
court order, been removed from unsuitable surroundings to a place of safety.[49]
This discretion may be exercised notwithstanding that the child may appear to
be over the age of 17.[50]

Duties of Local Authorities to Children in their Care

In addition to the general duties incumbent on persons having children in
their care, a local authority have a statutory duty in reaching any decision relating to a child in their care to give first consideration to the need to safeguard and
promote the welfare of the child throughout his childhood and, so far as practicable, to ascertain the wishes and feelings of the child regarding the decision and
give due consideration to them, having regard to his age and understanding.[51]
There is no counterpart in the Scottish legislation to the English provision that
absolves a local authority from that duty where necessary for the purpose of
protecting members of the public.[52] In providing for a child in their care, a local

---

[46] *i.e.* ss. 16–18, 20, 20A, 24–26, 28 and 29 of the Social Work (Scotland) Act 1968, and s. 18 of the
Adoption (Scotland) Act 1978.
[47] Children and Young Persons (Scotland) Act 1937, s. 79(4).
[48] *Post* at pp. 562–563.
[49] Adoption (Scotland) Act 1978, s. 34(3).
[50] *i.e.* in his 18th year. On attaining the age of 18 he ceases to be a child: Adoption (Scotland) Act
1978, s. 65(1).
[51] Social Work (Scotland) Act 1968, s. 20(1).
[52] Children Act 1989, s. 22(6).

authority are to make such use of facilities and services available for children in the care of their own parents as appears to the local authority reasonable.[53]

Transfer of Care—Effect

A local authority's statutory duty to children in its care applies in addition to the general duties incumbent on parents where a local authority have assumed parental rights and powers in respect of a child. If in such a case it appears to the local authority to be for the benefit of the child, the authority may allow, either for a fixed period or until they otherwise determine, the care of the child to be taken over by, and the child to be under the control of a guardian, relative or friend[54]; and on an application to determine a resolution assuming parental rights and powers the sheriff may in lieu of determining the resolution order the local authority to allow the care of the child to be taken over by, and the child to be under the control of, the applicant.[55] The statutory duty of care incumbent on the authority is not affected by such a take-over.[56]

Provision of Accommodation and Maintenance Contributions

The duty of a local authority towards children in their care extends to the provision of accommodation and maintenance for the child,[57] although contributions may be exacted from the father and mother of the child if he is under 16 and from the child himself if he is over 16.[58] Accommodation and maintenance are to be provided by the local authority either by boarding the child out or by maintaining him in a residential establishment managed by the authority, a voluntary organisation or other person providing residential accommodation for the purposes of the Social Work (Scotland) Act 1968.[59] The child may be boarded out in England or Wales or maintained in any accommodation in England or Wales which a local authority in those countries are authorised to use.[60] The statutory provisions on boarding out and maintenance in residential establishments do not derogate from the local authority's power to make such use of facilities and services available for children in the care of their own parents as appears to the authority reasonable, and for that purpose the authority may arrange for the child's accommodation and maintenance in any suitable manner.[61] Where a child is placed in a residential establishment, the local authority may, notwithstanding any agreement made in connection with the child's placing, remove the child at any time and must do so if so required by the Secretary of State or the person responsible for the establishment.[62]

Financial Assistance to Child Over School Age

Where a person, who is over school age but has not attained the age of 21, is

---

[53] Social Work (Scotland) Act 1968, s. 20(2).
[54] *Ibid.*, s. 17(3).
[55] *Ibid.*, s. 18(3).
[56] *Ibid.*, s. 20(3).
[57] *Ibid.*, s. 21(1).
[58] *Ibid.*, s. 78(1).
[59] *Ibid.*, ss. 21(1) and 94(1).
[60] *Ibid.*, s. 21(3).
[61] *Ibid.*, s. 21(2).
[62] *Ibid.*, s. 22.

or has at any time after ceasing to be of school age been in the care of a local authority, the authority may make contributions to the cost of his accommodation and maintenance in any place near the place where he may be employed or seeking employment or in receipt of education or training,[63] and the authority may make grants to such persons other than those still in care to enable them to meet expenses connected with their receiving suitable education or training.[64] These contributions or grants may be continued until the completion of any course of education or training on which a person was engaged when he attained the age of 21 or on which he had previously been engaged and which he resumes as soon as practicable after an interruption occasioned by any circumstance.[65]

Guarantee of Apprenticeship

A local authority may also undertake any obligation by way of guarantee under any indentures or other deed of apprenticeship or articles of clerkship entered into by a person in their care and where the authority have undertaken any such obligation they may at any time, whether or not the person concerned is still in their care, undertake the like obligation under any supplemental deed or articles.[66]

Emigration

A local authority or voluntary organisation may, with the consent of the Secretary of State, arrange or assist in arranging the emigration of any child in their care.[67] The consent of the Secretary of State is not, however, to be given unless he is satisfied that emigration would benefit the child, that suitable arrangements have been made or will be made for the child's reception and welfare in the country to which he is going, that the parent of the child has been consulted or that it is not practicable for that to be done and that the child consents.[68] If, however, the child is too young to form or express a proper opinion on the matter the Secretary of State may consent to his emigration notwithstanding that the child is unable to consent provided the child is to emigrate in company with a parent or relative or is to emigrate for the purpose of joining a parent, relative or friend.[69]

Visiting Expenses of Parents, etc.

A local authority may make payments to any parent, relative or other person connected with a person in the authority's care or receiving assistance from them in respect of travelling, subsistence or other expenses incurred in visiting the person in care if it appears to the authority that the parent, relative or other person would not otherwise be able to visit the person in care without undue hardship and that the circumstances warrant the making of the payment.[70] Like

---

[63] *Ibid.*, s. 24(1).
[64] *Ibid.*, s. 24(2).
[65] *Ibid.*, s. 24(3).
[66] *Ibid.*, s. 25.
[67] *Ibid.*, s. 23(1).
[68] *Ibid.*, s. 23(2).
[69] *Ibid.*
[70] *Ibid.*, s. 29(1).

payments may be made for the purpose of enabling a parent, relative or other person to attend the funeral of a person who was in the care of the local authority.[71]

Burial and Cremation

A local authority may cause to be buried or cremated the body of any deceased person who, immediately before his death, was in its care or receiving assistance from it.[72] The authority is not, however, to arrange for cremation where that is not in accordance with the practice of the person's religious persuasion.[73] Expenses incurred under this provision and not reimbursed under the Social Security legislation may be recovered from the estate of the deceased person or from any person who was liable to maintain the deceased immediately before his death.[74]

After-Care

Where it comes to the knowledge of a local authority that there is in its area any child over school age who at the time when he ceased to be of that age or at any subsequent time was, but no longer is, in the care of a local authority or voluntary organisation it is the duty of the authority, unless satisfied that the welfare of the child does not so require, to advise, guide or assist the child until he has attained the age of 18.[75] If, however, in the case of a child who has been in the care of a voluntary organisation the local authority are satisfied that that organisation has the necessary facilities, the authority may make arrangements whereby the child is to be advised, guided or assisted by the voluntary organisation instead of the local authority.[76] Where a child to whom these provisions apply ceases to be in the care of a local authority and proposes to reside in the area of another authority or ceases to be in the care of a voluntary organisation the authority or organisation in whose care the child was shall inform the local authority for the area in which the child proposes to reside[77] and where advice, guidance, or assistance has been provided to a child who proposes to transfer or has transferred his residence to the area of another local authority the authority or organisation which provided the advice, guidance or assistance shall inform the other local authority accordingly.[78]

---

[71] *Ibid.*, s. 29(2).
[72] *Ibid.*, s. 28(1). *Cf.* the English decision of *R.* v. *Gwynedd County Council, ex p. B and Anr.* [1992] 3 All E.R. 317.
[73] *Ibid.*
[74] *Ibid.*, s. 28(2).
[75] *Ibid.*, s. 26(1).
[76] *Ibid.*
[77] *Ibid.*, s. 26(2).
[78] *Ibid.*, s. 26(3).

CHAPTER 16

ASSUMPTION OF PARENTAL RIGHTS AND POWERS

INTRODUCTORY

Since 1948[1] local authorities[2] have been empowered, under certain conditions, to assume parental rights and powers in respect of children in their care. Such rights and powers may also now be vested by local authority resolution in a voluntary organisation.[3] This assumption has the effect of barring the parent in respect of whom the resolution is passed from exercising any of the relevant[4] rights and powers, and of vesting them in the local authority or the voluntary organisation. The relationship thus created between the authority or organisation and the child has been likened to adoption,[5] but there are a number of points of distinction, both practical and legal. An approximation to the natural relationship of parent and child, such as adoption seeks to promote, can be achieved by the body in which rights and powers are vested only indirectly by delegation to foster parents or, in a modified and necessarily incomplete form, by institutional care; the guarantee of permanency associated with adoption is lacking; the transfer of rights and powers, although considerable, is more limited than with adoption; the status of the child is unaffected and links with the natural parents may more often be maintained than with adoption. There is, moreover, a difference in purpose. The restructuring of the child's life on what is intended to be a secure basis is integral to the adoption process whereas the assumption of parental rights and powers is rather a device for the protection of the child while that restructuring takes place. Adoption is the creation of a (legal) parent-child relationship which is complete for almost all legal purposes, while the assumption of parental rights and powers on the other hand does not create that relationship, and the consequences of the parent-child relationship (most notably in relation to succession[6]) apply as ever to the parent, except that they are divested

---

[1] Children Act 1948, s. 2.

[2] *i.e.*, under present legislation, Regional and Islands Councils.

[3] Social Work (Scotland) Act 1968, s. 16(1)(*b*), as enacted by the Children Act 1975, s. 74. All references in this chapter are, unless otherwise stated, to the 1968 Act.

[4] See *post* at p. 432.

[5] *Re AB (An Infant)* [1954] 2 Q.B. 385.

[6] In the opinion of some commentators the wording of the English provisions contained in the Children Act 1975 was such as to give the local authority or voluntary organisation rights of succession on death to the child's estate (see Bevan and Parry, *The Children Act 1975*, p. 155, para. 333). (That conclusion was no longer apt on the wording of the Child Care Act 1980 (see Bevan, *Child Law* (1989) at p. 714) and is not apt on the wording of the Children Act 1989). It is submitted that this is an unacceptable conclusion, at least on the wording of the Scottish legislation. Despite the apparent generality of the words used, their construction is controlled by their context, and in particular by the protective purpose which is evident in the section. Any construction that led to succession rights being altered would be anomalous. A resolution vesting parental rights lapses on the occurrence of certain events, and it would be unacceptable for the local authority or voluntary organisation to benefit if the child died just before the occurrence of these events. Nor is it satisfactory that the existence of rights of succession should depend on the timing of local authority

of the relevant rights and powers. Likewise a parent who has been divested of parental rights and powers will remain a parent for the purposes of the law of incest and the forbidden degrees of marriage[7] and for the purposes of the prohibitions contained in, for example, the Child Abduction Act 1984 and the Child Abduction and Custody Act 1985. A parent will remain a parent for the purposes of aliment and, now, access. Again unlike adoption, the assumption of parental rights and powers does not affect the status of the child (*e.g.* in relation to its domicile or nationality) and its relationship to its actual parent is affected only in respect of the rights and powers that are removed from the parent and vested in the local authority or voluntary organisation. The purpose is not to destroy the parent-child relationship, but to ensure that that relationship does not unduly prejudice the child. An appreciation of its protective character is the key to an understanding of some of its features.

The assumption of parental rights and powers is now governed by section 16 of the Social Work (Scotland) Act 1968[8] and is effected by means of a resolution for that purpose passed by the local authority.[9] That is so whether the rights and powers are to be vested in the authority itself or in a voluntary organisation. Before passing the resolution the local authority is bound, unless the matter is urgent, to consider a report from its social work committee.[10] The local authority's functions cannot be delegated.[11]

CONDITIONS FOR PASSING THE RESOLUTION

Introduction

There is a discretion as to whether or not to pass a resolution, and in the exercise of that discretion the local authority must give first consideration to the need to safeguard and promote the welfare of the child throughout his childhood. It must also ascertain the wishes and feelings of the child so far as practicable and give due consideration to them having regard to his age and understanding.[12] Two conditions must, however, be satisfied before that discretion comes into play:

(a) The child must, at the time the resolution is passed, be in the care of the authority or organisation in which the rights and powers are to vest,[13] and

---

decisions on recision, or judicial decisions that a resolution should cease to have effect. Nor again is it satisfactory that a local authority should, by a resolution at its own hand which is unchallengeable by the voluntary organisation except on grounds of incompetence, be able to transfer from a voluntary organisation to itself rights of succession which *ex hypothesi* of the argument under consideration would have vested in that organisation. Clear words would be required to bring about the prejudice to the rights of third parties which a transfer of rights of succession to a local authority or voluntary organisation might create, and they are lacking.

[7] The same is true with adoption: see *post* at p. 521.

[8] As substituted by the Children Act 1975, s. 74 (and as amended a number of times since).

[9] This is now in contrast to the position in England, where this can only be done by means of a care order granted by the court under s. 31 of the Children Act 1989.

[10] Social Work (Scotland) Act 1968, s. 2(2).

[11] *Central Regional Council* v. *Mailley*, 1977 S.L.T. (Sh. Ct.) 36. Opinion was reserved on the competency of delegation to an officer, but it is submitted that the passing of a resolution is incapable of being so delegated (see sheriff principal's opinion at p. 38).

[12] Social Work (Scotland) Act 1968, s. 20(1), as substituted by Children Act 1975, s. 79.

[13] s. 16(1)(*a*).

  (b) one or more of the prescribed conditions considered later[14] for the
    passing of the resolution must exist.

Child must be "In Care"

Relevant Statutes

When the Children Act 1948 was passed, section 2 of that Act (the precursor
of section 16 of the Social Work (Scotland) Act 1968) had in its contemplation
only children who had come into care under section 1 thereof.[15] Section 1 had
been concerned with the duty of local authorities to receive and keep certain
children in their care. It was not concerned with compulsory measures of care.
Section 2 followed on section 1 by providing a framework for the assumption of
rights where that was necessary for the protection of the child. The simplicity of
this relationship between sections 1 and 2 has been disturbed by later legislation. Children taken into care under section 15 of the Social Work (Scotland)
Act 1968,[16] the successor to section 1 of the 1948 Act, still constitute the primary, but no longer the only, class in respect of whose members a resolution vesting parental rights and powers may be passed. Not only may a resolution now be
passed in respect of children in the care of a voluntary organisation but three additional classes of children have been engrafted on to the reference in section 16
of the 1968 Act to any child in care under section 15:

  (a) children who have been committed by the court to the care of a local
    authority under section 10 of the Matrimonial Proceedings (Children)
    Act 1958,[17]
  (b) children so committed under section 11 of the Guardianship Act
    1973,[18] and
  (c) children who are subject to a supervision requirement under section 44
    of the Social Work (Scotland) Act 1968.[19]

Children in these classes, together with children in care under section 15 of the
1968 Act, are all treated as being in the care of the local authority for the purposes of the assumption of parental rights and powers.[20]

---

[14] *Post* at pp. 426–430.
[15] Even then the 1948 Act was not the sole statutory source for parental rights and powers. A child
might be committed to the care of a fit person under the Children and Young Persons (Scotland)
Act 1937 and that person had parental rights and powers (ss. 66(2)(*b*) and 79(4)) but those rights
and powers were an incident of the court order and did not depend on any resolution by the local
authority.
[16] The local authority's duty to receive children into its care is considered in detail, *ante* at pp.
408–413.
[17] On which, see *ante* at pp. 250–251.
[18] On which, see *ante* at pp. 251–253.
[19] On which, see *post* at pp. 484–485.
[20] Matrimonial Proceedings (Children) Act 1958, s. 10(4), as substituted by the Social Work (Scotland) Act 1968, Sched. 8, para. 42; Guardianship Act 1973, s. 11(5) as extended by the Children
Act 1975, s. 17(4); Social Work (Scotland) Act 1968, s. 44(5), as amended by the Law Reform
(Miscellaneous Provisions) (Scotland) Act 1985, s. 28. S. 44(5) of the 1968 Act deems a child to
be in care for the purposes of s. 16 and not, as do the other provisions listed, expressly for the purposes of s. 15. However, in *Lothian Regional Council* v. *S*, 1986 S.L.T. (Sh. Ct.) 37 the sheriff
principal, reversing the sheriff, held that if s. 44(5) were to be made to work for the purposes of s.
16, it was unavoidable that it would also have to apply to s. 15, without which s. 16 could not get
off the ground. See also the Inner House decision in *Central Regional Council* v. *B*, 1985 S.L.T.

Duration of Care

There is no requirement that the child should have been in the care of the local authority or voluntary organisation for any length of time before the passing of the resolution. Nor is there any requirement that he continue in care thereafter, although, if the resolution is challenged, it may be necessary that he be in care at the time of the hearing on whether the resolution should lapse.[21] Accordingly a resolution may validly be passed although the child has been in care only for a very short time and has recently been brought into the area of the authority passing the resolution from another area.[22] In the main, difficulties have arisen not about whether care has commenced but about whether it has ended so as to render any resolution passed after its ending invalid. In the case of children committed to the care of a local authority by court order, that is under section 10 of the Matrimonial Proceedings (Children) Act 1958 or section 11 of the Guardianship Act 1973, or of children subject to a supervision requirement under section 44 of the Social Work (Scotland) Act 1968, it is clear that care endures as long as there is a valid court order or supervision requirement in force. Where, however, the child has been received into the care of a local authority under section 15(1) the question of when care ends is very much more complex.

The difficulties centre on the provisions of section 15(3) that "nothing in this section shall authorise a local authority to keep a child in their care under this section if any parent or guardian desires to take over the care of the child" and the interaction of these words with the local authority's duty under section 15(2) to keep the child in their care so long as the welfare of the child appears to them to require it.[23] The receiving of a child into care under section 15 is essentially a voluntary matter, as is made clear by the above-quoted words from section 15(3). It would follow that when a parent desires to take over the care of the child, the voluntariness disappears and indeed if the child has been in care for less than six months the child must be delivered back to the parent immediately. But if the child has been in care for more than six months, the parent must give the local authority not less than 28 days' written notice of his intention to resume care.[24] During the running of that period of notice the voluntariness of the local authority care is clearly lacking, but it may appear to the local authority that the child's welfare requires their care to continue. The question then is, whether care can be said to continue after such notice has been given but before the period of notice has ended. For if it does and the other conditions for the passing of a parental rights resolution are satisfied, such a resolution will be available, while if care ends on the receipt of the notice the power to pass the resolution will no longer exist. In *London Borough of Lewisham* v. *Lewisham Juvenile Court Justices*[25] a parent had given the 28 days' notice of intention to

---

413. It is suggested that this must be correct and that a possible explanation for the failure to refer expressly to s. 15 is that the express references are to sections that provide the consequences of a child being in "care," while s. 15 deals with the concept of care itself.

[21] *Post* at p. 438.

[22] *Barker* v. *Westmorland County Council* (1958) 56 L.G.R. 267.

[23] s. 15(2). It should be noted that this duty applies only to local authorities, and not to voluntary organisations.

[24] s. 15(3A).

[25] [1979] 2 All E.R. 297.

remove the child which required to be given, and the juvenile court held that this had the effect of terminating care. The House of Lords held instead that care persisted at least until the expiry of the period of notice, and that accordingly a resolution for the assumption of parental rights could be passed within that time. Certain problems, however, remain. In particular, it is uncertain (1) what effect an expression of parental desire to take over the care of the child has on the duration of care if the child has been in care for less than six months, and (2) what effect the giving of notice of intention to remove from care has, in the case of a child who has been in care for six months or more, if the child is not in fact removed on the expiry of the notice (*i.e.* whether a section 16 resolution can be passed at any time thereafter while the child in fact remains in care). There may also be problems of whether care is ended when a child runs away or is abducted.

A factual test has been suggested.[26] This would mean that a child is "in care under section 15" so long as he is in fact in care, that is being cared for by the local authority, with the result that a parental rights resolution can be passed at any time before care in fact ends. That test has the merit of simplicity, gives to the word "care" its ordinary meaning and therefore avoids superimposing on that meaning, which is clearly intended for some purposes of the statute, a further legal or notional concept of care. In one form or another such a factual test underlies three of the four speeches in the *Lewisham* case. For Viscount Dilhorne the desire of a parent to take over care of a child does not terminate the keeping of the child in local authority care. It merely prevents the local authority "from relying on section 1 [of the Children Act 1948; *i.e.* in Scottish terms, section 15 of the Social Work (Scotland) Act 1968] as authorising the retention by them of the care of the child." A parental rights resolution, in appropriate circumstances, may therefore still be passed.[27] The implication seems to be plain that care, for that purpose, persists until it in fact ends; at least, no other test for termination is suggested. Lord Keith is more explicit. In his opinion, the child continues to be in the "care" of the local authority (for the purposes of section 15) until delivered up.[28] Similarly, Lord Scarman considers that the child continues in care until the parent in fact removes him or a court order is made.[29] A factual test along those lines creates no difficulty on the particular *species facti* of the *Lewisham* case for which it affords a satisfactory basis of decision. However, pressed to its logical conclusion in other fact situations it may lead to anomalous or disturbing results. If it were consistently and strictly applied, a local authority would, on the one hand, be able to pass a parental rights resolution although it were retaining possession of a child wrongfully in the face of a parental demand for its return and, on the other hand, it would be unable to pass a resolution if the child ran away, was abducted by strangers or was removed by a parent without notice and in defiance of the prohibition of such removal where the child has been in care for six months or more. Unless these results are to be

---

[26] This was the argument for the local authority which was accepted by the Divisional Court but not by the Court of Appeal in *Johns* v. *Jones* [1978] 3 All E.R. 1222 (see *per* Orr L.J. at p. 1224).

[27] [1979] 2 All E.R. 297 at p. 304.

[28] *Ibid.*, at p. 316.

[29] *Ibid.*, at p. 320.

accepted, some modification of the factual test is necessary. Lord Keith may have had that in mind in saying that the child continued in care "until delivered up" (*i.e.* abscondment or clandestine or violent removal will not terminate care). A factual test was not, however, necessary for the decision in the *Lewisham* case, and indeed Lord Salmon reached the same result by an alternative route[30]; nor is the *Lewisham* case authority for extending that test beyond cases of the passing of a parental rights resolution in the circumstances with which it was concerned.[31]

It is submitted, consistently with the decision in the *Lewisham* case and with Lord Salmon's speech, that the better view is that care by a local authority for the purpose of passing a section 16 resolution persists as long as the authority is entitled under section 15 to keep the child in care. There is a duty, and, by implication, a corresponding right to keep the child in care as long as his welfare appears to require it. The only qualification to that is that retention in care is not authorised under section 15 in the face of the desire of a parent or guardian to take over care. These are the measures of the local authority's entitlement to keep a child in care. "Care" for the purposes of section 16, unless judicially determined, can therefore end short of the attainment of majority by the child, only if (1) care is surrendered by the local authority (a surrender which, if voluntary, cannot lawfully take place unless, in the authority's judgment, it consists with the welfare of the child)[32] or (2) a parent or guardian desires, consistently with the welfare of the child, to take over care. It is the second alternative that is problematic.

Parental Desire to Take Over Care—Ability to do so

In order to be effective a desire to take over care of a child must, it is submitted, be communicated and be capable of fulfilment. If the child's fate is not to be left in uncertainty and practical anomalies are to be avoided it must be capable of present fulfilment. Accordingly, the parental wish to take over care of the child brings care to an end and so excludes the passing of a parental rights resolution if, but only if, to the knowledge of the authority the parent or guardian is able and willing immediately to take over the care of the child.[33] Ability in this context refers only to the physical possibility of receiving the child and the absence of any legal constraint. It does not entitle the local authority to enter

---

[30] It appears from Lord Salmon's speech that a parental rights resolution could not competently be passed after a parent had demanded the immediate return of a child who had been in care for less than six months (at p. 306) and from his approval (at p. 309) of the judgment of the Divisional Court in *Wheatley* v. *London Borough of Waltham Forest* [1979] 2 All E.R. 289 that he considered care in the relevant sense to persist only so long as the child was lawfully in care.

[31] *i.e.* in respect of a child actually in care and within the 28 days' notice period applicable where a child has been in care for six months or more.

[32] The surrender of care is not, in principle, problematic. As care in its ordinary meaning consists in the provision of proper accommodation, maintenance and upbringing (*Re AB (An Infant)* [1954] 2 Q.B. 385, *per* Lord Goddard, C.J. at pp. 394 and 397, and *per* Hilbery J. at p. 400), and the exercise of such control as is necessary for the protection and care of the child (*cf.* Children and Young Persons (Scotland) Act 1937, s. 27), care is surrendered when the local authority voluntarily or under legal requirement substantially ceases to make such provision and exercise such control.

[33] See the references in the *Lewisham* case to a parent's demand "that the child be handed over to her immediately" and for "the immediate return of her child," *per* Lord Salmon [1979] 2 All E.R. at p. 306, and "instant will and readiness to take the child," *per* Lord Scarman, *ibid.* at p. 320.

into an assessment of the parent's or guardian's fitness.[34] Where a desire has been expressed to take over the care of the child in the future or notice of intention to do so at a fixed future date has been given, care will be terminated only when, whether at the expiry of the period of notice or at some other time intimated to the local authority, the parent or guardian is in fact able and willing immediately to take over care. As this analysis departs to some extent from a purely factual test there will be cases in which a child is treated as in care for the purposes of the passing of a section 16 resolution although in fact he is no longer being cared for (*e.g.* where he has run away or been abducted) and also cases in which "care" will be deemed for that purpose to have ceased although in fact the child remains in care (*i.e.* where a local authority wrongfully refuses to comply with a parental request for the immediate return of the child). (As a corollary of that a child may, if only exceptionally, be in the care of a local authority otherwise than under section 15.[35] In such a situation the authority, although unable to pass a parental rights resolution, has the rights and duties of any person in whose care a child is. These may include, where imminent danger to the child is anticipated, the right to withhold delivery pending an order of the court under section 3 of the Law Reform (Parent and Child) (Scotland) Act 1986 or the intervention of a children's hearing under Part III of the Social Work (Scotland) Act 1968).

Parental Desire to Take Over Care—Welfare of the Child

Section 15(3) of the Social Work (Scotland) Act 1968 provides that nothing in that section (*i.e.* in any part of section 15) shall authorise a local authority to keep a child in their care under section 15 if any parent or guardian desires to take over the care of the child. It follows that section 15(2), which imposes a duty on the local authority to keep the child in their care so long as the welfare of the child appears to them to require it, cannot authorise a local authority to keep a child in care under section 15 after a timeous parental demand for the child's return. Yet in the *Lewisham* case both Viscount Dilhorne[36] and Lord Salmon[37] considered that the child might be kept in care long enough to secure his welfare by judicial intervention (or alternatively, in the opinion of Viscount Dilhorne, by the passing of a parental rights resolution).[38] This was followed by the Court of Session in *Central Regional Council* v. *B*[39] in which Lord Robertson opined that if, knowing that the parent is able and willing immediately to take over care,

---

[34] *Ibid., per* Viscount Dilhorne at p. 301, Lord Salmon at p. 306, Lord Keith at p. 315.

[35] This, it is submitted, was the position of the child in *M* v. *Dumfries and Galloway Regional Council*, 1991 S.C.L.R. 481, where a local authority refused to return a child to its parents on the basis of the child's welfare under s. 3(2) of the Law Reform (Parent and Child) (Scotland) Act 1986: see comment on this case in the text, *post* at p. 425.

[36] at p. 304.

[37] at p. 306.

[38] For a discussion of the *Lewisham* case, see Freeman, "Who Cares?: Some Comments on the *Lewisham* Case" (1979) 129 New L.J. 648. There is also much pertinent comment on the statutory background although expressed before the *Lewisham* case in Clive, "Refusing to Return Children to Dangerous Homes," 1976 S.L.T. (News) 265. The view that a local authority can make a direct appeal to s. 20(1) of the Social Work (Scotland) Act 1968 for authority to retain a child in care is however, with respect, unsound. That subsection is not a source of power but is concerned with how power otherwise conferred should be exercised.

[39] 1985 S.L.T. 413.

the local authority is of the opinion that return of the child to the parent would be contrary to the interests and welfare of the child, the local authority "must keep the child against the wishes of the parent, under some other statutory power."[40] In the present case that other power was the making of a supervision requirement under section 44 of the Social Work (Scotland) Act 1968. A child subject to a supervision requirement is, of course, a child "in care" for the purposes of section 15,[41] with the result that a section 16 resolution would still be available in these circumstances. There are also other means by which judicial intervention can secure the child's welfare even in the face of a lawful parental request for his return, though not necessarily in such a way as preserves the availability of a section 16 resolution. In *M* v. *Dumfries and Galloway Regional Council*[42] the parents of a child requested return of their child from the local authority, and gave the proper notice, the child having been in care for more than six months. The local authority refused to return the child and, in an action for delivery of the child, opposed the parents' application on the basis that it was an "action relating to parental rights" under section 3(1) of the Law Reform (Parent and Child) (Scotland) Act 1986, and thus subject to the welfare test embodied in section 3(2) thereof. The sheriff (Barr) agreed with the local authority and held that the action for delivery should fail because "it has not been proved by the pursuers[43] that it is in [the child's] interests to change the present settled arrangements." This decision may be seen as rather disturbing in that it completely bypasses the statutory framework within which Parliament clearly intended local authorities to work. However, given the breadth of application of section 3—which is deliberate—the result in this case was perhaps inevitable.[44] Section 15(3) merely states that nothing in section 15 authorises the retention of the child in the face of a parental desire to take over the care of the child: it does not state that there is no such authority, and that authority can be found in section 3(2) of the Law Reform (Parent and Child) (Scotland) Act 1986. However, because the authority for holding the child was section 3(2) of the 1986 Act, the child could not be regarded as being in care under section 15 of the 1968 Act: the result of that is that a child so held cannot be the subject of a resolution vesting parental rights and powers in a local authority or voluntary organisation under section 16.

Care and Voluntary Organisations

The question of whether a child is, for the purposes of a parental rights resolution, in the care of a voluntary organisation is free from the statutory specialties that attach to local authority care. The result is, however, similar. Where the voluntary organisation's care depends, as will usually be the case, on the con-

---

[40] *Ibid.*, at p. 417.

[41] s. 44(5). See comments on this section, *ante* at note 20.

[42] 1991 S.C.L.R. 481 (Sh. Ct.).

[43] *i.e.* the burden is on the parents as pursuers.

[44] The case may well have to be restricted to its own particular facts, or at least to situations in which persons or bodies hold or originally held the children with legal sanction. A stranger could not, it is submitted, remove a child and throw the burden of proof in an action for delivery on to the parent to prove that delivery was in the interests of the child. Alternatively, Sheriff Barr may simply be mistaken in holding that an action for delivery is an action relating to parental rights.

sent, albeit tacit, of a parent, guardian or other person or body entitled to regulate care, the care of the voluntary organisation will end if that person makes alternative arrangements for the care of the child and seeks, again consistently with the child's welfare, to withdraw him for that purpose. In other cases the termination of care is entirely a question of fact except, it is thought, that care will not be terminated by the violent or clandestine removal of the child by a person with no title to do so or by a temporary absence.

Criteria for the Passing of the Resolution

Once it has been established that in the relevant sense the child is in care, consideration must be given to whether one of the various conditions for the passing of a section 16 resolution exists.

The Criteria

One of the following criteria must be satisfied before a resolution vesting parental rights and powers can competently be passed[45]:

(a) That the parents of the child are dead and he has no guardian.[46] The existence of a guardian excludes the operation of this condition absolutely and if someone is subsequently appointed to that office under section 3 or 4 of the Law Reform (Parent and Child) (Scotland) Act 1986 the resolution ceases to have effect.[47]

(b) That a parent or guardian has abandoned the child.[48] The meaning of abandonment is the same as in agreement to adoption.[49] In addition, however, a child is deemed to have been abandoned if the whereabouts of the parent or guardian have remained unknown for 12 months and throughout that period the child has been in the care of a local authority or of a voluntary organisation.[50] Where a child has been received into care, parents (but not guardians) have an obligation to keep the local authority informed of their address.[51]

(c) That a parent or guardian suffers from some permanent disability rendering him incapable of caring for the child.[52] The disability may be mental or physical but most cases of mental disability will fall more readily within condition (d) below.

(d) That a parent or guardian suffers from some mental disorder within the meaning of the Mental Health (Scotland) Act 1984 which renders him unfit to have the care of the child.[53] This is distinguished from cases of mental disability within the meaning of the preceding condition by the fact that the disorder may be temporary. Unfitness is also

---

[45] s. 16(1).
[46] s. 16(1)(i).
[47] s. 16(11)(c).
[48] s. 16(2)(a).
[49] See *post* at pp. 544–545.
[50] s. 16(12).
[51] s. 88(1).
[52] s. 16(2)(b).
[53] s. 16(2)(c).

probably a weaker test than incapability and wider in its scope (see condition (e) below).

(e) That a parent or guardian is of such habits and mode of life as to be unfit to have the care of the child.[54] The very width of this (it has been said that unfit "means no more than unsuited"[55]) may indicate the need for some caution in its application. Habitual drunkenness, sexual promiscuity, vagrancy and persistent criminal conduct of a serious kind are no doubt included. There is no requirement that the conduct complained of must have been directed to the child, but, to be relevant to unfitness to have care, it must at least have results, if only in its effects on the parent's character and his consequent influence on the child, that bear on the parent-child relationship. Habits and mode of life are to be distinguished from an isolated act. The latter points "to a single thing done, the other to a usage resulting from repeated action."[56] It does not matter in relation to the existence of this ground whether or not the parent is responsible for his lifestyle: it has been held that the ground must be interpreted in an objective rather than judgmental fashion.[57] So in the case cited the sheriff opined that a mother who is serving a life sentence of imprisonment for murder may not be unfit from habit, but that her mode of life though not voluntary, clearly brought her within this provision. It is to be noted that this condition is expressed in the present tense and that the parent may have reformed by the time of the hearing.[58] This may have significance in relation to whether the sheriff will order the resolution not to lapse.[59]

(f) That the parent or guardian has so persistently failed, without reasonable cause, to discharge the obligations of a parent or guardian as to be unfit to have the care of the child.[60] This condition resembles one of the grounds for dispensing with agreement to adoption[61] with, however, the addition of the words "so as to be unfit to have the care of the child." The difference in wording is probably immaterial.[62] In *Central Regional Council* v. *B*[63] it was held that "persistently" must be given its natural meaning without considering whether the persistent conduct was due to animus.[64] Lord Brand[65] considered that the adverb

---

[54] s. 16(2)(*d*).

[55] *Per* Sheriff Caplan in *Lothian Regional Council* v. *T* 1984 S.L.T. (Sh. Ct.) 74 at p. 80.

[56] *Bishop of Ely* v. *Close* [1913] P. 184 at p. 196. Evidence of past life may be taken into account: *Barker* v. *Westmoreland C.C.* (1958) 56 L.G.R. 267.

[57] *Lothian Regional Council* v. *T, supra,* at p. 79.

[58] *Per* Lord Stewart in *Central Regional Council* v. *B,* 1985 S.L.T. 413 at p. 423.

[59] See *post* at p. 437.

[60] s. 16(2)(*e*).

[61] See *post* at pp. 541–543.

[62] One would have expected adoption, as the more radical measure, to have required the more stringent test. The words used suggest the reversal of that so that in passing a parental rights resolution a local authority must be satisfied of present unfitness but in dispensing with agreement to adoption a court may rely merely on forfeiture from past conduct, but it is difficult to think of a sound policy on which such a distinction could be justified.

[63] 1985 S.L.T. 413.

[64] *Per* Lord Robertson at p. 419.

[65] *Ibid.,* at p. 421.

"connotes consistent or repeated behaviour which need not necessarily be wilful." This suggests that behaviour rather than circumstance is what is envisaged by this condition, and that conclusion is emphasised by the fact that the failure must be "without reasonable cause." Some element of blame, or, at the least, some element that will be antipathetic to sympathy, is therefore required. The words "without reasonable cause" would prevent, for example, temporary physical incapacity falling within this condition. This is probably as it should be, for while temporary illness may justify the local authority receiving the child into its care,[66] it will not normally on its own justify denying the parent his parental rights and powers.

(g) That a section 16 resolution is in force in relation to one parent and that parent is, or is likely to become, a member of the household comprising the child and his other parent.[67] In these circumstances a resolution may be passed on account of the other parent. This provision, which has its origins in one of the recommendations of the Houghton Committee[68] and which was introduced by the Children Act 1975, appears to be misconceived. The abuse that the committee intended to obviate was the withdrawal of a child from local authority care by the parent whose parental rights were unaffected by any resolution in order that the child might live with him and the parent on whose account a resolution had been passed. The example given was that of a father withdrawing a child so that it might live with him and a mentally-ill mother. The committee, therefore, recommended that "where parental rights had been assumed in respect of one parent, the local authority should be empowered to retain a child in care so as to prevent his return to the care of a parent in respect of whom parental rights had not been assumed" and that, to that end, "the grounds for assumption of parental rights should be extended to protect children where rights may be assumed in respect of one parent and not the other." It is doubtful if the committee's object has been achieved. As Bevan has pointed out[69] it is only on a strained construction that the language of the statute can be construed so as to cover a case where the child is not already a member of the household of which the parent on whose account parental rights and powers have already been assumed is likely to become a member. It is, therefore, inept to cover the case of apprehended withdrawal from care. If, however, that is so and the child is a member of such a household, he will almost certainly have passed out of the care of the local authority and so a fresh resolution cannot be passed.[70] The paragraph is therefore inept in that context as well.

---

[66] s. 15(1)(*b*).

[67] s. 16(1)(iii).

[68] Report of the Departmental Committee on the Adoption of Children, Cmnd. 5107 (1972), p. 45, para. 157, and p. 106, rec. 33.

[69] Bevan, *Child Law* (1989) at p. 698.

[70] A child in respect of whom parental rights and powers have vested in a local authority may pass out of the care of the authority into the care of *inter alios* a parent and subsequently be received back into the care of the authority (s. 17(3), (4) and (5)). Means are provided by which the return

(h) That throughout the three years preceding the passing of the resolution the child has been in the care of a local authority under section 15 or in the care of a voluntary organisation or partly the one and partly the other.[71] This too is a new provision introduced by the Children Act 1975 in implementation of a recommendation of the Houghton Committee.[72] The purpose was to "provide machinery for local authority intervention at the time when the parents, for whatever reason, had not been undertaking parental care for a considerable period, and at a stage in the history of a child in care where decisions as to his long-term future might be required." The underlying concern was with the problems of "children who wait"[73] with their future uncertain, and this provision is designed for the situation "where a parent has tacitly or expressly agreed to that state of affairs, or at all events has not objected thereto."[74] Assumption of parental rights can then be a means of arranging long-term fostering on a secure basis. Alternatively, although it does not remove the need for parental agreement to be given or dispensed with, it can facilitate adoption.[75]

The three-year period must have passed before litigation has commenced. So it was held in *Strathclyde Regional Council* v. *M*,[76] in which a section 16 resolution had been passed in respect of a child who had been in the local authority's care for 2½ years. The parent served a counter-notice and the case went to the sheriff on the application of the local authority that the care resolution should not lapse. The question was whether there still existed at the date of the hearing a ground upon which a resolution could be founded, and the sheriff principal held that the local authority could not rely upon the fact that, by the time of the hearing, the child had been in local authority care for more than three years. "To decide otherwise," he said,[77] "would result in the outcome of the case depending upon the length of the litigation."

If, as may sometimes happen, a child has spent intermittent spells with parents, friends or relatives, it may sometimes be difficult to determine whether he has been in care "throughout" the three-year period. Some assistance may be obtained from cases decided on the continuous care and possession provision of the Adoption Act 1958[78]

---

of the child can be compelled (s. 17(9) and (10)) but these would seem to be inapplicable to the return of a child from a parent on whose account no resolution has been passed because such a parent has a right to custody which, subject to judicial regulation, is in no way inferior to that of the local authority.

[71] s. 16(1)(iv).

[72] p. 45, para. 156, p. 106, rec. 32.

[73] The title of an important study by Rowe and Lambert (1973), Association of British Adoption Agencies.

[74] *Per* Sheriff Principal Bennet in *Strathclyde Regional Council* v. *M*, 1982 S.L.T. (Sh. Ct.) 106, at p. 107.

[75] But see the sheriff principal's comments in *Lothian Regional Council* v. *H*, 1982 S.L.T. (Sh. Ct.) 65 at p. 69.

[76] 1982 S.L.T. (Sh. Ct.) 106.

[77] *Ibid.* at p. 107.

[78] Repealed by the Adoption (Scotland) Act 1978, Sched. 4.

and earlier legislation[79] but the difference in context and time-scale makes the comparison an uncertain guide. These authorities are, however, in point to the extent that they show in general a willingness to look at questions of this kind as a matter of substance rather than of narrow technicality. Provision on proper accommodation, maintenance and upbringing, particularly and most importantly the last, require an element of continuity. So long as these matters are in the overall charge of the local authority or voluntary organisation, care is not, it is submitted, interrupted by spells spent in the immediate but temporary charge of others. On the other hand, once responsibility for these matters is taken over by a parent or other person, on what is intended to be a permanent basis, the period of care is broken even if the period so spent proves to be short.

It is to be noted that this condition may be satisfied in relation to children who are the subject of a supervision requirement under Part III of the Social Work (Scotland) Act 1968 if that supervision has lasted the requisite period.[80] There is, in these cases, as in the cases of children committed to care by court order, no problem about the continuity of care. In the case of a supervision requirement, however, while the child may have been in the actual care of a local authority if he has been required to reside in a residential establishment, the concept of local authority care will otherwise be largely notional in its application to him. Indeed the whole three year period may have been spent at home with his parents. The reasoning underlying the assumption of parental rights after a three year period of care has little relevance to these cases which seem therefore to require particular caution.

Meaning of "Parent" and "Guardian"

With one exception, the above conditions contain reference to a parent or guardian of the child. "Parent" for this purpose means either or both parents[81]; in relation to an adopted child it means adoptive parent to the exclusion of the natural parents[82]; and in relation to an illegitimate child[83] it means the child's mother to the exclusion of his father.[84] The father of a child who is not married to its mother is not a parent for this or any other purpose of the Social Work (Scotland) Act 1968, but if he has been appointed guardian of the child, by the court under section 3(1) of the Law Reform (Parent and Child) (Scotland) Act 1986 or by the mother's will under section 4 thereof, or if in the opinion of the court or children's hearing he has for the time being custody or charge of or con-

---

[79] *Post* at pp. 525–526.

[80] s. 44(5) expressly provides that a child subject to a supervision requirement will be in care for the purposes of, *inter alia*, s. 16. See *Central Regional Council* v. *B*, 1985 S.L.T. 413.

[81] s. 94(1).

[82] Adoption (Scotland) Act 1978, ss. 12 and 39(1).

[83] *i.e.* a child whose father was not married to its mother at any time from the conception of the child and whose father, consequently, does not have automatic parental rights under s. 2 of the Law Reform (Parent and Child) (Scotland) Act 1986.

[84] s. 94(1). This would change if the Scottish Law Commission's recommendations that fathers be given the same responsibilities and rights as mothers are accepted: see Scot. Law Com. No. 135, *Report on Family Law*, May 1992. "Parent" would consequently mean parent.

trol over the child, then he will be a guardian for the purposes of the 1968 Act.[85] The reference to charge or control suggests a factual test and it is not necessary that a custody order should be in force. Where, however, a custody order has been made, the custodian under that order will be a guardian for this purpose unless he has surrendered charge and control.[86]

Conditions for Vesting of Rights in Voluntary Organisation

A resolution vesting parental rights and powers in a voluntary organisation may be passed only in respect of a child in its care,[87] and only at the request of the organisation.[88] The child must be living, within the area of the local authority by which the resolution is passed, in a residential establishment or with foster parents with whom he has been boarded out by the organisation.[89] There must be grounds, in terms of one of the criteria already considered, for passing a section 16 resolution.[90] The local authority passing the resolution must, in addition, be satisfied that it is necessary in the interests of the welfare of the child for the parental rights and powers to be vested in the voluntary organisation and that the child is not in the care of any local authority under any enactment.[91] As an unincorporated association lacks any legal personality it is required that the voluntary organisation in which the rights and powers are to vest be an incorporated body, or a trust within the meaning of section 2(a) of the Trusts (Scotland) Act 1921.[92]

Transfer of Rights between Voluntary Organisations and Local Authorities

No provision is made for the transfer of parental rights and powers from a local authority to a voluntary organisation, and it seems that such a transfer cannot lawfully be effected unless by rescission of the original,[93] and the passing of a fresh, resolution. Rights and powers vested in a voluntary organisation may, however, in certain circumstances be transferred to the local authority. If it appears to the local authority, having regard to the interests of the welfare of a child within its area, that it is necessary that parental rights and powers vested in a voluntary organisation should no longer be so vested, the local authority is required to pass a resolution vesting the parental rights and powers in itself.[94] This is the only situation in which rights and powers may be vested in an authority which does not have the care of the child at the time of the passing of the resolution. It is also the only situation in which the passing of a resolution is mandatory.

---

[85] *Ibid.*; *C* v. *Kennedy*, 1991 S.L.T. 755.

[86] Thus in *Kennedy* v. *H*, 1988 S.L.T. 586 it was held that the respondents, who had been awarded interim custody of the child, were not "guardians" for the purpose of an appeal under s. 49 of the 1968 Act, because they did not have the care and control of the child at the relevant time.

[87] s. 16(1)(b).

[88] s. 16(4)(d).

[89] s. 16(4)(c).

[90] s. 16(1).

[91] s. 16(4)(a) and (b).

[92] s. 16(1)(b).

[93] See *post* at pp. 439–440.

[94] s. 16A, as inserted by Children Act 1975, s. 75.

EFFECT OF PARENTAL RIGHTS RESOLUTION

Parental Rights

On the passing of a section 16 resolution all the "relevant parental rights and powers" in relation to the child of the parent or guardian affected by the resolution vest in the authority or organisation.[95] The "relevant parental rights and powers" mean all the rights and powers which (if the resolution is passed because the parent is dead) the deceased parent would have if still living or which (if the resolution is passed because of another reason relating to the parent or guardian) the parent or guardian does have in relation to the child.[96] The only express exceptions are (1) that the rights of a parent or guardian in relation to agreement to the making of an adoption order, to consent to the making of an order freeing a child for adoption, or to consent to vesting parental rights and duties for the purpose of the adoption of a child abroad, are not affected[97]; (2) that the resolution does not authorise the local authority or voluntary organisation to cause a child to be brought up in any religious persuasion other than that in which he would have been brought up but for the resolution[98]; and (3) that the parent's right of access is preserved (subject to conditions to be discussed shortly).[99]

The rights which are assumed are, it is conceived, those incidental to, or associated with, the exercise of parental powers for the nurture and wellbeing of the child and the protection of his person and property. Although, in contrast with the English definition of parental responsibility,[1] there is no express reference to property in the Scottish provisions, the words used are wide enough to embrace administration of the child's property as well as care of his person. Accordingly, the rights and powers that parents have as guardians and legal representatives in respect of the patrimonial interests of their children under the age of 16 will be assumed from them as well as the rights and powers of the parents as custodians. It is likely that there is little if any difference between "parental rights and powers" subject to section 16 of the Social Work (Scotland) Act 1968, and the "parental rights" defined in section 8 of the Law Reform (Parent and Child) (Scotland) Act 1986: there the phrase is defined to mean "guardianship, custody and access." The contents of these particular rights are considered in detail elsewhere in this book, and reference should be made to the relevant chapters. The effect of a section 16 resolution is to extinguish the parental rights and powers of the parent affected.

Parental Duties

In contrast with the English legislation,[2] the Scottish provisions make no explicit reference to parental duties but, on the passing of a section 16 resolution,

---

[95] s. 16(1)(*a*) and (*b*).
[96] s. 16(3).
[97] *Ibid.*
[98] s. 17(7), as amended by the Children Act 1975, Sched. 3.
[99] s. 17A, as inserted by the Health and Social Services and Social Security Adjudications Act 1983, s. 7(2).
[1] Children Act 1989, s. 3(1).
[2] The Children Act 1989 s. 33(3), provides that a local authority will have "parental responsibility" for a child subject to a care order, and s. 3 defines that to include duties.

these are necessarily much abridged. In so far, however, as they are capable of fulfilment, they remain. Liability to maintain or contribute to the maintenance of the child is specifically preserved.[3] A parent's common law alimentary obligations and, if rights have been assumed on account *qua* guardian of a stepparent or other person who had charge or control, the statutory obligation of a person to maintain a child who has been accepted as one of the family,[4] are therefore unaffected. So long as the child remains in care, that is also true of the statutory obligation of a parent to contribute to the maintenance of a child in care.[5]

Access

As the effect of a section 16 resolution is to vest the parental rights and powers in the local authority or voluntary organisation to the exclusion of the parent or guardian affected, even the parent's title to sue for custody is extinguished and under section 16, as originally enacted, such a parent did not have any right of access to the child and could visit him only at the discretion of the local authority or voluntary organisation as the case might be.[6] It is, however, now provided that a local authority or voluntary organisation may not terminate arrangements for access by a parent or guardian or refuse to make such arrangements unless they have first given notice to that effect in the prescribed form.[7] That provision clearly applies to the parent or guardian on whose account the resolution was passed and is unnecessary in relation to any other parent or guardian. Notice does not require to be given where the authority or organisation proposes merely to substitute new arrangements for existing arrangements or where it postpones access for such reasonable period as appears to it to be necessary to enable it to consider what arrangements are to be made.[8] On receipt of a notice the parent or guardian may apply to the sheriff by way of summary application for an access order.[9] The order, if granted, may contain such conditions as it appears to the sheriff ought to be made, and may be varied or discharged on the application of the parent or guardian named in the order or of the local authority or voluntary organisation.[10] The sheriff may, moreover, if satisfied that continued access under the order will put the child's welfare seriously at risk, make an emergency order suspending the access order for a specified period not exceeding seven days;[11] but if during that period the local authority or voluntary organisation applies for variation or discharge of the access order the suspension remains in effect until the application for variation or discharge is determined or abandoned.[12] All applications for access orders or for their variation, discharge or suspension and all appeals in that connection are to

---

[3] Social Work (Scotland) Act 1968, s. 17(6).
[4] Family Law (Scotland) Act 1985, s. 1(1)(*d*).
[5] Social Work (Scotland) Act 1968, s. 78.
[6] *Beagley* v. *Beagley*, 1984 S.L.T. 202 (H.L.).
[7] Social Work (Scotland) Act 1968, ss. 17A–17E, as inserted by the Health and Social Services and Social Security Adjudications Act 1983, s. 7(2).
[8] s. 17A(4).
[9] s. 17B(1).
[10] s. 17B(2) and (3).
[11] s. 17C(1) and (2).
[12] s. 17C(3).

be determined with regard to the welfare of the child as the first and paramount consideration.[13] Although not so stated, the wishes and feelings of the child would seem to be entitled to respect according to his maturity and understanding: these are, it is submitted, inherent parts of the welfare test.

Rights of Other Parents and Judicial Intervention

The rights of a parent or guardian to whom the resolution does not relate are in no way impaired. So where a resolution relates to one parent but not to the other the latter is entitled to be fully consulted in decisions affecting the child and in the event of dispute may vindicate his rights by proceedings under section 3 of the Law Reform (Parent and Child) (Scotland) Act 1986 for an order relating to parental rights. Indeed the unaffected parent, if he or she has parental rights, may exercise these rights independently of the local authority and without its consent. This is a consequence of section 2(4) of the 1986 Act whose terms, though probably not intended to cover such cases, are clearly wide enough to do so. The father of a child who is not married to its mother, although not a parent in terms of the Act,[14] will be a guardian if he has been appointed as such or has custody or charge of or control over the child.[15] Even if he is not a guardian in these terms he may nevertheless pursue an application for custody of the child although parental rights and powers have been assumed in respect of the mother.[16] These are, however, the limits of judicial intervention. The court will not allow its jurisdiction to be invoked at the instance of persons who cannot qualify a right comparable to that of a parent or to the statutory right of the father of a child to claim custody, unless the body in which parental rights and powers have vested can be shown to have acted in breach or disregard of its statutory duty. In that respect the body in which parental rights and powers have vested may, as the body to which Parliament has specifically entrusted the decision as to the welfare of the child, be in a stronger position than an actual parent. Where, however, breach or disregard can be shown, the court will intervene, even, it is thought, at the instance of the parent to whom the resolution relates. The *nobile officium* of the Court of Session extends to the correction of such abuses no less than the wardship jurisdiction of the High Court in England. The court's intervention may also be justified where some positive advantage to the child which does not consist merely in the substitution of the court's view of its welfare for that of the local authority or voluntary organisation can be shown.[17]

Transfer of Care to Others and Return to Care

It might be thought that the vesting of parental rights and powers would, by it-

---

[13] s. 17D.

[14] s. 94(1).

[15] *C* v. *Kennedy*, 1991 S.L.T. 755.

[16] *R* v. *Oxford City Justices, ex p. H* [1975] Q.B. 1.

[17] *Re M (An Infant)* [1961] Ch. 328; *Re L (AC) (An Infant)* [1971] 3 All E.R. 743; *Re B (A Minor) (Wardship: Child in Care)* [1975] Fam. 36; *Re Y (A Minor) (Child in Care: Access)* [1976] Fam. 125, *per* Ormrod J. at p. 134; *Re DF (A Minor)* (1977) 76 L.G.R. 133; *Re D (A Minor)* (1978) 122 Sol.J. 193. *Cf. Re H. (A Minor)* [1978] Fam. 65. The last case goes beyond the correction of abuse and supports judicial intervention where circumstances are highly special. See also *Re W (Minors)* [1979] 3 W.L.R. 252.

self, authorise the entrusting of the care of the child to another person if that were consistent with the duty, laid on local authorities but not on voluntary organisations, to keep the child in care so long as his welfare requires it.[18] The matter is, however, put beyond doubt by a specific provision that a section 16 resolution shall not prevent the local authority or voluntary organisation from allowing, either for a fixed period or until the authority or organisation otherwise determine, the care of the child to be taken over by, and the child to be under the control of, a parent, guardian, relative or friend in any case where it appears to the authority or organisation to be for the benefit of the child.[19] As the competency of allowing the care of the child to be take over by a parent unaffected by the resolution, and with whom the parental rights and powers are therefore shared,[20] can scarcely be in doubt, the parent envisaged must be the parent to whom the section 16 resolution relates. "Relative" and "friend" are not defined but include, it is submitted, anyone with whom there is a relationship of blood or affinity in the former case, and anyone with whom there is a relationship of affection in the latter.[21] Where the care of a child in respect of whom parental rights and powers have vested in a local authority is taken over by another person and a child therefore ceases to be in the care of the local authority, that authority have, nonetheless, power to receive the child back into their care in circumstances in which it appears to them that their intervention is necessary in the interests of the welfare of the child.[22] Parental rights and powers remain with the local authority, even although care is transferred. There is no corresponding provision relating to voluntary organisations. The reason appears to be that the specific power is conferred for purposes internal to the local authority and is unnecessary in the case of a voluntary organisation. In a question with the person by whom care has been taken over, the power to secure the return of the child rests on the parental rights and powers themselves. Accordingly, summary means of securing the return of the child are made available to local authorities and voluntary organisations alike.[23] A child who is taken back into the care of a local authority is treated as if he had been received into care under section 15[24] but, as the section 16 resolution remains in force, the provisions of section 15(3), which restrict the power of a local authority to keep a child in care, do not apply.[25]

Offences

It is a criminal offence knowingly to assist, or induce, or persistently attempt

---

[18] Social Work (Scotland) Act 1968, s. 15(2).
[19] s. 17(3) and (3A) as amended and inserted by the Children Act 1975, Sched. 3, para. 52.
[20] Law Reform (Parent and Child) (Scotland) Act 1986, s. 2(4).
[21] In the Children Act 1948, s. 59(1), "relative" was defined as meaning a grandparent, brother, sister, uncle or aunt whether of the full blood or the half blood or by affinity, and included (a) where an adoption order was made in respect of the child, any person who would be a relative within the meaning of the definition if the adoptive person were the child of the adopter born in lawful wedlock, and (b) where the child was illegitimate the father of the child and any person who would be a relative within the meaning of the definition if the child were the legitimate child of its mother and father.
[22] s. 17(4), as amended.
[23] See following paragraph.
[24] s. 17(5).
[25] s. 16(9).

to induce, a child in respect of whom a section 16 resolution is in effect, to run away or, without lawful authority, to take him away, or knowingly to harbour or conceal him if he has run or been taken away, or to prevent him from returning.[26] Where the care of a child has been taken over by another person and the local authority or voluntary organisation in which parental rights and powers are vested has, by notice in writing, required the return of the child, it is also a criminal offence to harbour or conceal the child after the expiry of the notice or to prevent him from returning.[27] Where an offence has been, or is believed to have been, committed, a constable, or any person authorised by a court or by a justice of the peace, may take and return the child to the local authority or voluntary organisation.[28]

Commencement and Lapse of Resolution: Application to the Sheriff

It is implicit in the provisions on lapse[29] that a section 16 resolution comes into effect when it is passed. Sometimes such resolutions are passed with consent of the parent or guardian but whether or not there is consent the local authority must forthwith, after[30] the passing of the resolution, serve on the parent concerned notice in writing informing him of the passing of the resolution, of his right to object, and of the effect of any objection made by him.[31] The requirement to serve notice *forthwith* should be strictly observed but is directory rather than mandatory[32] and so failure to observe it does not affect the validity of the resolution. If, not later that one month thereafter, the parent or guardian serves a counter-notice in writing on the local authority objecting to the resolution, the resolution lapses on the expiry of 14 days from the service of the counter-notice unless, within that time, the local authority makes a summary application to the sheriff for an order that the resolution shall not lapse. Once the counter-notice is served, the onus is on the local authority to seek judicial confirmation of the resolution. On the making of such an application, the resolution remains in effect until the application is determined.

Conditions for the Sheriff's Order

The sheriff is precluded from ordering that the resolution shall not lapse unless he is satisfied on the following three conditions[33]:

(a) that it is in the interests of the child that it should not lapse, *and*
(b) that the grounds on which the local authority purported to pass the resolution were made out, *and*

---

[26] s. 17(8).

[27] s. 17(9).

[28] s. 17(10), as inserted by the Children Act 1975, s. 76.

[29] s. 16(7) and (8).

[30] Thomson sees it as a flaw in the present system that the parent need be informed of the resolution only after its passing, because "in many of these cases the parents will be amongst the more vulnerable in our society" (Thomson, at p. 237). Because now in England care orders are granted by the court under s. 31 of the Children Act 1989, parents there have a right to object before the order is made.

[31] s. 16(5), as amended by the Health and Social Services and Social Security Adjudications Act 1983, s. 7(1); s. 16(6).

[32] *Cf. Sloan* v. *B*, 1991 S.L.T. 530.

[33] s. 16(8).

(c) that at the time of the hearing there continued to be grounds (which need not be the grounds on which the resolution was in fact passed[34]) on which a section 16 resolution could be founded.

The conclusion is inescapable, although not so expressed, that if he is satisfied on these matters he must sustain the application and thus order that the resolution shall not lapse. Where the purported resolution is a nullity[35] the proper course must be to dismiss the application as incompetent on the ground that there is no resolution in respect of which the jurisdiction can be exercised.

The provision relating to the child's interests ((a) above) has been criticised as being equivocal and failing to make clear the weight to be given to those interests,[36] but its meaning, effect and consequent weight seem to be clear. Sheriff Principal O'Brien has said:

> "In every case this is the fundamental issue, and in each case it must be for the local authority to show, not just that children are in need of care, but that it is necessary in their interests for their parents' rights to be transferred to the authority."[37]

Each of the requirements for the confirmation of a resolution is determinative in the negative sense that, if it is not satisfied, the resolution will lapse. If, therefore, it cannot be shown that the resolution will serve the interests of the child, that is conclusive against the continuance of the resolution. Failure to satisfy either of the other two requirements is, of course, equally conclusive and it may be thought that as a result too little weight is attached to the interests of the child where these point to the continuance of the resolution; but there is no obscurity and, unless the basis of the statutory scheme is to be subverted, there is no alternative.

In relation to (b) the sheriff need not enter into a full examination of the case, in the sense of reviewing the merits of the original resolution: "all that it [is] necessary for the applicants to prove [is] that at the date of the passing of the resolution a state of facts existed which justified the passing of the resolution."[38] It is to be noted that this state of facts must have existed at the date of the passing of the resolution, and it is irrelevant, at least in relation to the satisfaction of condition (b), that the circumstances have since changed.

Condition (c) refers to present circumstances (*i.e.* those subsisting at the date of the hearing), and if the ground upon which the resolution was originally passed is no longer applicable, one or more of the other grounds can be used to satisfy this condition.

"The Grounds"

There is some uncertainty as to whether the reference to "the grounds" in sec-

---

[34] *W* v. *Nottinghamshire County Council* [1982] 1 All E.R. 1; *Central Regional Council* v. *B*, 1985 S.L.T. 413.

[35] As, for example, in *Central Regional Council* v. *Mailley* 1977 S.L.T. (Sh. Ct.) 36.

[36] Bevan *Child Law* (1989), at p. 709.

[37] *Lothian Regional Council* v. *S*, 1986 S.L.T. (Sh. Ct.) 37 at p. 40.

[38] *Per* Lord Robertson in *Central Regional Council* v. *B*, 1985 S.L.T. 413 at p. 418, citing with approval Sheriff Principal Gillies in *Strathclyde Regional Council* v. *T*, 1984 S.L.T. (Sh. Ct.) 18.

tion 16(8) (permitting the sheriff to order that the resolution shall not lapse) comprehends the whole content of section 16(1) or only the conditions specified in the enumerated paragraphs.[39] The latter view would accord with the terms of section 16 before the amendments made by the Children Act 1975 and there is no reason to think that there was any intention at that time to effect a change in this respect. Section 16(1) is applicable only when the child is "in care," but that in itself is not specified in the enumerated paragraphs as "a ground." The question centres on whether the child must still be in the care of the local authority or voluntary organisation at the time of the court hearing. The point is of some importance since, if proceedings are protracted, the child may have been returned to the care of the parent or guardian on a trial basis before the hearing takes place. There is some strain of language in describing the fact that the child was in care as a "ground" on which the resolution could be founded, and the interpretation which avoids that is probably to be preferred. It would follow that in determining whether condition (b) or (c) has been made out in relation to section 16(8), the question of whether the child is still in care or not is irrelevant (though whether the child was in care at the time the resolution was passed remains, of course, relevant to the competency of the resolution itself).

Cessation of Effect

If a resolution does not lapse for one of the reasons indicated above, the child remains subject to it until the attainment of the age of 18,[40] or until, on one of the prescribed grounds, the resolution ceases to have effect. A resolution ceases to have effect:

(a) If the child becomes the subject of an adoption order or of an order freeing him for adoption or vesting parental rights and duties for the purpose of adoption abroad.[41] The existence of a section 16 resolution is no barrier to an application for any of these orders.[42] As noted elsewhere, the agreement of the local authority or voluntary organisation is not required but it is submitted that they have a right to be heard.[43]

(b) If a guardian is appointed to the child under the Law Reform (Parent and Child) (Scotland) Act 1986[44] (application for such an appointment may be made despite the existence of a section 16 resolution[45]).

(c) If, where parental rights and powers have vested in a voluntary organisation, the local authority for the area in which the child is living passes a resolution that these rights and powers shall be vested in them. The local authority is obliged to pass such a resolution if it appears to

---

[39] paras. (i), (ii), (iii), and (iv) (para. (ii) including the conditions in s. 16(2)).
[40] s. 18(1).
[41] s. 16(11)(a) and (b).
[42] s. 18(4A).
[43] *Post*, at p. 532.
[44] s. 16(11)(c), as amended by the Law Reform (Parent and Child) (Scotland) Act 1986, Sched. 1, para. 9. Though it is not stated, the appointment has to be a court appointment since a testamentary appointment is available only to parents acting as guardians (s. 4(b)), which a parent in respect of whom a parental rights resolution is in force would not be.
[45] s. 18(4), as amended by the Children Act 1975, the Law Reform (Parent and Child) (Scotland) Act 1986, and the Age of Legal Capacity (Scotland) Act 1991.

them, having regard to the interests of the welfare of the child, that it is necessary that parental rights and powers should no longer be vested in the organisation.[46]

(d) If a child has been wrongfully removed, within the meaning of the Child Abduction and Custody Act 1985, from a person entitled to custody and an order under that Act has been made for its return; or if a custody decision made by an authority in a Contracting State to the Hague Convention on the Civil Aspects of International Child Abduction has been registered in an appropriate court in the United Kingdom.[47]

(e) If the resolution is determined by a court on the summary application of a parent or guardian affected by the resolution.[48] Because of the restricted class of those who may apply, a resolution passed on the purported ground that both parents were dead and there was no guardian will be open to review in this way only if it was, in fact, groundless and an applicant comes forward claiming to be a parent or guardian. Parents and guardians whose rights and powers are unaffected by the resolution and also relatives and others with an interest to have the resolution determined may bring it under review only by means of reduction. Jurisdiction summarily to determine the resolution is given to the sheriff court of the place where the applicant resides, with the result that parents or guardians affected by the resolution and residing outwith Scotland are excluded. They too, it seems, must have resort to reduction. It would have been more satisfactory if the statute had followed the principle *actor sequitur forum rei*, or at least admitted that as an alternative. The sheriff may determine the resolution if he is satisfied that there was no ground for making it *or* that it should, in the interests of the child, be determined.[49] Although the wording of the Act appears to admit of a discretion, there can be no justification for continuing, except perhaps as an interim measure, a resolution for which there were from the outset insufficient grounds or whose continuance is not in the interests of the child. The Act places no restriction on challenge for lack of grounds, but it is thought that only in compelling circumstances should objections be entertained which the applicant could have made by way of counter-notice at the time the resolution was passed or which were made and then rejected or abandoned. As an alternative to determining the resolution, the sheriff may order that the care of the child be taken over by the applicant either for a fixed period or until the court or, if the order so provides, the local authority otherwise directs.

(f) If the resolution is rescinded by the local authority. Rescission is open if it appears to the local authority that it will be for the benefit of the

---

[46] ss. 16(11)(*d*) and 16A(1).
[47] s. 16(11)(*e*), as inserted by the Child Abduction and Custody Act 1985, s. 25(6). On the Hague Convention, see *ante* at pp. 274–277.
[48] s. 18(3), as amended by the Children Act 1975, Sched. 3, para. 53.
[49] It is not a requirement, as it is in an application to the sheriff under s. 16(8), that both these conditions be satisfied.

child.[50] The power of rescission applies only to resolutions vesting parental rights and powers in a local authority. Accordingly a resolution vesting parental rights and powers in a voluntary organisation may not be rescinded either by the organisation or by the local authority. Where a voluntary organisation considers that the resolution vesting parental rights and powers in it should be terminated, the only expedient, unless a parent or guardian wishes to make an application to the sheriff, appears to be to request the local authority to pass a resolution vesting the rights and powers in itself, in place of the voluntary organisation, and then to rescind that resolution.

REVIEW OF JUDICIAL DECISIONS

The Children Act 1989[51] provides for an appeal to the High Court from decisions of magistrates' courts in England and Wales making orders placing children in the care of local authorities.[52] The Houghton Committee[53] had recommended a right of appeal from decisions upholding resolutions assuming parental rights, in terms which, if only by implication, suggested that fresh statutory provision was necessary in order to achieve that result in Scotland as well as in England and Wales. No right of appeal has, however, been enacted for Scotland. The omission of appeal provisions from Part II of the Social Work (Scotland) Act 1968 contrasts not only with the English provisions but also with the provisions in Part III of the 1968 Act.[54] There is difficulty only as regards appeals on the merits. Appeals to the sheriff principal have been entertained without the question of competency being raised,[55] but are difficult to reconcile with the principles generally applicable to appeals in summary applications. Despite the wide terms of section 27 of the Sheriff Courts (Scotland) Act 1907 by which appeals are governed, the statutory requirement that a matter is to be determined by the sheriff normally is taken to exclude by implication the appellate jurisdiction of the sheriff principal. A distinction is drawn for this purpose between "the sheriff" and "the sheriff court." Where the matter at issue is referred to the decision of the sheriff it may be decided by the sheriff or the sheriff principal but not, except in the sense that one may take over from the other, by both.[56] As sec-

---

[50] s. 18(2), as amended by the Children Act 1975, Sched. 3, para. 53(a).

[51] s. 94.

[52] Since the coming into force of the Children Act 1989 the vesting in local authorities of "parental responsibilities" has been done not by means of local authority resolution but by order of the court. Prior to 1989, when the English position was substantially similar to the Scottish, the Children Act 1975 provided for an appeal to the High Court from decisions of courts in England and Wales on the lapse or determination of resolutions assuming parental rights and duties (ss. 58 and 63(3)).

[53] Cmnd. 5107, p. 46, para. 159; p. 106, rec. 33.

[54] See *post*, at pp. 490–493.

[55] *Central Regional Council* v. *Mailley* 1977 S.L.T. (Sh. Ct.) 36. The application in that case, if properly analysed, raised, however, jurisdictional questions that are an exception to the general rule. No comment was made in the appeal in *Lothian Regional Council* v. *H*, 1982 S.L.T. (Sh. Ct.) 65. In *Strathclyde Regional Council* v. *McNair*, 1980 S.L.T. (Sh. Ct.) 16, and *Strathclyde Regional Council* v. *T*, 1984 S.L.T. (Sh. Ct.) 18 the appeal was heard under express reservation of the general question of competency.

[56] *Allen & Sons (Billposting) Ltd.* v. *Edinburgh Corporation*, 1909 S.C. 70, *per* Lord Justice-Clerk Macdonald at p. 74 and Lord Low at p. 75; *Ross-shire County Council* v. *Macrae-Gilstrat*, 1930

tion 16 requires "the sheriff" to be satisfied appeal to the sheriff principal would normally be regarded as incompetent. However, in *Central Regional Council* v. *B*,[57] the opinions of the judges clearly contemplated appeal from the sheriff to the sheriff principal, and in the case of Lord Stewart expressly so.[58] That case is also authority for the proposition that appeal from the sheriff court to the Court of Session is competent, unless expressly restricted (which it is not by the 1968 Act).[59]

There has never been the same doubt as to the competency of appeals other than on the merits of the case. Where the sheriff has exceeded his jurisdiction or failed to exercise it, there is a right of appeal to the sheriff principal.[60] That is probably also true of instances of incompetency, of breaches of natural justice, and of fundamental irregularity of procedure. Moreover, the jurisdiction of the Court of Session to review decisions both of administrative bodies and of inferior courts on grounds extrinsic to the merits remains unimpaired[61] and in the latter case may, where appropriate, be invoked by way of appeal as well as by reduction.[62] A decision of the sheriff or the sheriff principal on the competency of a resolution[63] necessarily involves, if it should be in error, a question either of excess of or failure to exercise jurisdiction and so is open to appeal to the Court of Session.

S.C. 808, *per* Lord Sands at p. 812; *Balderston* v. *Richardson* (1841) 3 D. 597; *Parish of Strichen* v. *Goodwillie*, 1908 S.C. 835. *Obiter dicta* to the contrary in *Leitch* v. *Scottish Legal Burial Society* (1870) 9 M. 40 cannot be reconciled with these authorities, while the decision in *Magistrates of Portobello* v. *Magistrates of Edinburgh* (1882) 10 R. 130 turns on its own statutory peculiarities and, in particular, on the fact that the statutory provisions on jurisdiction in Scotland were related to provisions conferring jurisdiction on "the county court" in England. Each statute must be considered on its own terms (*ibid.*, *per* Lord Justice-Clerk Moncreiff at p. 137; *Kaye* v. *Hunter*, 1958 S.C. 208 *per* Lord President Clyde at pp. 211–212). *Bone* v. *School Board of Parish of Sorn* (1886) 13 R. 768 and *Fleming* v. *Dickson* (1862) 1 M. 188 are authority for the view that the sheriff principal may intervene so as to take over the case where the sheriff has dealt with interlocutory matters but has not given final judgment. By s. 4(3) of the Sheriff Courts (Scotland) Act 1907 the word "sheriff," which formerly included "sheriff substitute" now includes "sheriff principal." The burden of the authorities is that the conferring of a new statutory jurisdiction on "the sheriff" excludes the appellate jurisdiction of the sheriff principal unless there is a peculiarity of the statute making it clear that "the sheriff court" was intended. The conferring of jurisdiction on the sheriff is also a factor tending to exclude the appellate jurisdiction of the Court of Session, but in that context it is not conclusive (*Arcari* v. *Dumbartonshire County Council* 1948 S.C. 62). The fact that it is the sheriff who has to be "satisfied" also tends to exclude review (*cf.* the interpretation of "in the opinion of the court or tribunal making the award" in *Todd* v. *Todd and Anr.*, 1966 S.L.T. 50). *Arcari* is not authority against that view as the point, although open, appears to have been neither argued nor considered). See also *Rodenhurst* v. *Chief Constable, Grampian Police*, 1992 S.L.T. 104 (Court of Five Judges) in which *Arcari* was followed, *Allen & Sons (Billposting)* was distinguished, and *Kaye* v. *Hunter* overruled.

[57] 1985 S.L.T. 413.

[58] *Ibid.* at p. 422.

[59] See also *Marr & Sons* v. *Lindsay* (1881) 8 R. 784; *Magistrates of Portobello* v. *Magistrates of Edinburgh* (1882) 10 R. 130.

[60] *Leitch* v. *Scottish Legal Burial Society*, *supra*; *Roxburgh County Council* v. *Dalrymple's Trs.* (1894) 21 R. 1063; *Leggat* v. *Burgh of Barrhead* (1902) 19 Sh. Ct. Rep. 7 at p. 11.

[61] *Dalgleish* v. *Leitch* (1889) 2 White 302; *Penny* v. *Scott* (1894) 22 R. 5; *Heddle* v. *Magistrates of Leith* (1898) 25 R. 801; *Moss's Empires* v. *Assessor for Glasgow*, 1917 S.C.(H.L.) 1, *per* Lord Kinnear at p. 6. See also Walker, *Civil Remedies*, at pp. 163–172.

[62] *Allen & Sons (Billposting) Ltd.* v. *Edinburgh Corporation*, *supra*.

[63] *i.e.* where it is alleged that the resolution was fundamentally null (as in *Central Regional Council* v. *Mailley*, 1977 S.L.T. (Sh. Ct.) 36).

EXTRA-TERRITORIAL AND INTERNATIONAL ASPECTS

The topics discussed in this chapter raise, for the most part, no extra-territorial question or questions of international private law. They are domestic in character, being concerned with the regulation within Scotland of the care of children. Some incidental questions of the application of foreign law and matters of jurisdiction, recognition and enforcement do, however, require consideration.

Application of Foreign Law

In the reception of a child into care and also in the assumption of parental rights and powers, it is necessary to ascertain who the child's parents or guardians are. That question, and also questions of legitimacy which may arise in association with it, are, subject to the statutory definition, referable to the law of the child's domicile as the personal law by which his status is determined.[64] Except for that purpose any reference to his domicile, or to his origin, residence or nationality, is irrelevant. The only territorial requirement relating to a local authority's duty to receive a child into care is the child's presence within the area of the authority. Parental rights and powers may be assumed in respect of any child in the care of the local authority passing the resolution, whether the child is still actually within the area of the authority or not, or in the care of a voluntary organisation and living within the local authority's area. In none of these situations is any foreign territorial factor relevant.

Extra-Territorial Enforcement—Criminal Jurisdiction

Problems may arise where a child who is in care or in respect of whom parental rights and powers have been assumed is outwith Scotland, as may happen legally (*e.g.* where he is boarded out or placed in residential accommodation in England or Wales[65] or where, while still the subject of a resolution assuming parental rights and powers, his care is taken over by a parent or other person[66]) as well as where he absconds or is illegally removed. The statutory provisions for direct enforcement of the return of a child[67] do not have extra-territorial effect even within the United Kingdom and whether his return can be effected must accordingly depend on the law of the place where the child is. Scottish criminal sanctions may, however, be applicable. As was noted earlier in this chapter,[68] it is an offence in the case of a child in respect of whom parental rights and powers have been assumed, or who has been in care for six months, knowingly to assist or induce him to run away, or, without lawful authority, to take him away, or knowingly to harbour or conceal him if he has run or been taken away, or to prevent him from returning. It is also an offence if a person who has taken over the care of a child in respect of whom parental rights and powers have been assumed has been given notice in writing requiring the return of the child to harbour or conceal the child after the expiry of the period of notice or

---

[64] See *ante* at pp. 158–160. The law of the domicile may, however, in the absence of proof to the contrary, be assumed to be the same as the law of Scotland.
[65] Social Work (Scotland) Act 1968, s. 21(3).
[66] *Ibid.*, s. 17(3).
[67] *Ibid.*, s. 17(10).
[68] *Ante*, at pp. 435–436.

prevent him from returning as required by the notice. The jurisdiction of the Scottish courts and the application of Scots law depend on whether the offence can be treated as having been committed in Scotland. If the child has been taken away, or induced or assisted to run away while in Scotland, the offence has clearly been committed there even if the destination to which the child has been taken is furth of Scotland. If, however, the acts take place for the first time when the child is already outwith Scotland (*e.g.* if he is taken away from foster parents with whom he has been boarded out in England, or if the offence consists solely in harbouring or concealing outside Scotland) the Scottish courts have no jurisdiction.[69]

Recognition and Enforcement of Analogous Rights arising outside Scotland

Although contained in separate statutes, and notwithstanding that in England and Wales assumption is now effected by court order,[70] legislative provision for the assumption of parental rights and powers follows a similar pattern throughout the United Kingdom. On the principle of reciprocity indicated in *Obers* v. *Paton's Trs.*,[71] a Scottish court would, it is submitted, be bound to recognise the vesting of parental rights and powers in an English, Welsh or Northern Irish authority or voluntary organisation and to grant appropriate remedies for their enforcement, by ordering delivery or otherwise, if the child were in Scotland. In the case of children who are in the care of a local authority without parental rights and powers having been assumed, the English, Welsh and Northern Irish courts may make recovery orders[72] when a child is removed or has run away from a responsible person or is missing: in that case the order has effect in Scotland as if it had been made by the Court of Session and as if that court had had jurisdiction to make it.[73] Such care is entitled to protection in a question with persons other than parents and guardians and in some circumstances after the expiry of six months in care, even against parents and guardians.[74] Some parallel may be drawn with the enforcement of custody orders but the arguments for the enforcement of rights arising under legislation in other parts of the United Kingdom corresponding to sections 15 and 16 of the Social Work (Scotland) Act 1968 lie *a fortiori*[75] of those applying to the recognition and enforcement of foreign custody orders and the jurisdictional tests on which the recognition of these orders largely depends are inept in the context of local authority care.

---

[69] *H.M.A.* v. *Witherington* (1881) 8 R.(J.) 41.

[70] Children Act 1989, s. 31.

[71] (1897) 24 R. 719. The existence of extra-judicial statutory remedies makes it, in general, unnecessary for a Scottish local authority which has assumed parental rights and powers to invoke the aid of the Scottish courts or to resort to common law remedies in Scotland, but there is little doubt that, if the exercise of these rights and powers were threatened, a Scottish court would be bound to grant its aid in their legitimate enforcement. Similar remedies should, therefore, be granted in respect of parental rights and powers assumed in England, Wales or Northern Ireland.

[72] Children Act 1989, s. 50.

[73] *Ibid.*, s. 50(13).

[74] *Ante* at p. 421.

[75] A custody order is always open to judicial review on a change of circumstances whereas, where a child is in the care of a local authority and especially where parental rights and powers have been assumed, the court will be slow to intervene and indeed in the latter case will do so only to prevent clear abuse or in other exceptional circumstances.

Institutions or legal régimes outside the United Kingdom may have features similar to the assumption of parental rights and powers or local authority care in this country but an exact parallel is not to be expected. In questions of recognition and enforcement much will turn on the particular features of the foreign system. Despite the lack of a common pattern and the impossibility of appeal to the intention of a common legislature, it is submitted that the principles applicable are, however, broadly similar to those applicable to cases arising within the United Kingdom except that the analogy with custody orders and, in some instances, with adoption, may be more apt than in the United Kingdom context. In general, and subject to the controls of public policy and the welfare test, there would seem to be no objection to giving effect to measures taken according to the law of the place where the child was at the time of the passing of the resolution or equivalent act, although restraints imposed by the law of the child's domicile may also require to be considered.

CHAPTER 17

COMPULSORY MEASURES OF CARE

INTRODUCTORY

Part III of the Social Work (Scotland) Act 1968 provides for the application of compulsory measures of care (i) to children who, under the former law, were treated as in need of care and protection, and (ii) to children who have committed offences. The underlying concept is that in both categories the fundamental need of the child is for measures of care which can be achieved only by compulsory intervention. The commission of an offence, no less than danger to the child's health, safety or wellbeing, is therefore seen as a symptom of need calling for a caring rather than a punitive response. Care is, however, widely defined. It includes "protection, control, guidance and treatment."[1] In offence cases the emphasis will often and inevitably be on control, while in the cases brought on non-offence grounds it will more often be on protection. In both categories guidance and treatment may, according to circumstances, be appropriate.

The changes introduced by the 1968 Act flow from the report of the departmental committee appointed to consider the law relating to children and young persons in Scotland (the Kilbrandon Committee).[2] Some of these changes were less radical than is sometimes represented. The measures of care actually available under the 1968 legislation, although different in form, are not materially different in substance from their predecessors. Even the use of measures of care, rather than of punishment, in relation to children who have committed offences is not a major innovation in principle. It was implicit in the obligation, previously laid upon courts dealing with offences committed by juveniles, to have regard to the welfare of the child.[3] The radical changes were in the personnel and machinery of administration, the composition of the decision-making tribunals, and procedures.

The Children's Hearing and the Reporter[4]

The key elements in the current system are a lay tribunal, known as the children's hearing, and an official charged with arranging and bringing cases before the children's hearing, known as the reporter.

A children's hearing consists of a chairman and two other members and must include both a man and a woman.[5] Its membership is chosen from the members

---

[1] Social Work (Scotland) Act 1968, s. 32(3). All references in this chapter are to this Act, unless otherwise stated.

[2] *Report on Children and Young Persons, Scotland*, Cmnd. No. 2306 (1964).

[3] Children and Young Persons (Scotland) Act 1937, s. 49(1), repealed by the Criminal Procedure (Scotland) Act 1975, Sched. 10.

[4] See generally Kearney, *Children's Hearings and the Sheriff Court* (1987).

[5] s. 34(2).

of children's panels constituted for each local authority area.[6] The members of panels are appointed by the Secretary of State who has an unfettered discretion as to whom he may appoint.[7] In practice, however, appointments are made from those nominated by children's panel advisory committees, upon whom a duty is laid to submit names of possible panel members and to advise the Secretary of State as required on the suitability of persons referred to him as possible members.[8] The selection of the chairman and members of any given hearing rests with the chairman of the children's panel, or, in his absence, the deputy chairman and may be effected by standing arrangements made by the chairman after consulting the reporter and such members of the panel as he may think fit.[9] No principles of selection are laid down, but the chairman of the panel is obliged to keep any standing arrangements which he has made under review and from time to time to engage in consultations about their operation.[10]

The reporter is appointed by the local authority after advertisement and the submission of copies of all applications to the Secretary of State who compiles a list of applicants considered by him to be suitable for appointment from which the appointment must be made.[11] Once appointed, the reporter cannot be removed from office or required to resign except with the consent of the Secretary of State.[12] The local authority is bound to secure the provision of adequate staff for assisting him in the performance of his functions and may appoint deputies.[13] It seems, however, that the special provisions for the appointment of the reporter and for protection against his removal from office do not apply to his deputies.

Restriction on Prosecution of Children

The policy of the Act is to take children out of the prosecution process. So the Act provides that no child is to be prosecuted for any offence except on the instructions of the Lord Advocate, or at his instance.[14] Private prosecution is, therefore, altogether excluded and a complaint by a procurator fiscal can be preferred only on the Lord Advocate's instructions. No court other than the High Court of Justiciary and the sheriff court has jurisdiction.[15] As all public prosecutions on solemn procedure are at the instance of the Lord Advocate, the indictment is, from this standpoint, itself conclusive of the competency of the proceedings. In summary cases, however, competency can be determined only by reference to the Lord Advocate's instructions. These may be verbal and in general terms covering various kinds of offences.[16] In the absence of challenge they are presumed to have been given and to embrace the case in question.[17]

---

[6] ss. 33(1) and 34(1).
[7] Sched. 3, para. 1.
[8] Sched. 3, para. 5.
[9] Children's Hearings (Scotland) Rules 1986 (S.I. 1986 No. 2291), r. 5(1).
[10] *Ibid.*, r. 5(2).
[11] s. 36(1) and (2)
[12] s. 36(4).
[13] s. 36(6).
[14] s. 31(1).
[15] *Ibid.*
[16] *M* v. *Dean*, 1974 S.L.T. 229.
[17] *Ibid.*

General instructions have, in fact, been issued[18] in relation to children of 13 years of age and over. They provide for prosecution of children of that age group if the case falls into any of the following categories and the procurator fiscal, in his discretion, decides to follow that course rather than to refer the case to the reporter:

(a) Offences which require by law to be prosecuted on indictment or which are so serious as normally to give rise to solemn proceedings on the instructions of the Lord Advocate in the public interest.

(b) Offences alleged to have been committed by children aged 15 years or over which in the event of conviction oblige or permit a court to order disqualification from driving.

(c) Offences alleged to have been committed by children as described in section 31(1) of the Social Work (Scotland) Act 1968.

As the matter is entirely one for the Lord Advocate's instructions, the above categories may, of course, be varied or withdrawn by him at any time either generally or in relation to a particular case. The sole question in relation to any prosecution is whether, at the time it is instituted, it comes within the terms of instructions by the Lord Advocate then in force. Children under the age of 13 are not to be prosecuted except with the prior express authority of the Lord Advocate.

Investigation and Transmission of Information

The satisfactory operation of any system of compulsory measures of care largely depends on the adequacy of the means for ascertaining cases in which such measures are needed and for the transmission of information so that action can be taken. The reporter's role is central but, although once information is received he has certain investigatory duties, he is, nearly always, dependent initially on information supplied by others. Accordingly the Act provides that where any person has reasonable cause to believe that a child may be in need of compulsory measures of care, he may give to the reporter such information about the child as he may have been able to discover.[19] Moreover, where a local authority receives information suggesting that a child is in need of compulsory measures of care, it is obliged, unless satisfied that they are unnecessary, to cause inquiries to be made into the case and, if it appears that the child may be in need of compulsory measures of care, to give to the reporter such information about the child as it has been able to discover.[20] The obligation appears to be incumbent on the local authority no matter from what source the information is received, and may be taken to have been imposed because Parliament envisaged a sifting function for local authorities where information came into their hands rather than directly into the hands of the reporter. As a consequence, however, there may be delay in information reaching the reporter while the authority investigates the information and considers, or even attempts, measures alternative

---

[18] Aug. 3, 1987.
[19] s. 37(1).
[20] s. 37(1A) as inserted by Children Act 1975, s. 83(a).

to compulsory measures of care. That consequence is somewhat mitigated if the statutory requirement that information must be transmitted whenever it appears that the child "may" be in need of compulsory measures of care is strictly observed. To the local authority is given the judgment, in cases in which it receives information, of whether there may be a need for compulsory measures but not of whether there is an actual need. Accordingly, it is obliged to transmit information whenever the view that compulsory measures are required could reasonably be entertained even if in its judgment alternative measures, or no action, would be preferable. The obligation is incumbent on the local authority as such and therefore on all its agencies which may become possessed of such information—*e.g.* not only the Social Work Department but also the Education Department, local authority schools and local authority medical services. The wording used is in contrast with that applied to the reporter, who is charged with taking a preliminary decision on whether a child "is" in need of compulsory measures of care.[21] The central role of the reporter is, therefore, preserved in cases in which information is first received by a local authority, as well as in other cases, but only if the limitations on the authority's function are scrupulously observed.

CONDITIONS OF NEED FOR COMPULSORY MEASURES OF CARE

The Grounds of Referral

A child may be in need of compulsory measures of care if certain conditions specified in the Act are satisfied.[22] The permissive form "may" is used to preserve the discretionary power of the reporter and of the hearing not to refer cases and to discharge referrals respectively. Although the matter could have been more clearly expressed, the conditions are, it is thought, exhaustive of the circumstances in which compulsory measures of care may be applied and there is no residual power to hold a child in need of compulsory measures of care on grounds extraneous to the specified conditions. These conditions apply (1) to children under the age of 16 years, (2) to children over that age but under the age of 18, in respect of whom a supervision requirement made by a children's hearing is in force, and (3) to children whose case has been referred to a children's hearing in pursuance of the provisions of the Act relating to the return and removal of children within the United Kingdom.[23] A hearing is obliged to inquire as to the age of anyone brought before it and any presumption or declaration it makes as to age is conclusive.[24] The conditions are as follows:

(a) *The child is beyond the control of his parent.*

"Parent" for this purpose means either or both parents[25]; in relation to an adopted child it means the adoptive parent or parents to the exclusion of the natural parents[26]; and in relation to an illegitimate child[27] means the

---

[21] s. 39(3).

[22] s. 32(1).

[23] s. 30(1).

[24] s. 55.

[25] s. 94(1).

[26] Adoption (Scotland) Act 1978, ss. 12 and 39(1).

[27] The statute continues to use this term, even although the concept of illegitimacy has all but disappeared. It would consist with the policy of the law if that term were now interpreted to mean the

mother to the exclusion of the father.[28] "Parent" also includes "guardian,"[29] which itself is defined to mean anyone appointed by deed or will or by order of a court of competent jurisdiction to be the guardian of the child and anyone who in the opinion of the court or children's hearing having cognisance of the case has for the time being the charge of, or control over, the child.[30] The opinion of a court or hearing concerning who has for the time being charge of or control over the child must, it is submitted, be formed in relation to the state of affairs existing so far as that is known or can be inferred at the time the question is considered. "For the time being" is to be understood as referring to that time.[31] Where, therefore, the "parent" has to be identified by reference to a person having charge or control, one looks to the person who ordinarily has overall charge or control as satisfying the description of parent rather than to someone such as a schoolteacher or child-minder into whose temporary charge or control the child may from time to time pass. The question is essentially one of fact.[32] Persons who have interim custody of a child do not thereby acquire charge and control and therefore are not to be regarded as guardians.[33] That a child is beyond the control of someone who has temporary charge of him may, however, be evidence, and, where the conduct is sustained or repeated over a substantial period, may be proof, that the child is beyond the control of his parent because a parent's interest in the care and therefore the appropriate control of his child obtains not only when the child is immediately in his charge but also when the child has been temporarily entrusted to others.

Problems may arise in applying this condition to older children, since the extent of control which a parent may exercise over a child becomes progressively more uncertain the older the child becomes.[34] In cases of older children it is thought that the child's conduct must not only show that there is an absence of control but must also be actually, or potentially, harmful to the child or to others so as to make the exercise of parental control appropriate.

(b) *The child is falling into bad associations or is exposed to moral danger.*
It is no longer necessary that this result should be caused "through lack of parental care."[35] Bad associations are not defined, nor is moral danger.

---

child whose father does not have automatic parental rights under s. 2 of the Law Reform (Parent and Child) (Scotland) Act 1986, rather than the child who, at common law, was illegitimate. This can be taken to be the modern equivalent of the concept of illegitimacy. The father of such a child can be brought within the definition of "parent" through his guardianship (as defined in the text) rather than through his paternity: *C* v. *Kennedy*, 1991 S.L.T. 755.

[28] s. 94(1). The Scottish Law Commission have suggested putting all fathers on an equal footing with all mothers, so that "parent" will, in future, mean parent: Scot, Law Com. No. 135, *Report on Family Law*, (May 1992), para. 2.50 and draft Bill, Sched. 1, para. 27.

[29] s. 30(2).

[30] ss. 30(2) and 94(1). This wider than normal definition of "guardian" for the purposes of the Act could include the father of an illegitimate child, otherwise excluded: *C* v. *Kennedy, supra.*

[31] *Kennedy* v. *H*, 1988 S.L.T. 586 at p. 590E–F. *Cf. Kennedy* v. *B*, 1972 S.C. 128.

[32] *Kennedy* v. *H, supra.*

[33] *Ibid.*

[34] See *ante*, at chap. 6.

[35] The words were removed by the Children Act 1975, Sched. 3, para. 54(*a*).

Any association which may be harmful to the child's welfare in any, not only in its moral, aspect may be regarded as bad. Moral danger is commonly equiparated with the risk of sexual corruption, but there is no warrant for restricting it to such cases. The mere commission of an offence does not, but the exposure to circumstances from which a habitual pattern of criminal conduct is likely to follow probably does, indicate moral danger.[36] There are obvious hazards and difficulties in going beyond recognised categories such as sexual corruption and criminality, but a wide scope is clearly intended. Thus, exposure of a child to scenes of habitual drunkenness may involve moral danger or at least indicate that the child is falling into bad associations. Similarly, circumstances in which the child is likely to indulge in solvent abuse or to develop the habit of taking drugs or drinking to excess may be regarded as obnoxious to this condition. Some regard must be had to the way of life in the community in which the child has been brought up. Thus, the English court has held that a 13-year-old girl domiciled in Nigeria, who lived in England with a Nigerian to whom she had been married in Nigeria under a form of marriage potentially polygamous, was not thereby to be regarded as exposed to moral danger.[37] While, however, it is wrong to ignore the way of life in which the child has been brought up, it is submitted that it is equally wrong to regard it as necessarily conclusive. The proper question is not one of what is permitted by the way of life in which the child has been brought up—the whole ground of complaint may be that he or she has been brought up in a way of life that involves moral danger—but whether the circumstances alleged to constitute exposure to moral danger are regarded as morally unobjectionable by the community to which by upbringing or present association the child is most closely connected. Even, however, if that question can be answered in the affirmative, it is no more than an element to be taken into account. In some cases it will be a strong factor and even conclusive. In others, the conduct in question may be so repugnant to the moral notions generally prevailing in the forum that the latter must prevail.

(c) *Lack of parental care is likely to cause the child unnecessary suffering or impair his health or development.*[38]

Parental care is undefined but is, it is submitted, to be understood in a sense consonant with the meaning of "parent" indicated in (a) above. Regard must be paid to the definition of "care" given in section 32(3), which states that it includes "protection, control, guidance and treatment."[39] Likelihood qualifies the whole condition and so, where it is likely that a child will suffer lack of parental care which is in turn likely to cause him unnecessary suffering or seriously to impair his health or development, the condition is satisfied even if the child has never been in the care of his

---

[36] *Cf. B* v. *Kennedy*, 1987 S.L.T. 765.

[37] *Mohamed* v. *Knott* [1968] 2 All E.R. 563.

[38] Amended by the Children Act 1975, Sched. 3, para. 54(*a*).

[39] *Per* Lord Justice-Clerk Ross in *Kennedy* v. *S*, 1986 S.L.T. 679 at p. 682K.

parents.[40] The likelihood of relevant lack of parental care may be inferred from past habits and mode of life of the parents which resulted in the neglect of other children if these habits and mode of life still persist.[41]

Impairment of health or development seems to be apt to cover mental or emotional conditions as well as physical. Parental refusal of consent to necessary medical or surgical treatment is clearly within this condition.[42]

Lack of parental care is to be assessed objectively from the standpoint of its effect on the child. The mental disposition of a parent does not require to be considered. The condition is concerned with defining circumstances in which a child may be in need of compulsory measures of care and that need is not affected by the fact that the lack of care does not flow from a blameworthy disposition on the part of the parent. Accordingly, this condition may be invoked where lack of care exists although the parent, by reason of psychosis, mental deficiency or illness, or other incapacity or circumstance over which he has no control, is unable to do better. A contrast may be drawn between lack of parental care in this context and "wilful neglect" which is the criterion in the Children and Young Persons (Scotland) Act 1937.[43]

(d) *Any of the offences mentioned in Sched. 1 to the Criminal Procedure (Scotland) Act 1975 has been committed in respect of the child or in respect of a child who is a member of the same household.*[44]

These offences are, generally speaking, those of a sexual nature and those causing bodily injury to a child. In determining membership of a household for this ground of referral (and for the following two grounds also) the test is membership of the household regarded as a family unit and not whether at a particular time the child has lived, or is likely to live, in the same house[45]: the test is "membership of" rather than "living in" the household. And a household continues to be the same household even if one of the original members has separated from it permanently, and even if new members join it, through birth or otherwise.[46] A child may be a member of the same household as another child even when the latter died some years before the former's birth,[47] so long as the household remains, in essence, the same as it was at the previous time: it is a question of circumstances whether the household is the same, and it is a matter of fact and degree.[48] Where grounds of referral under this heading have been es-

---

[40] *McGregor* v. *L*, 1981 S.L.T. 194.
[41] *Ibid.* And see the English House of Lords case of *D (A Minor)* v. *Berkshire County Council* [1987] 1 All E.R. 20.
[42] *Finlayson*, 1989 S.C.L.R. 601.
[43] s. 12.
[44] Amended by the Children Act 1975, Sched. 3, para. 54(*b*).
[45] *McGregor* v. *H*, 1983 S.L.T. 626.
[46] *A* v. *Kennedy*, 1993 S.C.L.R. 107. See Norrie, 1993 S.L.T. (News) 192.
[47] *Ibid.* The phrase "child who is a member" must be read to include "child who was a member" in order to give effect to the purpose of the statute and to provide protection when it is needed.
[48] *Ibid.* See also *Kennedy* v. *R.'s Curator ad litem*, 1993 S.L.T. 295 in which it was held that a temporary separation, or one designed purely to avoid the establishment of this ground, would not be sufficient to break up a household if the ties of affection and regular contact which hold the parties together still continue.

tablished in relation to one child in the household the certified copy interlocutor of the sheriff affords sufficient proof of the commission of the
offence for the purpose of proceedings relating to the other children in the
same household.

Where any person is convicted of having committed a Schedule 1 offence (or an offence under section 21 of the Children and Young Persons
(Scotland) Act 1937) the court may refer the child victim to the reporter
and certify that the commission of the offence shall be treated as a ground
established for the purposes of the Social Work (Scotland) Act 1968 relating to compulsory measures of care.[49] A conviction is not, however, a prerequisite for the existence of this ground and a child may be referred
under this paragraph as in need of compulsory measures of care although
a prosecution is pending,[50] or is not brought, or is brought and fails. Proceedings to find the ground established are, however, undesirable while a
prosecution is pending and so, in such cases, referral may be postponed if
the interim safety of the child can be otherwise secured. Postponement
must not, however, be for an unduly long or indefinite time, such as "until
after any criminal proceedings have taken place" and any decision to
postpone must take account of how the child is to be protected during the
delay.[51] If delay is undesirable from the point of view of the child, it is no
bar to the hearing, or to the sheriff deciding whether the ground of referral
is established, that the evidence will be rehearsed before being presented
in any criminal trial.[52]

Proof for the purpose of establishing this ground (and the following
two grounds also) is on the civil and not the criminal standard.[53] The identity of the offender is not in issue under this ground, and it is sufficient that
the commission of the offence be proved even if the perpetrator cannot be
identified.[54] The essence of this ground is whether the offence took place
in relation to the child and not who the perpetrator was: "it is concerned
with offences and not offenders"[55] (in contrast with the immediately following ground). Consequently it is unnecessary to identify the offender:
in *S* v. *Kennedy*[56] it was held that the sheriff was not entitled to make a
finding of fact that the offender was "probably" the child's stepfather.
Only the conditions for the existence of the offence, and the fact that it
was committed in relation to the child, need be shown.[57] Being civil proceedings, a husband or wife is, in principle, a compellable witness as to
the commission of the offence by the other spouse.[58] A conviction is

---

[49] Criminal Procedure (Scotland) Act 1975, ss. 168 and 364.

[50] As in *Ferguson* v. *P*, 1989 S.L.T. 681.

[51] *Ibid.*

[52] *Ibid.*

[53] *McGregor* v. *D*, 1977 S.C. 330.

[54] *Kennedy* v. *F*, 1985 S.L.T. 22; *McGregor* v. *K*, 1982 S.L.T. 293.

[55] *S* v. *Kennedy*, 1987 S.L.T. 667, *per* Lord Justice-Clerk Ross at p. 669I.

[56] *Ibid.*

[57] So in *B* v. *Harris*, 1990 S.L.T. 208 where the *mens rea* necessary for assault was missing, there
was no crime and therefore no ground for referral.

[58] Since spouses of parties became competent witnesses there is little doubt that in civil cases the
general rule that a witness who is competent is also compellable applies to them. See Wilkinson,

prima facie evidence of the commission of an offence[59] and may be used in circumstances in which the provisions for certification that the ground is established, noted above, do not apply.[60]

(dd) *The child is, or is likely to become, a member of the same household as a person who has committed any of the offences mentioned in Schedule 1 to the Criminal Procedure (Scotland) Act 1975.*[61]

For this ground, identification of the offender will normally be a practical necessity but if it can, in fact, be shown that the offence has been committed by someone in the household, then that will be sufficient even if the perpetrator cannot be identified. Under this ground it would be competent for the sheriff, in finding the ground established, to make a finding in fact concerning the identity of the offender.[62] The standard of proof was previously a matter of contention. Opinions were reserved in *S* v. *Kennedy*[63] as to whether the criminal standard of proof was required: it was argued that while the civil standard may be appropriate when identity is not in issue (as under ground (d) above) different considerations may well come into play when identity is in issue.[64] The matter was put beyond doubt in *Harris* v. *F*[65] in which it was held by the Second Division that the standard of proof to be applied in determining the existence of all grounds except that contained in section 32(2)(g) was the civil standard, *i.e.* balance of probability.[66] It is expressly provided that the criminal standard is to be applied in relation to s. 32(2)(g)[67]: "[T]he proper inference to be drawn from that provision is that a distinction is being taken between a ground of referral based on section 32(2)(g) and all other grounds of referral... The reasonable implication must be that a different and lesser standard of proof will be applicable in the case of all other grounds of referral...*expressio unius est exclusio alterius*."[68] It follows from this, and it has been held, that an acquittal is not conclusive proof of the absence of this ground: a failure to prove something beyond reasonable doubt does not mean that it cannot be established on a balance of probabilities.[69] "Household" is to be defined as in ground (d) above.

The Scottish Law of Evidence (1986) at p. 152. There is no rule of law that says that a husband or a wife who gives evidence cannot be asked questions that might tend to incriminate a spouse: *Bates* v. *H.M.A.*, 1989 S.L.T. 701 at p. 703D, *per* Lord Justice-Clerk Ross.

[59] Law Reform (Miscellaneous Provisions) (Scotland) Act 1968, s. 10. See *MacKenzie* v. *Mackay*, 1989 S.L.T. 810.

[60] *i.e.* where the child in respect of whom compulsory measures of care are sought is not himself a victim of the offence.

[61] Inserted by the Children Act 1975, Sched. 3, para. 54(c).

[62] *S* v. *Kennedy*, 1987 S.L.T. 667, *per* Lord Justice-Clerk Ross at p. 669E.

[63] 1987 S.L.T. 667.

[64] *Ibid.*, at pp. 669L and 671K.

[65] 1991 S.L.T. 242.

[66] Opinions were reserved on whether the standard of proof of the commission of a criminal offence was the civil or the criminal standard when such matters arose in ordinary civil proceedings.

[67] s. 42(6).

[68] *Harris* v. *F*, *supra*, *per* Lord Justice-Clerk Ross at p. 245F.

[69] *Kennedy* v. *B*, 1992 S.C.L.R. 55 (2nd Div.).

(e) The child being a female is a member of the same household as a female in respect of whom the crime of incest has been committed by a member of that household.

Many of the considerations noted in (d) and (dd) above apply to this condition also, but subsequent changes in the law have rendered it largely, if not entirely, otiose. The Act originally contained no provision (dd) but since its insertion in 1975 that paragraph has covered all children who become members of the same household as persons who commit schedule 1 offences. Until 1986 incest was a scheduled offence only if committed with a child under the age of 17, but since the Incest and Related Offences (Scotland) Act 1986 it is a scheduled offence regardless of age. Thus any child who is a member of the same household as a female child in respect of whom the crime of incest has been committed will fall under paragraph (d), and any child who is a member of the same household as the person who committed the crime of incest will fall under paragraph (dd) even if the female in respect of whom the offence was committed is not a child.

(f) *The child has failed to attend school regularly without reasonable excuse.*

The wording of this condition is perplexing not so much for what is said as for what is omitted. It can, it is submitted, apply only to children of school age but the absence of an express limitation to that effect is surprising (*cf.* the previous English provisions[70] which were in contrast on this point). Normally only children of school age can be the subject of compulsory measures of care but, exceptionally, they may be older.[71] The definitions of "school" and "reasonable excuse" given in the Education (Scotland) Act 1980 seem appropriate but are not expressly incorporated. The wording is, however, open to a construction that is at least as wide as these definitions. The condition can, it is submitted, apply only to a child for whom attendance at school is the means selected by his parent for providing efficient education; it is to be remembered that other means are open.[72] The onus of providing reasonable excuse probably rests on the child or parent.[73] It is a reasonable excuse that the child has been excluded from his school by an exclusion order issued by the rector which was made on the basis of an allegation of misconduct that was neither established nor admitted; a different conclusion might be reached if it is established that the exclusion order had been necessary due to the misconduct of the child.[74] Provision is made for the proof of attendance and other matters by documents.[75]

Where a child of school age has failed to attend a public school regu-

---

[70] Children and Young Persons Act 1969, s. 1(2)(*e*). This was repealed by the Children Act 1989, Sched. 15. The current English provisions do not contain a long and detailed list of conditions for a child being in need of compulsory measures of care, adopting instead a much more generally worded scheme: see Children Act 1989, s. 31.

[71] See *ante*, at p. 448.

[72] Education (Scotland) Act 1980, s. 30.

[73] *Kennedy* v. *Clark*, 1970 J.C. 55. See *ante* at pp. 325–327.

[74] *D* v. *Kennedy*, 1988 S.L.T. 55.

[75] Education (Scotland) Act 1980, s. 86 which applies to "any legal proceedings."

larly the education authority may refer the child to the reporter[76] who may then consider taking proceedings under this condition. Where a parent is prosecuted in respect of the failure of his child to attend school regularly without reasonable excuse, or failure to permit a medical examination where it is alleged that the child has been prevented by sickness from attending school or receiving education, the court may, if satisfied that the child has failed without reasonable excuse to attend regularly at school and whether or not the parent is convicted, direct that the case be referred to the reporter and, if it does so, must certify that failure as a ground established for the purposes of the application of compulsory measures of care.[77] In that event some of the difficulties of interpretation noted above are avoided.

(g) *The child has committed an offence.*

This is the most frequent ground on which children are referred to children's hearings. It differs from the others in that, in proceedings before the sheriff for a finding that the ground is established, the standard of proof is expressly that required in criminal procedure, *i.e.* beyond reasonable doubt.[78] It is, however, only the standard of proof that is affected. Proceedings under this condition, as under others, are not criminal proceedings; although essentially *sui generis* they are more akin to civil than to criminal proceedings.[79]

There is a conclusive presumption that no child under the age of eight years can be guilty of an offence.[80] It follows that no child under eight can be referred to a children's hearing under this heading.[81] Whether a child over that age has the *mens rea* necessary to commit an offence may sometimes be a question of difficulty. There is old authority for the view that a pupil child cannot be guilty art and part in a crime committed by his parent if he acted at his parent's command.[82] However, rules designed for the avoidance of punishment are not altogether apt in the context of measures of care, and in any case if the parent's guilt is established then ground (b)[83] will almost certainly be established and the child's case can be referred on that basis.

Except where the sentence for an offence is fixed by law, a court may remit a case for disposal by a children's hearing: (i) where a child who is not already subject to a supervision requirement pleads guilty to, or is found guilty of, an offence; (ii) after obtaining and considering the advice of a children's hearing as to the treatment of a child, whether or not already subject to a supervision requirement, who has pleaded guilty to, or

---

[76] Education (Scotland) Act 1980, s. 44(1).

[77] *Ibid.*

[78] s. 42(6).

[79] *McGregor* v. *T and Anr.*, 1975 S.L.T. 76.

[80] Criminal Procedure (Scotland) Act 1975, ss. 170 (solemn procedure) and 369 (summary procedure).

[81] *Merrin* v. *S*, 1987 S.L.T. 193.

[82] *John Rae*, Jan. 1, 1662; Mackenzie, I, v; Hume, *Comm.*, I, 49 and 50. The concept of pupillarity remains relevant for the criminal law: see Age of Legal Capacity (Scotland) Act 1991, s. 1(3)(*c*).

[83] *Ante* at pp. 449–450.

has been found guilty of, an offence; or (c) after obtaining and considering such advice in relation to a person not subject to a supervision requirement who is over the age of 16 and is not within six months of attaining the age of 18 and who, in summary proceedings, has pleaded guilty to, or been found guilty of, an offence.[84] Where such a remit is made the court's jurisdiction ceases and the case stands referred to the children's hearing. A certificate of the plea or finding of guilt signed by the clerk of court is conclusive evidence of the commission of the offence.[85] For the purposes of disposal of the case the Act applies to a person in category (c) above as if he were a child.[86]

(gg) *The child has misused a volatile substance by deliberately inhaling its vapour, other than for medical purposes.*[87]

(h) *The case has been referred to a children's hearing in pursuance of Part V of the Act.*

The relevant provisions of Part V are in section 73(1) and (2). Section 73(1) provides that where a juvenile (youth) court in England or Wales or Northern Ireland is satisfied that a child in respect of whom a probation order or a supervision order is in force proposes to reside or is residing in Scotland the court may either discharge the probation order or supervision order, or send notification of that order to the reporter of the local authority for the area in which the child proposes to reside or is residing. On receipt of such notification the reporter is obliged,[88] to arrange a children's hearing for the consideration and determination of the case. Similar provisions are made where the Secretary of State for Northern Ireland is satisfied that the parent of a child who is subject to a training school order or an order transferring a child to the care of the managers of a training school,[89] proposes to reside or is residing in Scotland and where a local authority in England or Wales, or a welfare authority in Northern Ireland, is so satisfied in relation to the parent of a child committed to its care.[90] In such a case the Secretary of State or the local authority or the welfare authority, as the case may be, may refer the case to the reporter of the local authority of the area in which the parent of the child is proposing to reside or is residing, and if the case is so referred the reporter is obliged to arrange a children's hearing for its consideration and determination. It is the duty of the managers of the welfare authority to ensure the transfer of the child to the place notified by the reporter.[91] Notification of an order, or the inclusion of particulars of an order when a case is referred, constitutes, for

---

[84] Criminal Procedure (Scotland) Act 1975, ss. 173, 372 and 373.

[85] Social Work (Scotland) Act 1968, s. 56(5).

[86] s. 57(2).

[87] Inserted by Solvent Abuse (Scotland) Act 1983, s. 1.

[88] Except in the case of a supervision order made by virtue of s. 7A(4) of the Criminal Justice (Scotland) Act 1949. In this case the reporter is obliged instead of arranging a children's hearing to notify the appropriate court, and to transmit to that court all documents relating to the case which the reporter has received.

[89] See s. 74(3).

[90] s. 75(1) and (2), amended by the Children Act 1989, Sched. 13, para. 22.

[91] s. 76(4).

the purposes of the children's hearing, conclusive evidence of the existence of the order in relation to the child.[92]

It is not clear whether a children's hearing which considers a referral under this condition exercises a jurisdiction under Part V of the Act. If it does, it may proceed in the absence of the child or his parents or both.[93] It is submitted, however, that the better view is that it is under Part V that the transfer of the case to the reporter is effected and that the jurisdiction of the hearing is exercised under Part III. That would seem to be the significance of the occurrence of this condition in Part III. In principle it is, therefore, open to the child or the parent to refuse to accept the ground of referral under this condition, as under others, with the result that an application must be made to the sheriff for a finding as to whether the grounds are established. In view of the provisions on proof, a challenge of the grounds can scarcely be successful unless on a question of identification. It is understood that where in cases under this condition the child is too young to understand the ground of referral or otherwise incapable of understanding it, it is the practice to proceed to consideration and disposal of the case without making an application to the sheriff. While that practice corresponds with good sense, it is difficult to reconcile with a strict reading of the statute, and probably ought not to be followed.

(i) *The child is in care of a local authority and his behaviour is such that special measures are needed for his adequate care and control.*[94]

PROCEDURES BEFORE THE HEARING

Interim Protection of the Child

While it is not required by the scheme of the Act that any interim measures be taken before the children's hearing convenes, this may sometimes be desirable, for need may arise to secure the safety of a child pending consideration of his case by the reporter and the children's hearing. This is achieved primarily by removing a child to a place of safety. A constable, or any person authorised by any court or by any justice of the peace, may take to a place of safety any child:

(a) in respect of whom any of the offences mentioned in Schedule 1 to the Criminal Procedure (Scotland) Act 1975 has been, or is believed to have been committed, or

(b) who is a member of the same household as a child in respect of whom such an offence has been, or is believed to have been, committed, or

(c) who is, or is likely to become, a member of the same household as a person who has committed, or is believed to have committed, such an offence, or

(d) in respect of whom an offence under s.21(1) of the Children and Young Persons (Scotland) Act 1937[95] has been, or is believed to have been committed, or

---

[92] ss. 73(2) and 75(3).
[93] s. 76(1).
[94] Inserted by the Health and Social Services and Social Security Adjudications Act 1983, s. 8(1).
[95] Vagrants preventing children from receiving education.

(e) who is likely to be caused unnecessary suffering or serious impairment of health because there is, or is believed to be, in respect of the
child a lack of parental care.[96]

Place of safety is widely defined. It means any residential or other establishment
provided by a local authority, a police station, or any hospital, surgery or other
suitable place, the occupier of which is willing temporarily to receive a child.[97]
"Other suitable place" is probably not to be construed *ejusdem generis* with the
whole of the preceding list or with hospital and surgery.[98] In view of the width of
the definition and of the absence of any need for a warrant to detain, there is in
principle, if not in practical probability of occurrence, a risk of abuse of the
power to detain by a person holding himself out to be an occupier of a place of
safety. A child may be taken to such a place of safety by a constable, who does
not require the authority of a court or a justice of the peace, or by any other person, though such other person does require the authority of a court or a justice of
the peace. It is not stated in whose judgment the conditions for taking a child to a
place of safety must be satisfied but the implication seems to be clear that the
question is referred to the judgment of the constable or of the authorising court
or justice, as the case may be. A summary application for the recall of the
court's authorisation to remove a child to a place of safety is incompetent.[99]

These provisions have been criticised as being in one respect too narrow in
that, with the exception of the likelihood of unnecessary suffering or serious impairment of health in respect of lack of parental care, they look to what has happened in the past rather than to the risk of future occurrences and, in another
respect, too wide in that they permit reference to the commission of offences in
the remote past, and, indeed, to mere belief in the commission of such offences,
which may have no continuing significance. They have also been criticised as
being unnecessarily complicated.[1] The intention clearly is, it is said, to provide
for children who are in danger and the statutory tests should have been specifically directed to that end. These criticisms have force, although practical constraints may have some mitigating effect. Thus, as a practical matter, it may
often be possible to bring a child who is in fact in danger within the protection of
a belief that one of the specified conditions exists. The risk that the width of the
provisions may lead to misuse or abuse of power is clear and has recently given
rise to some concern.[2]

A child who is taken to, or has taken refuge in, a place of safety may be detained there until arrangements can be made for him to be brought before a children's hearing. In that event the constable, or the authorised person, or the
occupier of the place of safety, as the case may be, must forthwith inform the re-

---

[96] Social Work (Scotland) Act 1968, s. 37(2).
[97] s. 94(1).
[98] The whole list does not readily yield a common *genus*, while to restrict "other suitable place" to
places comparable with a hospital or surgery is a strained construction when one looks to the list
as a whole.
[99] *L* v. *Strathclyde Regional Council*, 1991 S.C.L.R. 658 (Sh. Ct.).
[1] Clive, *Getting Children Out of Dangerous Homes*, 1976 S.L.T. (News) 201.
[2] The Clyde Report, published on Oct. 27, 1992, has suggested various changes to the law relating
to place of safety orders.

porter.[3] The detention under these provisions cannot last beyond the day on which the hearing first sits to consider the case.[4] Any further detention must be on warrant.[5] In any event it must not exceed seven days and if the reporter considers the child does not require compulsory measures of care detention must cease forthwith.[6]

"Taking Refuge"

The provisions for a child "taking refuge" in a place of safety give rise to some difficulties of interpretation which affect the power to detain. It is to be noted that the conditions which have to be satisfied before a child can be taken to a place of safety do not apply to a child's taking refuge there. The power to take a child to a place of safety, and if taken there to detain him, is exigible, if the conditions are satisfied, against both the child and his parents and so may be against the child's will. But a child cannot, it is submitted, be said to have taken refuge in a place of safety if he has been taken there or, when the need for his protection arose, constrained to remain there against his will. Accordingly, a child cannot be detained in a place of safety on the view that he has taken refuge there if, at the material times, he was unwilling to take refuge. A strict construction would, however, favour the view that once he has taken refuge he may be detained thereafter even if he becomes unwilling to remain. It is a doubtful point whether a child incapable of forming an intention can be said to take refuge, but it is submitted that intention is not essential and that he takes refuge when he is brought to a place of safety, or even chances to come. A mental element is implicit in the words "take refuge" only in the negative sense that he who repudiates a place as his refuge cannot be said to take refuge there.

It has been said[7] that the power to detain cannot easily be applied to a child who happens to be in a place of safety when the need to detain him there arises but who has not been taken there by a constable or authorised person and who has not had resort to it as a refuge—*e.g.* a child admitted to hospital with consent of his parents and for some reason unconnected with any neglect by them who is, nonetheless, likely to be caused unnecessary suffering because of lack of parental care if he is not kept in hospital. It is thought, however, that a child can be said to have taken refuge in a place of safety when the need for his detention there emerges, even if that was not the original purpose of his going there.

Return of The Child to a Place of Safety

A child who absconds or is unlawfully taken away from a place of safety in which he has been detained may be arrested without warrant in any part of the United Kingdom or Channel Islands and brought back. If the occupier of the place of safety is unwilling or unable to receive him, he must be detained in another place of safety until the reporter has considered whether he may be in need

---

[3] s. 37(2).
[4] s. 37(3).
[5] See *post*, pp. 460–462.
[6] s. 37(3).
[7] Clive, *supra*.

of compulsory measures of care or until he can be brought before a children's hearing.[8]

Powers of Search

The provisions on interim detention do not themselves give any powers of search and entry. The gap is partly filled by the Criminal Procedure (Scotland) Act 1975, ss. 14 (solemn procedure) and 323 (summary procedure), under which a justice (*i.e.* a sheriff, stipendiary magistrate, or justice of the peace) may issue a warrant authorising a constable to search for a child. The warrant may be granted on an application by any person who, in the opinion of the justice, is acting in the interests of the child. There must be information on oath from which it appears that there is reasonable cause to suspect either that the child has been or is being assaulted, ill-treated or neglected in a place within the jurisdiction in a manner likely to cause him unnecessary suffering or injury to health or that an offence mentioned in Schedule 1 to the 1975 Act has been or is being committed in respect of the child. The warrant may take one of two forms. It may first authorise a named constable to search for the child and, if it is found that he has been or is being assaulted, ill-treated or neglected in the manner described or that a scheduled offence has been or is being committed in respect of him, to take him to, and detain him in, a place of safety. It may secondly authorise any constable to remove the child with or without search to a place of safety and detain him there. The first form would seem to be appropriate where the grounds for granting the warrant are thought to require verification and the second form where they are well established. Whichever form is used the constable may enter (if need be by force) any house, building or other place specified on the warrant and may remove the child therefrom. The person making the application is, if he so desires, entitled to accompany the constable unless the justice directs otherwise and the justice may direct the constable to be accompanied by a duly qualified medical practitioner. It is not necessary to name the child. The justice may, by the same warrant, authorise the apprehension of any person accused of any offence in respect of the child.

Further Detention

Where the reporter considers that a child detained in a place of safety may be in need of compulsory measures of care, he must whenever practicable arrange a children's hearing to sit not later than in the course of the first lawful day after the commencement of the child's detention.[9] If the hearing are unable to dispose of the case and are satisfied that the child's further detention is necessary in his own interest, or have reason to believe that he will run away during the investigation of his case, they may issue a warrant requiring the child to be detained in a place of safety for such a period not exceeding 21 days as may be necessary.[10] In determining the child's interests for this purpose the hearing should take a broad approach. "The question in any case must simply be whether, in all the circumstances, it would be better for the child to remain in a place of safety than

---

[8] s. 69.
[9] s. 37(4).
[10] *Ibid.*

to be left to his own unprotected devices while the investigation is taking place."[11] On the application of the reporter that warrant may be renewed by the hearing on one occasion only for a further period of 21 days.[12] Thereafter the reporter may, if it appears to him that the children's hearing will not be able to dispose of the child's case before the expiry of the period required by the renewed warrant and that a further period of detention is necessary in the child's own interest, apply to the sheriff for a warrant requiring the child to be detained in a place of safety for such additional period not exceeding 21 days as may be necessary.[13] The sheriff may issue such a warrant if he is satisfied that detention is necessary in the child's own interest, and a warrant so granted by the sheriff may be renewed by him on the application of the reporter and on cause shown. The renewal may be granted on one occasion only and again may be for a period not exceeding 21 days.[14] It is to be noted that the sheriff, unlike the hearing, has no power to grant or renew a warrant because of a belief that the child might run away during the investigation of his case, but in many cases it may be possible to represent such a risk as indicating the necessity of further detention in the child's own interest.[15] The effect of these provisions is that if the requisite warrants and renewals are granted a child who has been detained in a place of safety may continue to be detained there for a maximum period of 84 days between his first appearance before a children's hearing and the hearing's ultimate disposal of his case.[16] In highly exceptional circumstances the period of detention may be further extended by the Court of Session in the exercise of its *nobile officium*.[17] There is no specific provision in the Act for the release of the child from detention where the reporter considers that compulsory measures of care may be necessary but considers his further detention unnecessary. There is, however, nothing that requires that the child should continue to be detained in these circumstances, and rules provide[18] that the reporter may liberate a child where he is satisfied that further detention is unnecessary and that the child will not run away during the investigation of his case.

Detention After Arrest

Where "a person who is apparently a child" has been arrested and detained in a place of safety in connection with criminal charges and it is decided not to proceed with these charges, the reporter for the area in which the child is detained must be informed and the child may continue to be detained until the reporter

---

[11] So said the First Division in *Humphries* v. *S*, 1986 S.L.T. 683 at p. 684K. It was held that a warrant ought to have been issued to detain a child who had already committed three offences of housebreaking, because of the risk that he would make his own position worse by committing further offences.

[12] s. 37(5).

[13] s. 37(5A).

[14] s. 37(5B).

[15] As in *Humphries* v. *S*, *supra*.

[16] Social Work (Scotland) Act 1968, s. 37(3), (4), (5), (5A) and (5B) as amended by the Children Act 1975, s. 83(*c*) and (*d*); Criminal Procedure (Scotland) Act 1975, ss. 14(2) and 323(2). See *Ferguson* v. *P*, 1989 S.L.T. 681. The period is 91 days if counted from the original taking to a place of safety: see *Sloan* v. *B*, 1991 S.L.T. 530 at p. 539K, *per* Lord President Hope.

[17] *Humphries, Petr.*, 1982 S.C. 79; *Ferguson* v. *P*, *supra*.

[18] Reporters' Duties and Transmission of Information Etc. (Scotland) Rules 1971 (S.I. 1971 No. 525).

has decided on the course that should be taken. The procedures that have been noted above and the limitations on the periods of his detention then apply as they do to a child who has been taken to, or has taken refuge in, a place of safety.[19]

Initial Action by Reporter

On receipt of information of a case that may require a children's hearing to be arranged (*i.e.* a case of a child who may be in need of compulsory measures of care) there are several ways in which, after making such initial investigation as he may think necessary, the reporter may proceed with the case.[20] As he is required to proceed only with cases that *may* require a children's hearing to be arranged, he must first decide whether any case on which information is received falls into that category. Unless it is clear that the information either does not disclose any case appropriate for action by him or is already sufficient to enable him to decide how to proceed, an initial investigation is then indicated so as to enable him to make a proper choice among the options which are open. It is, therefore, wrong to suggest[21] that investigation may be unnecessary because the information is unreliable. The test is whether the information received indicates a case which may require a children's hearing to be arranged. Vagueness and unreliability may bear on that question but do not decide it. If a case that may require a children's hearing is indicated, the reporter is bound to investigate until he has the information necessary to decide how he should proceed with the case. Having investigated the case, the reporter has three options:

(a) to take no further action,
(b) where he considers it to be the proper course, to refer the case to the local authority with a view to their making arrangements for the advice, guidance and assistance of the child and his family in accordance with Part II of the 1968 Act, or
(c) where it appears to him that the child is in need of compulsory measures of care, to arrange a children's hearing to whom the case will stand referred for consideration and determination.[22]

A decision to take no further action, or to refer the case to the local authority, precludes the subsequent arranging of a children's hearing in relation to the same facts.[23] A decision to take no further action does not, however, preclude a subsequent reference to the local authority.

The reporter's discretion is wide and unfettered. There is no means by which a case can be referred to a children's hearing except on his decision. He is not, however, master of the process in the way that a public prosecutor is. If it appears to him that a child is in need of compulsory measures of care, he must arrange a children's hearing "to whom the case shall stand referred for

---

[19] Social Work (Scotland) Act 1968, s. 37(4), as amended by Criminal Procedure (Scotland) Act 1975, s. 296(3) and (4).
[20] s. 38(1).
[21] *Children's Hearing; Note on Part III of the Social Work (Scotland) Act 1968* (Social Work Services Group (1970)).
[22] s. 39.
[23] s. 39(5).

consideration and determination."[24] It appears from these words that once a hearing has been arranged the case cannot be withdrawn or abandoned by the reporter. It is thought that this stage is reached as soon as there is an overt act indicating that a hearing has been arranged, such as notification to the child or his parent, or a request for the statutory report from a local authority.

CONDUCT OF THE HEARING

Privacy of Hearing: Persons Present

A children's hearing is conducted in private and the general rule is that no person other than one whose presence is necessary for the proper consideration of the case, or whose presence is permitted by the chairman, shall be present.[25] It appears that it is for the hearing as a whole to decide whether a person's presence is necessary for the proper consideration of the case, should that be in dispute, and that the chairman has a discretion to admit other persons. The general rule is, however, subject to some exceptions.

The Parent

A parent has a right to attend at all stages of a children's hearing.[26] The only express exception is that a hearing exercising jurisdiction under Part V of the Act may proceed in the absence of the parent.[27] "Parent" means either or both parents[28]; in relation to an adopted child it means the adoptive parent or parents to the exclusion of the natural parents; and in relation to an illegitimate[29] child includes a "guardian,"[30] which itself is defined to mean anyone appointed by deed or will or by order of a court of competent jurisdiction to be the guardian of the child and anyone who in the opinion of the court or children's hearing having cognisance of the case has for the time being the charge of, or control over, the child.[31] The father of an illegitimate child is entitled to be present at the hearing if he is a guardian within that wide definition,[32] this being essentially a question of fact.[33] If parental rights have been assumed by a local authority under section 16 of the Social Work (Scotland) Act 1968, all parental rights (except those specified) will vest in the local authority,[34] with the result that the right to attend the children's hearing will pass from the parents to the officers of the relevant local authority. Though the statute is not clear, it has been suggested that this will occur only after the vesting becomes absolute, that is after the time has elapsed for the parents to serve a counter-notice to the resolution assuming parental rights[35] or the sheriff has ordered that the resolution should not lapse after

---

[24] s. 39(3).
[25] s. 35(1).
[26] s. 41(1).
[27] s. 76(1).
[28] s. 94(1).
[29] See comments *ante* at p. 448 note 27.
[30] s. 30(2). This is not, of course, the normal definition of "guardian".
[31] ss. 30(2) and 94(1), as amended by the Age of Legal Capacity (Scotland) Act 1991, Sched. 2.
[32] *C* v. *Kennedy*, 1991 S.L.T. 755.
[33] *Ibid.*, at p. 757I.
[34] s. 16(3), and see *ante* at p. 432.
[35] s. 16(7).

such a counter notice has been served,[36] but it is doubtful if that is correct. The parental rights vest in the local authority by whom the resolution is passed and remain so vested until the resolution lapses or is otherwise brought to an end.

The parent's right to be present carries with it a duty to attend at all stages unless the hearing is satisfied that it would be unreasonable to require his attendance or that his attendance would be unnecessary for the consideration of the case.[37] It is an offence to fail to comply with that obligation.[38]

The Child

The child is obliged to attend[39] and provision is made for securing his attendance,[40] but the statute is remarkably silent on his right to attend. However, in *Sloan* v. *B.*, Sheriff Kelbie expressed himself "satisfied that the corollary of the obligation on the child to attend and listen to the explanation is a right to be there and to hear the explanation,"[41] and this is surely correct.

It is, however, provided that, where a hearing is satisfied in a case concerned with certain scheduled offences, the attendance of a child is not necessary for the just hearing of that case and, in any case, where the hearing is satisfied that it would be detrimental to the interests of the child to be present at the hearing, the case in whole or in part may be considered in the absence of the child.[42] Also, a children's hearing exercising jurisdiction under Part V of the Act may proceed in the absence of the child.[43] It is implicit in these provisions, and is required by natural justice,[44] that the child has in all other circumstances a right to attend when the merits of his case are being considered. Although not specifically provided for in the statute, it is necessary that certain decisions extrinsic to the merits (*e.g.* on the issuing of warrants) should be made in the absence of the child and also of the parent. It appears from the terms of the provisions on consideration of a child's case in his absence that, except in the cases for which specific statutory provision is made, such consideration may be incompetent even if the requisite measures to secure attendance have been taken and have failed or if the child has waived his right to attend and the hearing does not consider his attendance necessary.

The provision allowing the hearing to dispense with the presence of the child is expressly stated to be "without prejudice to the provisions of section 42(1)," which is the subsection that imposes a duty on the chairman of the hearing to explain to the child (and the parents) the ground or grounds of referral.[45] The duty to explain contained in section 42(1) does not supersede the power to exclude in

---

[36] *Lothian Regional Council* v. *S*, 1986 S.L.T. (Sh. Ct.) 37 at p. 42; Kearney at pp. 60–61, 77–78.

[37] s. 41(2).

[38] s. 41(3).

[39] s. 40(1).

[40] See *post* at pp. 467–469.

[41] 1991 S.L.T. 530 at pp. 534–535. This part of Sheriff Kelbie's judgment was not criticised by the First Division when the case reached that court.

[42] s. 40(2).

[43] s. 76(1).

[44] Though it is to be noted that in a clash between natural justice and the interests of the child, it is the latter that shall prevail: *Kennedy* v. *A*, 1986 S.L.T. 358. Attendance of the child was a matter at issue in the Clyde Report.

[45] See *post* at pp. 470–471.

section 40(2), because the exclusion ought to be after the explanation. Section 42(1) provides that the explanation must be given "*before* proceeding to the consideration of the case," while section 40(2) provides *not* that the hearing can taken place in the absence of the child but only that the case may be "considered" in the absence of the child. In other words, the explanation must be given before the case is considered, and the child may be excluded only from that consideration. That is what the Act clearly states. There is no statutory authority for excluding the child from the explanation, nor for omitting an explanation completely (except where the hearing are satisfied that the child is not capable of understanding the explanation[46]). However, the failure by the chairman of the hearing to give an explanation to the child because the child has been excluded before the explanation is given need not render the application to the sheriff incompetent. In *Sloan* v. *B*,[47] children were excluded by a children's hearing exercising their discretion to dispense with their presence under section 40(2), and no explanation was given under section 42(1). The sheriff (Kelbie) held that, section 42(1) not being satisfied, an application to the sheriff under section 42(2), which commences "thereafter...," was incompetent. This decision was overruled by the First Division. Lord President Hope, speaking for the court, held that the purpose of the obligation to explain the grounds of the referral to the child was to protect the child's right to dispute them and so to protect the right to have an application made to the sheriff.[48] But if the parent disputed the grounds of referral (as happened in the instant case) the hearing would have to direct the reporter to make an application to the sheriff in any case, and consequently the child would suffer no prejudice. It followed that when the parent accepts the grounds of referral it is necessary that the child attend the children's hearing and be given the opportunity to dispute the grounds (unless the child is not capable of understanding[49]) but that when the parent disputes the grounds the fact that the child is not present does not render the proceedings incompetent.[50] The fact that section 42(1) requires the child to be given an explanation before his presence can be dispensed with was dismissed as "a mere formality,"[51] because the purpose of the provision allowing the child's presence to be dispensed with was to protect the child from the harm that might be caused in some cases by coming face to face with the parents.[52]

A number of difficulties emerge from *Sloan* v. *B*. First, a mandatory statutory requirement even if merely formal must be followed. The court was of the clear opinion that the requirement to explain the grounds for referral to the child was mandatory where it applied but held that it did not apply where the parents did not accept the grounds. It is difficult to see how a requirement expressed in the statute without qualification as to the circumstances of its application can be

---

[46] s. 42(1) and (7). Whether the hearing are entitled to consider themselves so satisfied without seeing the child and accepting the judgment of the reporter remains a matter of some doubt, even after *Sloan* v. *B*, *infra*.

[47] 1991 S.L.T. 530; and see Thomson, "*Sloan* v. *B*—the Legal Issues," 1991 S.L.T. (News) 421; Sutherland, "The Orkney Case," 1992 J.R. 93.

[48] *Ibid.*, at p. 548F. On applications to the sheriff, see *post* at pp. 473–480.

[49] s. 42(7). See note 46 above.

[50] 1991 S.L.T. 530 at p. 549.

[51] *Ibid.*, at p. 548H.

[52] See also the Clyde Report, published on Oct. 27, 1992.

qualified in respect of its mandatory nature in that way[53]. Secondly, to say that the purpose of the child's presence is to ensure that he or she suffers no prejudice overlooks the equally important function of allowing the child to take an active part in the whole process and, at the very least, of keeping the child informed of what is happening. Thirdly, the result of the decision is that, in relation to the right of the hearing to dispense with the child's presence, a distinction must now be made between cases in which the parents accept the grounds of referral and cases in which they do not (or in which the child does not or cannot understand): in the former the child's presence may not be dispensed with, and it is only in the latter that this may be done. Yet the statute gives no authority for making this distinction. Fourthly and following on from the previous point, the protection from distress at having the child meet the parent, which the court was anxious to ensure, is thereby limited to cases in which the parents dispute the grounds of referral again there is no justification either in the statute or in principle to adopt that distinction. Fifthly, the decision to dispense with the child's presence will normally be taken before it is known whether or not the parents will dispute the grounds of referral, that is before it is known whether the child may suffer prejudice: in other words the decision to dispense with the child's presence will be taken before it is known whether or not the power to do so exists. That problem did not arise in *Sloan* because, due to the intense publicity the case generated, it was well-known beforehand that the parents would dispute the grounds of referral. But in cases in which the parents are silent until the hearing, it will not be known whether the parents will accept the grounds and therefore it will not be known whether the child can be excluded: consequently the coming together of the parent and child, the avoidance of which is the justification for the exclusion of the child, cannot be avoided. Finally, it is to be remembered that if a child is excluded from the hearing then he or she cannot accept the ground for referral and the case will always have to go before the sheriff: in other words, the child will never suffer the prejudice referred to by the court. If the court is right in its view that the purpose of the child's presence is to avoid that prejudice then the child's presence will never be necessary (because of the protection of the unavoidable referral to the sheriff) and every child could be excluded in every case. This is clearly not what the statute envisaged.

It is suggested that the way around these difficulties is to follow the wording in the Act. Section 42(1) demands that, "before proceeding to the consideration of the case," an explanation be given to the parents and the child. While the wording suggests that the explanation to both will be contemporary, there is nothing to prevent the reporter arranging that the child attends the explanation at a different moment, or in a different room, from the parent: thus the protection deemed essential in *Sloan* will be achieved. Section 40(2) allows the hearing to consider the case, in whole or in part, in the absence of the child, and it is only from that—*i.e.* the consideration of how the case is to be disposed of—that the child's presence can be dispensed with.[54] Though the matter is not entirely unambiguous, section 41(1) and (2) appears to confer on the parent the right to attend only the consideration of the case; section 42(1) gives the right to hear an

---

[53] See further, Norrie, "Excluding Children from Children's Hearings", 1993 S.L.T. (News) 67.
[54] See further the Clyde Report, published on Oct. 27, 1992.

explanation, but does not demand the contemporary presence of both parent and child.

Other Persons

In addition to the child and his parents, any member of the Council on Tribunals or of its Scottish committee and *bona fide* representatives of a newspaper or news agency have a right to attend,[55] and rules provide for the discretionary admission of certain other categories of persons.[56] The categories are:

(a) the chairman and members of the Children's Panel Advisory Committee and the clerk of the local authority;

(b) any members or possible members of Children's Panels whose attendance is required for the purpose of their training and their instructors;

(c) any student engaged in formal education or training in social work or any person engaged in research relating to children who may be in need of compulsory measures of care;

(d) any other person whose presence at the sitting may, in the opinion of the chairman, be justified by special circumstances; and

(e) any clerk, interpreter, janitor, messenger or other person whose attendance in a like executive capacity is required or expedient for the proper conduct of the proceedings.

The chairman must take all reasonable steps to ensure that the number of persons present at any one time is kept to a minimum[57] but as he cannot, of course, exclude the persons who have a right to attend, that injunction is little more than a guide as to the way in which he should exercise his discretionary powers of admission. It is an offence, unless in a case in which the Secretary of State has granted a dispensation, for any newspaper or broadcast report to reveal the name, address or school of any child in any way concerned in a hearing or to include any particulars calculated to lead to his identification or to publish a picture including a picture of the child.[58]

Securing the Attendance of the Child

The reporter is charged with the responsibility of securing the child's attendance at the hearing of his case, including hearings to which the case is continued subsequent to the first hearing.[59] The child must be notified that his case has been referred to a children's hearing, and must attend in accordance with the notification.[60] The requirement to notify is absolute regardless of age, despite its inevitably notional character in the case of very young children. Notification is not achieved by sending notice to the address from which the child has been removed to a place of safety.[61] The reporter has no discretion in respect of notification or of securing attendance, but if a hearing decides to consider the case at

---

[55] s. 35(3).
[56] Children's Hearings (Scotland) Rules 1986 (S.I. 1986 No. 2291), r. 14.
[57] s. 35(2).
[58] s. 58.
[59] s. 40(3).
[60] s. 40(1).
[61] *Sloan* v. *B*, 1991 S.L.T. 530, *per* Lord President Hope at p. 540I.

a subsequent hearing in the absence of the child the requirement to secure the attendance of the child is clearly superseded so far as the subsequent hearing is concerned. It is understood moreover that it is common practice, although without statutory authority, for reporters not to secure the attendance of a child at hearings at which they are satisfied it would be detrimental to the interests of the child to be present and have confidence that the hearing will endorse that view. This practice must, however, be seen in the light of the comments made above concerning the statutory requirement to explain the ground of referral to the child.

Warrants for Detention

In order to secure the attendance of a child, or in the event of the failure of a child to attend, a hearing may, if satisfied of the necessity for doing so, issue, either at the instance of the reporter on cause shown or of its own motion, a warrant for the apprehension of the child.[62] Such a warrant is authority both for bringing a child before a hearing and for his detention in a place of safety and, for the purposes of its execution and of the application of any enactments relating to execution, is treated with any necessary modification as if it were a warrant of apprehension issued by a court of summary jurisdiction.[63] Accordingly, it implies, where necessary for its execution, a warrant to officers of law to break open shut and lockfast places and to search for the child.[64] Where a child apprehended under a warrant cannot immediately be brought before a children's hearing, the reporter must, wherever practicable, arrange a hearing to sit not later than in the course of the first lawful day after the child's apprehension.[65] If, for whatever reason, a hearing is not arranged within seven days of the child's apprehension, the child cannot continue to be detained thereafter.[66] Moreover, he cannot continue to be detained after the day on which a children's hearing first sit to consider his case unless that hearing orders his continued detention.[67] That it may do, by issuing a warrant for that purpose, as may any hearing before whom a child is brought, if it is unable to dispose of the case *and* either (a) it has reason to believe that the child may not attend at a hearing or at any proceedings arising from the case, or (b) it is satisfied that detention of the child is necessary in his own interest.[68] A warrant so issued authorises the detention of the child in a place of safety for such period not exceeding 21 days as may be necessary,[69] and may, on the application of the reporter and on cause shown, be renewed by a hearing on one occasion only for the same period.[70] If it appears to the reporter that the hearing will not be able to dispose of the case before the expiry of the period of detention required by the warrant as renewed and that further detention of the child is necessary in the child's own interest, he may

---

[62] s. 40(4).
[63] s. 40(9).
[64] Criminal Procedure (Scotland) Act 1975, s. 14(4).
[65] Social Work (Scotland) Act 1968, s. 40(6).
[66] s. 40(5).
[67] *Ibid.*
[68] s. 40(7), as substituted by the Children Act 1975, s. 84.
[69] *Ibid.*
[70] s. 40(8), as substituted by the Children Act 1975, s. 84.

apply to the sheriff for a warrant requiring the child to be detained for such period not exceeding 21 days as may be necessary. The sheriff may issue such a warrant if he is satisfied that detention is necessary in the child's own interest, and a warrant so granted by the sheriff may be renewed by him on the application of the reporter and on cause shown. The renewal may be granted on one occasion only and again may be for a period not exceeding 21 days.[71]

The above provisions for the granting and renewal of warrants for securing the attendance of the child overlap and largely echo similar provisions noted earlier[72] concerning the issuing of warrants in cases which have their origin in the taking to a place of safety of a child in respect of whom any of certain offences has been, or is believed to have been, committed or in a child's taking refuge in a place of safety. The result of the duplication of provisions is, however, that two statutory codes, notionally distinct although largely coincident in function and subject matter, apply to such cases and may be applied cumulatively so that on the exhaustion of the facilities for granting warrants under the one code, the other may be invoked. As each code provides for detention under warrant for a continuous period of up to 84 days provided the appropriate renewals are obtained, in addition to an initial period of detention not exceeding seven days, it is possible in such cases for a child to be detained for a total period of as much as 182 days. It is doubtful if that was the legislature's intention and, although prolonged detention of the child may be necessary for his protection where criminal proceedings are pending against a person accused of an offence relevant to the child's case, 182 or even 168 days go beyond what is required for that purpose unless in the most exceptional circumstances.[73] The Court of Session will, in the exercise of its *nobile officium*, grant a prolongation where circumstances for which the statute has not provided make it necessary.[74] Once a warrant has been issued a fresh warrant issued even after an interval, while the case is still pending, is, it is submitted, a renewal and so subject to the applicable limitations. There is, however, no limitation on the number of occasions on which a warrant may be issued for the apprehension of a child so that he may be brought before a children's hearing and his detention for a maximum of seven days for that purpose.

Conflict of Interest between Parent and Child: Appointment of Safeguarder

The Act looks to the involvement of both parent and child throughout the proceedings. In the generality of cases parent and child may be supposed to have a community of interest. In some cases, however, a conflict of interest between parent and child will be evident and in others it may emerge as the case pro-

---

[71] s. 40(8A) and (8B), as substituted by the Children Act 1975, s. 84.

[72] *Ante*, at pp. 457–462.

[73] Detention for anything approaching this length of time would clearly breach Art. 37(*d*) of the UN Convention on the Rights of the Child, ratified by the UK on Dec. 16, 1991: "Every child deprived of his or her liberty shall have the right to *prompt* access to legal and other appropriate assistance, as well as the right to challenge the legality of the deprivation of his or her liberty before a court or other competent, independent and impartial authority, and to a *prompt* decision on any such action" (emphasis added). The UK, in ratifying the Convention, entered a reservation to this Article, to allow the present operation of Children's Hearings to continue.

[74] *Humphries, Petr.*, 1982 S.C. 79; *Ferguson* v. *P*, 1989 S.L.T. 681.

ceeds. In the event of such conflict separate representation for the child may be the only way of protecting his interests. Accordingly the Act provides that the chairman of the hearing is to consider whether it is necessary, for the purpose of safeguarding the interests of the child, because there is or may be a conflict between his interests and those of his parent on any matter relevant to the proceedings, to appoint a person to act for that purpose and, if he thinks fit, to make such an appointment.[75] The duty and the power are given to the chairman alone and although, no doubt, he may consult the other members of the hearing, he is not obliged to do so. The appointment may be made at any stage in the proceedings. A panel or panels of persons from which appointments may be made is to be established for each local authority area. The safeguarder's rights and powers are governed by rules.[76]

Commencement of the Hearing: Explanation of the Grounds

The hearing commences with an explanation given to the child and his parent of the grounds stated by the reporter for the referral of the case. It is the chairman's duty to give the explanation and he should do so before the hearing proceeds to a consideration of the case.[77] The purpose is to ascertain whether the grounds are accepted in whole or in part by the child and his parent. The Act is silent as to how the duty is to be discharged adequately where the grounds of referral raise legal issues of difficulty or complexity nor is any means provided for securing that such issues do not pass undetected.

Subsequent procedure depends on the response to the explanation of the grounds of referral. Where the child and his parents accept the grounds, the hearing proceeds.[78] If either (or both) the child or his parent does not accept the grounds, the hearing must, unless it decides to discharge the referral, direct the reporter to make an application to the sheriff for a finding as to whether the grounds are established.[79] That is required wherever there is not explicit acceptance; absence of dispute is not enough although a statement that the grounds are not disputed may be open to construction as an acceptance. It may, however, happen that the grounds are accepted by one or more of the parties only in part. In that situation, the hearing has a choice of:

(a) proceeding with the hearing if it considers it proper to do so in respect of the grounds accepted by the child and his parent, or
(b) directing the reporter to make an application to the sheriff for a finding as to whether such grounds as are not accepted are established, or
(c) discharging the referral.[80]

Grounds of referral are not defined but there is, by implication, a clear reference to the conditions which have to be satisfied if it is to be held that a child may be in need of compulsory measures of care,[81] and the relevant rules have been

---

[75] s. 34A, as inserted by the Children Act 1975, s. 66. See Kearney, at pp. 48–54, 204–214.
[76] Children's Hearings (Scotland) Rules 1986 (S.I. 1986 No. 2291), r. 12.
[77] s. 42(1). And see comments *ante* at pp. 464–467.
[78] s. 42(2).
[79] *Ibid.*
[80] *Ibid.*
[81] s. 32.

made on that basis.[82] The grounds of referral in any given case are the conditions which it is claimed are satisfied in respect of the child and the facts stated as supporting that claim. They are a composite of law and fact. If partial acceptance of the grounds is to be such as to enable the hearing, if it thinks it proper to do so, to proceed, it must, it is submitted, extend to an admission of both law and fact sufficient to justify the conclusion that the child may be in need of compulsory measures of care—*i.e.* the facts accepted must be sufficient to show that a condition on which the reporter relies is satisfied. Anything short of that means that the competency of the hearing's applying compulsory measures of care is not accepted or that facts sufficient to form a basis for disposal of the case, other than by discharge, are not accepted, or both. In any of these events, there is a clear barrier to the hearing's proceeding. It is not, however, necessary that the legal incidents of a condition should be accepted in the terms set out by the reporter. The emphasis is on the facts rather than on legal refinements although the facts must disclose that a condition is satisfied. Accordingly, if the grounds of referral relate to the commission by the child of an offence, the grounds are accepted in part if it is accepted that an offence was committed and stated facts sufficient to amount to the commision of an offence are also accepted. The case may then proceed before the hearing although it is not accepted that the particular offence libelled by the reporter was committed.[83] If, for example, the grounds of referral are that the child committed the offence of theft, and the child and parent accept that an offence was committed but claim it was reset, there is an acceptance in part which is sufficient to entitle the hearing to proceed provided facts sufficient to amount at least to reset are also accepted. Likewise, the hearing may proceed if assault is alleged but only breach of the peace and facts sufficient to support that offence are admitted. That hearings, as a result, may be faced with questions outwith the competence of a lay tribunal is a defect in the system for which the only remedy is that, whenever there is doubt, an application should be made to the sheriff.[84]

Lack of Understanding

It may also happen that a child is incapable of understanding the explanation of the grounds of referral, or in fact does not understand them. In either of these events the hearing must, unless it decides to discharge the referral, direct the reporter to make an application to the sheriff for a finding as to whether any of the grounds has been established.[85] This provision is supererogatory where the child does not accept a ground of referral. Its purpose would seem to be to require an application to be made where the child, although it did not understand the explanation, was nonetheless willing to accept the ground, and so to reduce the risk of acceptances based on deficient understanding. There is no corresponding provision for the case of a parent who is incapable of understanding or does not understand the explanation; but a parent who is incapable of under-

---

[82] Children's Hearings (Scotland) Rules 1986 (S.I. 1986 No. 2291), rr. 16 and 17.
[83] *Cf. McGregor* v. *D*, 1977 S.C. 330, which, although concerned with the sheriff's decision on whether grounds of referral are established, turns on issues which are largely similar.
[84] s. 42(2). On which, see *post* at pp. 473–480.
[85] s. 42(7).

standing cannot, it is submitted, accept and a parent who, although not lacking in capacity, does not understand must, unless he indicates to the contrary, be taken as not accepting.[86] Capacity to understand is to be presumed in the case of an adult and on the assumption that the explanation is adapted to the age and intellectual development of the child, the same is true of a child, other than a child clearly too young to understand any explanation. It is, however, desirable, if not mandatory, that the hearing should ascertain whether or not an explanation has in fact been understood by the child. There is no provision for the case where a child's lack of understanding relates to only part of the grounds of referral. It is attractive to regard such a case as one of non-acceptance of that part, but as the Act treats the explanation as a whole, it would appear, on a strict construction, that failure to understand any part of it affects the whole and so requires the making of an application to the sheriff for a finding as to whether any of the grounds has been established.

Non-Attendance

In the event of non-attendance by a parent, his acceptance is not required[87] and the hearing may proceed in his absence. Where the child does not attend it would in some cases be advantageous if the hearing could treat his non-attendance as indicating that he did not accept the grounds of referral and so direct the reporter to make an application to the sheriff forthwith. The Act, however, contemplates that acceptance or non-acceptance should follow on the chairman's explanation, and that before a hearing can either proceed with a case or make an application to the sheriff the child must have appeared before it, which can be secured by the issue of a warrant, and have had an opportunity of accepting or not accepting the grounds of referral. Except in cases falling within the *ratio* of *Sloan* v. *B*. (which, it is submitted ought to be narrowly construed), the hearing's power to exclude the child is limited, as explained above, to exclusion from the consideration of the case,[88] and an explanation cannot be avoided by excluding the child from that part of the proceedings before the consideration of the case. If the child is so excluded then, on the authority of *Sloan* v. *B*,[89] it can never be taken to have accepted the grounds of referral.

Transference of Case

A case may be transferred from a children's hearing in one local authority's area to a children's hearing in the area of another and, if that is done, grounds of referral accepted or established do not require to be further accepted or established.[90] This will normally be appropriate only before application has been made to the sheriff.[91]

---

[86] See Kearney at p. 110.
[87] s. 42(8).
[88] s. 40(2).
[89] 1991 S.L.T. 530.
[90] s. 54.
[91] *Sloan Petr.*, 1991 S.L.T. 527.

APPLICATION TO THE SHERIFF

Introduction[92]

The policy of the Act is to separate the body that decides what compulsory measures to take concerning the child, and the body that decides whether there are grounds on which such measures can lawfully be taken. Consequently, if either the child or the parent or both does not accept the ground or grounds of referral, or if the child does not or cannot understand the ground or grounds of referral, the hearing must direct the reporter to apply to the sheriff for a finding of whether or not the ground of referral is established.[93] If a hearing directs the reporter to make an application to the sheriff it is the duty of the chairman to explain to the child and his parent the purpose for which the application to the sheriff is being made and to inform the child that he is under an obligation to attend the hearing of the application.[94] The reporter must make the application within seven days. There is no prescription of the sheriff court to which application is to be made except that where the ground of referral is that the child has committed an offence the application must be made to the sheriff who would have jurisdiction if the child were being prosecuted for that offence.[95] In other cases, the matter would appear to be at the discretion of the reporter, or, if the hearing so directs, of the hearing. The court which will normally be appropriate is, however, that of the sheriff court district within which the hearing is held, or, at least, a sheriff court situated in the local authority area within which the hearing took place.[96] A plea of *forum non conveniens* may not be altogether apt in proceedings bounded by the confines of a self-contained statutory scheme but the court retains, it is submitted, power to control extreme instances of choice of forum which amount to an abuse of process. The sheriff has no statutory authority to conduct any part of the proceedings outside the sheriff court district within which the court is situated, but the reporter may apply to the *nobile officium* of the Court of Session for a direction that the hearing or part of it should be held elsewhere, if good reasons for the exercise of that power exists.[97] The hearing before the sheriff must commence within 28 days of the lodging of the application[98] but thereafter, in order to allow time for further inquiry or for any other necessary cause, the sheriff may, either on his own motion or on the motion of any party, continue the case for such reasonable time as he may in the circumstances consider necessary.[99] A hearing at which all parties are present or at

---

[92] See Kearney, at pp. 153–252.

[93] s. 42(2) and (7).

[94] s. 42(3).

[95] s. 42(2A), as inserted by the Criminal Justice (Scotland) Act 1980, Sched. 7, para. 21.

[96] *Sloan Petr.*, 1991 S.L.T. 527 at p. 529D, *per* Lord President Hope. In *L* v. *McGregor*, 1980 S.L.T. 17 it was held that it was competent for the reporter to apply to any court within, at least, the area of his local authority (Regional or Islands Council) and perhaps beyond.

[97] *Sloan Petr.*, *ibid.* at p. 529D, *per* Lord President Hope. In this case the application was refused, the grounds advanced (that it would be contrary to the interests of certain child witnesses, who had been removed from their home in Orkney to the mainland, to return to Orkney, and prejudicial to certain adult witnesses, including professional people, to require them to travel to Orkney) not being sufficient to persuade the court to direct that the proceedings before the sheriff be conducted elsewhere. Authority was however given for evidence of certain children to be taken elsewhere within the sheriffdom within which the sheriff was empowered to act.

[98] s. 42(4).

[99] Act of Sederunt, Social Work (Sheriff Court Procedure) Rules 1971, (S.I. 1971 No. 92), r. 9.

least have full opportunity of being present must take place within the prescribed time and accordingly the statutory requirement is not met if a diet fixed
for a competent time is adjourned to a date outwith the 28-day period in circumstances which effectively deprive a party of such opportunity.[1] It is essential to
such opportunity that there should be effective procedure at the diet fixed or at
least that the prospect of effective procedure should not be precluded by unilateral action in advance. It is not, however, necessary that a consideration of the
merits of the case should be commenced.[2] As the sheriff's power to continue the
case is subordinated to the requirement for a hearing within 28 days,[3] that requirement is, it is submitted, mandatory and cannot be waived by parties. At the
hearing, which must be in chambers, a reporter or deputy reporter[4] may appear
although not legally qualified, and the child and his parents may be represented.
Lay, as well as legal, representation appears to be competent for the child and
his parents.[5] The sheriff has the same duty and power as the chairman of the
hearing to consider and arrange separate representation for the child where
there is, or may be, a conflict of interest.[6] The role of a safeguarder appointed by
the sheriff probably comes to an end when the proceedings before the sheriff
end[7] (unlike the continuing role of a safeguarder appointed by the hearing). If
the child fails to attend the hearing before the sheriff, a warrant may be issued
for his apprehension which is authority for bringing him before the sheriff and
for his detention in a place of safety for a period not exceeding 14 days or until
disposal of the application by the sheriff, whichever is the earlier.[8] It is incompetent for the reporter to be represented by a lay representative other than his
deputy.[9] The powers of the reporter and his deputy are limited to those conferred by the statute and rules. He may cite witnesses and havers and attend to
the execution of such citations although he is not an enrolled solicitor.

Relevancy and Competency

There is no jurisdiction to dismiss an application as irrelevant[10] and, although
the reporter may abandon the application in part "as it relates to any ground of
referral" as well as a whole,[11] neither the reporter nor the court has any power to
amend.[12] It does not, however, follow from the lack of a preliminary jurisdiction
on relevancy, that where an application is tainted with radical incompetency apparent on the face of the record, a sheriff must hear evidence before dismissing
it. In such cases he is entitled *in limine* to refuse to exercise a jurisdiction which

---

[1] *H* v. *Mearns*, 1974 S.L.T. 184.
[2] *Ibid.*
[3] Act of Sederunt, Social Work (Sheriff Court Procedure) Rules 1971, (S.I. 1971 No. 92), r. 9.
[4] s. 36A, as inserted by the Children Act 1975, s. 82; Reporters (Conduct of Proceedings before the Sheriff) (Scotland) Regulations 1975 (S.I. 1975 No. 2251).
[5] s. 42(4).
[6] See further, Kearney at pp. 204–214.
[7] Kearney at p. 213.
[8] s. 42(3) (increased from seven days by the Law Reform (Miscellaneous Provisions) (Scotland) Act 1985, s. 25).
[9] See *Kennedy* v. *O*, 1975 S.C. 308, which although superseded by s. 36A in relation to the reporter and his deputy otherwise remains authoritative.
[10] *McGregor* v. *D*, 1977 S.C. 330.
[11] Act of Sederunt, Social Work (Sheriff Court Procedure) Rules 1971, r. 7.
[12] *McGregor* v. *D*, *supra*.

ex hypothesi of the incompetency he does not have, although reservation of the question of competency, until after the evidence has been heard, may often be convenient and desireable. In *L* v. *McGregor*[13] the sheriff entertained a plea on the grounds of no jurisdiction (and repelled it) and was not criticised for doing so by the Court of Session; and in *Merrins* v. *S*[14] the sheriff sustained a plea to the competency without hearing evidence on the basis that the child involved was under eight years of age and the ground of referral was that he had committed an offence. However, a sharp distinction arises between cases of this type, where the incompetency cannot be put right and the sheriff would be unable, whatever the evidence, to hold the ground of referral established, and other cases, where the alleged incompetency arises merely through a defect in procedure that can be put right. In all cases falling into the latter class it is the duty of the sheriff to hear all the evidence tendered by the reporter in respect of all the grounds so far as that evidence is competent and relevant to the statement of facts contained in the grounds of referral.[15] At the conclusion of the reporter's evidence the sheriff must, unless he considers that a *prima facie* case has not been made out, proceed to tell the child and his parent or representative and any safeguarder appointed under section 34A that they may give evidence or make a statement and call witnesses.[16]

Proof

The proceedings, which are essentially *sui generis*[17] and not in any proper sense adversarial, are governed by the statute[18] and Act of Sederunt.[19] They are civil rather than criminal in character even when the grounds relate to the commission of an offence, though they are "civil proceedings of a special type,"[20] and therefore the ordinary rules of civil procedure do not apply. The central consideration is, within the limits imposed by the Act and subordinate legislation, to achieve "a simplicity of procedure avoiding, as far as possible, technicalities of legal process which will, on the one hand, enable the requisite action in the interest and for the benefit of the child to be taken by panels of laymen while, at the same time, provide an effective and simple structure within which the purpose of the legislation can be secured."[21] Many of the basic rules of evidence apply.[22] However, it has been stated that the principles of natural justice have to yield to the interests of the child[23] and, even before the rule was statutorily altered, it had been held by the First Division that hearsay evidence should be admissible in a children's hearing case.[24] The court said this:

---

[13] 1980 S.L.T. 17. See also *H* v. *Mearns*, 1974 S.L.T. 184; *McGregor* v. *L*, 1983 S.L.T. (Sh. Ct.) 7.

[14] 1987 S.L.T. 193.

[15] *McGregor* v. *D*, 1977 S.C. 330; *Sloan* v. *B*, 1991 S.L.T. 530 at p. 546, *per* Lord President Hope. See Thomson, "*Sloan* v. *B*—The Legal Issues," 1991 S.L.T. (News) 421.

[16] Social Work (Sheriff Court Procedure) Rules 1971, r. 8(2).

[17] *McGregor* v. *D*, 1977 S.C. 330, *per* Lord Emslie at p. 336; *F* v. *Kennedy*, 1992 S.C.L.R. 750, *per* Lord Justice-Clerk Ross at p. 755A.

[18] Social Work (Scotland) Act 1968, P. III.

[19] *McGregor* v. *D*, *supra*, *per* Lord Cameron at p. 341. See also *Sloan Petr.*, 1991 S.L.T. 527.

[20] *Harris* v. *F*, 1991 S.L.T. 242 at p. 245B *per* Lord Justice-Clerk Ross.

[21] *McGregor* v. *D*, *per* Lord Cameron at p. 339.

[22] *Kennedy* v. *B*, 1973 S.L.T. 38, *per* Lord Justice-Clerk Grant at p. 41.

[23] *Kennedy* v. *A*, 1986 S.L.T. 358.

[24] *W* v. *Kennedy*, 1988 S.L.T. 583.

"The proceedings in front of the sheriff on referral are self-contained civil proceedings *sui generis* in which it must be borne in mind at all times that the principal purpose is to ascertain what is necessary to be done in the interests of the child. In our opinion it would be quite wrong for this objective to be thwarted by the application of rigid rules of evidence or procedure just because such rigidity may be appropriate in other kinds of proceedings."[25]

Statute has now provided that in any civil proceedings (which is defined to include any hearing by the sheriff under section 42 of the 1968 Act except in so far as the ground of referral is the commission by the child of an offence) evidence shall not be excluded solely on the ground that it is hearsay. Where, however, a child is rejected as a witness because of his inability to distinguish truth from falsehood evidence cannot be led of its extrajudicial hearsay statement.[26] It is also provided that facts can be held to be proved on the balance of probabilities even when the evidence is not corroborated.[27]

In so far as the rules against evidence of character and similar fact are in point, they apply as they would in civil rather than in criminal proceedings. When the ground of referral is that the child has committed an offence, proof is on the criminal standard[28] (*i.e.* proof beyond reasonable doubt). In any other case, as previously explained,[29] proof is on a balance of probability. Questions have however sometimes been raised of whether a higher standard applies where the ground of referral relates to the commission of offences by persons other than the child.[30] There is authority for the view that where allegations of certain types of criminal conduct are made in civil proceedings they require to be proved, if not on the criminal standard, at least by evidence of a clear and strongly persuasive kind.[31] The view taken in England[32] is that the gravity of an allegation may affect the degree of probability required for proof or that the

---

[25] *Ibid.* at pp. 585–586. See also *K* v. *Kennedy*, 1992 S.C.L.R. 386.

[26] Civil Evidence (Scotland) Act 1988, s. 2; *F* v. *Kennedy (No. 1)*, 1992 S.C.L.R. 139. See also *F* v. *Kennedy*, 1992 S.C.L.R. 750.

[27] *Ibid.*, s. 1. For a discussion, see *Harris* v. *F*, 1991 S.L.T. 242.

[28] s. 42(6).

[29] *Ante*, at pp. 452–453.

[30] s. 32(2)(*d*), (*dd*) and (*e*).

[31] *Arnott* v. *Burt* (1872) 11 M. 62, *per* Lord Neaves at p. 74, where the criminal standard was said to be applicable to cases of fraudulent conduct. *Cf.* "Fraud is a thing that must be clearly and conclusively established" (*Cullen's Tr.* v. *Johnston* (1865) 3 M. 935, *per* Lord President McNeill at pp. 937–938); and again in the case of fraud: "The case will require to be made out by very clear evidence" (*Wink* v. *Speirs* (1867) 6 M. 77, *per* Lord Justice-Clerk Patton at p. 80). It is clear, however, that these dicta cannot be applied to all instances of criminal conduct arising in the course of civil proceedings. It is, for example, an everyday incident of civil practice that contraventions of the Road Traffic Acts and the Factories Acts are proved on the ordinary civil standard. It is intelligible that a court should require strong evidence to prove allegations of conduct which would amount to the commission of a seriously reprehensible crime, but there is also justice in Sir Rupert Cross's observation that "very strong reason is required to justify the imposition of the standard of proof appropriate to a criminal charge in a civil case, and it is open to question whether that reason has ever been convincingly stated": *Evidence* (3rd ed.) at p. 99. See also *Buick* v. *Jaglar*, 1973 S.L.T. (Sh. Ct.) 6.

[32] *Hornal* v. *Neuberger Products Ltd.* [1957] 1 Q.B. 247, *per* Denning L.J. at p. 258 and Morris L.J. at p. 266.

very element of gravity becomes a part of the whole range of circumstances which have to be weighed in the scale when deciding as to the balance of probabilities. This was commented upon by the Second Division in *B* v. *Kennedy*,[33] in which the English approach was construed "as meaning that the weight of evidence required to tip the scales may vary with the gravity of the allegation to be proved. For example, the weight of evidence required to prove fraud in a civil case may be greater than that required to prove a breach of contract." But in the end, as was emphasised, "the standard of proof is fixed as 'the balance of probabilities'. [Apart from commission of an offence by the child] the ordinary civil law standard applies to all other grounds."[34] The appellant's contention that the sheriff should have applied a higher standard of proof than the balance of probabilities was expressly rejected. Clearly the trier of fact in a civil case may be more reluctant to believe an allegation of serious criminal conduct than an allegation of negligence or breach of contract, and that reluctance will enter into his assessment of the probabilities, but if at the end of the day the balance of probability is that the criminal conduct took place he must hold it proved. Such reluctance as may be appropriate in the ordinary civil case may not, however, be apt to an application to hold grounds of referral established. It is one thing to treat with caution or reserve allegations of crime made by one party against another; it is another and more questionable matter to entertain the same scruples where the protection of a third party—the child—is at issue. The purpose of the statute will be best achieved if attention focuses without further elaboration on proof on a balance of probabilities.

Fresh Matters

The grounds of referral are inevitably based on past events. It is to these events that the evidence will, in the main, be directed and on proof of which the establishment of the grounds of referral will depend. Where, however, a ground of referral involves consideration of an existing or future state of affairs, and in particular where it involves consideration of the future welfare of the child, it is competent to lead evidence of facts as at the date of the proof before the sheriff and such facts, if proved, must be taken into account.[35] In these circumstances, an adjournment should be granted if necessary to avoid prejudice caused by the introduction of new matter. The plea of *res judicata* has no place in applications of this kind and if an earlier episode is relied upon by the reporter, "the sheriff is entitled and indeed bound to hear evidence relating to it."[36] Where the grounds of referral relate to a state of affairs obtaining over a period of time and include incidents which had been finally disposed of in previous proceedings as well as

---

[33] 1987 S.L.T. 765.

[34] *Ibid.* at p. 768.

[35] *Kennedy* v. *B and Anr.*, 1972 S.C. 128. That case was concerned with a referal under s. 32(2)(*c*) (lack of parental care likely to cause unnecessary suffering or seriously to impair health or development), but its reasoning seems to be applicable to all the conditions in s. 32(2) that are expressed in the present or future, as opposed to the past tense, (*i.e.* conditions (*a*) to (*e*) and (*i*), but not (*f*), (*g*), (*gg*) and (*h*)). In *Kennedy* v. *R.'s Curator ad Litem*, 1993 S.L.T. 295 it was held that a parent was entitled to dispute the grounds of referral because circumstances had changed since the hearing, even if he or she had accepted the grounds at the hearing itself.

[36] *Per* Lord Hunter in *Kennedy* v. *S*, 1986 S.L.T. 679 at p. 681J, relying on the authority of *McGregor* v. *D*, 1981 S.L.T. (Notes) 97.

a later incident, evidence must be heard on all the facts stated, the earlier incidents cannot be treated as *res judicata*,[37] and the eventual decision must, it is submitted, be based on the totality of circumstances. A party is entitled to make an unsworn statement which may be taken into account and, if accepted, is entitled to have some weight given to it.[38]

Competency of Witnesses

A parent is a competent and compellable witness at the instance of the reporter where the ground of referral is that the child has committed an offence[39] and there is no reason that, subject where appropriate to a privilege against self-incrimination, he should not be similarly competent and compellable in relation to other grounds. Neither the common law rule that an accused person is not a competent witness for the prosecution or the defence in the proceedings against him nor its statutory modifications have any application in the context of proceedings for the establishment of a ground of referral and there is no barrier to the invocation of the principle that anyone is a competent witness unless of a class specifically excluded by law and, if competent, is compellable. Where, however, it is alleged that the child has committed an offence the privilege against self-incrimination would, unless waived, constitute an obstacle to the child's effective use as a witness for the reporter and the resemblance to criminal proceedings may, in any event, be thought to be sufficient to make such a course undesirable. There would seem to be no objection to the reporter's calling him as a witness in relation to any other ground. A spouse is a competent and compellable witness as to the commission of an offence by the other spouse, and there is no privilege to refuse to answer questions that might tend to incriminate one's spouse.[40]

Scope and Effect of Decisions

After hearing evidence the sheriff is required to give his decision orally.[41] A copy of the subsequent interlocutor embodying the decision must be transmitted by the sheriff clerk to the child and his parent, but there is no requirement that a note indicating the sheriff's reasons should be appended to the interlocutor, nor indeed that there should be any written communication with the reporter or the hearing. The absence of a note may in some cases deprive the hearing of information (*e.g.* on the truthfulness of statements by the child or his parent) that would be useful for the further consideration of the case. Where the sheriff decides that none of the grounds in respect of which the application was made has been established he must dismiss the application and discharge the referral in respect of these grounds.[42] The children's hearing can in that event proceed with the case only in respect of grounds, if any, which were accepted. Where the sheriff is satisfied on the evidence that any of the grounds in respect of which the application was made has been established, he must remit the case

---

[37] *Ibid.*

[38] *Kennedy* v. *B, supra.*

[39] *McGregor* v. *T and Anr.*, 1975 S.L.T. 71.

[40] *Ante* at p. 452.

[41] Social Work (Sheriff Court Procedure Rules) 1971, r. 11.

[42] s. 42(5).

to the reporter to make arrangements for a children's hearing for consideration and determination of the case.[43] It is noteworthy that the sheriff is not empowered in that event to discharge the referral in respect of any grounds which have not been established, and that it is the child's *case* that is remitted for consideration and determination. The inference would seem to be that consideration by the children's hearing is not to be too closely tied to the established ground or grounds of referral, although it would be anomalous if the hearing were entitled to put reliance on a ground which the sheriff had held not to be established. Where the grounds of referral are alleged to constitute an offence or offences or attempt thereat, the sheriff may find on the facts that any offence established by the facts has been committed provided it falls within the ambit of the conditions of section 32(2) to which the grounds relate notwithstanding that it is not the specific offence libelled in the grounds.[44] In *McGregor* v. *A* it was held that rule applies to offences committed by other persons, where these ground the referral, as well as to offences committed by the child, and it was said that the rule merely permits the sheriff to find that the facts establish some other offence and does not require him to do so. However, given the terms of the rule, it is difficult to conceive of any sound principle upon which, if the facts establish some relevant offence other than that libelled, the sheriff could, if invited to do so, decline so to find.[45]

Neither the Court of Session nor the sheriff has any power to direct the hearing as to how it should dispose of the case, and in *Kennedy* v. *A*[46] the Second Division held that the sheriff had no power even to indicate some of the factors which he considered that the hearing ought to take into account when coming to a decision on the merits of the case. The powers of the Court of Session are simiarly constrained. But neither court is, it is thought, precluded from drawing the hearing's attention to aspects of its decision or the reasons for it which may assist in the hearing's disposal and it may, in particular, sometimes be helpful for the sheriff to indicate evidence he has accepted or rejected and the weight he has attached to it. There is, however, no requirement to do so.

Further Application to the Sheriff

If the sheriff finds the ground of referral to be established the case is referred back to the children's hearing for consideration and disposal, and there is no provision in the Act for further applications to the sheriff to resolve matters of dispute which arise after the establishment of the grounds. It follows that it is for the hearing to resolve such disputes within the context of determining how to dispose of the case, and this is so even when the dispute concerns the original ground of referral. In *R* v. *Kennedy*[47] the ground of referral for three children was that the eldest girl had been the victim of the crime of incest, committed by her father. This was disputed by the parents but found established by the sheriff,

---

[43] s. 42(6).

[44] Social Work (Sheriff Court Procedure) Rules 1971, r. 10; *McGregor* v. *D*, 1977 S.C. 330; *McGregor* v. *A*, 1982 S.L.T. 45.

[45] It is a sufficient *ratio* for *McGregor* v. *A* that the reporter had not invited the sheriff to consider such a course and that on appeal the point was not raised in the stated case.

[46] 1986 S.L.T. 358.

[47] *Sub nom. R., Petr.*, 1993 S.L.T. 910.

primarily on the evidence of the girl herself. All three children were placed under supervision, with a condition that the father have only limited contact with them. The girl later retracted her evidence and the father petitioned the *nobile officium* for an order directing the sheriff to have the ground of referral reheard. The petition was dismissed as incompetent on the ground that the Act envisaged that the original finding was the prerequisite for the exercise of the hearing's jurisdiction and that once that jurisdiction was established all new matters were questions for the hearing alone to consider. Likewise, a retraction by the parent or the child of a previously given acceptance of the ground of referral does not take away the hearing's jurisdiction. However, a party who accepts a ground can dispute that ground before the sheriff if the case is sent to him for the establishment of the grounds because another party denies them or because the child is to young to accept.[48]

R v. *Kennedy* was distinguished in *L* v. *Kennedy*[48a] in which it was held that the Court of Session could, in the exercise of the *nobile officium*, order that a new hearing before the sheriff take place to determine whether the grounds of referral exist. The circumstances which had arisen in *L* v. *Kennedy* were exceptional and unforeseeable. A greater understanding had evolved since the original decision of the sheriff of the techniques for interviewing children in sexual abuse cases, and new medical evidence had come to light which cast doubt on the original finding that the grounds of referral were established.

CONSIDERATION AND DISPOSAL OF THE CASE BY THE HEARING

If grounds for referral are accepted or established, the children's hearing should proceed to a consideration of these grounds, the social background report which the local authority is obliged to furnish and such other relevant information including other reports as may be available; and, in discussion with the child, unless he is incapable of participating, his parent and any representative, and any safeguarder appointed under section 34A of the Act, they should consider on what course they should decide in the child's best interests.[48b] Three main options are open to the hearing:

> (a) to disharge the referral;
> (b) to continue the case to a subsequent hearing;
> (c) to make a supervision requirment.

The first of these options is appropriate where the hearing decides that no further action is required[49]; the second where it considers that further investigation in relation to the child and his history is necessary to complete the consideration of the case[50]; and the third where it decides that the child is in need of compulsory measures of care.[51] Where a case is continued for further investigation, the

---

[48] *Kennedy* v. *R's Curator ad Litem* 1993 S.L.T. 295.
[48a] June 18, 1993; July 15, 1993 (LEXIS).
[48b] s. 43(1); Children's Hearings (Scotland) Rules 1986 (S.I. 1986 No. 2291), rr. 19(2)(c) and 21(3)(b).
[49] s. 43(2).
[50] s. 43(3).
[51] s. 44(1).

child may be required to attend or reside at any clinic, hospital or establishment during a period not exceeding 21 days, and if he fails to fulfil that requirement, the reporter must arrange a hearing to consider the issue of a warrant for his detention.[52] The chairman is required to inform the child and his parents of the substance of any report provided that he considers that disclosure would not be detrimental to the interests of the child,[53] but there is no provision for resolution of disputes on the factual basis of reports. Ascertainment of facts as well as expression of opinion is, however, in so far as relevant to his report, within the province of the compiler of the report and the hearing is, it is submitted, entitled, if it thinks fit, to accept his findings as to the facts even if these have been challenged. Where, however, challenge raises doubts as to the accuracy of the report on an important matter, further investigation will be appropriate and, in any event, a hearing ought not to proceed on factual contents of a report that are inconsistent with grounds of referral accepted or established.

There has been some doubt as to the scope of the matter which a hearing is entitled to take into account in deciding whether a child is in need of compulsory measures of care and on the consequent disposal. In *K* v. *Finlayson*[54] it was contended on behalf of the reporter that, once the grounds of referral had been accepted or established, "the hearing then has absolute power to take any steps they considered to be in the child's best interests—and without having any further regard to any limitation in their discussion." The sheriff[55] held however that, where a ground of referral had been disputed and established, the hearing were bound to interpret the relevant statutory condition for the application of compulsory measures of care in the context of what had been held by the court to be established and were not entitled to look at other matters.[56] A decision of a hearing based on any grounds other than those accepted or established was, in her opinion, *ultra vires* of its powers.[57] It seems that the sheriff meant not merely that the hearing could not rely on facts which would appropriately have formed the subject-matter of an entirely different ground for referral involving another condition, but that it was illegitimate for the hearing to have regard to any facts and circumstances not stated in grounds of referral accepted or established. That view and the reporter's contention are both, it is submitted, somewhat extreme. The difficulty stems from some ambiguity in the statute about the role, in decisions on disposal, of the "grounds of referral" on the one hand and the wider aspects of the child's "case" on the other. At times the grounds of referral are stressed. Thus where the child and his parent accept grounds in part, the hearing is empowered if it considers it proper to proceed "in respect of the grounds so accepted"[58]; where a sheriff decides that none of the grounds has been established he discharges the referral "in respect of those grounds"[59] (leav-

---

[52] s. 43(4) and (5).
[53] Children's Hearings (Scotland) Rules 1986, rr. 19(3) and 21(4).
[54] 1974 S.L.T. (Sh. Ct.) 51: for comment and criticism see Grant, "More Bridges, but More Gaps," 1974 S.L.T. (News) 213.
[55] Isabel L. Sinclair, Q.C.
[56] at p. 53.
[57] at p. 54.
[58] s. 42(2)(*b*).
[59] s. 42(5).

ing, as already noted, the hearing to proceed in respect of the grounds, if any, which were accepted); and a hearing proceeds to consider on what course it should decide in the best interests of the child only after having considered *inter alia* "the grounds for the referral of a case, accepted or established."[60] On the other hand, where the sheriff is satisfied that any of the grounds has been established, it is the child's "case" that he remits for consideration and determination by a hearing[61] and it is after consideration of his "case" that a hearing may come to a decision that a child is in need of compulsory measures of care.[62] Facts unnecessary to ground the referral may, nonetheless, be relevant to a consideration of the child's case. If that were not so, the requirement that the hearing consider the social background report supplied by the local authority and such other relevant information as may be available[63] to them and the power given to continue a case for further investigation in relation to the child and his history[64] would scarcely be intelligible. The policy of the Act is that the hearing should explore what is in the interests of the child free from any narrow constraints. *K* v. *Finlayson* was disapproved by the First Division in *O* v. *Rae*,[65] in which Lord President Hope, speaking for the court, said:

> "The information to which [the hearing] must have regard in terms of s. 43(1) includes the grounds of referral accepted or established, but it may extend well beyond what may have been stated in these grounds. This is because the hearing must have regard also to a report obtained from the local authority under s. 39(4) on the child and his social background. As that subsection points out, this report may contain information from any such person as the reporter or the local authority may think fit. Furthermore they are entitled, in terms of s. 43(1), to have regard to 'such other relevant information as may be available to them.' [Counsel for the appellants] said that this information must be confined to information which was relevant to the grounds for the referral, but in our opinion that interpretation is not consistent with the express purpose of the subsection. Its purpose is to enable the children's hearing to consider what is in the best interests of the child. The test of relevancy in this context, therefore, is whether the information is relevant to a consideration of what course should be taken in the child's best interests."[66]

Nevertheless the grounds of referral have a central role. "While they [the hearing] have reports and submissions before them, the hard core of the material upon which their decision is based is the grounds of referral."[67] The grounds of referral should not be set in antithesis to the child's case or divorced from it. They are the grounds for referral "of the case." They indicate what the case referred is and if the hearing takes account of matters which have no substantial

---

[60] s. 43(1).
[61] s. 42(6).
[62] s. 44(1).
[63] s. 43(1).
[64] s. 43(3).
[65] 1992 S.C.L.R. 318.
[66] *Ibid.* at p. 323.
[67] *Kennedy* v. *B*, 1973 S.L.T. 38, *per* Lord Justice-Clerk Grant at p. 40.

connection with the grounds of referral accepted or established, or, *a fortiori*, elements of the grounds of referral that the sheriff has found not established,[68] it embarks on a consideration of what is essentially a different case. In that way the grounds of referral control the hearing's consideration but, within the limits as indicated, the hearing is free to explore all matters connected with the case and so take into account a wide range of facts and circumstances which are not detailed in, but flow from, or are related to, the grounds of referral. Moreover, facts and circumstances which are purely dispositive in character, in that they have no relevance to any ground on which the case was or might have been referred but bear only on the appropriate form of disposal, may be taken into account without restriction.

As a consequence of the grounds of referral being central to the hearing's consideration, an appeal by the reporter from a sheriff's finding that one or more grounds has not been established while another ground has been is not in any sense of the word "academic." The hearing is required by section 43(1) to consider the grounds of referral accepted or established in order to come to a decision as to what is best for the child. It is in light of that, and any reports obtained under section 39(4), that they proceed to consider how to dispose of the case of the child.[69] Likewise an application may be made to the sheriff to determine some incident of the ground, even although the ground itself is accepted, whenever that incident would be relevant to the subsequent disposal of the case. So in *M* v. *Kennedy*[70] the ground of referral (that the child had been the victim of unlawful sexual intercourse) was accepted by the parents, which was sufficient to allow the children's hearing to act, but an application was made to the sheriff to determine whether the unlawful act had taken place in the family home, since this was not accepted by the parents but would strongly influence the appropriate disposal of the case by the children's hearing.

Criteria of Decisions

Although the hearing is directed to consider on what course they should decide in the best interests of the child,[71] that direction relates in its terms only to decisions that no further action is required or that the case should be continued for further investigation. There is no explicit direction on the criteria to be employed in deciding that a child is in need of compulsory measures of care other than those inherent in that concept—*i.e.* the child is in need of protection, control, guidance and treatment.[72] "The scheme of the Act," however, "is the search for a solution which will be in the best interests of the delinquent child and other children in need of care,"[73] and there is no doubt that it is such a solution which the hearing must seek and which must guide its decision on this as on other matters. What is in the interests of the child will usually be the determining, and should never be a subordinate, consideration. It does not, however, follow that it

---

[68] *M* v. *Kennedy*, 1993 S.L.T. 431.
[69] *Per* Lord Justice-Clerk Ross in *Harris* v. *F*, 1991 S.L.T. 242 at p. 246F.
[70] *Supra*.
[71] s. 43(1).
[72] s. 32(3).
[73] *McGregor* v. *D*, 1977 S.C. 330, *per* Lord President Emslie at p. 336. *Cf. McGregor* v. *T and Anr.*, 1975 S.L.T. 76 at p. 82.

is the sole consideration and in some circumstances there may be need to reconcile the child's interests with other claims. Any other claim can, however, be
taken into account only as an aspect of the child's need for protection, control,
guidance and treatment and so conflict with the child's interest is likely to be
avoided. A child who has committed an offence (to take the strongest example,
although others do suggest themselves, *e.g.* where the child is beyond the control of his parents) may, however, be in need of control, not only in his own interests but in the interests of the protection of the public, and there is nothing in
the Act that excludes the latter factor from influencing the form which supervision should take.

Disposal other than Discharge: Supervision Requirements

Where, after consideration of the case, a hearing decides that the child is in
need of compulsory measures of care, it may make a supervision requirement.[74]
The form of words is apt to the conferment of a discretionary power but, as there
is no other measure that the hearing can take consistently with its decision that
the child is in need of compulsory measures of care, the effect is mandatory. The
supervision requirement may take one of two forms:

(a) requiring the child to submit to supervision in accordance with such
conditions as the hearing may impose, or

(b) requiring the child to reside in a residential establishment named in the
requirement and be subject to such conditions as the hearing may
impose.

A condition imposed by virtue of head (a) may be a condition as to the place,
other than a residential establishment, where the child is to reside and that place
may be in England or Wales where arrangements have been made in that behalf.[75] The reason for having two separate forms of requirement is at first sight
elusory but can be traced to a need to differentiate in the enforcement procedures applicable where a child absconds from the control of a person under
whose control he has been placed by virtue of a condition of a supervision requirement on the one hand, and from a residential establishment on the other.[76]
In making a supervision requirement requiring a child to reside in a residential
establishment, the hearing must have regard to the religious persuasion of the
child.[77] There is no such stipulation where a residential condition under head (a)
is imposed. A supervision requirement takes effect as from the date it is made
unless the hearing, where satisfied that such a course is proper, postpones its operation.[78] Where it appears to the hearing that the functions of the education authority relating to the ascertainment of handicapped children[79] may require to be

---

[74] s. 44(1).
[75] s. 44(1).
[76] See *post* at pp. 488–489. It has been thought necessary to make provision for interim detention
and consideration by a children's hearing if the person under whose control the child had been
placed was unwilling or unable to receive him back, but unnecessary to make such provision in
the case of a child being returned to a residential establishment.
[77] s. 44(2).
[78] s. 44(3).
[79] Education (Scotland) Act 1980, s. 60, as substituted by s. 4 of the Education (Scotland) Act 1981.

exercised, it must, in addition to any other course which it may take, send a re-port to that effect to the authority.[80] There may be circumstances in which it is appropriate in this connection to impose a condition that the child reside or at-tend an establishment providing special education but, as a rule, that will be jus-tified only after the assessment procedures of the education authority have been carried out. Where a hearing is of the opinion that an application for admission to hospital, or a guardianship application under Part V of the Mental Health (Scotland) Act 1984 should be made, it must make a report to that effect to the mental health officer concerned.[81]

The conditions attached to a supervision requirement may include provisions relating to access to the child by the parent. The parent's legal right of access is inhibited by and during the currency of the supervision requirement, and if dis-cretion to determine access is given to the local authority in whose residential care the child is put, a parent cannot claim access by any common law form of action.[82] However, it is competent for the parent to raise the question of access when the supervision requirement is reviewed.[83]

Implementation of Supervision Requirement

The carrying of supervision requirements into effect is entrusted to the local authority for the hearing's area[84] and for some purposes, including the assump-tion of parental rights and powers, a child subject to a supervision requirement is treated as being in the local authority's care.[85] Where for any of these pur-poses the performance of a function requires or would be facilitated by the vari-ation or discharge of the supervision requirement, the proper course is for the local authority to recommend a review.[86] There are some disadvantages in the placing of the duty to carry out the requirement on local authorities. There is a weakening of control by the hearing in that those responsible for the imple-mentation of the requirement are not directly answerable to it. While there is no difficulty in the placing of children in residential establishments managed by voluntary bodies, as these are in some degree subject to local authority supervi-sion,[87] there is a disincentive to the use of other voluntary agencies. Where, on the other hand, a placement is made with, or caring functions entrusted to, a vol-untary agency or private individual, or even where the child is placed in a resid-ential establishment managed by a voluntary organisation, problems may thereby be created for the effective discharge by the local authority of its duties. Such problems are mitigated in cases of urgent necessity by the power given to the Director of Social Work to direct in the interests of the child or of the other children in a place, that a child required to reside in that place be transferred elsewhere.[88] The power is personal to the director with the consequence that a

---

[80] s. 44(4).
[81] s. 46(1), as amended by the Mental Health (Scotland) Act 1984, Sched. 3, para. 16.
[82] *D* v. *Strathclyde Regional Council*, 1985 S.L.T. 114.
[83] *Kennedy* v. *A*, 1986 S.L.T. 358. On review, see *post* at pp. 486–487.
[84] s. 44(5).
[85] See *ante* at p. 420, note 20.
[86] See *post* at pp. 486–487.
[87] See *post* at pp. 504–508.
[88] s. 44(6).

direction given by anyone else other than his deputy is invalid. As the interests of the child, under the supervision requirement, and of the other children are alternatives, the power may be exercised where the interests of the child and the other children conflict provided it is in the interests either of the child or the other children for this to be done and provided, as always, there is urgent necessity. The reference to "place" is wide enough to cover any location in which the child is required to reside under the supervision requirement including his own home and it is immaterial whether or not he is actually residing there. No means, however, is provided for enforcing a direction if the place is outwith the control or supervision of the local authority. Where a transfer is made under this power, the child's case must be reviewed within seven days.[89]

Cessation or Variation of Supervision Requirement

It is consistent with the caring purposes for which supervision requirements are designed that they should not be of a determinate duration. The intention is that a child should remain under supervision so long as his need for care so requires.[90] The Act contains, however, no positive stipulation for determining that need. The matter is, instead, expressed negatively. No child shall continue to be subject to a supervision requirement for any time longer than is necessary in his interest.[91] Accordingly, where a local authority considers that a requirement should cease to have effect, or should be varied, it should refer the case to the reporter for review of the requirement by a children's hearing. On such a review, the hearing, if it thinks it proper, may terminate the requirement or continue or vary it. In the event of variation, the requirement as varied may take any form competent under the Act.[92] In addition a supervision requirement ceases to have effect when the child attains the age of 18 years[93] or, if it is not reviewed, within the period of one year from its making, or, if it has already been reviewed, from its continuation.[94] Within three months, ending on the day on which a child subject to a supervision requirement attains the age of 18 years, the local authority concerned must refer the case to the reporter so that a hearing may advise whether the child still requires supervision or guidance. In the event of the hearing so advising, the local authority is obliged to provide such supervision or guidance as the child is prepared to accept.[95] The Secretary of State may at any time terminate a supervision requirement if he is satisfied, having regard to all the circumstances of the case and the interests of the child, that that should be done.[96]

Review of Supervision Requirement

The hearing's control over the operation of supervision requirements is maintained by the provisions for review. As the decision of a hearing on review

---

[89] s. 44(7).
[90] See Report of the Kilbrandon Committee (Cmnd. 2306 (1964)), Chap. IX, para. 197.
[91] s. 47(1).
[92] Ibid.
[93] s. 47(2).
[94] s. 48(3).
[95] s. 47(2).
[96] s. 52.

is, like other decisions of the hearing, open to appeal, a safeguard is at the same time provided against the oppressive continuance of supervision requirements. A supervision requirement must be reviewed:

(1) Where a local authority so recommends.[97] This general provision supplements the obligation, already noticed, put on a local authority to refer a case to the reporter so that a review may be carried out where the authority considers that a supervision requirement should cease to have effect or should be varied.

(2) Within a year of the making of the requirement or of a previous decision continuing the requirement after review.[98] The sanction for failure is that the requirement ceases to have effect. That result appears to be mandatory as the Act contains no provision for excuse or failure.

(3) At the request of the child or his parent after the expiration of (a) a period of three months from the date of the making of the supervision requirement or the date of a previous review where that review has varied the requirement, or (b) a period of six months from the date of a previous review which has continued the supervision requirement.[99] The six rather than the three-month limitation applies although the review at which the requirement was continued was at the request of the local authority.

It is the duty of the reporter to ensure that any review is duly made and to make any necessary arrangements.[1] He may arrange for the requirement to be reviewed in accordance with the above provisions during the period of nine months following the date when it was made or last reviewed.[2] The provisions of the Act on disposal other than by discharge apply to disposal on review as they do to an original disposal.[3] There is no express power to terminate the requirement except where the review results from a reference by a local authority,[4] but it is implicit that it may be allowed to lapse.

Implementation of Residential Requirement

Where as a result of the making or variation of a supervision requirement, a child is required to reside in a residential establishment or other place specified in the requirement, the local authority may, if it is unable forthwith to make arrangements for the child's reception in that establishment or place, arrange for the child to be temporarily accommodated in some other suitable place for any period not exceeding 21 days.[5] If these arrangements cannot be made before the expiry of the 21-day period, the local authority must, before the period expires, recommend to the reporter that a children's hearing review the supervision re-

---

[97] s. 48(2).
[98] s. 48(3).
[99] s. 48(4).
[1] s. 48(5).
[2] s. 48(4A), as amended by the Law Reform (Miscellaneous Provisions) (Scotland) Act 1985, s. 29.
[3] s. 48(6).
[4] Under s. 47(1).
[5] Reporter's Duties and Transmission of Information Etc. (Scotland) Rules 1971 (S.I. 1971 No. 525), r. 12(1).

quirement. In that event the reporter is obliged to arrange a children's hearing to sit to review the requirement as soon as may be and, in any event, before the expiry of seven days commencing on the date on which the recommendation was received. If the sitting of the children's hearing occurs after the expiry of the period of 21 days from the making or varying of the supervision requirement, that period is deemed to extend until the hearing sits.[6] It is the duty of the local authority to ensure that the child is conveyed to the place where he is required to reside and for that purpose the authority may place the child under the control of any person authorised by them.[7] The person who thus has control over the child has all the powers, protection and privileges of a constable so far as these are necessary for that control while he is conveying the child to the residential establishment or other place.[8] A child who absconds or is unlawfully taken away from that person's control may be arrested without warrant in any part of the United Kingdom or the Channel Islands[9] and then brought back to the person under whose control he had been placed.[10] It appears from the absence of any other relevant provision that these provisions are intended to cover the case of the child who *ab initio* refuses to surrender himself to, or is withheld by his parents or others from, the control of the person authorised by the local authority, but they are ill-expressed for that purpose.

Abscondment or Unlawful Removal of Child

Child Subject to a Supervision Requirement
   The above provisions on arrest and return of a child apply *mutatis mutandis* to a child who absconds or is unlawfully taken away from the control of a person under whose control he has been placed by a supervision requirement.[11] If the person under whose control he has been placed is unwilling or unable to receive the child, the child must be detained in a place of safety until he can be brought before a children's hearing for review of the supervision requirement. A hearing must meet for that purpose within a period of seven days from the date of the commencement of the detention of the child.

Child Subject to a Residential Requirement
   If a child who is required by a supervision requirement to reside in a residential establishment absconds or is unlawfully taken away[12] from the establishment, or from any hospital or other institution in which he is temporarily residing, or if he fails to return to the establishment at the end of a period of leave, he may be arrested without warrant in any part of the United Kingdom or the Channel Islands and brought back to the residential establishment, or, if he absconds from a hospital or other institution, to that institution.[13] Similarly if he

---

[6] *Ibid.*, r. 12(2).
[7] *Ibid.*, r. 13(1).
[8] *Ibid.*, r. 13(2).
[9] s. 69(1).
[10] s. 69(2).
[11] s. 69.
[12] s. 69(5).
[13] s. 70.

runs away, or is unlawfully taken away, from a person in whose charge he is during a period of leave, he may be arrested and brought back to that person.

Offences in Connection with Abscondment or Unlawful Removal

It is an offence knowingly to assist or induce or persistently attempt to induce a child so to act as to be liable to be brought back in pursuance of any of the provisions on abscondment or unlawful removal or to harbour or conceal a child who is so liable or to prevent him from returning.[14]

Transfer where Child or Parent moves to Other Part of United Kingdom

Where a children's hearing is satisfied that a child who is subject to a supervision requirement proposes to reside, or is residing, in England or Wales or Northern Ireland, the hearing may either discharge the requirement or send notification of the requirement to a juvenile court acting for the area in which the child proposes to reside or is residing.[15] In the latter event, the juvenile court may make a supervision order placing the child under the supervision of a probation officer for a period not exceeding one year beginning with the day on which notification was sent, and the requirement then ceases to have effect.[16] It is the duty of the reporter to ensure that all documents relating to the case or certified copies of them are transmitted to the juvenile court.[17] The juvenile court may proceed in the absence of the child or his parent, or both.[18]

Where a children's hearing is satisfied that the parent of a child who is required to reside in a residential establishment under a supervision requirement proposes to reside, or is residing, in England or Wales or Northern Ireland, it must review the requirement and on such review may, as it thinks proper,

(a) discharge the requirement, or

(b) continue the requirement, or

(c) vary the requirement so that the child is no longer required to reside in a residential establishment but instead is required to submit to supervision under such conditions as the hearing imposes, or

(d) make a report on the case to the Secretary of State with a recommendation for the transfer of the child to the care of the managers of an approved school in England or Wales or a training school in Northern Ireland.[19]

If the requirement is varied so that the child is no longer required to reside in a residential establishment, notification must be sent to the juvenile court for the area in which the child is to reside as noted above. Where a report is made to the Secretary of State, he may, if for any reason he is unable to accept the recommendation for transfer, refer the matter back to the children's hearing for their reconsideration or himself discharge the supervision requirement.[20] He may

---

[14] s. 71.
[15] s. 72(1).
[16] s. 72.
[17] s. 76(2).
[18] s. 76(1).
[19] s. 74(1).
[20] s. 74(2).

also, instead of transferring the child to an approved school or training school, commit him, if he thinks fit, to the care of the local authority or in Northern Ireland of the welfare authority in whose area the parent of the child proposes to reside or is residing.[21] Where a child is transferred from a residential establishment in Scotland to any place in England or Wales or Northern Ireland, it is the duty of the local authority responsible for him to ensure his transfer to that place.[22]

APPEALS

Appeal to Sheriff[23]

Jurisdiction and Procedure

An appeal to the sheriff lies at the instance of the child or his parent or both but not of the reporter against any decision of a children's hearing.[24] The appeal must be taken within a period of three-weeks beginning with the date of the decision appealed against and is to be heard in chambers. The date of the hearing is to be included in the computation of the three week period with the result that it terminates at midnight on the 20th day after the date of the decision.[25] Despite the apparent generality of the words "any decision," appeals may be taken only against decisions disposing of a referral or reviewing a supervision requirement or on the issue or renewal of a warrant for apprehension or detention. Decisions that relate merely to steps in procedure may not be appealed. Accordingly there is no appeal against a direction to make an application to the sheriff for a finding as to whether the grounds of referral are established rather than to discharge the referral,[26] nor against a decision to dispense with the presence of the child.[27] A decision to discharge a referral is, however, an appealable decision[28]; and, although normally neither parent nor child would have an interest or wish to appeal such a decision, cases are conceivable, especially where there is a conflict of interest between parent and child, in which the child, in particular, might competently use the appellate process to secure the protection of compulsory measures of care which the hearing, by a decision to discharge the referral, had denied him; and a parent might likewise seek such measures where a child was beyond his control. Appeals against decisions taken after remit from the sheriff on disposal of a previous appeal are subject to a seven-day limit.[29] An appeal in respect of the issue of a warrant must be disposed of within three days of the

---

[21] s. 74(3).

[22] s. 76(3).

[23] See Kearney, at pp. 299–344.

[24] s. 49(1).

[25] *S Applicants*, 1979 S.L.T. (Sh. Ct.) 37.

[26] *H* v. *McGregor*, 1973 S.C. 95.

[27] See Thomson, "*Sloan* v. *B*—The Legal Issues," 1991 S.L.T. (News) 421 at p. 423, who suggests that such a decision might be challenged by means of a judicial review of the hearing's decision. But see *R* v. *Kennedy*, March 26, 1993 (LEXIS).

[28] *H* v. *McGregor*, *supra* at p. 100, *per* Lord Wheatley.

[29] s. 51(2).

lodging of the appeal and if that is not done the warrant forthwith ceases to have effect.[30]

The Act provides that the child, or his parent, or both, shall be heard as to the reasons for the appeal.[31] The correct interpretation of that is, it is submitted, that both must be heard if they so wish. The sheriff again has a duty and power to consider and arrange separate representation for the child if there is or may be a conflict of interests.[32] It appears to be accepted that the reporter is the contradictor in an appeal,[33] and that is consistent with the right given to the reporter, acting on behalf of a children's hearing, to initiate an appeal from the sheriff's decision to the Court of Session.[34] If that is correct the reporter must also be heard. The duty is laid on the reporter of ensuring that all reports and statements available at the hearing, along with the reports of the proceedings and the reason for the decision of the hearing, are lodged with the sheriff clerk.[35] The duty of making, or causing to be made, a report of the hearing's decision and a statement in writing of the reasons for it is laid upon the chairman.[36] The statement of reasons must disclose the reasoning which influenced the hearing's decision and it is not sufficient merely to refer to the information and recommendations before, and the procedure at, the hearing, to state that the decision was taken on that basis.[37] The sheriff may examine the reporter and the authors or compilers of any reports or statements and may call for any further report which he considers may assist him in deciding the appeal.[38] Under that power there is no warrant for examining any member of the hearing other than the chairman, but it may sometimes be useful to do so and, although no means of compulsion are available, there is nothing in the Act which excludes it.

Disposal

Where the sheriff is satisfied that the decision of the hearing is not justified in all the circumstances of the case, he must allow the appeal[39]; otherwise he must hold that it has failed. There is said to be controversy about the scope of the ground on which a sheriff may reverse a hearing's decision, one view being that the matter is at large for the sheriff, the other that some error on the part of the hearing going beyond what may be the legitimate subject-matter of difference of opinion must be shown.[40] The former view derives some support from the powers of examination and of calling for further reports given to the sheriff and from the requirement that he be satisfied that the decision was not justified "in

---

[30] s. 49(7). "Three days" means three calendar days and not three court days: *B* v. *Kennedy*, 1992 S.L.T. 870 (2nd Div.).

[31] s. 49(1).

[32] See *ante* at pp. 469–470 and 474. Kearney at pp. 325–327.

[33] See the role placed by the reporter in *K* v. *Finlayson*, 1974 S.L.T. (Sh. Ct.) 51.

[34] s. 50(1). See *post* at pp. 492–493.

[35] s. 49(2).

[36] Children's Hearings (Scotland) Rules 1986, r. 9(3).

[37] *K* v. *Finlayson*, *supra* at p. 54.

[38] s. 49(3).

[39] s. 49(5).

[40] See Grant, "The Legal Safeguards for the Rights of the Child and Parents in the Children's Hearing System," 1975 J.R. 209.

all the circumstances of the case," but it is submitted that the latter view is to be preferred. In *D* v. *Sinclair*[41] Sheriff Mowat said:

> "a sheriff should not interfere with the determination simply because he felt another form of treatment might be preferable..... Accordingly, I consider that a sheriff should not allow an appeal unless there was some flaw in the procedure adopted by the hearing or he was satisfied that the hearing had not given proper consideration to some factor in the case."

The key is the words "not justified," as they appear in section 49(5). The sheriff cannot merely substitute his own opinion for that of the hearing but must, if the appeal is to be allowed, have some grounds on which the hearing's decision can justly be impugned.

Where the appeal fails, the sheriff confirms the decision of the hearing.[42] If the appeal is against the issue of a warrant and he allows the appeal, he must recall the warrant. In any other case in which an appeal is allowed, the sheriff may, as he thinks fit, remit the case with reasons for his decision to the children's hearing for reconsideration of their decision or discharge the child from any further hearing or other proceedings in relation to the grounds for referral.[43] Criminal proceedings arising out of the same *species facti* are not, it is submitted, "proceedings in relation to the grounds for referral."

Frivolous Appeals

Although decisions at the review of a supervision requirement are appealable, there is a risk that repeated appeals against such decisions might become an abuse. Accordingly, if the sheriff is satisfied that an appeal against the decision of the hearing at a review is frivolous, he may order that no appeal against a decision, made on a subsequent review, to continue the supervision requirement which was the subject of the appeal, shall lie until the expiration of a period of 12 months beginning with the date of the order.[44]

Effect of Pending Appeal

A supervision requirement, if made, remains in force pending an appeal unless the hearing, on the application of the child or parent, suspends it.[45] The considerations which militate against appeals from decisions on mere steps in procedure do not, in the main, apply to decisions not to suspend a requirement pending appeal and these are, it is submitted, themselves appealable.

Appeal to Court of Session[46]

An appeal on a point of law, or in respect of any irregularity in the conduct of the case, lies to the Court of Session from any decision of the sheriff.[47] The sher-

---

[41] 1973 S.L.T. (Sh. Ct.) 47 at p. 48.
[42] s. 49(4).
[43] s. 49(5).
[44] s. 49(6).
[45] s. 49(8).
[46] See Kearney, at pp. 347–361.
[47] s. 50(1).

iff's decisions, not only on applications for findings in relation to the grounds of referral but also on appeals from decisions of hearings, may therefore be brought under review in this way. Appeal is by way of stated case and may be at the instance of a child or his parent or both or of a reporter acting on behalf of a children's hearing. The application to the sheriff to state a case must be made within a period of 28 days beginning with the date of his decision.[48] On deciding the appeal, the Court of Session must remit the case to the sheriff for disposal in accordance with such directions as it may give.[49] It is specifically enacted that no appeal to the Court of Session shall lie in respect of a decision imposing a supervision requirement where the sole ground of objection is that the treatment prescribed is inappropriate for the child.[50] As such a question is essentially a question of fact, that provision is redundant. No other, or further, appeal is competent beyond the Court of Session.[51]

---

[48] s. 50(2).
[49] s. 50(3).
[50] s. 50(4).
[51] s. 50(1).

CHAPTER 18

FOSTERING AND TEMPORARY CARE OF CHILDREN

Scope of this Chapter

Previous chapters have examined how parental rights and powers are assumed and vested in local authorities or voluntary organisations,[1] in what circumstances compulsory measures of care can be exercised over children,[2] and how statutory (and other) relationships of care with children are created.[3] The chapters following this one will examine the creation of a new legal parent-child relationship through the process of adoption. This chapter is concerned with the control of temporary arrangements for the care and wellbeing of children, through fostering and other forms of temporary care. Fostering is always, and the temporary care may be, on a residential basis, but the law controls both that and the non-residential care of children.

This chapter will examine, first, private fostering arrangements, secondly different forms of local authority provision for the care of children (including fostering as an aspect thereof), and thirdly the controlled forms of non- residential child care, that is child minding and day care of young children.

PRIVATE FOSTERING OF CHILDREN

Introduction

Fostering may take one of two forms: (1) it may be the subject of private arrangement, or (2) it may be the means by which a local authority or voluntary organisation looks after children in its care. Each form is the subject of separate statutory regulation. In both cases it is convenient to speak of "foster children" and "foster parents," although in the case of private arrangements the relevant statute employs the term "foster child" but not "foster parent" while the reverse is true of the boarding-out of children by local authorities or voluntary organisations. Private arrangements will be considered immediately hereafter, while fostering as a feature of local authority care or care by voluntary organisations is considered later under the heading "Boarding Out of Children."[4]

Private arrangements for the care, on a residential but temporary or at least uncertain basis, of children by those who have no parental rights in relation to the child, hereinafter referred to as "fostering," are governed by the Foster Children (Scotland) Act 1984.[5] Before 1968, the legislation dealing with the fostering of children had been concerned with the control of fostering only where it was undertaken for reward. That concern had its origin in the gross abuses asso-

---

[1] *Ante*, Chap. 16.
[2] *Ante*, Chap. 17.
[3] *Ante*, Chap. 15.
[4] *Post* at pp. 503–504.
[5] This Act consolidates legislation, most of which was previously contained in the Children Act 1958, as amended. The 1958 Act was repealed by the 1984 Act.

ciated in the nineteenth century with "baby farming." Experience had, however, shown that abuses might arise even where the care of a child is undertaken without reward or provision for reward. Moreover, difficulties might often occur in ascertaining whether or not there was an element of reward in a fostering arrangement. The Social Work (Scotland) Act 1968[6] remedied these defects by removing most of the references to reward. The only remaining relevance of "reward" is that a person who maintains a foster child for reward is deemed for the purposes of the Life Assurance Act 1774 to have no interest in the life of the child (with the result that any policy taken out by him on the life of the child is void).[7]

Meaning of "Foster Child"

A "foster child," within the meaning of the Foster Children (Scotland) Act 1984, is a child below the upper limit of compulsory school age whose care is undertaken by a person who is not a relative or guardian of the child.[8] "Relative" means a grandparent, brother, sister, uncle or aunt, whether of the full blood or half blood or by affinity, and includes, where the child is illegitimate, the father of the child and any person who would be a relative if the child were the legitimate child of his mother and father.[9] "Guardian" is not defined, but, in the absence of indication to the contrary, may be taken to mean a person who has the right of guardianship under the Law Reform (Parent and Child) (Scotland) Act 1986.[10] This definition of "foster child" is wide and would, if unqualified, embrace many who would not in ordinary usage be so described. It is, however, qualified in a number of respects. First, a child is not a foster child for the purpose of the statutory provisions at present under consideration while he is in the care of a local authority or a voluntary organisation or is boarded out by an education authority.[11] Secondly, a child is not a foster child:

(1) while he is in the care[12] of any person[13]
  (a) in premises in which any parent, adult relative or guardian of his is, for the time being, residing;

---

[6] Sched. 1, para. 2(1), amending the Children Act 1958, s. 2(1).

[7] Foster Children (Scotland) Act 1984, s. 18.

[8] Foster Children (Scotland) Act 1984, s. 1, as amended by the Children Act 1989, Sched. 12, para. 41.

[9] *Ibid.* s. 21(1). The reference to the father of an illegitimate child would be removed if Parliament legislated along the lines suggested by the Scottish Law Commission to give full parental responsibilities and rights to all fathers and all mothers: see Scot. Law Com. No. 135, *Report on Family Law*, (May 1992), para. 2.50 and draft Bill, Sched. 2.

[10] See *ante*, Chaps. 13 and 14. Any other definition of "guardian", such as is found, for example, in s. 94 of the Social Work (Scotland) Act 1968, would require express statutory authority.

[11] Foster Children (Scotland) Act 1984, s. 2(1). Education authorities in England and Wales appear to be contemplated. The provision for children in care covers children boarded-out by Scottish local authorities.

[12] Care is undertaken when it is in fact provided but the continuity of a period of care is not interrupted by a weekend break spent at the parents' home: *Surrey County Council* v. *Battersby* [1965] 2 Q.B. 194.

[13] Foster Children (Scotland) Act 1984, s. 2(2).

(b) in any residential establishment within the meaning of the Social Work (Scotland) Act 1968[14];

(c) in any school within the meaning of the Education (Scotland) Act 1980 (where, however, a child below the upper limit of the compulsory school age resides, during school holidays, in a school other than a local authority school for a period exceeding one month, he is, for most purposes of the Act, a foster child[15]);

(d) in any hospital or in any nursing home registered, or exempt from registration, under the Nursing Homes Registration (Scotland) Act 1938;

(e) in any home or institution maintained by a public or local authority.

(f) if he has been in that person's care for a period of less than 28 days and that person does not intend to undertake his care for any longer period.[16] The effect of this is that, subject to the other qualifications, a child falls into the category of a foster child if his care is undertaken by another person for 28 days or more. Control of foster parents, and thus protection of foster children, is available before the completion of 28 days if the foster parent's intention is to care for the child beyond that time. Otherwise the provisions of the Act do not apply, so preserving the general policy that casual short-term arrangements should not be subject to local authority supervision.

(2) while he is in the care of any person in compliance with a supervision order within the meaning of the Children and Young Persons Act 1969 in England and Wales, or a supervision requirement (under Part III of the Social Work (Scotland) Act 1968), or a probation order.[17]

(3) while he is liable to be detained, or subject to guardianship, under the Mental Health (Scotland) Act 1984.[18]

(4) while he is placed in the care and possession of prospective adopters under arrangements made by an adoption agency, or is a protected child within the meaning of section 32 of the Adoption (Scotland) Act 1978.[19]

The Child's Age

Although it is only children below the upper limit of compulsory school age who come within the statutory definition of "foster child," a child who is already a foster child and who has attained that age will remain subject to the protection of the Act unless (a) he would, apart from the age limit, have ceased to be a foster child; or (b) he has reached the age of 18; or (c) he is living elsewhere than with the person with whom he was living when he attained the upper age limit.[20]

---

[14] *i.e.* an establishment by whomsoever managed which provides residential accommodation for the purposes of the 1968 Act: Social Work (Scotland) Act 1968, s. 94(1).
[15] Foster Children (Scotland) Act 1984, s. 16.
[16] para. (f) was substituted by the Children Act 1989, Sched. 12, para. 42.
[17] Foster Children (Scotland) Act 1984, s. 2(3).
[18] *Ibid.*, s. 2(4).
[19] *Ibid.*, s. 2(5).
[20] *Ibid.*, s. 17.

Disqualification

Unless the disqualifying fact has been disclosed to the local authority and their written consent obtained, no-one may maintain a foster child if[21]

(a) an order has been made against him under the Foster Children (Scotland) Act 1984 or the Foster Children Act 1980 removing a child from his care;

(b) a child has been removed from his care by virtue of an order made under the Children and Young Persons legislation[22] or a supervision requirement made under the Social Work (Scotland) Act 1968;

(c) he has been convicted of any of certain specified offences against children and young persons,[23] or has been placed on probation or discharged absolutely or conditionally for any such offence;

(d) his parental rights and powers with respect to a child have been vested in a local authority[24];

(e) a local authority has made an order under the Nurseries and Child-Minders Regulation Act 1948[25] refusing or cancelling his registration under the Act or the registration of any premises occupied by him;

(f) an order has been made under any of the Adoption Acts[26] for the removal of a protected child who was being kept or was about to be received by him; or

(g) he is disqualified from fostering a child privately, within the meaning of the Children Act 1989, by regulations made under section 68 of that Act.[27]

The disqualification extends to any person living in the same premises as the person disqualified or in premises at which he is employed.[28] Any disqualified person who maintains a foster child commits an offence,[29] but it is a defence for anyone disqualified by virtue of living in premises in which a disqualified person lives or is employed to show that he did not know and had no reasonable ground for believing that a disqualification applied to that person.[30]

Visiting of Foster Children

The duty is laid upon the local authority of securing the welfare of foster children within their area.[31] Presence within the area is sufficient to give rise to the duty and there is no additional residential or other qualification. In order to fulfil

---

[21] *Ibid.*, s. 7, as amended by the Children Act 1989, Sched. 12, para. 43.

[22] Children and Young Persons Acts 1933 and 1969 or the Children and Young Persons (Scotland) Act 1937.

[23] Specified in Sched. 1 to the Criminal Procedure (Scotland) Act 1975, or in the corresponding statutory provisions for England and Wales (Children and Young Persons Act 1933, Sched. 1).

[24] Under s. 16 of the Social Work (Scotland) Act 1968 or under s. 2 of the Children Act 1948 or ss. 2 or 3 of the Child Care Act 1980.

[25] s. 1(3) or (4) or s. 5.

[26] Adoption Act 1958, s. 43; Adoption (Scotland) Act 1978, s. 34; Adoption Act 1976, s. 34.

[27] Sched. 15 of the Children Act 1989 repeals many of the English statutory provisions mentioned above. Orders made under them remain valid.

[28] Foster Children (Scotland) Act 1984, s. 7(2).

[29] *Ibid.*, s. 15(1)(c).

[30] *Ibid.*, s. 15(2).

[31] *Ibid.*, s. 3(1).

their duty, the local authority are required to cause the children to be visited from time to time by their officers where they consider such a course to be necessary or expedient. The officers making such visits are required to give such advice as to care and maintenance as may appear to be necessary.[32] Regulations[33] provide that a foster child is to be visited within one week of the placement or within one week of notice being given to the local authority under section 5(2),[34] and thereafter (i) in the case of a child who has lived with the foster parent for less than one year at intervals of not more than three months, (ii) in any other case at intervals of not more than six months, (iii) and in all cases on such occasions as the local authority consider necessary.

It is an offence to refuse to allow the visiting of any foster child by a duly authorised officer of a local authority,[35] and such refusal affords reasonable cause for suspicion of assault, ill-treatment or neglect, or of the commission of a scheduled offence so as to give grounds on which a warrant may be issued.[36]

Notification

By Prospective Foster Parents

A prerequisite of the discharge by the local authority of its duty in relation to foster children is that it should have sufficient knowledge of private fostering arrangements. Accordingly, anyone who proposes to maintain as a foster child a child not already in his care is required to give written notice not less than two weeks before he receives the child unless he receives him in an emergency.[37] The notice must be given to the local authority in whose area the premises in which the child is to be kept are situated and must specify these premises.[38] If a foster child is received in an emergency, the foster parent must give written notice not later than one week after reception.[39] Similarly, anyone who has in his care a child previously outwith the statutory definition of a foster child who becomes a foster child (e.g. if there has been a parent, or adult relative, or guardian residing in the premises and he leaves) must give written notice not later than one week after that event. The duty to give notice does not apply if the child has within the last three months been maintained as a foster child by the same foster parent but ceased to be a foster child while in his care or on removal from his care.[40]

By Foster Parents

Certain additional duties of notification are laid on foster parents. If there is a permanent change of address, or of the premises in which a foster child is kept, written notice must be given not less than two weeks before or, in the case of

---

[32] *Ibid.*, s. 3(2).

[33] Foster Children (Private Fostering) (Scotland) Regulations 1985 (S.I. 1985 No. 1798), reg. 7.

[34] *Post* at pp. 498–500.

[35] Foster Children (Scotland) Act 1984, s. 15(1)(*b*)(i).

[36] *Ibid.*, s. 13 and Criminal Procedure (Scotland) Act 1975, ss. 14 and 323.

[37] Foster Children (Scotland) Act 1984, s. 5(1).

[38] *Ibid.*, s. 5(3).

[39] *Ibid.*, s. 5(2).

[40] *Ibid.*, s. 5(6).

emergency, not later than one week after the change.[41] The new address or premises must be specified. The notice must be given to the local authority for the area in which the premises in which the child was kept before the change were situated. If, however, the new premises are in the area of another local authority, the authority to which notice was given must pass on such particulars as are known to it of the name, sex and date and place of birth of the child and the name and address of every person who is a parent or guardian, or acts as a guardian, of the child, or from whom the child was received. Any person maintaining or proposing to maintain a foster child is required to furnish these particulars so far as known to him, at the request of the local authority.[42] Written notice must be given within 48 hours of the death of a foster child or of his removal from the care of the foster parent, and that notice must be given to the person from whom the child was received as well as to the local authority. It must state, if known, the name and address of the person, if any, into whose care the child has been removed or received. The duty to give such notice applies in cases where the child removes himself as well as to cases where he is taken away by another but it does not apply if, on removal, the child ceases to be a foster child. In the latter event the foster parent must, however, at the request of the local authority, give them the same particulars as would have been required to be stated in the notice.[43]

By Parents

As well as the statutory obligation on foster parents to notify the local authority, Regulations[44] also provide that, except in an emergency, the parent of a child whom it is proposed will become a foster child must give notice of the proposed fostering to the local authority in whose area the premises in which the child is to be kept are situated not less than two weeks before the date on which the child becomes a foster child.[45] Where a child is placed with a foster parent in an emergency, or becomes a foster child while in the care and possession of a person with whom he has been placed, the parent of the child must give notice thereof to the local authority in whose area the premises in which the child is to be kept are situated not later than one week after the child is placed with the foster parent or becomes a foster child.[46] The notice must specify in writing the premises in which the child is to be or is being kept, and the local authority may require any additional information it considers necessary to determine whether the placement is or will be appropriate to the child's needs.[47] "Parent" in this context includes a guardian or relative of the child who has care and possession of the child and who is proposing to place the child with a foster parent.

Exemptions and Offences

A local authority may exempt anyone from the duty of giving notice. The ex-

---

[41] *Ibid.*, s. 5(4).
[42] *Ibid.*, s. 5(5).
[43] *Ibid.*, s. 6.
[44] Made under the Foster Children (Scotland) Act 1984, s. 4.
[45] Foster Children (Private Fostering) (Scotland) Regulations 1985 (S.I. 1985 No. 1798), reg. 3(1).
[46] *Ibid.*, reg.3(2).
[47] *Ibid.*, reg.3(3).

emption may be granted as regards all or any such notices for a specified period and may be revoked at any time by notice in writing.[48] It is an offence for anyone to fail to give notice or information or to fail to give the notice timeously or to fail to give the information within a reasonable time, or knowingly to make or to cause or procure another to make any false or misleading statement in the notice or information.[49] It is also an offence to cause to be published or knowingly to publish an advertisement indicating that a person will undertake or will arrange for the care and maintenance of a child which does not state that person's name and address.[50]

Requirements and Prohibitions

Where anyone keeps or proposes to keep foster children in premises used, while the children are kept there, wholly or mainly for that purpose, the local authority may impose on him requirements as to:

(a) the number, age and sex of the foster children who may be kept at any one time on the premises or any part thereof;

(b) the accommodation and equipment to be provided for the children;

(c) the medical arrangements to be made for protecting the health of the children;

(d) the giving of particulars of the person for the time being in charge of the children;

(e) the number, qualifications or experience of the persons employed in looking after the children;

(f) the keeping of records.[51]

These requirements must, after such time as the authority may specify, be complied with whenever a foster child is kept on the premises. Requirements imposed under (b) to (f) above may, however, be limited by the authority so as to apply only if the number of foster children kept on the premises exceeds a specified number.[52] If, within the specified time, a requirement is not complied with, the local authority may prohibit the keeping of foster children in the premises thereafter.[53]

Under the above provisions a prohibition is competent only after a requirement has been imposed and there has been failure to comply with it within the time specified. Where foster children are already being kept in the premises, that is the only way in which a prohibition can be made against keeping these children there. In the case, however, of a child who is not already kept as a foster child in the premises, the local authority may, without the necessity of imposing any requirements in advance, prohibit the keeping of that child there as a foster child if it is of the opinion that it would be detrimental to the child to be kept there by the person proposing to do so.[54] Similarly, if the premises are not for the

---

[48] Foster Children (Scotland) Act 1984, ss. 5(7) and 6(4).
[49] *Ibid.*, s. 15(1)(*a*).
[50] *Ibid.*, ss. 14 and 15(1)(*f*).
[51] *Ibid.*, s. 9(1).
[52] *Ibid.*, s. 9(2).
[53] *Ibid.*, s. 10(2).
[54] *Ibid.*, s. 10(1).

time being used for the keeping of a foster child by the person who proposes to keep a foster child there, a prohibition, on like grounds, may be made against keeping any foster child there.[55] It is to be noted that the question of detriment to the child is to be considered in relation not only to the premises but also to the foster parent. Both the physical suitability of the premises and the capacity and resources of the foster parent to care for a child there may therefore be taken into account.

Any requirement or prohibition must be imposed by a notice in writing addressed to the person on whom it is imposed.[56] Failure to comply with a requirement or contravention of a prohibition is an offence.[57]

Inspection

The power to impose requirements and make prohibitions would be largely nugatory without a power of inspection; so any officer of a local authority authorised to visit foster children may inspect any premises in the area of the authority in which foster children are to be, or are being kept.[58] He must, if asked to do so, produce a document showing his authorisation. The document must be duly authenticated, but the manner of authentication is not specified. It is an offence to refuse to allow inspection[59] and such refusal affords grounds for the issue of a warrant on the same basis and with the same effect as refusal to allow a foster child to be visited.[60]

Appeal Against Requirement or Prohibition

Within 14 days from the date on which he was notified of a requirement or prohibition an aggrieved person may appeal to the sheriff.[61] Where the appeal is against a requirement, the requirement shall not have effect while the appeal is pending. The notice of a requirement or prohibition must contain a statement informing the person to whom it is directed of his right to appeal and of the time within which he may do so. If the court allows the appeal it may, instead of cancelling the requirement or prohibition, vary it or allow more time for compliance, or, where an absolute prohibition has been imposed, substitute a prohibition against use of the premises, after a time specified by the court, unless there is compliance with such specified requirements as the local authority had power to impose. Any requirement or prohibition specified or substituted by the court shall be deemed for the purposes of the Act other than appeal to have been imposed by the local authority. In England and Wales provision is made for an appeal to the High Court,[62] but there is no Scottish provision for an appeal from the sheriff's decision. Such an appeal may, however, be open on

---

[55] *Ibid.*
[56] *Ibid.*, s. 10(3).
[57] *Ibid.*, s. 15(1)(*d*).
[58] *Ibid.*, s. 8.
[59] *Ibid.*, s. 15(1)(*b*)(ii).
[60] *Ante*, p. 498.
[61] Foster Children (Scotland) Act 1984, s. 11.
[62] Children Act 1989, s. 94.

principles already discussed,[63] even in the absence of express statutory provision, either to the sheriff principal or direct to the Court of Session.

Cancellation of Requirement or Prohibition

It has been specifically enacted for England and Wales that a local authority may, if it thinks fit, cancel, on the ground that it is no longer justified, a prohibition (other than a prohibition made in respect of non-compliance with a requirement) and may do so either of its own motion or on the application of the person on whom the prohibition was imposed.[64] There is no corresponding provision for Scotland. Accordingly, there can be no right to apply for a cancellation and no right to appeal against refusal to accede to an application for cancellation. It is thought, however, that the power to make a prohibition carries with it, as a facultative power, an implied power to revoke.

Removal of Foster Children

The sanctions attaching to the maintaining of foster children by disqualified persons and to non-compliance with requirements and contravention of prohibitions do not give any direct protection to the child. As has been noticed already, refusal to allow the visiting of a foster child, or the inspection of premises, may, however, give ground for a warrant to search for, and remove, the child. A child so removed may be kept in a place of safety within the meaning of the Social Work (Scotland) Act 1968.[65] Moreover, a warrant may, of course, be issued if circumstances justifying it appear when a visit or inspection is carried out. The statutory grounds for the issue of a warrant do not, however, embrace all the circumstances in which the removal of a child may be expedient for his protection. Provision is accordingly made that if a sheriff is satisfied on the complaint of a local authority that a foster child is being kept, or is about to be received (a) by any person who is unfit to have his care, or (b) in contravention of a disqualification imposed by the Act or of a prohibition from keeping foster children or a foster child imposed by a local authority, or (c) in any premises or any environment detrimental or likely to be detrimental to the child, he may make an order for removal of the child to a place of safety until he can be restored to a parent, relative or guardian, or until other arrangements can be made with respect to him.[66] On proof that there is imminent danger to the health or wellbeing of the child, the power to make such an order may be exercised by a justice of the peace acting on the application of a person authorised to visit foster children.[67] Where an order is made on the ground that a prohibition imposed by a local authority has been contravened, it may require the removal from the premises of all the foster children kept there.[68] It is an offence to refuse to comply with an order for the removal of any child or obstruct any person in the execution of such an order.[69] Any child removed under these provisions may be

---

[63] *Ante*, at pp. 440–441.
[64] Children Act 1989, s. 69(4).
[65] Social Work (Scotland) Act 1968, s. 94(1).
[66] Foster Children (Scotland) Act 1984, s. 12(1).
[67] *Ibid.*, s. 12(2).
[68] *Ibid.*, s. 12(3).
[69] *Ibid.*, s. 15(1)(*e*).

received into care by the local authority under section 15 of the Social Work (Scotland) Act 1968 whether or not the conditions otherwise applicable to reception into care are satisfied[70] and notwithstanding that the child appears to be over the age of 17.[71] In any event, the local authority must, if practicable, inform a parent or guardian of the child, or any person who acts as his guardian, of his removal.[72] Where a child has been detained in a place of safety and the reporter appointed under section 36 of the Social Work (Scotland) Act 1968 considers that he may be in need of compulsory measures of care the reporter must, wherever practicable, arrange a children's hearing to sit not later than in the course of the first lawful day after the commencement of the child's detention.[73] The implication must be that if the reporter does not consider that the child is in need of compulsory measures of care, detention in a place of safety should cease.

LOCAL AUTHORITY CARE

Boarding Out of Children

The only kind of fostering so far considered has been the private fostering arrangement. The term may, however, also be used to describe the boarding-out of children by local authorities and voluntary organisations. It is one of the ways in which a local authority may discharge their duty to provide accommodation and maintenance for children in their care.[74]

The Boarding Out and Fostering of Children Regulations 1985

The Social Work (Scotland) Act 1968 provides for the making of regulations regarding the boarding out of persons, including children, by local authorities and voluntary organisations. It is noteworthy and in contrast to the legislation on private fostering, which is applicable to a variety of residential arrangements including those in which the element of a domestic setting is lacking,[75] that the scope of the regulations here under consideration is confined to cases where the child lives as a member of the family of the person with whom he is boarded. Residential care by local authorities or voluntary organisations otherwise than by boarding in a domestic familial context is the subject of separate statutory treatment, considered shortly.[76]

The regulations,[77] which came into force on April 1, 1986, make provision for the appointment and composition of fostering panels,[78] whose functions are to consider the suitability of prospective foster parents and to make recommendations to the care authority[79] thereupon[80]; for the approval of foster parents by a care authority[81]; for the entering into agreements by the care authority with

---

[70] *Ante*, at pp. 420–426.
[71] *Ibid.*, s. 12(5).
[72] *Ibid.*, s. 12(6).
[73] Social Work (Scotland) Act 1968, s. 37(4).
[74] *Ibid.*, s. 21(1).
[75] *Ante*, at p. 494.
[76] *Post*, at pp. 504–508.
[77] The Boarding Out and Fostering of Children (Scotland) Regulations 1985 (S.I. 1985 No. 1799).
[78] regs. 4 and 5.
[79] *i.e.* the local authority or voluntary organisation responsible for the welfare of the child.
[80] reg. 6.
[81] reg. 7.

the foster parents regarding the care to be provided to the child[82]; and for the payment of allowances to the foster parent, which may be subject to such conditions as the care authority considers necessary, taking into account the needs and circumstances of the foster parent with whom the child is placed.[83] The regulations also detail the arrangements to be made by a care authority for the placing of a foster child[84]; the limitations on the composition of the household of the prospective foster parent[85]; the obligation to ensure that the person with whom the child is fostered is of the same religious persuasion as the child or, if that is not practicable, that the person undertakes that the child will be brought up in accordance with the child's religious persuasion[86]; the notifications to be made by the care authority to the local authority, education authority, health authority and the parent or guardian of the child[87]; the monitoring of placements[88]; and the termination of placements.[89]

Restrictions on Removal

The freedom with which a placing authority or organisation may terminate boarding out reflects the view that foster parents are the agents or delegates of the authority or organisation in whose care the child is and that restrictions on the power to secure the return of the child would fetter the authority's or organisation's exercise of their responsibility to those in their care and so put the welfare of the child at risk. The criticism may, on the other hand, be made that the way is open to arbitrary disturbance of long-standing arrangements and to administrative abuse and that the legitimate interests of foster parents are insufficiently protected. It is submitted, however, that arbitrary action or abuse of powers is open to judicial review on application to the Court of Session.

Residential Care

Residential Establishments

Maintaining a child in a residential establishment is the principal alternative to boarding out by which a local authority may discharge its duty to provide accommodation and maintenance for a child in its care.[90] It is a means of care also used by voluntary organisations. The term "residential establishment" means an establishment, by whomsoever managed, which provides residential accom-

---

[82] reg. 8.

[83] reg. 9.

[84] regs. 10–16.

[85] reg. 14: the household must comprise a man and a woman living together and acting jointly, or a man or a woman living alone and acting alone, or a person living with relatives who are not concerned with the care of the child.

[86] reg. 15. This applies only so far as consistent with the care authority's duty to further the best interests of the child and to afford opportunities for his proper development, and after having ascertained the child's own wishes and feelings so far as practicable.

[87] reg. 17.

[88] reg. 18.

[89] reg. 19.

[90] Social Work (Scotland) Act 1968, s. 21(1). Other options may be open under the general power to arrange accommodation and maintenance in any suitable manner for the purpose of making use of such facilities and services as are available for children in the care of their own parents (s. 21(2))

modation for the purposes of the Social Work (Scotland) Act 1968.[91] These purposes include promoting social welfare in Scotland, and in the present context a residential establishment may be classed as an establishment that provides residential accommodation for the purpose of promoting the welfare of children (including children in need of compulsory measures of care within the meaning of Part III of the Act).

Duty to Provide

It is the duty of a local authority to provide and maintain such residential and other establishments as may be required for their functions under the Act.[92] These functions include the care of children.[93] A local authority is not, however, obliged to provide all such establishments itself but may join with another local authority in so doing, or may secure the provision of such establishments by voluntary organisations or other persons, including other local authorities.[94] In any event local authorities, in providing accommodation for children in their care, are not restricted to residential establishments that they themselves manage, but, by arrangement with the managers, may use establishments managed by others.[95]

Regulations

Under the Social Work (Scotland) Act 1968[96] the Secretary of State has made regulations for the conduct of residential and other establishments and for securing the welfare of persons resident and accommodated in them.[97] These regulations, which came into force in June 1, 1988, make provision concerning the conduct of residential establishments[98]; the making of decisions to place a child in residential care[99]; notifications by the care authority on the placement of a child[1]; the monitoring of placements[2]; and the termination of placements.[3]

Registration

Anyone other than a local authority or government department who carries on a residential establishment must be registered with the local authority,[4] or, if the Secretary of State so directs, in respect of any establishment or class of es-

---

[91] Social Work (Scotland) Act 1968, s. 94(1).
[92] *Ibid.*, s. 59(1).
[93] See, *e.g.* ss. 1(5) and 15, and P. III.
[94] *Ibid.*, s. 59(2).
[95] *Ibid.*, ss. 21(1)(*b*) and 94(1).
[96] *Ibid.*, s. 60.
[97] Social Work (Residential Establishments—Child Care) (Scotland) Regulations 1987 (S.I. 1987 No. 2233).
[98] regs. 3–16.
[99] regs. 18–21.
[1] reg. 22: nofication must be given to the local authority, education authority, health authority and to the parent or guardian of the child.
[2] reg. 23.
[3] reg. 24.
[4] Social Work (Scotland) Act 1968, s. 61, as amended by the Registered Establishments (Scotland) Act 1987, s. 1. Any grant-aided school or independent school which performs the functions of a residential establishment may, but is not required to, apply for registration: s. 61A, as inserted by the Registered Establishments (Scotland) Act 1987, s. 2(1).

tablishments, with the Secretary of State.[5] Unless there are grounds for refusal the authority must, on receipt of an application, register the applicant in respect of the establishment named. The registration authority, whether the local authority or the Secretary of State, may refuse to register the applicant if they are satisfied:

(a) that he, or any person employed or proposed to be employed by him in the management of the establishment, is not a fit person whether by reason of age or otherwise to carry on or be employed by an establishment of that description; or

(b) that for reasons connected with situation, construction, state of repair, accommodation, staffing or equipment, the establishment or any premises used in connection with it are not fit to be used for an establishment of that description; or

(c) that the way in which it is proposed to conduct the establishment is such as not to provide services or facilities reasonably required by persons resorting to an establishment of that kind.[6]

Registration may be cancelled at any time, (a) on any ground that would entitle the authority to refuse an application for registration; or (b) on the ground that the registered person has either failed to notify the local authority of a change in manager[7] or been convicted of an offence under the present section or under any of the regulations made under Part III of the 1968 Act relating to the conduct of an establishment; or (c) on the ground that any other person has been convicted of such an offence in respect of that establishment; or (d) on the ground that the annual fee[8] for the continuation of registration has not been paid on the due date.[9] The person in respect of whom an establishment is registered must comply with such reasonable conditions with regard to the proper operation of the establishment as the local authority may impose, and these conditions must include conditions as to the maximum number of persons who may be accommodated at any one time in the establishment and the categories of person who may be admitted to the establishment.[10] The local authority may impose new conditions or vary any existing conditions.[11] Provision is made for appeal to an appeal tribunal[12] against the imposition of conditions on registration or subsequently.[13]

In the event of the death of the registered person, his executor or widow or any other member of his family may, for a period not exceeding four weeks from his death or such longer period as the authority may sanction, carry on the establishment without being registered.[14]

Notice stating the grounds on which it is intended to refuse or cancel registra-

---

[5] Ibid., s. 63.
[6] Ibid., s. 62(3).
[7] Which he is obliged to do under s. 62(4).
[8] For which see s. 64A, as added by the Registered Establishments (Scotland) Act 1987, s. 6(1).
[9] Ibid., s. 62(4C), as similarly added (s. 3).
[10] Ibid., s. 62(5), as similarly amended.
[11] Ibid., s. 62(5A), as similarly added.
[12] Established under Sched. 5.
[13] Ibid., s. 63A, as inserted by the Registered Establishments (Scotland) Act 1987, s. 4.
[14] Ibid., s. 62(8).

tion must be given to the person affected who may, within 14 days, inform the authority in writing of his desire to show cause why the registration should not be refused or cancelled, and if that is done an opportunity of being heard must be given.[15] Provision is made for appeal to an appeal tribunal[16] against refusal or cancellation of registration.[17]

Removal of Occupants

Where an establishment is carried on by an unregistered person, other than the person authorised to carry it on at the death of a registered person, or where notice to cancel a registration has been given, the local authority with which the person carrying on the establishment is registered, or ought to be registered, may remove all, or any, of the persons for whom accommodation is being provided.[18] That power may be exercised although the time for appeal has not expired or although an appeal is pending. The Secretary of State may, where the person carrying on the establishment is, or ought to be, registered with him, require the local authority in whose area the establishment is situated to act and he may, in any case of urgent necessity, exercise that power in respect of any establishment. Any person authorised by the local authority may, on producing, if required, a duly authenticated document showing his authority, enter premises in which the establishment in question is being carried on in order that the local authority's function in removing the persons accommodated may be performed.[19] It is an offence to obstruct the exercise of that power.[20]

Particulars to be Furnished, Visitation and Inspection

A person in charge of an establishment is obliged to furnish such particulars of the establishment and the persons accommodated, or to be accommodated, in it as the Secretary of State may prescribe.[21] A duly authorised officer of a local authority may enter any establishment where the person carrying it on is registrable for the purpose of making such examination as he thinks necessary into the state and management of the place and the condition and treatment of the persons in it and for the purpose of inspecting any records or registers which are required to be kept there. Like powers of entry and inspection may be exercised at all reasonable times in respect of any place in the area of the local authority which is used, or which the officer has reasonable cause to believe is being used, as an establishment in respect of which the person carrying it on is registrable.[22] Any person authorised by a local authority is similarly empowered to enter any establishment for the purpose of visiting the persons in the establishment and that power extends to entering establishments outside the area of the authority for the purpose of visiting children who are in the care, or under the supervision,

---

[15] *Ibid.*, s. 64(1), (2) and (3).
[16] Established under Sched. 5.
[17] *Ibid.*, s. 64(4).
[18] *Ibid.*, s. 65.
[19] *Ibid.*, s. 65(3).
[20] *Ibid.*, s. 65(4), as amended by the Registered Establishments (Scotland) Act 1987, s. 7.
[21] *Ibid.*, s. 66(1) and (2).
[22] *Ibid.*, s. 67.

of the authority, or who are receiving assistance from it.[23] The local authority has a duty to see that persons in establishments in their area are visited from time to time in the interests of their well-being. It is the duty of a local authority to review the case of a child in their care at intervals of approximately six months and in reaching any decision relating to the child to give first consideration to the need to safeguard and promote his welfare throughout his childhood, and, so far as is practicable, to ascertain his wishes and feelings regarding any decision and give due consideration to them, having regard to his age and understanding[24]; and so the visitation of children who are in the care of the local authority must be at least as frequent as to enable the local authority to carry out its duty of review on an informed basis in relation to the matters which it has a duty to consider on such a review. It is an offence to obstruct the exercise of the powers of inspection and visitation.[25]

CHILD MINDING AND DAY CARE OF YOUNG CHILDREN

Child minding and day care (*i.e.* any form of care or activity supervised by a responsible person and provided for children during the day, whether or not it is provided on a regular basis[26]) may take a wide variety of forms. Some are free from statutory control, for example where children are cared for during the day in a dwelling-house under a private arrangement that makes no provision for reward or where children over eight are so cared for even if for reward. Establishments provided for the purpose of the Social Work (Scotland) Act 1968 that receive children on a non-residential basis are subject to the same controls in respect of the registration of the person by whom they are carried on, of their management and conduct and of the treatment of persons in them as have just been noted in connection with residential establishments.[27] Child minding and day care of children under eight (other than local authority day care but including care in certain voluntary establishments, carried on by persons also registrable under the Social Work (Scotland) Act 1968) is, however, regulated by Part X of the Children Act 1989.[28] It effects control through a system of registration and inspection, which forms the subject matter of the following paragraphs.

Register of Child Minders and Register of Persons who Provide Care

Every local authority is required to keep a register (which must be open to inspection by members of the public at all times and which may be kept by means of a computer[29]) of (a) persons who act as child minders on domestic premises within the authority's area, and (b) persons who provide day care for children under the age of eight on premises other than domestic premises within that

---

[23] *Ibid.*, s. 68.

[24] ss. 20A(1) and 21, as inserted and substituted by Children Act 1975, ss. 79 and 80.

[25] *Ibid.*, ss. 67(1), 6(5) and 68(3).

[26] Children Act 1989, s. 79(*b*).

[27] Social Work (Scotland) Act 1968, s. 61(1), as substituted by the Registered Establishments (Scotland) Act 1987, s. 1(1).

[28] As applied to Scotland by s. 108(11). And see Sutherland, "Child Law: Radical Change or Woeful Neglect?" 1991 S.L.T. (News) 447.

[29] Children Act 1989, s. 71(15).

area.[30] A child minder is a person who looks after, in a domestic setting,[31] one or more children under the age of eight for reward for more than two hours in any day[32]; though excluded from this definition are parents, relatives, persons in whom parental rights and duties relating to the child are vested, foster parents, and nannies[33] employed for the child.[34] Anyone who provides day care for one or more children under the age of eight for more than two hours in any day in other than a domestic setting, and whether or not for reward, is registrable as a person who provides day care for children.[35] Every local authority shall, at least once every three years, review the provision of day care within their area made for children under the age of eight by the local authority and by persons required to register as persons who provide day care.[36]

Refusal of Registration

A local authority may refuse to register an applicant for registration as a child minder if:

(a) the applicant, or any person looking after or likely to be looking after any children in any premises on which the applicant is or is likely to be child minding, is not fit to look after children under the age of eight[37]; or

(b) any person living or likely to be living at any premises on which the applicant is or is likely to child minding, or any person employed or likely to be employed on those premises, is not fit to be in the proximity of children under the age of eight[38]; or

(c) the local authority are satisfied that any premises on which the applicant is or is likely to be child minding are not fit to be used for looking after children under the age of eight, whether because of their condition or the condition of any equipment used on the premises or for any reason connected with their situation, construction, or size.[39]

A local authority may refuse to register an applicant for registration as a person who provides day care for children if:

(a) they are satisfied that any person looking after, or likely to be looking after, any children on the premises to which the application relates is not fit to look after children under the age of eight;[40] or

---

[30] *Ibid.*, s. 71(1).
[31] "Domestic premises" means any premises which are wholly or mainly used as a private dwelling; and "premises" includes any vehicle: s. 71(12).
[32] *Ibid.*, s. 71(2)(a).
[33] "A person acts as a nannie for a child if she is employed to look after the child by (a) a parent of the child, (b) a person who is not a parent of the child but in whom parental rights and duties relating to the child are vested, or (c) a person who is a relative of the child and who has assumed responsibility for his care": *ibid.*, s. 71(13), as applied to Scotland by s. 79(e).
[34] *Ibid.*, ss. 71(4), (5) and (6) and 79.
[35] *Ibid.*, s. 71(1)(b) and (2)(b).
[36] *Ibid.*, s. 19(3) and (5).
[37] *Ibid.*, s. 71(7).
[38] *Ibid.*, s. 71(8).
[39] *Ibid.*, s. 71(11).
[40] *Ibid.*, s. 71(9).

(b) they are satisfied that any person living or likely to be living at the premises to which the application relates, or any person employed or likely to be employed, at these premises, is not fit to be in the proximity of children under the age of eight[41]; or

(c) they are satisfied that the premises to which the application relates are not fit to be used for looking after children under the age of eight, whether because of their condition or the condition of any equipment used on the premises or for any reason connected with their situation, construction, or size.[42]

Requirements that May be Imposed

Either at the time of registration or at any time thereafter the local authority may impose requirements upon applicants to be child minders or persons providing day care. The requirements in both cases shall be such reasonable requirements as the local authority consider appropriate, and they may be added to, varied, or removed at any time.[43] If the local authority consider it appropriate to impose requirements on the applicant, they must impose certain specified requirements, described below; and if in addition they impose other requirements, those other requirements must not be incompatible with any of those that must be imposed.[44]

Specified Requirements for Child Minders[45]

In imposing requirements on a registered child minder, the local authority shall:

(a) specify the maximum number of children, or the maximum number of children within specified age groups, whom he may look after when acting as a child minder. In determining the maximum number of children under this provision the authority shall take account of the number of other children who may at any time be on any premises on which the person concerned acts, or is likely to act, as a child minder[46];

(b) require him to secure that any premises on which he looks after any child, and the equipment used in those premises, are adequately maintained and kept safe;

(c) require him to keep a record of the name and address of any child looked after by him on any premises within the authority's area, and of any person who assists in looking after any such child, and of any person living or likely to be living at those premises; and

(d) require him to notify the authority in writing of any change in the persons mentioned above.

---

[41] *Ibid.*, s. 71(10).
[42] *Ibid.*, s. 71(11).
[43] *Ibid.*, s. 72(1) and (6), and s. 73(1) and (8).
[44] *Ibid.*, s. 72(5) and s. 73(7).
[45] *Ibid.*, s. 72(2).
[46] *Ibid.*, s. 72(4).

Specified Requirements for Persons Providing Day Care[47]

In imposing requirements on a person registered as a person providing day care the local authority shall:

(a) specify the maximum number of children, or the maximum number of children within specified age groups, who may be looked after on the premises. In determining the maximum number of children to be specified the authority shall take account of the number of other children who may at any time be on the premises[48];

(b) require him to secure that the premises, and the equipment used in them, are adequately maintained and kept safe;

(c) require him to notify the authority of any change in the facilities which he provides or in the period during which he provides them;

(d) specify the number of persons required to assist in looking after children on the premises;

(e) require him to keep a record of the name and address of (i) any child looked after on the registered premises, (ii) any person who assists in looking after any such child, and (iii) any person who lives, or is likely at any time to be living, at those premises; and

(f) require him to notify the authority of any change in the persons mentioned above.

Cancellation of Registration

Registration of child minders or of persons providing day care may be cancelled by the local authority at any time if,

(a) it appears to them that the circumstances of the case are such that they would be justified in refusing to register the person in the first place,

(b) the care provided is, in the opinion of the authority, seriously inadequate having regard to the needs of the child or children,[49]

(c) the person has contravened or failed to comply with any requirement imposed,[50] or

(d) the person has failed to pay any annual fee under Schedule 9 within the prescribed time.[51]

In addition, registration of persons providing day care may be cancelled if it appears to the local authority that the circumstances of the case are such that they would be justified in refusing to register the applicant with respect to any premises.[52]

---

[47] *Ibid.*, s. 73(3).
[48] *Ibid.*, s. 73(6).
[49] In relation to this provision the local authority must have regard, amongst other things, to the child's religious persuasion, racial origin, and cultural and linguistic background: s. 74(6).
[50] Registration may not be cancelled on this ground where the requirement is to carry out repairs or make alterations or additions, and they have not been carried out or made, but the time set for complying with the requirements has not expired: s. 74(4).
[51] *Ibid.*, s. 74(1) and (2).
[52] *Ibid.*, s. 74(3).

Protection of Children in an Emergency

The sheriff has the power to make an order, on the application of the local authority, cancelling registration, or varying, removing or imposing any additional requirements on a registered person, if it appears to the sheriff that a child being looked after by that person is suffering or is likely to suffer significant harm.[53] Any such cancellation, variation, removal or imposition shall have effect from the date on which the order is made.[54] Notice must be served by the local authority on the registered person.[55]

Inspection

Any person authorised by a local authority may at any reasonable time enter (a) any domestic premises in the area of the authority on which child minding is at any time carried on, or (b) any premises within their area on which day care for children under the age of eight is at any time provided,[56] or (c) any premises within their area in which the local authority have reasonable cause to believe that a child is being looked after in contravention of the provisions of the Act.[57] Such a person may inspect the children being looked after there, the arrangements for their welfare, and any statutory records relating to them.[58] Every local authority must exercise their power to inspect at least once a year.[59] A duly authenticated document showing authority to enter and inspect must be produced if required.[60] It is an offence to obstruct the exercise of the power of inspection.[61]

In addition to the power of the local authority, the Secretary of State may also cause to be inspected premises on which any person is acting as a child minder or in respect of which a person is registered as a person who provides day care.[62]

Appeals

Not less than 14 days before taking any of the steps described above, the authority concerned shall send to the applicant for registration or registered person notice of their intention to take the step, with reasons and a statement of their rights to object or appeal.[63] Where the recipient of the notice wishes to object he must be afforded the opportunity to do so.[64] If the step is nevertheless taken the person aggrieved thereby may appeal to the sheriff.[65] If he allows the appeal, the sheriff may impose requirements, cancel requirements, or vary those appealed

---

[53] *Ibid.*, s. 75(1) and s. 79(*a*).

[54] *Ibid.*, s. 75(2).

[55] *Ibid.*, s. 75(4).

[56] *Ibid.*, s. 76(1).

[57] *Ibid.*, s. 76(2).

[58] *Ibid.*, s. 76(3). The right to inspect records includes the right to have access to, inspect and check the operation of any computer in use in connection with the records in question: s. 76(5).

[59] *Ibid.*, s. 76(4).

[60] *Ibid.*, s. 76(6).

[61] *Ibid.*, s. 76(7).

[62] *Ibid.*, s. 80, as applied to Scotland by s. 108(11).

[63] *Ibid.*, s. 77(1) and (2).

[64] *Ibid.*, s. 77(3).

[65] *Ibid.*, s. 77(6) and 79(*a*).

against.[66] The appeal is by way of summary application to the sheriff and must be brought within 21 days of the date of the step to which the appeal relates.[67]

Offences

It is an offence for a person, without reasonable cause, to provide day care for children under the age of eight on any premises within the area of a local authority without being registered.[68] If a person acts as a child minder on domestic premises within the area of a local authority without being registered, the local authority may serve an enforcement notice on him,[69] which will have effect for a period of one year beginning with the date on which it is served[70]; if a person to whom an enforcement notice relates continues, without reasonable excuse, to act as a child minder, he shall be guilty of an offence,[71] this whether or not the subsequent contravention occurs within the area of the authority who served the enforcement notice.[72] It is also an offence to contravene any requirement imposed.[73]

[66] *Ibid.*, s. 77(8) and (9).
[67] *Ibid.*, s. 77(10).
[68] *Ibid.*, s. 78(1) and (2).
[69] *Ibid.*, s. 78(3) and (4).
[70] *Ibid.*, s. 78(5).
[71] *Ibid.*, s. 78(6).
[72] *Ibid.*, s. 78(7).
[73] *Ibid.*, s. 78(8).

CHAPTER 19

ADOPTION OF CHILDREN

INTRODUCTORY

History of Adoption in Scotland

Before the Adoption of Children (Scotland) Act 1930 there was no legally secured means by which, during the lifetime of the father of a legitimate, or the
mother of an illegitimate, child the role of parent in relation to the child could be
permanently undertaken by someone else. Informal arrangements by which relatives or others took a child into their care and acted as substitute parents were
not uncommon and, where they were intended to be permanent, that intention
may often, in fact, have been respected. However, an intention of permanency,
even if expressed in the most solemn and apparently binding terms, lacked legal
sanction. These arrangements were in principle revocable and the natural parents could at any time reassert their parental rights including, in the case of a pupil child, the right to custody.[1] This lack of any equivalent in Scots law for the
Roman law *adoptio* or *adrogatio* has sometimes been thought remarkable in a
system which has been heavily influenced by Roman law institutions. The
omission is, however, consistent with other legal systems within the Civil law
tradition. Adoption was not in use in the Roman/Dutch law[2] which was the principal vehicle for the mediation of the Civil to Scots law during its formative
period and it was virtually unknown to pre-Napoleonic French law even within
the *pays de droit écrit*.[3] Moreover, in the Civil law tradition, including modern
systems into which adoption has been introduced, adoption was until quite recent times seen principally as a means of providing heirs and thereby overcoming some of the consequences of the restraints on freedom of testation typical of
the Civil law. Although Scots law is closer to the Civil law than is the law of
England in the restraints that it imposes on freedom of testation, none of these
restraints is of a kind that gives rise to the need for adoption as a means of

---

[1] *Kerrigan* v. *Hall* (1901) 4 F. 10; *Macpherson* v. *Leishman* (1887) 14 R. 780, *per* Lord President
Inglis at p. 782. *Cf. Humphreys* v. *Polak* [1901] 2 K.B. 385. Even at common law, however, the
court would not order redelivery of the child where to do so would involve serious danger to his
health or morals (*Sutherland* v. *Taylor* (1887) 15 R. 224; *Mackenzie* v. *Keillor* (1892) 19 R. 963;
Campbell v. *Croall* (1895) 22 R. 869; *Alexander* v. *McGarrity* (1903) 5 F. 654; *Mitchell* (1903)
43 S.L.R. 429), and a parent's claim might be weakened if the child had been abandoned to the
care of others (*Harvey* v. *Harvey* (1860) 22 D. 1198). The revocability of arrangements entrusting
children to the care of persons other than the parents is, short of adoption, still true today, but
where a child has been for a long time in the care of someone other than his parents the effect of
modern statute is to present much more formidable obstacles to recovery of custody by parents
than existed at common law.
[2] Grotius, *Jurisprudence of Holland*, I, vi, 1; Voet I, vii, 7.
[3] Amos and Walton, *Introduction to French Law* (3rd ed.) at p. 78.

ameliorating its effects[4]; and when adoption was eventually introduced by statute it had, until the Succession (Scotland) Act 1964, practically no consequences in the law of succession. More remarkable than any departure from Roman law roots is that the prevalence and antiquity of fostering in Scotland did not give rise to any recognition at common law of the custodial rights of foster parents or of the need for at least some degree of permanency in *de facto* adoptions. The introduction of adoption in 1930 was a radical statutory innovation.

Changes in the law subsequent to the Adoption of Children (Scotland) Act 1930 were consolidated in the Adoption Act 1950 which was in turn replaced by the Adoption Act 1958. The 1958 Act comprehended at the time it was passed practically all the statute law applicable to adoption but additions and amendments were made, in respect of the revocation of adoption orders in the event of legitimation, by the Adoption Act 1960 and the Legitimation (Scotland) Act 1968[5] and, in respect of certain international questions of adoption, by the Adoption Acts 1964 and 1968. The most important changes effected since 1958 were, however, those contained in the Children Act 1975 by which large parts, but not all, of the 1958 Act were repealed. The whole of the 1958 Act and the relevant Part of the 1975 Act were themselves repealed by the Adoption (Scotland) Act 1978,[6] which, as subsequently amended, now contains most of the law of adoption in Scotland.[7]

Legal Character of Adoption

It is a common feature of the present statutory provisions and their predecessors that adoption involves a radical divestiture of the rights and obligations of the natural parents brought about by operation of law in favour of the adoptive parents. The status of the child and his rights and obligations are also thereby affected. A new relationship of parent and child is created which, for practically all legal purposes, replaces the previous natural relationship. As Lord President Cooper said in *J and J* v. *C's Tutor*:

> "The Adoption of Children (Scotland) Act 1930 made a serious innovation upon the common law by introducing a novel institution which cannot easily be fitted into its setting...The chief elements of the previously inalienable *patria potestas* were made assignable—not by a contract between natural parent and adopter, but by an act of the adopter authorised

---

[4] The testamentary incapacity of bastards had, so long as it subsisted, other remedies, and the rule that heritage could not be the subject of a proper testament could be overcome by the use of a disposition to take effect on death (see Erskine, III, viii, 20). The most important restriction of Scots law on freedom of testation is that constituted by the legal rights of spouses and children. Adoption can and does affect the distribution of the bairns' part in that it brings in a stranger to the rateable prejudice of the children and so to that limited extent may be seen as a possible means of reducing the effects of restriction on the freedom of testation. On the other hand, if a childless couple adopt a child, a right to legitim is thereby created at the expense of the *jus relicti* or *jus relictae* as well as of the dead's part available for testamentary disposal.

[5] See *ante* at pp. 23–24.

[6] Adoption (Scotland) Act 1978, Sched. 4. References in this chapter are to this Act, unless otherwise stated.

[7] The Adoption (Scotland) Act 1978 was brought into force on Sept. 1, 1984 by the Adoption (Scotland) Act 1978 Commencement Order 1984 (S.I. 1984 No. 1050).

by the court. All that is required from the natural parent is his consent, and even that consent may be dispensed with."[8]

Adoption is, therefore, not a matter of contract but an act of law.

Competency of Revocation

The statutory purpose is that adoption should be permanent, and this differentiates it from, for example, custody.[9] It has been described as irrevocable. There are, however, limited circumstances in which specific provision is made for the revocation or supersession of an adoption order.

First, an adoption order may be made notwithstanding that the child is already an adopted child,[10] and so an existing adoption order may be effectively superseded by a later order. Secondly, an adoption order made in favour of one natural parent may be revoked by the court which made it if that parent subsequently marries the other natural parent.[11] So too an adoption order in favour of both natural parents, made before the commencement of the Legitimation (Scotland) Act 1968, in respect of a child legitimated by virtue of the terms of that Act, may be revoked.[12] Thirdly, there are special rules (discussed later) for the annulment of overseas adoptions. It is undecided whether these statutory provisions and the ordinary provisions for review, by appeal or reclaiming motion, within the prescribed time limits, exhaust the means by which an adoption order can be set aside.

Reduction will not be open at the instance of adopters who allege essential error or misrepresentation as to the health, physical state or other qualities of the child.[13] It is thought that that will be the case even if the misrepresentation is deliberate. Indeed, any ground that treats adoption as essentially a contract between the natural parents and the adopters will be excluded, for that is to mistake the nature of adoption. Nor will reduction be open where adopters allege a neglect of the statutory prerequisities for the making of an order.[14] In *Skinner* v. *Carter*[15] doubts were expressed by the Court of Appeal as to whether there were any appropriate proceedings as a result of which an adoption order could be set aside, but in subsequent English cases a remedy has been allowed.

---

[8] 1948 S.C. 637 at pp. 641–642.
[9] *F* v. *F*, 1991 S.L.T. 357, *per* Lord President Hope at p. 360E.
[10] s. 12(7).
[11] s. 46(1).
[12] Legitimation (Scotland) Act 1968, s. 6. The natural parents must at the time of adoption have been married to each other because only the parties to a marriage can adopt jointly.
[13] *J and J* v. *C's Tutor*, 1948 S.C. 636. It is interesting to compare the situation in some states in the U.S.A. Many statutes previously allowed for annulment on grounds of essential error, or because, for example, the child developed a disability as a result of some condition existing at the time of the adoption. For a discussion, see LeMay, "Wrongful Adoption" (1989) 27 J. Fam. L. 475. Most of these statutes have now been repealed and annulments are granted only if this is in the best interests of the child. An interesting modern development is to allow the parents to sue in tort the adoption agency which arranged the adoption, if the agency fraudulently conceals some "defect" in the child: see for example *Burr* v. *Board of County Commissioners* (1986) 491 N.E. 2d 1101. Such an action can only be based on the theory that adoption is designed to confer some benefit on the parents, which the negligence or fraud denied, and is therefore unlikely to be successful in Scotland or England where adoption is seen as being designed for the benefit of the child.
[14] *J & J* v. *C's Tutor, supra*.
[15] [1948] Ch. 387.

Certiorari issued in *R* v. *Leeds City Justices, ex p. Gilmartin*[16] to quash an adoption order on grounds which, in the only report of the case, are obscure, and in *R* v. *Liverpool City Justices, ex p. W*[17] on the ground that the statutory provisions had not been properly considered by the justices making the order. In *Re F (R) (An Infant)*[18] leave to appeal out of time was granted where the natural mother's consent had been dispensed with on the ground that she could not be found and the foster parents, on whose application the order had been made, had not taken all reasonable steps to ascertain her whereabouts. In the last-mentioned case it was said that the Court of Appeal had an inherent jurisdiction to set aside an adoption order in such circumstances. There can be no doubt that the Court of Session has a similar jurisdiction although exercised in a different way. Only in the case of reclaiming motions from the Outer House is there an equivalent of allowing leave to appeal out of time. After the time for appeal has elapsed sheriff court decrees can be set aside only by reduction, or perhaps, where reduction is not open, by petition to the *nobile officium*.[19]

"The right of review by reduction is," it has been said, "a common law right which has existed for a very long time, and is a mode of review which cannot be taken away except by statutory enactment,"[20] and that right will not readily be held to have been taken away by implication.[21] There is no express statutory exclusion of reduction in relation to adoption and no ground on which such exclusion can be said to be necessarily implied. Yet the unique character of adoption proceedings, including the fact that the process of investigation and certification proceeds largely, and in many cases entirely, at the court's own hand, may point to a severe limitation of the grounds on which reduction will be entertained and perhaps to its virtual exclusion.[22] Considerations appropriate to adversarial procedure are not apt to an inquisitorial procedure which, moreover, must turn on the welfare of the child rather than on issues of a kind properly justiciable between parties such as arise in most other types of case. Some assistance may be obtained from the legislation of jurisdictions which deal with this problem by specific enactment. In Australia discharge of adoption orders is a matter of express statutory provision in all the States.[23] Section 16(1) of the Victorian Adoption of Children Act 1964 is typical:

> "(1) A law officer may apply to the Supreme Court for an order discharging an order for the adoption of a child made under this Act or under any corresponding previous enactment, and the court may make such an

---

[16] [1951] C.L.Y. 1629.

[17] [1959] 1 All E.R. 337.

[18] [1969] 3 W.L.R. 853.

[19] Formerly reduction was not open if the defender was not subject to the jurisdiction (*Acutt* v. *Acutt*, 1936 S.C. 386; *Longworth* v. *Yelverton* (1868) 7 M. 70; *Jack* v. *Jack*, 1940 S.L.T. 122). The enlargement of the jurisdiction to actions of reduction effected by the Law Reform (Miscellaneous Provisions) (Scotland) Act 1980, s. 20 virtually removes any need for petition to the *nobile officium* in these cases.

[20] *Mathewson* v. *Yeaman* (1900) 2 F. 873, *per* Lord Trayner at p. 881.

[21] *Marr & Sons* v. *Lindsay* (1881) 8 R. 784, *per* Lord President Inglis at p. 785; *Mathewson* v. *Yeaman, supra, per* Lord Justice-Clerk Macdonald at p. 880.

[22] Lord Cullen accepted counsel's submission that an attempt to vary an adoption order was "incompetent" in *W* v. *R* 1987 S.L.T. 369 at p. 370H.

[23] See Finlay and Bissett-Johnson at p. 230.

order if it is satisfied that the adoption order, or any consent for the purposes of the adoption order, was obtained by fraud, duress, or other improper means or that there is some exceptional reason why, subject to the
welfare and interests of the child, the adoption order should be
discharged."

It is noteworthy that the initiative of a law officer is required. In the absence of
statutory requirement the Lord Advocate's concurrence cannot be a prerequisite of reduction, but it is arguable that there is an element of public interest
which requires that he be convened as a party. It is submitted that in Scotland the
reasoning of *J and J* v. *C's Tutor*[24] requires that a conservative view be taken of
fraud and improper means as a ground of reduction where these have been exercised against the adopters. It may be otherwise in cases of duress. There is a difference between cases in which the will does not go with the act of application
for adoption and cases in which the act is willed even if on the basis of expectations falsely induced by another. It is submitted, moreover, that the welfare of
the child and also, where practicable, his wishes and feelings, are factors to be
taken into account in all cases including cases of fraud, duress and improper
means. A decision on reduction is a decision relating to the adoption of a child
within the meaning of section 6 of the Adoption (Scotland) Act 1978, which requires that first consideration must be given to the need to safeguard and promote the welfare of the child throughout his childhood and that the wishes and
feelings of the child regarding the decision must, so far as is practicable, be ascertained and receive due consideration having regard to his age and understanding.[25] The view of a child's welfare, taken in the Australian case of *Re S*[26]
should not, however, be followed. In that case McInerney J., on facts not materially different from those in *J and J* v. *C's Tutor*, held that an adoption order
should be discharged as the adoptive parents were emotionally and economic-
ally unable to provide for the child and that his welfare would be better provided
for if he were left in the care of the State. That is to confuse reasons for taking a
child, perhaps compulsorily, into the care of the State with reasons for the discharge of an adoption order. There is no reason why adoptive parents should,
any more than natural parents, be discharged of their responsibilities merely because the child requires special care. In any question of the reduction of an adoption order, the child must be called as a party,[27] and if still under the age of
majority a curator *ad litem* should be appointed. An adoption order is not, so
long as it stands unreduced, a nullity because a condition essential to its making
(*e.g.* that joint adopters be husband and wife) was not in fact fulfilled and, even
on admitted facts, no court can disregard it on that ground.[28]

---

[24] 1948 S.C. 636.

[25] Although it is manifest that there are decisions relating to the adoption of a child to which such a
test cannot be applied (*Re P (An Infant) (Adoption: Parental Consent)* [1977] Fam. 25), the wide
wording of the statute should not be denied effect where, as here, there is no absurdity or inconsistency in doing so.

[26] [1969] V.R. 490.

[27] *Skinner* v. *Carter* [1948] Ch. 387.

[28] *Ibid.* See also *Re F (Infants) (Adoption Order: Validity)* [1977] 2 W.L.R. 488 in which the Court
of Appeal held voidable but not void adoption orders in favour of joint adopters whose marriage
turned out to be void. The court refused to set aside the voidable adoption orders because no one

Effects of Adoption

Restricted Impact on Status Under Earlier Legislation

Although it is clear that adoption affects status it was not, until the Children Act 1975, clear what the exact nature of that impact on status was. Previous legislation had referred to the transfer of "all rights, duties, obligations and liabilities of the parent or parents in relation to the future custody, maintenance and education of the adopted child" so that they should "vest in and be exercisable by and enforceable against the adopter as though the adopted child was a child born to the adopter in lawful wedlock" and had further provided that "*in respect of the same matters* and in respect of the liability of a child to maintain its parents" the adopted child should stand to the adopter exclusively in the position of a child born to the adopter in lawful wedlock.[29] The 1930 Act did not, but later legislation did, place the adopters and the adopted child within the forbidden degrees of relationship for marriage.[30] Later still, legislation placed the adopter and the adopted child within the forbidden degrees of relationship for the purposes of the crime of incest.[31] The equiparation of the adopted child's status to that of a legitimate child of the adopters was therefore restricted to questions of custody, maintenance, education and marriage and was, moreover, restricted to questions between adoptive parent and adopted child *inter se* and had no wider familial consequences. Questions therefore arose of whether an adopted child might correctly be described as retaining his original status, be that legitimate or illegitimate, subject only to some modifications resulting from his adoption, or whether he might more aptly be described as the legitimate child of the adopters, subject again to certain modifications, or of whether he was the subject of some new kind of status, *e.g.* adoptive or *quasi*-legitimate status. All three descriptions were viable, but the first was closest to the immediate legal effects of the statutes, the second closest to common understanding, while the third represented an attempt to do justice to the essentially distinct character of adoption. The question of description was not of importance and in any doubtful practical issue it was unnecessary to do more than to echo or adopt the words of Lord Atkin in *Coventry Corporation* v. *Surrey County Council*[32] (on a question of construction of a statute in order to ascertain whether it affected adopters and adopted children):

> "It is only necessary to consider whether the statute purports to deal with the rights or obligations of parents or the position of a child in relation to the matters of custody, maintenance, or education. If it does the adopter has the same rights and obligations as though he were the natural parent, and the child is in the same position as though he were the legitimate child of the adopters."

---

had been aggrieved by them and the interests of justice would not be served by setting them aside.

[29] Adoption Act 1958, s. 13(1); Adoption Act 1950, s. 10(1); Adoption of Children (Scotland) Act 1930, s. 5(1).

[30] Adoption Act 1958, s. 13(3); Adoption Act 1950, s. 10(3). See now Marriage (Scotland) Act 1977, Sched. 1.

[31] Incest and Related Offences (Scotland) Act 1986, Sched. 1(5), amending Adoption (Scotland) Act 1978, s. 41(1).

[32] [1935] A.C. 199 at p. 206.

There were, however, practical consequences of the restricted scope of the statutory transfer of rights and obligations. Under the original adoption legislation neither adoptive parent nor adopted child had the right to sue for damages or *solatium* on the death of the other, although that defect was cured by the Law Reform (Miscellaneous Provisions) (Scotland) Act 1940.[33] It seems that adoptive parents did not have the rights and duties of tutors and curators in relation to the property, contracts and legal acts of their adopted children although in practice this limitation may often have been ignored.[34] The adopted child had no obligation to aliment, nor right to be alimented by, his adoptive parents' ascendants. Accordingly, on the death of his adoptive parents his only recourse for aliment was against those who were *lucrati* by their succession to the adoptive parents' estate.[35] Equally, the child's natural grandparents retained an obligation to aliment him and the right to claim aliment from him if need arose.

Status Under Current Legislation

The anomalies of the previous law were removed by the Children Act 1975 and the current legislation is now the Adoption (Scotland) Act 1978, which provides, by section 39(1), that an adopted child shall be treated in law, where the adopters are a married couple, as if he had been born a legitimate child of the marriage and, in any other case, as if he had been born a legitimate child of the adopter (but not as a child of any actual marriage of the adopter).[36] Rights and duties vested in any other person are extinguished, and the child is to be treated as if he were not the child of any person other than the adopters or adopter.[37] The child's previous status is eliminated and he becomes the child of his adoptive parents with all the familial consequences, including for most purposes relationship to siblings and grandparents, which flow from that. Typically therefore adoption substitutes new parents for the child's biological parents and a new nexus of family relationships for the old. Where a child has been adopted by one of his natural parents as sole adoptive parent and the adopter thereafter marries the other natural parent, the child will be treated in law as the child of both his natural parents.[38]

The creation of the relationship of child and parent between adopted child and adopter is not, however, complete. The facts about the child's natural relationships are not altered so that, for example the natural grandparents of the child are entitled to claim custody after an order freeing the child for adoption, so long as they can claim an interest on grounds relating to the welfare of the child, and they are not disabled from doing so simply because they were previ-

---

[33] s. 2(1). See now Damages (Scotland) Act 1976.

[34] Somewhat anomalously, adoptive parents had the right to appoint guardians, but the rights and duties of such guardians must, it is submitted, have been construed as being confined to those which the adoptive parents themselves had enjoyed unless, perhaps, where the natural parents were dead.

[35] See *Hutchison* v. *Hutchison's Trs.*, 1951 S.C. 108.

[36] All references to legitimacy and illegitimacy will disappear on the enactment of the Scottish Law Commission's proposals to equate all fathers with all mothers and rid the law completely of the concept of illegitimacy: see Scot. Law Com. No. 135, *Report on Family Law* (May 1992) para. 17.9 and draft Bill, Sched. 1, para. 61 and Sched. 2.

[37] *Ibid.*

[38] s. 39(2).

ously related in law to the child.[39] Likewise, the adopter and adopted child come within the forbidden degrees of consanguinity and affinity in relation to the crime of incest and for the purposes of marriage[40]; but the adopted child is not brought within the forbidden degrees with any other adoptive relative. In other words, an adopted child may not marry nor have sexual intercourse with the adoptive parent, but may (in the absence of any other legal prohibition) do so with any of that parent's natural relatives.[41] The adopted child remains within the forbidden degrees in relation to his or her natural parents and other relatives. Also, the operation of the British Nationality Act 1981, the Immigration Act 1971, instruments having effect under either, and any other laws determining British citizenship, British Dependent Territories citizenship, or British Overseas citizenship, is unaffected by the status conferred by section 39.[42] However, by section 1(5) and (6) of the British Nationality Act 1981, an adopted child who is not a British citizen acquires British citizenship if that is the citizenship of the adopter or, in the case of joint adoption, of one of the adopters. The child does not lose his British citizenship when the adoption order ceases to have effect.[43] British citizenship carries with it the right of abode in the United Kingdom.[44]

Effect on Parental Responsibilities, Rights and Duties

An adoption order has the effect of vesting the parental responsibilities, rights and duties relating to a child in the adopters, except that such responsibilities, rights and duties are not affected so far as they relate to any period before the making of the order.[45] The order will also result in the child being treated in law as if he had been born the child of the adopters, although this will have no effect on things done or events occurring before the adoption order, or in any case before January 1, 1976.[46] Conversely, the order will have the effect of extinguishing parental responsibilities, rights and duties which before it was made were vested in the child's parent or guardian appointed by deed or order of a court.[47] This is broad enough to cover parental responsibilities, rights and duties arising from custody orders or from orders freeing a child for adoption and vesting parental responsibilities, rights and duties in an adoption agency.[48] The adoption order will also extinguish any obligation on the natural parent to pay aliment or make any payment arising out of parental rights and duties, owed to or by the child, in respect of any period occurring after the making of the order.[49] However, these obligations will not be terminated where they have arisen from a deed or agreement which constitutes a trust or which expressly provides that

---

[39] *F* v. *F*, 1991 S.L.T. 357, *per* Lord President Hope at pp. 361–362.
[40] Marriage (Scotland) Act 1977, Sched. 1, as amended by the Marriage (Prohibited Degrees of Relationship) Act 1986, Sched. 2; Adoption (Scotland) Act 1978, s. 41, as amended by the Incest and Related Offences (Scotland) Act 1986, Sched. 1, para. 5.
[41] See Norrie, "Incest and the Forbidden Degrees of Marriage in Scots Law" (1992) 37 J.L.S. 216.
[42] s. 41(2).
[43] British Nationality Act 1981, s. 1(6).
[44] Immigration Act 1971, s. 2(1)(*a*), as amended by s. 39(2) of the British Nationality Act 1981.
[45] Adoption (Scotland) Act 1978, s. 12(1) and (2).
[46] s. 39(1) and (4).
[47] s. 12(3)(*a*), as amended by the Age of Legal Capacity (Scotland) Act 1991, Sched. 2.
[48] s. 18(5).
[49] s. 12(3)(*b*).

the obligation is not to be extinguished by the making of an adoption order.[50] Also extinguished are parental rights and powers that are vested in a local authority or voluntary organisation as a result of a resolution under section 16 of the Social Work (Scotland) Act 1968.[51] A right of action under the Damages (Scotland) Act 1976 for the death of a natural parent that accrues before the date of the adoption order is not extinguished by the adoption, but a claim for loss of support under that statute cannot take account of any period after the adoption, since the adoptive parent's obligation of support will replace that which is lost.[52]

Effect on Succession

Until the coming into force of the Succession (Scotland) Act 1964 the questions of succession to, and of legal rights in, the estate of a deceased person, were unaffected by adoption. The adopted person retained rights of succession and the right to legitim which arose from his relationship with his natural parents and he acquired no right to succeed or to claim legitim from the estate of his adoptive parents or of his adoptive parents' relatives. Any reference to "child," "children" and "issue" in a will or *inter vivos* deed was construed as not including an adopted person or his issue unless the contrary intention appeared. Likewise the adoptive parents, or persons claiming through them, had no rights of succession to the estate of an adopted person. This has been wholly altered by the Succession (Scotland) Act 1964, which, for successions opening on or after September 10, 1964, now regulates the law relating to adopted persons in respect of (i) the succession, whether testate or intestate, to a deceased person, (ii) legal rights in the estate of a deceased person and (iii) the disposal of property by virtue of any *inter vivos* deed. Under that Act, for all purposes relating to succession, whether testate or intestate, to any person who has died on or after September 10, 1964, adopted children are treated as children of the adopter and not as the children of any other person. The rights of succession so conferred extend to claims for legitim from the moveable estate of a deceased adoptive parent and to representing the adoptive parent in a claim for legitim to which he would have been entitled by survivance.[53] If a person has been adopted by a married couple, he is treated as a brother or sister of the full blood of any other child or adopted child of that couple; but in any other cases, where the relationships between an adopted child and another child or adopted child of an adopter is in issue, the children are treated as brothers or sisters of the half blood only.[54] Any reference in a deed to a "child" or "children" is construed as including an adopted child,[55] unless the contrary be expressed or necessarily implied.[56] These provisions have the effect of equiparating the position of an adopted child to that of a child of the adopters for all purposes of succession including succession to the estate of the adopted person. But where any right is conferred or ob-

---

[50] s. 12(4)(*a*).
[51] Social Work (Scotland) Act 1968, s. 16(11)(*a*) and (*b*), as substituted by the Children Act 1975, s. 74.
[52] *Watson and Ors.* v. *Willmot* [1991] 1 All E.R. 473.
[53] Succession (Scotland) Act 1964, s. 23(1).
[54] *Ibid.*, s. 24.
[55] *Ibid.*, s. 23(2).
[56] As in *Spencer's Trs.* v. *Ruggles*, 1982 S.L.T. 165.

ligation imposed by reference to the relative seniority of the members of a class of persons then, except in the case of an illegitimate child adopted by one of his parents, any member of that class who is an adopted person shall rank as if he had been born on the date of his adoption. (Where a right or obligation arises under a deed, this rule shall apply only if the deed came into operation on or after January 1, 1976). If two or more members of the class are adopted persons whose dates of adoption are the same they rank between themselves in accordance with their respective times of birth.[57] In only one situation do adopted children retain full rights of succession in the estate of their natural parents. Where the natural parent has died after August 3, 1966 and the adoptive parent or parents died before September 10, 1964 an adopted person has rights of succession in, and may claim legitim from, the estate of his natural parents.[58] The law prior to September 10, 1964, however, still regulates the succession to titles, honours and coats of arms,[59] but not now to the tenancy of crofts.[60]

JURISDICTION AND QUALIFICATIONS OF PARTIES

The Child's Qualifications

Age and Status

Any person who is at least 19 weeks old (if the adopter is a parent, step-parent or relative of the child, or if the child is placed with the applicant by an adoption agency) or at least 12 months old (in all other cases),[61] who has not attained the age of 18,[62] and who is not and has not been married[63] may be adopted. Both the upper age limit[64] and the lower age limit[65] are to be ascertained at the time the order is made. A person who has already been adopted may be readopted.[66] There is no need to wait until the child is 19 weeks old before presenting the petition and as expedition is in the interest of all concerned, not least of the child, it will usually be desirable that the petition should be presented at the earliest opportunity.[67]

---

[57] Succession (Scotland) Act 1964, s. 24(1A).

[58] Law Reform (Miscellaneous Provisions) (Scotland) Act 1966, s. 5.

[59] Succession (Scotland) Act 1964, s. 37(1)(*a*).

[60] Law Reform (Miscellaneous Provisions) (Scotland) Act 1968, s. 8 and Sched. 2, para. 28.

[61] s. 13(1) and (2).

[62] s. 65(1). The adoption order is available even a few days short of the child's 18th birthday: see *Re D (A Minor) (Adoption Order: Injunction)* [1991] 3 All E.R. 461. The order's effect on status survives, of course, the attainment of majority.

[63] s. 12(5).

[64] *M, Petr.*, 1953 S.C. 227. The earlier case of *TB, Petrs.*, 1950 S.L.T. (Sh.Ct.) 74, in which it was held that the date of the application was the relevant date, was decided on the rather different wording of the Adoption of Children (Scotland) Act 1930.

[65] s. 13(1).

[66] s. 12(7).

[67] Except in cases where it is intended to dispense with agreement, it will usually be prudent to wait until the necessary agreements have been given. The agreement of the mother of the child cannot be given less than six weeks after birth (s. 16(4)). Subject to that, the petition may be presented immediately after the child is placed. S. 6 of the Adoption of Children (Regulation) Act 1939 (which required in effect that a petition for adoption might not be presented where arrangements for the placing of the child had been made by a registered adoption society until the expiration of three months from the time when the child was delivered into the care and possession of the prospective adopters but must be made within the following three months if the child had not been

Domicile and Nationality

There is no requirement as to the domicile or nationality of the child. The express jurisdictional tests relating to the domicile of the applicants and the presence of the child within the jurisdiction,[68] discussed shortly, are exhaustive of the questions of jurisdiction and there is no room for implying a further jurisdictional requirement in relation to the child's domicile. In *Re B(S) (An Infant),*[69] however, Goff J. treated recognition of the adoption by the law of the child's domicile as a factor to be taken into account in considering whether the making of an adoption order would be for the welfare of the child. Goff J.'s reasoning has been criticised[70] and his views on the ascertainment of domicile and foreign laws are obscure, but it may be accepted that recognition by the law of the domicile is a factor which, in some circumstances, may bear on the welfare of the child. Any importance to be attached to this factor is, however, much reduced by the current provisions. Under the previous law the child's domicile did not change on adoption but since 1975,[71] due to changes in the law affecting status of an adopted child, the child acquires on adoption a new domicile of dependency which, it seems, will be treated as if it were his domicile of origin. Recognition of the adoption by the law of the country in which the child was domiciled before the adoption can, therefore, be relevant only on the footing that the courts of that country will take a different view of the child's domicile from that which courts within the United Kingdom are bound to take. That is a consideration to which ordinarily the courts of the forum should pay no regard, but on a question of welfare there may, of course, be the exceptional case in which it cannot be ignored.

Child's Residence

Residence is not a jurisdictional test, but at all times during the 13 weeks preceding the making of the adoption order the child must have had his home with the applicants or one of them.[72] Where the placement has not been by an adoption agency and if the applicant or one of the applicants is not a parent, stepparent or relative of the child, the 13-week period is extended to 12 months.[73] It is an offence for anyone other than an adoption agency to make arrangements for the adoption of a child, or to place a child for adoption except where the proposed adopter is a relative of the child; and it is also an offence for anyone other than a relative of the child to receive a child for adoption otherwise than from an adoption agency.[74] Adoption may, however, still follow such illegal placements provided the 12-month requirement is satisfied. In order to gain advantage of the shorter period, it is not required that the original placing should have been for the purposes of adoption and, accordingly, foster parents with whom a child

---

returned to the society) has been repealed, but its ghost lingers with detrimental effect.
[68] ss. 14(2) and 15(2).
[69] [1968] Ch. 204.
[70] Morris, *The Conflict of Laws* (3rd ed.) at p. 255.
[71] Children Act 1975, Sched. 2, para. 1. See now Adoption (Scotland) Act 1978, s. 39(1).
[72] s. 13(1).
[73] s. 13(2).
[74] s. 11(1) and (3).

has been placed by a local authority or approved adoption society[75] may apply for adoption, and an order may be made in their favour, provided the child has had his home with them for the 13 weeks preceding the making of the order even if adoption was not contemplated when the child was placed. Where, however, the fostering arrangement has been made by someone other than a local authority or approved adoption society, the 12-month period applies. This causes no hardship as, in the ordinary case of a genuine fostering arrangement, more than 12 months will have expired before the question of adoption arises. There is, however, a danger that placings may be made under cover of fostering so as to defeat the policy of the Act against illegal placements for adoption. The only safeguard is that courts should examine critically, from the standpoint of the child's welfare, all cases in which the applicants are not relatives of the child and the placing has not been by an adoption agency, and particularly so where it appears either that the placing was illegal or that it was done under cover of fostering with a view to circumventing the prohibitions of the Act.

The requirement in section 13(1) of the 1978 Act that the child should have had his home with the prospective adopters contrasts with the requirement of the 1958 Act that he should have been in their continuous care and possession.[76] Although under the previous law a fairly liberal interpretation was allowed of continuous care and possession, the new provisions admit of applications being entertained where formerly they were refused.[77] It may now be possible to make a case that the person to be adopted has had his home with the applicants in circumstances in which the making of an adoption order would formerly have been incompetent because of the lack of continuous care and possession (*e.g.* due to absence on military service). It remains essential that the applicants should stand *in loco parentis* to the child to be adopted.[78] They may do so where they exercise quasi-parental control even if the day-to-day care is delegated to others.[79] Continuous care and possession has been held to be interrupted when the child was allowed, in the course of the statutory period, to stay overnight with his natural mother,[80] but such absence today will affect the competency of the adoption order only if it shows vacillation concerning the home of the child.[81] In the case of applications by spouses an order may competently be made although one of the applicants has been absent (*e.g.* in the course of his employment on business or on military or other public service) during the 13-week period, because it is sufficient that the child should have had his home

---

[75] *i.e.* by an adoption agency (s. 1(4)).

[76] Adoption Act 1958, s. 3.

[77] *M, Petr.*, 1953 S.C. 227; *F, Petr.*, 1955 S.L.T. (Sh.Ct.) 12. Cases of absence for treatment in hospital (*G, Petr.*, 1955 S.L.T. (Sh.Ct.) 27) and for the purposes of vocational training with return to the home at weekends and for holidays (*A, Petr.*, 1953 S.L.T. (Sh.Ct.) 45) in which the statutory requirements were held to have been satisfied will continue to qualify under the current test.

[78] *Re B (An Infant)* [1964] Ch. 1; *Re A (An Infant)* [1963] 1 W.L.R. 231.

[79] *Re B (An Infant), supra.*

[80] *Re CSC* [1961] 1 W.L.R. 304.

[81] Any substantial contact with the natural parents during the period leading up to the making of an adoption order may, however, make it difficult to assess whether the child has settled down satisfactorily with the proposed adopters and will be, with the possible exception of some adoptions by relatives, from that standpoint a consideration adverse to the making of an adoption order. See *post.* On care and possession see also *XY, Petrs.*, 1954 S.L.T. (Sh.Ct.) 86.

with one of the applicants.[82] The court must, however, be satisfied that the adoption agency which placed the child, or in any other case the local authority, has had sufficient opportunities, which need not be within the 13 weeks preceding the order, to see the child with the applicant in the home environment and, where husband and wife jointly apply for adoption, the child must be seen with them both together.[83]

Appropriate Court Determined by Child's Presence

If the child is in Scotland an application for an adoption order may be made to the Court of Session or to the sheriff court of the sheriffdom within which the child is.[84] The physical presence of the child within the jurisdiction at the time the petition is presented is all that is required: domicile and residence are irrelevant. Prospective adopters have an unfettered choice between the Court of Session and the appropriate sheriff court, but past experience has been that nearly all adoption applications are made in the sheriff court. If the child is in England or Wales no Scottish court has jurisdiction.[85] If, however, the child is not in Great Britain, the Court of Session, but not the sheriff court, has jurisdiction.[86]

Capacity of Applicants to Adopt

Age and Domicile of Applicants

An adoption order may be made on the application of any person who is domiciled in a part of the United Kingdom or in the Channel Islands or the Isle of Man[87] and who has attained the age of 21,[88] or, in the case of a natural parent seeking to adopt jointly with his or her spouse, the age of 18.[89] Domicile and age are to be ascertained at the time when the order is made. There is no requirement that the applicant should be domiciled in Scotland. Provided he or she is domiciled in a part of the United Kingdom or in the Channel Islands or the Isle of Man, the jurisdiction of the Scottish court is determined by the whereabouts of the child.[90] In the case of applications by a married couple, each of them must satisfy the relevant age requirement,[91] but it is sufficient if only one of them has the requisite domicile.[92]

Individuals and Married Couples as Applicants

Although applications by married couples are the norm, applications by individuals are competent. Only, however, in the case of an application by a married

---

[82] Adoption (Scotland) Act 1978, s. 13(1). Under the previous law continuous care and possession had been held *dubitante* to be consistent with absences of one applicant on military service: *A, Petr.*, 1958 S.L.T. (Sh.Ct.) 61.

[83] s. 13(3).

[84] s. 56(2).

[85] The Adoption Act 1976, s. 62, gives exclusive jurisdiction to stated courts in England and Wales in relation to children present there.

[86] s. 56(3).

[87] ss. 14(2) and 15(2).

[88] s. 14(1A), as substituted by the Children Act 1989, Sched. 10, para. 33.

[89] s. 14(1B), as inserted by the Children Act 1989, Sched. 10, para. 33.

[90] above.

[91] *i.e.* 18 or 21.

[92] s. 14(2)(*a*).

couple may an order be made on the application of more than one person.[93] Where an application is made by an individual, he must either be unmarried, or, if married, he must satisfy the court that (1) his spouse cannot be found, or (2) the spouses have separated and are living apart and the separation is likely to be permanent, or (3) his spouse is, by reason of ill-health (whether physical or mental) incapable of making an application for an adoption order.[94] Where reliance is placed on the fact that the spouse cannot be found, the court will require that every reasonable step to trace the spouse has been taken.[95] Separation connotes the putting into effect of an intention on the part of at least one of the spouses to cease cohabitation, and "living apart" is the maintenance of that separation. The twin elements of intention and act are essential. The act of separation involves withdrawal from the society of the other but not necessarily living under separate roofs.[96] Cohabitation may have ceased where each is living as if a single person to whom the other is a stranger although their separate accommodation is under the same roof.[97] An adoption application by a spouse who, although separated from the other spouse, is living under the same roof, is, however, unlikely to be successful as such an arrangement almost inevitably would involve some hazard to the welfare of the child.

Parents as Applicants

When a child is born its mother will have parental rights over it whether or not she is or was married to the child's father[98]; the father will have parental rights if he is married to the mother or was married to her at the date of the child's conception or at any time subsequently,[99] or if he has obtained an order relating to parental rights.[1] When both parents have parental rights, any adoption order obtained at the instance of one or other of the child's natural parents will have the effect of extinguishing the parental responsibilities and rights that were vested in the other,[2] and the child will be treated in law as the child of the adopter and of no other person.[3] In other words, adoption by one parent will effectively exclude the other parent from any legal relationship with the child. Consequently there is a risk that such an adoption might be used as a weapon designed to hurt the other parent by denying parental responsibilities and rights rather than to benefit the child; there is also the risk that the adoption will be used to hide from the child the true facts about his origins, which may in the long run prove damaging to him; and in general it will often be socially and psychologically undesirable to exclude the other parent from contact with the child.

---

[93] s. 14(1), (1A), and (1B), as substituted and inserted by the Children Act 1989, Sched. 10, para. 33.
[94] s. 15(1).
[95] *Cf. Re F. (R) (An Infant)* [1970] 1 Q.B. 385.
[96] Clive, *Husband and Wife* (3rd ed.) at p. 430.
[97] See *Lennie* v. *Lennie*, 1950 S.C.(H.L.) 1, *per* Lord Normand at p. 5 and Lord Reid at p. 16. *Cf. Macdonald* v. *Macdonald*, 1948 S.L.T. 380.
[98] Law Reform (Parent and Child) (Scotland) Act 1986, s. 2(1)(a).
[99] *Ibid.*, s. 2(1)(b).
[1] *Ibid.*, s. 3(1). This will change in the event of the enactment of the Scottish Law Commission's proposals that fathers be treated equally with mothers: see Scot. Law Com. No. 135, *Report on Family Law* (May 1992), para. 2.50.
[2] Adoption (Scotland) Act 1978, s. 12(3).
[3] s. 39(1).

There are few valid reasons for doing so today, and single-parent adoptions will therefore normally be inappropriate, especially since parental rights can be acquired in ways that do not exclude the other parent, such as obtaining an order for parental rights under section 3 of the Law Reform (Parent and Child) (Scotland) Act 1986.[4]

The law therefore tries to discourage adoption applications by one of the child's natural parents. By section 15(3) of the Adoption (Scotland) Act 1978,[5] an adoption order is not to be made on the application of the mother or father of the child alone unless the court is satisfied that (1) the other natural parent is dead, or cannot be found, or there is no other parent by virtue of section 28 of the Human Fertilisation and Embryology Act 1990,[6] or (2) there is some other reason justifying the exclusion of the other natural parent. These provisions are directed to applications by an unmarried parent or, in the limited circumstances in which one spouse alone can apply, a parent who although married is not married to the other parent of the child. "Other natural parent" necessarily includes fathers of children born out of wedlock. There is, in these circumstances, a risk that where paternity has neither been admitted nor established in other proceedings, the aim of section 15(3) may be circumvented by falsely attributing paternity to someone who is dead or who cannot be found. There is also a question of what will amount to "some other reason" that will justify excluding the other parent? This would, it is thought, include for example a failure to discharge parental responsibilities, failure by either parent to discharge their alimentary obligations,[7] and abandonment, neglect or ill-treatment of the child. There is a clear overlap with the conditions allowing the court to dispense with parental agreement to adoption, but the phraseology used in the present context is significantly less precisely drawn and may well be taken, for that reason, to be wider.

Nor is it clear what "the exclusion of the other natural parent" means. As section 15(3) applies to applications by unmarried mothers and fathers, it cannot mean exclusion from the adoption process because such natural parents could not make a joint application. The meaning seems to be exclusion from the legal incidents of the relationship between father or mother and child. Where the court is satisfied that there is reason justifying the exclusion of the other natural parent, that reason must be recorded.[8]

CONSENT AND AGREEMENT

Consent of the Child

Children Over 12

If the person to be adopted is of or over the age of 12 years his consent is re-

---

[4] The position is different when a parent seeks to adopt jointly with a new spouse, and it is reported that around 40 per cent. of all applications in Scotland disclose this situation (Thomson at p. 216).

[5] As amended by the Human Fertilisation and Embryology Act 1990, Sched. 4, para. 6.

[6] Which defines when a man will be "father" of a child born as a result of an artificial reproduction technique: see *ante* at pp. 136–141.

[7] Family Law (Scotland) Act 1985, s. 1(1)(c).

[8] s. 15(3).

quired.[9] A requirement that minor children consent to their own adoption has
been a consistent feature of adoption legislation in its application to Scotland[10]
and reflects the personal competence and capacity for legal acts previously imputed by law to a minor as distinct from a pupil child; the requirement was preserved when pupils' incapacities were extended to all children under the age of
16,[11] but the ages equalised at 12 for boys and girls. The court may dispense
with the child's consent where it is satisfied that the child is incapable of giving
his consent.[12] Subject to that exception the requirement of consent is mandatory.[13] The Adoption Act 1958[14] had required, as had the earlier legislation,[15] that
the court should be satisfied that the minor had understood the nature and effect
of the adoption order for which application was made, but that requirement was
repealed by the Children Act 1975[16] and is not repeated in the Adoption (Scotland) Act 1978. However, where the child is of or above the age of 12 and
capax, the court cannot discharge its statutory duty[17] to ascertain the wishes and
feeling of the child without inquiring as to his understanding of the nature and
effect of the proposed adoption order. Under the previous law the court had refused to give effect to a minor's consent granted in ignorance of his illegitimacy
until he had been made acquainted with the whole circumstances, including his
illegitimacy, set forth in the petition. Only after that had been done, and he had
not withdrawn his consent, was the adoption order made.[18] It is thought that it
will still, in general, be sound practice to ensure that the child is aware of his
parentage.[19]

Children Under 12

The consent of the child is not required if he or she is under the age of 12 years

---

[9] s. 12(8), as substituted by the Age of Legal Capacity (Scotland) Act 1991, s. 2(3).

[10] Adoption of Children (Scotland) Act 1930, s. 2(3); Adoption Act 1950, s. 2(4); Adoption Act
1958, s. 4(1); Children Act 1975, s. 8(6).

[11] Age of Legal Capacity (Scotland) Act 1991, s. 1(2).

[12] Adoption (Scotland) Act 1978, s. 12(8). The Adoption of Children (Scotland) Act 1930 had contained a similar power of dispensation (s. 2(4)), but it was omitted from the 1950 and 1958 Acts.
In *PQ and RQ, Petrs.*, 1965 S.C. 45 it was held, in a question under the 1958 Act, that no adoption
order could be granted where the minor child was mentally retarded and unable to understand the
circumstances of adoption or sign a form of consent. The omission was supplied by the Law
Reform (Miscellaneous Provisions) (Scotland) Act 1966, s. 4 and the 1978 Act repeats what was
then enacted.

[13] *PQ and RQ, Petrs., supra; McD and McD, Petrs.*, (1949) 65 Sh. Ct. Rep. 42.

[14] s. 7(1)(*a*).

[15] Adoption of Children (Scotland) Act 1930, s. 3(*a*); Adoption Act 1950, s. 5(1)(*a*).

[16] Sched. 4.

[17] s. 6.

[18] *A, Petr.*, 1936 S.C. 255. See, however, *A, Petr.*, 1953 S.L.T. (Sh.Ct.) 45.

[19] In the absence of a statutory direction there is room for judicial discretion, but it will only be in
highly exceptional circumstances that the court can be satisfied that proper consideration has
been given to the wishes and feelings of the child when the child is in ignorance of his true status
or parentage and it is practicable to dispel that ignorance. In considering what is practicable it
may, however, be right to give weight to any adverse effect that knowledge of his origins would
have on the child. That he should be kept in ignorance is undesirable but an adoption process may
not afford the best occasion for telling him the true facts. In *C, Petrs.*, 1993 S.C.L.R. 14 Sheriff
Gow held that it was impracticable to ascertain the wishes and feelings of a six year old child
when the prospective adopters refused to allow her to be interviewed, because they did not want
the child to know she was adopted – the wife was the child's natural mother and the husband had
married the wife two weeks after the birth. The adoption application was granted.

on the date the order is made, but the provision[20] requiring the court to ascertain the wishes and feelings of the child regarding the decision and to give due consideration to them, having regard to his age and understanding, has no age limit attached to it and it will be appropriate for the court, or the reporting officer, to consult the child even under the age of 12. Indeed the statutory obligation could hardly be fulfilled without doing so, except in the case of the very young child. In *AB and CB, Petrs.*,[21] the sheriff was criticised for not having satisfied this statutory obligation when he failed to take account of the view of two children aged 11 and 12.

Parental Agreement

Except where the procedure of freeing a child for adoption under section 18 of the 1978 Act,[22] or the English or Northern Irish equivalent, has been used, it is a prerequisite to the making of an adoption order either that the court should be satisfied that each parent or guardian of the child to be adopted has freely and with full understanding of what is involved agreed unconditionally to the making of the adoption order (whether or not he knows the identity of the applicant) or that his agreement to the making of the adoption order should be dispensed with on one of the specified statutory grounds.[23] It is the stress laid on parental agreement that, along with permanence, points the character of adoption as distinct from applications for custody or other proceedings regulating the care of children. As Lord Hailsham of St Marylebone L.C. said in *Re W (An Infant)*[24]:

> "In custody cases what is in question is the custody, care or control of the child, or perhaps the administration of his property, and that is why his interest is the first and paramount consideration. But in adoption cases what is in issue is the parent-child relationship itself and in that relationship the parent as well as the child has legitimate rights."

While the welfare of the child may be relevant to some aspects of dispensing with parental agreement,[25] the withholding of parental agreement may constitute a barrier to the granting of an adoption order even if it can be shown that to grant the order would promote the child's welfare. The primary purpose of the obligation to obtain agreement is to give a right of objection to the parents, rather than to protect the welfare of the child.

Meaning of "Parent" and "Guardian"

Unlike the word "guardian," the word "parent" is not defined in the Adoption (Scotland) Act 1978, and it is not initially clear whether the requirement of consent applies to all natural parents or only those who have parental rights. In a

---

[20] s. 6.

[21] 1990 S.C.L.R. 809.

[22] See *post* at pp. 546–550.

[23] s. 16(1), as amended by Children Act 1989, Sched. 10, para. 34. "Agreement" is the term used in place of "consent" in the previous legislation. The purpose is to provide a distinct terminology for the procedure for freeing for adoption. A parent agrees to the making of an adoption order but consents to freeing for adoption. It is, however, obscure why "agreement" was not used for the new process and "consent" retained in the context in which it had hitherto been used.

[24] [1971] A.C. 682 at p. 693.

[25] See *post* at pp. 534–546.

case decided under the Adoption Act 1950[26] it was held that a putative father who was not a guardian of an illegitimate child was not a "parent" within the meaning of the agreement requirement. The decision rested on the basis that the law clearly distinguished between the legitimate and the illegitimate child and that it was only in the case of the former that the term parent could in the full legal sense be applied to a father. That distinction has been modified by subsequent legislation but in relation to parental rights of fathers important distinctions remain between children of married parents, on the one hand, and of unmarried parents, on the other; and in the definition section of the 1978 Act "guardian" and "relative" are given special meanings in relation to the "illegitimate" child. The position of the putative father has not been expressly altered by legislation and it may therefore be inferred that Parliament has not intended to grant the right to withhold agreement to putative fathers.[27] That inference is fortified by the definition of guardian in the 1978 Act, parts of which would be otiose if the father of a child born out of wedlock were a parent for the purposes of the Act, and that it is correct is implicit in a decision of the First Division, who have indicated that it would be entirely improper for a reporting officer to ask the father of a child over whom he has no parental rights whether he agrees to the adoption.[28] There are, moreover, practical advantages in not burdening the adoption process with a requirement of agreement from putative fathers who may have had little or no contact with the child or who may be difficult to trace or whose paternity of the child may be uncertain. Putative fathers who have sought and obtained parental rights are guardians for the purposes of the Act and their agreement in that capacity is required. Other putative fathers may be able to assert a right to be heard and so achieve some protection for their legitimate interests in so far as these are consistent with the welfare of the child. Parent for the purposes of the Act may therefore be taken to mean the child's mother and the child's father if married to the mother at the time of conception or subsequently.[29]

"Guardian" is defined by section 65 of the Adoption (Scotland) Act 1978 to mean a person appointed by deed or will or by a court of competent jurisdiction to be the guardian of the child, and in the case of a child whose father is not married to the mother[30] includes the father where he has, in relation to the child, guardianship, custody, access or any other parental right by virtue of an order by a court of competent jurisdiction.

Other Person's Agreement

Persons other than parents or guardians who obtain parental rights and pow-

---

[26] *A* v. *B*, 1955 S.C. 378.

[27] *Per* Sheldon J. in *Re TD (A Minor) (Wardship: Jurisdiction)* (1986) 16 Fam. L. 18, discussing similar English statutory provisions and the English case of *Re M (An Infant)* [1955] 2 Q.B. 479.

[28] *Per* Lord President Emslie in *A and B* v. *C*, 1987 S.C.L.R. 514. See also *A and B, Petrs.*, 1971 S.C.(H.L.) 129.

[29] If the Scottish Law Commission's proposals, that all fathers be treated equally with all mothers, and be given automatic parental responsibilities and rights, are given legislative effect, this position will change and agreement of both parents will be required, irrespective of their marital status. See Scot. Law Com. No. 135, *Report on Family Law* (May 1992), at para. 2.50, and draft Bill, Sched. 1, para. 65.

[30] See n. 29 above, and draft Bill, Sched. 2.

ers other than under the Law Reform (Parent and Child) (Scotland) Act 1986 have no right to grant or withhold agreement to the making of an adoption order, and consequently their agreement should not be sought. For example, a local authority that has resolved that there shall vest in them parental rights and powers under section 16 of the Social Work (Scotland) Act 1968[31] do not thereby obtain the right to grant or withhold agreement to the making of an adoption order, for that right is expressly excluded by section 16(3) of the 1968 Act.[32] Likewise a local authority into whose care a child has been received under section 15 of the 1968 Act, or in whose care a child is by virtue of a supervision requirement made under section 44(5) of the 1968 Act, has no right to grant or withhold agreement. Nor does a foster parent, a custodian of the child, or the husband of a woman whose child is not his and is the subject of the proceedings. This last case may cause difficulty since the husband will be the presumptive father,[33] and that presumption would have to be overturned before his agreement is not required.

There is no necessary connection between agreement to adoption and the right to be heard in the adoption process, except, of course, that a parent or guardian has a right to be heard if there is a question of dispensing with his agreement. Persons whose agreement is not required, including some in the categories mentioned in the previous paragraph, may nonetheless have a right to be heard.[34]

Agreement to be given freely and with full understanding

The requirement that parental agreement should have been given "freely and with full understanding of what is involved" replaces the requirement in the Adoption Act 1958[35] that the court should be satisfied that the parent understood the nature and effect of the adoption order for which application was made and, in particular, that the effect of it would be permanently to deprive him of his parental rights. The new wording seems to be both less precise and wider than the old, but the question remains of what knowledge is necessary to constitute understanding. What must the parent know about the adopters and the environment in which the child, if adopted, is to be brought up? In some cases the identity of the proposed adopters is already known to the natural parents, as in most cases of adoption by relatives, and in others, particularly of adoption of older children, there is increasing recognition that the maintenance of some contact with biological parents may be advantageous. In many circumstances,

---

[31] As substituted by the Children Act 1975, s. 74, and as amended by the Adoption (Scotland) Act 1978, Sched. 3, paras. 13 and 14. An application for adoption may be made notwithstanding that parental rights and powers are vested in a local authority or voluntary organisation (Social Work (Scotland) Act 1968, s. 18(4A), and Adoption (Scotland) Act 1978, Sched. 3, para. 15).

[32] A resolution vesting parental rights and powers ceases to have effect if the child becomes the subject of an adoption order (Social Work (Scotland) Act 1968, s. 16(11)(a)).

[33] See ante, at pp. 128–133.

[34] See post at pp. 567–568.

[35] s. 7(1)(a). The Adoption of Children (Scotland) Act 1930, s. 3(a) and the Adoption Act 1950, s. 5(1)(a) had been to the same effect.

however, it is sound and usual practice that the identity of the adopters should not be disclosed, and the rules make provision for achieving that result.[36]

The reasons for anonymity in most cases are obvious. As Lord President Normand said in *H and H, Petrs.*: "On both sides it may be recognised that it is best for the future welfare of the child that the natural mother should not have the temptation or the power to interfere between the child and its adoptive parents."[37] The requirement that agreement should have been given freely and with full understanding implies, however, as did the earlier law, that the mother should

> "have had as real an opportunity of making a decision as she would have had if the identity of the adopters had been disclosed to her, and of this also the Court must be satisfied. The names and designations of the adopters are not in themselves material, but it is material that the mother should have such information about their character and circumstances and about the kind of home into which it is proposed to adopt her child as she may desire."[38]

Although the adopters need not, and often should not, be identified, it is essential to the validity of parental agreement that it should have been given in relation to an adoption by proposed adopters distinguished in accordance with the satutory requirements. In *YZ, Petrs.*[39] it was held that a form of consent which neither named nor distinguished the petitioners was invalid. Under the law as it then stood[40] that result was inescapable and although the requirements of the principal Act have changed the subsidiary rules in their present form point to the same result.[41] A person proposing to present a petition for an adoption order may, before presenting the petition, apply for a serial number to be assigned to him and he is sufficiently distinguished for the purposes of the agreement to the making of an order if the document signifying agreement refers to him as the petitioner to whom that serial number has been assigned and specifies the year in which, and the court by which, it was assigned. It is, therefore, no objection to agreement to adoption that it was given before the presentation of the petition.[42] The requirement that agreement be freely given strikes at the validity of any agreement obtained by pressure, but the mere existence of pressure will not have that result if it did not in fact affect the agreement.[43] A mother is protected against her ill-considered giving of agreement in the aftermath of birth by the provision that agreement is ineffective if given by the mother less than six weeks after the child's birth.[44] Agreement must be unconditional and a parent

---

[36] For the Court of Session see Rules of Court, r. 222, as amended by Act of Sederunt (Rules of Court Amendment No. 6) (Adoption Proceedings) 1984 (S.I. 1984 No. 997); and for the sheriff court see Act of Sederunt (Adoption of Children) 1984 (S.I. 1984 No. 1013).

[37] 1944 S.C. 347 at p. 352.

[38] *Ibid. Cf.* C and C, Petrs., 1936 S.C. 257 and *Re Carroll* [1931] 1 K.B. 317.

[39] 1954 S.L.T. (Sh.Ct.) 98.

[40] Adoption Act 1950, s. 4(1). *Cf.* Adoption Act 1958, s. 6(1).

[41] r. 222 of the Rules of Court (Court of Session) and s. 18 of the Act of Sederunt (Adoption of Children) (sheriff court).

[42] *Ibid.*

[43] *Re T (An Infant)* (1954) 118 J.P. 139.

[44] s. 16(4).

can no longer, therefore, as he or she could under the previous law,[45] impose conditions as to the religious upbringing of the child. An adoption agency in placing a child must, however, "have regard (so far as is practicable) to any wishes of the child's parents and guardians as to the religious upbringing of the child,"[46] and the court may still, in so far as it can do so consistently with its duty under section 6 of the Adoption (Scotland) Act 1978,[47] impose such conditions as it thinks fit,[48] which might concern the child's religious upbringing. The wisdom of imposing such restraints on the conscience of adopters is, however, to be doubted, and in the normal case the condition is unenforceable.

Form of agreement and withdrawal

All agreements to the making of an adoption order require to be in writing and in the form prescribed by the rules.[49] Agreement must be operative at the very moment when the adoption order is made. Accordingly, it may be withdrawn at any time before then.[50] Cases in which parental agreement once given is subsequently withdrawn, constitute, in fact, the typical contested case in which the court is asked to dispense with parental agreement.

Dispensing with Agreement

The modern legislation does not confer on the court any general discretion to dispense with parental agreement such as had been given by the Adoption of Children (Scotland) Act 1930.[51] A similar discretion had been given in England and Wales by the Adoption Act 1926,[52] but in neither jurisdiction does it appear to have been frequently invoked. Where agreement has not been given, dispensing with it is a judicial act which bears directly not only on the propriety but on the validity of an adoption order and so ought to be recorded in the court's order, preferably as a substantive part of it.[53] If none of the statutory grounds is established there can be no dispensation, while, on the other hand, if a ground is established the facts will often, subject to what is said below in relation to the welfare of the child, compel a decision in favour of dispensation. An appellate court can, however, interfere with the decision of the court of first instance, not only where there is an error of law but where, on other grounds, it is clear that it

---

[45] Adoption Act 1958, s. 4(2).

[46] Adoption (Scotland) Act 1978, s. 7.

[47] i.e. that first consideration be given to the need to safeguard and promote the welfare of the child throughout his childhood and that due consideration be given to the wishes and feelings of the child having regard to his age and understanding.

[48] s. 12(6).

[49] r. 222 of the Rules of Court (Court of Session) and s. 18 of the Act of Sederunt (Adoption of Children) (sheriff court).

[50] Re Hollyman [1945] 1 All E.R. 290; Re F (An Infant) [1957] 1 All E.R. 819.

[51] s. 2(3). Under that subsection the court could dispense with consent if satisfied that the person whose consent was to be dispensed with was a person whose consent ought (in the opinion of the court and in all the circumstances of the case) to be dispensed with. The discretion was probably aimed primarily at dispensing with the consent of persons other than parents who were liable to contribute to the support of the child (and whose consent was required under the 1930 Act although they were not parents or guardians) but the wording was wide enough to comprehend dispensation with the consent of parents.

[52] s. 2(3).

[53] S v. Huddersfield Borough Council [1975] Fam. 113.

has reached a wrong conclusion[54] and where the court of first instance has refused to dispense with agreement an appellate court may do so if, in its view, the
facts justify that course.[55] Nevertheless, both because of the experience that
courts of first instance commonly have in dealing with questions of adoption
and because of the critical role necessarily played by matter of impression, great
importance will be attached to the decision of the court of first instance and in
the absence of some clear error of fact or law an appellate court will be slow to
reverse that decision.[56] Although questions of dispensing with agreement and of
whether, given that agreement, an adoption order should be made, may often
arise in association, and involve some common factors, they are essentially distinct. The welfare of the child, although central to the decision on the merits of
making the adoption order and relevant to the decision of whether to dispense
with parental agreements,[57] is not relevant to the determination of whether a
ground of dispensation exists, except when agreement is allegedly being unreasonably withheld and even then only in the limited sense that it is a matter
which the reasonable parent may be supposed to take into account.[58] It has been
said:

> "A judge considering whether parental consent to the making of an adop-
> tion order should be dispensed with ... must proceed by way of two steps.
> In the first place he must decide whether a ground set out in s. 16(2) of the
> Act has been established. If no such ground is established that is an end of
> the matter. The application of necessity must be refused. On the other
> hand, if the necessary ground is established the judge must then proceed
> to the next stage which is to consider whether in the light of the considera-
> tions set out in section 6 of the 1978 Act the order applied for ought to be
> made".[59]

Questions of dispensation should, however, usually be considered along with
the merits. In Re C(L) (An Infant)[60] the view had been expressed that a common
feature of all the grounds for dispensing with agreement, with the exception of
incapacity, and the basis of each of them, was "a callous or self-indulgent indifference [on the part of the parent] to the welfare of the child" using "welfare" in
the broad sense and not of mere material advantage; but if by that it was intended to postulate that such indifference was a necessary criterion for invoking
any of the grounds, that view must now be rejected.[61]

The grounds for dispensing with the agreement of a parent or guardian to ad-

[54] A and B, Petrs., 1971 S.L.T. 258, per Lord Reid at p. 259 and Lord Guest at p. 260.
[55] S v. Huddersfield Borough Council, supra; L v. Central Regional Council, 1990 S.L.T. 818.
[56] A and B, Petrs., supra, per Lord Reid at p. 259, Lord Guest at p. 260 and Lord Simon of Glaisdale
at p. 264.
[57] That decision being one "relating to the adoption of a child" and so activating the welfare test in s.
6: per Lord Justice-Clerk in P v. Lothian Regional Council, 1989 S.L.T. 739 at p. 741G (disapproving the English decision of Re P (An Infant) (Adoption: Parental Consent) [1977] Fam.
25).
[58] Post at pp. 536–541. Cf. Re PB (A Minor) (1985) 15 Fam. L. 198, in which Sheldon J, held the
welfare test relevant to a determination of whether the ill-treatment ground existed or not.
[59] Per Lords Wylie, Murray and Caplan in L v. Central Regional Council, 1990 S.L.T. 818 at p. 821,
approved and reiterated by the 1st Division in Lothian Regional Council v. A, 1992 S.L.T. 858.
[60] Per Diplock L.J. [1965] 2 Q.B. 449 at p. 471.
[61] Re W (An Infant) [1971] A.C. 682 , esp. Lord Hailsham of St Marylebone L.C. at p. 697.

option are now contained in section 16(2) of the Adoption (Scotland) Act 1978. These are that he or she:

(a) cannot be found or is incapable of giving agreement;
(b) is withholding agreement unreasonably;
(c) has persistently failed without reasonable cause to discharge the parental duties in relation to the child;
(d) has abandoned or neglected the child;
(e) has persistently ill-treated the child;
(f) has seriously ill-treated the child, and[62] the rehabilitation of the child within the household of the parent or guardian is unlikely.

Disappearance or incapacity[63]

It is normally a prerequisite of holding that a person cannot be found that his whereabouts should be unknown after every reasonable step, by reasonable means, has been taken to trace him.[64] Knowledge of the whereabouts of the person whose agreement is required[65] or the failure to use all reasonable means to ascertain them normally therefore excludes dispensation on this ground. Exceptionally, however, it may be held that a person cannot be found although his whereabouts are known. The true test is the reasonable practicability of communication. Thus, in *Re R (Adoption)*[66] it was held that the parents of the person in respect of whom an adoption was sought could not be found when, although their whereabouts were known, they lived under a totalitarian regime in a country from which the person to be adopted had recently escaped.

Incapacity might be shown in a medical report on the mental and physical condition of the person whose agreement is to be dispensed with. Though it does not say so, the terms of the statute imply that the incapacity be permanent or at least long-term. The deprivation of the right to withhold agreement to an adoption is so significant that it should not be allowed because of a mere temporary or short-term incapacity at the critical time. Although the adoption process is often urgent, it must, it is submitted, await the outcome of an incapacity from which there is a prospect of recovery within a reasonably short space of time, as, for example, until a parent, unconscious after a road accident, recovers consciousness and ability to understand the consequences of agreeing or withholding agreement.

Unreasonable Withholding of Consent[67]

By far the most common ground upon which parental agreement is dispensed is that it is being unreasonably withheld. Where dispensation is sought on this ground, it is commonly the case, at any rate where the proposed adoption is by strangers, that agreement has been once given and subsequently withdrawn.

---

[62] s. 16(5).
[63] s. 16(2)(a).
[64] *Re C, The Times*, April 2, 1957; *Re F(R)* [1970] 1 Q.B. 385; *cf. Clark-Kennedy* v. *Clark-Kennedy* (1908) 15 S.L.T. 844.
[65] *Re B* [1958] 1 Q.B. 12.
[66] [1966] 2 All E.R. 613.
[67] s. 16(2)(b).

Agreement is in principle revocable until the adoption order is made and an undertaking not to oppose the making of an order, however solemnly given, is not binding.[68] The statutory test is whether at the time of the hearing[69] or, if fresh evidence has been admitted on appeal, at the time of the appeal[70] agreement is being unreasonably withheld and not whether it has been unreasonably withdrawn. The fact that agreement has been given and then withdrawn is, however, relevant to whether agreement is being unreasonably withheld. Vacillation is an element evidencing unreasonable withholding of agreement[71] although little weight will be attached to vacillation under stress.[72]

In determining what is reasonable in the circumstances, regard must be had to the interests of the child, of the natural parents, and of the prospective adopter.[73] It follows that whether this ground exists or not is not a matter that is absolutely governed by the welfare test embodied in section 6 of the 1978 Act. The existence of any of the grounds for dispensing with parental agreement is primarily a question of fact.[74] However, the welfare of the child is one factor that is always relevant to the reasonableness or otherwise of the withholding of consent, and thus always relevant to the question of whether this ground exists: it has been said that "a reasonable mother would put the welfare of her child first."[75] This means that "the welfare of the child is a matter to which the reasonable parent must be presumed to give first consideration."[76] It has indeed been held that the question of whether a parent's consent is being unreasonably withheld is not a separate issue from the question of whether adoption would be in the child's best interests.[77] It is submitted that this is to confuse the question of the existence of the ground for dispensing with agreement with the question of whether agreement should be dispensed with. While closely related, the two issues are essentially distinct. An Extra Division of the Inner House has said this:

> "It is, no doubt, a difficult matter for the judge to stand back from his section 6 judgment [concerning whether to dispense with agreement] and make a separate, independent and different judgement from the standpoint of the reasonable parent [concerning whether the ground exists], but that is what the law requires."[78]

The welfare test set out in section 6 is directly relevant only to the issue of whether dispensation should be granted, but the same considerations as those

---

[68] *Re F* [1957] 1 All E.R. 819.

[69] *Re L (An Infant)* [1974] 5 Fam. Law 24.

[70] *Re S (An Infant) (Adoption: Parental Consent)* [1973] 3 All E.R. 88.

[71] *AB* v. *CB* 1963 SC 125, *per* Lord President Clyde at p. 137 and Lord Sorn at p. 138.

[72] *Re W (An Infant]* [1971] A.C. 682; [1971] 2 All E.R. 49, *per* Lord Hailsham of St Marylebone at pp. 56 and 57.

[73] *Per* Lord Justice-Clerk Ross in *P* v. *Lothian Regional Council*, 1989 S.L.T. 739, at p. 741K. *Cf.* Lord Reid in *A and B, Petrs., supra.*

[74] *Re P (An Infant) (Adoption) (Parental Consent)* [1977] Fam. 25.

[75] *Per* Lord Justice-Clerk Ross in *P* v. *Lothian Regional Council, supra*, at p. 742H.

[76] *Per* Sheriff Stewart in *A* v. *B*, 1987 S.L.T. (Sh.Ct.) 121 at p. 125J.

[77] *AB and CB, Petrs.*, 1990 S.C.L.R. 809 at p. 811A.

[78] *Per* Lord McCluskey in *Central Regional Council* v. *M*, 1991 S.C.L.R. 300 at pp. 302–303.

which that section describes are matters to be taken into account in determining the reasonableness of the parent's refusal.[79]

It is clear that dispensation will not be granted merely because it is in the child's interests to be adopted, for otherwise the court could dispense with agreement every time it considered that adoption was advisable, and "the right of the parent or guardian to refuse to agree to the adoption of the child would be rendered nugatory."[80] "It is perfectly feasible that the court will reach its own view that it would be better that the adoption order should proceed but none the less arrive at the view that a reasonable parent was perfectly entitled to withhold his or her consent to the making of such an order."[81]

There have been a number of cases on this ground,[82] but the two leading cases are the House of Lords decisions of *A & B Petitioners*[83] and *Re W (An Infant)*.[84] The central feature of the law as laid down in these two cases is that the reasonableness of the withholding of parental agreement is to be measured by the objective test of whether or not a reasonable parent would have withheld agreement in the circumstances. The objective nature of the test means that the matter has to be viewed in the light of all the circumstances of the case even if these were not known to the actual parent. Because *inter alia* of the prospective adopters' right to remain anonymous important features of the proposed adoption may in fact be unknown to the parent, but the reasonableness of his or her withholding agreement will nonetheless be assessed as if these features, along with all the circumstances of the case, had been known. An objective assessment will be made of how the interests of the child may be served. These interests will then be held in just balance with the interests of the prospective adopters and of the biological parent, because the reasonable parent, to whose judgment the matter is entrusted, would have regard to all these factors and would, in particular, attach great weight to the interests of the child. The question is viewed through the eyes of the parent but these eyes are endowed with a vision and perspective which the natural parent, by reason of ignorance or otherwise, may have lacked. On the other hand, it does not follow from the objectivity of the test that the court is entitled simply to substitute its own view for that of the natural parent.

> "Two reasonable parents can perfectly reasonably come to opposite conclusions on the same set of facts without forfeiting their title to be re-

---

[79] *Per* Lord President Hope in *Lothian Regional Council* v. *A*, 1992 S.L.T. 858 at p. 863B.

[80] Thomson, at p. 225. See also Lord Hodson in *Re W (An Infant)*, *supra*, at p. 718: "it has been repeatedly held that the withholding of consent could not be held unreasonable merely because the [adoption] order, if made, would conduce to the welfare of the child."

[81] *Per* Lord McCluskey in *Central Regional Council* v. *M*, *supra*, at p. 302.

[82] See *B and B, Petrs.*, 1946 S.L.T. (Sh.Ct.) 36; *AB and CB* v. *X's Curator*, 1963 S.C. 124; *Re W (An Infant)* [1971] A.C. 682; *A and B, Petrs.*, 1971 S.C.(H.L.) 129; *Re P (An Infant) (Adoption) (Parental Consent)* [1977] Fam. 25; *Re F (A Minor) (Adoption: Parental Consent)* [1982] 1 W.L.R. 102; *AB* v. *CB*, 1985 S.L.T. 514; *Re V (A Minor) (Adoption: Consent)* [1986] 1 All E.R. 752; *Re A (A Minor) (Adoption: Parental Consent)* [1987] 1 W.L.R. 153; *Re V (Adoption: Parents' Consent)* (1987) 15 Fam. L. 55; *A* v. *B*, 1987 S.L.T. (Sh.Ct.) 121; *P* v. *Lothian Regional Council*, 1989 S.L.T. 739; *L* v. *Central Regional Council*, 1990 S.L.T. 818; *AB and CB, Petrs.*, 1990 S.C.L.R. 809; *Central Regional Council* v. *M*, 1991 S.C.L.R. 300.

[83] 1971 S.C. (H.L.) 129, 1971 S.L.T. 258.

[84] [1971] A.C. 682, [1971] 2 All E.R. 49.

garded as reasonable. The question in any given case is whether a parental veto comes within the band of possible reasonable decisions and not whether it is right or mistaken. Not every reasonable exercise of judgment is right, and not every mistaken exercise of judgment is unreasonable. There is a band of decisions within which no court should seek to replace the individual's judgment with its own".[85]

In, but only in, that way and to that extent *A & B Petitioners* represents a vindication of what has been called the primacy of the natural parent's right.[86] It is better, however, that attention should be concentrated on the words of the statute than on concepts such as primacy of right which, although legitimate as a gloss on the statute, create a risk of introducing extraneous considerations. The statutory extent of the parent's right is that adoption cannot be effected without the parent's agreement unless, on one of the prescribed grounds, the court dispenses with that agreement. That parental agreement is required, is doubtless a reflection of the primary right of parents to order the upbringing of their own children. That their agreement can be dispensed with is a qualification of that right. It is not, however, necessary to refer to the concepts of right which may lie behind the statute in order to determine whether a statutory ground for dispensation exists. If the parental withholding of agreement comes within the band of decisions open to a reasonable parent, acting with the knowledge and objectivity mentioned above, there can be no dispensation on this ground and, if it falls outwith that band, the way to dispensation is open.

Certain further propositions emerge from *A & B Petitioners* and *Re W (An Infant)*. These are to be read in the context of the objective test for assessing the reasonableness of the parental decision and, in the main, as describing, elaborating or explaining that test. The following are the principle among them:

> (1) The interests or claims of the child, the natural parents and the prospective adopters all require to be considered.[87]
>
> (2) The child's interests come first and great weight is to be attached to them. They require consideration inferior in importance to no other. They are not necessarily the paramount consideration, as they are in actions relating to parental rights, but in some cases they may be so.[88] Other things being equal, it may be in the best interests of a child to be with his natural parents but that consideration may be outweighed by other factors, including the merits of his new environment with the prospective adopters and, if a substantial time has invervened since the child was placed for adoption, the disruption necessarily involved in removing him from a home in which he is happy and well cared for and into which he has been integrated.[89]

---

[85] *Re W (An Infant)* [1971] 2 All E.R. at p. 56, *per* Lord Hailsham of St Marylebone.

[86] *A & B Petrs.*, 1971 S.L.T. at p. 263, *per* Lord Simon of Glaisdale.

[87] *Ibid.*

[88] *A & B, Petrs., per* Lord Reid at p. 259, *per* Lord Simon of Glaisdale at p. 279; *Re W (An Infant), per* Lord Donovan at p. 78.

[89] *A & B, Petrs., per* Lord Guest at p. 260. Great stress was laid by Lord Guest on the fact that the child's parents had married after the child was placed for adoption although other factors were held to outweigh that. The main relevance of marriage in the context of the child's welfare is that

(3) The child's welfare is not to be considered exclusively or even primarily in a material sense but extends to all factors which will affect his future.[90] Although these factors are not spelt out in *A & B Petitioners* it seems that the prospect of a stable home environment where he enjoys affection and care and may be expected to be happy is foremost among them.

(4) The right of natural parents to bring up their own children is reciprocal on the responsibility which they have to do so.[91] Their affection for a child and their natural claim as parents should not, however, be ignored if they have given up these responsibilities and agreed to adoption under the stress of adverse circumstances and on a change of circumstances have withdrawn that agreement.[92]

(5) The interests of the prospective adopters should not be ignored. By volunteering to perform the duty of bringing up the child they acquire a right to be considered and once they actually enter upon the performance of responsibility towards the child they acquire thereby a further right to be considered. If as a result of the natural parent's actings, they have been brought into a quasi-parental role towards the child they ought not to be displaced without good reason.

(6) The fact that what will, in the long run, be the child's best interests may often be uncertain is an additional reason for giving considerable weight in proper cases to the claims of the biological parents and of the prospective adopters.

The question of whether or not agreement is being unreasonably withheld is primarily one of fact to be determined by the court of first instance according to the circumstances of the particular case.[93] The question is, however, open for review by an appellate court which is entitled to come to a contrary conclusion to that of the court of first instance if the latter is plainly wrong.[94] As a description of how the onus lies, it is still correct to say that it is *prima facie* reasonable for a parent to withhold agreement to adoption[95] but cases of this kind will rarely be decided on onus. Cases in which, in the absence of culpability, parental agreement is unreasonably withheld, are likely to be exceptional[96] but the reasonableness of the decision and not the exceptionality or otherwise of the circumstances remains the test.[97]

That the position of the biological parent has improved in the interval between agreeing to adoption and withdrawing that agreement is a relevant factor but where, as in *Re W (An Infant)* and *A & B Petitioners*, a significant period of time has elapsed, that will require to be weighted against the adverse con-

---

it may indicate the stability of the home which the natural parents will be able to provide.

[90] *Re W (An Infant)*, *per* Lord Donovan at p. 80. *Cf. A & B v. C*, 1977 S.C. 27.

[91] *A & B, Petrs.*, *per* Lord Simon of Glaisdale at p. 262.

[92] *Ibid.*, *per* Lord Reid at p. 259.

[93] *Re W (An Infant)*, *per* Lord Hailsham of St Marylebone at p. 56 and Lord Guest at p. 77.

[94] *A & B, Petrs.*, *per* Lord Guest at p. 260.

[95] *Re W (An Infant)*, *per* Lord Hailsham of St Marylebone at p. 55; *Re K (An Infant)* [1953] 1 Q.B. 117, *per* Jenkins L.J. at pp. 129–130.

[96] *Re K (An Infant)*, *supra*; *Re F (An Infant)* [1957] 1 All E.R. 819, *per* Harman J. at p. 825.

[97] *Re W (An Infant)*.

sequences which may follow from disrupting the life of the child.[98] The stability of the home which adoptive parents are able to provide will usually indicate the unreasonableness of withholding agreement if the biological parents have a history of instability or, on other grounds, the child's future with them seems insecure.[99] Other instances of unreasonable withholding of agreement are where it is withheld by one parent in order to spite the other,[1] where the decision is not truly that of the parent[2] and where the decision is based on sentiment rather than substantive considerations.[3] A reasonable parent would not withhold agreement to adoption when he or she has nothing to offer the child,[4] nor any prospect of contact with the child in the foreseeable future,[5] nor when he or she has no accommodation in which to keep the child.[6] Nor would a reasonable parent withhold agreement simply in order to protect his or her own access rights, when all other factors point towards adoption being in the interests of the child.[7] Parents who have not cared for their child for some years and who remained emotionally unstable were held to be unreasonable in withholding agreement to the child's adoption.[8]

Persistent Failure to Discharge Parental Duties[9]

The parent's or guardian's agreement may be dispensed with if the court is satisfied that he has persistently failed without reasonable cause to discharge the parental duties in relation to the child. "Parental duties" are not defined in the Act, but it is envisaged that the phrase includes the duty of nurture and education and the duty to aliment the child. In *Re P (Infants)*[10] the obligations of a parent or guardian were held to include "first the natural and moral duty of a parent to show affection, care and interest towards his child; and second, as well, the common law or statutory duty of a parent to maintain his child in the financial or economic sense." There may, therefore, be a failure to discharge parental duty where the emotional nurture of the child is neglected no less than when there is defective provision for his material needs. Failure to maintain contact with the child may well found this ground also.[11]

The failure must be persistent. "Persistently" has been glossed as the equivalent of "permanently"[12] and it has been said that more than "a temporary drifting apart" is envisaged, for the failure must be

> "of such gravity, so completely, so convincingly proved, that there can be

---

[98] *Cf. Re L (An Infant)* (1962) 106 S.J. 611 and *Re W (Infants)* [1965] 3 All E.R. 231.

[99] *Re P (An Infant)* [1976] 3 W.L.R. 924.

[1] *L v. M* (1955) 120 J.P. 27.

[2] *Re P (An Infant)* (1962) 107 S.J. 55.

[3] *S v. B* (1973) 4 Fam. Law 75.

[4] *Re D (An Infant) (Adoption) (Parent's Consent)* [1977] A.C. 602.

[5] *Re F (A Minor) (Adoption: Parental Consent)* [1982] 1 W.L.R. 102.

[6] *Re H and Anr. (Minors) (Adoption: Putative Father's Rights) (No. 3)* [1991] 2 All E.R. 185. See also *Re A (A Minor) (Adoption: Parental Consent)* [1987] 1 W.L.R. 153.

[7] *AB v. CB*, 1985 S.L.T. 514; *AB and CB, Petrs.*, 1990 S.C.L.R. 809; *Re H and Anr. (Minors) (Adoption: Putative Father's Rights) (No. 3) supra.*

[8] *A and B, Petrs.*, 1971 S.C.(H.L.) 129.

[9] s. 16(2)(c).

[10] [1962] 1 W.L.R. 1296, *per* Pennycuick J. at p. 1302.

[11] *A v. B*, 1987 S.L.T. (Sh.Ct.) 121, *per* Sheriff Stewart at p. 123.

[12] *Re D* [1973] 3 All E.R. 1001, *per* Sir George Baker, P. at p. 1005.

> no advantage to the child in keeping continuous contact with the natural
> parent, who has so abrogated his duties that he for his part should be de-
> prived of his own child against his wishes."

It is, however, submitted that to say this is to read words into the statute that are
not there. A drifting apart, temporary or otherwise, may be associated with a
failure in parental duty, but is not in itself in point. Nor is it relevant that there
would be advantage to the child in keeping continuous contact with his natural
parent. That is a matter which arises on a consideration of whether, on the merits
as a whole, an adoption order should be made and not in relation to dispensing
with agreement. Nor is there any warrant for requiring a higher standard of
proof on this than on other matters. The *de quo* is that the court should be satisfied that there has been persistent failure, without reasonable cause, to discharge
the parental duties. The ground clearly refers to past behaviour rather than future prospects: so in *L* v. *Central Regional Council*[13] the sheriff was overruled
for holding that this ground did not exist because the mother had recently established herself in a more settled environment and was now better able to provide
properly for her children.[14] Again, this is a matter relevant to whether consent
should be dispensed with because of the ground, rather than to the existence of
the ground itself.

In order to be characterised as persistent, failure must endure over a substantial period of time, but it need not be permanent. Unlike some Commonwealth
legislatures,[15] Parliament has not prescribed a minimum period and so the
length of time required to constitute persistent failure must be a question of circumstances,[16] but if there has been failure over what can properly be regarded as
a substantial period, it is submitted that it is irrelevant that it lacks or has lacked
permanency because of interruption by periods of virtue or because of the prospect of reformation.

In relation to a local authority's powers to assume parental rights and obligations under section 16 of the Social Work (Scotland) Act 1968, it has been held
that no mental element is required to establish the existence of "persistent failure" as the phrase was used in that statute. In *Central Region Council* v *B*[17] the
sheriff was overruled by an Extra Division of the Inner House because, *inter
alia*, he had held that the adverb "persistently" imports animus. If this were also
the case in the present context—and the statutory wording is so similar that a
different construction could hardly be justified—then it would be irrelevant
whether the parent's failure were deliberate or wholly outwith his control. The
only expressed qualification is that the failure be "without reasonable cause,"
and the word "reasonable" might in some situations justify a consideration of

---

[13] 1990 S.L.T. 818.
[14] *Cf. R* v. *Lothian Regional Council*, 1987 S.C.L.R. 362 (Sh.Ct.) in which a mother claimed that her
alcoholism was being beaten.
[15] *e.g.* the various states of Australia, which require that there should be a failure to discharge the
obligations of a parent or guardian for a period of not less than one year: Finlay and Bisset-
Johnson at p. 226.
[16] In *Re M (An Infant)* (1965) 109 Sol. J. 574 it was doubted if six months was long enough to constitute persistent failure.
[17] 1985 S.L.T. 413.

the parent's intention. In *A* v. *B*[18] the sheriff held that a failure to aliment the child was not without reasonable cause when the parent had no earnings with which to fulfil the obligation. The position might, however, be different if the lack of resources had come about deliberately, for then the cause of the lack of care could hardly be described as being reasonable. In this connection the case of a parent serving a long term of imprisonment is problematic. The lack of opportunity to discharge parental duty is imputable to the prisoner's fault; however, against that it can be said that he has not willed the lack of opportunity of which the proximate cause is his imprisonment and any fault on his part is therefore too remote to characterise his failure as being without reasonable cause. There is much to be said for the view that this ground of dispensing with agreement is designed to deal with the parent who has forfeited the right to give consent through lack of caring. This may not necesssarily be the case with the imprisoned parent. Dispensing with an imprisoned parent's agreement may often come more appropriately under the heading of unreasonable withholding of agreement.

Whether there has been persistent failure to discharge parental duties has been discussed in a number of cases. A father who, after separation from his wife, saw the young children of the marriage only occasionally and who, after divorce, did not see or maintain them, although he maintained some contact by sending presents, has been held by the Divisional Court in England not to have persistently failed to discharge the obligations of a parent.[19] There was no persistent failure without reasonable cause where a mother, in a six-month period following the placing of the child for adoption, did not maintain contact with him,[20] and it is generally reasonable for a parent not to maintain contact with a child placed for adoption[21] although it may be reasonable to make inquiries if, after a lapse of time, steps in the adoption process are not taken. Where, however, a mother handed her children over to foster parents soon after their birth, and thereafter, although for much of the time she had accommodation for them, showed little interest in them, visiting them only seldom and paying little towards their maintenance although drawing family allowances for them, it was held that there was persistent failure without reasonable cause.[22] A father who neither claims custody nor aliments a child of his marriage born after separation from his wife and placed by her for adoption may be said to have persistently failed in his duty.[23]

---

[18] 1987 S.L.T. (Sh.Ct.) 121.

[19] *Re D (Minors) (Adoption by Parent)* [1973] 3 W.L.R. 595. As noted above, it is to be doubted if this proceeds on a sound view of the law.

[20] *Re M (An Infant), supra.*

[21] Where the child has been placed with strangers, it will usually be impracticable to maintain contact and, even in other cases, it may be desirable that the child should be given an opportunity to settle down in his adoptive home without the conflict which may ensue from maintaining contact with the natural parent.

[22] *Re P (Infants) (Adoption) (Parental Consent)* [1962] 1 W.L.R. 1296.

[23] *Re B (S) (An Infant)* [1968] 1 Ch. 204. See further *Re H (Minors), The Times*, Nov. 26, 1974; *Re M and M* (1976) 6 Fam. L. 172; *H and H, Petrs.*, 1976 S.L.T. 80; *A and B* v. *C*, 1977 S.L.T. (Sh.Ct.) 55; *L* v. *Central Regional Council* [1990] S.L.T. 818.

Abandonment[24]

A child is abandoned when he is left to his fate.[25] When, therefore, by an arrangement freely entered into, a parent entrusts the care of a child to others, there is no abandonment.[26] It is, moreover, not abandonment to leave a child in the hands of a person who has the right of custody of the child and therefore the corresponding duties, even if that is done against the person's will,[27] unless perhaps where there is evident physical impossibility in his arranging for the welfare of the child. Accordingly if one parent of a child hands the child over to the other, there is, unless the other has been deprived of custody by an order of the court, normally no abandonment.[28] It is thought, however, that it is abandonment to leave a child, without the agreement of the recipient freely given, with a person (or body), (*a*) who has no duty to care for the child even if it is known that the child will, in fact, be cared for; (*b*) who (as, *e.g.* a local authority) has a duty to care for the child only in the event of failure by the parent, and the child is left with that person because the parent refuses to provide a home or to aliment the child when in a position to do so.[29] In *Watson* v. *Nikolaisen*[30] it was held that abandonment connotes such conduct as would attract the sanctions of the criminal law under, in England and Wales, section 27 of the Offences Against the Person Act 1861 or section 1 of the Children and Young Persons Act 1933. That view was not, however, necesssary for the decision of the case and it is submitted that, in any event, it involves a misconstruction of the statute which a Scottish court should not follow. Abandonment may have the same meaning in criminal as in adoption legislation but neither of the statutes to which reference was made penalised abandonment as such. Under section 1 of the Children and Young Persons Act 1933, as under its Scottish equivalent,[31] it is an offence to abandon a child in a manner likely to cause him unnecessary suffering or injury to health, and under section 27 of the Offences against the Person Act 1861 it must be shown that the abandonment was such that the life of the child was endangered or his health had been or was likely to be permanently injured. Under neither statute, therefore, does abandonment in itself attract the sanctions of the criminal law. However, for the purposes of dispensing with parental agreement to adoption, it is abandonment as such which the court requires to consider and the qualifications of that concept contained in the criminal legislation are miss-

---

[24] s. 16(2)(*d*).

[25] *Mitchell* v. *Wright* (1905) 7 F. 568, *per* Lord President Dunedin at p. 574.

[26] *Ibid.* See also *McLean* v. *Hardie*, 1927 S.C. 344.

[27] *McLean* v. *Hardie, supra.*

[28] At common law there could be abandonment if the father handed over the child to the mother when she was unwilling or unable to receive him. This rule probably no longer applies since the mother will always now have obligations to the child, for example that of aliment (under the Family Law (Scotland) Act 1985).

[29] *Cf. New Monkland Parish Council* v. *Erskine*, 1926 S.C. 835 in which it was held that a mental defective was a person found abandoned in the poorhouse for the purposes of the Mental Deficiency and Lunacy (Scotland) Act 1931 when she had been placed there by her parents who had refused to give her a home or to pay for her keep although able to do so. The decision was influenced by the consideration that the humane objects of the Act pointed to a "liberal and not jesuitical construction," but it is nonetheless capable of an application wider than the statute in issue.

[30] [1955] 2 Q.B. 286.

[31] Children and Young Persons (Scotland) Act 1937, s. 12(1).

ing. Accordingly, conduct that would fail to attract sanctions under section 12(1) of the Children and Young Persons (Scotland) Act 1937 because there was no likelihood that it would cause the child unnecessary suffering or injury to health, may, nonetheless, amount to abandonment for the purposes of section 16(2)(d) of the Adoption (Scotland) Act 1978. A child may therefore be abandoned for the purposes of dispensing with parental agreement to adoption when he is left to his own fate, even if, to the knowledge of the abandoning parent, that fate is unlikely to entail unnecessary suffering or injury to health and even if it is likely to be beneficial. To leave a child in a court room, as was done in R v. Whibley,[32] may not be to abandon the child in a manner likely to cause him unnecessary suffering or injury to health but it may, nonetheless, be abandonment.

Neglect[33]

A parent neglects a child when he shows

> "want of reasonable care—that is, the omission of such steps as a reasonable parent would take, such as are usually taken in the ordinary experience of mankind . . . provided the parent had such means as would enable him to take the necessary steps."[34]

Where, however, a parent lacks the necessary means, he may nonetheless be guilty of neglect if he does not take reasonable steps to remedy that defect (as, e.g. by taking advantage of the provisions of welfare legislation). Neglect, like abandonment, is unqualified by any reference in the statute to the likelihood of unnecessary suffering or injury to health but, unlike abandonment, the word connotes some contemplation of consequences. What might have been foreseen, in the way of suffering or injury, necessarily enters into what constitutes neglect. Conduct constituting neglect for the purposes of dispensing with parental agreement to adoption will, therefore, often be assimilable to conduct attracting criminal sanctions. Nonetheless, the omission of any references to unnecessary suffering or likelihood of injury to health means that conduct which would not be criminal is not excluded in principle from the category of neglect in the context of adoption. In order to be obnoxious to the statute, neglect must be significant in kind and degree; it must relate to an aspect of the child's well-being to which a reasonable parent would attach importance and be of such seriousness as reasonably to cause concern for its adverse effect on the child. Not only neglect of physical welfare but also emotional neglect and rejection may be in point. Although there is in the adoption legislation no express provision corresponding to section 12(2)(a) of the Children and Young Persons (Scotland) Act 1937 relating to failure to provide adequate food, clothing, medical aid or lodging such failure falls, it is submitted, within the ordinary meaning of neglect.

---

[32] (1938) 26 Cr. App. Rep. 184.
[33] s. 16(2)(d).
[34] R v. Senior [1899] 1 Q.B. 283, per Lord Russell C.J. at p. 291.

Ill-Treatment[35]

Ill-treatment is also an echo of section 12(1) of the Children and Young Persons (Scotland) Act 1937. Ill-treatment is not separated by any precise boundary from neglect or, indeed, from assault, abandonment or exposure. These are not mutually exclusive categories.[36] Ill-treatment may also be criminal at common law. Ill-treatment that does not result in the likelihood of unnecessary suffering or injury to health, or which is not so gross as to offend against the common law, may nonetheless give grounds for dispensing with parental agreement. Conduct resulting in "agitation of mind, astonishment and disgust,"[37] may be ill-treatment for this purpose although not for the purposes of a criminal offence. There need not be a physical element in the conduct and threats. Language or conduct calculated to create terror in the child, or verbal abuse, may be enough. The age, health and constitution of the child and his or her past history require to be taken into consideration and what may be innocuous in the case of a healthy, well cared-for child, may be ill-treatment "if applied to a child already enfeebled and suffering from previous ill-usage."[38]

The contrast between paragraph (e) (persistent ill-treatment) and paragraph (f) (serious ill-treatment) in section 16(2) of the Adoption (Scotland) Act 1978 might suggest that for the purposes of paragraph (e) the ill-treatment need not be serious. It is thought, however, that some significant degree of seriousness is implicit in persistent ill-treatment, although in paragraph (e) the emphasis is on the persistent nature of the course of conduct, whereas in paragraph (f) it is on the serious nature of the ill-treatment, which may consist of an isolated incident. For paragraph (f) there must be something that justifies the explicit qualification of ill-treatment by the epithet "serious." It is only where the rehabilitation of the child within the household of the parent or guardian is unlikely that paragraph (f) applies,[39] and, while it is not necessary that the unlikelihood of rehabilitation should be because of the ill-treatment, the prospects of rehabilitation will in most cases afford a good index of whether or not the ill-treatment was serious.

Freeing for Adoption

The question of the parent's or guardian's agreement to adoption, or dispensation therefrom, can be dealt with in the same process as the making of the adoption order itself, and the discussion so far has assumed that this will be so. However, it has been possible since the coming into force of the Adoption (Scotland) Act 1978 for the issue of the parent's or guardian's agreement to be examined and, if appropriate, dispensed with in a separate and earlier process in which the court makes an order declaring the child free for adoption.[40] This has the practical advantage that the parent's agreement can be obtained earlier than otherwise, thus reducing the risk of the parent changing his or her mind at a late stage: for while in the normal case agreement is not binding and can be withdrawn at any time until the adoption order is made, its retraction after a freeing

---

[35] s. 16(2)(e) and (f).
[36] R v. Hayles [1969] 1 Q.B. 364.
[37] R v. Hatton [1925] 2 K.B. 322 at p. 324.
[38] Farquharson v. Gordon (1894) 21 R.(J.) 52, per Lord Justice-Clerk Macdonald at p. 53.
[39] s. 16(5).
[40] See 1985 S.L.T. (News) 1 at pp. 1–4.

order is without effect and the only way the parent can later prevent the adoption is to have the freeing order revoked. It has the further advantage that the natural parent can give his or her final agreement earlier and so drop out of the picture earlier and thus be free of prolonged trauma and further inquiry. Prospective adopters, with whom the child is placed, obtain thereby a greater sense of security.

The court may make an order freeing a child for adoption on an application by an adoption agency (and only then), if satisfied either (1) that each parent or guardian[41] of the child has freely and with full understanding of what is involved agreed generally[42] and unconditionally to the making of an adoption order, or (2) that the parent's or guardian's agreement to the making of an adoption order should be dispensed with on any of the grounds listed in section 16(2) and described above.[43] The application to free the child for adoption requires the consent of a parent or guardian of the child, or alternatively, when the child is in the care of the adoption agency, the adoption agency must be applying for dispensation of the agreement of each parent or guardian of the child.[44] Though the grounds of dispensation are the same as under section 16(2), there is a further requirement in the freeing process, that is, that no agreement can be dispensed with unless the child is already placed for adoption or the court is satisfied that it is likely that the child will be placed for adoption.[45] As with an application for adoption, the agreement of a mother to the making of an adoption order is ineffective if given less than six weeks after the child's birth but her consent to the freeing application may be given earlier;[46] and the consent of a child of or over the age of 12 years is required, except that where the court is satisfied that the child is incapable of giving consent to the making of the order, it may dispense with that consent.[47]

Before making an order freeing a child for adoption, the court must satisfy itself, in relation to each parent or guardian of the child who can be found, that he has been given an opportunity of making, if he so wishes, a declaration that he prefers not to be involved in future questions concerning the adoption of the child.[48] In the case of a child whose father is not married to the mother and who does not have any parental right in relation to the child (and is not considered a parent in the adoption process itself[49]), the court must, before making the order, satisfy itself in relation to any person claiming to be the father that either (1) he has no intention of applying for any parental right under section 3 of the Law Reform (Parent and Child) (Scotland) Act 1986 or (2) if he did so apply for any parental right the application would be likely to be refused.[50] The decision to

---

[41] Defined as above, *ante* at pp. 530–531.

[42] s. 12(1) (agreement to adoption) does not require "general" agreement, and it is thought that this word in s. 18(1) (agreement to freeing for adoption) has little, if any, substantive content.

[43] s. 18(1).

[44] s. 18(2).

[45] s. 18(3).

[46] s. 18(4).

[47] s. 18(8), as amended by the Age of Legal Capacity (Scotland) Act 1991, s. 2(3).

[48] s. 18(6).

[49] *A* v. *B*, 1955 S.C. 378. But see the comments concerning future changes in the law at n. 29 above.

[50] s. 18(7). This section will be repealed on the enactment of the proposals contained in Scot. Law Com. No. 135, *Report on Family Law* (May 1992), draft Bill, Sched. 2.

free a child for adoption is one to which the welfare principle in section 6 of the 1978 Act[51] applies.

Effect of a Freeing Order

On the making of an order freeing a child for adoption the parental rights and duties relating to the child vest in the adoption agency as if the order were an adoption order and the agency were the adopters.[52] Thereafter, when the adoption application itself comes to be considered, there is no need to obtain the further agreement of the parent or guardian, or to dispense with their agreement[53]: apart from that feature, the effect of a freeing order is very similar to the vesting of parental rights and duties in a local authority or voluntary organisation under section 16 of the Social Work (Scotland) Act 1968.[54]

Within 14 days following the date 12 months after the making of the freeing order the adoption agency shall, if it has not already done so, inform the former parent[55] whether an adoption order has been made in respect of the child and, if no such order has been made, whether the child has his home with a person with whom he has been placed for adoption.[56] If an adoption order has not been made at the time when the former parent is to be given notice, the agency must thereafter give notice to the natural parent of the making of an adoption order and meanwhile give notice whenever the child is placed for adoption or ceases to have his home with a person with whom he has been placed for adoption.[57] None of these requirements applies if, before the expiry of the 12-month period, the agency has informed the parent that an adoption order has been made[58] or if the parent has made a declaration that he does not wish to be involved in further questions concerning the adoption of the child.[59]

Revocation of Freeing Order

An order freeing a child for adoption may be revoked on the application of the natural parent or guardian at any time more than 12 months after the making of an order, on the ground that the parent or guardian wishes to resume parental rights and duties.[60] An application is competent, however, only if no adoption order has been made in respect of the child *and* the child does not have his home with a person with whom he has been placed for adoption. It is sufficient that the applicant is willing to resume parental rights and duties and there is no requirement that he should himself be able to provide a home for the child. The court is not, however, bound to grant the application and in reaching its decision it must

---

[51] See *post* at pp. 550–558.

[52] s. 18(5).

[53] s. 16(1)(a).

[54] See *ante* at pp. 418–419.

[55] *i.e.* each parent or guardian who must be given the opportunity under s. 18(6) of declaring that he prefers not to be involved in future questions concerning the adoption of the child: s. 19(1).

[56] s. 19(2).

[57] s. 19(3). For a discussion of the analogous English provision (s. 19(3) of the Adoption Act 1976) and in particular the meaning of "having his home," see *R* v. *Derbyshire County Council, ex p. T and Anr.* [1990] 1 All E.R. 792.

[58] s. 19(2)(a).

[59] s. 19(4)(b).

[60] s. 20(1).

have regard to all the circumstances and give first consideration to the need to safeguard and promote the welfare of the child.[61]

The effect of revocation is that the parental rights and duties relating to the child are vested in the person in whom they were vested immediately before the order freeing the child for adoption was made.[62] There is, however, one exception to that rule: if, when the order was made, parental rights and duties were vested in a local authority or voluntary organisation, they vest, on revocation, in the person in whom they vested immediately before vesting in the local authority or organisation.[63] The reason for this exception appears to be that the granting of an application for revocation carries the connotation that parental rights and duties can properly vest in the applicant. In that situation it is undesirable that resolutions passed or orders made for the protection of the child in different circumstances should revive so as to exclude the rights of the natural parent or guardian making the application. Any duty to make payments in respect of the maintenance of the child which was extinguished by the order freeing the child for adoption revives on revocation.[64] While the application is pending the adoption agency retains the parental rights and duties but is prohibited from placing the child for adoption without the leave of the court.[65] There is no indication of what the consequences of the granting of leave are in relation to the application for revocation but it seems that it does not automatically fall when leave is granted or even if the child is thereafter placed for adoption. It is, of course, superseded by an adoption order which might competently be made following such a placement and before the revocation proceedings were completed, for a child remains free for adoption although such proceedings are pending. It is, however, unlikely that a court would grant an adoption order in these circumstances, and still less so if a child were placed without leave and therefore in contravention of the statutory prohibition.

If an application for revocation is dismissed on the ground that to allow it would contravene the principle embodied in section 6 of the Adoption (Scotland) Act 1978, the applicant is precluded from making any further application for revocation without leave of the court.[66] The court may grant such leave only if it appears that, because of a change in circumstances, or for any other reason, it is proper to allow the application to be made. Unless the court grants leave to make a further application, the adoption agency is released from the duty of complying with the statutory requirement on progress reports, so far as the applicant in question is concerned. Leave is not required for a further application if the application is dismissed on grounds other than those embodied in section 6. Leave will not therefore be required when the application is dismissed on ground of incompetency (*e.g.* because the required period of time has not elapsed since the freeing order was made, or because, when the application is made, the child has his home with a person with whom he has been placed for adoption), or when the application is dismissed of consent or is abandoned.

---

[61] s. 6.
[62] s. 20(3).
[63] s. 20(3)(*b*).
[64] s. 20(3)(*c*), as amended by Children Act 1989, Sched. 10, para. 36.
[65] s. 20(2).
[66] s. 20(4) and (5).

Leave will, however, be required whenever an application is dismissed on its merits as every such decision to dismiss must be governed by section 6.[67]

DECISION ON MERITS OF ADOPTION

The Importance of Section 6

When the conditions precedent to the making of an adoption order have been satisfied, the decision on the merits of whether or not an order should be made is governed by section 6 of the Adoption (Scotland) Act 1978, which provides:

> "In reaching any decision relating to the adoption of a child, a court or ad-
> option agency shall have regard to all the circumstances, first considera-
> tion being given to the need to safeguard and promote the welfare of the
> child throughout his childhood; and shall so far as practicable ascertain
> the wishes and feelings of the child regarding the decision and give due
> consideration to them, having regard to his age and understanding."

Although large claims have been made for the importance and novelty of this section (repeated from section 3 of the Children Act 1975) it is doubtful if, so far as decisions by courts on the merits of making an adoption order are concerned, it makes any significant addition to the previous law. The Adoption Act 1958 had required, as had its predecessors, that a court before making an adoption order should be satisfied that the order if made would be for the welfare of the child[68] and that due consideration should be given to the wishes of the child, having regard to his age and understanding.[69] There was, it is true, no specific requirement to relate a consideration of the child's welfare to the duration of his childhood but, despite the difficulties of prediction which were experienced and will remain, it had never been supposed that, in a case of adoption, welfare could be judged on a short-term basis. The present provisions may even detract from the stress hitherto placed on the welfare of the child. Under the previous legislation an adoption order could not be made if it were not for the welfare of the child. That is no longer so. The welfare of the child is no more than the first among any number of considerations, none of which, apart from the child's welfare and his wishes and feelings, is named in the statute. It follows, and has been held in England,[70] that the child's welfare is not a condition precedent to the making of an adoption order, in the sense that the court is not obliged to make a positive finding that the order will be in the child's interests before making it.[71]

The freedom to take considerations other than the child's welfare into account is unfettered. The meaning of "first consideration" is, moreover, obscure.

---

[67] The principles embodied in s. 6 are, it is thought, exhaustive of the principles governing a decision on the merits. It is to be noted that these principles include having regard to all the circumstances.

[68] Adoption Act 1958, s. 7(1) and (6).

[69] *Ibid.*, s. 7(2).

[70] *Re D (A Minor) (Adoption Order: Injunction)* [1991] 3 All E.R. 461.

[71] This contrasts with an order relating to parental rights made under s. 3 of the Law Reform (Parent and Child) (Scotland) Act 1986. For a comparison of the place of welfare in the two processes, see Lord President Hope in *F* v. *F*, 1991 S.L.T. 357 at p. 360; and Lord Justice-Clerk Ross in *Borders Regional Council* v. *M*, 1986 S.L.T. 222 at p. 225.

It does not mean paramount.[72] It may mean that the need to safeguard and promote the welfare of the child is not to be given greater weight than any other
single consideration, but the weight so given will not necessarily be greater than
that given to all other considerations taken together, because, if that were so, the
welfare of the child would then become paramount.[73] That interpretation has,
however, the disadvantage that the weighting is left uncertain and conditioned
by the arbitrary circumstances of the number of other considerations there may
be (which may in turn depend on the subtlety which can be exercised in separat-
ing one consideration from another).[74] So to argue may be to place too much
stress on exactitude of language and perhaps the courts will, and should, adopt a
broader interpretation. In *P* v. *Lothian Regional Council*[75] the Second Division
denied that the effect of section 6 was to give "paramount" consideration to the
welfare of the child. In Lord Cowie's words[76]:

> "that is not the meaning of section 6, which merely requires the court to
> give first consideration to the need to safeguard and promote the welfare
> of the child throughout his childhood while at the same time having re-
> gard to all the circumstances including. . .the claims of the natural parents
> and the adoptive parents."

Since the United Kingdom ratification of the UN Convention on the Rights of
the Child[77] the Scottish court may be inclined to interpret section 6 to consist
with Article 21 of that Convention, which provides that in adoption "the best interests of the child shall be the paramount consideration." It would, however, be
wrong to regard the child's welfare as the sole relevant consideration because,
as Lord Cowie indicates, the natural parents have interests which ought not to be
ignored. These interests require that the child's welfare is not determinative and
a proper interpretation of section 6 should take that into account.[78] It will be difficult, on any view, to put the first consideration test higher than an exhortation
to attach considerable importance to the welfare of the child. Where, however,
the welfare of the child so considered would be served by adoption, that is a factor which the court is bound to take into account as an indicator in favour of
making the order. To that extent there is a change in the law laid down by, if not
from the practice, under earlier legislation which had given no direction on the
importance to be attached to the welfare of the child as a positive factor pointing
to adoption. The court could not make an order unless satisfied that it was for the

---

[72] See *A and B, Petrs.*, 1971 S.C.(H.L.) 129, *per* Lord Reid at p. 141; and *P* v. *Lothian Regional
Council*, 1989 S.L.T. 739 in which the Second Division disapproved the sheriff for holding that
the child's welfare was the paramount rather than simply the first consideration. See also *Borders
Regional Council* v. *M, supra* at p. 225.

[73] See Lord Simon of Glaisdale, H.L., vol. 359, col. 544.

[74] *Cf.* the Lord Chancellor's memorandum of Feb. 19, 1975: "To make the child's welfare the 'first
consideration' is clearly intended to mean that the child's interest is to be weighed—but the question of weighted by how much is not answered."

[75] 1989 S.L.T. 739.

[76] at p. 745D.

[77] 28 *International Legal Materials* 1448, ratified Dec. 16, 1991.

[78] Some writers consider that the child's welfare ought to be determinative, but doing so ignores the
rights and interests of persons other than the child: see, for example, Bridge, "Changing the
Nature of Adoption: Law Reform in England and New Zealand" (1993) 13 Leg. Stud. 81 at pp.
98–101.

welfare of the child but if it was disposed to refuse to make an order the child's welfare did not, as a matter of law, require to be considered. Such niceties were, however, usually ignored, and in all cases the child's welfare was a major, and usually the dominant, consideration. Under the present legislation, the fact that "first consideration" is given to the child's welfare would seem to indicate that the child's welfare will *always* be relevant, but that other considerations *may*, in the circumstances of any particular case, also be relevant. Overall, the practical result probably is that decisions on the merits of making or refusing an adoption order will continue to be determined by considerations similar to those that prevailed under the previous law.

Terms and Conditions Attached to the Order

Section 6 is to be read in conjunction with section 12(6), which provides that "an adoption order may contain such terms and conditions as the court thinks fit." These words give the court a wide discretion, for as Lord Ackner said,

> "it seems to me essential that, in order to safeguard and promote the welfare of the child throughout his childhood, the court should retain the maximum flexibility given to it by the Act and that unnecessary fetters should not be placed upon the exercise of the discretion entrusted to it by Parliament."[79]

The English courts have frequently used the analogous English provisions[80] to impose a condition of access in favour of a natural parent or other relative, where this has been shown to be in the interests of the child,[81] and the House of Lords have accepted this as a proper, and unqualified, usage to which section 12(6) can be put.[82] The discretion of the court is unfettered in relation to the terms or conditions the court can impose, though no doubt any condition imposed must not be inconsistent with the fundamental concept of adoption itself. Thus it would not be a valid exercise of the power to make an adoption order subject to the condition that the child should remain in or be passed into the care and control of some person other than the adopter.[83] The terms and conditions must, the English Court of Appeal has held, concern the parental rights and duties affected by the adoption order itself, and cannot concern something entirely extrinsic thereto. So in *Re D (A Minor) (Adoption Order: Injunction)*[84] it was held that the court had no power to issue an injunction under the Adoption Act 1976 to restrain the natural mother of the child from having contact with it

---

[79] *Re C (A Minor) (Adoption Order: Conditions)* [1989] A.C. 1 at p. 17.

[80] Adoption Act 1976 ss. 6 and 12(6) (and previously the Children Act 1975, ss. 3 and 8(7)).

[81] *Re J (A Minor) (Adoption Order: Conditions)* [1973] Fam. 106 (access granted in favour of putative father); *Re G (DM) (An Infant)* [1962] 1 W.L.R. 730 (natural mother); *Re B (MF) (An Infant)* [1972] 1 W.L.R. 102 (parents); *Re S (A Minor) (Adoption Order: Access)* [1976] Fam. 1 (natural father); *Re C (A Minor) (Wardship and Adoption)* [1981] 2 F.L.R. 177 (elder brother and grandparents).

[82] *Re C (A Minor) (Adoption Order: Conditions), supra.* In *AB* v. *CB*, 1985 S.L.T. 514 the sheriff had considered it incompetent to impose such a condition, and the Inner House did not consider it necessary to decide the point. In the light of the House of Lords decision in *Re C (A Minor) (Adoption Order: Conditions)* on identical statutory wording, the sheriff's view must now be considered mistaken.

[83] *Per* Lord Ackner in *Re C*, [1989] A.C. 1 at pp. 14–15.

[84] [1991] 3 All E.R. 461.

after it reached the age of majority.[85] The Court also held that the appropriate procedure in relation to a child before majority when it was considered necessary to protect it from a third party was to make a wardship order. In Scotland an adoption order has the effect of depriving the natural parents of any parental responsibilities and rights and conferring such responsibilities and rights on the adoptive parents. It hardly seems appropriate to qualify the adoptive parents' rights and duties with conditions attached to the natural parents, and it is submitted that section 12(6) of the Adoption (Scotland) Act 1978 gives no authority to impose an interdict on persons other than the adopters. Doubtless, however, if the adoptive parents' or the child's interests are being threatened, they can be protected by interdict at common law against apprehended wrong at the hands of a natural parent or third party.

Meaning of Welfare

In deciding the merits of making an order, as in assessing the reasonableness of the withholding of parental agreement, a broad view should be taken of the child's welfare.

> "One must look at the whole future of the child; not to mere temporary unhappiness or grief, however acute, if it is transient; not to mere material affluence in childhood or a better chance through educational advantages, to achieve affluence later."[86]

Disruption in a child's life should not, however, be lightly dismissed as likely to be transient in its effects, and has to be regarded in the light of the increased recognition given to the importance of continuity for the secure and stable upbringing of a child.[87] Medical evidence may be of assistance in assessing the effects of disruption,[88] but even in the absence of such evidence the court is entitled to reach the conclusion that disruption is likely to have serious adverse effects.[89] Welfare comprehends every factor likely to affect the physical, mental and emotional development of the child, including "educational, general surroundings, happiness, stability of home and the like,"[90] and is not restricted, or even mainly directed, to material considerations.[91] A principal merit of adoption—indeed its primary aim—is that it provides the child with a normal family background which, in most cases, it would otherwise lack, and it is usually thought that that can be achieved only if there is a complete break of links with the natural parents.[92] In some instances, especially of adoption by relatives, there may, however, be benefits in maintaining contact with the natural par-

---

[85] Cf. Re F (A Minor) (Adoption Order: Injunction) [1990] 3 All E.R. 580, which may now be taken to be overruled.

[86] Re C(L) [1965] 2 Q.B. 449, per Diplock L.J. at p. 471.

[87] See J v. C [1970] A.C. 668; A and B, Petrs., 1971 S.C.(H.L.) 129; Re B (MF) (An Infant) supra; Re D (SL) (An Infant) [1972] 1 W.L.R. 102; Re M (An Infant) (No. 2) (1964) 108 Sol. J. 1031.

[88] As in Re B(MF) (An Infant) supra.

[89] Re W (An Infant) [1971] A.C. 682 per Lord Hailsham of St Marylebone at pp. 703–704.

[90] Re B [1971] 1 Q.B. 437, per Davies L.J. approved in Re W (An Infant), per Lord Hodson at p. 719.

[91] A and B v. C, 1977 S.C. 27.

[92] Re B (MF), supra.

ents,[93] and even where there are no specialties pointing to the advantage of maintaining contact the fact that contact will be maintained is not necessarily a factor that is conclusive against adoption.[94] The court is no longer required, as it had been by the Adoption Act 1958[95] but not by previous legislation, to have regard to the health of the applicants. Serious chronic illness affecting capacity to care for the child, or of an infectious character, are, however, obvious factors to be taken into account.[96] Stress was previously laid on the advantage of adoption in removing the stigma of illegitimacy,[97] which was commonly considered to be its practical effect, although until the Children Act 1975 it did not in the full sense legitimise an illegitimate child.[98] This is probably a less potent consideration now that the legal status of illegitimacy has all but disappeared, though the continuance (if diminished) of a social stigma means that the consideration may still be of some force. The character of the applicants is necessarily an important consideration, but a conviction for an offence against a child is not an automatic disqualification if a long interval of time during which the applicant had a blameless record has elapsed since the conviction.[99] In custody cases it has been held that a religious upbringing is essential to the welfare of a child[1] and the reasoning adduced in support of that view is in the main also applicable to adoption. It is not, however, in practice applied to questions of custody where there is no dispute and it seems to be equally inapplicable to uncontested adoptions. When regard is had to other factors affecting the welfare of the child its role, even in contested cases, will usually be small. In placing a child for adoption, an adoption agency is required to have regard, so far as is practicable, to any wishes of the child's parents and guardians as to the religious upbringing of the child[2] and, if the matter is raised, the court should be satisfied that that duty has been conscientiously discharged. When a parent with strong religious conviction withholds agreement to adoption because the child is to be brought up in a different system of religious belief, or in none, it will usually be right to respect these convictions and give them considerable weight in assessing the reasonableness of the parental attitude. Where a child has been accustomed to a pattern of religious observance it will often be desirable that that should be continued and, in matters of this kind, the wishes of older children are entitled to particular respect. If these considerations have been taken into account the scope for questions of religious upbringing in decisions on adoption, if not exhausted, is very largely fulfilled.[3]

While section 6 is limited in its terms to "the welfare of the child throughout

---

[93] *Re J (Adoption Order: Conditions)* [1973] Fam. 106; *Re S (A Minor) (Adoption Order: Conditions)* [1975] 1 All E.R. 109.
[94] *Re G(DM) (An Infant)* [1962] 1 W.L.R. 730.
[95] s. 7(2).
[96] See *G and G, Petrs.*, 1949 S.L.T. (Sh. Ct.) 60.
[97] *Re E(P)* [1969] 1 All E.R. 323; *Re C* (1969) 113 Sol. J. 721.
[98] See *ante* at pp. 519–520.
[99] *Re G(DM) (An Infant), supra.*
[1] See *ante* at pp. 221–224.
[2] s. 7.
[3] On some of the problems of religious upbringing which may arise see, however, *Re E (An Infant)* [1964] 1 W.L.R. 51; *Re G (An Infant)* [1962] 2 Q.B. 141; and *H and H, Petrs.*, 1949 S.L.T. (Sh. Ct.) 68.

his childhood," the broad approach that has to be taken will allow the court to take into consideration a benefit accruing after the child reaches majority. The English Court of Appeal held in *Re D (A Minor) (Adoption Order: Injunction)*[4] that a benefit during minority was not a condition precedent to the making of an adoption order, but simply a first consideration: it followed that the fact that the child in the case was six days short of majority did not preclude the making of an adoption order, if in all the circumstances it was appropriate to make the order. The benefit in that case was the fact that the child would be fully integrated into the family circle,[5] and would continue to receive the special care he needed due to severe mental disabilities.[6]

Merits of Applications by Parents

As has been seen,[7] special restrictions apply to applications by the mother or father of the child alone. Applications by both parents are incompetent if they are unmarried because only a married couple may present a joint application and, in the case of married parents, a joint application will usually be refused because adoption will have no effect on the legal relationships between parent and child. The latter objection will apply even where some collateral benefit is to be achieved by adoption, as where the child has been registered as illegitimate in a foreign register of births.[8] Where, however, the child's status is to be determined by the law of a country that does not recognise legitimation *per subsequens matrimonium*, or which imposes restrictions which would prevent legitimation in the particular case, it is submitted that an adoption application by parents who have married since the birth of the child may be entertained[9] if its effect, if granted, would be to confer legitimate status by the law of that country.

Merits of Applications by Relatives or Step-Parents

Adoption applications at the instance of relatives or step-parents are common, especially with the latter (normally in conjunction with a natural parent), but they require particular caution as they may be influenced by considerations ulterior to the welfare of the child or lack the assurance of permanency characteristic of adoption. In these circumstances contact with the other natural mother or father is often maintained and, although that is not necessarily inimical to adoption, it may produce tensions that will be harmful for the child or prevent the child forming a satisfactory relationship either with his natural or with his adoptive parents. In most cases in which relatives seek adoption, both the welfare of the child and the objects which the relatives have in view can be best served by the making of a custody order rather than by adoption. Accordingly, where an application for an adoption order is made by a relative or step-

---

[4] [1991] 3 All E.R. 461.

[5] *Cf. Re R (Adoption)* [1966] 2 All E.R. 613.

[6] *Cf. Re A (An Infant)* [1963] 1 All E.R. 531, in which an order was refused when the child was one month short of majority but in which avowedly the only reason for the adoption was to confer British nationality on the child.

[7] *Ante* at pp. 527–528.

[8] *Y and Y, Petrs.*, (1950) 66 Sh. Ct. Rep. 22; *M & M, Petrs.*, 1950 S.L.T. (Sh. Ct.) 3.

[9] Accordingly, there may be circumstances in which it will be competent to entertain applications for a Convention adoption order (see *post* at pp. 577–579) at the instance of a married couple who are the parents of the child.

parent of the child and the court is of the opinion (1) that the child's welfare would not be better safeguarded and promoted by the making of an adoption order than it would be by the making of a custody order, and (2) that it would be appropriate to make a custody order, the court is required to direct that the application for adoption be treated as if it had been made for the custody of the child.[10] The result is that, in such cases, the adoption application must be treated as a custody application unless the court is of the opinion that the child's welfare would be better safeguarded and promoted by the making of an adoption order. A relative for this purpose means a grandparent, brother, sister, uncle or aunt, whether of the full blood or half blood or by affinity.[11] The court may be of the opinion that an adoption order would further the child's welfare rather than a custody order if, for example, the child were settled with its grandparents and there is no likelihood of the child going to live with someone else.[12] The permanence of adoption may then be preferred over a variable or revocable award of custody. Applications for adoption at the instance of the relatives of the child sometimes follow the breakdown of the marriage of the child's parents and it has been said that the test in such cases is whether the separation of the parents is final[13]; but the sound view, it is submitted, is that that is only one of the factors to be taken into account in determining what is for the welfare of the child. Where a step-parent has become the real "father figure" or "mother figure" in the child's life[14] and has been so from an early age, it may be right to give formal recognition to the actual relationship by means of an adoption order, in favour of the step-parent and the parent who is his spouse; though it should be noted that in such cases adoption will confer little tangible advantage and its intangible results will often be either vague and uncertain or ambivalent.[15]

Specialties Affecting Applications by One Applicant Alone

The law in force before 1975 had required that an adoption order should not be made in respect of a female child if the sole applicant were a man unless the court was satisfied that there were special circumstances justifying the making of the order as an exceptional measure.[16] That requirement was repealed in

---

[10] Children Act 1975, s. 53, as amended by the Law Reform (Parent and Child) (Scotland) Act 1986, Sched. 2 and the Family Law Act 1986, Sched. 2.

[11] Children Act 1975, s. 55(1), as amended by the Law Reform (Parent and Child) (Scotland) Act 1986, Sched. 1. Under the same definition given in the Adoption Act 1976 the English court has held that "uncle" does not include "great-uncle": *Re C and Anr. (Minors) (Wardship: Adoption)* [1989] 1 All E.R. 395.

[12] This was the state of affairs in *Re O (Minor) (Adoption of Grandparents)* (1984) 15 Fam. L. 305.

[13] *LH, Petrs.*, 1951 S.L.T. (Sh. Ct.) 46.

[14] As in *Re S (A Minor)* [1975] 5 Fam. L. 88.

[15] *Re S (Infants)* [1977] 2 W.L.R. 919, although decided on statutory provisions that have no Scottish counterpart, contains a useful discussion of the issues which the court requires to take into account in cases of step-parent adoptions. Thomson is of the view (see *Family Law in Scotland* at p. 217) that the Scottish courts are somewhat too ready to grant adoption orders when custody orders would be appropriate, and are therefore ignoring s. 53 of the Children Act 1975, and he notes that the equivalent English provisions have been repealed: Children Act 1989, Sched. 15. See also *Glasgow Herald*, June 27, 1988.

[16] Adoption of Children (Scotland) Act 1930, s. 2(2); Adoption Act 1950, s. 2(2); Adoption Act 1958, s. 2(3). See *R* v. *Liverpool City Justices, ex p. W* [1959] 1 W.L.R. 149; *AB, Petr.*, 1959 S.L.T. (Sh. Ct.) 49; *H, Petr.*, 1960 S.L.T. (Sh. Ct.) 3.

1975[17] and has not been re-enacted in the Adoption (Scotland) Act 1978. Its intention seems to have been to provide special safeguards against sexual corruption although, if so, it overlooked the risk of homosexual corruption and indeed of corruption (heterosexual or homosexual) by a sole female applicant. All such risks are now subsumed into a consideration of the need to safeguard and promote the welfare of the child throughout his childhood[18] which will often be best served by his being brought up in a home in which he has adoptive parents with whom he can identify as fulfilling the role of father and mother respectively. Adoptions at the instance of one person may nonetheless be conducive to the child's welfare where a connection already exists between that person and the child. It will be more difficult (though not impossible) to reconcile with the child's welfare adoption on the application of a sole applicant who is a stranger to the child[19] but the making of an adoption order may be justified, for example, where the child has been placed with a married couple one of whom has died in the interval between the placement and the hearing of the adoption application[20] or a sole applicant is relevant to a child with special needs.

Collateral Considerations

It is against public policy to make an adoption order where the applicants do not truly stand *in loco parentum* to the person to be adopted and the application is made solely for the purpose of conferring on him British nationality.[21] It is, however, no objection that one of the objects of the application is to secure British nationality for the person to be adopted, if there is a genuine intention to create the relationship of parent and child and the order would confer social, legal and psychological benefits as well as the benefit of British nationality.[22] The fact that the main object of the application is a collateral one is not, it is thought, a reason for refusing to make an order if the collateral object is consistent with the welfare of the child and there is no public policy objection.[23] In an application by a mother and step-father it is not a sufficient reason for refusing to make an order that the main object of the application is to promote the welfare of the mother if there is no possibility of conflict between her welfare and the interests of the child.[24] Where the child to be adopted is domiciled abroad, that is a factor to be taken into account in assessing the welfare of the child but it has no further significance and that is so even if adoption is not possible by the law of the domicile.[25] The *bona fides* of a proposed adoption requires careful scrutiny where it is associated with the intention of one of the parents of a child to enter

---

[17] Children Act 1975, Sched. 4.
[18] See *ante* at pp. 550–552.
[19] At one time it was not the practice of adoption agencies to make placements with one person alone, but, except in the case of very young children, such placements are no longer uncommon.
[20] *AB, Petr.*, 1976 S.L.T. (Sh. Ct.) 49.
[21] *Re A (An Infant)* [1963] 1 W.L.R. 231.
[22] *Re R (Adoption)* [1967] 1 W.L.R. 34.
[23] See *W, Petrs.* (1945) 61 Sh. Ct. Rep. 130.
[24] *Re S (A Minor)* (1975) 5 Fam. L. 88.
[25] *Re B (S) (An Infant)* [1968] 1 Ch. 204.

into a second marriage.[26] Similar scrutiny requires to be applied to the use of adoption as a means of "shifting about," as part of a family arrangement, a child who has already been adopted. The duties owed by adoptive parents to the child in such circumstances are the same as they would owe to their biological child.[27]

---

[26] *F, Petr.*, (1951) 67 Sh. Ct. Rep. 12; *EO, Petrs.*, 1951 S.L.T. (Sh. Ct.) 11. See also *Re DX (An Infant)* [1949] Ch. 320.

[27] *B, Petr.*, 1951 S.L.T. (Sh. Ct.) 48.

CHAPTER 20

PROCEDURAL AND INTERNATIONAL ASPECTS OF ADOPTION

INTRODUCTORY

The Scottish Adoption Service

The Adoption (Scotland) Act 1978 contemplates, and in large measure prescribes, that except where the child is to be adopted by one of its relatives, placement for adoption should be made by an adoption agency (*i.e.* a local authority or an approved adoption society).[1] The aim is that throughout Scotland there should be a comprehensive adoption service known as "The Scottish Adoption Service" to be provided by local authorities acting in conjunction with approved adoption societies in their areas, so that help may be given where needed in a co-ordinated manner and without duplication, omission or avoidable delay.[2] The service is designed to meet the needs of children who have been or may be adopted, parents and guardians of such children and persons who have adopted or may adopt a child. The facilities to be provided include temporary board and lodgings where needed by pregnant women, mothers and children, arrangements for assessing children and prospective adopters and placing children for adoption, and counselling for persons with problems relating to adoption.[3] Duty is placed on local authorities to provide these facilities or secure that they are provided by approved adoption societies[4] and this is to be done in conjunction with the local authorities' other social services so that the whole social work functions of a local authority, and in particular its functions concerning the care of children,[5] are integrated with the adoption service.[6] Although the duties are laid on local authorities the service is seen as national in its extent, and accordingly the approval of adoption societies is entrusted to the Secretary of State who must be satisfied, before giving approval, that a society is making, or is likely to make, an effective contribution to the Scottish Adoption Service.[7]

Placement of Child by Adoption Agency

In arranging the placement of a child for adoption and in taking any other decisions relating to the adoption of a child, an adoption agency is under the same duty as is the court in deciding the merits of making an adoption order. It must

---

[1] Adoption (Scotland) Act 1978, ss. 1(4) and 65(1). All references in this Chapter are to this Act, unless otherwise stated.

[2] s. 1(3).

[3] s. 1(2).

[4] s. 1(1).

[5] See s. 2.

[6] s. 1(3).

[7] See ss. 3, 4 and 5 for the detailed provisions on approval, and withdrawal of approval, and s. 8 for the Secretary of State's power to give directions in relation to the care of any child who is or was in the care of an inactive or defunct society.

have regard to all the circumstances and give first consideration to the need to safeguard and promote the welfare of the child throughout its childhood; and it must, so far as practicable, ascertain the wishes and feelings of the child and give due consideration to them, having regard to the child's age and understanding.[8] There are, moreover, special statutory regulations with which it must comply.[9] It must ensure that the parent or guardian of the child is furnished with a memorandum in the prescribed form explaining the effect of the making of an adoption order on his rights as parent or guardian and calling attention to the statutory provisions relating to the agreement of parents or guardians to the making of adoption orders and also to the provisions relating to the sending or taking of children abroad. Before the child can be regarded as having been placed at the disposition of the agency for adoption the parent or guardian must sign a document in the prescribed form certifying that he has read and understood the memorandum.

Inquiries

Inquiries must be made and reports obtained in relation to the child and the proposed adopters for the purpose of ensuring, so far as may be possible, the suitability of the child and the proposed adopters respectively. The matters to be covered include the religious persuasion of the parties; the prospective adopters' educational attainments, past and present occupations and interests; details of their financial circumstances and living standards; particulars of all the members of the household of the prospective adopters and of their attitudes to the adoption; the prospective adopters' previous experience in caring for children as step-parent, foster parent, child-minder or prospective adopter, and assessment of ability in this respect, together where appropriate with assessment of ability to bring up their own children, and details of their previous fostering and adoption experience. An interview with the prospective adopters is obviously necessary for many of these purposes and must, in any event, be held. A medical report on the child and the adopters must be obtained, the premises where he and the prospective adopters are permanently to reside must be inspected and, where the agency is not the local authority, inquiries must be made of the local authority as to whether there is any reason to believe that the premises would be detrimental to the child. Where the agency is an approved adoption society, the inquiries and interviews are carried out by or on behalf of an adoption panel of the agency, which must consist of not less than six persons, and include at least one man and one woman, and they must consider the particulars relating the parties described above. In the case of a local authority, the corresponding responsibilities rest with the Social Work Committee.[10]

---

[8] s. 6. For an examination of this section, see *ante* at pp. 550–558.

[9] Made under s. 9 of the 1978 Act. See the Adoption Agencies (Amendment) Regulations 1981 (S.I. 1981 No. 1818), and Adoption Agencies (Scotland) Regulations 1984 (S.I. 1984 No. 988).

[10] Social Work (Scotland) Act 1968, s. 2(2), as amended by the Adoption (Scotland) Act 1978, Sched. 3, para. 8.

Protection Against Undesirable Placements

Illegal Placements

It is illegal for anyone other than an adoption agency to make arrangements for the adoption of a child or place a child for adoption except where the proposed adopter is a relative of the child.[11] It is also an offence to receive a child placed in contravention of the statutory prohibitions. This represents a tightening of the previous law which had prohibited arrangements for adoption made by any body of persons other than an adoption agency but had permitted them when made by individuals (*e.g.* the parents themselves, friends, relatives, doctors, ministers of religion, etc.). Such arrangements (commonly called "third party placements") were thought to be undesirable for at least two reasons: (1) the persons who made them did not usually have the knowledge, experience or means of investigation necessary to ensure, so far as possible, the welfare of the child; and (2) the placements were sometimes made in circumstances which left open the possibility of contact between the natural parent and child when that was undesirable and thus endangered the security of the child and adoptive parents which is normally necessary for the success of adoption and the well-being of the child. The same objection can in some degree be made where the child is placed with a relative, but the character of such adoptions is necessarily rather different from that of adoption by strangers and there is less need to guard against the maintenance of contact with the natural parent which, in these cases, may sometimes be beneficial. Third party arrangements are illegal only where they are for adoption and, in any given case, it may be difficult to prove that adoption rather than some arrangement for care or fostering was the original purpose. Moreover, where there has been illegal placement or where there has been a placement which is legal only because adoption was not its original purpose, an adoption application may nonetheless be made and an order granted. In such cases, however, the child must have had his home with the adopters for a period of 12 months preceding the making of the adoption order.[12]

Further Prohibitions

Further protection against undesirable placements is provided by the prohibition against the giving or receiving of any payment or reward in consideration of an adoption,[13] against any advertisement indicating that the parent or guardian of the child desires the child to be adopted or that anyone desires to adopt a child, or that anyone other than an adoption agency is willing to make arrangements for adoption[14]; and against taking or sending a child who is a British subject, or a citizen of the Republic of Ireland, to any place outside the United Kingdom, the Channel Islands or the Isle of Man, with a view to his adoption by any person who is not a parent, guardian or relative of the child, except where an order vesting the parental rights and duties relating to the child in the person tak-

---

[11] Adoption (Scotland) Act 1978, s. 11.

[12] s. 13(2).

[13] s. 51(1). Payments may, however, be made to an adoption agency in respect of expenses reasonably incurred (s. 51(3)) and provision is made for the payment of allowances to adopters under schemes to be approved by the Secretary of State (s. 51(5) and (6)).

[14] s. 52.

ing or sending him has been made under section 49 of the Adoption (Scotland) Act 1978[15] or its English or Northern Irish equivalent.[16] These matters are more fully described later.[17]

Non-Agency Placements

If the placement has not been by an agency the prospective adopter must give notice to the local authority within whose area he has his home of his intention to apply for an adoption order. No adoption order can be made until after the expiry of three months from the giving of notice.[18] This requirement applies not only to illegal third-party placements and to non-agency placements which were originally for some purpose other than adoption but to all non-agency placements including placements with relatives and cases where parents or step-parents wish to adopt. The local authority to which notice has been given must then investigate the matter and submit to the court a report of its investigation.[19] That investigation shall, in particular, include (a) so far as is practicable, the suitability of the applicant and any other matters relevant to the operation of section 6 of the 1978 Act (*i.e.* the duty of the court in relation to the welfare, wishes and feelings of the child), and (b) whether the child was placed in contravention of the statutory prohibitions contained in section 11.[20]

Protected Children

A child in respect of whom notice has been given becomes a protected child and the local authority has a duty to secure that he is visited from time to time by its officers, who shall satisfy themselves as to the well-being of the child and give such advice as to his care and maintenance as may appear to be needed.[21] Persons who have a protected child in their custody are required to give to the local authority notice of change of address and, if the child should die, notice of his death.[22] There is power to have protected children removed from persons unfit to have their care or from unsuitable surroundings.[23]

Under the Adoption Act 1958 a child who had been placed for adoption by an adoption agency was, no less than a child placed by individuals, a protected child,[24] and it was the duty of the local authority to secure that he was visited from time to time by their officers who had to satisfy themselves as to his well-being.[25] There was a resultant duplication of effort between local authorities and adoption societies, which sometimes had confusing and detrimental results for prospective adopters. Children placed by adoption agencies are no longer protected children,[26] and are therefore no longer the subject of local authority vis-

---

[15] s. 50, as amended by the Children Act 1989, Sched. 10, para. 43.
[16] Adoption Act 1976, s. 55; Adoption (Northern Ireland) Order 1987, art. 57.
[17] *Post* at pp. 572–574.
[18] s. 22(1).
[19] s. 22(2).
[20] s. 22(3).
[21] ss. 32 and 33.
[22] s. 35.
[23] s. 34.
[24] Adoption Act 1958, s. 37.
[25] *Ibid.*, s. 38.
[26] 1978 Act ss. 32(1) and 22(1).

itation. It is, however, expected that the adoption agency will visit the prospective adopters and supervise the child's welfare between his being placed for adoption and the making of an adoption order; and a duty of reporting to the court is now placed on the agency.[27]

THE ADOPTION APPLICATION

Petitions—Productions

Applications for adoption are made by petition in the prescribed form.[28] In a sheriff court petition[29] the petitioner must state (a) the date upon which the child was received into his care and possession, (b) whether the child has, since that date, been continuously in his care and possession, (c) the date upon which he notified the local authority of his intention to apply for an adoption order, (d) whether he has received or given any reward or payment for, or in consideration of, the adoption of the child or for giving agreement to the making of the adoption order, (e) what persons have taken part in the arrangements for placing the child, and (f) particulars of any order freeing the child for adoption.[30] Along with the petition there require to be lodged:

(1) An extract of the entry in the Register of Births relating to the birth of the child.

(2) In the case of a joint petition by spouses, an extract of the entry in the Register of Marriages relating to their marriage.

(3) A medical certificate of the health of the petitioners, except where the petitioner or one of the joint petitioners is a parent of the child.

(4) Any report by the adoption agency required by section 23 of the 1978 Act (*i.e.* on the suitability of the applicant).

(5) Any report by the local authority required by section 22(2) of the Act (*i.e.* on the investigation upon receipt of notice of intent to apply for an adoption order).

(6) Any consent required from the child, or agreement required from the parent.[31]

(7) Any other document founded upon by the petitioner in support of the terms of his petition.[32]

Anonymity

Anonymity as between adoptive parents and the natural parents or guardians is usually an advantage. Any petitioner who desires that his identity should not be disclosed to the parent or guardian of the child may apply for a serial number to be assigned to him for the purpose of the petition and, in that event, the docu-

---

[27] Adoption (Scotland) Act 1978, s. 23.

[28] Rules of Court—hereinafter R.C.—222(1) and Appendix Form 36 (Court of Session); Act of Sederunt (Adoption of Children) 1984 (S.I. 1984 No. 1013) (sheriff court)—hereinafter A.S.—s. 16 and Forms 7 and 8.

[29] Most adoption petitions are sheriff court petitions, and the details in the text relate thereto. Differences in the Court of Session are identified in the footnotes.

[30] A.S., s. 16(2). The petition in the Court of Session is in different form: see Appendix Form 36.

[31] There are special provisions for the witnessing of these agreements or consents from persons furth of Scotland; A.S., s. 18(3).

[32] A.S., s. 16. R.C. 220(5) requires only the first and last-mentioned from the petitioner.

ment signifying the agreement of the parent or guardian shall not name the petitioner but shall identify him by reference to the serial number.[33]

Appointment of Reporting Officer and Curator Ad Litem

On presentation or lodging of the petition for adoption, a reporting officer must in all cases be appointed to the child. If the petition is in the sheriff court a curator *ad litem* must also be appointed; and if in the Court of Session, the court has a discretionary power to appoint a curator *ad litem* where it appears desirable in the circumstances of the case in order to safeguard the interests of the child, and in any case must appoint a curator *ad litem* where the child is not free for adoption and it appears that a parent or guardian of the child is unwilling to agree to the making of the adoption order.[34] Where reasonably practicable, the same person must be appointed as curator *ad litem* and reporting officer in the same petition.

Duties of Curator Ad Litem[35]

The curator's duty is to investigate as fully as possible and to report to the court on all the circumstances of the child and petitioners and all other matters relevant to the proposed adoption. No time limit is fixed within which the report must be made but the court may give the curator directions on this as on other matters. Expedition is important and six weeks should normally be regarded as a maximum. Nothing in the more specific points of investigation which are entrusted to the curator is intended, or should be taken, to detract from the generality of his duty as just described or from the centrality of the safeguarding of the interests of the child as the viewpoint from which his investigations are to be directed. His investigations and report must, however, include the following[36]:

(1) Whether the statements in the petition are true and, if not, what the true facts are.

(2) Particulars of the accommodation in the home of the petitioner and the condition of the home.

(3) Particulars of all members of the household of the petitioner and their relationship to the petitioner.

(4) Why, in the case of a petition by one of two spouses, the other spouse does not join in the petition. (This information is required not only because it may bear on the interests of the child but because an application by one of two spouses is incompetent unless certain conditions are satisfied.[37] The curator should therefore direct his attention, in particular, to matters on which the court has to be satisfied if the competency of the petition is to be sustained.)

(5) Whether the means and status of the petitioner are sufficient to enable

---

[33] A.S., s. 19; R.C. 222(3).

[34] A.S., s. 20; R.C. 222(5).

[35] A.S., s. 21; R.C. 224.

[36] The duties listed in the text are those under the sheriff court rules; the Court of Session rules are differently worded, though substantially similar.

[37] Adoption (Scotland) Act 1978, s. 15. See *ante* at p. 527.

him to maintain and bring up the child suitably; and what right or interest in property the child has.

(6) Whether the petitioner understands the nature and effect of an adoption order, and in particular that the making of the order will render him responsible for the maintenance and upbringing of the child.

(7) When the mother of the child ceased to have the care and possession of the child, and to whom care and possession was transferred.

(8) Whether any payment or other reward in consideration of the adoption has been given or agreed upon.

(9) Whether the adoption is likely to safeguard and promote the welfare of the child throughout his childhood.

(10) What insurance, if any, has been effected on the life of the child.

(11) Whether it is in the interests of the welfare of the child that the court should be asked to make (a) an interim order, or (b) to impose, in making an adoption order, particular terms or conditions, or (c) to require the petitioner to make any particular provision for the child and, if so, what provision.

(12) Whether, if the petitioner is not ordinarily resident in Great Britain, a report has been obtained on his home and living conditions from a suitable agency in the country in which he is ordinarily resident.

(13) Why the petitioner wishes to adopt the child.

(14) The petitioner's religious persuasion, if any.

(15) The considerations arising from the difference in age between the petitioner and the child if such difference is less than the normal difference in age between parents and their children. (Difference in age greater than the normal difference between parents and their children is not specifically mentioned, but the curator's general duty to report on all the circumstances with a view to safeguarding the interests of the child requires him to comment on that aspect if he conceives that it would have an adverse effect on the child's interests.)

(16) Such other questions or matters, including the assessment of the petitioner's personality and, where appropriate, of that of the child, as have a bearing on the mutual suitability of the petitioner and the child for the relationship created by adoption and on the ability of the petitioner to bring up the child.

(17) The ascertainment, so far as is practicable, of the wishes and feelings of the child regarding the proposed adoption.

When the petition is one for an order declaring the child free for adoption, the curator *ad litem* has the following duties:[38]

(1) To safeguard the interests of the child generally and to ensure that section 6 of the 1978 Act is given proper consideration.

(2) To ascertain whether the facts stated in the petition are correct (except where such facts fall within the duties of the reporting officer).

(3) To confirm that the child, if over 12, consented to the application.

---

[38] A.S., s. 6.

(4) To ascertain whether an order freeing the child for adoption would promote the child's well-being.

(5) To report on the current circumstances and care of the child.

Duties of Reporting Officer

When he is appointed by the sheriff[39] the reporting officer (who will usually be the same person as the curator *ad litem*) has the following duties:

(1) To witness any agreement executed within the United Kingdom by a parent or guardian to the making of an adoption order in respect of his child and to lodge the agreement in process.

(2) To ascertain that each parent or guardian whose agreement is required or may be dispensed with understands that the effect of the adoption order would be to deprive him permanently of his parental rights. The previous rules imposed this duty on the curator, but that was somewhat anomalous since the curator was and is appointed to the child and it is the child's interests that the curator has to protect. The present rule would seem to oblige the reporting officer to communicate with the parent or guardian to ascertain their understanding.

(3) To ascertain whether there is any person other than those mentioned in the petition upon whom notice of the petition should be served.

(4) To ascertain, where a parent or guardian whose agreement is required or may be dispensed with can be found, whether alternatives to adoption have been discussed with him.

(5) To confirm that each parent or guardian whose agreement is required understands that he may withdraw his agreement at any time before the adoption order is made.

The reporting officer has certain further duties in addition to the above, when the petition is one for an order declaring the child free for adoption:

(6) To investigate the giving by a parent or guardian of his consent to the lodging of the petition.

(7) To confirm that each parent or guardian who can be found understands the implications of an order freeing the child for adoption.

(8) To confirm that each parent or guardian who can be found is aware that he may in certain circumstances apply to the court for revocation of the order freeing the child for adoption and the appropriate procedure for such an application.

(9) To confirm that each parent or guardian who can be found has been given an opportunity to make a declaration of preference not to be involved in further questions concerning the adoption of the child.

(10) In the case of a child of parents who are not married, to consider the likelihood of any person reputed to be the father of the child successfully raising proceedings for custody of, or access to, the child.

---

[39] A.S., s. 21. The duties of a reporting officer appointed by the Court of Session are slightly different, and are laid out in R.C. 224(1), (2) and (3).

Intimation and Service

Intimation on the walls and in the Minute Book ordinarily required for Court of Session petitions is not required for an adoption petition and accordingly, in the Court of Session, there is a prayer for dispensation with intimation. The corresponding crave in the sheriff court form is superfluous. The rules are silent on service, but it appears from the prescribed forms that service of notice of the petition is intended to take the place of service of the petition in common form.[40] In practice it is understood that service of notice of the petition is seldom required and the convening of interested parties to the process is deferred until the service of notice of hearing is considered on receipt of the reports of the reporting officer and the curator *ad litem*.

The Statutory Hearing

Upon receipt by the court of the reports of the reporting officer and the curator *ad litem* a date for the hearing will be fixed. Before the 1978 Act came into force a hearing was not essential and it was unusual in uncontested cases. Now, however, there must be a hearing in any petition to adopt a child where the child has not previously been freed for adoption, and to free a child requires a hearing:[41] the result is that no child can ever be adopted without some form of court hearing. The petitioner must intimate the diet to every person who can be found and whose agreement or consent to the making of such an order is required to be given or dispensed with. In the Court of Session the petitioner must also intimate the date of the hearing to the local authority or adoption agency which lodged a report, the reporting officer and, where one was appointed, the curator *ad litem* and any other person the court requires. In relation to this last category, what is required for the welfare of the child, and the effect which the making of an adoption order may have on the interests (which need not in this context be construed in a narrow patrimonial sense) of third parties, should be the guiding consideration. It is a question of circumstances including such connection with, and interest in, the child, as the putative father has maintained, as to whether the court should under this general power order notice to be served on a man who is not married to the child's mother but who is the putative father and who does not fall under one of the specific headings considered above. Some circumstances will be strong for service of notice, *e.g.* where he has *de facto* custody, where he has applied or wishes to apply for custody, or where, although willing to contribute to the child's maintenance, his contributions have been refused by the mother. In other cases a putative father's continuing connection with the child may have been so tenuous that he can have no representations of value to make on the child's welfare or claims to put forward which can be given practical effect. Even so, service of notice on him may be prudent unless there is some contrary indication or it is shown that he acquiesces in the petition, but delay should

---

[40] Contrast on this point A.S. (Adoption of Children) 1930, App. No. 1 of which contemplated service on interested parties in common form. What is meant by service of notice of the petition is not, however, clear and no form of notice is prescribed. The interlocutor ordering service of notice may direct what form the notice should take but in the absence of such direction, although it is within the power of the court to order answers, answers do not seem to be contemplated and in that situation it is obscure what response to the notice the interlocutor should require.

[41] s. 18.

not be caused by attempts to trace putative fathers whose identity or where-abouts is unknown.[42]

Form and Conduct of Hearing

There is no rule about the form which the hearing should take.

> "Adoption proceedings are *sui generis*, uniquely devised to effectuate a new statutory institution, and incapable of being forcibly compressed into any of our pre-existing categories of forms of action."[43]

Natural justice must be observed but there is no right to a proof at large. If, how-ever, the court is not satisfied with the certification of the statement in the peti-tion provided by the documents lodged or by the report of the reporting officer or the curator *ad litem* the court may order further production of documents or appoint oral evidence to be led.[44] It may interview privately the petitioner and the child or either of them, or any person on whom a notice of the hearing has been served. It may remit to a reporter to investigate facts[45] and may rely on re-ports, documents and interviews in substitution for the ordinary methods of proof. In general, the court may adopt any form of inquiry which is consistent with the maintenance of justice to the parties and with the statutory objects to which the inquiries must be directed and among which the need to safeguard and promote the welfare of the child is first. Parties have no right to see re-ports,[46] but where a report contains allegations against a party which are mater-ial to the determination of the case, justice requires that he be informed of the nature of the allegations and given an opportunity of meeting them.[47] Where the child has been placed by an adoption agency, the agency must submit to the court a report on the suitability of the petitioners and any other matters relevant to the operation of section 6 of the Adoption (Scotland) Act 1978[48] and shall as-sist the court in any manner the court may direct.[49] Where the child is not placed by an adoption agency a report must be submitted to the court by the local au-thority to which notice of intention to apply for an adoption order was given, covering the same matters and also whether the child was placed in contraven-tion of the statutory prohibition against anyone other than an adoption agency making arrangements for adoption, or placing a child for adoption, otherwise than with relatives of the child.[50] Where anyone claiming, contrary to what ap-pears *ex facie* of the petition, to be a parent or guardian of the child, is heard in support of that claim, the consequence of success is of course that his agreement to the making of an adoption order must either be given or be dispensed with on

---

[42] *Re Adoption Application (41/1961)* [1962] 1 W.L.R. 866, *per* Wilberforce J.

[43] *J and J* v. *C's Tutor*, 1948 S.C. 636, *per* Lord President Cooper at p. 642; approved in *A and B, Petrs.*, 1971 S.L.T. 258, *per* Lord Reid at p. 259.

[44] A.S., s. 23; R.C. 230(5). See *AB* v. *CD*, 1970 S.C. 268.

[45] *A and B, Petrs., supra.*

[46] *Re G (An Infant)* [1963] 2 Q.B. 73, *per* Ormrod and Pearson L.JJ. at pp. 93 and 99.

[47] *Ibid., per* Donovan L.J. at pp. 97–98.

[48] The duty *inter alia* to give first consideration to the need to safeguard and promote the welfare of the child throughout his childhood and to ascertain and give due consideration to his wishes and feelings.

[49] s. 23.

[50] s. 22(2) and (3).

one of the statutory grounds. With that exception, the fact that a person is heard, even of right, in an adoption proceeding, is in no sense to be equiparated with a requirement for his agreement. Any objections he offers to the making of an adoption order, or support for it, will, unless in so far as they bear on proof of one of the prerequisites, be relevant only in the context of the child's welfare or as one of the other circumstances to which the court may give consideration in reaching a decision on the merits of whether or not an adoption order should be made.

Restrictions on Removal of Child

It is essential, both for the orderly disposal of adoption applications and also, as a general rule, for the welfare of the child, that the child should, while the proceedings are pending, remain undisturbed in the home of the prospective adopters. Except where the child has had his home with the prospective adopters for the five years preceding the application, parents or guardians who have not agreed to adoption may, however, seek to recover a child during that time. A general prohibition against their so doing would create the hazard that an adoption application would be used as a weapon in a custody dispute or as a means of preventing or delaying the recovery of a child illegally removed. These considerations do not, however, apply where a parent has agreed to adoption even if he subsequently withdraws that agreement. In these circumstances it is undesirable that he should be able to embarrass or frustrate the proceedings by removing the child. Accordingly, while proceedings are pending, a parent or guardian who has agreed to the making of an adoption order may not, against the will of the person with whom the child has his home, remove the child from the custody of that person except with the leave of the court.[51] To do so is to commit a criminal offence.[52] Where parents authorise others to remove the child they no doubt commit an offence no less than if they remove the child themselves, but there is no statutory prohibition against the removal of the child by third parties (e.g. grandparents or other relatives) who may act without the parent's authority even if in what they conceive to be the parent's interests; nor is it clear that in these circumstances the crime of *plagium* is committed.[53]

A prohibition against removal of the child also applies while an application for an order freeing the child for adoption is pending. In that event, if the child is in the care of the adoption agency making the application, and the application was not made with the consent of each parent or guardian of the child, no parent or guardian of the child who did not consent to the application is entitled, against the will of the person with whom the child has his home, to remove the child from the custody of that person except with the leave of the court.[54] Al-

---

[51] s. 27(1). In considering applications for leave, the court will, it is thought, require to have regard to s. 6 and it will only be in exceptional circumstances that leave will be granted. The previous legislation had required the court to have regard to the child's welfare and that requirement is now replaced by s. 6.

[52] *Ibid.* It would also be an offence under s. 6 of the Child Abduction Act 1984 for a parent or guardian of a child to take or send the child outside the U.K. if custody has been awarded to some other person.

[53] See *ante* at pp. 262–264.

[54] s. 27(2).

though in such a case the child will be in the care of an adoption agency,[55] there is no requirement that consent of the agency must be obtained before the child is removed. It is removal against the will of the person with whom the child has his home that constitutes the offence, and that person need not be the prospective adopter but may be a temporary foster parent. Anomalously, and in contrast with pending adoption proceedings, there is no restraint, while proceedings for freeing a child for adoption are pending, against the removal of the child by a parent who has consented to the application.

The prohibition against removal of a child from prospective adopters is more extensive where the child has had his home with them for the five years preceding the application. In these circumstances no person is entitled, against the will of the prospective adopters, to remove the child from their custody without the leave of the court or under authority conferred by any enactment or on the arrest of the child.[56] The protection applies not only while the application is pending but also in the interval between the giving of notice of intention to apply for an adoption order and the presentation of the petition.[57] The purpose is to strengthen the position of foster parents who have had children in their long-term care and wish to adopt but are inhibited from doing so by parental unwillingness to agree. In such cases there may be a strong *prima facie* case for adoption. The prohibition is against removal by any person and that extends to the local authority in whose care the child is.[58] Removal "under authority conferred by any enactment" is ostensibly far-reaching but it does not extend to the statutory provisions relating to the return of the child placed for adoption by adoption agencies.[59] Children may, however, be removed where the removal is authorised by a justice of the peace or a children's hearing in terms of Part III of the Social Work (Scotland) Act 1968. Foster parents or others who have had a child in their care for less than five years have, in a question with natural parents who do not agree to adoption, no direct means of securing the continued residence of the child with them while the adoption application is pending other than by first making an application for custody. Foster parents with whom a child has been boarded out by a local authority may, however, with the co-operation of the authority, obtain security against the removal of the child if the local authority has assumed parental rights and powers.[60]

Where a child has been removed in contravention of the statutory prohibition, the court before whom the application for an adoption order or for an order freeing the child for adoption is pending may, on the application of a person from

---

[55] s. 18(2).

[56] s. 28(1).

[57] s. 28(2).

[58] s. 28(3). Questions arise as to the consequences of this. If a child is in the care of a local authority, the authority may be impeded from making decisions for the welfare of the child and thus discharging its statutory duties. If the authority has assumed parental rights the exercise of these rights may also be frustrated. If a foster parent refuses to return a child, pending an adoption application, he may be in breach of the fostering agreement but if the local authority seeks to enforce its rights it will be in contravention of the statutory prohibition and will commit an offence.

[59] *Ibid.*

[60] Social Work (Scotland) Act 1968, s. 16(1)(*b*)(iv), under which a local authority may assume parental rights and powers where, throughout the three years preceding the passing of the resolution, the child has been in the care of the local authority or voluntary organisation, may prove particularly useful for this. See *ante* pp. 429–430.

whose custody the child has been removed, order the return of the child to the applicant. Where there is no pending application but the child has been removed after the giving of notice of intention to adopt by a person with whom the child has had his home for the preceding five years, the Court of Session or the sheriff court of the sheriffdom within which the child is may make such an order.[61] The order must be directed to the person who has removed the child and so, where that person has handed on the child to another, an action of delivery may be necessary in order to secure the return of the child. Where there are reasonable grounds for believing that someone intends to remove a child in contravention of the statutory prohibition, an order may be made directing that person not to do so.[62] This does not seem to add anything to the remedy of interdict which would, in any event, be available, but when proceedings are pending there may be some convenience in seeking an order in the adoption process rather than making a separate application for interdict.

Interim Orders

Instead of making a final adoption order, the court may make an interim order. The effect of an interim order is to vest the custody of the child in the petitioners for a probationary period not exceeding two years upon such terms for the aliment of the child, and otherwise, as the court thinks fit.[63] Where an interim order specifies a period of less than two years the court may, by a further order, extend the period to a duration not exceeding two years in all.[64] Such orders are rare. They appear to be used where the court is not fully satisfied but it is felt that doubts or difficulties may be resolved after the passage of time. A better course may often be to adjourn the application. Such need as there has been for interim orders may be largely obviated by the power which the court now has to make a custody order on an application for adoption,[65] but an interim order has the advantage that the matter remains subject to automatic review by the court and that during the probationary period the adoption agency and the reporting officer and the curator *ad litem* may remain in touch with the prospective adopters. It is a prerequisite of the making of an interim order either that the child should be free for adoption or that parental agreement to adoption has been given or dispensed with.

FURTHER PROCEDURAL MATTERS

Return of Child to Agency

Once a child has been placed in the care and possession of prospective adopters by an adoption agency, the return of the child to the agency is subject to statutory control. On the one hand, the prospective adopters may give notice in writing to the adoption agency of their intention not to retain the care and pos-

---

[61] ss. 29(1) and 56(2).
[62] s. 29(2).
[63] s. 25(1). *Cf.* Adoption Act 1958, s. 8. For a case in which conditions were imposed, see *S* v. *Huddersfield Borough Council* [1974] 3 All E.R. 296, in which a condition of access by a natural parent was imposed.
[64] s. 25(2).
[65] Children Act 1975, s. 53.

session of the child. On the other hand, the agency may give notice in writing to the prospective adopters of their intention not to allow the child to remain in the prospective adopter's care and possession.[66] However, once an application for an adoption order has been made the agency cannot give such notice except with the leave of the court.[67] Where notice is given, whether by the agency or by the prospective adopter, or where an application for an adoption order is refused or withdrawn, or where the probationary period under an interim order expires without an adoption order having been made, then the prospective adopter must, within seven days, return the child to the adoption agency and the agency must receive the child.[68] Where an adoption order is refused the seven day period may, if the court thinks fit, be extended to a period not exceeding six weeks[69] but with that exception there is no jurisdiction to extend the period within which the child must be returned.[70] Where notice of intention to apply for an adoption order is given in respect of a child who is, for the time being, in the care of a local authority but who has not been delivered into the care and possession of the person by whom the notice is given in pursuance of an adoption placement, *i.e.* where the child has been placed with the applicant for a purpose other than adoption the provisions affecting return of the child apply as if the child had been so delivered except that where the adoption application is refused or withdrawn the child need not be returned to the local authority unless the local authority so require.[71] Once such notice has been given, any right of the local authority to require the child to be returned, otherwise than in pursuance of the above provisions, is suspended pending disposal of the adoption application and, while the child remains in the care and possession of the person by whom the notice is given, the liability of any person to make contributions in respect of the child as being a child in care[72] is suspended until the expiry of 12 weeks since the giving of the notice without the application being made or until the application is refused or withdrawn.[73]

Prohibition on Payments

In order to prevent trafficking in children for gain it is necessary to prohibit the exchange of money or other valuable consideration in relation to an adoption. It is, accordingly, unlawful to give to anyone any payment or reward in respect of (1) the adoption by that person of a child, or (2) the granting by him of any agreement or consent required in connection with the adoption of a child, or (3) the transfer by him of the care and possession of a child with a view to adoption, or (4) the making by him of any arrangements for the adoption of a child.[74] The prohibition does not apply to any payment by a parent or guardian or prospective adopter made to an adoption agency in respect of expenses reasonably

---

[66] Adoption (Scotland) Act 1978, s. 30(1).
[67] s. 30(2).
[68] s. 30(3) and (4).
[69] s. 30(6).
[70] *Re CSC (An Infant)* [1960] 1 All E.R. 711, *per* Roxburgh J. at p. 715.
[71] s. 31(1).
[72] Social Work (Scotland) Act 1968, s. 78.
[73] Adoption (Scotland) Act 1978, s. 31(3).
[74] s. 51(1).

incurred by the agency in connection with the adoption, or to any payment or re-ward authorised by the court.[75] Nor does the prohibition apply to any payment made by an adoption agency to (1) the prospective adopter in respect of legal or medical expenses incurred by that person in connection with the adoption ap-plication, (2) another adoption agency in consideration of the placing of the child for adoption, or (3) an approved voluntary organisation as a fee for ser-vices in putting the agency in contact with another agency for the making of an adoption arrangement.[76] The prohibition, being a matter of criminal law, does not have extra-territorial effect.[77] It has been held that payments made under a surrogacy arrangement[78] before the possibility of adoption was considered do not fall within the prohibition.[79] Special allowances paid to adopters for the ali-ment of the child are, however, generally thought to fall within the prohibition. That special allowances should not be paid is consistent with the general prin-ciple of adoption law that the relationship between adoptive parents and their adopted children should, so far as possible, be the same as that between natural parents and their children. The rigid application of that doctrine has, however, the unfortunate result that handicapped children and other children who are "hard to place," including large families of children, remain in institutional care when adoptive homes might be found for them if payments to compensate the adopters for the exceptional expenditures which they will incur could be made. Foster parents who wish to adopt a child who has been in their care for a long time may, moreover, not be able to do so because they cannot afford to be with-out the boarding-out allowance, although adoption would be in the best interests of the child. Provision is accordingly made for the approval by the Secretary of State of schemes submitted to him by adoption agencies for the payment by the agency of allowances to persons who have adopted, or intend to adopt, a child. Payments made under such schemes will not offend against the prohibition.[80]

Restrictions on Advertising

Further protection against trafficking and other abuses in connection with ad-option is provided by the restriction on advertisements. It is unlawful to publish any advertisement indicating that the parent or guardian of a child desires to cause the child to be adopted or that anyone desires to adopt a child or that any-one, other than an adoption agency, is willing to make arrangements for the ad-option of a child.[81] Advertisements by an adoption agency that it has children, or even specified children, whom it wishes to place for adoption is not, it is thought, a contravention of this restriction because such an advertisement does not carry any necessary implication that the parent or guardian of a child desires to cause the child to be adopted. Such advertisements, although controversial, may be of assistance in finding homes for children who are hard to place.

---

[75] s. 51(3). Authorisation may be prospective or retrospective: *Re An Adoption Application (Sur-rogacy)* [1987] 2 All E.R. 826.

[76] s. 51(4).

[77] *Re A (Adoption: Placement)* [1988] 1 W.L.R. 229.

[78] See *ante* at pp. 142–145.

[79] *Re An Adoption Application (Surrogacy), supra.*

[80] s. 51(5) and (11).

[81] s. 52(1).

Restrictions on Removal of Children for Adoption Abroad

Except under the authority of an order vesting the parental rights and duties relating to a child in a person who is not domiciled in England and Wales or Northern Ireland or Scotland, it is unlawful to take or send a child who is a British subject out of Great Britain to any place outside the United Kingdom, the Channel Islands, and the Isle of Man with a view to the adoption of the child by anyone who is not a parent or guardian or relative[82] of the child; and it is also unlawful to take part in any arrangement for transferring the care and possession of a child to any person for that purpose.[83] This prohibition does not apply to a child in the care of a local authority.[84]

Appeals

Formerly adoptions in the Court of Session were Inner House petitions and so the only appeal was to the House of Lords. They are now heard in the Outer House[85] and interlocutors in an adoption process may be reclaimed to the Inner House and appeal taken from there to the House of Lords in accordance with the rules generally applicable to Court of Session causes. Appeals in cases originating in the sheriff court also follow the ordinary rules. Decisions in adoption cases, and in particular decisions on dispensation with parental agreement are not properly discretionary and so review is not confined to the well-recognised grounds on which an appellate court may interfere with the exercise of a discretion.[86] At any rate where the decision depends on facts ascertained by reporters the matter is at large on appeal. Great importance is, however, to be attached to the opinion of the trial judge and while the appellate court is well entitled to come to a contrary conclusion if it thinks he is wrong, it will be slow to do so unless he has misdirected himself in law or is otherwise clearly in error.[87] Because adoption proceedings are not essentially adversarial and because of the primacy attached to the need to safeguard and promote the welfare of the child, additional evidence will be admitted on appeal with greater liberality than in ordinary causes and that may include evidence of facts occurring since the date of the order.[88] The power to direct that proceedings be heard in open court, which in fact is never exercised in proceedings at first instance may often, without disadvantage, be exercised for the hearing of an appeal.

Registration and Disclosure

Every adoption order must contain a direction to the Registrar General to

---

[82] "Relative" is defined in s. 65(1) of the Adoption (Scotland) Act 1978. It includes "uncle" and has been held in this context under the equivalent English legislation not to include a great-uncle: *Re C and Anr. (Minors) (Wardship: Adoption)* [1989] 1 All E.R. 395.

[83] s. 50(1), as amended by the Children Act 1989, Sched. 10, para. 43.

[84] Social Work (Scotland) 1968, s. 23.

[85] R.C. 220(1).

[86] *A and B, Petrs.*, 1971 S.L.T. 258, *per* Lord Guest at p. 260. On the appellate court's power to interfere with the trial judge's discretion in custody cases, see *Jordan* v. *Jordan*, 1983 S.L.T. 539; *Britton* v. *Central Regional Council*, 1986 S.L.T. 207; *Early* v. *Early*, 1990 S.L.T. 221.

[87] *A and B, Petrs.*, *ibid.*; *cf. per* Lord Reid at p. 259 and Lord Simon of Glaisdale at p. 264.

[88] *Re Adoption Act 1950, The Times*, July 29, 1958.

make in the Adopted Children Register an entry recording in prescribed form the adoption.[89]

The entry in the Adopted Children Register is, without further or other proof, received as evidence of the adoption to which it relates and of the date of birth and country of birth of the adopted person.[90] The original entry of the child's birth in the Register of Births is marked "Adopted" and where the child has been previously adopted the entry then made in the Adopted Children Register is marked "Re-adopted."[91] The Registrar General must keep registers and books so as to record and make traceable the connection between any entry in the Register of Births which has been marked "Adopted" and any corresponding entry in the Adopted Children Register, but these registers and books are not to be open to public inspection or search and no information contained in them may be furnished to any person unless a court so orders or an adopted person who has attained the age of 17 years seeks such information relating to himself.[92] The right of an adopted person, who has attained the age of 17, to trace the records of his birth has been a feature of the Scottish legislation on adoption since it was introduced in 1930. On furnishing information from the Register of Births to an adopted person, the Registrar General is now obliged to advise him that counselling services are available from the local authority for the area where he lives or, if his adoption was arranged by an approved adoption society, from that society; and it is the duty of local authorities and approved adoption societies to provide counselling in these circumstances.[93] Where counselling is provided, an extract of the entry relating to the adopted person in the Register of Births may be furnished from the Register of Births to the authority or society carrying out the counselling as well as to the adopted person.[94]

The court has power (1) to amend an adoption order within one year from the date of the order by adding any new name given to, or taken by, the adopted person or substituting such a name for a name in the order, and (2) to revoke any direction for the marking of an entry in the Register of Births or the Adopted Children Register where that direction has been wrongly included in the order.[95] If an adoption order is so amended, or a direction revoked, the entry in the Adopted Children Register or in the Register of Births is to be amended or cancelled accordingly.[96] The power to revoke is a wide one which is not restricted to the correction of clerical errors.[97]

No extract of an adoption order may be issued except by authority of the court obtained by petition setting forth the reasons for which the extract is required.[98] Where such an extract is issued then immediately on its issue, or otherwise immediately after the communication to the Registrar General of any adoption order or its amendment or revocation, the adoption process must be sealed and

---

[89] Sched. 1, para. 1(1).
[90] s. 45(2).
[91] Sched. 1, para. 1(5) and (6).
[92] s. 45(4) and (5).
[93] s. 45(6), (6A), and (6B), as substituted and inserted by the Children Act 1989, Sched. 10, para. 41.
[94] s. 45(5) and (7), as amended by the Children Act 1989, Sched. 10, para. 41.
[95] Sched. 1, para. 4(1).
[96] Sched. 1, para. 4(2).
[97] See R v. Chelsea Juvenile Court (Re An Infant) [1955] 1 W.L.R. 52.
[98] A.S., s. 27(2) and (3); R.C. 230(3).

cannot thereafter be opened up or made accessible to any person within 100 years after the date of the order except:

(1) to an adopted person to whom the order refers and who has attained the age of 17 years or, in relation to Court of Session petitions, to a solicitor, local authority, or adoption agency so authorised in writing by the adopted person;

(2) on the written application of an adoption agency made with the agreement of the adopted person for the purpose of ascertaining the name of the agency, if any, responsible for the placement of that person;

(3) by the authority of the court in which the order was pronounced obtained on petition specifying precisely the reasons for which access to the process is required. (This provision applies in particular to giving authority for making the process accessible to another court, public authority or an administrative board (none of which need be within the United Kingdom) having power to authorise an adoption, which has requested that information be made available for the purpose of the discharge of its duties in considering an application for adoption); and

(4) to a person who is authorised in writing by the Secretary of State to obtain information from the process for the purposes of such research as is designed to improve the working of adoption law and practice.[99]

INTERNATIONAL ASPECTS OF ADOPTION

Adoption of Children Abroad

The general rule is that a child who is a British subject may not be taken out of the country in order to be adopted abroad.[1] However, where a person who is not domiciled in England and Wales or Scotland or Northern Ireland intends to adopt a child under the law of, or within, the country in which he is domiciled, the court may make an order vesting in him the parental rights and duties relating to the child.[2] The result of this order is to enable the child to be taken out of the country for the purpose of adoption. "Parental rights and duties" are not defined in the Adoption (Scotland) Act 1978, but the meaning of the phrase cannot be substantially different from the definition of parental rights given in the Law Reform (Parent and Child) (Scotland) Act 1986: "guardianship, custody or access, as the case may require, and any right or authority relating to the welfare or upbringing of a child conferred on a parent by any rule of law," taken together with the parental duties of nurture, education and aliment.[3] The main provisions of the adoption legislation apply to such orders but they do not have the full effect on status which an adoption has and they do not affect citizenship and rights

---

[99] A.S., s. 28(2); R.C. 230(4).

[1] s. 50.

[2] s. 49, as amended by the Children Act 1989, Sched. 10, para. 42.

[3] *Cf.* the definition of "parental responsibilities" given for England in the Children Act 1989, s. 3(1): "all the rights, duties, power, responsibility and authority which by law a parent of a child has in relation to the child and his property."

of succession.[4] An interim order cannot be made.[5] A petitioner must, in addition to complying with the other requirements relating to an adoption petition, adduce evidence of the law of adoption in the country in which he is domiciled. Such evidence may take the form of an affidavit sworn by a person conversant with that law and who practises, or has practised, law in that country or is a duly accredited representative of the government of that country in the United Kingdom.[6] For purposes of registration the words "proposed foreign adoption" or "proposed foreign re-adoption" take the place of "adopted" or "re-adopted."[7]

The prerequisites for the making of these orders differ from those of adoption orders in that the child must be at least 32 weeks old (rather than 19 weeks) and have had his home with the applicants, or one of them,[8] for at least 26 weeks (rather than 13 weeks) preceding the making of the order.[9]

Convention Adoption Orders

Convention adoption orders were introduced by the Adoption Act 1968 following the Hague Convention on Adoption of Children 1965,[10] and the law applicable to them is now contained in section 17 of the Adoption (Scotland) Act 1978[11] which substantially re- enacts the provisions of the 1968 Act. Their purpose is to facilitate adoption where the nationality or country of habitual residence of the prospective adopters is different from that of the child. As the test for jurisdiction in adoption is ordinarily that of the domicile of the prospective adopters and not of their nationality or habitual residence, cases may occur where there is jurisdiction to make both a convention order and an order in ordinary form. The extent of that overlap is restricted by the exclusion of a convention order where the applicant or applicants and the child are all United Kingdom nationals living in British territory[12] but that in turn leaves a gap where the applicants and the child all fall into that category and the applicants are domiciled abroad. In such a case there is no jurisdiction to make an adoption order although an order, discussed in the preceding section, vesting parental rights for the purposes of adoption in the country of the prospective adopters' domicile may be made.[13] Where there is an overlap of jurisdiction the applicants can choose which type of order to apply for. However, if the application is for a convention order then a convention order must be made so long as the conditions

---

[4] The definition of "adoption order" given in s. 65(1), *i.e.* the orders which have the effects mentioned in the text, does not include orders under s. 49.

[5] And there is no equivalent for an order freeing a child for adoption (see further s. 49(2)).

[6] A.S., s. 17(2); R.C. 224(3)(*b*). The Rule of Court requires only a "statement from a qualified person...whether there is any legal impediment to the adoption taking place."

[7] s. 49(3).

[8] See *Re M (An Infant) (Adoption: Child's Removal from Jurisdiction)* [1973] Fam. 66.

[9] s. 49(2).

[10] The Hague Convention on Jurisdiction, Applicable Law, and Recognition of Decrees Relating to Adoption, signed on Nov. 15, 1965.

[11] For comment on the Hague Convention, see Graveson, Cmnd. 2615, also printed at (1965) 14 I.C.L.Q. 558; Graveson, *Conflict of Laws* (7th ed.), 1974, at pp. 532–538; Lipstein, [1965] Camb. L.J. 224; Unger, (1965) 28 M.L.R. 463. For comment on the 1968 Act see McClean and Patchett, (1970) 19 I.C.L.Q. 1 and Blom, (1973) 22 I.C.L.Q. 109.

[12] s. 17(3).

[13] s. 49.

for making it are satisfied both at the time of application and at the time the order is made.[14]

Apart from the rule that the applicants and the child must not all be United Kingdom nationals living in British territory the conditions relating to nationality and residence are:

(1) The child must be a United Kingdom national or a national of a convention country and must habitually reside in British territory or a convention country.[15]

(2) If the application is by a married couple *either* (a) each must be a United Kingdom national or a national of a convention country and both must habitually reside in Great Britain, *or* (b) both must be United Kingdom nationals and each must habitually reside in British territory or a convention country.[16]

(3) If the application is by one person, *either* (a) he must be a United Kingdom national or a national of a convention country and habitually reside in Great Britain, *or* (b) he must be a United Kingdom national and habitually reside in British territory or a convention country.[17]

A convention country is any country outside British territory designated by an order of the Secretary of State as a country in which the Hague Convention is in force.[18] "British territory" means the United Kingdom, the Channel Islands, the Isle of Man and any colony, unless the Secretary of State has designated any countries as British territory for the purposes of adoption legislation in which case British territory means countries so designated. "United Kingdom national" means a citizen of the United Kingdom and colonies satisfying such conditions, if any, as the Secretary of State may specify for the purpose of a convention order.[19] The term "habitual residence" is not defined, but it will have the meaning ascribed to it in other areas of international private law.[20]

In order to make a convention adoption order, the following further conditions must be satisfied:

(1) The child must not be or have been married.[21]

(2) If, in the case of an application by a married couple, they are both nationals of the same convention country, or if, in the case of an application by one person, he is a national of a convention country, the adoption must not be prohibited by a specified provision of the internal law of that country. By specified provision is meant a provision of the law of the foreign country which has been notified to the United Kingdom government in pursuance of one of the provisions of the Hague

---

[14] s. 17(1).
[15] s. 17(2).
[16] s. 17(4).
[17] s. 17(5).
[18] To date, only the U.K., Austria, and Switzerland have ratified the Hague Convention: see Convention Adoption (Austria and Switzerland) (Scotland) Order 1978 (S.I. 1978 No. 1442).
[19] s. 65(1).
[20] See *ante*, at pp. 241.
[21] s. 17(2)(*c*).

convention and has, as a result, been specified in a statutory instrument.[22]

(3) If the child is not a United Kingdom national the consents and consultations required by the internal law of its nationality must be carried out and the court must be satisfied that each person who consents in accordance with that internal law does so with full understanding of what is involved. This restriction does not, however, apply to any provision of the foreign law requiring consents by, or consultations with, the family of the prospective adopter, including his or her spouse. Where the foreign law provides for dispensation with consent, the court shall be treated as the authority by whom that dispensation may be made and the adoption effected.[23]

Only the Court of Session has jurisdiction to make a convention adoption order.[24]

A convention adoption order is an adoption order in the statutory sense and not an independent species of order. Accordingly, with the exception of the statutory requirements on the domicile of applicants,[25] the general law of adoption applies, subject to the conditions noted above, to applications for a convention adoption order as it does to other applications. Among the advantages of the provision for convention adoption orders is that the jurisdiction of British courts is enlarged to comprehend cases with an international aspect which would not otherwise be open while, at the same time, the simplicity of retaining the internal rules of the forum for such cases is largely maintained. As has been seen, the law of the nationality of the child is, however, respected so far as questions of consent and consultation are concerned, as is the law of the nationality of prospective adopters in relation to prohibitions on adoption.

Recognition of Foreign Adoptions

An adoption order made in England and Wales, Northern Ireland, the Isle of Man or the Channel Islands is an adoption order within the meaning of the same statutory provisions as is a Scottish adoption order,[26] and is entitled to the same recognition. Beyond that, the recognition of non-Scottish adoptions depends in part on special statutory provisions, and in part on the common law. The statutory and common law rules constitute independent systems and the fact that recognition is not available under statute is no bar to recognition at common law.

Statutory Recognition

All adoptions that take place outside British jurisdiction are entitled to be recognised by the Scottish courts as long as they come within the definition of "overseas adoptions."[27] Recognition entails that the adoption is to be treated in every way as if it had been granted under the domestic legislation in Scotland.

---

[22] s. 17(4), (5) and (6).
[23] For questions of proof, etc., see further, s. 17(6) and (7).
[24] s. 56(4).
[25] ss. 14(2)(*b*) and 15(2)(*b*).
[26] s. 38(1)(*c*).
[27] ss. 38(1)(*d*) and 65(2).

The result is that the effect given to an overseas adoption may be different from that which it would have received in the country in which the adoption took place. Where the succession to an estate is governed by the law of Scotland a child adopted under an overseas adoption will, therefore, have the succession rights which a Scottish adopted child would have even if the system of law under which he was adopted did not confer such rights on him.[28]

An overseas adoption is an "adoption of such a description as the Secretary of State may by order specify, being a description of adoptions of children appearing to him to be effected under the law of any country outside Great Britain."[29] In effect, therefore, provided the description specified by the Secretary of State is one that can be applied to the adoption of children, any order falling within that description is an overseas adoption. Determinations of competent overseas authorities in relation to overseas adoption, whether authorising, reviewing or annulling the adoption, must receive effect.[30]

While the general rule is that overseas adoptions will be recognised and determinations in relation to overseas adoptions will be given effect, this suffers an exception in terms of section 47(2) of the Adoption (Scotland) Act 1978, which allows the Court of Session to order that the adoption or determination shall cease to be valid on the ground that it is contrary to public policy or that the authority which purported to authorise the adoption or make the determination was not competent to entertain the case. Similarly any court may, for the purposes of proceedings before it, treat an overseas adoption as invalid on either of these grounds.[31] In addition, where the overseas adoption is regulated by the Hague Convention (*i.e.* broadly, was effected in a country which is a party to the convention under provisions corresponding to those laid down for convention adoption orders in this country) it may be annulled by the Court of Session on any ground on which it could be impugned in the country in which it was effected or on the ground that it was prohibited by a notified provision of the law of the adopters' nationality or could have been impugned as contravening the consent requirements of the internal law of the nationality of the adopted person.[32] With these exceptions the validity of an overseas adoption or determination may not be impugned in any court.

Statutory (or indeed common law) recognition of overseas adoptions does not depend on reciprocity nor is it necessary that the country whose adoptions are recognised should have been a party to the Hague Convention from which the legislation flows. Adoptions made in and under the law of many Commonwealth countries, the United States of America, the Republic of South Africa and all western European countries, have now been specified as overseas adoptions.[33]

Overseas adoptions have effect as respects anything done or any event occurring on or after February 1, 1973. An exception however must be made in

---

[28] Succession (Scotland) Act 1964, s. 23, amended by the Adoption (Scotland) Act 1978, Sched. 3, para. 4. See *Salvesen's Trs., Petrs.*, 1992 S.C.L.R. 729.
[29] s. 65(2).
[30] s. 53(1), as amended by the Children Act 1989, Sched. 10, para. 44.
[31] s. 47(2).
[32] s. 47(1).
[33] Adoption (Designation of Overseas Adoptions) Order 1973 (S.I. 1973 No. 19).

questions of succession: an overseas adoption will be recognised for the purpose of successions opening before, as well as on or after, that date (provided they do not open before 10th September 1964) because section 23 of the Succession (Scotland) Act 1964, which puts adopted children in the same position, for succession purposes, as natural children, includes "overseas adoptions" in its definition of "adoption order"[34] and consequently no distinction is to be made between overseas adoptions and domestic adoptions for this purpose.[35] The date when the adoption took place is immaterial provided, in a question of succession, it preceded the death.[36]

Common Law Recognition

There is no Scottish authority directly in point on questions of common law recognition and no English authorities other than in relation to succession. The Adoption (Scotland) Act 1978 assumes that adoptions can be recognised in Scotland by means other than that discussed in the preceding paragraph,[37] but it gives no indication of the grounds upon which such recognition is based. A number of propositions are, however, open in principle and these are discussed in the following paragraphs.

Jurisdictional Parity

A foreign adoption will, it is submitted, be recognised if it took place in a country in which, had rules corresponding to the Scottish rules for jurisdiction being applied, there would have been jurisdiction to make an adoption order. As Lord President Robertson said in a different but relevant context: "It seems difficult to the degree of impossibility for this Court to decline on principle to recognise if done abroad, what it is itself bound to do and does daily at home."[38] It is sufficient that the jurisdictional basis should be substantially the same[39]; and it is not required that principles of recognition must be "a mirror image of our own law or that the pace of recognition must be geared to the haphazard movement of our legislative process."[40] A broad correspondence will take account of the general trend of legislative development.

The ordinary jurisdictional requirement for a Scottish adoption order is that the applicant or, in the case of a joint application, one of the applicants should be domiciled in the United Kingdom, the Channel Islands or the Isle of Man. A foreign adoption should therefore be recognised if the adoptive parent, or one of

---

[34] Succession (Scotland) Act 1964, s. 23(5).
[35] *Salvesen's Trs., Petrs.*, 1992 S.C.L.R. 729, *per* Lord President Hope at p. 733D and E.
[36] See Blom, (1973) 22 I.C.L.Q. 109 at p. 146.
[37] Adoption (Scotland) Act 1978, s. 38(1)(e).
[38] *Obers v. Paton's Trs.* (1897) 24 R. 719 at p. 732. This view is difficult to reconcile with *Warden v. Warden*, 1951 S.C. 508, in which Lord Strachan said: "I doubt whether Scots law recognises without qualification the general proposition thus contended for, *viz.*, that in the recognition of foreign decrees the Scots Courts must concede to foreign Courts any ground of jurisdiction which they claim for themselves." *Warden* v. *Warden* is, however, in turn difficult to reconcile with *Travers v. Holley* [1953] P. 246, which was approved in *Indyka v. Indyka* [1969] 1 A.C. 33. See also *Galbraith v. Galbraith*, 1971 S.C. 65; *Bain v. Bain*, 1971 S.L.T. 141; Anton and Beaumont, *Private International Law* (2nd ed.) at p. 468. For a criticism of *Warden* v. *Warden* see Gow, (1954) 3 I.C.L.Q. 152.
[39] *Travers v. Holley, supra.*
[40] *Indyka v. Indyka, supra, per* Lord Wilberforce at p. 106.

two adoptive parents, were domiciled, at the time the adoption took place, in the country in which it took place[41] (or, where that country forms part of a larger national unit, were domiciled in one of the component parts of that unit). As a Scottish adoption order, other than a convention adoption order, may be made irrespective of the child's domicile or nationality and, so far as the Court of Session's jurisdiction is concerned, largely irrespective of his whereabouts, there is no need to import any of these factors into a decision on recognition where the adopters satisfy the domiciliary test for jurisdiction.

That attention should be directed to the domicile of the adopters is supported by authority and borne out by the statutory provisions on vesting parental rights and duties for the purpose of adoption abroad.[42] These provide for an order being made in favour of an applicant who intends to adopt a child under the law of, or within, the country in which he (the applicant) is domiciled. It would be anomalous if recognition were to be denied to adoptions following on such orders and valid by the law of the domicile. The fundamental reason for using the law of the adopter's domicile as the basis for recognition is, however, that the domicile of the applicants for adoption is the basis upon which Scottish courts ordinarily exercise jurisdiction.[43] Where, therefore, as is now the case in relation to convention adoption orders, alternative grounds of jurisdiction may be invoked, recognition of foreign adoptions should follow if jurisdictional tests corresponding to those for a convention adoption order are satisfied in the country in which the adoption took place.

Questions remain as to whether on the principles under discussion recognition can be granted where, although on Scottish grounds of jurisdiction there would have been jurisdiction in the courts of a foreign country, (1) the foreign court, in fact, exercised jurisdiction on other grounds, or (2) the adoption was not the subject of judicial proceedings but was effected in that country by an administrative agency or by contract, or (3) the adoption did not take place in, but would be recognised by the law of, the country in question. There are arguments against recognition in all these cases. That the Scottish courts claim jurisdiction on one ground is, it may be said, no reason that they should recognise the jurisdiction of a foreign court claimed on another. A fortiori of that, there is no reason to recognise the results of administrative procedures to which jurisdictional tests in the proper sense do not apply at all, while contract is both alien to Scottish principles of adoption and invites the application of international private law rules in which the observance of jurisdictional parity plays no part. And to say that one should recognise an adoption recognised by, as distinct from taking place in, the country, for example, of the domicile, is illogical (though accepted, for example, in relation to recognition of divorce[44]). That recognition is accorded to an adoption under the law of the adopters' domicile because that law is indicated by Scottish jurisdictional tests is no reason for recognising an adoption which that law would recognise by invoking other tests. These arguments

---

[41] It was assumed in *Spencer's Trs.* v. *Ruggles*, 1982 S.L.T. 165 that a Scottish adoption granted when the adopter was domiciled in Scotland would be given effect in a Scottish succession.

[42] s. 49.

[43] "Our courts should recognise a jurisdiction which *mutatis mutandis* they claim for themselves": *Re Valentine's Settlement* [1965] Ch. 831, *per* Lord Denning M.R. at p. 842.

[44] *Armitage* v. *Att.-Gen.* [1906] P. 135.

have force but under none of the heads under consideration is the argument against recognition conclusive. Considerations of policy, that is a favour which the law may show to adoption as it did to legitimacy because of the beneficial results which follow, point to a more liberal view. An analogy with recognition of foreign divorces at common law[45] is again of assistance. In *Robinson-Scott* v. *Robinson-Scott* it was said:

> "It is not essential for recognition by this court that the foreign court should assume jurisdiction on the grounds laid down [by English domestic legislation]. It is sufficient that facts exist which would enable the English courts to assume jurisdiction."[46]

So when divorce was recognised on the ground of its validity according to the law of the husband's domicile, a basis of recognition which had for long been accepted, it was never required as a condition of recognition that the foreign court should, in fact, have asserted jurisdiction on that ground. The foreign basis of jurisdiction is irrelevant. It is, therefore, submitted that it is sufficient for the recognition of a foreign adoption that the adopters were domiciled where the adoption took place, or that another relevant Scottish jurisdictional test[47] could have been satisfied, regardless of the basis for jurisdiction actually invoked in the foreign country. As in the case of extra-judicial divorces (at common law)[48] the extra-judicial character of the adoption process, whether contractual or administrative, is also, it is submitted, irrelevant. In the case of an administrative process that argument takes added force from the fact that the court's function in a Scottish adoption bears a ministerial as well as a judicial aspect. The comparison with divorce also supports the view that adoptions recognised in the foreign country should be regarded in the same light as adoptions which actually take place there.[49]

The general view of recognition indicated above can be reconciled with *Re Marshall*[50] and *Re Valentine's Settlement*[51] and derives considerable support from the latter. It can also be reconciled with *Re Wilson*[52] in which it seems that Vaisey J. would have recognised the adoption had it taken place according to the law of the adopters' domicile. It cannot be reconciled with *Re Wilby*,[53] which was however overruled by *Re Valentine's Settlement*.

Child's Domicile

In addition to the ground for recognition considered above, a foreign adoption will, it is submitted, also be recognised if made according to the law of the child's domicile at the time the adoption took place. It is no objection that Scottish jurisdictional rules make no requirement regarding the child's domicile.

---

[45] See now Family Law Act 1986.
[46] [1958] P. 71 at p. 88, *per* Karminski J.
[47] *e.g.* the tests for Convention orders.
[48] *Har-Shefi* v. *Har-Shefi (No. 2)* [1953] P. 220.
[49] *Armitage* v. *Att.-Gen.*, *supra*.
[50] [1957] Ch. 263, affirmed *ibid.*, at 507.
[51] [1965] Ch. 831.
[52] [1954] Ch. 733.
[53] [1956] P. 174.

The absence of such a requirement is a positive feature, enlarging the scope of adoption, which should not be given the negative effect of denying recognition which the law of the domicile would confer.

The reason for this is that adoption affects status,[54] and that will be so in practically all legal systems, although the exact nature of the impact on status may vary greatly from one system to another.[55] The grand rule in questions of status is that they should be determined by the law of the domicile of the *propositus*. It therefore follows that adoption valid by the law of the child's domicile should be recognised because, and in so far as, it affects his status. It has been suggested that before this can be done the adoption must also be valid by the law of the adopter's domicile.[56] It is, however, the child's status that is primarily in issue and the child should not, because of conflict with the law of the adopters' domicile, be denied the protection which adoption confers on him by the law of his domicile or the benefit of rights enforceable by that law against adopters who have freely entered into an adoptive relationship with him. Similarly there is no reason that the child should not be subject to obligations imposed by the law of his domicile.

Succession may be thought to be a special case pointing to the adopter's domicile but that view is increasingly difficult to maintain in the light of the availability of British adoption processes to petitioners who are not domiciled in this country.[57] It is therefore submitted that reference should not be made to the law of the adopters' domicile as an additional requirement.[58] There is also no reason for taking into account jurisdiction over the natural parents of the child. Scottish domestic law makes no jurisdictional requirements in relation to the natural parents, and there is no reason that its rules of international private law should do otherwise. The legitimate interests of natural parents are sufficiently protected by considerations of morality and public policy which, if contravened, would lead to refusal of recognition and also by the coincidence that will usually obtain between their domicile and the domicile of the child.

The proposition which is here put forward can be reconciled with *Re Valentine's Settlement*[59] and *Re Wilson*[60] only on the view that in these cases the domicile of the child was not proved. There is nothing in the opinions to suggest that that was the controlling factor, and in both cases it seems likely that the child was, in fact, domiciled in the country in which the adoption took place. In *Re Valentine's Settlement*, moreover, Lord Denning M.R. expressly rejected the domicile of the child as even among the criteria to be considered: "You do not" he said, "look to the domicile of the child; for that has no separate domicile of its

---

[54] *J and J* v. *C's Tutor*, 1948 S.C. 636.

[55] The effect of a Scottish adoption on status is now practically complete, but has not always been so. See *ante* at pp. 519–520.

[56] See Cheshire and North, *Private International Law* (11th ed., 1987), at p. 762.

[57] Convention adoption orders (for which see *ante* at pp. 577–579). Moreover, where an adoption in ordinary form is by a married couple only one of them need have the requisite domiciliary qualification. It is therefore difficult to argue that the requirements of the law of an adopter's domicile must be met before adoption can impinge on succession, or indeed, on other rights.

[58] See *Re Valentine's Settlement, supra, per* Salmon J. at pp. 850–851.

[59] *Supra.*

[60] *Supra.*

own. It takes its parent's domicile. You look to the [adopting] parents' domicile only."[61]

There is, however, a fallacy in that reasoning. It is true that a child will not normally have a domicile separate from that of one or other of its parents, but its domicile may well not coincide with that of its adoptive parents. That may be so after as well as before adoption if, under the relevant legal régime, adoption does not effect a change in domicile. Even where that change takes place, it is only if the adoption is recognised that the child's domicile can, in the contemplation of the forum, become the same as that of the adopters; and to exclude consideration of the child's domicile because it will be the same as theirs is therefore to beg the question of recognition. It is submitted that the proposition is, despite the conflict with *Re Valentine's Settlement*, sound in principle.

Real and Substantial Connection

Lastly, it is further submitted that a foreign adoption may be recognised where any of the parties had, at the time of the adoption, a real and substantial connection with the jurisdiction under which the adoption took place. This proposition is derived, by analogy with the common law on recognition of foreign decrees of divorce, from *Indyka* v. *Indyka*.[62] "Real and substantial connection" is not defined and, indeed, it is of the essence of its utility that it should be at large for the court. As Lord Wilberforce said:

> "The courts are well able to perform the task of examining the reality of the connection...In so acting, I am convinced that they are more likely to reach just, and to avoid artificial, results."[63]

Among the factors that may play a part are, however, nationality, domicile (although not necessarily in the technical sense of the forum), or residence, which again need not be in the sense of "habitual residence or ordinary residence" as these have come to be understood in the forum. *Indyka* has been superseded so far as recognition of foreign divorces is concerned but similar thinking underlies the Law Commissions' proposals on domicile,[64] whereby the domicile of an individual is to be determined by looking at the place with which he is most closely connected and is also reflected in the rules relating to the inferred proper law of the contract[65]; and the principle of the proper law of the trust whereby if the truster has not chosen a legal system to govern the trust, it will be governed by the law with which it is most closely connected.[66]

As a test for recognition of foreign adoptions this outlook accords well with

---

[61] [1965] Ch. at p. 842.

[62] [1969] 1 A.C. 33. For a discussion of this case and the principle of recognition on the ground of real and substantial connection which emerges from it, see Graveson, *Conflict of Law* (7th ed.) at pp. 311–318. The case was followed in Scotland in *Galbraith* v. *Galbraith and Ors.*, 1971 S.C. 65 and in *Bain* v. *Bain and Ors.*, 1971 S.C. 146.

[63] [1969] 1 A.C. at pp. 106–107.

[64] Scottish Law Commission No. 107; Law Commission No. 168 (1987).

[65] See Anton and Beaumont at pp. 268–270.

[66] Hague Convention on the Law Applicable to Trusts and their Recognition, Art. 7, imported into Scots and English domestic law by the Recognition of Trusts Act 1987.

the dissenting judgment of Salmon L.J.[67] in *Re Valentine's Settlement*, where he said:

> "Our law...develops in accordance with the changing needs of man. These have always been ascertained by experience rather than by the rigid application of abstract theory. Experience has shown that there are sound sociological reasons for recognising an adoption in circumstances such as these. Adoption—providing that there are proper safeguards—is greatly for the benefit of the adopted child and of the adoptive parents, and also, I think, of civilised society, since this is founded on the family relationship. It seems to me that we should be slow to refuse recognition to an adoption order made by a foreign court which applies the same safeguards as we do and which undoubtedly had jurisdiction over the adopted child and its natural parents."[68]

The last words, if taken out of their context, may seem to beg some questions of jurisdiction, but, read in context, it seems that Salmon L.J. had in mind the domicile of the child and its natural parents and the real connection with the country where the adoption took place which arose from that. A *caveat* may, however, be entered against too strict an interpretation of Salmon L.J.'s reference to the application of "the same safeguards as we do." In the United Kingdom the safeguards are as stringent as almost anywhere else in the world, and if an exact equivalence were required there would be little scope for recognition of foreign adoptions at common law with the exception of a few countries whose adoptions are, in any event, recognised under statute. In so far as the safeguards relate to the welfare of the child their importance may, moreover, vary according to the purpose for which recognition is sought. It is an important matter where the purpose is the assertion of parental rights and powers, but in questions of succession it can often be discounted.

Limitations on Recognition

Limitation by Reference to Purpose

As has been seen, an overseas adoption to which statutory recognition is accorded is valid in this country for all purposes. The same is not true of common law recognition. Whether or not a foreign adoption should be recognised at common law may vary according to the purpose for which recognition is sought.[69] Thus, an objection on the grounds of public policy may be apt for certain purposes of recognition and inept in others. What is offensive where parental responsibilities and rights are at stake may not be so in relation to succession or property. The limits of adoption under the foreign law may also limit purposes for which it should be recognised in this country. To take any other view is to become a prisoner of terminology. There is, despite some similarities, no common international understanding of the nature and effects of adoption such as there is, say, of marriage (other than polygamous marriage), and

---

[67] See Anton and Beaumont at p. 507.
[68] [1965] Ch. at p. 852.
[69] *Re Wilson* [1954] Ch. 733, *per* Vaisey J. at p. 738.

the basis for all-purpose recognition that exists in relation to marriage is therefore lacking in the case of adoption. The foreign adoption should receive recognition only to the extent, broadly conceived and with regard to substance rather than technicality or form, that it corresponds with the Scottish understanding of adoption (or the understanding of the appropriate *lex causae* if not Scottish), for it is only to the extent that it reflects that understanding that the label adoption can properly be applied to it. That is consistent with and, it is submitted, a correct interpretation of what was said on a question of testate succession in *Re Marshall*,[70] that "only those who are placed by adoption in a position, both as regards property rights and status, equivalent, or at all events substantially equivalent, to that of the natural children of the adopter can be treated as being within the scope of the testator's contemplation." That does not derogate from but gives effect to, the primacy of the law governing the succession. That law determines whether or not an adopted child should succeed (or whether claims to succession should transmit through him), but the law of the adoption determines whether or not the *propositus* has for the purposes of succession been adopted.

An inevitable consequence of recognition according to purpose is a piecemeal effect and the creation of "limping adoptions," good for one purpose but not for another. Carried to excess that would be a serious disadvantage but, at some cost in consistency and flexibility, the scope for that is much reduced by the Adoption (Scotland) Act 1978. Part IV, which regulates the status conferred by adoption for practically all purposes other than succession and property, applies to any adoption recognised by the law of Scotland.[71] Within the boundaries of the Act discrimination according to purpose is, therefore, excluded. It is doubtful whether the result is restrictive or enlarging. Does a foreign adoption which satisfies the principles for common law recognition but by its own law effects only a very limited transfer of parental rights and duties still qualify for recognition? If it does qualify it must, despite the limitations imposed by its own law, receive effect for all the purposes of the Act; for the only alternative is to deny it recognition altogether. The question of what is meant by adoption where the Act refers to "any other adoption recognised by the law of Scotland" cannot be answered merely by reference to whether "adoption" or its foreign language equivalent, is the name employed, but must involve some consideration of the incidents and effects of the foreign institution. It is thought that the statute envisages a broad correspondence between the effects of adoption under the foreign law and the scope of the Act as a condition of recognition.

As questions of succession and property are excluded from Part IV of the 1978 Act room for discrimination remains between recognition decisions affecting succession and property on the one hand, and the other features of status, including parental responsibilities and rights, on the other. That distinction is preserved if the relevant provisions of the Succession (Scotland) Act 1964 and Part IV of the Adoption (Scotland) Act 1978 are construed in a restrictive but, it

---

[70] [1957] Ch. 507 at p. 523.
[71] s. 38(1).

is submitted, correct sense.[72] In view of the disparate nature of the issues raised in questions of succession and property and in questions of parental responsibilities and rights the distinction accords with sound policy.

Other Limitations on Recognition

One general constraint on recognition of foreign adoptions remains to be noticed. Foreign adoptions which are *contra bonos mores* or contrary to public policy in the forum will not be recognised.[73] The principles which have been discussed are to be read subject to that qualification. Nor will a foreign adoption be recognised at common law if to do so would offend against section 6 of the Adoption (Scotland) Act 1978. A decision on recognition is, it is submitted, "a decision relating to the adoption of a child" so as to bring section 6 into operation, and the considerations which have led to a restrictive application of that section do not in general apply to questions of common law, as distinct from statutory, recognition. Accordingly first consideration must be given to the need to safeguard and promote the welfare of the child throughout his childhood and also due consideration must be given to his wishes and feelings. There are, however, two qualifications. First, there is a fundamental inconsistency between the welfare test contained in section 6 and the principles governing the law of succession and property. So section 6 is excluded if recognition is sought in that context. Second, the operation of section 6 is purely negative. Positive principles of recognition are, it is thought, like principles of jurisdiction, anterior to the operation of section 6 which serves only to exclude recognition which would otherwise be accorded. So if the grounds of recognition discussed above are lacking, regard for the welfare of the child or his wishes and feelings cannot in itself supply the gap.

---

[72] Adoption (Scotland) Act 1978, s. 44. Succession (Scotland) Act 1964, s. 23(5), as amended by the 1978 Act, Sched. 3, para. 4; Adoption (Scotland) Act 1978, s. 38.
[73] See *Re Valentine's Settlement* [1965] Ch. 831, *per* Lord Denning M.R. at p. 842.

INDEX

589